BOUNTY AND DONATION LAND GRANTS IN BRITISH COLONIAL AMERICA

Lloyd deWitt Bockstruck

GENEALOGICAL PUBLISHING Co., Inc

Published by Genealogical Publishing Company
3600 Clipper Mill Rd., Suite 260
Baltimore, MD 21211-1953
Library of Congress Catalogue Card Number 2007927674
ISBN-13: 978-0-8063-1780-9
Made in the United States of America

Bounty and Donation Land Grants in British Colonial America

At the quad-centenary of the successful founding of the British Empire at Jamestowne in Virginia in 1607, it seems appropriate to recognize those colonials who served in the armed forces of the Crown by defending and extending the Empire first on the North American continent and later around the globe. In return the Kingdom recognized their services with land.

The English colonies in North America had an abundance of land, but they seldom had the financial resources to accomplish many of their objectives. Accordingly, they gave land bounties for various purposes including the establishment of military outposts on the frontier and for military service. The recipients were the soldiers and sailors who served in various colonial wars or, in the event of death, their next of kin. All levels of government–municipal, colonial, and imperial–resorted to the practice. At times land was offered in advance of service; at other times, it was offered retroactively.

The definitions of the terms "bounty land grant" and "donation land grant" have become blurred over time. A bounty land grant was offered as an inducement to military service. It was a policy already in place whose terms were public knowledge when an individual enlisted in the military. A donation land grant was a reward to a veteran or his heirs after the conflict when government made such benefits available–sometimes as an afterthought.

The granting of lands to veterans or their heirs was not necessarily altruistic. Such a practice allowed governments to create buffers on the frontier against the enemy. Veterans of military conflicts were more skilled in warfare than ordinary citizens and often possessed the equipment for defending those outposts. Their physical presence offered some reassurance to others who might have been reluctant to settle farther inland. In the more populous colonies the military grants also helped to alleviate the population pressures on coastal settlements by locating veterans on the frontiers. In those areas of the New World where one colony was in competition with another for territory, land grants to veterans were also viewed as one way of strengthening a colony's claims, as in the cases of the rivalry between Massachusetts and New Hampshire and between Pennsylvania and Connecticut.

America's colonial conflicts fall into several categories. Firstly, there were the wars waged against hostile Indians. Secondly, there were the wars waged against other European powers and, incidentally, their Indian allies in the New World. Lastly, there were conflicts directed at armed rebellions against colonial governments.

By an order of the Council, Virginia authorized the granting of land on the frontier for protection against Indian incursions on 8 October 1630. It was not, however, until 1646 following the peace with Necotowance that Virginia authorized the granting of forts with surrounding lands to the captains who had commanded them. The captains had to fulfill the requirement of garrisoning the forts for three years at their own expense.

Massachusetts Bay and Connecticut after the Pequot War in 1637 parceled out some of their winnings to their soldiers.

In King Philip's War, 1675-1676, the English managed to break the power of the Narraganset Indians in southern New England and freed up land to be granted to the troops. When the soldiers were mustered at Dedham, Massachusetts in December 1675, they were told that "... if they played the man, took the fort, and drove the enemy out of the Narraganset country, which is their great seat, they should have a gratuity of land, beside their wages." The troops came from the colonies of Plymouth,

Massachusetts Bay, and Connecticut.

The town of Voluntown, Connecticut, as its name suggests, was awarded to the Connecticut soldiers who had volunteered for the conflict. Massachusetts granted seven townships in an arc from Springfield to Portland, Maine to veterans of King Philip's War. The seven townships were Narraganset #1 Buxton, Maine; Narraganset #2 Westminster, Massachusetts; Narraganset #3 Amherst, New Hampshire; Narraganset #4 Greenwich, Massachusetts; Narraganset #5 Merrimac and Manchester, New Hampshire; Narraganset #6 Templeton, Massachusetts; and Narraganset #7 Gorham, Maine. Each of these was considered to be a military outpost on the frontier, and each one had to have a minimum of thirty settlers with a minister within four years. There was a lapse of some forty years, however, before the grants materialized. Many of the veterans were no longer alive so it was often the heirs of the veterans who made good their claims. The records, therefore, aptly demonstrate filiation. The Narraganset township grants were made to soldiers who had served together and had been recruited from the same towns. Those land grants, therefore, reveal group migrations from the coastal New England settlements into the interior.

There were four wars waged between the English and the French between 1689 and 1763 for dominance in North America. The first was known as King William's War (1689-1697). The French forces destroyed Schenectady, New York, burned Salmon Falls on the New Hampshire border, and forced the capitulation of the outpost at Fort Loyal (Portland, Maine). In 1690 Sir William Phips led a naval expedition which captured Port Royal, Nova Scotia. Massachusetts promised its soldiers pay in loot and plunder from the citadel. The expedition failed to take Quebec and ended in disaster, and those who survived returned home without compensation. For a number of years thereafter the General Court of Massachusetts was besieged with petitions for bounty land from the veterans.

The second was Queen Anne's War, 1702-1713, which was the American counterpart of the War of the Spanish Succession in Europe.

Introduction

The most significant territorial exchange in America was the capture of Port Royal in October 1710, causing Acadia to fall to Great Britain. The British renamed the city, Annapolis, in honor of Her Majesty.

The third war was the War of Jenkins' Ear, 1739-1748, which merged into King George's War, 1740-1748. The former was a struggle between England and Spain for supremacy on the seas and ownership of Georgia. From North America the conflict extended into Europe where it was known as the War of Austrian Succession. In the New World it was a struggle over the boundaries of Acadia and northern New England and the Ohio River Valley.

The last of the major colonial conflicts was the French and Indian War, 1754-1763. It was overshadowed by the Seven Years' War in Europe, 1756-1763. France's policy was to encircle the English Atlantic seaboard colonies by extending her fur-trading outposts along the St. Lawrence River up to the Great Lakes and southward along the Mississippi River via Saint Louis, Missouri to New Orleans, Louisiana. In that way the French would confine the English in North America to cis-Appalachia.

It was the French and Indian War that generated the greatest number of claimants for bounty land. The conflict erupted in the Ohio River Valley in 1754 when several militia companies from Virginia under the command of Colonel Joshua Fry and Lt. Colonel George Washington set out into the interior to expel the French. Following Fry's accidental death, the command devolved upon Washington, who was forced to surrender Fort Necessity near present-day Pittsburgh, Pennsylvania to a superior French force. In an attempt to resist the French, Governor Robert Dinwiddie of Virginia issued a proclamation on 19 February 1754 authorizing bounty land grants to those who would volunteer for military service, over and above their regular pay.

At the end of the French and Indian War, King George III by proclamation of 7 October 1763 authorized his governors on the continent to grant bounty land without fee as a reward to reduced officers who had served in North America and to private soldiers disbanded in America. The land was to be free of quit rents for ten years, and the acreage was proportional with the rank of the soldier. The Royal Proclamation also extended coverage to reduced officers of the Royal Navy who had served at the reduction of Louisbourg and Quebec. The formula was:

Field Officers	5,000 acres
Captains	3,000 acres
Subalterns	2,000 acres
Noncommissioned officers	200 acres
Privates	50 acres.

An uprising of Indians followed the French and Indian War. The Ottawa chief, Pontiac, laid the war plan for a systematic destruction of British fortifications and settlements. Pontiac's War, 1763-1764, was unsuccessful in part because Pontiac did not receive the aid he expected from the French and because of the defection of some of his Indian allies. For the purposes of awarding bounty land, Pontiac's War was seemingly appended to the French and Indian War. The final Indian colonial conflict was Dunmore's War in 1774, when the Shawnee opposed the encroachment of the colonists into the Ohio River Valley. Lord Dunmore was the Royal Governor of Virginia, and it was his troops who waged the successful campaign.

The Royal Proclamation of 1763 declared off limits the parts of the British Empire in trans-Appalachia. Accordingly, Nova Scotia, New York, and the recently acquired colony of West Florida were favored locations for land grants. Veterans from colonies with no vacant lands available to be awarded had to locate in other colonies, and their land grants provide the clues for such migrations. For example, Samuel Clarkpaine, Thomas Cowdon, John Fry, Jeremiah Learned, Daniel McFarland, and Samuel Ward served under Col. Abijah Willard from Massachusetts in the French and Indian War but received their bounty lands in Virginia.

There is a question as to the integrity of some of the recipients. A veteran of the French and Indian War with the same name and rank might claim bounty land for the same service in two different colonies. Perhaps he had learned that his initial choice in upper New York had been a poor one, so he resubmitted his petition for land in a much more desirable colony such as West Florida. It is also possible that a veteran was attempting to double his holdings, and governmental officials were unaware of the fraud.

While racial designations of veterans do not necessarily appear in the records, there are examples of such. Matthew Roberts was a black veteran. Toby was an Indian. Both received land, but Solomon Uhahurinausaussmit, also an American Indian, was deemed ineligible for bounty land. Hannah Bradley was a female who received land in her own right.

The source material, both manuscript and published literature, for the respective colonies pertinent to this subject follows.

CONNECTICUT

The Public Records of Connecticut (Millwood, N.Y.: Kraus Reprint, 1977), volumes I, II, IV, and V contain references to the bounty lands awarded to veterans and heirs of veterans of the Pequot War of 1637. Voluntown, Connecticut was the location for the bounty land granted to Connecticut volunteers in the Narraganset War.

Charles Bancroft Gillespie's *An Historic Record and Pictorial Description of the Town of Meriden, Connecticut and Men Who Have Made It* (Meriden: Journal Publishing Company, 1906) and Charles H. S. Davis's *History of Wallingford, Conn., from Its Settlement in 1670 to the Present Time, Including Meriden* (Meriden: n.p., 1870) are two town histories whose military history sections mention several veterans and their land grants. James Shepard's *Connecticut Soldiers in the Pequot War of 1637* (Meriden: Journal Publishing Company, 1913) sought to identify those land grand recipients in soldiers' field.

GEORGIA

Residents in the colony of Georgia who applied for bounty land appear in the four-volume set by Mary Bondurant Warren, *Georgia Governor and Council Journals* (Athens, Ga.: Heritage Papers, 1991-2004) for the years 1753-1773. *An Index to English Crown Grants in Georgia, 1755-1775* (Spartanburg, S.C.: Reprint Co., 1989) provides the best access to the original patents, although Silas Emmett Lucas's *Index to the Headright and Bounty Grants of Georgia 1756-1909* (Easley, S.C.: Southern Historical Press, 1970) revised edition, does likewise. It should be noted that neither index identifies bounty land recipients as such. Such designations appear in the original records. The Georgia Surveyor General grants 1756-1775, volumes A-M, are on microfilm.

MARYLAND

John Kilty, *Land-Holder's Assistant and Land Office Guide* (Baltimore: G. Dobbin and Murphy, 1802), was the first publication to indicate the earliest bounty land grants issued to those loyal to Lord Baltimore in suppressing the rebellion led by the pirate, Richard Ingle, in 1645. The records are in the third volume of land patents of the colony on microfilm. Maryland had no vacant lands to award veterans of the French and Indian War so her veterans elected to take their bounty lands in other colonies.

MASSACHUSETTS

On 9 December 1675 Massachusetts offered a grant of land to each man who should engage in the war against the Narraganset.

Sir William Phips led a naval expedition to Quebec in 1690 in King William's War. The colony of Massachusetts promised its soldiers pay in loot and plunder from the citadel. The expedition ended in disaster, and those who survived returned home without compensation. For a number of years thereafter the General Court was besieged with petitions for their bounty land.

It was not until a period of relative tranquility from 1727 to 1739 that Massachusetts could begin granting land to veterans in the eastern and western parts of the province. The areas on the frontier were deliberately chosen in order to create a buffer to protect the towns in the older settled areas. Massachusetts also hoped to strengthen its claim to lands which New Hampshire claimed. Finally, these new towns would relieve the population pressures on the coastal settlements.

On 15 June 1728 the General Court granted two townships of six miles square each to the officers and soldiers or their legal representatives who were in the Narraganset War. Because there was insufficient land to satisfy the requests, the General Court granted another township of six miles square.

Nathaniel B. Shurtleff's *Records of the Governor and Company of the Massachusetts Bay in New England* (reprint, New York: A. M. S. Press, 1971), George M. Bodge's *Soldiers in King Philip's War, Being a Critical Account of That War, with a Concise History of the Indian Wars of New England from 1620-77, Official Lists of the Soldiers of Massachusetts Colony Serving in Philip's War ...*, and *Records of the Colony of New Plymouth in New England* (New York: A. M. S. Press, 1967) contain innumerable references to lands awarded for military service. *The Journals of the House of Representatives of Massachusetts, 1715-1776* (Boston: Massachusetts Historical Society, 1919 ff.) in 51 volumes, although inconsistently indexed, offer many details of military grants not found elsewhere.

Walter Kendall Watkins's *Soldiers in the Expedition to Canada in 1690 and Grantees of the Canada Townships* (Boston: printed for the author, 1898) was the groundbreaking work for bounty land grants from Massachusetts for King William's War. Abijah P. Marvin's *History of the Town of Winchendon, (Worcester County, Mass.,) from the Grant of Ipswich Canada in 1735 to the Present Time* (Winchendon: published by the author, 1868) and the proprietors' records of Winchendon 1735-1794, pp. 3-5, constitute the records of the town. Ezra S. Stearns, *History of Ashburnham, Massachusetts from the Grant of Dorchester Canada to the Present Time, 1734-1886* (Ashburnham: published by the town, 1887) and the proprietors' records 1739-1798 of the town of Poland contain the names of those on the Canada Expedition for what is Bakerstown, Maine today.

William F. Goodwin's *Records of the Proprietors of Narraganset Township No. 1, now the Town of Buxton, York County, Maine from August 1st, 1733 to January 4th, 1811 with a Documentary Introduction* (Medford, Mass.: Tufts College Press, 1906) details the records of the grantees in Township Number 1. His text gives the names of veterans by their towns of origin in Massachusetts.

Narraganset Township Number 2 grantees appear in the records of Westminister, Massachusetts. The proprietors' records, pp. 6-9, contain their names.

Narraganset Township Number 3 became Amherst, New Hampshire.

Narraganset Township Number 4 became Greenwich, Massachusetts. The proprietors' records identify the names of the grantees. [Family History Library film #1902753].

Narraganset Township Number 5 became Bedford, New Hampshire and parts of Merrimac and Manchester, New Hampshire.

Narraganset Township Number 6 became Templeton, Massachusetts. The proprietors' records [Family History Library film #864109] contain the names of the grantees.

Narraganset Township Number 7 was Gorham, Maine. The proprietors' town records, pp. 1-8, contain the names of the original grantees.

Surviving veterans of the 1725 "Lovewell's Battle" against the Maine Indians in 1725 received their bounty land in Lovell and Sweden in Oxford County, Maine in 1727. Ezra Scolley Stearns's "Lovewell's Men" appeared in *The Register of the New England Historic Genealogical Society*, LXIII (July 1909), pp. 288-96. Mabel Cook Coolidge's *The*

History of Petersham, Massachusetts Incorporated April 20, 1754, Volunteerstown or Voluntown, 1730-1733, Nichewaug, 1733-1754 (n.p.: Petersham Historical Society, 1948) and N. F. Carver and T. L. Fowler's *History of Pembroke, New Hampshire 1730-1895* (Allenstown, N.H.: Allenstown-Pembroke Bicentennial Committee, 1976) are the local histories discussing the grantees at Voluntown [now Petersham] and Suncook [now Pembroke], New Hampshire.

In 1740 a Royal Commission settled the boundary dispute between Massachusetts and New Hampshire. Eight Canadian townships fell within the limits of New Hampshire, and the grantees, therefore, found their titles from Massachusetts invalid. The year before the Anglo-French rivalry had erupted; it continued until the end of the French and Indian War and Pontiac's Conspiracy, so activity ceased in regard to military land grants. In 1768 Massachusetts resumed making a series of compensatory grants inside its borders to those with invalid New Hampshire grants. The township of Bethel was awarded to the veterans or their heirs of the Canada Expedition in 1690. In 1771 there was a similar grant in the towns of Canton and Jay. In that same year James Otis and others received a compensatory grant to replace the lands they had originally been awarded. In 1774 the heirs of Captain Gardner's Company received a compensatory grant in what is Waterford, Maine today for their forfeited earlier grant in Henniker, New Hampshire.

Volumes 45 and 46 of *The Massachusetts Archives* contain petitions of residents of Massachusetts seeking the lands to which they themselves or their forbears were entitled. These records are available on microfilm.

NEW HAMPSHIRE

In the forty-volume series *The New Hampshire Provincial and State Papers* (imprint varies, 1867-1943) are some of the richest published materials pertaining to lands in the colony. D. Donovan and Jacob A. Woodward's *The History of the Town of Lyndeborough, New*

Hampshire, 1735-1905 (Medford, Mass.: Tufts College Press, 1906) identifies many veterans with military grants.

NEW YORK

The patents of the State of New York, 1649-1912, contain three volumes of colonial military patents, 1764-1775. The records are on microfilm. They are complemented by the *Calendar of Council Minutes 1668-1783* (Harrison, New York: Harbor Hill Books, 1987) compiled by Berthold Fernow and E. B. O'Callaghan's *Calendar of N.Y. Colonial Manuscripts Indorsed Land Papers in the Office of the Secretary of State of New York 1643-1803* (Harrison, New York: Harbor Hill Books, 1987).

NORTH CAROLINA

Records of the Executive Council 1755-1775 (Raleigh: Division of Archives and History, 1994), which is volume IX of *The Colonial Records of North Carolina [Second Series]* contain the only mention of bounty land grantees under the Royal Proclamation of 1763. Unfortunately, the records of the colonial land office and the Court of Claims of North Carolina do not indicate which lands were awarded to veterans of the French and Indian War. The Secretary of the Colony's patent books, the Deputy Auditor General's patent books, the registers of warrants sued for and the patents sued for are likewise silent. While there was also a suspension of quit rents for a decade, the land records do not contain any such notation. The few land grants for military service which can be identified as such involved those grantees who had lost their warrants and had to reapply for duplicates.

NOVA SCOTIA

The Nova Scotia Crown Land Grant Registers, books 1-15, contain the records of those receiving land grants under the terms of the

Royal Proclamation following the French and Indian War, interspersed with other land grants. These records have been microfilmed.

PENNSYLVANIA

In the aftermath of the French and Indian War, the colony of Pennsylvania was anxious to block the Connecticut settlers of the Susquehannah Company at the forks of the Susquehannah River, so the proprietors encouraged former officers who had served in the First and Second Battalions of the Pennsylvania Regiment in 1764 to apply for a special application of land. Their grant was for 24,000 acres, not to be laid out in more than three 8,000-acre tracts in the New Purchase. The Bald Eagle Creek Tract lies within present-day Clinton and Centre Counties, the Buffalo Valley Tract in Union County, and the Susquehanna River Tract in Union, Snyder, Northumberland, and Montour Counties. There was a second group of officers who had served in Pennsylvania regiments between 1756 and 1760. They were known as the gentlemen. They were allowed 50,000 acres. Several of them are mentioned in the "Minutes of the Board of Property," *The Pennsylvania Archives,* 3rd Series, I, 253-54. The muster rolls appear in Land Office Microfilm 21.2. The New Purchase applications numbered 1 to 46 list the names of the veterans in the officers' and gentlemen's tracts. They appear in Land Office Microfilm roll 1.9, pp. 1-7. Kenneth McCrea's *Pennsylvania Land Applications*, volume II: *New Purchase Applications, 1769-1773* (Philadelphia: Genealogical Society of Pennsylvania, 2005), pp. xxviii-xxxv, also lists the officers of the French and Indian War who received land for their military service.

RHODE ISLAND & PROVIDENCE PLANTATIONS

In May 1677 the General Assembly awarded 5,000 acres, 500 of which were laid out as the town of East Greenwich in 50 house lots, to fifty men for their services rendered during King Philip's War. The town was to be located in the former Narraganset lands. The grantees were those who had been driven and forced out of their habitations with the loss of all or most parts of their estates. The grant was made 31 October 1677. Three versions with slight variations appear in D. H. Greene's *History of the Town of East Greenwich and Adjacent Territory, from 1677 to 1877* (Providence: J. A. & R. A. Reid, 1877), pp. 2-11, John Russell Bartlett's *Records of the Colony of Rhode Island and Providence Plantations, in New England* (Providence: A. Crawford Greene and Brothers, 1857), II, 573-75 & 584-89, and John D. Cushing's *The Earliest Acts and Laws of the Colony of Rhode Island and Providence Plantations 1647-1719* (Wilmington, Del.: Michael Glazier, Inc., 1977), 87-88.

SOUTH CAROLINA

The grants for military service are in Records of the Secretary of State of South Carolina's *Land Grants, Colonial Series, Copies, Royal Grants, 1732-1775,* on microfilm. The South Carolina Council Journals include names of veterans and their heirs seeking bounty land. They too are on microfilm. Brent H. Holcomb's seven-volume work, *Petitions for Land from South Carolina Council Journals* (Columbia, S.C.: SCMAR, 1996-99) contains some mentions of land grants on the King's Bounty. His other series, *South Carolina's Royal Grants* (Columbia, S.C.: SCMAR, 2006-), is even more valuable. South Carolina's military grants bear the notation "King's Bounty" in the actual land grant volumes as opposed to those with the notation "Bounty." The latter term had a definition peculiar to the colony of South Carolina where it indicated bounty or assistance provided colonists from the British Isles and Europe as an inducement to settling in South Carolina, and did not pertain to military service in any way. It is important to bear in mind this distinction. The notations "Bounty as to the King's quit rents" and "free of quit rents for ten years" likewise in no way indicate military service.

VIRGINIA

A Calendar of the Warrants for Land in Kentucky, Granted for

Service in the French and Indian War (Baltimore: Genealogical Publishing Company, Inc., 1975) abstracted by Philip Fall Taylor is certified to be a calendar of the surveys made for the officers and soldiers of the French and Indian War whose bounty lands lay in trans-Appalachian Virginia [*i.e.* Kentucky]. Neal O. Hammon's work, *Early Kentucky Land Records, 1773-1780* (Louisville, Ky.: The Filson Club, 1992), pp. 250-66, contains corrections to the former. Lloyd de Witt Bockstruck's *Virginia's Colonial Soldiers* (Baltimore: Genealogical Publishing Company, 1988) has abstracts of bounty land applications and bounty land warrants for French and Indian War veterans. Barbara Vines Little's series, "Land Office Warrants Issued for Service in the French and Indian War," *Magazine of Virginia Genealogy*, XXXI-XXXVIII (1993-99), is especially useful for the details contained in the warrants. The Virginia Land Office's *Old Military and Importation Warrants; Land Bounty Certificates, French and Indian War; Index, Land Bounty Books, French and Indian War* are on two rolls of microfilm [Family History Library #29661 and #29634]. Mary B. Kegley and F. F. Kegley's *Early Adventurers on the Western Waters* (Orange, Va.: Green Publishers, Inc., 1980), I, 71-80, treats the first surveys recorded in the Fincastle County Survey Book A. County courts certified the military service of veterans of the French and Indian War, Pontiac's Conspiracy, and Dunmore's War. The entries appear in the various county court order and minute books, and these have been microfilmed.

Milo M. Quaife's *The Preston and Virginia Papers of the Draper Collection of Manuscripts* (Hartford, Ky.: Cook & McDowell Publications, 1979) contains abstracts of some of Governor Dunmore's warrants for lands in Fincastle County. *Cavaliers and Pioneers: Abstracts of Virginia Land Patents and Grants,* volumes I-III (v. I: Richmond: 1934 and vols. II and III: Richmond, Virginia State Library, 1977-79), edited by Nell Marion Nugent and volumes IV-VIII (Richmond: Virginia Genealogical Society, 1994-2005), edited by Dennis Ray Hudgins, treat the colonial patents plus the Commonwealth grants from the first six grant books. The original records are on microfilm. Fairfax Harrison's *Virginia Land Grants: A Study of Conveyancing in Relation to Colonial Politics* (Westminister, Md.: Willow Bend Books, 1998) explains and exemplifies many of the lesser known military grants.

The application process began at the local level so the county and hustings court order books constitute the richest source for land awarded for military service in the colony. While many of the claims were filed in 1779 and 1780, some were as late as the second decade of the nineteenth century.

WEST FLORIDA

Gordon M. Wells's "British Land Grants–William Wilton Map, 1774," *Journal of Mississippi History*, XXVIII (1966), 152-160, indicates the officers who received bounty lands for their service at the reduction of Louisbourg and Quebec in 1758 and 1759. Several of the land warrants are to be found in the National Archives in the Records of the General Land Office, Record Group 49, Division D (Private Land Claims Division), *British West Florida Papers,* Micro-publication NNFN 468, 3 rolls. Photostats of records from the British Public Record Office, Colonial Office Series 5:574-635 are the richest primary source material. They are located at the Library of Congress in the Manuscripts Division. Abstracts from them appear in three articles by Mary A. Petersen, "British West Florida: Abstracts of Land Petitions," *Louisiana Genealogical Register*, XVIII (1971), 318-37, XIX (1972), 86-89, 162-67, 239-48, 339-48, and XX (1973), 1-8, "British West Florida Abstracts of Land Petitions The Mobile-Pensacola-Tombigbee-Biloxi Area," *Louisiana Genealogical Register* XXXI (1984), 136-54, and "British West Florida Land Petitions of Particular Interest," *Louisiana Genealogical Register* XXXI (1984), 263-71. Clinton N. Howard's *The British Development of West Florida 1763-1769* (Berkeley: University of California Press, 1947) and Winston De Ville's *English Land Grants in West Florida: A Register for the States of Alabama, Mississippi & Parts of Florida and Louisiana 1766-1776* (Ville Platte, La: W. De Ville, 1986) are pioneer works which, though broader in scope, also include grants for colonial military service.

Introduction

I am especially grateful to those scholars who clarified many complex points and offered suggestions to inquiries I made of them. Among them are David Dumas of East Greenwich, Rhode Island; Gordon Remington, FASG, of Salt Lake City, Utah; Patricia Law Hatcher, FASG, of Dallas, Texas; Brent H. Holcomb of Columbia, South Carolina; Conley Edwards, Archivist of the Commonwealth of Virginia; Elizabeth Shown Mills, FASG, of Tuscaloosa, Alabama; Margaret Hofmann of Roanoke Rapids, North Carolina; Dr. A. Bruce Pruitt of Whitakers, North Carolina; and George Stevenson, Private Manuscripts Archivist, of the North Carolina State Archives, Raleigh, North Carolina.

In such a compilation it is inevitable that errors and omissions exist. I invite any additions and corrections.

Lloyd de Witt Bockstruck, FNGS
Dallas, Texas
A.D. MMVII

BOUNTY AND DONATION LAND GRANTS IN BRITISH COLONIAL AMERICA

Bounty and Donation Land Grants in British Colonial America

—, —. He served on the expedition to Canada in 1690. He was a servant of John King. Samuel King was admitted to his land in Lyndeboro, Maine in 1735.

—, —. He served on the expedition to Canada in 1690. He was a servant of Mr. Knowlton whose son, John Knowlton, received his land in Winchendon, Massachusetts in 1736.

—, —. He served on the expedition to Canada in 1690. His daughter, Rachel Rust, received his land in 1736 in Winchendon, Massachusetts.

—, —. He served on the expedition to Canada in 1690. Edward Chapman received his land in Winchendon, Massachusetts in 1736.

—, —. He served on the expedition to Canada in 1690. John Goodhue received his land in Winchendon, Massachusetts in 1736.

—, Bartholomew. He served on the expedition to Canada in 1690. He received his land in Bethel, Maine in 1767.

—, Toby. He was an Indian and served under Capt. John Lovewell from Massachusetts and was in battle at Pigwacket 8 May 1725. He received his land in Pembroke, New Hampshire.

Abbet, Thomas. He served in the Narraganset War from Wenham, Massachusetts. His son, Thomas Abbet, received his land in Amherst, New Hampshire in 1734.

Abbott, James. He served as a soldier in the French and Indian War and had his service certified in Montgomery County, Virginia 8 March 1780 for his 50 acres of land.

Abbott, John. He served in the Narraganset War from Salem, Massachusetts. Ephraim Ingalls drew his land in Amherst, New Hampshire in 1734.

Abbott, Matthias. He served as a sergeant in the Virginia Battalion of Regulars under Col. William Byrd in the French and Indian War in 1758 and received his 200 acre warrant in Virginia.

Abbott, Nathan. He served as a noncommissioned officer in the Virginia Regiment under Col. William Byrd in the French and Indian War. He was from Hanover County, Virginia and assigned his 200 acre land warrant.

Abell, Joshua. He served in the Narraganset War from Connecticut and received his land in Voluntown, Connecticut in 1701.

Able, John. He served as a sergeant in the French and Indian War and petitioned for his land in New York 8 July 1765.

Able, William. He was granted 200 acres in Albany County, New York for his service as a sergeant in the 60th Regiment of Foot in the French and Indian War 15 August 1765.

Abott, Garret. He received 2,000 acres in West Florida for his service as a staff officer in the French and Indian War 17 October 1776.

Ackland, Christopher. He was entitled to 50 acres for his service in a Virginia Ranging Company under Capt. Robert Rutherford in the French and Indian War. His claim was certified in Washington County, Virginia 15 May 1781.

Ackland, Dudley. He served as deputy adjutant general in the West Indies in the French and Indian War and had his service certified in New York 31 May 1769.

Acoff, John. He served as a sergeant under Col. Robert Mumford in Col. William Byrd's Regiment in 1760 in the French and Indian War. He received his warrant for 200 acres 27 April 1780 in Henry County, Virginia.

Acre, Andrew. He served as a corporal in the French and Indian War and petitioned for his 200 acres in New York 19 January 1775. He assigned it to John Antill.

Acres, James. He served as a soldier for six months in the 1st Virginia Regiment of Foot under Col. William Byrd in 1758 or 1759 for six months in the French and Indian War. He next enlisted in the Regiment of Col. Adam Stephen. He received his 50 acre warrant 13 March 1780 in King and Queen County, Virginia.

Adams, Charles. He served in the French and Indian War and received 700 acres in Nova Scotia 29 March 1779.

Adams, James. He served as a soldier in Capt. John Smith's Company of Regulars on the Cherokee Expedition in 1760 in the French and Indian War. He received his 50 acre warrant in April 1780 in Montgomery County, Virginia.

Adams, John. He served in the Narraganset War from Sudbury, Massachusetts. He received his land in Westminster, Massachusetts in 1733.

Adams, John. He served in the Narraganset War and received land in Templeton, Massachusetts in 1733.

Adams, John. He served as a private in Capt. Thomas Woodford's Company of the 1st Virginia Regiment in the French and Indian War. He assigned his 50 acres in Virginia.

Adams, John. He served as a soldier under Col. William Byrd in the French and Indian War in 1760. He proved his service in Bedford County, Virginia 23 August 1779.

Adams, John. He served as a sergeant in Capt. John Smith's Company on the Cherokee Expedition in 1760 under Col. William Byrd in the French and Indian War. He received his 200 acre warrant in April 1780 in Montgomery County, Virginia.

Adams, Simon. He was a veteran of the Narraganset War from Massachusetts in 1685. His land was located in Buxton, Maine.

Adams, William. He served as a sergeant in Lt. Col. Campbell's Company in the French and Indian War and petitioned for his 200 acres in New York 12 April 1770.

Adkins, Gardner. He served as a private in a company of rangers in 1757 in the French and Indian War. He assigned his 50 acre warrant in Virginia.

Adkins, John. He served as a soldier in the 1st Virginia Regiment under Col. William Byrd in the French and Indian War. He proved his right to 50 acres in Augusta County, Virginia 19 October 1779.

Adkins, Joseph. He served as a soldier in the 1st Virginia Regiment under Col. William Byrd in the French and Indian War. He assigned his right to 50 acres in Virginia.

Adley, William. He served as a soldier in the 46th Regiment in the French and Indian War and had his service certified 30 January 1767 in New York.

Adlington, Daniel. He was granted 50 acres in Charlotte County, New York for his service as a soldier in the Inniskilling Regiment of Foot in the French and Indian War 18 October 1775.

Adye, Stephen Payne. He served as a captain in the Royal Regiment of Artillery as fire master in the French and Indian War. His service was certified 5 November 1774 in New York.

Affleck, Philip. He was granted 5,000 acres in West Florida for his service as a captain in the navy in the French and Indian War 15 May 1778.

Aggaton, John. He was granted 50 acres in Albany County, New York for his service as a soldier in the 55th Regiment of Foot in the French and Indian War 27 September 1769.

Ahern, William. He served as a soldier in Capt. Samuel Overton's Company of Rangers in 1756 in the French and Indian War. He assigned the warrant for 50 acres in Virginia.

Airey, Joseph. His widow, Mary Airey, was granted 2,000 acres in Tryon County, New York for his service as a lieutenant in an independent company of foot in the French and Indian War 7 October 1774.

Akers, Uriah. He served as a soldier in the French and Indian War and had his service certified in Montgomery County, Virginia for his 50 acres of land 8 March 1780.

Albey, Abraham. He was granted 200 acres in Albany County, New York for his service as a sergeant in the 46th Regiment of Foot in the French and Indian War 29 October 1765.

Albro, John, Jr. He shared in the grant of East Greenwich, Rhode Island made to those who had rendered service in King Philip's War. The grant was made 31 October 1677.

Albro, Samuel. He shared in the grant of East Greenwich, Rhode Island made to those who had rendered service in King Philip's War. The grant was made 31 October 1677.

Alcorn, James. He served as a soldier in Capt. William Preston's Company of Rangers in 1759 in the French and Indian War. He received his 50 acre warrant in April in 1780 Montgomery County, Virginia.

Alcorn, John. He served as a soldier in the 1st Virginia Regiment in the Cherokee Expedition of 1760 under Col. William Byrd. No warrant was issued to him in May 1780 in Montgomery County, Virginia.

Alden, John. He was from Duxbury, Plymouth County, Massachusetts and received 200 acres of land in Massachusetts 24 June 1737.

Alden, John. He served as captain of a vessel. In 1690 enroute to Port Royal he was taken prisoner by a French ship of war and held in captivity for five years. His heir, Nathanael Alden of Boston, applied for his land in Massachusetts 26 March 1736.

Alder, John. He was granted 50 acres in Albany County, New York for his service as a soldier in the 60th Regiment of Foot in the French and Indian War 14 April 1772.

Alexander, Archibald. He served as a captain in the expedition against the Shawnee in the French and Indian War. His heir, William Alexander, received his 3,000 acre warrant in Virginia.

Alexander, Daniel. He served in the Narraganset War from Northampton, Massachusetts. His brother, John Alexander, claimed his land in Greenwich, Massachusetts in 1737.

Alexander, John. He served in the Narraganset War from Northampton, Massachusetts. He claimed his land in Greenwich, Massachusetts in 1737.

Alexander, Robert. He served as a corporal in the Royal Regiment in the French and Indian War and petitioned for his 200 acres in New York 27 April 1765.

Alexander, William. He served as a sergeant in the 2nd Virginia Regiment under Col. William Byrd in the French and Indian War. He received a warrant for 200 acres in November 1779 in Rockbridge County, Virginia.

Allaz, James. He was granted 3,000 acres in Albany County, New York for his service as a captain in the 60th Regiment of Foot in the French and Indian War 23 August 1764.

Allen, —. He served on the expedition to Canada in 1690. Samuel Allen received his land in Dumbarton, New Hampshire in 1735.

Allen, Andrew. He was granted 2,000 in Northumberland County, Pennsylvania and 3,000 acres in Pennsylvania for his service in the French and Indian War 4 February 1769.

Allen, Benjamin. He served in the Narraganset War from Barrington, Massachusetts. His son, Joseph Allen, claimed his land in Greenwich, Massachusetts in 1737.

Allen, Hugh. He served as a subaltern in the French and Indian War. His heir at law, John Allen, received his 2,000 acres of land warrant in Virginia.

Allen, John. He served on the expedition to Canada in 1690. Henry Hale petitioned for his land in Raymond, Maine in 1735.

Allen, John. He served on the expedition to Canada in 1690. John Allen received his land in Warwick, Massachusetts in 1738.

Allen, John. He was granted 29 acres in Ulster County, New York for his service as a soldier in the 40th Regiment of Foot in the French and Indian War 27 September 1765.

Allen, John. He served as a subaltern in the French and Indian War and received 2,000 acres in Nova Scotia 14 December 1783.

Allen, John. He was granted 10,000 acres in Pennsylvania for his service in the French and Indian War 4 February 1769.

Allen, John. He served as a subaltern in the French and Indian War. He was deceased when his representative, James Allen, received his 2,000 acre land warrant in New York.

Allen, Joseph. He served on the expedition to Canada in 1690. William Coolidge, Jr. received his land in Alstead, New Hampshire in 1771.

Allen, Matthew. He served as a soldier in the French and Indian War and received 50 acres in Nova Scotia 9 October 1776.

Allen, Richard. He served in the Narraganset War from Barrington, Massachusetts. His nephew, Joseph Allen, claimed his land in Greenwich, Massachusetts in 1737.

Allen, Robert. He was granted 200 acres in Albany County, New York for his service as a sergeant in the 60th Regiment of Foot in the French and Indian War 25 May 1771.

Allen, Samuel. He served in the Narraganset War from Barnstable, Massachusetts. He received land in Gorham, Maine in 1733.

Allen, Samuel. He served as a captain in Col. Wyser's Regiment in Pennsylvania and also as a captain under Col. William Byrd in the French and Indian War and received his 3,000 acre warrant in Virginia.

Allen, Thomas. He served as a subaltern in the French and Indian War and received 3,000 acres in Nova Scotia 5 July 1769.

Allen, William. He served as a subaltern in the French and Indian War and received 2,000 acres in Nova Scotia 3 November 1771.

Allin, Nicholas. He served in the Narraganset War from Boston, Massachusetts. His son, Daniel Allin, received his land in Bedford, New Hampshire in 1733.

Allin, Richard. He was a veteran of the Narraganset War from Massachusetts in 1685. His land was located in Buxton, Maine.

Allin, William. He was a veteran of the Narraganset War from Massachusetts in 1685. His land was located in Buxton, Maine.

Allison, Francis. He was a physician. He was granted 1,500 acres in Cumberland County, Pennsylvania for his service in the French and Indian War 4 February 1769.

Allison, Hector. He was granted 2,000 acres on the north side of the Pedee River in South Carolina on the King's bounty 21June 1765. He served as a chaplain in the French and Indian War.

Allison, Patrick. He served as a lieutenant in the French and Indian War and received 2,000 acres of land in Virginia which he assigned.

Allman, John. He was granted 50 acres in Albany County, New York for his eight years of service as a soldier in Capt. Bradstreet's Company in the 40th Regiment of Foot in the French and Indian War 15 August 1766. He also appeared as John Almann.

Aloon, Christian. He served as a private in the French and Indian War and petitioned for land in New York 5 February 1772.

Alpin, Giles: He was granted 50 acres in Albany County, New York for his service as a soldier in the 80th Regiment of Foot in the French and Indian War 26 July 1765.

Alson, Christian. He was granted 50 acres in Albany County, New York for his service as a soldier in the 60th Regiment of Foot in the French and Indian War 14 April 1772.

Alsup, John. He served as a soldier in the Virginia Regiment about three years until it was disbanded by Col. Adam Stephen. He received his 50 acre warrant in May 1780 in Montgomery County, Virginia.

Alvard, Benedict. He was granted 50 acres in Connecticut for his service as sergeant in the Pequot War 11 May 1671. He resided at Windsor. He also appeared as Benedict Aluard.

Ames, Jacob. He served in Lovewell's War in Massachusetts and received his land in Petersham, Massachusetts. He also appeared as Jacob Eames.

Ames, Jethro. He served in Lovewell's War in Massachusetts and received his land in Petersham, Massachusetts. He also appeared as Jethro Eames.

Amos, Francis. He served as a corporal under Capt. Thomas Fleming and one year under Capt. Charles Scott in Col. William Peachey's Regiment in the French and Indian War and assigned his 200 acre warrant. He was from Buckingham County, Virginia.

Amsden, Isaac. He served in the Narraganset War. Thomas Amsden received his land in Templeton, Massachusetts in 1733.

Amsden, Jacob. He served in the Narraganset War. Thomas Amsden received his land in Templeton, Massachusetts in 1733.

Anderson, Andrew. He served as an assistant surgeon in the French and Indian War and prayed for a grant of 2,000 acres in New York 26 June 1767.

Anderson, James. He served as a captain in the New Jersey Regiment of Col. John Johnson in the French and Indian War in 1756 for six months. He received his 3,000 acre warrant in Frederick County, Virginia 8 March 1780. His unit was in the Jersey Blues.

Anderson, John. He was granted 200 acres in Albany County, New York for his service as a drummer in the 55th Regiment of Foot in the French and Indian War 1 April 1772.

Anderson, John. He served as a sergeant in the 2nd Virginia Regiment under Col. William Byrd in the French and Indian War. He was entitled to 200 acres which he assigned.

Anderson, Joseph. He was granted 50 acres in Albany County, New York for his service as a soldier in the 17th Regiment of Foot in the French and Indian War 1 July 1771.

Anderson, Matthew. He served as a sergeant under Col. John Hickman in 1750 in the French and Indian War. He assigned his warrant for 200 acres in Virginia.

Anderson, Peter. He received his 50 acres of land in West Florida for his service as a soldier in the French and Indian War 21 September 1776.

Anderson, Robert. He was granted 200 acres in Albany County, New York for his service as a corporal in the 1st Regiment of Foot in the French and Indian War 18 February 1775.

Anderson, William. He served as a sergeant in the 77th Regiment in the French and Indian War and petitioned for his 200 acres in New York 19 January 1775.

Anderson, William. He served as a soldier in Capt. William Preston's

Company of Rangers from 1758 to 4 May 1759 in the French and Indian War. He received a warrant for 50 acres in April 1780 in Montgomery County, Virginia.

Anderton, James. He served on the expedition to Canada in 1690 and received bounty land in Poland, Maine in 1739.

Andrew, John. He was granted 200 acres in Albany County, New York for his service as a sergeant in the 80th Regiment of Foot in the French and Indian War 16 July 1765.

Andrews, John. He was a veteran of the Narraganset War from Massachusetts in 1685. His land was located in Buxton, Maine.

Andrews, John. He served on the expedition to Canada in 1690. John Gyles was admitted to his land in Lyndeboro, Maine in 1736.

Andrews, John. He was granted 200 acres in Albany County, New York for his service as a sergeant in the French and Indian War 8 June 1771.

Andrews, Robert. He served in the Narraganset War from Boxford, Massachusetts. His son, John Andrews, claimed his land in Amherst, New Hampshire in 1734. Thomas Andrews drew the land.

Andrews, Robert. He served in the Narraganset War from Boxford, Massachusetts. His son, John Andrews, received his land in Amherst, New Hampshire in 1734.

Andrews, Thomas. He was a veteran of the expedition to Canada in 1690. His brother, John Andrews of Stoughton, Massachusetts, received his land in Ashburnham, Massachusetts in 1736.

Andrews, Thomas. He served as a captain on the expedition to Canada in 1690. Thomas Andrews received his land in Chesterfield, Massachusetts in 1739.

Andrews, William. He served as a soldier in the French and Indian War and had his service certified in New York in November 1766.

Andrus, John. He served in the expedition to Canada in 1690 and claimed his land in Dumbarton, New Hampshire in 1735.

Angier, Oakes. He received bounty land in Alstead, New Hampshire in 1771 for the service of an unidentified veteran in the expedition to Canada in 1690.

Annets, Joseph. He was granted 200 acres in Albany County, New York for his service as a corporal in the 55th Regiment of Foot in the French and Indian War 1 April 1772. He also appeared as Joseph Aunets.

Annett, Joseph. He served as a soldier in Capt. Thomas Bullet's Company and received a warrant for 50 acres in Virginia 19 October 1779. He also appeared as Joseph Annet.

Anslow, Thomas. He served as a sergeant in the 80th Regiment in the French and Indian War and had his service certified 8 October 1766 in New

York.

Anterbush, Philip. He was granted 50 acres in Albany County, New York for his service as a soldier in the 4th Battalion in the 60th Regiment of Foot in the French and Indian War 18 July 1770.

Anthony, John. He served as a captain of a company of rangers in 1759 in the French and Indian War. His heir, John Anthony, received his warrant for 3,000 acres in March 1780 in Bedford County, Virginia.

Anthony, Joseph. He was granted 50 acres in Gloucester County, New York for his service as a soldier in the 4th Battalion of the 60th Regiment of Foot in the French and Indian War 5 April 1770.

Appleton, Samuel. He served as a major in the Narraganset War from Massachusetts in 1685. His land was located in Buxton, Maine.

Arbuthnot, Charles. He served as a noncommissioned officer in the French and Indian War and received 200 acres in Nova Scotia, 4 March 1777.

Arbuthnot, John. He served as ensign in a regiment of foot in the French and Indian War and received 200 acres in Nova Scotia 4 March 1777.

Arbuthnot, Mariot. He served as a captain in the Royal Navy in the French and Indian War and received 5,000 acres in Nova Scotia 4 March 1777.

Archer, John. He served on the expedition to Canada in 1690. Jonathan Very was admitted to his land in Lyndeboro, Maine in 1736.

Archer, Joseph. He received 150 acres of land in West Florida for his service as a soldier in the French and Indian War 21 September 1776.

Archdeacon, Maurice. He was granted 50 acres in Albany County, New York for his service as a soldier in the 35th Regiment of Foot in the French and Indian War 26 September 1765.

Arison, William. He was granted 200 acres in Orange County, New York for his service as a corporal in a company of rangers in the French and Indian War 15 May 1770.

Armantrout, George. He served as a soldier in Capt. Peter Hogg's Company of Rangers until 1758 in the French and Indian War. He received his 50 acre warrant 24 April 1780 in Rockingham County, Virginia.

Armstrong, John. He was granted 200 acres in Charlotte County, New York for his service as a corporal in the 80th Regiment of Foot in the French and Indian War 8 August 1774.

Armstrong, John. He was granted 200 acres in Charlotte County, New York for his service as a noncommissioned officer in the 18th Regiment of Foot in the French and Indian War 12 October 1774.

Armstrong, John. He served as a sergeant in the French and Indian War and received his 200 acre land warrant in Virginia.

Armstrong, Jonathan. He served in the Narraganset War from Connecticut and received land in Voluntown, Connecticut in 1701.

Armstrong, Lanty. He served as a subaltern in the French and Indian War and had his service certified in Montgomery County, Virginia 8 March 1780 for his 2,000 acres of land.

Armstrong, Thomas. He was granted 200 acres in Albany County, New York for his service as a corporal in the 55th Regiment of Foot in the French and Indian War 6 August 1765.

Armstrong, Thomas. He was granted 200 acres in Gloucester County, New York for his service as a noncommissioned officer in the Royal Regiment of Artillery in the French and Indian War 3 February 1775.

Armstrong, William. He served as a corporal in a company of rangers under Capt. Peter Hogg in the French and Indian War and received a warrant for 200 acres 28 October 1779 in Virginia.

Arnold, Charles. He served in the French and Indian War as a soldier. He assigned his 50 acre land warrant in Virginia.

Arnold, James. He was granted 50 acres in Craven County, South Carolina on the King's bounty in the French and Indian War 15 February 1770.

Arnold, James. He served as a soldier in the French and Indian War until 1759. He proved his right in Caroline County, Virginia in February 1780. He assigned his right to 50 acres in Virginia.

Arnold, John. He served in the Narraganset War from Boston, Massachusetts. His heirs received land in Bedford, New Hampshire in 1733.

Arnold, John. He served in the Narraganset War from Hingham, Massachusetts. His heirs received land in Bedford, New Hampshire in 1733.

Arnold, Matthew. He was granted 50 acres in Albany County, New York for his service as a soldier in the 60th or Royal American Regiment of Foot in the French and Indian War 28 March 1771.

Arnold, Stephen. He shared in the grant of East Greenwich, Rhode Island made to those who had rendered service in King Philip's War. The grant was made 31 October 1677.

Arnott, John. He was granted 2,000 acres in West Florida for his service as a warrant officer at the reduction of Louisbourg in the French and Indian War 11 March 1778.

Arnurne, Albertus. He was a soldier in the 80th Regiment in the French and Indian War and petitioned for his land in New York 22 October 1766.

Asa, John. He was a veteran of the Narraganset War from Massachusetts in 1685. His land was located in Buxton, Maine.

Ashby, Jabez. He was granted 50 acres in Ulster County, New York for his service as a soldier in the 28th Regiment of Foot in the French and Indian War 2 May 1776.

Ashby, John. He served as a captain in the French and Indian War. He received 3,000 acres of land in Kentucky Co.,Virginia.

Ashcraft, John. He served in the Narraganset War from Connecticut. His heirs received land in Voluntown, Connecticut in 1701.

Ashfield, Christopher. He was granted 200 acres in Albany County, New York for his service as a soldier in the 60th Regiment of Foot in the French and Indian War 13 February 1767.

Ashman, Daniel. He was granted 200 acres in Charlotte County, New York for his service as a noncommissioned officer in the 4th Battalion of the 60th Regiment of Foot in the French and Indian War 12 October 1774.

Aske, Thomas. He was granted 50 acres in Albany County, New York for his service as a soldier in the 80th Regiment of Foot in the French and Indian War 17 September 1765.

Askew, James. He served as a soldier in the French and Indian War under Col. William Byrd and received his 50 acre warrant in Virginia.

Askey, Thomas. He was granted 288 ½ and 348 acres in Berks County, Pennsylvania for his service as a lieutenant in the French and Indian War 3 February 1769.

Askill, Martin. He was granted 50 acres in Albany County, New York for his service as a private in a regiment of foot in the French and Indian War 19 May 1770.

Askins, John. He was a soldier in the 1st Virginia Regiment under Col. William Byrd and assigned his right to 50 acres in Virginia. His service was proved in Augusta County, Virginia 19 October 1779.

Aspinwall, Peter. He served on the expedition to Canada in 1690. Peter Aspinwall received land in Warwick, Massachusetts in 1738.

Aspinwall, Richard. He served as a soldier in the 47th Regiment in the French and Indian War and petitioned for his 50 acres in New York 27 April 1765.

Atherton, Benjamin. He served in the Narraganset War and received land in Templeton, Massachusetts in 1733.

Atherton, Consider. He was a veteran of the expedition to Canada in 1690. His son, Humphrey Atherton, received his land in Ashburnham, Massachusetts in 1736.

Atherton, Joseph. He was a veteran of the expedition to Canada in 1690. His nephew, James Atherton of Harvard, Massachusetts, received his land in Ashburnham, Massachusetts in 1736.

Atherton, Phineas. He was granted 2,000 acres in Tryon County, New York for his service as a lieutenant in an independent company of foot in the French and Indian War 20 January 1775.

Atkin, William. He served as a soldier in the 4th Battalion of the Royal Americans in the French and Indian War and petitioned for land 22

October 1766 in New York.

Atkins, —. He served in the expedition to Canada in 1690. Nathaniel Atkins received his land in Dumbarton, New Hampshire in 1735.

Atkins, James. He served in the Narraganset War from Sandwich, Massachusetts. He received land in Gorham, Maine in 1733.

Atkins, Samuel. He served in the Narraganset War from Barnstable, Massachusetts. He received land in Gorham, Maine in 1733.

Atkins, Stephen. He served as a soldier in the French and Indian War and had a warrant for 50 acres which he assigned in Virginia.

Atkinson, John. He served as a private in the company of Capt. John Posey under Col. William Byrd in the French and Indian War and received his 50 acre warrant in Virginia.

Atkinson, Joseph. He received land in Richmond, New Hampshire in 1765 for the service of an unidentified veteran of the expedition to Canada in 1690.

Atkinson, Joseph. He served in a Virginia Regiment in the French and Indian War. He proved his service in Essex County, Virginia 21 February 1780.

Atkinson, Richard. He served as a noncommissioned officer in the 55th Regiment of Foot in the French and Indian War and received 200 acres in Charlotte County, New York 12 October 1774.

Auchinlek, John. He was granted 3,000 acres in West Florida for his service as a master in the navy in the French and Indian War 18 April 1779.

Auchmuty, Arthur. He was granted 250 acres in Berks County, Pennsylvania for his service in the French and Indian War 1 April 1769.

Austin, Abiel. He served under Capt. John Lovewell from Massachusetts and was in the battle at Pigwacket 8 May 1725. He was from Haverhill, Massachusetts and received his land at Pembroke, New Hampshire.

Austin, Benjamin. He served as a corporal in the Col. George Washington's Regiment in the French and Indian War. His heir at law, John Wilson Austin, assigned his land in Virginia.

Austin, Francis. He served as a sergeant in the 1st Virginia Regiment in the French and Indian War and assigned his right to 200 acres. He was from Frederick County, Virginia 7 September 1779.

Austin, Henry. He served as a sergeant in Col. George Washington's Regiment in the French and Indian War. His heir at law, John Wilson Austin, assigned his 200 acre warrant in Virginia.

Austin, John Wilson. He served as a sergeant in the French and Indian War and received a warrant for 200 acres which he desired to locate in Fincastle County, Virginia 15 March 1774.

Austin, Thomas. He served as a staff officer of Ordnance in the French and

Indian War and petitioned for his 2,000 acres in New York 9 January 1775.

Austin, Zebediah. He served under Capt. John Lovewell from Massachusetts and was in battle 8 May 1725 at Pigwacket. He was from Haverhill, Massachusetts and received his land in Pembroke, New Hampshire.

Avery, James. He was a captain in the Narraganset War from Connecticut and received land in Voluntown, Connecticut in 1701.

Avery, James. He was in the Narraganset War from Connecticut and received land in Voluntown, Connecticut in 1701.

Avery, John. He was in the Narraganset War from Connecticut and received land in Voluntown, Connecticut in 1701.

Avery, Thomas. He was in the Narraganset War from Connecticut and received land in Voluntown, Connecticut in 1701.

Avery, William. He served as a soldier in Capt. John McNeil's Company in the French and Indian War. He proved his right in Mecklenburg County, Virginia 13 March 1780. He assigned his right to 50 acres in Virginia.

Axdill, Thomas. He served on the expedition to Canada in 1690. Daniel Walker received his land in Bethel, Maine in 1767.

Axtence, James. He was granted 50 acres in Albany County, New York for his service as a soldier in the 60th Regiment of Foot in the French and Indian War 3 September 1771.

Ayer, Ebenezer. He served under Capt. John Lovewell from Massachusetts and was in battle at Pigwacket 8 May 1725. He was from Haverhill, Massachusetts and received his land in Pembroke, New Hampshire.

Ayer. William. He served as surgeon under Capt. John Lovewell from Massachusetts and was in battle at Pigwacket 8 May 1725. He was from Haverhill, Massachusetts and received his land in Pembroke, New Hampshire.

Ayers, Peter. He served on the expedition to Canada in 1690 and received land in Poland, Maine in 1739.

Ayres, John. He served on the expedition to Canada in 1690. Samuel Ayres requested Thomas Norton, Jr. to receive his land in Winchendon, Massachusetts in 1736.

Ayres, Thomas. He served as a sergeant in the French and Indian War until he was discharged in 1758. He petitioned for his 200 acres 10 February 1780 in Caroline County, Virginia.

Ayscough, James. He served in the French and Indian War and received 3,000 acres of land in Nova Scotia 17 July 1776.

Babcock, John. He served in the Narraganset War from Connecticut and received his land in Voluntown, Connecticut in 1701.

Babington, Charles. He was granted 2,000 acres in Albany County, New York for his service as a lieutenant in the 55th Regiment of Foot in the French and Indian War 22 May 1770.

Babson, Thomas. He served in the Narraganset War from Salem, Massachusetts. His brother, John Babson, claimed his land in Amherst, New Hampshire. Joseph Williams drew the land.

Bacheler, John. He served in the Narraganset War from Malden, Massachusetts. William Willis received his land for the heirs in Westminster, Massachusetts in 1733.

Bacheler, Joseph. He served in the Narraganset War from Wenham, Massachusetts. His nephew, John Bacheler, received his land in Amherst, New Hampshire in 1734.

Backer, William. He served in the French and Indian War. His service was certified in New York 1 March 1769.

Bacon, Edmund. He served as a corporal in the French and Indian War in Virginia and assigned his warrant for 200 acres.

Badger, John. He served on the expedition to Canada in 1690 and received his land in Poland, Maine in 1739.

Badley, Joseph. He served as a private in the French and Indian War and petitioned for his land in New York 8 July 1765.

Bagley, Jonathan. He received 500 acres of land in Massachusetts for his extraordinary services and for being an engineer in 1755.

Bagnell, John. He served as a private in the 44th Regiment in the French and Indian War and petitioned for a grant of 50 acres in New York 10 October 1766.

Bagnell, William. He served as a sergeant in the French and Indian War and received 200 acres of land in Nova Scotia 7 June 1783.

Bailey, Andrew. He sought land for himself as major and for his servant under Col. Hugh Waddle in the French and Indian War from North Carolina 28 February 1775.

Bailey, Henry. He served as a sergeant in the Virginia Regiment of Regulars in the French and Indian War. He assigned his warrant of 200 acres. He was from Henrico County, Virginia 4 October 1779.

Bailey, Joseph. He served in the Narraganset War from Bridgewater, Massachusetts. His nephew, Ebenezer Hill, claimed his land in Greenwich, Massachusetts in 1737.

Bailey, Peter. He served in the 2nd Virginia Regiment of Regulars in the French and Indian War as a corporal from Virginia. He disposed of his 200 acre warrant. He was from Hanover County, Virginia.

Bailey, Richard. He served as a soldier in one of the Virginia Regiments under Col. William Byrd in the French and Indian War and received his 50 acre warrant. His service was proved in Amherst County, Virginia 6 March 1780.

Bailey, Roger Cock. He served as a corporal in Capt. James Gunn's Company of the Virginia Regiment in the French and Indian War and was in Charlotte County, Virginia 6 March 1780. He assigned his 200 acre warrant in Virginia.

Bailey, William. He served in the French and Indian War and took his land in Fincastle County, Virginia 15 December 1772.

Bain, James. He was granted 2,000 acres in Albany County, New York for his service as a lieutenant in an independent company of foot in the French and Indian War 12 July 1765.

Baines, Hugh. He served as a drummer in the French and Indian War and petitioned for his land in New York 2 May 1768.

Baken, Richard. He was granted 50 acres in Albany County, New York for his service as a soldier in the 80th Regiment of Foot in the French and Indian War 26 July 1765.

Baker, Christian. She was taken prisoner and carried captive to Canada where she was held for twenty-five years. She sought 500 acres for herself and her seven children by her present husband. She was instrumental in regaining several persons who had been carried captive to Canada. She was granted 500 acres in York County, Massachusetts 25 June 1734. The land was to be held in trust for her.

Baker, Daniel. He served in the Narraganset War from Yarmouth, Massachusetts and received land in Gorham, Maine in 1733.

Baker, James. He served as a lieutenant in the 1st Virginia Regiment under Col. George Washington in the French and Indian War and died in the service. His 2,000 acre warrant was delivered to his son and heir, Lawrence Baker, 25 April 1780 in Surry County, Virginia.

Baker, John. He was a veteran of the Narraganset War from Massachusetts in 1685. His grandson, John Baker, received his land in Buxton, Maine.

Baker, John. He served in the Narraganset War from Roxbury, Massachusetts and received land in Bedford, New Hampshire in 1733.

Baker, John. He was granted 200 acres in Albany County, New York for his service as a corporal in the 60th or Royal American Regiment of Foot in the French and Indian War 8 June 1771.

Baker, John. He served as a lieutenant in the French and Indian War from Virginia. His heir, Lawrence Baker, received his 2,000 acres of land.

Baker, Joseph. He served in the Narraganset War from Rehoboth,

Massachusetts. His son, John Baker, claimed his land in Greenwich, Massachusetts in 1737.

Baker, Joshua. He served in the Narraganset War from Connecticut and received land in Voluntown, Connecticut in 1701.

Baker, Richard. He served as a soldier in the 28th Regiment in the French and Indian War and had his service certified 28 January 1767 in New York.

Baker, Samuel. He served in the Narraganset War from Yarmouth, Massachusetts. His son, Samuel Baker, received his land in Gorham, Maine in 1733.

Baker, Samuel. He served in the Narraganset War from Eastham, Massachusetts. He received land in Gorham, Maine in 1733.

Baker, Thomas. He served in the Narraganset War from Lynn, Massachusetts. He claimed his land in Amherst, New Hampshire in 1734.

Baker, Thomas. He served in the Narraganset War from Roxbury, Massachusetts. His brother, John Baker, received his land in Bedford, New Hampshire in 1733.

Baker, Thomas. He served as a soldier for nearly seven years in the French and Indian War under different commanders and had his service certified in Montgomery County, Virginia for his 50 acres of land 3 May 1780.

Baker, William. He was a veteran of the expedition to Canada in 1690. His nephew, Josiah Baker of Boston, Massachusetts, received his land in Ashburnham, Massachusetts in 1736.

Baker, William. He served in the Narraganset War from Eastham, Massachusetts and received land in Gorham, Maine in 1733.

Baker, William. He was granted 200 acres in Albany County, New York for his service as a sergeant in the 28th Regiment of Foot in the French and Indian War 8 October 1771.

Baker, William. He served as a sergeant in the 1st Virginia Regiment under Col. George Washington in the French and Indian War. He petitioned for his 200 acres 17 February 1780 in King William County, Virginia. His service was also proved in Richmond County, Virginia 6 February 1780.

Balch, Samuel. He served as an ensign in the expedition to Canada in 1690. Samuel Balch received his land in Raymond, Maine in 1735.

Baldock, Levy. He served as a soldier in the Virginia Regiment under Col. William Byrd in the French and Indian War and received his 50 acre warrant in February 1780 in Amherst County, Virginia.

Baldock, Richard. He served as a sergeant in the Virginia Regiment under Col. Adam Stephen in the French and Indian War. Levy Baldock, his heir, received his 200 acre warrant in February 1780 in Amherst County, Virginia.

Baldwin, Benjamin. He served under Capt. Noah Wiswall at the battle of Lamprey River and received 150 acres of land from Massachusetts in 1735.

Baldwin, Henry. He served in the Narraganset War and received his land in Templeton, Massachusetts in 1733.

Baldwin, Thomas. He served in the Narraganset War and received his land in Templeton, Massachusetts in 1733.

Ball, Conrad. He served as a non-commissioned officer in the French and Indian War. He was named in New York 8 May 1765.

Ball, Thomas. He served in the Narraganset War and received his land in Templeton, Massachusetts in 1733.

Ball, William. He served in the Virginia Regiment under Col. George Washington in the French and Indian War as a soldier. He received his 50 acre warrant in Rockbridge County, Virginia 7 September 1779.

Ballard, John. He served in the Narraganset War from Lynn, Massachusetts. His son, John Ballard, received his land in Amherst, New Hampshire in 1734.

Ballard, John. He served in the Narraganset War from Andover, Massachusetts. His son, John Ballard, in Amherst, New Hampshire claimed his land in 1734. The land was delivered to Sherebiah Ballard.

Ballard, Nathaniel. He served in the Narraganset War from Lynn, Massachusetts. He applied for his land 4 June 1685. His son, William Ballard, received his land in Amherst, New Hampshire in 1734.

Baller, John. He served as a sergeant in Capt. John Dickenson's Company of Rangers on the Frontier in 1756 and 1757 in the French and Indian War and received his 200 acre warrant in Virginia. He proved his service in Botetourt County, Virginia 11 February 1780.

Ballew, Leonard. He served as a soldier under Col. William Byrd in the French and Indian War. He proved his service in Bedford County, Virginia 27 March 1780.

Baltimore, Christopher. He served as a soldier in Capt. Thomas Fleming's Company under Col. William Peachey in 1756 in the French and Indian War. He received his 50 acre warrant 6 April 1780 in Fluvanna County, Virginia. He also appeared as Christopher Bollimore.

Bane, Joseph. He served as interpreter at Richmond Fort and was upwards of thirty years in the service sometimes as a guide or pilot. He was granted 4,000 acres in York County by Massachusetts.

Banks, Benoni. Unlocated land was granted to him as a reduced officer in New

York 26 June 1773.

Banks, Josiah. He was granted 2,000 acres in Albany County, New York for his service as a lieutenant in an independent company of foot in the French and Indian War 8 June 1771. He also appeared as Josias Banks.

Banks, James. He was granted 200 acres in West Florida for his service as a noncommissioned officer in the French and Indian War 8 September 1777.

Banks, Linn. He served as a sergeant in 1759 and as a sergeant in 1760 under Col. William Byrd in the French and Indian War. He received his 200 acre warrant in February 1780 in Amherst County, Virginia.

Banks, William. He served in the French and Indian War from Virginia. His legal representative, Tunstall Banks, received his 1,000 acres of land in Ohio County, Virginia 20 November 1779.

Banton, William. He served as a soldier in 1760 in Col. William Byrd's Regiment of Regulars in the French and Indian War. He received his 50 acre warrant 7 April 1780 in Chesterfield County, Virginia.

Barber, Edward. He was granted 50 acres in Charlotte County, New York for his service as a soldier in the 27th Regiment of Foot in the French and Indian War 25 January 1773.

Barbour, Philip. He served as a captain under Col. Adam Stephen in the French and Indian War. He also served as a captain on an expedition to the westward under Col. Henry Bouquet and received two 3,000 acre warrants in Virginia.

Barbutt, James. He served as Paymaster General of the Works and Troops in the French and Indian War and received a warrant for 500 acres 23 May 1774 in West Florida. He was granted 500 acres and 1,000 acres in West Florida for his service as a captain on 13 June 1774 and 13 September 1775. He also received 2,000 acres for his service as captain of the batteaus at the reduction of Louisbourg in Quebec in the French and Indian War on 26 July 1774 in West Florida.

Bard, William. He served as an ensign in the 80th Regiment in the French and Indian War and was granted land in New York 13 November 1771.

Bardwell, Robert. He served against the Indians in Massachusetts. On 6 November 1733 his eldest surviving son, Samuel Bardwell, was granted 100 acres on behalf of the heirs for his father, late of Hatfield, deceased.

Barefoot, William. He served as a soldier in the 1st Virginia Regiment under Col. George Washington in the French and Indian War. His service was certified in Essex County, Virginia 21 February 1780. Richard

Barefoot assigned his right to 50 acres.

Barker, Benjamin. He served in Lovewell's War in Massachusetts and received his land in Petersham, Massachusetts.

Barker, Ebenezer. He served in the Narraganset War from Andover, Massachusetts. He received his land in Amherst, New Hampshire in 1734. Edward Phelps drew it.

Barker, Jacob. He served as a subaltern officer in the French and Indian War and received 2,000 acres of land in Nova Scotia 26 July 1782.

Barker, James. He was granted 200 acres in Albany County, New York for his service as a corporal in the 60th Regiment of Foot in the French and Indian War 11 August 1768.

Barker, John. He was granted 50 acres in Amelia Township, South Carolina on the King's bounty for his service in the French and Indian War 21 June 1765.

Barker, Joseph. He was in the Crown Point Expedition and at the battle of Lake George was dangerously wounded. He was from Westfield, Hampshire County, Massachusetts and applied for his land 22 April 1758.

Barker, Robert. He served in the Narraganset War from Duxbury, Massachusetts and received land in Gorham, Maine in 1733.

Barker, Thomas. He served as a soldier for nearly seven years under different commanders in the French and Indian War. He received his 50 acre warrant in May 1780 in Montgomery County, Virginia.

Barksdale, John. He served as a sergeant in the 1st Virginia Regiment in the French and Indian War and petitioned for his 200 acres in February 1780 in Stafford County, Virginia.

Barlow, John. He was granted 50 acres in Albany County, New York for his service as a soldier in the 60th Regiment of Foot in the French and Indian War 6 July 1771.

Barlow, Moses. He served in the Narraganset War from Rochester, Massachusetts. He claimed his land in Greenwich, Massachusetts in 1737.

Barlow, William. He served as a soldier under Col. William Byrd in the 2nd Virginia Regiment in the French and Indian War in 1758. He received a warrant for 50 acres 18 November 1779 in King William County, Virginia.

Barnam, Samuel. He served in the Narraganset War from Barnstable, Massachusetts and received land in Gorham, Maine in 1733.

Barnam, Thomas. He served in the Narraganset War from Norton, Massachusetts. His son, John Barnam, claimed his land in Greenwich,

Massachusetts in 1737.

Barnard, James. He served in the Narraganset War from Watertown, Massachusetts. His nephew-in-law, Joseph Bowman, received his land in Westminster, Massachusetts in 1733.

Barnard, John. He served in the Narraganset War from Watertown, Massachusetts. His son-in-law, Joseph Bowman, received his land in Westminster, Massachusetts in 1733.

Barnard, John. He served in the Narraganset War from Watertown, Massachusetts. He received his land in Westminster, Massachusetts in 1733.

Barnard, Thomas. He served in the Narraganset War from Boston, Massachusetts. His son, Thomas Barnard, received his land in Bedford, New Hampshire in 1733.

Barnes, Francis. He served as a soldier in 1758 under Gen. Forbes in the French and Indian War. He was in Culpeper County, Virginia 17 January 1780. His assigned his 50 acre warrant in Virginia.

Barnes, Henry. He was granted 200 acres in Albany County, New York for his service as a noncommissioned officer in the 4th Battalion in the Royal American or 60th Regiment in the French and Indian War 27 September 1769.

Barnes, Hugh. He served in the French and Indian War. His service was certified in New York 22 November 1766. He was granted 200 acres in Albany County, New York 27 September 1769.

Barnes, Joseph. He was in command of the Marines on board the man-of-war, *Epivier,* under Peter Blake. He sought his land in Georgia 4 October 1763.

Barnes, Joseph. He was granted 50 acres in Albany County, New York for his service as a soldier in the 55th Regiment of Foot in the French and Indian War 27 September 1769.

Barnes, Richard. He shared in the grant of East Greenwich, Rhode Island made to those who had rendered service in King Philip's War. The grant was made 31 October 1677.

Barnes, Samuel. He was granted 50 acres in Albany County, New York for his service as a drummer in a regiment of foot in the French and Indian War 19 May 1770.

Barnes, Thomas. He was granted 50 acres in Connecticut for his service in the Pequot War 11 May 1671.

Barnes, Thomas. He served as a quartermaster sergeant in the French and Indian War and assigned his land warrant for 2,000 acres in Virginia.

Barnet, Fisher. He served as a soldier in the French and Indian War from

Virginia and proved his service for a warrant for 50 acres in King William County, Virginia 18 November 1779.

Barnett, James. He served as a sergeant in Capt. Christian's Company of Regulars on the Cherokee Expedition under Col. William Byrd in 1760 in the French and Indian War. He received his warrant for 200 acres in April 1780 in Botetourt County, Virginia.

Barnett, James. He served as a soldier under Col. William Peachey in the French and Indian War for six months and assigned his 50 acre warrant in Virginia. He was from Buckingham County, Virginia 8 November 1779.

Barnett, Lemuel. He served as a captain in the French and Indian War and received a land warrant for 1,000 acres in Virginia.

Barr, William. He was granted 3,000 acres in Albany County, New York for his service as surgeon in a military hospital in the French and Indian War 28 October 1765.

Barrass, Ralph. He was granted 200 acres in Albany County, New York for his service as a miner in the Royal Regiment of Artillery in the French and Indian War 21 October 1765.

Barrat, Lemuel. He served as a captain in the French and Indian War. He assigned his right to 3,000 acres in Virginia. He also appeared as Lemuel Barnett.

Barrel, John. He was a veteran of the Narraganset War and was from Cambridge, Massachusetts. His brother-in-law, Peter Hay, received his land in Westminster, Massachusetts in 1733.

Barrell, Joseph. He served in the Narraganset War from Lynn, Massachusetts. His grandson, Ebenezer Barrell, received his land in Amherst, New Hampshire in 1734.

Barret, John. He served in the Narraganset War from Plympton, Massachusetts. He claimed his land in Greenwich, Massachusetts in 1737.

Barrett, Charles. He served as a sergeant in Capt. William Phillips's Company of Volunteers in 1763 in the French and Indian War. He petitioned for his 200 acres 14 February 1780 in Louisa County, Virginia.

Barrett, James. He had his service in the French and Indian War certified in New York 28 January 1767.

Barrett, John. He served in the Narraganset War and received land in Templeton, Massachusetts in 1733.

Barrett, Nathaniel. He served in the French and Indian War and took his land in Fincastle County, Virginia 15 December 1772.

Barron, Andrew. He was granted 50 acres in Albany County, New York for his service as a soldier in the 80th Regiment of Foot in the French and

Indian War 5 April 1771.

Barron, Earnest. He was granted 200 acres in Albany County, New York for his service as a noncommissioned officer in the 60th Regiment of Foot in the French and Indian War 5 April 1771.

Barron, Edward. He was granted 2,000 acres in Albany County, New York for his service as a lieutenant in the 60th Regiment of Foot in the French and Indian War 23 August 1764.

Barron, Edward. He served as a subaltern in the French and Indian War and received 2,000 acres in Nova Scotia 29 October 1772.

Barron, Ellis. He served under Capt. John Lovewell from Massachusetts and was killed in May 1725. He was from Concord, Massachusetts, and his land was located in Pembroke, New Hampshire. He also appeared as Elias Barron.

Barron, James. He was granted 200 acres in Gloucester County, New York for his service as a corporal in the 80th Regiment of Foot in the French and Indian War 5 April 1770.

Barron, John. He was granted 200 acres in Charlotte County, New York for his service as a noncommissioned officer in Major Fuller's corps in the French and Indian War 12 October 1774.

Barron, Thomas. He served as a sergeant in the French and Indian War and received his land warrant for 200 acres in Virginia.

Barron, William. He was granted 2,000 acres in Charlotte County, New York for his service as a lieutenant in a corps of rangers in the French and Indian War 23 November 1775.

Barron, William. He was granted 50 acres in Albany County, New York for his service as a soldier in the 44th Regiment of Foot in the French and Indian War 1 April 1772.

Bartee, William. He served as a sergeant under Capt. John Smith in Col. William Byrd's Regiment in the French and Indian War and received his 200 acre warrant in Virginia.

Bartel, Robert. He served on the expedition to Canada in 1690. John Bartel was admitted to his land in Lyndeboro, Maine in 1735.

Bartlet, Christopher. He served in the Narraganset War from Massachusetts in 1685. His son, Christopher Bartlet, received his land in Buxton, Maine.

Bartlet, David. He served on the expedition to Canada in 1690 and received his land in Poland, Maine in 1739.

Bartlet, Samuel. He served on the expedition to Canada in 1690 and received his land in Poland, Maine in 1739.

Bartlett, Henry. He served in the Narraganset War and received his land in

Templeton, Massachusetts in 1733.

Bartlett, Joseph. He was from Almsbury, Massachusetts and petitioned for 200 acres of land 18 March 1735.

Bartlett, Joseph. He served on the expedition to Canada in 1690 and received his land in Bethel, Maine in 1767.

Bartlett, Nathaniel. He received land in Richmond, New Hampshire in 1765 for the service of an unidentified veteran of the expedition to Canada in 1690.

Bartley, Thomas. He was granted 50 acres in Albany County, New York for his service in the 60th or Royal American Regiment in the French and Indian War 8 June 1771.

Barton, Samuel. He served as a corporal on the expedition to Canada in 1690. Samuel Barton petitioned for his land in Raymond, Maine in 1735.

Barton, William. He served as a soldier in the 1st Virginia Regiment under Col. George Washington in the French and Indian War and assigned his warrant for 50 acres in Virginia. He proved his right in Caroline County, Virginia 21 February 1780.

Basdel, John. He served as a sergeant in the French and Indian War. He proved his service for 200 acres in February 1780 in Stafford County, Virginia.

Bason, Edward. He served as a noncommissioned officer in the French and Indian War from Virginia. He received a warrant for 200 acres.

Bass, Robert. He was granted 3,000 acres in Albany County, New York for his service as senior apothecary in a military hospital in the French and Indian War 28 June 1765.

Bass, Samuel. He served in the Narraganset War from Braintree, Massachusetts. He received his land in Bedford, New Hampshire in 1733.

Bassett, William. He served in the Narraganset War from Lynn, Massachusetts. He applied for his land 4 June 1685. His grandson, William Bassett, received his land in Amherst, New Hampshire in 1734.

Bateman, Eleazer. He served in the Narraganset War and received land in Templeton, Massachusetts in 1733.

Bateman, John. He served on the expedition to Canada in 1690. His brother, Eleazer Bateman, received his land in Woburn, Massachusetts in 1738.

Bateman, Nathaniel. He was granted 5,000 acres in West Florida for his service as a captain in the navy at the reduction of Quebec, in the French and Indian War 13 February 1778.

Bates, —. He served on the expedition to Canada in 1690. Benjamin Bates received land in Dumbarton, New Hampshire in 1735.

Bates, Benjamin. He served in the Narraganset War from Hingham,

Massachusetts. His heirs received land in Bedford, New Hampshire in 1733.

Bates, Jacob. He served as a private in the French and Indian War and was granted land in New York 1 April 1767.

Bathrick, Thomas. He was a veteran of the Narraganset War from Cambridge, Massachusetts. His son, Jonathan Bathrick, received his land in Westminster, Massachusetts in 1736.

Baton, Malcolm. He was granted 50 acres in Charlotte County, New York for his service as a soldier in the Royal Highland Regiment of Foot in the French and Indian War 12 July 1775.

Battey, James. He shared in the grant of East Greenwich, Rhode Island made to those who had rendered service in King Philip's War. The grant was made 31 October 1677.

Battey, Sampson. He shared in the grant of East Greenwich, Rhode Island to those who had rendered service in King Philip's War. The grant was made 31 October 1677. He also appeared as Samson Balloo.

Battle, Arthur. He served as a lieutenant of Marines in the French and Indian War and received 2,000 acres in Nova Scotia 4 March 1777.

Baughan, James. He was a soldier in the 2nd Virginia Regiment in the French and Indian War. His heir and brother, John Baughan, assigned his right to 50 acres. He was from Goochland County, Virginia 20 September 1779. John Baughan had the service proved in Essex County, Virginia 21 February 1780. His name may have been James Baugham.

Baughman, Jacob. He served as a soldier in the 1st Virginia Regiment in the French and Indian War and received a warrant for 50 acres in Kentucky County, Virginia. He also appeared as Jacob Bowman.

Bauman, Wilhelm. He was granted 200 acres in Albany County, New York for his service as a noncommissioned officer in the 60th Regiment of Foot in the French and Indian War 30 May 1765.

Baws, John. He served as a corporal in the French and Indian War and had his service certified 22 January 1767 in New York.

Baxter, Alexander. He served as a private in the 42nd Regiment in the French and Indian War and petitioned for land in New York 8 July 1772.

Baxter, Simon. He served as lieutenant and adjutant in General Lyman's Regiment in Connecticut in the French and Indian War and received 2,000 acres of land in Nova Scotia 9 October 1781.

Baxter, Thomas. He served in the Narraganset War from Yarmouth, Massachusetts and received land in Gorham, Maine in 1733.

Bay, Andrew, Rev. Dr. He was a reduced staff officer in the French and Indian

War and received a warrant for 2,000 acres in West Florida 19 July 1774.

Bayard, Daniel. He served as a private in the French and Indian War and petitioned for his land in New York 8 July 1765.

Bayer, George. He served as a subaltern in the French and Indian War and received his land in Nova Scotia 12 October 1771.

Bayley, Henry. He served in the Narraganset War from Beverly, Massachusetts. He claimed his land in Amherst, New Hampshire in 1734.

Baylie, William. He served as storekeeper in H. M.'s hospitals in the French and Indian War and petitioned for a grant of 2,000 acres in New York 23 December 1775.

Bayne, Duncan. He was granted 50 acres in Albany County, New York for his service as a soldier in the 42nd Regiment of Foot in the French and Indian War 7 October 1771.

Beach, Joseph. He served on the expedition to Canada in 1690. Samuel Whitney received his land in Bethel, Maine in 1767.

Beach, Richard. He served in the Narraganset War from Newton, Massachusetts. His brother, Isaac Beach, received his land in Westminster, Massachusetts in 1733.

Beadle, Thomas. He served on the expedition to Canada in 1690. Joseph English was admitted to his land in Lyndeboro, Maine in 1736.

Beal, Caleb. He served on the expedition to Canada in 1690. Caleb Beal received land in Chesterfield, Massachusetts in 1739.

Beal, John. He served on the expedition to Canada in 1690. John Beal received land in Chesterfield, Massachusetts in 1739.

Beal, John. He served on the expedition to Canada in 1690. Samuel Wells was admitted to his land in Lydeboro, Maine in 1736.

Beal, Nathaniel. He served in the Narraganset War from Hingham, Massachusetts. His heirs received land in Bedford, New Hampshire in 1733.

Beal, Zacheriah. He served on the expedition to Canada in 1690 and received land in Poland, Maine in 1739.

Beamass, Ephraim. He served in the Narraganset War from Windham, Massachusetts. He claimed his land in Greenwich, Massachusetts in 1737.

Beamos, Joseph. He served in the Narraganset War from Cambridge, Massachusetts. His son, Joseph Beamos, received his land in Westminster, Massachusetts in 1733.

Bean, James. He served as a soldier and petitioned for his land in Massachusetts 14 April 1761.

Bean, James. He was granted 50 acres in Albany County, New York for his service as a soldier in the 42nd Regiment of Foot in the French and Indian War 30 October 1765.

Beane, Lewis. His heir, Jonathan Beane, was granted 300 acres in York County, Massachusetts 18 December 1735 for his service.

Beard, John. He served as a soldier in an independent company under Col. Henry Bouquet in an expedition against the Indians in 1764. He received a warrant for 50 acres 17 November 1779 in Augusta County, Virginia.

Beard, William. He was granted 200 acres in Albany County, New York for his service as a sergeant in the 17th Regiment of Foot in the French and Indian War 25 October 1765.

Beard, William. He served as an ensign in the 80th Regiment in the French and Indian War and petitioned for 2,000 acres of land in New York 12 November 1771.

Bearmore, George. He served from New Jersey for six months in the French and Indian War. He proved his service in Prince William County, Virginia 11 April 1780.

Bears, James. He was granted 50 acres in Albany County, New York for his service as a soldier in the 60th Regiment of Foot in the French and Indian War 27 September 1769.

Bearse, Joseph. He served in the Narraganset War from Barnstable, Massachusetts and received land in Gorham, Maine in 1733.

Beartman, Godlyr. He served as a private in the 60th Regiment in the French and Indian War and was granted his land in New York 11 November 1772.

Beatie, Robert. He was granted 50 acres in Albany County, New York for his service as a soldier in the 17th Regiment of Foot in the French and Indian War 30 October 1765. He also appeared as Robert Beattey.

Beatley, Robert. He served as a sergeant in the French and Indian War. He was named in New York 1 April 1767.

Beckham, Elijah. He served as a soldier under Capt. John Field in Gen. Forbes's expedition in 1758 in the French and Indian War. He received a warrant for 50 acres which he assigned in Virginia.

Becket, Joseph. He served as a lieutenant under Lord Dunmore in 1772. His service was proved in Yohogania County, Virginia 28 March 1780.

Beckley, Joseph. He served as a lieutenant in the French and Indian War. His 2,000 acre warrant was issued to his heir, Joseph Beckley, in Virginia.

Bedford, William. He served as a corporal in the 4th Battalion of the Royal American Regiment in the French and Indian War. His service was certified in New York 17 October 1766.

Bedortha, Samuel. He was from Springfield, Massachusetts and sought 100 acres in Massachusetts in consideration of his former service. His application was rejected 27 August 1726.

Beebe, Nathaniel. He served in the Narraganset War from Connecticut and received land in Voluntown, Connecticut in 1701.

Beedle, Thomas. He served in the Narraganset War from Boston, Massachusetts. His son, Thomas Beedle, received his land in Bedford, New Hampshire in 1733.

Beeler, Joseph. He commanded a company at Fort Cumberland and was in Col. Henry Bouquet's campaign. He also served as wagon master in Gen. Forbes's campain in the French and Indian War. He assigned his 3,000 acre warrant in Virginia. He was in Ohio County, Virginia 6 March 1780.

Beers, Richard. He served as a lieutenant in the campaign against the Pequot and received 300 acres of land in Massachusetts 19 October 1664. Capt. Richard Beers was slain at Northfield by the Indians in 1675. His relict, Elizabeth Beers, sought his 300 acres of land 19 October 1697.

Beggs, James. He served as surgeon's mate in the French and Indian War and petitioned for a grant of 2,000 acres in Albany County, New York 17 July 1766.

Beirs, Elnathan. He served in the Narraganset War from Watertown, Massachusetts. His son, Richard Beirs, received his land in Westminster, Massachusetts in 1733.

Belcher, Andrew. He served in the Narraganset War from Boston, Massachusetts. His son, Jonathan Belcher, received his land in Bedford, New Hampshire in 1733.

Bell, David. He served as a sergeant in the 55th Regiment in the French and Indian War. He sought his 200 acres of land in New York 15 February 1765.

Bell, David. He served as a captain in the 1st Virginia Regiment in the French and Indian War, and his heir, Henry Bell, received his 3,000 acre warrant in Virginia.

Bell, James. He served in the Narraganset War from Taunton, Massachusetts. His heirs claimed his land in Greenwich, Massachusetts in 1737.

Bell, James. He served as a soldier in an independent company under Col. Henry Bouquet in an expedition against the Indians in 1764. He received a warrant for 50 acres 17 November 1779 in Augusta County, Virginia.

Bell, Robert. He was granted 200 acres in Albany County, New York for his service as a sergeant in the 43rd Regiment of Foot in the French and Indian War 8 July 1771.

Bell, Thomas. He served in the Narraganset War from Connecticut. His heirs received land in Voluntown, Connecticut in 1701.

Bell, Thomas. He served in the Narraganset War from Salem, Massachusetts. He claimed his land in Amherst, New Hampshire in 1734. Samuel Bell drew the land.

Bell, William. He served in the French and Indian War as a sergeant. He assigned his 200 acres of land in Virginia.

Bellamy, James. He was granted 200 acres in Albany County, New York for his service as a sergeant in the 55th Regiment of Foot in the French and Indian War 1 April 1772.

Bellew, Henry. He served as a subaltern in the French and Indian War and received 5,000 acres in Nova Scotia 26 May 1769.

Bellows, —. He served on the expedition to Canada in 1690. His nephew, Moses Bellows, received his land in Bethel, Maine in 1767.

Belshire, Robert. He was granted 100 acres in Albany County, New York for his service as a noncommissioned officer in the 2nd Battalion in the 60th Regiment of Foot in the French and Indian War 1 June 1770. He also appeared as Robert Belsier.

Bemis, Jonathan. He served on the expedition to Canada in 1690. Seth Stone received his land in Alstead, New Hampshire in 1771.

Benham, Joseph. He was a soldier in the Narraganset War. The town of Wallingford, Connecticut granted him five acres of land 27 December 1687.

Bennet, Fisher. He served as a soldier in the 2nd Virginia Regiment under Col. William Byrd in 1758 in the French and Indian War. He received a warrant for 50 acres 28 November 1779 in King William County, Virginia. His name may have been Fisher Barnet.

Bennet, Peter. He served in the Narraganset War from Boston, Massachusetts. His son-in-law, Owen Harris, received his land in Bedford, New Hampshire in 1733.

Bennet, William. He was granted 50 acres in Albany County, New York for his service as a soldier in the 55th Regiment of Foot in the French and Indian War 18 April 1769.

Bennett, Henry. He served in the Narraganset War from Connecticut and received land in Voluntown, Connecticut in 1701.

Bennett, John. He served in the Narraganset War from Connecticut. His heirs received land in Voluntown, Connecticut in 1701.

Bennett, John. He served in Lovewell's War from Massachusetts and received his land in Petersham, Massachusetts.

Bennett, Richard. He was a soldier in the 2nd Virginia Regiment in the French and Indian War and assigned his 50 acres. He was from Goochland County, Virginia.

Bennett, Samuel. He served as chaplain to the garrison at Montreal in the French and Indian War and petitioned for his land in New York 3 March 1767.

Bennett, William. He served in the Narraganset War from Connecticut and received land in Voluntown, Connecticut in 1701.

Bennett, William. He served in the French and Indian War and had his service certified in August 1767 in New York.

Bennis, Simon. He served as a corporal in the 1st Regiment in the French and Indian War and petitioned for his 200 acres of land in New York 18 March 1768. He also appeared as Simon Bemis.

Benson, Joseph. He served in the Narraganset War from Hull, Massachusetts. His son, Joseph Benson, received land in Bedford, New Hampshire in 1733.

Benson, Richard. He was granted 50 acres in Albany County, New York for his service as a soldier in the 80th Regiment of Foot in the French and Indian War 29 October 1765.

Bent, Hopestill. He served on the expedition to Canada in 1690. Peter Bent received his land in Bethel, Maine in 1767.

Bentley, Samuel. He served as a soldier in Capt. Samuel Meredith's Company under Col. William Byrd in the French and Indian War in Virginia. He assigned his right to 50 acres.

Benzell, Adolphus. He was granted 2,000 acres in Charlotte County, New York for his service as a lieutenant in the 50th Regiment of Foot in the French and Indian War 4 July 1772.

Bernard, Nathaniel. He served on the expedition to Canada in 1690 and received his land in Poland, Maine in 1739.

Berry, —. He served on the expedition to Canada in 1690. His son, Thomas Berry of Ipswich, received his land in Winchendon, Massachusetts in 1736.

Berry, George. He served as a sergeant in a ranging company under Lord Dunmore in 1774. His service was proved in Yohogania County, Virginia 28 March 1780.

Berry, John. He was a soldier under Maj. Gen. Jeffery Amherst in the French and Indian War and assigned his right to 50 acres in Virginia. He was in Augusta County, Virginia 19 October 1779.

Berry, Samuel. He served in the Narraganset War from Eastham, Massachusetts. Joseph Doan and Samuel Doan received the land for their father in Gorham, Maine in 1733.

Bessey, Nehemiah. He served in the Narraganset War from Rochester, Massachusetts. His son, Robert Bessey, claimed his land in Greenwich, Massachusetts in 1737.

Best, Christopher. He served as a soldier in the 1st Virginia Regiment under Col. William Byrd and Col. Adam Stephen in the French and Indian War and proved his right to 50 acres of land in December 1779 in Botetourt County, Virginia.

Bethel, John. He served as a soldier in the 1st Virginia Regiment under Col. George Washington in the French and Indian War. He received his 50 acre warrant in May 1780 in Montgomery County, Virginia.

Betkie, John. He served as a sergeant in the 60th Regiment in the French and Indian War and petitioned for his 200 acres in New York 24 October 1764. He also appeared as John Bertkie.

Betts, Abraham. He was granted 50 acres in Albany County, New York for his service as a private in the 60th or Royal American Regiment of Foot in the French and Indian War 30 May 1771.

Betts, John. He was granted 50 acres in Albany County, New York for his service as a private in the 46th Regiment of Foot in the French and Indian War 8 March 1771.

Bevan, John. He was granted 200 acres in Albany County, New York for his service as a sergeant in the 46th Regiment of Foot in the French and Indian War 8 March 1771.

Bevan, John. He was granted 50 acres in Albany County, New York for his service as a private in the 46th Regiment of Foot in the French and Indian War 8 June 1771.

Bevan, William. He was granted 200 acres in Albany County, New York for his service as a sergeant in the 46th Regiment of Foot in the French and Indian War 18 February 1775.

Beyerly, Andrew. He was granted 300 acres in Pennsylvania for his service in the French and Indian War 1 April 1769.

Bibb, Thomas. He served as a 1st lieutenant in Capt. Joseph Fox's Company of Volunteer Rangers in 1755 in the French and Indian War. His 2,000 acres were issued to his executor, Richard Phillips, 13 March 1780 in Louisa County, Virginia.

Bibb, William. He served as a soldier in Capt. Joseph Fox's Company of Volunteer Rangers in 1755 in the French and Indian War. He assigned his 50 acre warrant in Virginia.

Bicker, Henry. He received 1,000 acres of land in West Florida for his service as a subaltern in the French and Indian War 18 April 1776.

Bickerton, Solomon. He was granted 50 acres in Albany County, New York for his service as a soldier in the 47th Regiment of Foot in the French and Indian War 1 April 1772.

Bickley, Joseph. He served as a lieutenant in Capt. William Phillips's Company of Volunteer Rangers in 1763 in the French and Indian War in Virginia. His heir was Joseph Bickley.

Bicknerd, Samuel. He served in the Narraganset War from Boston, Massachusetts. His son, Benjamin Bicknerd, received his land in Bedford, New Hampshire in 1733.

Biddeford, Samuel. He was from York, Massachusetts and served as a captain. He was taken captive and held prisoner in Canada for eight years. He was granted 3,000 acres 6 December 1734 by Massachusetts.

Biddeford, Thomas. He served as a private in the 27th or Inniskilling Regiment in the French and Indian War and petitioned for his land in New York 11 September 1771.

Bigby, John. He served as a soldier in the French and Indian War and received 50 acres in Nova Scotia 9 October 1776.

Biglow, Joshua. He served in the Narraganset War from Watertown, Massachusetts and received his land in Westminster, Massachusetts in 1733.

Bill, John. He served on the expedition to Canada in 1690. Edward Trask petitioned for his land in Raymond, Maine in 1735.

Bill, Philip. He served in the Narraganset War from Connecticut. His heirs received land in Voluntown, Connecticut in 1701.

Bill, Philip. He served in the Narraganset War from Connecticut and received land in Voluntown, Connecticut in 1701.

Bill, Richard. He served in the Narraganset War from Boston, Massachusetts. His son, Richard Bill, received his land in Bedford, New Hampshire in 1733.

Billing, Nathaniel. He served in the Narraganset War. Daniel Billing received his land in Templeton, Massachusetts in 1733.

Billings, Ebenezer. He served in the Narraganset War from Connecticut and received land in Voluntown, Connecticut in 1701.

Billings, William. He served in the Narraganset War from Connecticut and received land in Voluntown, Connecticut in 1701.

Billot, Daniel. He served as a soldier in the 2nd Virginia Regiment in the French and Indian War until it was disbanded. He was dead when his son proved his service in Frederick County, Virginia 3 May 1770.

Billson, Samuel. He served as a soldier in the French and Indian War and petitioned for his 50 acres in New York in 1772.

Bingley, Samuel. He served in the Narraganset War from Braintree, Massachusetts. His son-in-law, Samuel Whitt, received his land in Bedford, New Hampshire in 1733.

Bingley, Thomas. He served in the Narraganset War from Braintree, Massachusetts. His heirs received land in Bedford, New Hampshire in 1733.

Bingman, Christian. He served as a soldier in the French and Indian War and had his service certified in Montgomery County, Virginia 8 March 1780 for his 50 acres of land.

Biram, Henry. He was granted 200 acres in Albany County, New York for his his service as a corporal in the 28th Regiment of Foot in the French and Indian War 25 May 1771.

Bird, Thomas. He was a veteran of the expedition to Canada in 1690. His nephew, Benjamin Bird, Jr., of Dorchester, Massachusetts received his land in Ashburnham, Massachusetts in 1736.

Birdinwinck, Joseph. He was granted 50 acres in Albany County, New York for his service as a soldier in the 60th Regiment of Foot in the French and Indian War 26 September 1765.

Birtch, Thomas. He was granted 200 acres in Albany County, New York for his service as a corporal in the 55th Regiment of Foot in the French and Indian War 1 July 1771.

Bisco, Thomas. He served on the expedition to Canada in 1690. Josiah Bisco received his land in Alstead, New Hampshire in 1771.

Bishop, John. He served as a soldier in the Virginia Regiment under Col. William Byrd in the French and Indian War and assigned his 50 acre warrant in Virginia. He was from Frederick County, Virginia 2 May 1780.

Bishop, Thomas. He served in the Narraganset War from Roxbury, Massachusetts. His son-in-law, Zachariah Chandler, received his land in Bedford, New Hampshire in 1733.

Bixbe, Joseph. He served in the Narraganset War from Boxford, Massachusetts. His son, John Bixbe, claimed his land in Amherst, New Hampshire in 1734.

Blachfield, Thomas. He served in the Narraganset War from Beverly, Massachusetts. His son, Thomas Blachfield, claimed his land in Amherst, Massachusetts in 1734. Robert Hale drew the land.

Black, Henry. He was a soldier under Col. William Byrd in the French and Indian War and was awarded 50 acres in Rockbridge County,

Virginia 7 September 1779.

Black, James. He was granted 100 acres in Albany County, New York for his service as a soldier in the 42nd Regiment of Foot in the French and Indian War 27 March 1775.

Black, James. He served as a captain in Malcolm's Regiment in the French and Indian War and sought his land in New York 5 May 1785.

Black, James. He served as a soldier under Gen. Braddock in 1758 in the French and Indian War. His warrant of 50 acres was issued to his son-in-law, Reubin Long, who had married his daughter and heiress, Anne Black, 21 February 1780 in Culpeper County, Virginia.

Black, John. He served as a private in the 78th Regiment in the French and Indian War and petitioned for his 50 acres in New York.

Black, John. He was granted 200 acres in Albany County, New York for his service as a corporal in the 55th Regiment of Foot in the French and Indian War 11 August 1768.

Black, John. He served as a private in the 63rd Regiment in the French and Indian War and was granted land in New York 13 November 1771.

Black, Robert. He was granted 200 acres in Charlotte County, New York for his service as a noncommissioned officer in the 1st or Royal Regiment of Foot in the French and Indian War 2 October 1774.

Black, William. He served as a soldier in Capt. William Preston's Company of Rangers in 1758 in the French and Indian War and received a warrant for 50 acres 15 February 1780 in Augusta County, Virginia.

Blackburn, Christopher. He served as a sergeant in the Virginia Regiment under Col. William Byrd in the French and Indian War. He received warrants totaling 200 acres 19 November 1779 in King William County, Virginia and on 10 February 1780 in Caroline County, Virginia. He or one of the same name assigned 200 acres.

Blackburn, Edward. He served as an ensign in the Virginia Regiment under Col. George Washington. His heir was his son, George Blackburn, who assigned the warrant for 2,000 acres in Virginia and was in Greenbrier County, Virginia 18 November 1779. He also appeared as Edmund Blackburn.

Blackford, Peter. His heirs were granted 50 acres in Connecticut for his service in the Pequot War 11 May 1671. He also appeared as Peter Blatchford.

Blackwood, Alexander. He was granted 50 acres in Albany County, New York for his service as a soldier in the 46th Regiment of Foot in the French and Indian War 8 June 1771.

Blagg, John. He served as a captain in the French and Indian War. He assigned his right to 3,000 acres of land in Virginia.

Blair, James. He served as a private in the 66th Regiment in the French and Indian War and had his service certified in New York in January 1767.

Blair, John. He proved his service in Capt. Peter Hogg's Company in 1758 in the French and Indian War in Augusta County, Virginia 18 May 1780.

Blair, Samuel. He served in the French and Indian War and proved his service in Berkeley County, Virginia 23 March 1780.

Blair, William. He was granted 50 acres in Albany County, New York for his service as a soldier in a regiment of foot in the French and Indian War 19 May 1770.

Blaisdell, John. He was from Almsbury, Massachusetts. He was in service against the Indians when thirty-one of them were killed or captured. He was awarded 300 acres by Massachusetts 4 December 1734. He had found the land so poor that he asked for an additional 100 acres.

Blaisdell, Jonathan. He served on the expedition to Canada in 1690 and received land in Poland, Maine in 1739.

Blake, Jeremiah. He served in the Narraganset War from Connecticut and received land in Voluntown, Connecticut in 1701.

Blake, William. He was a veteran of the 1690 expedition to Canada. His nephew, Samuel Blake of Taunton, Massachusetts, received his land in Ashburnham, Massachusetts in 1736.

Blake, William. He was granted 200 acres in St. Matthew's Parish, South Carolina on the King's bounty for his service in the French and Indian War 21 July 1775.

Blakeney, Edward. He served as a soldier in the 17th Regiment in the French and Indian War and petitioned for his 50 acres in New York 24 October 1764.

Blakeny, Nicholas. He served as a sergeant in the 60th Regiment in the French and Indian War and returned the survey of his 200 acres in Albany County, New York 14 August 1766.

Blanch, John. He served as a private in the 2nd Troop of Rangers under Capt. James Edward Powell in the French and Indian War and requested 50 acres in Georgia. His application was rejected 5 May 1767.

Blanch, Richard. He served on the expedition to Canada in 1690. Daniel Epes was admitted to his land in Lyndeboro, Maine in 1736.

Blanchard, Stephen. He served in the French and Indian War and petitioned for his land 2 February 1769.

Blane, Archibald. He was granted 2,000 acres in Albany County, New York for his service as a lieutenant in the 60th Regiment of Foot in the French and Indian War 3 May 1765.

Blane, David. He served as a soldier in the French and Indian War and received 50 acres in Nova Scotia 9 October 1776.

Blankenship, Stephen. He served as a soldier in the 1st Virginia Regiment in the French and Indian War. He was taken prisoner and held by the enemy to the end of the war. He received his 50 acre warrant 27 March 1780 in Chesterfield County, Virginia.

Blankford, James. He was a soldier in the 2nd Virginia Regiment in the French and Indian War and assigned his right to 50 acres.

Blankingship, William. He served as a soldier in the Virginia Regiment of Regulars under Col. William Byrd in the French and Indian War. He received his 50 acre warrant 7 April 1780 in Chesterfield County, Virginia. He also appeared as William Blankinship.

Blanton, William. He enlisted in June 1760 and served under Capt. Scott and Col. William Byrd in the French and Indian War until disbanded. He proved his service in Chesterfield County, Virginia 7 April 1780.

Blanton, William. He served as a sergeant in the 1st Virginia Regiment in the French and Indian War and received his 200 acre warrant 15 February 1780 in Greenbrier County, Virginia.

Blany, Joseph. He served on the expedition to Canada in 1690. Joseph Blany was admitted to his land in Lydeboro, Maine in 1736.

Blare, John. He served as a private in the 16th Regiment in the French and Indian War. He was named in New York 16 May 1774.

Blashfield, Thomas. He served on the expedition to Canada in 1690. Henry Blashford petitioned for his land in Raymond, Maine in 1735.[*n.b.* the similarity of the two surnames.]

Blaylock, William. He served as a corporal in the 4th Battalion 60th Regiment in the French and Indian War and petitioned for his land in New York 24 October 1764.

Bledsoe, Joseph. He served as a sergeant in the 1st Virginia Regiment under Col. George Washington and later as an ensign in the French and Indian War. He petitioned for his land in February 1780 in Spotsylvania County, Virginia. He assigned his right to his 2,000 and his 200 acre warrants.

Blewford, Jeremiah. He served in the regiment under Col. William Byrd in the French and Indian War. He was a native of Virginia and was from King George County, Virginia. He assigned his right to 50 acres in Virginia. He also appeared as Jeremiah Blinford and Jeremiah Blueford.

Blinkinsop, Matthew. He was granted 50 acres in Albany County, New York for his service as a soldier in the 46th Regiment of Foot in the French and Indian War 30 October 1765.

Blish, Joseph. He served in the Narraganset War from Barnstable, Massachusetts and received his land in Gorham, Maine in 1733.

Bliss, Thomas. He served in the Narraganset War from Connecticut. His heirs received land in Voluntown, Connecticut in 1701.

Blockson, Richard. He served as a drummer in the Virginia Regiment under Col. William Byrd in the French and Indian War and assigned his 200 acre warrant in Virginia. He also appeared as Richard Bloxom and Richard Boxsom.

Blommart, John. He was granted 2,000 acres in West Florida for his service as a warrant officer in the navy in the French and Indian War 29 April 1776.

Bloomer, Joshua. He served as a major in the French and Indian War and petitioned for his land 30 December 1765 in New York.

Blumfield, William. He served in the Pequot War. He received a grant of land in Soldiers' Field in Hartford, Connecticut.

Blundel, Stephen. He served as a soldier in the 44th Regiment in the French and Indian War. He petitioned for 50 acres in New York 26 May 1772.

Blundell, Christopher. He was granted 2,000 acres in Albany County, New York for his service as storekeeper of Fort George in New York in the French and Indian War 27 July 1765.

Blunkall, William. He served as a corporal in the French and Indian War. He assigned his right to 200 acres in Virginia.

Board, James. He served as a soldier under Col. William Byrd in 1761 and 1762 in the French and Indian War. He was in Bedford County, Virginia 27 March 1780. He assigned his 50 acre warrant.

Bodkin, Henry. He served as a corporal in the French and Indian War and petitioned for his 200 acres in New York 30 January 1775.

Bodkin, Hugh. He proved his service in the French and Indian War in Augusta County, Virginia 21 March 1780.

Bodkin, James. He proved his service in Capt. William Preston's Company of Rangers in the French and Indian War in Augusta County, Virginia 21 March 1780.

Bodkin, John. He proved his service in the French and Indian War in Augusta County, Virginia 21 March 1780.

Bodwell, Henry. He served in the Narraganset War from Massachusetts in 1685. His land was located in Buxton, Maine.

Boen, John. He served on the expedition to Canada in 1690. Daniel Epes was admitted to his land in Lyndeboro, Maine in 1736.

Bogan, John. He served as a private in the 45th Regiment in the French and

Indian War and received his land in New York 17 March 1767.

Boggs, James. He was granted 2,000 acres in Albany County, New York for his service as a surgeon's mate in His Majesty's hospital in the French and Indian War 25 May 1771.

Boits, Jacob. He served in the French and Indian War and petitioned for his land in New York in November 1766.

Bole, George. He was granted 200 acres in Albany County, New York for his service as a corporal in the 28th Regiment of Foot in the French and Indian War 8 June 1771.

Boll, Conrad. He served as a soldier and corporal in the 3rd Battalion 60th Regiment in the French and Indian War and petitioned for his 200 acres in New York 26 April 1765. He also appeared as Conrad Ball and Conrad Bale.

Bolton, —. He served on the expedition to Canada in 1690. Hannah Bolton received his land in Poland, Maine in 1739.

Bolton, Henry. He served as a soldier in one of the Virginia Regiments in 1758 in Capt. Hancock Eustace's Company in the French and Indian War and received a warrant for 50 acres which he assigned in Virginia.

Bolton, Hugh. He served in an independent company of rangers in the French and Indian War and petitioned for land in New York 12 April 1769.

Bolton, John. He served in an independent company of rangers in the French and Indian War and petitioned for land in New York 12 April 1769.

Bolton, Richard. He served in the French and Indian War and took his land in Fincastle County, Virginia 15 December 1772.

Bolton, William. He was granted 50 acres in Albany County, New York for his service as a soldier in the 60th Regiment of Foot in the French and Indian War 3 September 1771.

Bomgardner, Christian. He served in the French and Indian War and took his land in Fincastle County, Virginia 15 December 1772.

Bond, Benjamin. He received land in Alstead, New Hampshire in 1771 for the service of an unidentified veteran of the expedition to Canada in 1690.

Bond, Daniel. He served on the expedition to Canada in 1690. Daniel Bond received his land in Alstead, New Hampshire in 1771.

Bond, James. He served in the French and Indian War from Virginia and assigned his warrant.

Bond, Jonas. He served on the expedition to Canada in 1690. Jonas Bond received his land in Bethel, Maine in 1767.

Bond, Walter. He was granted 50 acres in Gloucester County, New York for his service as a soldier in Capt. Cornelius Cuyler's Company in the 46th Regiment of Foot in the French and Indian War 5 April 1770.

Bonney, Thomas. He served in the Narraganset War from Duxbury, Massachusetts and received his land in Gorham, Maine in 1733.

Bonny, Alexander. He served in the French and Indian War and received his land in Botetourt County, Virginia.

Bootson, —. He served on the expedition to the Canada in 1690. William Bootson claimed his land in Dumbarton, New Hampshire in 1735.

Booth, Thomas. He served as a subaltern in the French and Indian War and assigned his 2,000 acre land warrant in Virginia.

Borrey, David. He was granted 2,000 acres in Albany County, New York for his service as a lieutenant in the 60th Regiment of Foot in the French and Indian War 23 August 1764.

Bottom, Henry. He served in Capt. Hancock Eustace's Company in 1758 in the French and Indian War in Virginia. He received his 50 acres of land 21 October 1779

Boucher, Conrad. He was granted 570 and 619.7 acres in Berks County, Pennsylvania for his service as a captain in the French and Indian War 3 February 1769.

Boudger, John. He was granted 50 acres in Albany County, New York for his service as a soldier in the 55th Regiment of Foot in the French and Indian War 29 October 1765.

Boulware, Newman. He served as a soldier until 1760 in the French and Indian War. His co-heiresses were Margaret Boulware, Jannet Boulware, and Elizabeth Boulware who received his warrant for 50 acres in March 1780 in Caroline County, Virginia and assigned same.

Bourke, William. He was granted 200 acres in Albany County, New York for his service as a corporal in the 55th Regiment of Foot in the French and Indian War 1 April 1772.

Bourne, Richard. He served as a captain and was in the battle at Norridgewock in August 1724 plus other service. He was granted 100 acres in York County, Massachusetts 21 June 1727.

Bouse, John. He served as a sergeant in Capt. Robert Rutherford's Company of Rangers in 1758 and 1759 in the French and Indian War. He received his 200 acre warrant in March 1780 in Berkeley County, Virginia.

Bowden, Thomas. He was granted 200 acres in Albany County, New York for his service as a sergeant in the Royal Regiment of Artillery in the French and Indian War 18 February 1775.

Bowditch, William. He served on the expedition to Canada in 1690. Capt. Joseph Bowditch was admitted to his land in Lyndeboro, Maine in 1736.

Bowen, Andrew. He served as a corporal in the French and Indian War and petitioned for his land in New York 2 May 1768.

Bowen, Henry. He served in the Narraganset War from Woodstock, Connecticut. His grandson, Henry Bowen, claimed his land in Greenwich, Massachusetts in 1737.

Bowen, John. He was granted 2,000 acres in Albany County, New York for his service as a lieutenant in the 45th Regiment of Foot in the French and Indian War 25 May 1771.

Bowen, William. He was granted 50 acres in Gloucester County, New York for his service as a soldier in the 28th Regiment of Foot in the French and Indian War 5 April 1770.

Bower, Nicol. He served as a subaltern in the French and Indian War and received 2,000 acres in Nova Scotia 3 August 1769.

Bower, Nicol. He was granted 2,000 acres in West Florida for his service as a warrant officer in the navy in the French and Indian War 2 March 1778.

Bower, William. He served in the 80th Regiment in the French and Indian War and had his service certified in New York 19 September 1766.

Bowers, Jonathan. He served as a captain in the Narraganset War and received land in Templeton, Massachusetts in 1733.

Bowin, Richard. He served as a soldier in 1758 and 1759 in Capt. Robert Rutherford's Company of Rangers in the French and Indian War. He received his 50 acre warrant 23 March 1780 in Berkeley County, Virginia. He also appeared as Richard Bowen.

Bowles, Charles. He served as a soldier in the French and Indian War and received his land warrant for 50 acres in Virginia.

Bowles, John. He was granted 200 acres in Albany County, New York for his service as a noncommissioned officer in the 28th Regiment of Foot in the French and Indian War 8 March 1771.

Bowles, William. He served as a private in the 2nd Virginia Regiment under Col. William Byrd in the French and Indian War. His heir, Charles Tyler, assigned his 50 acre warrant.

Bowls, Henry. He served as a soldier in Col. William Byrd's Regiment of Regulars in the French and Indian War. He received his 50 acre warrant 5 May 1780 in Chesterfield County, Virginia. He also appeared as Henry Bowles.

Bowman, Edmond. He served as a sergeant in the 80th Regiment in the French and Indian War and petitioned for his land in New York 26 April 1765.

Bowman, Nathanael. He served on the expedition to Canada in 1690 and petitioned for his land in Massachusetts in 1735.

Bowtel, John. He served in the Narraganset War from Reading, Massachusetts. His son, John Bowtel, claimed his land in Amherst, New Hampshire in 1734. Samuel Lampson drew the land.

Bowyer, John. He served as an officer and was entitled to 2,000 acres for his service in the French and Indian War in Virginia. He assigned the warrant.

Bowyer, Thomas. He served as a lieutenant under Col. William Byrd in 1760; he also served in 1762 in the French and Indian War and received his 3,000 acres of land in Virginia. He proved his service in Augusta County, Virginia 24 March 1780.

Bowyer, William. He served as a subaltern in the French and Indian War and had his service certified in Montgomery County, Virginia for his 2,000 acres of land 8 March 1780.

Boyd, Alexander. He served from 31 March 1755 under General Braddock. He was paymaster from 1 May 1756, muster master from February 1757 to May 1759, and lieutenant in the 1st Virginia Regiment 2 May 1759 to March 1762, in the French and Indian War. His service for 13,000 acres of land was certified in Montgomery County, Virginia 3 May 1780. Andrew Boyd, his heir at law, received his 2,000 acre land warrant in 1774.

Boyd, Robert. He served as a mate in H. M.'s Hospital in the French and Indian War and petitioned for his 2,000 acres of land in New York 3 January 1775.

Boyden, John. He served as a lieutenant in Abijah Willard's Regiment in Massachusetts under Gen. Jeffery Amherst in the French and Indian War and assigned his 2,000 acre warrant in Virginia.

Boyle, Charles. He served as a soldier in the 4th Battalion of the Royal Americans in the French and Indian War and petitioned for his land in October 1766 in New York.

Boynton, Benoni. He served in Lovewell's War from Massachusetts and received his land in Petersham, Massachusetts in 1733.

Boynton, Hilkiah. He served on the expedition to Port Royal and was granted his land in Massachusetts 3 December 1735.

Boynton, John. He was a veteran of the Narraganset War from Massachusetts in 1685. His land was located in Buxton, Maine.

Boynton, John. He was a veteran of the Narraganset War from Bradford, Massachusetts. His son, Ichabod Boynton, claimed his land in Amherst, New Hampshire in 1734.

Boynton, Joshua. He was a veteran of the Narraganset War from Massachusetts in 1685. His son, William Boynton, received his land in Buxton,

Maine.

Bozorth, John. He served in the Narraganset War from Bristol, Massachusetts. His son, John Bozorth, claimed his land in Greenwich, Massachusetts in 1737.

Brabstone, Nicholas. He served as a noncommissioned officer in the French and Indian War and received a warrant for 200 acres which he intended to locate in Fincastle County, Virginia 9 February 1774.

Bradbury, Joseph. He served as a soldier under Capt. John Lightfoot in Col. William Byrd's Regiment in 1760 in the French and Indian War. He received his 50 acre warrant 25 May 1780 in Henry County, Virginia. He also appeared as Joseph Bradberry.

Bradbury, William. He received his land in Massachusetts 3 December 1735.

Bradford, John. He served as a corporal in the 2nd Virginia Regiment under Col. William Byrd in the French and Indian War. He petitioned for his 200 acres 16 February 1780 in King William County, Virginia.

Bradford, Joseph. He was granted 250 acres in Amelia Township, South Carolina on the King's bounty for his service in the French and Indian War 21 June 1765. He served as a private.

Bradford, Richard. He served in the 47th Regiment in the French and Indian War. His service was certified in New York 13 April 1774.

Bradford, William. He served in the Narraganset War from Kingston, Massachusetts. His son, John Bradford, claimed his land in Greenwich, Massachusetts in 1737.

Bradley, Daniel. He served on the expedition to Canada in 1690 and received land in Poland, Maine in 1739.

Bradley, Hannah. She lived in Haverhill, Essex County, Massachusetts and received 250 acres for her extraordinary sufferings and services in the former Indian wars 20 June 1738. Her son, Daniel Bradley, and other heirs sought 160 acres out of the 250 which fell into New Hampshire from Massachusetts 3 June 1766. They received 225 acres 6 June 1766.

Bradley, James. He served as a soldier in the French and Indian War and petitioned for 50 acres in New York in 1771.

Bradley, Joseph. He served from Massachusetts and went to Canada with Ensign Sheldon from Massachusetts. His widow received 250 acres.

Bradley, Joseph. He served as a soldier in the French and Indian War from Virginia and received 50 acres of land.

Bradley, Manasses. He was granted 50 acres in Tryon County, New York for his service as a private in the Royal American Regiment of Foot in the French and Indian War 10 September 1774.

Bradley, William. He served in the French and Indian War as an ensign and captain and received 2,000 acres of land in Virginia which he assigned.

Bradshaw, James. He was granted 200 acres in Albany County, New York for his service as a noncommissioned officer in the 60th Regiment of Foot in the French and Indian War 5 April 1771.

Bradstreet, John. He served as a major general in the French and Indian War. He had his petition granted in New York 31 August 1773.

Brady, John. He was granted 393 ½ , 144 ½ , and 629 ½ acres in Berks County, Pennsylvania for his service as a captain in the French and Indian War 3 February 1769.

Brady, William. He served as corporal in the 80th Regiment in the French and Indian War and had his service certified in April 1767 in New York.

Bragdon, Arthur. He served more than forty years in Massachusetts against the Indians and French. He was from Scarborough. He received 100 acres in York County 29 July 1728

Branan, Thomas. He served as a sergeant in the 1st Virginia Regiment under Col. George Washington in the expedition against Fort DuQuesne in 1755 under Gen. Braddock in the French and Indian War. He was in Hampshire County, Virginia 19 August 1779.

Brand, Thomas. He served in the Narraganset War from Connecticut and received his land in Voluntown, Connecticut in 1701.

Brandon, John. He served as a subaltern in the French and Indian War and petitioned for his 2,000 acres in New York 15 January 1775.

Branham, Nathaniel. He served as a soldier in Capt. William Phillips's Company of Volunteer Rangers in 1763 in the French and Indian War and assigned his warrant for 50 acres in Virginia. He was from Louisa County.

Branham, Richard. He served as a sergeant in Col. William Byrd's Regiment in the French and Indian War in 1758 and petitioned for his 200 acres of land in February 1780 in Spotsylvania County, Virginia.

Brannan, Patrick. He was granted 50 acres in Albany County, New York for his service as a private in the 80th Regiment of Foot in the French and Indian War 5 April 1771.

Brannan, Peter. He served as a soldier in Capt. Stewart's Company of Regulars in the French and Indian War in Virginia. He assigned his warrant for 50 acres.

Brattle, Thomas. He served in the Narraganset War from Cambridge, Massachusetts. His grandson, William Brattle, received his land in Westminster, Massachusetts in 1733.

Brecken, Archibald. He was granted 200 acres in Orange County, New York for his service as a sergeant in the 28th Regiment of Foot in the French and Indian War 15 May 1770.

Breckenridge, Robert. He was the captain of a company of soldiers incorporated with a detachment of the 1st Virginia Regiment in 1756 in the expedition under Col. Andrew Lewis against the Shawnee in the French and Indian War. His heir was Alexander Breckenridge of Botetourt County, Virginia in December 1779.

Breden, Joseph. He served on the expedition to Canada in 1690. Joshua Breden received his land in Chesterfield, Massachusetts in 1739.

Breed, John. He served in the Narraganset War from Cambridge, Massachusetts. His son, Ebenezer Breed, received his land in Westminister, Massachusetts in 1733.

Breed, Joseph. He served in the Narraganset War from Massachusetts and petitioned for his land 4 June 1685. He also appeared as Joseph Brade.

Breed, Timothy. He served in the Narraganset War from Lynn, Massachusetts and applied for his land 4 June 1685. His son, Timothy Breed, received his land in Amherst, New Hampshire in1734. He also appeared as Timothy Brade.

Breedlove, Philip. He served as a soldier in an independent corps under Maj. John Field in 1764 in Col. Henry Bouquet's expedition against the Indians. He received a warrant for 50 acres 15 November 1779 in Culpeper County, Virginia.

Breese, John. He served as a corporal in the French and Indian War. He was named in New York 16 May 1774.

Bremner, George. He was granted 50 acres in Albany County, New York for his service as a soldier in the 42nd Regiment of Foot in the French and Indian War 13 February 1767.

Bresler, Robert. He served as a private in the 60th Regiment in the French and Indian War and was granted land in New York 30 May 1779.

Brewer, Daniel. He served on the expedition to Canada in 1690 and received his land in Bethel, Maine in 1767.

Brewer, David. He served as a captain in the French and Indian War and petitioned for 3,000 acres of land 5 May 1766 in Albany County, New York.

Brewer, George. He served as a private in the French and Indian War and petitioned for 50 acres on the King's bounty in South Carolina 8 July 1774. He received the land in Ninety Six District 4 May 1775. He also appeared as George Bruer.

Brewer, Jonathan. He was granted 3,000 acres in Albany County, New York for his service as a captain in an independent company of foot in the French and Indian War 24 November 1770.

Brewer, Jonathan. He was granted 3,000 acres in Albany County, New York for his service as a captain in an independent company of foot in the French and Indian War 25 May 1771.

Brewerton, George, Sr. He served as a captain in the French and Indian War and petitioned for land 30 December 1765 in New York.

Brewerton, George, Jr. He served as a colonel in the French and Indian War and petitioned for land 30 December 1765 in New York.

Breyton, Rev. John. He served as a subaltern in the French and Indian War and received 2,000 acres in Nova Scotia 25 September 1770.

Briant, John. He served in the Narraganset War from Plympton, Massachusetts. He claimed his land in Greenwich, Massachusetts in 1737.

Brick, Thomas. He served in the Narraganset War from Bellingham, Massachusetts. His son, Thomas Brick, claimed his land in Greenwich, Massachusetts in 1737.

Bridge, John. He served as a private in the French and Indian War in Virginia. He assigned his 50 acres.

Bridgeman, John. He served as a soldier in the 60th Regiment in the French and Indian War and petitioned for land in New York 4 April 1768.

Bridges, John. He served on the expedition to Canada in 1690. Caleb Bridges received his land in Bethel, Maine in 1767.

Bridgitts, James. He served as a soldier in the 1st Virginia Regiment under Col. William Byrd in the French and Indian War and assigned his 50 acres warrant in Virginia. He proved his service in Augusta County, Virginia 21 March 1780.

Bridgman, John. He was granted 50 acres in Albany County, New York for his service as a soldier in the 60th Regiment of Foot in the French and Indian War 1 April 1772.

Brier, Richard. He served in the Narraganset War from Massachusetts in 1685. His land was located in Buxton, Maine.

Bright, John. He served in the Narraganset War from Watertown, Massachusetts. His nephew, John Bright, received his land in Westminster, Massachusetts in 1733.

Bright, Thomas. He served as a soldier in Capt. Robert Rutherford's Company of Rangers in 1758 in the French and Indian War. He received his 50 acre warrant in March 1780 in Berkeley County, Virginia.

Brightman, Henry. He shared in the grant of East Greenwich, Rhode Island made to those who had rendered service in King Philip's War. The grant was made 31 October 1677.

Brigs, Joseph. He served in the Narraganset War from Scituate, Massachusetts. His heirs received his land in Bedford, New Hampshire in 1733.

Britton, Edward. He served on the expedition to Canada in 1690. Daniel Epes, Jr. was admitted to his land in Lyndeboro, Maine in 1736.

Broadie, Robert. He was granted 50 acres in Gloucester County, New York for his service as a soldier in the 55th Regiment of Foot in the French and Indian War 5 April 1770.

Brock, George. He served in the 74th Regiment in the French and Indian War. His service was proved in Yohogania County, Virginia 28 February 1780.

Brock, William. He served as a soldier in Capt. William Phillips's Company of Volunteers in the French and Indian War in 1763. He received his warrant for 50 acres 14 February 1780 in Louisa County, Virginia.

Brock, William. He served in Col. Adam Stephen's Regiment in 1762 in the French and Indian War. He was in Orange County, Virginia 23 December 1779.

Brockenbrough, Austin. He served as a subaltern in the French and Indian War and received his 2,000 land warrant in Virginia.

Brockett, Jabez. He was a veteran of the Narraganset War. The town of Wallingford, Connecticut granted him 5 acres for his service 9 April 1688.

Brockett, Samuel. He was a veteran of the Narraganset War. The town of Wallingford, Connecticut granted him 5 acres for his service 16 November 1687.

Brocklebank, Samuel. He served in the Narraganset War in 1685 from Massachusetts. His land was located in Buxton, Maine.

Broddie, Robert. He was granted 50 acres in Albany County, New York for his service as a soldier in the 55th Regiment of Foot in the French and Indian War 27 September 1769.

Brodie, James. He served as a lieutenant in the French and Indian War. His service was certified in New York 25 January 1764.

Brodie, John. He was granted 200 acres in Albany County, New York for his service as a sergeant in a regiment of foot in the French and Indian War 19 May 1770.

Broghghart, Conraet. He applied for a grant of a tract of land on the west side of Sheffields bound for his sundry services in Massachusetts in 1741.

Bromby, Thomas. He served as a soldier in the Virginia Regiment under Col. William Byrd and assigned his 50 acres. He was in Washington County, Virginia 18 January 1780. He also appeared as Thomas

Bromley.

Bronaugh, William. He was an officer in the French and Indian War and received a warrant for 3,000 acres which he assigned in Virginia.

Bronson, John. He served in the Pequot War. He received a grant of land in Soldiers' Field in Hartford, Connecticut.

Brookman, Godlieb. He served in the French and Indian War and petitioned for his land in New York 29 June 1774.

Brooks, Ebenezer. He served on the expedition to Canada in 1690. His nephew, Jonathan Brooks, received his land in Bethel, Maine in 1738.

Brooks, George. He served as a lieutenant in Capt. Marcus Rankin's Company under Maj. Gen. Sir John Irvin, Colonel of His Majesty's 74th Regiment of Foot in the French and Indian War. He received his 2,000 acre warrant in Virginia.

Brooks, Isaac. He served on the expedition to Canada in 1690. His kinsman, John Brooks, received his land in Woburn, Massachusetts in 1738.

Brooks, John. He served on the expedition to Canada in 1690. His grandson, Jonathan Brooks, received his land in Woburn, Massachusetts in 1738.

Brooks, William. He served as a soldier in the French and Indian War and petitioned for 50 acres in New York in 1771.

Broomley, Augustine. He served as a soldier under Capt. John Blagg in the Regulars in the French and Indian War. He was in Botetourt County, Virginia 9 March 1780. He assigned his warrant for 50 acres. He also appeared as Augustine Brumley.

Broughton, William. He served as a sergeant in Capt. Stewart's Company in the French and Indian War and assigned his 200 acre warrant in Virginia.

Browall, Henry. He was granted 200 acres in Albany County, New York for his service as a corporal in the 4th Battalion in the Royal American or 60th Regiment in the French and Indian War 27 September 1769.

Brower, Andrew. He served in the French and Indian War and had his service certified 28 January 1767 in New York.

Brown, Andrew. He served as a soldier in the French and Indian War and petitioned for 50 acres in New York in 1771.

Brown, Andrew. He received his 50 acres of land in West Florida for his service as a private in the French and Indian War 9 April 1777.

Brown, Cornelius. He served as a soldier in the French and Indian War and petitioned for land in New York in November 1766.

Brown, Cornelius. He served in the French and Indian War and petitioned for 250 acres on the King's bounty in South Carolina 2 June 1767.

Brown, David. He was granted 50 acres on Twelve Mile Creek in South

Carolina on the King's bounty for his service in the French and Indian War 25 September 1766.

Brown, Ebenezer. He received land in Alstead, New Hampshire in 1771 for the service of an unidentified veteran in the expedition to Canada in 1690.

Brown, Edmond. He served in the Narraganset War from Reading, Massachusetts. His nephew, Richard Brown, received his land in Westminster, Massachusetts in 1733.

Brown, Edmund. He was a veteran of the Narraganset War from Massachusetts in 1685. His land was located in Buxton, Maine.

Brown, Edward. He served as a soldier in the French and Indian War until he was discharged in 1758. He received his warrant for 50 acres in February 1780 in Caroline County, Virginia.

Brown, George. He served in the Narraganset War from Eastham, Massachusetts. His son, George Brown, received his land in Gorham, Maine in 1733.

Brown, George. He shared in the grant of East Greenwich, Rhode Island made to those who had rendered service in King Philip's War. The grant was made 31 October 1677.

Brown, Gershom. He served in the Narraganset War from Massachusetts in 1685. His land was located in Buxton, Maine.

Brown, Henry. He served as a soldier in Col. William Byrd's Regiment in the French and Indian War in 1758 and received 50 acres. He was in Culpeper County, Virginia 29 September 1779.

Brown, Hercules. He served as a private in the 47th Regiment in the French and Indian War and petitioned for land in New York 10 March 1774.

Brown, James. He served on the expedition to Canada in 1690 and received land in Poland, Maine in 1739.

Brown, James. He served as a corporal in the 80th Regiment in the French and Indian War and had his service certified 30 January 1767 in New York.

Brown, James. He served as a sergeant in the artillery in the French and Indian War. His service was certified in New York 2 May 1774.

Brown, John. He was a veteran of the Narraganset War from Massachusetts in 1685. His land was located in Buxton, Maine. He was from Haverhill.

Brown, John. He was a veteran of the Narraganset War from Massachusetts in 1685. His son, John Brown, received his land in Buxton, Maine.

Brown, John. He was a veteran of the Narraganset War from Swanzy, Massachusetts. His son, John Brown, claimed his land in Greenwich, Massachusetts in 1737.

Brown, John. He was granted 200 acres in Albany County, New York for his service as a drummer in the 16th Regiment of Foot in the French and Indian War 8 October 1765.

Brown, John. He served as a private in the 45th Regiment in the French and Indian War and was granted land in New York 16 April 1767.

Brown, John. He served as a soldier in the 2nd Virginia Regiment of Regulars under Col. William Byrd in 1758 in the French and Indian War. He petitioned for his 50 acres 14 February 1780 in King and Queen County, Virginia.

Brown, John. He had a warrant for 200 acres for his service in the French and Indian War to be surveyed in Augusta County, Virginia in 1774.

Brown, Joseph. He was a veteran of the Narraganset War from Massachusetts in 1685. His land was located in Buxton, Maine.

Brown, Joseph. He served as a captain in many tedious marches against the enemy. He was from Attleborough, Massachusetts. He was granted 100 acres 16 June 1727.

Brown, Michael. He served as a subaltern in the French and Indian War and received his land in Nova Scotia 12 October 1771.

Brown, Peter. He was granted 2,000 acres in Albany County, New York for his service as a lieutenant fireworker in the Royal Regiment of Artillery in the French and Indian War 19 October 1765.

Brown, Peter. He was granted 2,000 acres in Albany County, New York for his service as a surgeon's mate in the French and Indian War 25 May 1771.

Brown, Philip. He received his land in West Florida for his service as a lieutenant in the French and Indian War 11 May 1774.

Brown, Robert. He served in the Narraganset War from Topsfield, Massachusetts. Samuel Kneeland claimed his land in Amherst, New Hampshire in 1734.

Brown, Swanson. He served as a sergeant under Col. William Byrd in the French and Indian War. He proved his service in Fauquier County, Virginia 27 March 1780.

Brown, Thomas. He was a veteran of the Narraganset War from Massachusetts in 1685. His land was located in Buxton, Maine.

Brown, Thomas. He was a veteran of the Narraganset War and was from Cambridge, Massachusetts. His heirs received his land in Westminster, Massachusetts in 1736.

Brown, Thomas. He served in the Narraganset War. His son, Ephraim Brown, received his land in Templeton, Massachusetts in 1733.

Brown, Thomas. He served as deputy chaplain in the 60th Regiment in the French and Indian War and petitioned for 2,000 acres of land in New

York 5 December 1768.

Brown, Thomas. He served as a corporal in the 60th Regiment in the French and Indian War and was granted land in New York 5 February 1772.

Brown, William. He was a veteran of the Narraganset War from Massachusetts in 1685. His land was located in Buxton, Maine.

Brown, William. He served on the expedition to Canada in 1690. Josiah Brown received his land in Alstead, New Hampshire in 1771.

Brown, William. He was granted 50 acres in Albany County, New York for his service as a soldier in the 55th Regiment of Foot in the French and Indian War 28 October 1765.

Brown, William. He was granted 2,000 acres in Albany County, New York for his service as a lieutenant in the Royal American Regiment in the French and Indian War 20 February 1775.

Brown, William. He served as a corporal in the French and Indian War and assigned his 200 acre warrant in Virginia.

Browne, John. He was granted 50 acres in Albany County, New York for his service as a soldier in a regiment of foot in the French and Indian War 19 May 1770.

Browne, John. He was granted 3,000 acres in West Florida for his service as a captain in the French and Indian War 20 February 1772.

Browne, Montfort. He served as an officer in the French and Indian War and received 2,000 acres in West Florida 18 December 1768.

Browne, Thomas. He was granted 200 acres in Albany County, New York for his service as a soldier in the 28th Regiment of Foot in the French and Indian War 14 April 1772.

Bruce, James. He received his land for his service as a warrant officer in the navy in the French and Indian War 21 October 1774 in West Florida.

Bruce, John. He was granted 50 acres in Albany County, New York for his service as a private in the 18th Regiment of Foot in the French and Indian War 8 June 1771.

Bruce, John. He served as a sergeant in the 55th Regiment in the French and Indian War and had his service certified in New York 22 May 1769.

Bruce, Thomas. He had his service in the French and Indian War certified in January 1767 in New York. He served in the 18th Regiment and received 50 acres in Albany County, New York 8 June 1771.

Bruce, William. He served under Capt. Noah Wiswall at the battle at Lamprey River and received 150 acres from Massachusetts in 1735.

Bruckley, John. He was granted 50 acres in Albany County, New York for his service as a soldier in the 28th Regiment of Foot in the French and Indian War 1 April 1772.

Brumley, John. He served as a soldier in the 2nd Virginia Regiment under Col. William Byrd in the French and Indian War and proved his service 21 February 1780 in Culpeper County, Virginia. He was entitled to 50 acres of land.

Bruyer, John. He was granted 2,000 acres in Gloucester County, New York for his service as a lieutenant in the 56th Regiment of Foot in the French and Indian War 4 October 1775. He also appeared as John Desbruyeres.

Bryan, Thomas. He was granted 200 acres in Charlotte County, New York for his service as a noncommissioned officer in the 28th Regiment of Foot in the French and Indian War 12 October 1774.

Bryant, Abraham. He served on the expedition to Canada in 1690. Isaac Baldwin received his land in Bethel, Maine in 1767.

Bryant, Samuel. He served in the Narraganset War from Barnstable, Massachusetts. He received land in Gorham, Maine in 1733.

Bryant, Nathaniel. He received land in Richmond, New Hampshire in 1765 for the service of an unidentified veteran of the expedition to Canada in 1690.

Bryant, William. He served as surveyor to His Majesty's Hospital in the West Indies during the French and Indian War per certificate in West Florida 23 November 1777.

Buchanan, James. He received 200 acres of land in West Florida for his service as a noncommissioned officer in the Royal Regiment of Artillery in the French and Indian War 17 October 1774.

Buchanan, James. He served as a lieutenant under Capt. Alexander and Col. Thomas Nash in the campaign against the Shawnee in the French and Indian War in 1757. He served for four months until the corps was disbanded. His eldest brother and heir, Alexander Buchanan, received his 2,000 acre warrant in May 1780 in Montgomery County, Virginia.

Buchanan, John. He served as a captain of a company on the frontiers of Augusta County from April 1758 to May 1759 in the French and Indian War. His warrant for 3,000 acres was issued to his son, James Buchanan, in April 1780 in Montgomery County, Virginia.

Buchanan, Robert. He served as a soldier in the French and Indian and had his service certified in Montgomery County, Virginia for his 50 acres of land 5 April 1780.

Buckanan, Archibald. He served as a sergeant in Capt. William Preston's Company of Rangers about ten months in 1756 and 1757 in the French and Indian War. He received his 200 acre warrant in April 1780 in Montgomery County, Virginia. He also appeared as

Archibald Buchanan.

Buck, Robert. He received land in Richmond, New Hampshire in 1765 for the service of an unidentified veteran of the expedition to Canada in 1690.

Buckler, Robert, Jr. He served as a soldier in 1758 in Capt. Robert Rutherford's Company of Rangers in the French and Indian War. He received his 50 acre warrant in March 1780 in Berkeley County, Virginia. [His identity had been interpreted as Robert Buckles, but that does not seem to the correct rendering.]

Buckley, Butler. He served as a soldier in Capt. Thomas Fleming's Company in the 1st Virginia Regiment in the French and Indian War and assigned his warrant for 50 acres in Virginia.

Buckley, John. He served as a soldier in the 28th Regiment in the French and Indian War and petitioned for his land in New York 4 April 1768.

Buckley, Peter. He served in the Narraganset War. His son, Joseph Buckley, received his land in Templeton, Massachusetts in 1733.

Buckner, Mordecai. He served as a captain in the Virginia Regiment under Col. Adam Stephen in 1758 in the French and Indian War. He was also quartermaster in 1755. He assigned his right to 3,000 acres in Virginia. He had another warrant for 2,000 acres for his service as captain and quartermaster. He proved his service in Essex County, Virginia 20 March 1780.

Budd, John. He served as a soldier in the French and Indian War from Virginia and received a warrant for 50 acres.

Buetz, Francis. He was granted 50 acres in Craven County, South Carolina on the King's bounty for his service in the French and Indian War 21 June 1765.

Buffington, David. He was granted 2,000 acres in Albany County, New York for his service as a conductor in the Royal Regiment of Artillery in the French and Indian War 13 July 1770.

Buffington, Thomas. He served in the Narraganset War from Swanzy, Massachusetts. He claimed his land in Greenwich, Massachusetts in 1737.

Buford, James. He served as a sergeant in Capt. John Field's Company under Col. William Byrd in the French and Indian War and died in 1758. His 200 acres of land were awarded to his heir, John Buford, 26 October 1779 in Petersburg, Virginia.

Buford, John. He served as a soldier in the French and Indian War and received a land warrant for 50 acres in Virginia.

Buford, Thomas. He served as a captain in the French and Indian War and was entitled to 3,000 acres which he desired to locate in Fincastle County,

Virginia. The land was issued to his children, William Buford and Nancy Buford.

Buford, Thomas. He served as a sergeant under Gen. Braddock in the French and Indian War from 1754 to 1755 and again in 1756. He was a lieutenant under Col. George Washington. He was a lieutenant under Col. William Byrd in 1758 and in another regiment under Col. George Washington in 1759. His heir was John Buford whose guardian was James Buford who was also executor of the said Thomas Buford. Five warrants for 2000, 2000, 2000, 200, and 200 acres were issued in Feb. 1780 in Bedford County, Virginia.

Bugbee, Benjamin. He served on the expedition to Canada. Benjamin Bugbee received land in Warwick, Massachusetts in 1738.

Bugg, John. He was granted 50 acres in Albany County, New York for his service as a soldier in the 46th Regiment of Foot in the French and Indian War 30 October 1765.

Bull, John. He served in the Narraganset War from Hingham, Massachusetts. He applied for his land 4 June 1685. Thomas Vickers received his land in Bedford, New Hampshire in 1733.

Bull, John. He served as a captain in the 3rd Pennsylvania Regiment under Col. Hugh Mercer in the French and Indian War until the unit was disbanded in December 1759. He moved to Virginia in May 1779 and applied for his bounty land in Frederick County, Virginia 6 February 1781.

Bull, Joseph. He served as a lieutenant in the French and Indian War and petitioned for his land 30 December 1765 in New York.

Bull, Thomas. He was granted a share of land in Connecticut for his service as a lieutenant in the Pequot War 2 March 1651/2. He received another grant in exchange for same 12 October 1671.

Bullard, Jacob. He served in the Narraganset War from Watertown, Massachusetts. His nephew, Joseph Ball, received his land in Westminster, Massachusetts in 1733.

Bullard, John. He served a soldier in the 1st Virginia Regiment under Col. George Washington in the French and Indian War. He assigned his right to 50 acres in Virginia. He was in Essex County, Virginia 21 February 1780.

Bullen, Thomas. He served in the Narraganset War from Horseneck, Massachusetts. His son, Thomas Bullen, claimed his land in Greenwich, Massachusetts in 1737.

Bullet, Benjamin. He served as an ensign in a Virginia Regiment in the French and Indian War and was slain about April 1757. His heir, Cuthbert

Bullet, was due his 2,000 acres of land.

Bullett, Thomas. He served as an officer in the French and Indian War and received his land in Botetourt County, Virginia. He devised the land to Cuthbert Bullett who patented the land in Greenbrier County, Virginia 20 November 1779.

Bullman, Dr. Alexander. He served against the Indian enemy from Massachusetts. He sought 100 acres in York County, but his application was rejected 25 August 1727.

Bullock, James. He served as an ensign in a volunteer company under Capt. William Phillips in 1763 in the French and Indian War. He petitioned for 2,000 acres 2 March 1780 in Hanover County, Virginia.

Bullock, John. He served in the Narraganset War from Salem, Massachusetts. His son, John Bullock, claimed his land in Amherst, New Hampshire in 1734.

Bullock, Richard. He served as a soldier in the regiment under Col. William Byrd in the French and Indian War in 1758. He assigned his right to 50 acres in Virginia. He was in Orange County, Virginia 25 November 1779.

Bumstead, Jeremiah. He was wounded in the Indian War and was granted 200 acres by Massachusetts 6 May 1685 at which time he was also authorized to maintain an ordinary.

Bunce, Thomas. He was granted 60 acres in Connecticut for his service in the Pequot War 11 May 1671.

Bunteel, John. He was granted 200 acres in Albany County, New York for his service as a corporal in the 28th Regiment of Foot in the French and Indian War 1 April 1772.

Burdon, George. He served as a lieutenant in the French and Indian War and petitioned for 600 acres as other officers of supply in West Florida 17 May 1779.

Burdue, Moses. He served in the Narraganset War and received land in Templeton, Massachusetts in 1733.

Burg, —. He served on the expedition to Canada in 1690. Joseph Burg received land in Dumbarton, New Hampshire in 1735.

Burk, John. He served as a drummer in the French and Indian War and petitioned for land in New York 4 April 1768.

Burk, Thomas. He served as a soldier in the French and Indian War. His 50 acre warrant was issued to his heir, Richard Burk, in Essex County, Virginia where the service was proved 21 February 1780.

Burke, Edward. He served as a noncommissioned officer in the 80th Regiment in the French and Indian War and had his service certified in New

York 5 March 1767. He assigned his right to his land.

Burke, John. He was granted 200 acres in Albany County, New York for his service as a drummer in the 55th Regiment of Foot in the French and Indian War 1 April 1772.

Burke, William. He served in the French and Indian War and had his service certified in New York in 1768.

Burly, Simon. He served as a soldier in the French and Indian War and received his land in New York 17 March 1767.

Burmley, John. He served as a soldier in the 2nd Virginia Regiment under Col. William Byrd in the French and Indian War. He assigned his right to 50 acres in Virginia.

Burnet, James. He served as a soldier in Col. William Peachey's Virginia Regiment for six months in the French and Indian War. He sought his 50 acre warrant 8 November 1779 in Buckingham County, Virginia.

Burnett, Thomas. He served as a captain in the Royal Navy in the French and Indian War and received 5,000 acres in Nova Scotia 13 October 1780.

Burnham, Richard. He served in the Narraganset War from Bridgewater, Massachusetts. His daughter, Abigail Hubbard, claimed his land in Greenwich, Massachusetts in 1737.

Burnom, James. He served in Narraganset War from Massachusetts in 1685. His son, Thomas Burnom, received his land in Buxton, Maine.

Burns, George. He served as a subaltern officer in the French and Indian War and received 2,000 acres of land in Nova Scotia.

Burns, Thomas. He was granted 50 acres in Ulster County, New York for his service as a soldier in the 4th Battalion of the 60th Regiment of Foot in the French and Indian War 2 May 1775.

Burns, William. He was granted 50 acres in Albany County, New York for his service as a private in the 18th Regiment of Foot in the French and Indian War 8 June 1771.

Burr, Jonathan. He served on the expedition to Canada in 1690. Jonathan Burr received land in Chesterfield, Massachusetts in 1739.

Burridge, John. He served on the expedition to Canada in 1690. Ephraim Burridge received his land in Alstead, New Hampshire in 1771.

Burrill, John. He served in the Narraganset War from Lynn, Massachusetts. His brother, Ebenezer Burrill, received his land in Amherst, New Hampshire in 1734.

Burrill, John. He served in the Narraganset War from Weymouth, Massachusetts and received land in Bedford, New Hampshire in 1733.

Burros, Joseph. He was granted 50 acres in Albany County, New York for his service as a soldier in the Inniskilling Regiment of Foot in the French and Indian War 30 May 1772.

Burt, Thomas. He served on the expedition to Canada in 1690. Richard Burt received his land in Bethel, Maine in 1767.

Burt, William. He served in the Narraganset War from Massachusetts. His heirs from Charleston, Massachusetts received his land in Westminster, Massachusetts in 1733.

Burtch, Jonathan. He served in the Narraganset War from Connecticut and received land in Voluntown, Connecticut in 1701.

Burton, John. He served as a soldier in the 1st Virginia Regiment under Col. William Byrd in the French and Indian War and received his 50 acre warrant 21 March 1780 in Augusta County, Virginia.

Burton, Ralph. He served as a major general in the French and Indian War. He was named in New York 15 April 1767.

Burton, Robert. He served as colonel commanding the 95th Regiment in the French and Indian War in New York and qualified for 5,000 acres of land 22 October 1764.

Burton, Samuel. He served as a private under Col. William Byrd in the French and Indian War in Virginia and petitioned for his 50 acres in March 1780 in Prince Edward County, Virginia.

Busbee, Elisha. He served in the Narraganset War from Pembrook, Massachusetts. His son, Elisha Busbee, claimed his land in Greenwich, Massachusetts in 1737.

Busbee, Hopestill. He served in the Narraganset War from Pembrook, Massachusetts. His nephew, Elisha Busbee, claimed his land in Greenwich, Massachusetts in 1737.

Bush, John. He served in the Narraganset War. John Overing received his land for him in Templeton, Massachusetts in 1733.

Bushnell, Richard. He served in the Narraganset War from Connecticut and received land in Voluntown, Connecticut in 1701.

Buss, Joseph. He served in the Narraganset War. Samuel Chandler claimed his land in Templeton, Massachusetts in 1733. Chandler called him his father.

Butler, John. He was granted 2,000 acres in Albany County, New York for his service as a lieutenant in an independent company of foot in the French and Indian War 24 November 1770.

Butler, John. He was granted 200 acres in Albany County, New York for his service as a corporal in the 28th Regiment of Foot in the French and Indian War 25 May 1771.

Butler, Zebulon. He was granted 3,000 acres in West Florida for his service as a captain in the French and Indian War 15 April 1775.

Butrick, George. He was granted 2,000 acres in Albany County, New York for his service as Quartermaster in the 46th Regiment of Foot in the French and Indian War 9 January 1768. He also appeared as George Buttrick.

Butt, Richard. He was a veteran of the expedition to Canada in 1690. His nephew, Samuel Butt of Dorchester, Massachusetts, received his land in Ashburnham, Massachusetts in 1735.

Butt, William. He was a soldier in the Virginia Regiment under Col. George Washington in the French and Indian War and assigned his warrant for 50 acres.

Buttle, Arthur. He served as a lieutenant in the French and Indian War and received 2,000 acres of land in Nova Scotia 28 February 1777.

Buttrick, Samuel. He served in the Narraganset War. Jonathan Buttrick for the heirs received his land in Templeton, Massachusetts in 1733.

Buxton, Daniel. He served as a soldier in the 80th Regiment in the French and Indian War and petitioned for his 50 acres in New York 27 April 1765.

Buzzard, Peter. He was granted 200 acres in Albany County, New York for his service as a drummer in the 4th Battalion in the 60th Regiment of Foot in the French and Indian War 18 July 1770.

Byels, Jonathan. He served in the Narraganset War from Beverly, Massachusetts. He claimed his land in Amherst, New Hampshire in 1734.

Byrd, William. He was a captain from Henrico County, Virginia and was to assemble 50 armed men on the south side of James River one mile and a half below the falls in return for a tract of land continuing five miles upriver and a mile back into the woods and also land on the north side of River half a mile below the falls continuing five miles up the river and two miles into the woods by act of April 1679.

Byrd, William. He served in the 2nd Virginia Regiment of Regulars until 1758. In his lifetime he received a warrant for 5,000 acres for his service as colonel in the Virginia Regiment in 1759, 1760, and part of 1762 in the French and Indian War. His executrix, Mary Byrd, petitioned for warrants for 1,000, 1,000, 1,000, 1,000, 1,000, and 5,000 acres 9 February 1780 in Williamsburg, Virginia and 1 March 1780 in Charles City County, Virginia.

Byrn, Barnaby. He was granted 2,000 acres in Albany County, New York for his service as a lieutenant in an independent company in the French and Indian War 7 February 1765.

Byrns, James. He served as a soldier in the French and Indian War and received his 50 acre land warrant in Virginia which he assigned.

Byrnsides, James. He served as a sergeant in one of the Virginia regiments in the French and Indian War. He received a warrant for 200 acres 17 November 1779 in Greenbrier County, Virginia.

Cadare, John. He served as a soldier in Capt. William Preston's Company of Rangers from the fall of 1755 to June 1756 in the French and Indian War. His warrant for 50 acres was issued to his legal representative, Israel Christian, in April 1780 in Montgomery County, Virginia. His name may have been John Codare.

Cage, Benjamin. He served as a soldier in Capt. Richard Dogget's Company of the Virginia Regiment in the French and Indian War. He received his 50 acre warrant in Virginia.

Cahoon, Robert. He was granted 200 acres in Albany County, New York for his service as a noncommissioned officer in an independent company of foot in the French and Indian War 8 March 1771.

Calbreath, Thomas. He served as a soldier in Capt. Peter Hogg's Company of Rangers in 1758 in the French and Indian War and received his 50 acre warrant in Virginia.

Calder, James. He served as a captain in the French and Indian War. His widow, Mary Calder, married secondly Lloyd Danberry. In behalf of the veteran's son, William Coventry Calder, they petitioned for 3,000 acres land in New York 5 October 1772.

Caldwell, Dilingham. He served on the expedition to Canada in 1690. He requested that Capt. Edward Eveleth to receive his land in Winchendon, Massachusetts in 1736.

Caldwell, William. He served on the expedition to Canada in 1690. His brother, Nathaniel Caldwell of Ipswich, Massachusetts claimed his land in Winchendon, Massachusetts in 1736.

Calhoun, Robert. He was granted 200 acres in Albany County, New York for his service as a sergeant in an independent company of foot in the French and Indian War 8 June 1771.

Callaghan, John. He was granted 50 acres in Albany County, New York for his service as a private in the 44th Regiment of Foot in the French and Indian War 8 June 1771.

Callaghan, Timothy. He was granted 50 acres in Albany County, New York for his service as a soldier in the 60th Regiment of Foot in the French and Indian War 17 September 1765.

Callahan, John. He served as a soldier in the 1st Virginia Regiment under Col. George Washington in the French and Indian War. He proved his service in Middlesex County, Virginia 22 May 1780.

Callane, John. He served in the French and Indian War and was entitled to 50 acres which he desired to locate in Fincastle County, Virginia in 1774.

Callannan, John. He served as a soldier in the French and Indian War and petitioned for his land in New York 6 February 1764.

Callow, Daniel. He served in 80th Regiment in the French and Indian War and petitioned for land in New York 22 October 1766.

Calvery, Edward. He shared in the grant of East Greenwich, Rhode Island made to those who had rendered service in King Philip's War. The grant was made 31 October 1677.

Cameron, Allen. He was granted 200 acres in Albany County, New York for his service as a corporal in the 78th Regiment of Foot in the French and Indian War 22 May 1765.

Cameron, Allen. He was granted 200 acres in Albany County, New York for his service as a sergeant in the 77th Regiment of Foot in the French and Indian War 29 May 1765.

Cameron, Donald. He was granted 50 acres in Albany County, New York for his service as a soldier in the 77th Regiment of Foot in the French and Indian War 13 May 1765.

Cameron, Donald. He served as a soldier in the French and Indian War and received 50 acres in Nova Scotia 8 February 1775.

Cameron, Duncan. He served as a corporal in the 42nd Regiment in the French and Indian War and petitioned for his 200 acres of land in New York 20 March 1770.

Cameron, Evan. He was granted 50 acres in Albany County, New York for his service as a soldier in the 77th Regiment of Foot in the French and Indian War 13 May 1765.

Cameron, Evan. He was granted 200 acres in Albany County, New York for his service as a corporal in the 78th Regiment of Foot in the French and Indian War 26 July 1765.

Cameron, John. He was granted 50 acres in Albany County, New York for his service as a soldier in the 42nd Regiment of Foot in the French and Indian War 7 October 1771.

Cameron, John. He served as a private in 2nd Battalion of the 60th Regiment in the French and Indian War and petitioned for a grant of an island of about 30 acres in Lake George, New York 21 September 1773.

Cameron, John. He served as a soldier in the French and Indian War. He assigned his right to 50 acres to William McDonald who received same in Nova Scotia 7 January 1781.

Cameron, John. He was granted 150 acres in Craven County, South Carolina on the King's bounty 21 June 1765. He served as a private in the French and Indian War.

Cammock, John. He was granted 50 acres in Albany County, New York for his service as a private in the 46th Regiment of Foot in the French and Indian War 25 May 1771.

Camp, Wolf. He served as a private in the 60th Regiment in the French and Indian War and petitioned for land in New York 22 May 1769.

Camp, William. He served as a corporal in the 1st Virginia Regiment in Capt. Christopher Hudson's company under Col. George Washington in the French and Indian War and assigned his right to 50 acres in Virginia. He also appeared as William Cempt. He was in Hanover County, Virginia 3 February 1780.

Campbell, Alexander. He was granted 2,000 acres in Albany County, New York for his service as a subaltern in the 77th Regiment of Foot in the French and Indian War 19 October 1765.

Campbell, Alexander. He was granted 200 acres in Albany County, New York for his service as a quartermaster sergeant for five years in the 80th Regiment of Foot in the French and Indian War 30 October 1765. He had previously served in the 42nd Regiment for a decade.

Campbell, Alexander. He was granted 50 acres in Albany County, New York for his service as a soldier in the 42nd Regiment of Foot in the French and Indian War 30 October 1765.

Campbell, Alexander. He was granted 50 acres in Charlotte County, New York for his service as a soldier in the 42nd Regiment of Foot in the French and Indian War 1 April 1775.

Campbell, Alexander. He was granted 1,000 acres in West Florida for his service as a captain in the French and Indian War 19 March 1779.

Campbell, Allen. He was granted 5,000 acres in Albany County, New York for his service as a field officer in the 2nd Battalion of the Royal Highland Regiment of Foot in the French and Indian War 11 July 1764.

Campbell, Andrew. He served as a private in the French and Indian War and petitioned for 50 acres on the King's bounty in South Carolina 3 March 1767.

Campbell, Archibald. He was granted 2,000 acres in Albany County, New York for his service as a lieutenant in the 42nd Regiment of Foot in the French and Indian War 11 October 1765.

Campbell, Archibald. He was granted 50 acres in Albany County, New York for his service as a soldier in the 42nd Regiment of Foot in the French and Indian War 30 October 1765.

Campbell, Arthur. He served as a subaltern and was entitled to a warrant for 2,000 acres which he desired to locate in Fincastle County, Virginia 15 December 1773.

Campbell, Daniel. He served as a soldier in the 28th Regiment in the French and Indian War and petitioned for his land 18 October 1766 in New York.

Campbell, Daniel. He was granted 50 acres in Gloucester County, New York for his service as a soldier in the 46th Regiment of Foot in the French and Indian War 5 April 1770.

Campbell, Donald. He was granted 2,000 acres in Albany County, New York for his service as a lieutenant in the 77th Regiment of Foot in the French and Indian War 19 October 1765.

Campbell, Duncan. He was granted 3,000 acres in Albany County, New York for his service as a lieutenant in the 42nd Regiment of Foot in the French and Indian War 21 June 1770.

Campbell, Duncan. He was granted 2,000 acres in Tryon County, New York for his service as quartermaster in the 42nd or Royal Highland Regiment in the French and Indian War 5 April 1774.

Campbell, Duncan. He served as a corporal in the 77th Regiment in the French and Indian War and returned his survey 5 November 1764.

Campbell, James. He was granted 200 acres in Albany County, New York for his service as a sergeant in the 77th Regiment of Foot in the French and Indian War 29 October 1765.

Campbell, James. He was granted 50 acres in Albany County, New York for his service as a soldier in the 42nd Regiment of Foot in the French and Indian War 30 October 1765.

Campbell, John. He was granted 50 acres in Albany County, New York for his service as a soldier in an independent company of foot in the 60th or Royal American Regiment of Foot in the French and Indian War 30 May 1772.

Campbell, John. He served as a captain in the French and Indian War. He petitioned for his 2,000 acres in New York 17 December 1762. He also petitioned for 5,000 acres in behalf of his brothers german, Capt. Archibald Campbell and Lt. Alexander Campbell, 30 May 1767 in New York.

Campbell, John. He was granted 200 acres in Charlotte County, New York for for his service as a sergeant in the 77th Regiment of Foot in the French and Indian War 12 October 1774.

Campbell, John. He was granted 200 acres in Charlotte County, New York for his service as a corporal in the 77th Regiment of Foot in the French and Indian War 12 October 1774.

Campbell, John. He was granted 300 acres in Pennsylvania for his service in the French and Indian War 1 April 1769.

Campbell, John. He was a soldier in the Virginia Regiment under Col. William Byrd in the French and Indian War. He was in Rockbridge County, Virginia in 1779. He assigned his 50 acres.

Campbell, John. He served as an officer in the French and Indian War and assigned his 2,000 acre warrant in Virginia.

Campbell, Moses. He was granted 200 acres in Albany County, New York for his service as a sergeant in the 2nd Battalion of the 42nd Regiment of Foot in the French and Indian War 30 March 1765.

Campbell, Robert. He was granted 3,000 acres in Albany County, New York for his service as a captain in the 60th Regiment of Foot in the French and Indian War 23 August 1764.

Campbell, Robert. He served as a soldier in Capt. William Christian's Company of Regular Additional Troops under Col. William Byrd on the Cherokee Expedition in 1760. He was also in Capt. John Blagg's Company of Regulars in the Virginia Regiment commanded by Col. Adam Stephen at Fredericksburg in 1762 in the French and Indian War. He received his 50 acre warrant in April 1780 in Montgomery County, Virginia.

Campbell, Samuel. He served as a soldier in Capt. William Preston's Company in 1758 in the French and Indian War and received his 50 acre warrant 15 February 1780 in Greenbrier County, Virginia.

Campbell, Tamberlain. He served as a subaltern officer in the French and Indian War and received 2,000 acres in Nova Scotia 3 August 1782.

Campbell, William. He was granted 200 acres in Albany County, New York for his service as a corporal in the 55th Regiment of Foot in the French and Indian War 18 February 1775.

Camron, Alexander. He was granted 2,000 acres in Granville County, South Carolina on the King's bounty for his service in the French and Indian War 25 September 1766.

Cane, —. He served on the expedition to Canada in 1690. Joseph Cane received the land in Dumbarton, New Hampshire in 1735.

Cane, John. He served in the Narraganset War from Massachusetts. His daughter, Jane Cane, received land in Templeton, Massachusetts in 1733.

Canterbury, Cornelius. He served in the Narraganset War from Hingham, Massachusetts. His heirs received his land in Bedford, New Hampshire in 1733.

Cantley, John. He served as a soldier in Capt. Christian's Company of Regulars in 1760 in the French and Indian War. He proved his service in Botetourt County, Virginia 10 December 1779.

Carden, John. He was granted 3,000 acres in Albany County, New York for his service as a captain in the 2nd Battalion of the 60th Regiment of Foot in the French and Indian War 21 October 1765.

Cargill, Abernethy. He was granted 2,000 acres in Gloucester County, New York for his service as a lieutenant in an independent company of foot in the French and Indian War 6 April 1770.

Cargill, John. He was granted 200 acres in Albany County, New York for his service as a corporal in the 55th Regiment of Foot in the French and Indian War 25 May 1771.

Carleton, Dennis. He was granted 2,000 acres in Cumberland County, New York for his service as a lieutenant in the 28th Regiment of Foot in the French and Indian War 9 February 1770.

Carlile, John. He served as a soldier in Capt. William Preston's Company of Rangers in 1758 in the French and Indian War and received a warrant for 50 acres 15 February 1780 in Augusta County, Virginia.

Carmichal, Miles. He served as a private in the 77th Regiment in the French and Indian War and petitioned for his 50 acres in New York in 1765.

Carmon, John. He served in the Narraganset War from Barnstable, Massachusetts and received land in Gorham, Maine in 1733.

Carnes, William. He served in the French and Indian War and took his land in Fincastle County, Virginia 15 December 1772.

Carney, Edmond. He was granted 50 acres in Albany County, New York for his service as a soldier in the 18th Regiment of Foot in the French and Indian War 8 June 1771. He also appeared as Edward Carney.

Carothers, James. He served in the French and Indian War from Virginia and assigned his warrant.

Carpenter, John. He served as a soldier in the Old Virginia Regiment in the French and Indian War. He proved his service in Ohio County, Virginia 6 March 1780.

Carpenter, Joseph. He served in the Narraganset War from Woodstock, Connecticut. His son, Eliphalet Carpenter, received his land in Greenwich, Massachusetts in 1737.

Carpenter, Joseph. He was granted 200 acres in Granville County, South Carolina on the King's bounty 4 May 1775. He served as a corporal in the French and Indian War.

Carpenter, Joseph. He served in Capt. John Dickenson's Company of Rangers in the French and Indian War. His heir at law was John Carpenter, son of Thomas Carpenter. His service was proved in Botetourt County, Virginia 10 February 1780.

Carpenter, Robert. He served as a subaltern in the French and Indian War and received 5,000 acres in Nova Scotia 27 October 1767.

Carpenter, Solomon. He served as a soldier in Capt. John Dickerson's Company of Rangers in 1758 and 1759 in the French and Indian War. John Carpenter, the son of Thomas Carpenter, and heir at law of Solomon Carpenter, petitioned for his 50 acres February 1780 in Botetourt County, Virginia.

Carpenter, Thomas. He served as a soldier in Capt. John Dickerson's Company of Rangers in 1759 in the French and Indian War. He petitioned for 50 acres in February 1780 in Botetourt County, Virginia.

Carpenter, Thomas. He served as a soldier in the rangers under William Preston in 1759 in the French and Indian War. He proved his service in Botetourt County, Virginia 10 February 1780.

Carpenter, Zopher. He served as a drummer in Capt. John Dickenson's Company of Rangers in the French and Indian War and proved his service in Botetourt County, Virginia 11 November 1779.

Carr, Andrew. He was granted 200 acres in West Florida for his service as a petty officer in the French and Indian War 19 April 1779.

Carr, Dabney. He served as a soldier in Capt. William Phillips's Company of Volunteer Rangers in 1763 in the French and Indian War in Virginia. His warrant for 50 acres was issued to his heirs, Peter Carr, Samuel Carr, and Dabney Carr, 14 February 1780 in Louisa County, Virginia.

Carr, Martin. He received 50 acres of land in West Florida for his service as a private in the French and Indian War 9 April 1777.

Carr, Thomas. He served as a private in the 4th Battalion of the Royal American Regiment in the French and Indian War. His service was certified in New York 17 November 1766.

Carr, Thomas. He was granted 50 acres in Albany County, New York for his service as a soldier in the 55th Regiment of Foot in the French and Indian War 27 September 1769.

Carr, William. He served on the expedition to Canada in 1690. Benjamin Trask petitioned for his land in Raymond, Maine in 1735.

Carr, William. He served a soldier under Col. William Byrd from Virginia in the French and Indian War in 1759. He proved his service in Orange County, Virginia 24 February 1780 and received a warrant for 50 acres.

Carrigan, Patrick. He served as a soldier in Capt. John Dickerson's Company of Rangers in 1758 in the French and Indian War in 1757. He was in Botetourt County, Virginia in February 1780. He assigned his right to 50 acres in Virginia.

Carrin, Edward. He served as a subaltern officer in the French and Indian War.

He proved his service in Montgomery County, Virginia 7 March 1780.

Carroll, John. He was granted 150 acres on a branch of Broad River in South Carolina on the King's bounty for his service in the French and Indian War 21 June 1765.

Carroll, William. He was granted 50 acres in Albany County, New York for his service as a soldier in the 55th Regiment of Foot in the French and Indian War 18 April 1769.

Carter, Daniel. He served in the French and Indian War and had his service certified in January 1767. He was granted 200 acres in Albany County, New York for his service as a drummer in the 80th Regiment of Foot in the French and Indian War 8 June 1771.

Carter, John. He served as an assistant surgeon in the French and Indian War and prayed a grant of 2,000 acres in New York 26 June 1767.

Carter, John. He served as a soldier in the French and Indian War and was discharged in 1758. He applied for his 50 acres in Caroline County, Virginia in March 1780. He assigned his right.

Carter, Thomas. He served as an ensign in the French and Indian War and assigned his 2,000 acres of land in Virginia.

Carter, Thomas. He served as a subaltern in the French and Indian War. His representative, James Carter, received his 2,000 acre land warrant in Virginia at which time the veteran was deceased.

Carver, James. He had his service as a corporal in the French and Indian War certified 12 December 1766 in New York. He assigned his right to land to Robert Buchanan 20 January 1767.

Carvin, William. He served a soldier in Capt. John Montgomery's Company of Volunteers incorporated into the Virginia Regiment in 1756 under Maj. Andrew Lewis. He also served as a sergeant in Capt. William Christian's Company from July 1763 to March 1764 in the French and Indian War. He received his warrant in April 1780 in Montgomery County, Virginia.

Cary, Edward. He served as a officer in the French and Indian War and assigned his right to 4,000 acres in Virginia.

Cary, James. He served in the Narraganset War from Bridgewater, Massachusetts. His son, James Cary, claimed his land in Greenwich, Massachusetts in 1737.

Case, Ebenezer. He served on the expedition to Canada in 1690. Ebenezer Case received land in Warwick, Massachusetts in 1738.

Casper, Joseph. He was granted 200 acres in Albany County, New York for his service as a sergeant in the 60th Regiment of Foot in the French and Indian War 13 October 1767.

Cassady, Thomas. He served as a soldier in the Virginia Regiment under Col. George Washington in the French and Indian War. His heir, Thomas Cassady, received his 200 acre warrant in Virginia. The service was proved in Botetourt County, Virginia 10 February 1780.

Castles, Philip. He served as a private in the French and Indian War and petitioned for his land in New York in November 1766.

Castroft, John Andrew. He was awarded 200 acres in Albany County, New York for his service as a sergeant in a regiment of foot in the French and Indian War 19 May 1770.

Catton, John. He served as a private in the French and Indian War and received 50 acres in Virginia.

Cats, Manuel. He served as a private in the 60th Regiment in the French and Indian War and was granted land in New York 16 April 1767.

Causel, Michael. He served in the French and Indian War and received a warrant for 50 acres which he desired to locate in Fincastle County, Virginia in 1774. He also appeared as Michael Cousel.

Cave, William. He served as a soldier in the Col. William Byrd's Regiment in 1759 in the French and Indian War. He assigned his right to a 50 acre warrant in Virginia.

Cawley, John. He served in the French and Indian War and petitioned for his land in New York 2 February 1769.

Cawthen, James. He was granted land for his service in the French and Indian War in Virginia. He proved he was a soldier in Goochland County, Virginia 6 September 1779. He disposed of his warrant.

Cearns, Thomas. He was granted 200 acres in Albany County, New York for his service as a corporal in the 55th Regiment of Foot in the French and Indian War 1 April 1772.

Chadwell, Joseph. He served on the expedition to Canada in 1690. His nephew, Benjamin Chadwell of Ipswich, Massachusetts, claimed his land in Winchendon, Massachusetts in 1736.

Chadwick, Thomas. He was granted 200 acres in Craven County, South Carolina on the King's bounty 21 June 1765. He served as a corporal in the French and Indian War.

Chaisty, William. He served as an ensign in Capt. Samuel Scott's Company of the 1st Battalion of Pennsylvania troops in the French and Indian War and received his 2,000 acre warrant in Virginia.

Challis, Thomas. He served on the expedition to Canada in 1690 and received land in Poland, Maine in 1690.

Chamberlain, Benjamin. He served in the Narraganset War from Colchester, Connecticut. He claimed his land in Greenwich, Massachusetts in

1737.

Chamberlain, Henry. He served in the Narraganset War from Boston, Massachusetts. His son, John Chamberlain, received his land in Bedford, New Hampshire in 1733.

Chamberlain, John. He served under Capt. John Lovewell from Massachusetts and was in the battle of Pigwacket in May 1728. He was from Groton, Massachusetts and received his land in Pembroke, New Hampshire.

Chamberlain, Joseph. He served in the Narraganset War from Oxford, Massachusetts. His son, Joseph Chamberlain, claimed his land in Greenwich, Massachusetts in 1737.

Chamberlain, Samuel. He served on the Canada Expedition of 1690 and sought land 10 December 1735 in Massachusetts.

Chamberlayne, Thomas. He served as a soldier in Capt. James Gunn's Company in the French and Indian War in Virginia. He was in Mecklenburg County, Virginia 14 February 1780. He assigned his right to 50 acres.

Champlin, William. He served in the Narraganset War from Connecticut and received land in Voluntown, Connecticut in 1701.

Champlin, William. He served in the Narraganset War from Connecticut and received land in Voluntown, Connecticut in 1701. [second of the name]

Champney, Samuel. He served in the Narraganset War from Cambridge, Massachusetts. His son, Downing Champney, received his land in Westminster, Massachusetts in 1733.

Chandler, Joseph. He received 50 acres of land for his service as a private in the French and Indian War 9 April 1777.

Chandler, Moses. He served in Lovewell's War in Massachusetts and received his land in Petersham, Massachusetts in 1733.

Chandler, Samuel. He was a veteran of the expedition to Canada in 1690. His brother, Jonathan Chandler of Dorchester, Massachusetts, received his land in Ashburnham, Massachusetts in 1736.

Chapin, Samuel. He was of Springfield, Massachusetts and received 200 acres for his services 18 May 1664.

Chaplin, Moses. He was a veteran of the expedition to Canada in 1690. His brother, Joseph Chaplin of Roxbury, Massachusetts received his land in Ashburnham, Massachusetts in 1736.

Chapman, Nathan. He served in the French and Indian War and took his land in Fincastle County, Virginia 15 December 1773.

Chapman, Peter. He was granted 50 acres in Albany County, New York for his service as a soldier in the 60th Regiment of Foot in the French and

Indian War 3 September 1771.

Chapman, Richard. He served as a soldier in the Virginia Regiment under Col. William Byrd in the French and Indian War. He petitioned for his 50 acres 18 January 1780 in Washington County, Virginia.

Chappell, George. He served in the Narraganset War from Connecticut and received land in Voluntown, Connecticut in 1701.

Charhore, John. He was a veteran of the expedition to Canada in 1690. His nephew, John Charhore of Milton, Massachusetts, received his land in Ashburnham, Massachusetts in 1736.

Charles, John. He served in the Narraganset War from Connecticut. His heirs received land in Voluntown, Connecticut in 1701.

Chase, John. He served in the Narraganset War from Yarmouth, Massachusetts and received land in Gorham, Maine in 1733.

Chase, Moses. He served in the Narraganset War from Massachusetts in 1685. His son, Samuel Chase, received his land in Buxton, Maine.

Chase, Stephen. He served on the expedition to Canada in 1690 and received land in Poland, Maine in 1739.

Chase, William. He served in the Narraganset War from Yarmouth, Massachusetts and received land in Gorham, Maine in 1733.

Chasy, Stephen. He was granted 50 acres in Albany County, New York for his service as a soldier in a regiment of foot in the French and Indian War 19 May 1770.

Cheak, James. He served in the Narraganset War from Malden, Massachusetts. His heirs received his land in Westminster, Massachusetts in 1733.

Cheaver, James. He served in the Narraganset War from Cambridge, Massachusetts. His nephew, Daniel Cheaver, received his land in Westminster, Massachusetts in 1733.

Cheeck, John. He was granted 50 acres in Albany County, New York for his service as a soldier in the 80th Regiment of Foot in the French and Indian War 17 September 1765. He also appeared as John Chuuck.

Cheek, John. He served as a soldier in the French and Indian War from Virginia and received 50 acres of land. [Compare with John Chick.]

Cheesebro, Nathaniel. He served in the Narraganset War from Connecticut and received land in Voluntown, Connecticut in 1701.

Cheever, Solomon. He served in the Narraganset War from Bridgewater, Massachusetts. Josiah Edson claimed his land in Greenwich, Massachusetts in 1737.

Cheney, Josiah. He served on the expedition to Canada in 1690. Josiah Cheney received land in Warwick, Massachusetts in 1738.

Cheney, William. He was a veteran of the expedition to Canada in 1690. His brother, Benjamin Cheney, of Dorchester, Massachusetts, received his land in Ashburnham, Massachusetts in 1736.

Cherry, James. He was granted 200 acres in Albany County, New York for his service as a corporal in the 3rd Battalion of the 60th Regiment of Foot in the French and Indian War 30 May 1765.

Cherry, John. He served as a sergeant in the 60th Regiment in the French and Indian War and returned his survey for 200 acres in Albany County, New York 14 August 1766.

Cherry, Thomas. He was granted 50 acres in Albany County, New York for his service as a soldier in the 80th Regiment of Foot in the French and Indian War 28 October 1765.

Cheshire, John. He was granted 50 acres in Craven County, South Carolina on the King's bounty for his service in the French and Indian War 6 February 1773.

Chester, Peter. He was granted 3,000 acres in West Florida for his service as Major of Brigade in the French and Indian War 28 July 1772.

Chester, William. He received a warrant for 2,000 of land in West Florida for his service as a lieutenant in the French and Indian War 8 October 1774.

Chew, Coleby. He served as a lieutenant in the Virginia Regiment under Col. George Washington in 1758 in the French and Indian War. He was wounded by the Indians and drowned in the Ohio River. He was a native of Virginia. His warrant for 2,000 acres was issued to his legal representative, Joseph Chew, 21 February 1780 in Culpeper County, Virginia.

Chew, John. He was granted 500 acres in Charles River County, Virginia 6 July 1636 for defending the frontier of the colony against the King of the Pamunky and his warriors.

Chew, Larkin. He served as an ensign in the 2nd Virginia Regiment in 1758 and later as a lieutenant in the 1st Virginia Regiment under Col. William Byrd in the French and Indian War. He assigned his right to 2,000 acres. He also served as lieutenant under Col. Adam Stephen. He petitioned for his land in February 1780 in Spotsylvania County, Virginia. He received two warrants for 4,000 acres which he also assigned.

Chick, James. He served as a soldier in the Virginia Regiment until 1760 in the French and Indian War. His heir, John Chick, assigned the 50 acre warrant. [Compare with John Cheek.]

Chickchester, Jeremiah. He was granted 50 acres in Charlotte County, New York for his service as a soldier in the 80th Regiment of Foot in the

French and Indian War 18 October 1775.

Childs, Richard. He served in the Narraganset War from Deerfield, Massachusetts. His sons, Samuel Childs and Timothy Childs, claimed his land in Greenwich, Massachusetts in 1737.

Childs, Samuel. He served in the Narraganset War from Barnstable, Massachusetts and received land in Gorham, Maine.

Childs, Timothy. He served as a lieutenant from Deerfield, Massachusetts and was granted 300 acres for his many wounds and grievous misfortunes 13 June 1733.

Chinn, John. He served as a soldier in 1758 under Capt. John Field in Gen. Forbes's expedition in the French and Indian War and assigned his his 50 acres in Virginia.

Chinnery, George. He was granted 50 acres in Albany County, New York for his service as a matross in the 2nd Battalion of the Royal Regiment of Artillery in the French and Indian War 13 February 1767.

Chisholm, John. He was granted 200 acres in Craven County, South Carolina on the King's bounty for his service in the French and Indian War 1 June 1767.

Chism, John. He served as a soldier in 1758 under Capt. John Field in Gen. Forbes's Expedition against the Indians in the French and Indian War. He was in Culpeper County, Virginia 18 October 1779. He assigned his 50 acre warrant.

Christian, Israel. He served as commissary to the battalion commanded by Col. William Peachey in 1759 and afterwards occasionally to the troops in the 1st Virginia Regiment in the French and Indian War. He received his 2,000 acre warrant in April 1780 in Botetourt County, Virginia.

Christian, Israel. He served as a captain of a company of volunteers against the Shawnee under Col. Thomas Nash for about four months until the corps was disbanded in the French and Indian War. He received his 3,000 acre warrant in May 1780 in Montgomery County, Virginia.

Christian, William. He served in the French and Indian War as a captain of a company of volunteers in 1757, a captain of a company on the frontier of Augusta in 1756, and a captain of a company on the frontier from July 1763 until the autumn when he was discharged by Col. Andrew Lewis who commanded the troops on duty in Augusta County. In April 1780 in Montgomery County, Virginia his sons and legatees, Gilbert Christian and Patrick Christian, received 1,000 acre warrants apiece in Virginia. His daughters and legatees, Margaret Christian, Mary Christian, and Elizabeth Christian, received his other 1,000 acre warrant in Virginia.

Christie, Gabriel. He was granted 4,086 and 850 acres in West Florida for his service as a field officer in the French and Indian War 19 November 1777.

Christie, Hugh. He was granted 200 acres in Albany County, New York for his service as a corporal in the 42nd Regiment of Foot in the French and Indian War 30 October 1765.

Christie, James. He was granted 1,435 acres and 565 acres in West Florida for his service as a subaltern in the French and Indian War 19 November 1777 and 8 September 1779.

Christie, William. He was granted 200 acres in Albany County, New York for his service as a noncommissioned officer in the 80th Regiment of Foot in the French and Indian War 18 July 1770.

Christie, William. He was granted 200 acres in Albany County, New York for his service as a sergeant in the 80th Regiment of Foot in the French and Indian War 8 June 1771.

Christy, William. He served as an ensign in the 1st Battalion in the Pennsylvania troops in 1760 under Capt. Samuel Scott in the French and Indian War. He proved his service in Yohogania County, Virginia 28 March 1780. He received 2,000 acres of land in Virginia.

Chubbuck, John. He served as a lieutenant on the expedition to Canada in 1690. John Chubbuck received land in Chesterfield, Massachusetts in 1739.

Church, Benjamin. He served in the Narraganset War from Little Compton, Rhode Island. His son, Thomas Church, claimed his land in Greenwich, Massachusetts in 1737.

Church, David. He served in the Narraganset War from Killingly, Connecticut. He claimed his land in Greenwich, Massachusetts in 1737.

Cissel, Henry. He served as a soldier in the French and Indian War in 1755. His heir, William Cissel, received his warrant for 50 acres in Caroline County, Virginia in February 1780.

Cissel, James. He served as a soldier in the French and Indian War in 1755. His heir, William Cissel, received his warrant for 50 acres in Caroline County, Virginia in February 1780.

Cissel, William. He served as a soldier in the French and Indian War and was discharged in 1755. He received a warrant for 50 acres in Caroline County, Virginia in February 1780.

Claghorn, —. He served in the expedition to Canada in 1690. Ens. James Claghorn received land in Dumbarton, New Hampshire in 1735.

Claghorn, —. He served in the expedition to Canada in 1690. Robert Claghorn received land in Dumbarton, New Hampshire in 1735.

Claghorn, James. He served in the Narraganset War from Yarmouth, Massachusetts and received land in Gorham, Maine in 1733.

Clancy, George. He served as a corporal in Capt. Stewart's Company in the Old Virginia Regiment under Col. William Byrd in the French and Indian War. He proved his service in Botetourt County, Virginia 11 February 1780.

Clap, Edward. He was a veteran of the expedition to Canada in 1690. His brother, Nehemiah Clap of Milton, Massachusetts, received his land in Ashburnham, Massachusetts in 1736.

Clap, Edward. He served on the expedition to Canada in 1690. Palmer Golding received his land in Bethel, Maine in 1767.

Clap, Eleazer. He served in the Narraganset War from Barnstable, Massachusetts and received land in Gorham, Maine in 1733.

Clap, Increase. He was a veteran of the Narraganset War from Barnstable, Massachusetts and received land in Gorham, Maine in 1733.

Clark, Adam. He was from Rutland and in 1724 was captivated and carried by Indians to Canada in 1724. He was granted 150 acres in Massachusetts 24 June 1737.

Clark, Alexander. He was granted 200 acres in Albany County, New York for his service as a corporal in the 80th Regiment of Foot in the French and Indian War 15 June 1765.

Clark, Alexander. He was granted 200 acres in Albany County, New York for his service as a noncommissioned officer in the 60th or Royal American Regiment of Foot in the French and Indian War 28 March 1771.

Clark, Charles. He served as a soldier in the 2nd Virginia Regiment under Col. William Byrd in the French and Indian War. He petitioned for 50 acres 21 February 1780 in Essex County, Virginia.

Clark, Daniel. He served in the Narraganset War from Connecticut and received land in Voluntown, Connecticut in 1701.

Clark, Daniel. He was awarded 3,000 acres of land in West Florida for his service as a captain in Pennsylvania during the French and Indian War 15 January 1768.

Clark, Ephraim. He served in the Canada Expedition in 1690 in Capt. Thomas Andrews's Company. His brother, Samuel Clark of Medfield, Massachusetts, was granted 400 acres 15 February 1766.

Clark, Freeman. He was a veteran of the expedition to Canada in 1690. His nephew, Nathaniel Clark of Ipswich, Massachusetts, claimed his land in Winchendon, Massachusetts in 1736.

Clark, George. He was a veteran of the expedition to Canada in 1690. His brother, Nathaniel Clark of Ipswich, Massachusetts, claimed his land in Winchendon, Massachusetts in 1736.

Clark, George. He was granted 3,000 acres in Albany County, New York for his service as a captain in the 77th Regiment of Foot in the French and Indian War 18 October 1765.

Clark, George. He was granted 200 acres in Granville County, South Carolina on the King's bounty for his service in the French and Indian War 28 August 1767.

Clark, Henry. He served in the Narraganset War from Duxbury, Massachusetts. His nephew, Thomas Standish, received land in Gorham, Maine in 1733.

Clark, James. He served in the French and Indian War and petitioned for 50 acres of land 15 December 1773 in New York.

Clark, James. He was granted 2,000 acres in Albany County, New York for his service as a lieutenant in the a corps of rangers under Maj. Robert Rogers in the French and Indian War 22 May 1770.

Clark, James. He served as a soldier in the French and Indian War until he was discharged in 1760. He assigned his warrant for 50 acres in Virginia.

Clark, James. He served as a lieutenant in the French and Indian War and assigned his land warrant for 2,000 acres in Virginia.

Clark, John. He served in the Pequot War. He received a grant of land in Soldiers' Field in Hartford, Connecticut.

Clark, John. He served in the Narraganset War from Boston, Massachusetts. William Clark for the heirs received his land in Bedford, New Hampshire in 1733.

Clark, John. He served on the expedition to Canada in 1690. John Clark received his land in Bethel, Maine in 1767.

Clark, John. He was granted 200 acres in Albany County, New York for his service as a sergeant in the 77th Regiment of Foot in the French and Indian War 4 April 1770.

Clark, John. He served as a quartermaster in the 60th Regiment in the French and Indian War and petitioned for land 9 October 1765 in New York.

Clark, John. He was granted 2,000 acres in Albany County, New York for his service as an ensign in a corps of rangers under Maj. Robert Rogers in the French and Indian War 9 March 1771.

Clark, John. He served as a sergeant in a company of rangers under Col. Henry Bouquet in the 1st Virginia Regiment in 1764 against the Indians. He requested his 200 acres 17 November 1779 in Augusta County, Virginia.

Clark, Josiah. He served in the Narraganset War from Topsfield,

Massachusetts. His heirs claimed his land in Amherst, New Hampshire in 1734.

Clark, Nathaniel. He served in the Narraganset War from Massachusetts in 1685. His land was located in Buxton, Maine.

Clark, Nathaniel. He served on the expedition to Canada in 1690 and received land in Poland, Maine in 1739.

Clark, Nicholas. He was granted 50 acres in Hartford, Connecticut for his service in the Pequot War 11 May 1671.

Clark, Percival. He served on the expedition to Canada in 1690 and received land in Poland, Maine in 1739.

Clark, Samuel. He served on the expedition to Canada in 1690. Samuel Clark received land in Warwick, Massachusetts in 1738. His heirs, David Clark and Samuel Clark of Medfield, received his land from Massachusetts 21 January 1766.

Clark, Samuel. He served as a sergeant in one of the ranging companies under Capt. Charles Lewis in the French and Indian War. He was in Greenbrier County, Virginia 18 Nov. 1779 and assigned his warrant for 200 acres in Virginia.

Clark, Thomas. He served as a soldier in the Canada Expedition in 1690. His nephew, David Clark of Medfield, Massachusetts received his 400 acres of land in Massachusetts 15 February 1766.

Clark, William. He served in the Narraganset War from Massachusetts.

Clark, William. He served in an independent company of rangers in the French and Indian War and petitioned for his land in New York 12 April 1769.

Clarke, Arthur. He received his 2,000 acres of land in West Florida for his service as a lieutenant in the navy in the French and Indian War 13 June 1774.

Clarke, John. He served in the Narraganset War from Barnstable, Massachusetts and received land in Gorham, Maine in 1733.

Clarke, John. He served as a sergeant in the French and Indian War and received a warrant for 200 acres of land in Virginia.

Clarke, Samuel. He petitioned for 250 acres in St. Mark's Parish on the King's bounty in South Carolina for his service in the French and Indian War 3 May 1768.

Clarke, William. He was granted 50 acres in Albany County, New York for his service as a private in the 61st Regiment of Foot in the French and Indian War 8 March 1771.

Clarke, William. He shared in the grant of East Greenwich, Rhode Island made to those who had rendered service in King Philip's War. The grant was made 31 October 1677.

Clarkpaine, Samuel. He served as a captain in Col. Abijah Willard's Regiment in Massachusetts under Gen. Jeffery Amherst for the reduction of Canada in 1759 in the French and Indian War and assigned his 3,000 acre warrant in Virginia.

Clarkson, Anselm. He served as a soldier in Capt. Samuel Overton's Company of Rangers in 1755 in the French and Indian War. He assigned his warrant for 50 acres in Virginia. He also served as a second enlistment as sergeant in the same unit in 1756. He was in Louisa County, Virginia 11 October 1779. He assigned the two warrants for 50 and 200 acres respectively.

Clarkson, Peter. He served as a soldier in 1755 in Capt. Samuel Overton's Company of Rangers in the French and Indian War and assigned his warrant for 50 acres in Virginia.

Clarkson, William. He was granted 200 acres in Albany County, New York for his service as a noncommissioned officer in the 46th Regiment of Foot in the French and Indian War 8 March 1771.

Claus, Daniel. He was granted 3,000 acres in Albany County, New York for his service as a captain in the 60th or Royal American Regiment of Foot in the French and Indian War 29 September 1770.

Clay, Christian. He served as a sergeant in the French and Indian War and petitioned for 200 acres of land 31 May 1766 in New York.

Clayton, Asher. He was a colonel from Pennsylvania in the French and Indian War, but there is no evidence that he was granted land on 3 February 1769.

Clayton, David. He was granted 50 acres in St. Matthew's Parish, South Carolina on the King's bounty for his service in the French and Indian War 1 December 1773.

Clayton, George. He served as a soldier in the 44th Regiment in the French and Indian War and petitioned for a grant of 50 acres in Ulster County, New York 19 August 1766.

Cleaveland, Samuel. He was granted 5,000 acres in Charlotte County, New York for his service as Lieutenant Colonel in the Royal Regiment of Artillery in the French and Indian War 5 July 1774.

Cleek, James. He served as a soldier under Col. William Byrd in the 2nd Virginia Regiment in 1760 in the French and Indian War. He was dead by February 1780 when John Cleek received his warrant of 50 acres in Caroline County, Virginia. [There is some confusion in the warrant between the forenames of the soldier and the heir.] The veteran's name also appears as Jacob Cleek.

Clegg, Joseph. He served as a soldier in the French and Indian War and received 50 acres in Nova Scotia 9 October 1776.

Clements, Benjamin. He served as a private in Capt. William Temple's Company in the 1st Virginia Regiment in the French and Indian War. He was in Charlotte County, Virginia 7 February 1780. He assigned his right to 50 acres.

Clements, Newell. He was granted 50 acres on a branch of the Edisto River in South Carolina on the King's bounty for his service in the French and Indian War 21 June 1765.

Clency, George. He served as a corporal in Capt. Stewart's Company under Col. William Byrd in the French and Indian War. His service was proved in Botetourt County, Virginia 11 February 1780.

Clesson, Joseph. He was from Deerfield, Massachusetts. He was awarded 300 acres for his service by Massachusetts 12 December 1735.

Cleveland, Moses. He served in the Narraganset War from Freetown, Massachusetts. His son, John Cleveland, claimed his land in Greenwich, Massachusetts in 1737.

Cleveland, Samuel. He served in the Narraganset War. His son-in-law, William Ward, of Southborough, sought his land in Massachusetts. His grandson, Hezekiah Ward, continued the petition.

Clifford, John. He was granted 50 acres in Albany County, New York for his service as a soldier in the 60th Regiment of foot in the French and Indian War 19 May 1770.

Clinton, Charles, Jr. He was granted 2,000 acres in Albany County, New York for his service as an apothecary's mate in a military hospital in the French and Indian War 6 April 1771.

Cobb, Charles. He was awarded 2,000 acres of land in West Florida for his service as a warrant officer in the navy in the French and Indian War 29 November 1776.

Cobright, John. He served as a soldier in the French and Indian War and received 50 acres in Nova Scotia 9 October 1776.

Cochran, Edward. He served as a soldier upwards of three years in the 1st Virginia Regiment under different commanders in the French and Indian War. He received his 50 acre warrant in May 1780 in Montgomery County, Virginia.

Cochran, John. He served as a surgeon's mate in the French and Indian War and petitioned for 2,000 acres of land in New York 6 October 1774.

Cochran, Thomas. He petitioned for 200 acres on the Little River on the King's bounty in South Carolina for his service as a noncommissioned officer in the French and Indian War 3 May 1768.

Cockburn, John. He was granted 200 acres in Albany County, New York for his service as a corporal in the 28th Regiment of Foot in the French and Indian War 8 June 1771.

Cocke, William. He served as a lieutenant in the French and Indian War and received a warrant for 2,000 acres in Virginia.

Cockheart, James. He served as a soldier in Capt. Alexander Sayers's Company of Rangers in the French and Indian War. He proved his right to 50 acres in Greenbrier County, Virginia 21 March 1780.

Cockroft, William. He served as a colonel in the French and Indian War and petitioned for his land 30 December 1765 in New York.

Codner, Christopher. He served on the expedition to Canada in 1690. Benjamin Codner was admitted to his land in Lyndeboro, Maine in 1736.

Coffee, William. He was granted 200 acres in Granville County, South Carolina on the King's bounty for his service in the French and Indian War 4 May 1775.

Coffey, John. He served as a sergeant in the Virginia Regiment under Col. William Byrd in the French and Indian War and received a warrant for 200 acres in Virginia.

Cofland, William. He served in the French and Indian War and took his land in Fincastle County, Virginia 15 December 1772.

Cogin, John. He served on the expedition to Canada in 1690. John Cogin received his land in Bethel, Maine in 1767.

Cogswell, —. He served on the expedition to Canada in 1690. His son, William Cogswell, claimed his land in Winchendon, Massachusetts in 1736.

Cogswell, Adam. He served on the expedition to Canada in 1690 and claimed his land in Winchendon, Massachusetts in 1736.

Cogswell, Edward. He served in the Narraganset War from Massachusetts in 1685. His land was located in Buxton, Maine.

Colburn, Robert. He served on the expedition to Canada in 1690. Robert Baker petitioned for his land in Raymond, Maine in 1735.

Colburn, Samuel. He served in the Narraganset War from Dedham, Massachusetts. Ephraim Colburn received his land in Bedford, New Hampshire in 1733.

Colcut, Edward. He served in the Narraganset War from Massachusetts in 1685. His land was located in Buxton, Maine.

Colder, John. He was granted 200 acres in Albany County, New York for his service as a corporal in the 55th Regiment of Foot in the French and Indian War 15 August 1765.

Colden, Richard. He served as a corporal in the French and Indian War and petitioned for 200 acres of land 23 May 1766 in New York.

Cole, Daniel. He served in the Narraganset War from Eastham, Massachusetts. His son-in-law, Jonathan Grew, received land in Gorham, Maine in 1733.

Cole, Daniel. He served on the expedition to Canada in 1690 and received land in Dumbarton, New Hampshire in 1735.

Cole, Jacob. He served in the Narraganset War from Charlestown, Massachusetts. His heirs received his land in Westminster, Massachusetts in 1733.

Cole, Timothy. He served in the Narraganset War from Eastham, Massachusetts. His son, Timothy Cole, received land in Gorham, Maine in 1733.

Coleman, George. He served as a soldier in the 2nd Virginia Regiment of Regulars under Col. William Byrd in the French and Indian War and petitioned for his 50 acres 14 February 1780 in King and Queen County, Virginia.

Coleman, James. He was granted 200 acres in Albany County, New York for his service as a sergeant in the 60th Regiment of Foot in the French and Indian War 11 August 1768.

Coleman, William. He served in the French and Indian War and took his land in Fincastle County, Virginia 15 December 1772.

Colhoun, Alexander. He was granted 2,000 acres in Albany County, New York for his service as a lieutenant in an independent company of foot in the French and Indian War 7 October 1770.

Colhoun, Alexander. He was granted 2,000 acres in Albany County, New York for his service as a subaltern in an independent company of foot in the French and Indian War 1 June 1770.

Collier, John. He served as a soldier in Capt. Christian's Company of Rangers in 1760 under Col. William Byrd against the Cherokee in the French and Indian War. He received his warrant for 50 acres in December 1779 in Botetourt County, Virginia. He also appeared as John Colyer.

Collier, Moses. He served as a soldier in Col. William Byrd's Regiment in the French and Indian War and received 50 acres. He was in Rockbridge County, Virginia 5 August 1779.

Collier, Peter. He served on the expedition to Canada in 1690. Benjamin Lynde, Jr. was admitted to his land in Lyndeboro, Maine in 1735.

Collier, Richard. He was granted 200 acres in Albany County, New York for his service as a corporal in the 44th Regiment of Foot in the French and Indian War 15 August 1766.

Collier, Thomas. He served as an ensign under Col. Samuel Meredith in the 2nd Virginia Regiment in the French and Indian War and received a warrant for 2,000 acres 4 October 1779 in Henrico County, Virginia.

Collins, —. He served against the Indians in Massachusetts. His son, Nathaniel Collins, sought 200 acres for his father's service in December 1734.

Collins, Henry. He served in the Narraganset War from Lynn, Massachusetts. He claimed his land in Amherst, New Hampshire in 1734.

Collins, Henry. He served in the French and Indian War and received a 3,000 acre land warrant in Virginia.

Collins, Joseph. He served in the Narraganset War from Lynn, Massachusetts. He applied for his land 4 June 1685. His son, William Collins, claimed his land in Amherst, New Hampshire in 1734.

Collins, Joseph. He served on the expedition to Canada in 1690. Joshua Collins received land in Chesterfield, Massachusetts in 1739.

Collins, Peter. He served as a soldier in the Royal American Regiment in the French and Indian War. He was at the siege of Louisbourg and Ticonderoga. He petitioned for 50 acres at Ketch Harbor, Nova Scotia in 1779.

Collins, Robert. He was granted 2,000 acres in Gloucester County, New York for his service as a first lieutenant in the Royal Regiment of Artillery in the French and Indian War 3 February 1775.

Collins, Thomas. He served as a sergeant in one of the Virginia Regiments in Capt. Charles Lewis's Company in the French and Indian War in 1755. His 200 acres of land were awarded to his heir, Bartlett Collins, in Spotsylvania County, Virginia 16 September 1779.

Colly, John. He was granted 200 acres in Albany County, New York for his service as a sergeant in the 80th Regiment of Foot in the French and Indian War 17 September 1765.

Colquhond, James. He served as a soldier under Col. William Byrd in 1758 in the French and Indian War and received his 50 acre warrant in Virginia.

Colquohoun, Alexander. He served as a lieutenant in the French and Indian War and had his service certified in New York 21 December 1763.

Colton, Thomas. He served as a captain in engagements with the Indians and French at the time of Sir William Phipps's expedition to Canada. He was from Springfield, Massachusetts and received 200 acres in Hampshire County 13 September 1728. He also appeared as Thomas Colten.

Colvin, Elkin. He served as a soldier in the French and Indian War from Virginia in 1758 or 1759 and died in the service. His eldest brother, Mason Colvin of Culpeper County, Virginia, sought his land in October 1811. He believed that his brother served under Captain John

Blagg.

Colvin, James. He served as an ensign in a company of rangers in 1764 in Col. Henry Bouquet's campaign. He received a warrant for 2,000 acres in February 1780 in Yohogania County, Virginia.

Commack, James. He served in the French and Indian War and took his land in Fincastle County, Virginia 15 December 1772.

Comstock, Daniel. He served in the Narraganset War from Connecticut and received land in Voluntown, Connecticut in 1701.

Conachar, Donald. He was granted 50 acres in Albany County, New York for his service as a soldier in the 42nd Regiment of Foot in the French and Indian War 30 October 1765.

Conant, Caleb. He was from Eastham, Massachusetts. He was impressed into the service when Port Royal was taken. He was taken prisoner by the Indians and held captive for many years. He was awarded 300 acres by Massachusetts 20 June 1735.

Conant, Exercise. He served as a lieutenant on the expedition to Canada in 1690. Nehemiah Porter petitioned for his land in Raymond, Maine in 1735.

Conant, Lot. He served in the Narraganset War from Barnstable, Massachusetts and received land in Gorham, Maine in 1733.

Conant, Lott. He served in the Narraganset War from Beverly, Massachusetts. He claimed his land in Amherst, Massachusetts in 1733. Joshua Conant drew the land.

Coney, Richard. He served on the expedition to Canada in 1690. David Coney received his land in Bethel, Maine in 1767.

Connel, Dennis. He was granted 50 acres in Albany County, New York for his service as a soldier in the 44th Regiment of Foot in the French and Indian War 21 April 1768.

Conner, James. He served as a corporal in the 55th Regiment in the French and Indian War and had his service certified in New York in February 1767.

Conner, John. He served as a soldier in Col. Adam Stephen's Regiment in the French and Indian War and petitioned for his 50 acres in February 1780 in Spotsylvania County, Virginia.

Conner, John. He served as a soldier in the Virginia Regiment under Col. George Washington in the French and Indian War and received a warrant for 50 acres in Bedford County, Virginia in August 1779.

Conner, Samuel. He served as a soldier in the Virginia Regiment in Capt. George Mercer's Company in the French and Indian War. He was in Botetourt County, Virginia in April 1780. He assigned his 50 acre warrant in Virginia.

Connolly, Daniel. He was granted 50 acres in Albany County, New York for his service as a soldier in the 80th Regiment of Foot in the French and Indian War 26 July 1765.

Connolly, John. He was granted 2,000 acres in Albany County, New York for his service as a surgeon's mate in a military hospital in the French and Indian War 13 April 1765.

Connolly, John. He served as a surgeon's mate in the General Hospital in the French and Indian War and received 2,000 acres of land in Fincastle County, Virginia which he patented 16 December 1773.

Connolly, Matthew. He served as a private in the French and Indian War and petitioned for his 50 acres on the King's bounty in South Carolina 7 October 1766.

Connolly, Terence. He was granted 50 acres in Albany County, New York for his service as a soldier in the 80th Regiment of Foot in the French and Indian War 28 June 1765.

Connor, Fitzmaurice. He served as a captain in the French and Indian War and received 1,000 acres of land in West Florida 18 January 1773.

Connor, Samuel. He served as a soldier in the Old Virginia Regiment in the French and Indian War and assigned his right to 50 acres in Virginia.

Connor, Timothy. He served as a private in the French and Indian War and petitioned for 50 acres in South Carolina 3 September 1765.

Constable, John. He served as a surgeon in the French and Indian War and petitioned for his land 30 December 1766 in New York.

Converse, Samuel. He served on the expedition to Canada in 1690. His son, Samuel Converse, received his land in Woburn, Massachusetts in 1738.

Converse, Zachariah. He served on the expedition to Canada in 1690 and received his land in Woburn, Massachusetts in 1738.

Conway, John. He was granted 200 acres in Albany County, New York for his service as a noncommissioned officer in the 60th Regiment of Foot in the French and Indian War 8 March 1771.

Conway, Joseph. He served as a lieutenant in the Royal Marines in the French and Indian War and petitioned for his 2,000 acres of land in New York 8 May 1772.

Conway, Timothy. He served as a private in the Virginia Regiment in the French and Indian War and received a warrant for 50 acres which he assigned.

Cook, Caleb. He served in the Narraganset War from Plympton, Massachusetts. His heirs claimed his land in Greenwich, Massachusetts in 1737.

Cook, Josiah. He served in the Narraganset War from Eastham, Massachusetts and received land in Gorham, Maine in 1733.
Cook, Richard. He served in the Narraganset War from Connecticut. His heirs received land in Voluntown in 1701.
Cook, Stephen. He served in the Narraganset War from Newton, Massachusetts. He received his land in Westminister, Massachusetts in 1733.
Cook, William. He was a veteran of the expedition to Canada in 1690. His brother, Robert Cook of Needham, Massachusetts, received his land in Ashburnham, Massachusetts in 1736.
Cooke, John. He served as deputy commissary in the French and Indian War and petitioned for land 25 February 1767 in New York.
Cookoone, James. He served on the expedition to Canada in 1690 and received land in Dumbarton, New Hampshire in 1735.
Coolidge, David. He received land in Alstead, New Hampshire in 1771 for service of an unidentified veteran of the expedition to Canada in 1690.
Coolidge, John. He served on the expedition to Canada in 1690. William Coolidge received his land in Alstead, New Hampshire in 1771.
Coolidge, Jonas. He served on the expedition to Canada in 1690. Jonas Coolidge received his land in Alstead, New Hampshire in 1771.
Coolidge, Joseph. He received land in Alstead, New Hampshire in 1771 for the service of an unidentified veteran of the expedition to Canada in 1690.
Coolidge, Richard. He served on the expedition to Canada in 1690. James Hay received his land in Alstead, New Hampshire in 1771.
Coolidge, Thaddeus. He served on the expedition to Canada in 1690. Nathaniel Coolidge received his land in Alstead, New Hampshire in 1771.
Coolidge, William. He received land in Alstead, New Hampshire in 1771 for the service of an unidentified veteran of the expedition to Canada in 1690.
Cooling, John. He served in the French and Indian War and petitioned for his land 2 February 1769 in New York.
Coombs, John. He served in the Indian war and was awarded 150 acres in Massachusetts 23 March 1735/6.
Coomes, Michael. He served on the expedition to Canada in 1690. John Gardner was admitted to his land in Lyndeboro, Maine in 1735.
Cooper, James. He served as a soldier in Col. William Byrd's Regiment in 1758 in the French and Indian War. He was in Louisa County, Virginia 14 February 1780. He assigned his right to 50 acres in Virginia.
Cooper, James. He served as a soldier in Capt. Gist's Company of Light Infantry in the French and Indian War. He was in Botetourt County,

Virginia in March 1780. He assigned the warrant for 50 acres in Virginia.

Cooper, Robert. He was awarded 200 acres by Massachusetts for his service 3 December 1735.

Cooper, Thomas. He served as a soldier in the Virginia Regiment under Col. William Byrd in the French and Indian War until it was disbanded. His heir and brother, James Cooper, was in Essex County, Virginia 21 February 1780. He assigned his right to the 50 acres.

Cooper, William. He served in the Virginia Regiment under Col. William Byrd in the French and Indian War until it was disbanded. His heir and brother, James Cooper, was in Essex County, Virginia 21 February 1780 and assigned his right to the 50 acre warrant.

Coplen, Joseph. He served in the French and Indian War and petitioned for his land in New York 17 March 1767.

Coplin, Thomas. He served in the Narraganset War from Braintree, Massachusetts. His son, Thomas Coplin, received his land in Bedford, New Hampshire in 1733.

Coppney, Joseph. He served as a private the French and Indian War and was granted land in New York 16 April 1767.

Cops, Samuel. He served in the Narraganset War from Barnstable, Massachusetts and received land in Gorham, Maine in 1733. His name was later corrected to Samuel Cobb on 25 March 1740 due to a clerical error.

Corbett, John. He served as a soldier in the French and Indian War and received 50 acres in Nova Scotia 9 October 1776.

Corbin, Daniel. He served as a sergeant in the French and Indian War and petitioned for his land in New York in November 1766.

Corbin, John. He served in the Narraganset War from Pomfret, Connecticut. His son-in-law, Nathaniel Sessions, claimed his land in Greenwich, Massachusetts in 1737.

Corey, Jacob. He served in Lovewell's War in Massachusetts and received his land in Petersham, Massachusetts.

Corey, Thomas. He served in the expedition to Canada in 1690. Ebenezer Corey received his land in Bethel, Maine in 1767.

Corkings, Samuel. He was granted 50 acres on the Little Pee Dee River, South Carolina on the King's bounty for his service in the French and Indian War 14 September 1771.

Cornwell, William. He served in the Pequot War and received a grant in Soldiers' Field in Hartford, Connecticut.

Corsa, Isaac. He served as a colonel in the French and Indian War and petitioned for his land 30 December 1765 in New York.

Corsa, Teunis. He served as a lieutenant in the French and Indian War and petitioned for his land 30 December 1765 in New York.

Cory, Thomas. He served in the Narraganset War from Weston, Massachusetts. His son, Thomas Cory, received his land in Westminster, Massachusetts in 1733.

Cosby, Philip. He served as a soldier in Capt. William Phillips's Company of Volunteer Rangers in 1763 in the French and Indian War. His heir, David Cosby, was in Louisa County, Virginia 4 February 1780 and assigned his right to 50 acres.

Cosby, Zaccheus. He served as a soldier under Capt. William Phillips in a volunteer company in 1763 in the French and Indian War. He was in Caroline County, Virginia 14 February 1780. He assigned his warrant of 50 acres.

Cotten, John. He served as a corporal in the French and Indian War and petitioned for his land in New York 8 July 1765.

Cotter, John. He served on the expedition to Canada in 1690. Peter Grout received his land in Bethel, Maine in 1767.

Cotteril, Isaac. He was granted 50 acres in Albany County, New York for his service as a soldier in the 55th Regiment of Foot in the French and Indian War 18 April 1769.

Cotton, Nathaniel. For his service as a chaplain aboard the ship of war, *Princess Amelia*, at the reduction of Quebec in the French and Indian War he was eligible for 2,000 acres. In his will of 27 April 1769 he devised his right to land to Edmund Rush Wegg who in turn received the survey 15 May 1778 in West Florida.

Cottrell, Nicholas. He served in the Narraganset War from Connecticut and received land in Voluntown, Connecticut in 1701.

Coulter, Andrew. He was granted 200 acres in Albany County, New York for his service as a corporal in the 46th Regiment of Foot in the French and Indian War 5 July 1765.

Coulter, John. He was granted 200 acres in Albany County, New York for his service as a corporal in the 80th Regiment of Foot in the French and Indian War 15 August 1765.

Coutt, Daniel. He served as a lieutenant in the French and Indian War and received 2,000 acres in Nova Scotia 15 February 1776.

Cowan, Duncan. He was granted 50 acres in Charlotte County, New York for his service as a soldier in the 42nd Regiment of Foot in the French and Indian War 12 October 1774.

Cowan, Thomas. He was granted 200 acres in Albany County, New York for his service as a drummer in the 55th Regiment of Foot in the French and Indian War 11 August 1768.

Cowdon, Thomas. He served as a captain in Col. Abijah Willard's Regiment in Massachusetts under Gen. Jeffery Amherst for the reduction of Canada in 1759 in the French and Indian War and assigned his 3,000 acre warrant in Virginia.

Cowen, William. He served as a soldier in Capt. John Montgomery's Company under Maj. Andrew Lewis in the French and Indian War in 1756. He was also a sergeant in Capt. William Christian's Company from July 1763 to March 1764. He proved his right to 50 acres in Montgomery County, Virginia in April 1780.

Cowherd, James. He served as an ensign in Col. Henry Bouquet's Regiment. His warrant for 2,000 acres was issued to his heir, Jonathan Cowherd, 28 October 1779 in Orange County, Virginia.

Cowper, James. He enlisted under Richard Johnson of Caroline County, Virginia in 1760 in the French and Indian War and served in Capt. Charles Scott's Company of Rangers. He petitioned for his 50 acres 13 March 1780 in Louisa County, Virginia.

Cowper, William. He received his 1,000 acres of land in West Florida for his service as a staff officer in the French and Indian War 6 May 1776.

Cox, David. He served as a soldier in the French and Indian War and had his service certified in Montgomery County, Virginia 5 April 1780 for his 50 acres of land.

Cox, Isaac. He served as an ensign in a corps of rangers under Col. Henry Bouquet in 1764. He was in Yohogania County, Virginia in October 1779. He assigned his right to 2,000 acres.

Cox, John. He served as a soldier in the French and Indian War and had his service certified in Montgomery County, Virginia for his 50 acres of land 5 April 1780.

Cox, Joshua. He served as a soldier in Capt. John Smith's Company of Regulars under Col. William Byrd in 1760 in the French and Indian War. He received his 50 acre warrant in April 1780 in Montgomery County, Virginia.

Cox, Matthew. He served in the French and Indian War and took his land in Fincastle County, Virginia 15 December 1773.

Coyce, Jeremiah. He was granted 50 acres in Albany County, New York for his service as a private in the 80th Regiment of Foot in the French and Indian War 5 April 1771.

Coyne, Barne. He was granted 50 acres in Albany County, New York for his service as a private in the 46th Regiment of Foot in the French and

Indian War 8 March 1771.

Cox, Paul. He was granted 200 acres in Charlotte County, New York for his service as a noncommissioned officer in the 4th Battalion in the 60th Regiment of Foot in the French and Indian War 12 October 1774.

Crabtree, John. He was granted 200 acres in Albany County, New York for his service as a sergeant in the 35th Regiment of Foot in the French and Indian War 28 June 1770.

Craddock, Thomas. He served as a fifer in the French and Indian War and desired to locate his 200 acres in Fincastle County, Virginia 2 June 1774.

Craft, Ebenezer. He served on the expedition to Canada in 1690. Ebenezer Craft received his land in Warwick, Massachusetts.

Craft, Nathaniel. He served on the expedition to Canada in 1690. He received his land in Warwick, Massachusetts in 1736.

Craige, John. He served on the expedition to Canada in 1690. Benjamin Trow petitioned for his land in Raymond, Maine in 1735.

Craighead, George. He served as lieutenant under Maj. Andrew Lewis in the French and Indian War and received his 2,000 acre warrant in Virginia. His brother was William Craighead of Hanover County, Virginia. George Craighead later resided in New Castle County, Delaware.

Craik, James. He served as a lieutenant under Col. William Byrd in the Virginia Regiment in the French and Indian War and was entitled to 2,000 acres which he intended to locate in Fincastle County, Virginia in 1773. He was a doctor.

Crampton, Adam. He served in the French and Indian War and petitioned for his land in New York 20 May 1767.

Crandal, John. He shared in the grant of East Greenwich, Rhode Island made to those who had rendered service in King Philip's War. The grant was made 31 October 1677.

Crane, Benjamin. He served in the Narraganset War from Dighton, Massachusetts. His heirs claimed his land in Greenwich, Massachusetts in 1737.

Crane, Ebenezer. He was a veteran of the expedition to Canada in 1690. Ebenezer Crane of Braintree received his land in Ashburnham, Massachusetts in 1736.

Crane, Peter. He served as a soldier in the French and Indian War and petitioned for his 50 acres in New York 26 April 1769.

Craney, John. He was granted 200 acres in Albany County, New York for his service as a corporal in the 3rd Regiment of Foot in the French and

Indian War 27 March 1775.

Craton, William. He served as a soldier in the French and Indian War and was entitled to 50 acres. He assigned his warrant in Virginia.

Craty, Peter. He served as a soldier in the 46th Regiment in the French and Indian War. Cathren Craty was certified as his widow 13 December 1766 in New York.

Crause, Charles. He served as a lieutenant in the French and Indian War and received 2,000 acres in Nova Scotia 2 April 1774.

Crawford, Hugh. He served as a captain in the French and Indian War and petitioned for land in New York 28 February 1770.

Crawford, John. He served as a soldier under Capt. William Piper in 1763 and in a troop of Light Horse under Capt. John Piper in the French and Indian War in Pennsylvania. He moved to Virginia in 1772. He proved his service in Berkeley County, Virginia 21 March 1780.

Crawford, William. He was granted 200 acres in Albany County, New York for his service as a sergeant in the 55th Regiment of Foot in the French and Indian War 1 July 1771.

Crawford, William. He served as a lieutenant of light horse in 1758 in the French and Indian War and as a major or rangers under Lord Dunmore in 1774. He proved his service in Yohogania County, Virginia 28 March 1780.

Crawley, John. He was granted 200 acres in Albany County, New York for his service as a noncommissioned officer in the 80th Regiment of Foot in the French and Indian War 8 March 1771.

Creagh, James. He was granted 50 acres in Ulster County, New York for his service as a soldier in the 28th Regiment of Foot in the French and Indian War 2 May 1775.

Creagh, John. He served as a sergeant in the French and Indian War and assigned his right to 200 acres in Virginia.

Crean, Daniel. He was granted 200 acres in Albany County, New York for his service as a sergeant in the 40th Regiment of Foot in the French and Indian War 15 May 1770.

Crean, Peter. He served as a private in the French and Indian War and petitioned for his land in New York 26 April 1767.

Crebbin, Thomas. He served as surgeon aboard H.M.S. *Race Horse* at the reduction of Quebec in 1759 in the French and Indian War and petitioned for his 2,000 acres of land in New York 8 May 1771.

Cregg, John. He was granted 200 acres in Gloucester County, New York for his service as a corporal in the 55th Regiment of Foot in the French and Indian War 5 April 1770.

Creighton, John. He served as a noncommissioned officer in the French and Indian War and petitioned for 200 acres on the King's bounty in South Carolina 11 November 1773.

Cremore, Henry. He served as a soldier in the French and Indian War and assigned his warrant for 50 acres in Virginia.

Crews, David. He served as a corporal under Col. William Byrd in 1760 in the French and Indian War and received a warrant for 200 acres in March 1780 in Bedford County, Virginia.

Crocker, Jonathan. He served in the Narraganset War from Marshfield, Massachusetts. He claimed his land in Greenwich, Massachusetts on 1737.

Crocker, Josiah. He served in the Narraganset War from Barnstable, Massachusetts and received land in Gorham, Maine in 1733.

Crockett, John. He served as a sergeant during the French and Indian War in Capt. John Montgomery's Company in the Shawnee Expedition in 1756 which was incorporated with part of the Virginia Regiment under Maj. Andrew Lewis. He received his 200 acre warrant in April 1780 in Montgomery County, Virginia.

Crockett, Walter. He served as a soldier in the French and Indian War and had his service certified in Montgomery County, Virginia for his 50 acres of land 8 March 1780.

Crockford, James Edward. He received his 2,000 acres of land in West Florida for his service as purser on the sloop *Saltash* in the French and Indian War 7 October 1776.

Crogan, —. He served as a colonel in the French and Indian War. Matthew Ridley of Baltimore, Maryland received his warrant for 3,000 acres in Virginia 2 April 1774. [Compare with the following entry.]

Croghan, George. He was awarded 1500, 400, 400, 400, 600, 400, 500, and 500 acres in Cumberland and Westmoreland Counties, Pennsylvania for his service in the French and Indian War 1 April 1769.

Croghan, George. He served as a captain in the French and Indian War and received 4,000 acres of land in Virginia.

Cromwell, William. He served as a subaltern in the French and Indian War from Virginia and received 300 acres in Augusta County, Virginia.

Cronin, Dennis. He was granted 200 acres in Albany County, New York for his service as a sergeant in the 94th Regiment of Foot in the French and Indian War 26 July 1765. He also appeared as Dennis Croner.

Crooks, John. He was granted 200 acres in Albany County, New York for his service as a noncommissioned officer in the 60th Regiment of Foot in the French and Indian War 5 April 1771.

Crooks, William. He was granted 200 acres in Albany County, New York for his service as a sergeant in an independent company in the French and Indian War 14 June 1765.

Cross, —. He served on the expedition to Canada in 1690. His son, Robert Cross, claimed his land in Winchendon, Massachusetts in 1736.

Cross, George. He served in the Narraganset War from Massachusetts in 1685. His son, William Cross, received his land in Buxton, Maine.

Cross, John. He served as a private in the French and Indian War and petitioned for his land in New York 17 March 1767.

Cross, Peter. He served in the Narraganset War from Connecticut and received land in Voluntown, Connecticut in 1701.

Cross, William. He served in the 1st Virginia Regiment under Col. William Byrd and Col. Adam Stephen in the French and Indian War. He received his warrant for 50 acres in Botetourt County in December 1779.

Crossby, Joseph. He was from Braintree and petitioned for his land in Massachusetts 12 January 1735/6.

Crossthwait, Isaac. He was a soldier in Col. William Byrd's Regiment in 1758 in the French and Indian War. He was in Orange County, Virginia 28 October 1779. He assigned his 50 acres.

Crossthwait, Jacob. He was a soldier in Col. William Byrd's Regiment in 1758 in the French and Indian War and was awarded 50 acres in Orange County, Virginia 26 August 1779.

Croucher, Charles. He served as a soldier in the Virginia Regiment under Col. Adam Stephen in the French and Indian War. He assigned his warrant of 50 acres.

Crow, Isam. He served as a sergeant in the 2nd Virginia Regiment of Regulars under Col. William Byrd in 1758 in the French and Indian War. He petitioned for his warrant for 200 acres 28 February 1780 in Middlesex County, Virginia.

Crow, Richard. He was granted 2,000 acres in Tryon County, New York for his service as a lieutenant in the 48th Regiment of Foot in the French and Indian War 20 January 1775.

Crowe, Robert. He served as a lieutenant in the 48th Regiment in the French and Indian War and petitioned for a grant of 2,000 acres of land in New York 19 April 1769.

Crowell, John. He served in the Narraganset War from Yarmouth, Massachusetts and received land in Gorham, Maine in 1733.

Crowell, Yelverton. He served in the Narraganset War from Yarmouth, Massachusetts and received land in Gorham, Maine in 1733.

Cruickshanks, John. He was granted 2,000 acres in Albany County, New York for his service as a lieutenant in the 47th Regiment of Foot in the French and Indian War 25 May 1771.
Cruckshank, Hugh. He was granted 200 acres in Albany County, New York for his service as a sergeant in the 42nd Regiment of Foot in the French and Indian War 30 October 1765. He also appeared as Hugh Cruikshank.
Crumb, Daniel. He served in the Narraganset War from Connecticut and received land in Voluntown, Connecticut in 1701.
Crumpton, Benjamin. He was granted 50 acres in Albany County, New York for his service as a soldier in the 60th Regiment of Foot in the French and Indian War 6 July 1771.
Culbert, John. He was granted 200 acres in Albany County, New York for his service as a sergeant in the 80th Regiment of Foot in the French and Indian War 28 June 1765.
Cullum, John. He served in the French and Indian War and petitioned for 50 acres of land 15 December 1773 in New York.
Culver, Edward. He served in the Narraganset War from Connecticut and received land in Voluntown, Connecticut in 1701. He also appeared as Edward Colver.
Culver, Ephraim. He served in the Narraganset War from Connecticut and received land in Voluntown, Connecticut in 1701. He also appeared as Ephraim Colver.
Culver, Joseph. He served in the Narraganset War from Connecticut and received land in Voluntown, Connecticut in 1701. He also appeared as Joseph Colver.
Cummin, Lawrence. He was granted 350 acres on the north side of the Santee River in South Carolina on the King's bounty 21 August 1765. He was a private in the French and Indian War.
Cummings, Jeremiah. He served as a subaltern in the French and Indian War and had his service certified in Montgomery County, Virginia for his 2,000 acres of land 8 March 1780.
Cummings, John. He served in the Narraganset War and received land in Templeton, Massachusetts in 1733.
Cummings, Jonathan. He served under Capt. John Lovewell from Massachusetts and was in battle at Pigwacket in May 1728. He was from Dunstable, Massachusetts and received his land in Pembroke, New Hampshire.
Cummings, Josiah. He served as a corporal in the French and Indian War and assigned his right to 200 acres in Virginia. He also appeared as Josiah

Cunningham (*quo vide*).

Cummings, Peter. He was granted 50 acres in Gloucester County, New York for his service as a soldier in the 28th Regiment of Foot in the French and Indian War 5 April 1770.

Cummings, Robert. He served in the Narraganset War and received land in Templeton, Massachusetts in 1733.

Cummings, William. He served under Capt. John Lovewell from Massachusetts and was in battle at Pigwacket in May 1728. He was from Dunstable, Massachusetts and received his land in Pembroke, New Hampshire.

Cunningham, Henry. He served as a soldier in the 45th Regiment in the French and Indian War. His service was certified 15 September 1763.

Cunningham, Josiah. He served in the French and Indian War as a corporal in Virginia. His representative, William Preston, received his 200 acres.

Cunningham, Miles. He was granted 50 acres in Gloucester County, New York for his six years of service as a soldier in the 2nd Battalion of the 60th Regiment of Foot in the French and Indian War 5 April 1770.

Cunningham, Samuel. He was granted 50 acres in Gloucester County, New York for his service as a soldier in the 46th Regiment of Foot in the French and Indian War 5 April 1770.

Cunningham, Samuel. He served in the 80th Regiment in the French and Indian War. His service was certified in New York 14 July 1766.

Cunningham, Walter. He served as a lieutenant in 1st Virginia Regiment under Col. William Byrd in the French and Indian War and received a warrant for 2,000 acres. He also served as a captain of an independent company on the expedition against the Shawnee Indians under Col. Henry Bouquet in 1765 and received another warrant for 1,000 acres 17 November 1779 in Augusta County, Virginia.

Currant, James. He was granted 50 acres in Albany County, New York for his service as a soldier in the 55th Regiment of Foot in the French and Indian War 1 July 1771.

Curriour, Richard. He served in the Narraganset War from Massachusetts in 1685. His son, Timothy Curriour, received his land in Buxton, Maine.

Curry, Daniel. He served in the 80th Regiment in the French and Indian War and petitioned for his land in New York 22 October 1766.

Curry, Joseph. He requested 3,000 acres for his service as a captain in provincial service from South Carolina. He was granted 2,000 acres 15 December 1768 but not for his provincial service.

Curry, William. He served as a soldier in the French and Indian War and petitioned for 50 acres on the King's bounty in South Carolina 7 August 1764.

Curten, John. He was granted 200 acres in Albany County, New York for his service as a sergeant in the 48th Regiment of Foot in the French and Indian War 30 October 1765.

Curtice, Joseph. He was a veteran of the expedition to Canada in 1690. His cousin, Isaac How of Dorchester, Massachusetts, received his land in Ashburnham, Massachusetts in 1736.

Curtice, William. He served in the Narraganset War from Salem, Massachusetts. His son, William Curtice, claimed his land in Amherst, New Hampshire in 1734.

Curtis, John. He served on the expedition to Canada in 1690. John Curtis received land in Warwick, Massachusetts in 1738.

Curtis, William. He served in the expedition to Canada in 1690. He petitioned for his land in Raymond, Maine in 1735.

Cushing, Theophilus. He served on the expedition to Canada in 1690. Theophilus Cushing received land in Chesterfield, Massachusetts in 1739.

Cuthbert, Donald. He served as a soldier in the 78th Regiment in the French and Indian War and petitioned for his 50 acres in New York 27 April 1765.

Cutler, Ephraim. He served in the Narraganset War from Watertown, Massachusetts. He received his land in Westminster, Massachusetts in 1733.

Cutler, John. He served in the Narraganset War from Boston, Massachusetts. His heirs received the land in Bedford, New Hampshire in 1733.

Cutler, Timothy. He served in the Narraganset War from Charlestown, Massachusetts. His heirs received his land in Westminister, Massachusetts in 1733.

Cutt, Richard. He was from Kittery and was an officer in the expedition against Louisbourg in 1745 and applied for his land in Massachusetts 24 November 1761.

Cutter, Gershom. He served in the Narraganset War from Cambridge, Massachusetts. He received his land in Westminster, Massachusetts in 1733.

Cutting, James. He served in the Narraganset War from Watertown, Massachusetts. His son, Jonas Cutting, received his land in Westminster, Massachusetts in 1733.

Cutting, John. He served in the Narraganset War from Watertown, Massachusetts. His son, John Cutting, received his land in Westminster, Massachusetts in 1733.

Cutting, Zacheriah. He served in the Narraganset War from Charlestown,

Massachusetts. He received his land in Westminster, Massachusetts in 1733.

Cuttler, John. He served in the Narraganset War and received land in Templeton, Massachusetts in 1733.

Cuyler, Abraham. He was granted 2,000 acres in Albany County, New York for his service as a lieutenant in an independent company of foot called the Queen's Rangers in the French and Indian War 29 October 1765.

Cuyler, Henry. He was granted 3,000 acres in Albany County, New York for his service as a commissioner of stores and provisions in the French and Indian War 26 May 1767.

Daggett, Joseph. He served in the Narraganset War from Rehoboth, Massachusetts. His son, John Dagget, claimed his land in Greenwich, Massachusetts in 1734.

Daingerfield, William. He served as a captain in the 1st Virginia Regiment under Col. George Washington in 1755 and in Col. Adam Stephen's Regiment in 1758 in the French and Indian War. He petitioned for his land in 21 February 1780 in Culpeper County, Virginia and in February 1780 in Spotsylvania County, Virginia. He had three warrants for 3,000, 2,000, and 2,000 acres. He assigned all three warrants. He also appeared as William Dangerfield.

Daland, Benjamin. He served in the expedition to Canada in 1690. George Daland petitioned for his land in Raymond, Maine in 1735.

Dalley, Thomas. He served as a drummer under Thomas Elliott in Col. William Byrd's Regiment in the French and Indian War. His warrant for 200 acres was issued to his heir, John Dalley, 20 March 1780 in Essex County, Virginia.

Dalling, John. He was granted 5,000 acres in West Florida for his service as a lieutenant colonel in the French and Indian War 6 October 1773.

Dalrymple, John. He served as a captain in the French and Indian War and petitioned for his land in New York 18 April 1764.

Dalton, John. He served in Lovewell's War in Massachusetts and received his land in Petersham, Massachusetts in 1733. He also appeared as John Dolton.

Dalton, John. He served as a soldier in Capt. Hubberd's Company of Rangers in 1759 in the French and Indian War. He was in Louisa County, Virginia 14 February 1780. He assigned his right to 50 acres in Virginia.

Dalton, John. He served as a soldier in Capt. Thomas Bullet's Company of Rangers in 1762 in the French and Indian War and was in Louisa County, Virginia 8 November 1779. He assigned his warrant for 50 acres. He also appeared as John Dolton.

Dalway, Henry. He served as a lieutenant in Capt. Alexander Rigby's Company under Maj. Gen. Sir John Irvin, Colonel of His Majesty's 74th Regiment of Foot in the French and Indian War. He assigned his 2,000 acre warrant in Virginia.

Dalziel, Archibald. He was granted 2,000 acres in West Florida for his service as a warrant officer in the navy in the French and Indian War 10 August 1778.

Damon, Samuel. He served in the Narraganset War from Reading, Massachusetts and petitioned for his land 4 June 1685.

Dana, William. He received land in Alstead, New Hampshire in 1771 for the service of an unidentified veteran of the expedition to Canada in 1690.

Danal, Stephen. He served as armourer in the French and Indian War and petitioned for 200 acres of land in New York 4 February 1767. He also appeared as Stephen Dannal.

Dane, Philemon. He served in the Narraganset War from Massachusetts in 1685. His son, Philemon Dane, received his land in Buxton, Maine.

Daniel, —. He served on the expedition to Canada in 1690. Joseph Daniel received land in Dumbarton, New Hampshire in 1735.

Daniel, Joseph. He served on the expedition to Canada in 1690. Joseph Daniel received land in Warwick, Massachusetts in 1738.

Daniel, Robert. He served on the expedition to Canada in 1690. Robert Daniel received land in Warwick, Massachusetts in 1738.

Daniel, Samuel. He served as a soldier in the French and Indian War until 1758. He received his 50 acre warrant in April 1780 in Caroline County, Virginia.

Daniel, Stephen. He served on the expedition to Canada in 1690. Stephen Daniel, Jr. was admitted to his land in Lyndeboro, Maine in 1736.

Danielson, James. He served in the Narraganset War from Connecticut and received land in Voluntown, Connecticut in 1701.

Danks, Benoni. He had his service as a captain of rangers in the French and Indian War certified in New York 27 May 1773.

Dannall, Stephen. He served as an armorer in the French and Indian War. He was named in New York 12 November 1766.

Dannavan, John. He served as a soldier in the 45th Regiment and returned the survey of his 50 acres in Albany County, New York 15 August 1766.

Darby, John. He was granted 50 acres in Albany County, New York for his service as a soldier in the 86th Regiment of Foot in the French and Indian War 28 October 1765.

Dark, John. He served as a soldier in Capt. Robert Rutherford's Company of

Rangers in 1758 and 1759 in the French and Indian War. A warrant for 50 acres was issued to his representative in March 1780 in Berkeley County, Virginia. He was deceased.

Dark, William. He served as a corporal in a company of rangers under Capt. Robert Rutherford in 1758 and 1759 in the French and Indian War. He was a prisoner in New York when his 50 acre warrant was issued in March 1780 in Berkeley County, Virginia.

Darling, William. He was granted 50 acres in Albany County, New York for his service as a soldier in the 60th Regiment of Foot in the French and Indian War 25 May 1771.

Dart, Richard. He served in the Narraganset War from Connecticut and received land in Voluntown, Connecticut in 1701.

Daulton, Philip. He was granted 50 acres in Albany County, New York for his service as a soldier in the 46th Regiment of Foot in the French and Indian War 8 June 1771.

Davenport, Joseph. He served as a sergeant in the French and Indian War. He assigned his 200 acre land warrant in Virginia.

Davenport, Nathaniel. He served as a captain in the Narraganset War from Boston, Massachusetts. His nephew, Addington Davenport, claimed his land in Bedford, New Hampshire in 1733.

Davenport, Solomon. He served as a corporal in the 60th Regiment in the French and Indian War and had his service certified 28 January 1767 in New York.

Davenport, Thomas. He served in the Narraganset War from Dorchester, Massachusetts. His heirs received land in Bedford, New Hampshire in 1733.

Davenport, William. He served in the Narraganset War from Dorchester, Massachusetts. His nephew, Richard Davenport, received his land in Bedford, New Hampshire in 1733.

Davidson, Adam. He was granted 200 acres in Albany County, New York for his service as a corporal in the 47th Regiment of Foot in the French and Indian War 15 August 1765.

Davidson, David. He was granted 200 acres in Charlotte County, New York for his service as a noncommissioned officer in the 42nd Regiment of Foot in the French and Indian War 12 October 1774.

Davidson, Robert. He was granted 200 acres in Albany County, New York for his service as a sergeant in the 55th Regiment of Foot in the French and Indian War 10 March 1772.

Davies, Robert. He served as a soldier in the French and Indian War and had his service certified in Montgomery County, Virginia for his 50 acres of land 5 April 1780.

Davies, Thomas. He was granted 50 acres in Albany County, New York for his service as a soldier in the 18th Regiment of Foot in the French and Indian War 30 May 1771.

Davis, —. He served on the expedition to Canada in 1690. His son, Moses Davis, received his land in Winchendon, Massachusetts in 1736.

Davis, Benjamin. He served in the Narraganset War from Reading, Massachusetts. His heirs received his land in Westminster, Massachusetts in 1733.

Davis, Cornelius. He served in the Narraganset War from Massachusetts in 1685. His land was located in Buxton, Maine.

Davis, David. He served as a soldier in Capt. John Montgomery's Company of Volunteers on the Shawnee Expedition in 1756 under Maj. Andrew Lewis in the French and Indian War. His representative, Robert Montgomery, received his 50 acre warrant in April 1780 in Montgomery County, Virginia.

Davis, Edward. He was granted 200 acres in Charlotte County, New York for his service as a noncommissioned officer in the 4th Battalion of the 60th Regiment of Foot in the French and Indian War 12 October 1774.

Davis, Eleazer. He was from Harvard, Massachusetts. He served in Capt. John Lovewell's company at Pigwacket. He was awarded 200 acres by Massachusetts 25 March 1736 which was located in Pembroke, New Hampshire. He was from Concord, Massachusetts.

Davis, Gershom. He served on the expedition to Canada in 1690. Gershom Davis received land in Warwick, Massachusetts in 1783.

Davis, Henry. He served as a soldier in the 2nd Virginia Regiment in the French and Indian War and received his 50 acre warrant 13 April 1780 in Albemarle County, Virginia.

Davis, Hopestill. He served in the Narraganset War from Charlestown, Massachusetts. His nephew, Zechariah Davis, received his land in Westminster, Massachusetts in 1733.

Davis, James. He served as collar maker in the royal artillery in the French and Indian War and petitioned for 200 acres of land in New York 13 June 1771.

Davis, James. He served in the Royal Artillery in the French and Indian War and petitioned for his land in New York 7 April 1769.

Davis, James. He served as a soldier in Col. William Byrd's Regiment in 1761 in the French and Indian War and received a warrant for 50 acres 1 February 1780 in Kentucky County, Virginia.

Davis, John. He served in the Narraganset War from Massachusetts. He applied for his land 4 June 1685. His son, Jonathan Davis, received his land in Buxton, Maine.

Davis, John. He served in the Narraganset War from Lynn, Massachusetts. His son-in-law, Michael Bowden, received his land in Amherst, New Hampshire in 1734.

Davis, John. He was granted 200 acres in Albany County, New York for his service as a sergeant in the 60th Regiment of Foot in the French and Indian War 13 February 1767.

Davis, John. He served as a sergeant in Capt. William Preston's Company of Rangers in 1758 in the French and Indian War. He received his 200 acre warrant 17 May 1780 in Greenbrier County, Virginia.

Davis, Jonathan. He was granted 50 acres in Albany County, New York for his service as a soldier in the 80th Regiment of Foot in the French and Indian War 6 June 1765.

Davis, Joseph. He served on the expedition to Canada in 1690 and received land in Poland, Maine in 1739.

Davis, Josiah. He served under Capt. John Lovewell from Massachusetts and was killed at Pigwacket in May 1725. His land was located in Pembroke, New Hampshire.

Davis, Josiah. He served in the Narraganset War from Barnstable, Massachusetts and received land in Gorham, Maine in 1733.

Davis, Samuel. He served in the Narraganset War from Barnstable, Massachusetts and received land in Gorham, Maine in 1733.

Davis, Samuel. He served on the expedition to Canada in 1690. Samuel Davis received land in Warwick, Massachusetts in 1738.

Davis, Samuel. He served as a soldier under Capt. John Montgomery in a company of volunteers on the Shawnee Expedition in 1756 incorporated with the Virginia Regiment under Maj. Andrew Lewis in the French and Indian War. He received his 50 acre warrant in April 1780 in Montgomery County, Virginia.

Davis, Simon. He served in the Narraganset War and received land in Templeton, Massachusetts in 1733.

Davis, Thomas. He served in the Narraganset War from Topsfield, Massachusetts. His heirs received his land in Amherst, New Hampshire in 1734 and sold same to Capt. Stephen Peabody.

Davis, Thomas. He served as a sergeant in the 2nd Virginia Regiment of Regulars under Col. William Byrd in 1756 in the French and Indian War. He petitioned for his 200 acres 14 February 1780 in King and Queen County, Virginia.

Davis, Thomas. He served as a sergeant in the 1st Virginia Regiment under Col.

William Byrd in 1756 in the French and Indian War. He assigned his 200 acre warrant in Augusta County, Virginia 21 March 1780.

Davis, William. He was granted 50 acres in Albany County, New York for his service as a soldier in the 60th Regiment of Foot in the French and Indian War 26 September 1765.

Davis, William. He served as a soldier in Capt. John Dickinson's Company of Rangers in the French and Indian War in 1758. He received his warrant for 50 acres 1 February 1780 in Kentucky County, Virginia.

Davis, William. He served as a sergeant in Capt. William Preston's Company of Rangers from July 1755 to June 1756 and for nine months in 1758 and 1759 in the French and Indian War. He received his 200 acre warrant in April 1780 in Montgomery County, Virginia.

Davis, Zacheriah. He served in the Narraganset War from Massachusetts in 1685. His land was located in Buxton, Maine.

Dawes, Ambros. He served in the Narraganset War from Boston, Massachusetts. His son, Thomas Dawes, received his land in Bedford, New Hampshire in 1733.

Daweze, John. He was granted 50 acres in Gloucester County, New York for his service as a soldier in the 80th Regiment of Foot in the French and Indian War 5 April 1770.

Dawson, Frederick. He was granted 50 acres in Gloucester County, New York for his service as a soldier in the 4th Battalion of the 60th Regiment of Foot in the French and Indian War 5 April 1770.

Dawson, Henry. He served as a captain in the French and Indian War and petitioned for his land 30 December 1766 in New York.

Dawson, Henry. He served as a soldier under Col. William Byrd in 1760 in the French and Indian War. He received his 50 acre warrant in Virginia. His service was proved in Amherst County, Virginia 6 March 1780.

Dawson, John. He was granted 200 acres in Albany County, New York for his service as a corporal officer in the 80th Regiment of Foot in the French and Indian War 15 August 1765.

Dawson, John. He petitioned for 500 acres on the King's bounty in South Carolina on the north side of the Santee River for his service in the French and Indian War 3 May 1768.

Day, John. He served in the Narraganset War from Gloucester, Massachusetts. He claimed his land in Amherst, New Hampshire in 1734.

Day, John. He served in the Narraganset War from Wrentham, Massachusetts. His son, John Day, claimed his land in Greenwich, Massachusetts in 1737.

Day, Joseph. He was granted 50 acres in Albany County, New York for his service as a private in the 18th Regiment of Foot in the French and Indian War 8 June 1771.

Deacon, Peter. He served as a sergeant in the French and Indian War and had his service certified in New York in January 1767.

Dean, Daniel. He served in the Narraganset War. His son-in-law, Daniel Adams, received his land in Templeton, Massachusetts in 1733.

Dean, Joseph. He served as a subaltern in the French and Indian War and received 5,000 acres in Nova Scotia 16 January 1767.

Dean, Thomas. He served as a sergeant in the French and Indian War and received his 200 acres of land from Virginia. His heir at law, Thomas Dean, assigned the warrant.

Dean, William. He served on the expedition to Canada in 1690. His brother, John Dean, received his land in Woburn, Massachusetts in 1737.

Dean, William. He served in the Narraganset War from Dedham, Massachusetts. He died at Lebanon. His heirs received his land in Bedford, New Hampshire in 1733.

Deane, John. He served as a sergeant in the 49th Regiment in the French and Indian War and petitioned for his land in New York 29 June 1774.

DeBernier, John. He was granted 2,000 acres in Albany County, New York for his service as a lieutenant in the 44th Regiment of Foot in the French and Indian War 22 May 1770.

Debnam, Mordecai. He served as a subaltern in the French and Indian War from Virginia and assigned his land warrant for 2,000 acres in Virginia.

DeConti, Peter. He was granted 2,000 acres in Albany County, New York for his service as a lieutenant in a corps of rangers under Major Joseph Gorham in the French and Indian War 5 September 1774. He also appeared as Peter Marquis de Conty.

Dee, Richard. He served as a corporal in the 47th Regiment in the French and Indian War and petitioned for his 200 acres of land in New York 24 January 1775.

Deen, William. He served as a corporal under Col. William Byrd in the Virginia Regiment in the French and Indian War and assigned his warrant for 200 acres in Virginia. He also appeared as William Dean.

DeForge, Peter. He served as a sergeant in the French and Indian War and received 200 acres in West Florida 18 January 1777.

Dehass, John Philip. He was granted 809 and 922.62 acres in Berks County, Pennsylvania for his service as a major in the French and Indian War 3 February 1769.

Deimer, James. He received his 2,000 acres of land in West Florida for his service as a staff officer in the French and Indian War 17 October 1774.

Dekeyser, Leckamyes. He was granted 200 acres in Albany County, New York for his service as a sergeant in the 80th Regiment of Foot in the French and Indian War 17 September 1765.

Delafons, John. He was granted 1,100 acres in West Florida for his service as a warrant officer in the navy in the French and Indian War 29 October 1778.

Delano, John. He received land in Richmond, New Hampshire in 1765 for the service of an unidentified veteran of the expedition to Canada in 1690.

Delashmet, John. He petitioned for 200 acres on Little River on the King's bounty in South Carolina for his service as a noncommissioned officer in the French and Indian War 3 May 1768.

Delleway, John. He served on the expedition to Canada in 1690. John Delleway received land in Chesterfield, Massachusetts in 1739.

Demetral, Louis. He served as a lieutenant in the 4th Battalion of the Royal American Regiment in the French and Indian War. His widow, Marie Lavoyne, petitioned for 3,000 acres of land in New York 9 August 1773.

Demler, George. He was granted 2,000 acres in Albany County, New York for his service as a lieutenant in the 60th Regiment of Foot in the French and Indian War 24 May 1771.

Demmick, Joseph. He was wounded in his back by a bullet at the fight at Nerridgawock. He had five sons but no land on which to settle them. He was from Barnstable, Massachusetts and sought 250 acres 30 November 1727.

Dempsey, William. He served as a soldier in Capt. Smith's Regular Company in the French and Indian War and assigned his 50 acre land warrant in Virginia.

Dempsy, Charles. He served in the 48th Regiment in the French and Indian War and petitioned for his land in New York 20 May 1771.

Denhard, Thomas. He served as a corporal in the 4th Battalion 60th Regiment in the French and Indian War and petitioned for his 200 acres in New York 24 October 1764.

Denio, Aaron. He was taken prisoner by the Indians in 1702 and carried to Canada. He was from Deerfield and was awarded 200 acres by Massachusetts 28 November 1735.

Dension, D. He served on the expedition to Canada in 1690. His nephew, John Dension, by his guardian, Nathaniel Rogers, received his land in Winchendon, Massachusetts in 1736.

Denison, George. He served as a captain in the Narraganset War from Connecticut and received land in Voluntown, Connecticut in 1701.

Denison, George. He served in the Narraganset War from Connecticut and received land in Voluntown, Connecticut in 1701.

Denison, John. He served in the Narraganset War from Connecticut and received land in Voluntown, Connecticut in 1701.

Denison, John. He served in the Narraganset War from Massachusetts in 1685. His son, John Denison, received his land in Buxton, Maine.

Denison, William. He served in the Narraganset War from Connecticut and received land in Voluntown, Connecticut in 1701.

Dennis, James. He served in the expedition to Canada in 1690. Thomas Pitman petitioned for his land in Raymond, Maine in 1735.

Dennis, John. He served as Chaplain at St. George's Fort and prayed for a grant of land in Massachusetts 12 June 1740. He was awarded 200 acres on 21 June following.

Dennis, Lawrence. He served in the expedition to Canada in 1690. Thomas Pitman petitioned for his land in Raymond, Maine in 1735.

Dennis, Peter. He was granted 50 acres in Albany County, New York for his service as a soldier in the 60th Regiment of Foot in the French and Indian War 26 September 1765.

Dennis, William. He served in the expedition to Canada in 1690. Thomas Pitman petitioned for his land in Raymond, Maine in 1735.

Dennison, John. He was granted 200 acres in Albany County, New York for his service as a noncommissioned officer in the 46th Regiment of Foot in the French and Indian War 8 March 1771.

Denwood, Cornelius. He served in the French and Indian War and petitioned for land in New York 2 February 1769.

Dent, Arthur. He served as a non-commissioned officer in the Virginia Regiment under Col. George Washington in the French and Indian War until disbanded after which he served under Col. Adam Stephen. He proved his service 4 April 1780 in Frederick County, Virginia.

DePeyster, Pierre William. He served as a midshipman on board H.M.S. sloop *Hunter* in the French and Indian War and petitioned for his land in New York 9 March 1768.

Derby, William. He served on the expedition to Canada in 1690. Roger Derby was admitted to his land in Lyndeboro, Maine in 1736.

Desbarres, Joseph Frederick Wallet. He served in the French and Indian War and received 2,000 acres in Nova Scotia 5 April 1769.

Desbruyeres, John. He served as a lieutenant in the 56th Regiment in the French and Indian War from New York and petitioned for his 2,000 acres of land in 1764.

Devell, Jonathan. He shared in the grant of East Greenwich, Rhode Island made to those who had rendered service in King Philip's War. The grant was made 31 October 1677.

Dever, William. He served in the French and Indian War from Virginia under Col. William Byrd. His heir, Edward Dever, received the warrant for 50 acres 19 October 1779.

Devericks, Nicholas. He was granted 50 acres in Albany County, New York for his service as a soldier in the 80th Regiment of Foot in the French and Indian War 4 July 1770.

Devine, William. He was granted 200 acres in Albany County, New York for his service as a sergeant in the 60th Regiment of Foot in the French and Indian War 13 May 1765.

Dewolf, Edward. He served in the Narraganset War from Connecticut and received his land in Voluntown, Connecticut in 1701.

Dewolf, Stephen. He served in the Narraganset War from Connecticut and received land in Voluntown, Connecticut in 1701.

Dexter, Philip. He served in the Narraganset War from Falmouth, Massachusetts. He claimed his land in Amherst, New Hampshire in 1734.

Dick, Charles. He served as commissary of provisions and stores for the Virginia troops in 1754 in the French and Indian War. He was also on the expedition of British troops against Fort DuQuesne. He received four warrants for 1,000 acres 27 March 1780 in Richmond, Virginia.

Dick, Samuel. He was granted 2,000 acres in Albany County, New York for his service as a surgeon's mate in a military hospital in the French and Indian War 7 October 1771.

Dickenson, John. He served as a captain in the French and Indian War and received a land warrant for 3,000 acres in Virginia.

Dickerson, Charles. He served as a captain in the French and Indian War and received 3,000 acres in Nova Scotia 23 October 1779.

Dickerson, James. He served as a soldier in the French and Indian War and received 50 acres in Nova Scotia 9 October 1776.

Dickerson, Thomas. He served as a soldier in 1758 in the French and Indian War. He assigned his right to 50 acres in Virginia. He was in Caroline County, Virginia in February 1780. He also appeared as Thomas Dickinson.

Dickinson, Samuel. He served from Deerfield, Massachusetts against the Indians. For his great sufferings in captivity he was granted 200 acres 16 June 1733.

Dickson, Benjamin. He was granted 200 acres in Albany County, New York for his service as a corporal in the 3rd Battalion in the 60th Regiment of Foot in the French and Indian War 1 June 1770.

Dickson, Charles. He served in the French and Indian War and received 3,000 acres in Nova Scotia 1 October 1770.

Dickson, David. He was granted 1,000 acres in West Florida for his service as a major of a brigade on 27 September 1773 and 3,000 acres as a captain during the French and Indian War.

Dickson, David. He was granted 3,000 acres in West Florida for his service as a captain in the 64th Regiment of Foot in the French and Indian War 21 October 1774.

Dike, Nathaniel. He served on the expedition to Canada in 1690. Palmer Golding claimed his right to land in Bethel, Maine in 1767.

Dimmock, Samuel. He served in the Narraganset War from Mansfield, Massachusetts. He claimed his land in Greenwich, Massachusetts in 1737.

Dimmock, Thomas. He served as a captain and was slain at the memorable Winnegance fight in 1697. His only son, Edward Dimmock of Barnstable, was awarded 300 acres by Massachusetts.

Dingwall, Alexander. He was granted 200 acres in Albany County, New York for his service as a sergeant in the 55th Regiment of Foot in the French and Indian War 6 June 1765.

Dinsdell, William. He served in the Narraganset War from Boston, Massachusetts. His son, William Dinsdell, received his land in Boston, Massachusetts in 1733.

Dinsley, John. He was granted 50 acres in Albany County, New York for his service as a soldier in the 60th Regiment of Foot in the French and Indian War 25 May 1771.

Disborough, Nicholas. He was granted 50 acres in Connecticut for his service in the Pequot War 11 May 1671. He also appeared as Nicholas Desborough.

Disney, Daniel. He served as a captain in the 80th Regiment in the French and Indian War and petitioned for 3,000 acres of land in New York 2 June 1767.

Dix, James. He received land in Alstead, New Hampshire in 1771 for the service of an unidentified veteran of the expedition to Canada in 1690.

Dixey, Samuel. He served on the expedition to Canada in 1690. William Dixey was admitted to his land in Lyndeboro, Maine in 1736.

Dixon, Alexander. He was granted 50 acres in Albany County, New York for his service as a soldier in the 60th Regiment of Foot in the French and

Indian War 28 October 1765.

Doan, Daniel. He served in the Narraganset War from Eastham, Massachusetts and received land in Gorham, Maine in 1733.

Doan, John. He served in the Narraganset War from Eastham, Massachusetts and received land in Gorham, Maine in 1733.

Dobbs, John. He was granted 50 acres in Albany County, New York for his service as a private in the 60th or Royal American Regiment of Foot in the French and Indian War 8 June 1771.

Dobson, Henry. He served in the French and Indian War and received 3,000 acres in Nova Scotia 7 October 1771.

Dodd, John. He served on the expedition to Canada in 1690. John Dodd was admitted to his land in Lydeboro, Maine in 1736.

Dodd, Morris. He was granted 200 acres in Charlotte County, New York for his service as a corporal in the 35th Regiment of Foot in the French and Indian War 4 August 1774.

Dodding, John. He was granted 50 acres near Fort Charlotte, South Carolina on the King's bounty for his service in the French and Indian War 13 May 1768.

Dodds, John, Jr. He served in the Narraganset War from Beverly, Massachusetts and petitioned for his land in Massachusetts 4 June 1685.

Dodds, William. He served in the Narraganset War from Beverly, Massachusetts and petitioned for his land in Massachusetts 4 June 1685.

Dodge, John. He served in the Narraganset War from Beverly, Massachusetts. His heirs claimed his land in Amherst, New Hampshire in 1734. Jonathan Dodge and John Dodge drew the land.

Dodge, John. He served in the expedition to Canada in 1690. John Dodge petitioned for his land in Raymond, Maine in 1735.

Dodge, Jonathan. He sought land for his service against the Indians in Massachusetts. His application was rejected 10 March 1735. He was from Beverley.

Dodge, William. He served in the Narraganset War from Beverly, Massachusetts. His heirs claimed his land in Amherst, New Hampshire in 1734.

Dodgin, William. He was granted 200 acres in Craven County, South Carolina on the King's bounty 21 June 1765. He served as a corporal in the French and Indian War.

Doe, John. He was granted 50 acres in Gloucester County, New York for his service as a soldier in the 80th Regiment of Foot in the French and

Indian War 5 April 1770.

Dolway, Henry. He served as a lieutenant in Capt. Alexander Regley's Company in the 74th Regiment of Foot under Maj. Gen. Sir John Irvin in 1759 until the end of the French and Indian War and received his 2,000 acre warrant in Virginia. He proved his service in Yohogania County, Virginia 28 February 1780.

Domini, John. He was granted 50 acres in Albany County, New York for his service as a soldier in the 48th Regiment of Foot in the French and Indian War 25 May 1771.

Donald, Robert. He was granted 50 acres in Albany County, New York for his service as a soldier in the 42nd Regiment of Foot in the French and Indian War 30 October 1765.

Donaldson, Alexander. He was granted 2,000 acres in Charlotte County, New York for his service as a lieutenant in the 42nd Regiment of Foot in the French and Indian War 12 October 1774.

Donaldson, John. He served as a sergeant in the 55th Regiment in the French and Indian War and had his service certified in New York 1 October 1773.

Donaldson, Joseph. He served as an ensign in the 1st Virginia Regiment under Col. William Byrd in the French and Indian War. He was from Greenbrier County, Virginia. His administrator, John Stuart, assigned his 2,000 acre warrant in Virginia. He also appeared as Joseph Donnelson.

Doncan, John. He served in the Narraganset War from Barnstable, Massachusetts and received land in Gorham, Maine in 1733.

Donelly, John. He was granted 50 acres in Albany County, New York for his service as a private in the 80th Regiment of Foot in the French and Indian War 8 June 1771.

Donnavan, Cornelius. He was granted 50 acres in Colleton County, South Carolina on the King's bounty for his service in the French and Indian War 1 June 1767.

Donnelly, John. He served as a noncommissioned officer in the Virginia Regiment under Col. William Byrd in the French and Indian War. He was in Washington County, Virginia 18 January 1780. Arthur Campbell proved that he was entitled to 200 acres.

Donnolly, Thomas. He was granted 200 acres in Albany County, New York for his service as a corporal in the 28th Regiment of Foot in the French and Indian War 10 May 1770.

Donnoly, John. He was granted 50 acres in Gloucester County, New York for his service as a soldier in the 28th Regiment of Foot in the French and

Indian War 5 April 1770.

Donnoway, William. He served as a soldier from 1759 to 1762 under Col. William Byrd in the French and Indian War and assigned his 50 acre warrant in Virginia.

Doolittle, John. He was a veteran of the Narraganset War. The town of Wallingford, Connecticut granted him 5 acres for his service 27 December 1687.

Dooly, Henry. He served as a soldier in the Virginia Regiment under Col. William Byrd in the French and Indian War. He petitioned for 50 acres 18 January 1780 in Washington County, Virginia.

Dopler, Frederick. He served as a private in the 60th Regiment in the French and Indian War and returned the survey for his 50 acres in Albany County, New York 14 August 1766.

Doran, Matthew. He served in the French and Indian War. He was entitled to a warrant of 50 acres which his widow, Elizabeth Doran, assigned in Virginia.

Dorins, James. He served as a soldier in Capt. Woodward's Company of Regulars in the French and Indian War. He applied in Botetourt County, Virginia in March 1780. He assigned his warrant for 50 acres in Virginia.

Dormon, Dennis. He served in the French and Indian War and had his service certified 22 January 1767 in New York and assigned his right to the land the following day.

Dorrington, Richard. He was granted 50 acres in Tryon County, New York for his service as a private in the 40th Regiment of Foot in the French and Indian War 10 September 1774.

Douener, —. He served in the Narraganset War from Barnstable, Massachusetts. Mary Douener received his land in Gorham, Maine in 1733.

Dougel, Thomas. He was granted 50 acres in Orange County, New York for his service as a soldier in the 28th Regiment of Foot in the French and Indian War 15 May 1770.

Dougherty, Charles. He was granted 50 acres in Gloucester County, New York for his eight years and four months of service as a soldier in the 44th Regiment of Foot in the French and Indian War 5 April 1770.

Dougherty, Felix. He was granted 200 acres in Albany County, New York for his service as a drummer in the 55th Regiment of Foot in the French and Indian War 15 May 1770.

Dougherty, Jeremiah. He was granted 200 acres in Albany County, New York for his service as a corporal in the 4th Battalion of the Royal American or 60th Regiment of Foot in the French and Indian War 27 September 1769.

Doughirty, James. He was granted 50 acres in Albany County, New York for his service as a soldier in the 17th Regiment of Foot in the French and Indian War 1 April 1771.

Douglas, Thomas. He served as a noncommissioned officer in the French and Indian War and received a land warrant for 200 acres which he assigned.

Douglass, George. He served as a captain in the 51st Regiment in the French and Indian War. His son, David Douglass, petitioned for his late father's land in New York 19 June 1773.

Douglass, John. He served as a soldier in the French and Indian War and petitioned for his land in New York in November 1766.

Douglass, Skeen. He was granted 200 acres in Albany County, New York for his service as a miner in the Royal Regiment of Artillery in the French and Indian War 21 October 1765.

Douglass, William. He served in the Narraganset War from Connecticut and received land in Voluntown, Connecticut in 1701. He also appeared as William Douglace.

Douglass, William. He was granted 200 acres in Albany County, New York for his service as a sergeant in the 60th Regiment of Foot in the French and Indian War 1 April 1772.

Douglass, William. He was granted 50 acres in Albany County, New York for his service as a soldier in the 2nd Battalion 60th Regiment of Foot in the French and Indian War 14 April 1772.

Douglass, William. He was commissioned a major of a regiment of foot under Col. Peter Schuyler by Gov. Francis Barnard in New Jersey on 15 March 1759 and served in the French and Indian War. He applied in Prince Edward County, Virginia 4 April 1780. His warrant for 5,000 acres was issued in Virginia and assigned.

Douthalt, Michael. He applied for his 100 acre land grant for his service as a soldier in Georgia. His application was rejected 1 November 1759.

Dow, Archibald. He served as a lieutenant in the French and Indian War and petitioned for his 2,000 acres of land in New York 8 March 1764.

Dow, Thomas. He served in Narraganset War from Massachusetts in 1685. His son, Ephraim Dow, received his land in Buxton, Maine.

Dowd, Michael. He was granted 50 acres in Albany County, New York for his his service as a soldier in the 80th Regiment of Foot in the French and Indian War 29 October 1765.

Dowe, Alexander. He served as a lieutenant in the 60th Regiment in the French and Indian War from New York. He was the son of James Dowe.

Dowe, Henry. He served on the expedition to Canada in 1690 and received land in Poland, Maine in 1739.

Dowe, James. He served as a lieutenant in the 60th Regiment in the French and Indian War. His son, Alexander Dowe, petitioned for his father's grant of 2,000 acres 19 July 1766 in New York.

Dower, John. He was granted 50 acres in Albany County, New York for his service as a soldier in the 55th Regiment of Foot in the French and Indian War 28 October 1765.

Dowse, Lodwick. He served on the expedition to Canada in 1690. Joshua Kibby received his land in Bethel, Maine in 1767.

Dowlin, William. He was granted 200 acres in Charlotte County, New York for his service as a noncommissioned officer in the 4th Battalion of the 60th Regiment of Foot in the French and Indian War 12 October 1774.

Down, Robert. He served in the Narraganset War from Massachusetts in 1685. His land was located in Buxton, Maine.

Downe, Edward. He was granted 200 acres in Albany County, New York for his service as a sergeant in the 28th Regiment of Foot in the French and Indian War 1 April 1772.

Downes, James. He served in the French and Indian War and petitioned for his land in New York in November 1766.

Downie, John. He was granted 50 acres in Albany County, New York for his service as a soldier in the 55th Regiment of Foot in the French and Indian War 18 April 1769.

Downing, —. He served on the expedition to Canada in 1690. John Downing by his attorney received his land in Winchendon, Massachusetts in 1736.

Downings, Benjamin. He served in the Narraganset War from Eastham, Massachusetts and received land in Gorham, Maine in 1733.

Downings, Joseph. He served in the Narraganset War from Eastham, Massachusetts and received land in Gorham, Maine in 1733.

Downs, James. He was granted 200 acres in Albany County, New York for his service as a corporal in the 28th Regiment of Foot in the French and Indian War 25 May 1771.

Dowse, Joseph. He served in the Narraganset War from Charlestown, Massachusetts. His daughter, Margery Dowse, received his land in Westminster, Massachusetts in 1733.

Doyen, Francis. He served in the campaign against the Indians from Penacock, Massachusetts in or about 1728. He received his land in Pembroke, New Hampshire.

Doyle, Charles. He was granted 50 acres in Albany County, New York for his service as a soldier in the 80th Regiment of Foot in the French and Indian War 28 October 1765.

Dozier, Timothy. He was granted 50 acres in Fredericksburg Township, South Carolina on the King's bounty for his service in the French and Indian War 21 June 1765.

Drake, Francis. He served as a corporal in the French and Indian War and received his 200 acre land warrant in Virginia.

Draper, John. He served as a lieutenant in the French and Indian War and was entitled to 2,000 acres of land in Virginia which he assigned. He may have been the one of the name who proved his service in Botetourt County, Virginia 10 February 1780.

Driggen, Thomas. He served as a soldier under Col. William Byrd in 1760 in the French and Indian War and received a warrant for 50 acres in July 1779 in Bedford County, Virginia. He also appeared as Thomas Drigger.

Driskill, Daniel. He served as a soldier under Gen. Forbes in the French and Indian War in 1758. He proved his service in Bedford County, Virginia 28 February 1780.

Driver, John. He served on the expedition to Canada in 1690. His heirs received land in Chesterfield, Massachusetts in 1739.

Driver, Robert. He served in the Narraganset War from Lynn, Massachusetts. He applied for his land 4 June 1685. His daughter, Ruth Driver, claimed his land in Amherst, New Hampshire in 1734.

Driver, William. He was a soldier under Col. William Byrd in one of the Virginia Regiments in the French and Indian War. Edward Driver, relationship not specified, assigned the 50 acres.

Drummond, Gregor. He was granted 200 acres in Charlotte County, New York for his service as a corporal in the 55th Regiment of Foot in the French and Indian War 14 February 1775.

Drummond, Hugh. He was granted 200 acres in Albany County, New York for his service as a noncommissioned officer in the 42nd Regiment of Foot in the French and Indian War 30 October 1765.

Drummond, John. He was granted 50 acres in Albany County, New York for his service as a soldier in the 80th Regiment of Foot in the French and Indian War 26 July 1765.

Drummond, Norman. He served as a sergeant in the French and Indian War in the 42nd Regiment. He had a survey in Albany County, New York 29 October 1765.

Duane, Cornelius. He served as a lieutenant in the French and Indian War and petitioned for his land 30 December 1765 in New York.

Dubois, Peter. He served as a captain in the French and Indian War and petitioned for his land 30 December 1766 in New York.

Dudley, Joseph. He served in the Narraganset War from Roxbury, Massachusetts. His son, Paul Dudley, received his land in Bedford, New Hampshire in 1733.

Duff, Bartholomew. He served in the French and Indian War and petitioned for his land in New York 2 February 1769.

Duff, David. He assigned his right to land for service in the French and Indian War to Robert Buchanan 9 January 1767 in New York.

Dugan, Christopher. He served as a corporal in the 47th Regiment in the French and Indian War and petitioned for his 200 acres in New York 27 April 1765.

Dugan, Dennis. He was granted 50 acres in Albany County, New York for his service as a soldier in the 60th Regiment of Foot in the French and Indian War 29 October 1765.

Duggin, John. He served as a private in the 43rd Regiment in the French and Indian War and petitioned for 50 acres in Ulster County, New York 19 August 1766.

Dumprey, William. He served as a soldier in the French and Indian War and assigned his 50 acre warrant in Virginia.

Dun, William. He served as a corporal under Col. William Byrd in the Virginia Regiment in the French and Indian War and received 200 acres of land in Fincastle County, Virginia in 1774.

Dunbar, Donald. He was granted 50 acres in Albany County, New York for his service as a soldier in the 77th Regiment of Foot in the French and Indian War 13 May 1765.

Dunbar, George. He served as a captain in the French and Indian War and petitioned for his land 30 December 1765 in New York.

Duncan, James. He was granted 200 acres in Charlotte County, New York for his service as a corporal in the 55th Regiment of Foot in the French and Indian War 25 January 1773.

Duncan, John. He served in Lovewell's War in Massachusetts and received his land in Petersham, Massachusetts in 1733.

Duncan, Joseph. He served a soldier under Capt. John Field in Gen. Forbes's expedition in 1758 in the French and Indian War. He was in Culpeper County, Virginia 8 October 1779. He assigned his warrant of 50 acres in Virginia.

Duncan, William. He served as a soldier in Capt. Charles Lewis's Company of Regulars in the French and Indian War and received his 50 acre warrant in Virginia.

Duncanson, James. He served as a lieutenant under Col. George Washington in the Virginia Regiment in the French and Indian War and assigned his land warrant for 2,000 acres in Virginia.

Dunkin, Thomas. He shared in the grant of East Greenwich, Rhode Island made to those who had rendered service in King Philip's War. The grant was made 31 October 1677.

Dunham, John. He served in the Narraganset War from Mansfield, Massachusetts. His son, Isaac Dunham, claimed his land in Greenwich, Massachusetts in 1737.

Dunkham, James. He served as a soldier under Capt. Robert Mumford in Col. William Byrd's Regiment in 1758 in the French and Indian War. He received his 50 acre warrant 27 March 1780 in Cumberland County, Virginia. He also appeared as James Durham.

Dunlap, James. He served as a lieutenant in Capt. Peter Hogg's Company of Rangers destroyed by the savages at the fort in the upper tract of the South Branch of the Potomac in 1758 in the French and Indian War. His heirs and nephews, James Brown and Adam Guthery, requested his 2,000 acres 21 December 1779 in Augusta County, Virginia. He served as a captain of a company of rangers from 8 June 1757 to December 1757 and was killed by the Indians in 1758. His 3,000 acres were issued to his heirs James Brown, Adam Guthrie, and George Armstrong in April 1780 in Montgomery County, Virginia.

Dunn, John. He was granted 200 acres in Ulster County, New York for his service as a sergeant in the 49th Regiment of Foot in the French and Indian War 6 December 1774.

Dunn, Patrick. He received his land in West Florida for his service as a soldier in the French and Indian War 27 March 1776.

Dunn, Richard. He was granted 50 acres in Amelia Township, South Carolina on the King's bounty for his service in the French and Indian War 21 August 1765.

Dunn, Thomas. He was granted 50 acres in Albany County, New York for his service as a matross in the 2nd Battalion of the Royal Regiment of Artillery in the French and Indian War 13 February 1767.

Dunnavon, John. He was granted 50 acres in Albany County, New York for his service as a soldier in the 45th Regiment of Foot in the French and Indian War 15 August 1765.

Dunning, Thomas. He was granted 50 acres in Albany County, New York for his service as a private in the 60th or Royal American Regiment of Foot in the French and Indian War 8 June 1771.

Duperon, Philip. He was granted 2,000 acres in Albany County, New York for his service as a lieutenant in the 60th Regiment of Foot in the French and Indian War 23 August 1764.

Durgan, John. He served as a private in the French and Indian War and petitioned for his land in New York 8 July 1765.

Durgee, —. He served on the expedition to Canada in 1690. His son-in-law, John Martin, received his land in Winchendon, Massachusetts in 1736.

Durham, James. He served as a soldier under Capt. Robert Mumford and Col. William Byrd in 1758 in the French and Indian War. He applied for his 50 acres in Cumberland County, Virginia 27 March 1780.

Durnford, Elias. He received land in West Florida for his service as aide de camp to Lord Albemarle in the French and Indian War 30 July 1772.

Durrell, Moses. He served in the Narraganset War from Massachusetts in 1685. His son, Nathaniel Durrell, received his land in Buxton, Maine.

Durrell, Peter. He received land in Alstead, New Hampshire in 1771 for the service of an unidentified veteran of the expedition to Canada in 1690.

Dutton, William. He was granted 50 acres in Gloucester County, New York for his service as a soldier in the 44th Regiment of Foot in the French and Indian War 5 April 1770.

Dutton, William. He was granted 50 acres in Granville County, South Carolina on the King's bounty for his service in the French and Indian War 24 August 1770.

Dwelly, Samuel. He received land in Richmond, New Hampshire in 1765 for the service of an unidentified veteran of the expedition to Canada in 1690.

Dyer, Benjamin. He served in the Narraganset War from Boston, Massachusetts. His son, Benjamin Dyer, received his land in Bedford, New Hampshire in 1733.

Dyre, Henry. He shared in the grant of East Greenwich, Rhode Island made to those who had rendered service in King Philip's War. The grant was made 31 October 1677.

Eaby, Thomas. He served as an artificer in the French and Indian War. His discharge was signed by Lt. Col. Adam Stephen. He assigned his right to Thomas Patterson in Yohogania County, Virginia 22 May 1780.

Ealey, Thomas. He was a soldier under Col. William Byrd in the French and Indian War and received a warrant for 50 acres 8 November 1779 in James City County, Virginia.

Eames, Nathaniel. He served on the expedition to Canada in 1690. Nathaniel

Eames received his land in Bethel, Maine in 1767.

Eams, Henry. He served in the Narraganset War and received land in Templeton, Massachusetts in 1733.

Eams, John. He served in the Narraganset War and received land in Templeton, Massachusetts in 1733.

Earle, John. He served as a lieutenant in the French and Indian War and assigned his 2,000 acre warrant in Virginia.

Earles, Thomas. He served as a sergeant in Capt. Gist's Company under Col. William Byrd in the French and Indian War and received his 200 acre warrant in Virginia.

Early, Thomas. He served as a soldier in the 1st Virginia Regiment in the French and Indian War and assigned his 50 acre warrant in Virginia.

Earlybush, Michael. He was granted 50 acres in Craven County, South Carolina on the King's bounty for his service in the French and Indian War 6 February 1773.

Easley, John. He served as a soldier for eight months under Col. William Peachey in 1759 in the French and Indian War and assigned his 50 acre warrant to William Easley 14 February 1780 in Buckingham County, Virginia.

Easley, Thomas. He served as a soldier in the 1st Virginia Regiment in the French and Indian War and received a warrant for 50 acres.

Easley, William. He served as a soldier under Col. William Peachey for eight months in 1759 in the French and Indian War and received his warrant 14 February 1780 in Buckingham County, Virginia.

Easmon, Thomas. He served in the Narraganset War from Massachusetts in 1685. His son, Jonathan Easmon, received his land in Buxton, Maine.

East, Josiah. He was a soldier in the Virginia Regiment under Col. George Washington in the French and Indian War. He was in Rockbridge County, Virginia in October 1777 and assigned his 50 acres in Virginia.

Eatherinton, James. He served as a sergeant in the Virginia Regiment under Col. George Washington in the French and Indian War and assigned his warrant for 200 acres.

Eaton, Thomas. He was granted 50 acres in Albany County, New York for his service as a soldier in the 46th Regiment of Foot in the French and Indian War 28 June 1770.

Eaton, William. He received land in Richmond, New Hampshire in 1765 for the service of an unidentified veteran of the expedition to Canada in 1690.

Eberhard, Augustus Charles. He served in the French and Indian War and received 500 acres in Nova Scotia 11 October 1771.

Eberhard, George. He was granted 500 acres in West Florida for his service as a staff officer in the French and Indian War 30 March 1778. He was also granted 500 acres 24 November 1778.

Eckley, Arthur. He was granted 50 acres in Albany County, New York for his service as a soldier in the 80th Regiment of Foot in the French and Indian War 28 October 1765.

Ecuyier, Simon. He was granted 3,000 acres in Albany County, New York for his service as a captain in the 60th Regiment of Foot in the French and Indian War 28 October 1765.

Eddington, James. He was granted 2,000 acres in Cumberland County, New York for his service as a lieutenant in the 42nd Regiment of Foot in the French and Indian War 22 October 1766.

Edlington, William. He served in the French and Indian War and assigned his 50 acre warrant in Virginia.

Edmiston, Robert. He served as a lieutenant in the French and Indian War and received 5,000 acres of land in Albany County, New York. The survey was returned 3 March 1770.

Edmiston, Samuel. He served as a sergeant in the French and Indian War and received 200 acres of land in Virginia. He also appeared as Samuel Edmondson.

Edmiston, William. He served as a captain in the French and Indian War and received 5,000 acres of land in Cumberland County, New York. The survey was returned 3 March 1770.

Edmiston, William. He served as an ensign in the French and Indian War and was entitled to 2,000 acres of land which he took in Fincastle County, Virginia 5 July 1774. He also appeared as William Edmondson.

Edmonds, Samuel. He served in the Narraganset War from Lynn, Massachusetts. His land was in Amherst, New Hampshire in 1734. John Jenks drew same.

Edmunds, John. He served in the Narraganset War from Lynn, Massachusetts and petitioned for his land 4 June 1685.

Edmundson, Thomas. He served as a noncommissioned officer in the French and Indian War and assigned his 200 acre warrant in Virginia. He also appeared as Thomas Edmiston.

Edwards, James. He served as a surgeon's mate in the French and Indian War and petitioned for his 2,000 acres of land in New York 27 March 1765.

Edwards, Jeremiah. He served as a soldier in the 1st Virginia Regiment under Col. William Byrd in the French and Indian War and received his 50 acre warrant in Virginia. He proved his service in Augusta County, Virginia 21 March 1780.

Edwards, John. He served as a soldier in Capt. Mercer's Company of Regulars in the 1st Virginia Regiment in the French and Indian War. He was in Botetourt County, Virginia in April 1780. He assigned his 50 acre warrant in Virginia.

Edwards, William. He served as a soldier in Capt. Walter Steward's Company of Rangers in 1758 in the French and Indian War. He was in Louisa County, Virginia 13 March 1780. He assigned his 50 acres.

Eggleston, James. He was granted 50 acres in Connecticut for his service in the Pequot War 11 May 1671.

Ekshaw, John. He commanded one of H.M.'s vessels on the lakes in the French and Indian War and petitioned for 3,000 acres in New York 14 14 December 1767.

Elamus, —. He served on the expedition to Canada in 1690. Jabez Elamus received land in Dumbarton, New Hampshire in 1735.

Elbing, John. He was granted 50 acres in Ulster County, New York for his service as a soldier in the 60th or Royal American Regiment of Foot in the French and Indian War 2 May 1775.

Eldridge, George. He served as a private sentinel in the independent companies in the French and Indian War and sought his 50 acres of land in Georgia 21 March 1769.

Eldridge, Jehosophat. He served in the Narraganset War from Sandwich, Massachusetts and received land in Gorham, Maine in 1733.

Eldridge, Rolfe. He served as a sergeant for eight months under Col. William Peachey in 1759 in the French and Indian War. He assigned his 200 acre warrant in Virginia.

Elisha, John. He was granted 50 acres in Albany County, New York for his service as a soldier in the 60th Regiment of Foot in the French and Indian War 17 September 1765.

Elkins, John. He was granted 5,000 acres in Albany County, New York for his service as a major in the 60th Regiment of Foot in the French and Indian War 19 October 1765.

Elkintorn, John. He served as a soldier in the 28th Regiment in the French and Indian War and petitioned for his land in New York 6 August 1774.

Elinwood, John. He served in the Narraganset War from Beverly, Massachusetts. Andrew Dodge claimed his land in Amherst, New Hampshire in 1734.

Elinwood, Ralph. He served in the Narraganset War from Beverly, Massachusetts and claimed his land in Amherst, New Hampshire in

1734.

Ellerson, Charles. He served as a corporal in Capt. Roote's Company of Regulars in the French and Indian War and received his 200 acre warrant in April 1780 in Botetourt County, Virginia. He also appeared as Charles Ellison.

Ellery, Isaac. He served in the Narraganset War from Gloucester, Massachusetts. Samuel Stevens claimed his land in Amherst, New Hampshire in 1734.

Ellet, Richard. He served as a soldier in Capt. Samuel Meredith's Company in 1758 under Col. William Byrd in the French and Indian War. He was too infirm to appear in court to make his application for his 50 acre warrant. His petition was presented 6 April 1780 in Hanover County, Virginia.

Ellingham, Richard. He served in the Narraganset War from Barnstable, Massachusetts and received land in Gorham, Maine in 1733.

Ellinwood, David. He served on the expedition to Canada in 1690. Ebenezer Ellinwood petitioned for his land in Raymond, Maine in 1735.

Elliot, Francis. He was granted 200 acres in Albany County, New York for his service as a sergeant in the 55th Regiment of Foot in the French and Indian War 15 May 1770.

Elliot, Henry. He served in the Narraganset War from Connecticut. His heirs received land in Voluntown, Connecticut in 1701.

Elliott, George. He served as a noncommissioned officer in the French and Indian War and assigned his 200 acre land warrant in Virginia.

Elliott, James. He received his land in West Florida for his service as a commissary in the French and Indian War 27 August 1776.

Elliott, Joseph. He received his 200 acres of land in West Florida for his service as a noncommissioned officer in the French and Indian War 17 October 1774.

Elliott, Hamilton. He was granted 50 acres in Albany County, New York for his service as a soldier in the 44th Regiment of Foot in the French and Indian War 27 September 1769.

Elliott, Thomas. He served as an officer in the French and Indian War and was entitled to 2,000 acres which he desired to locate in Augusta County, Virginia in 1773.

Elliott, Thomas. He served as a lieutenant Col. William Peachey's Battalion in the 2nd Virginia Regiment in 1759 in the French and Indian War and received a warrant for 1,000 acres 18 November 1779 in King William County, Virginia. He also received 3,000 acres for serving as paymaster.

Elliott, William. He served in the Capt. Dunlop's Company of Rangers in 1758 in the French and Indian War. He was dead when his service was proved in Augusta County, Virginia 15 February 1780.

Ellis, Alexander. He was granted 2,000 acres in West Florida for his service as commander of the armed schooner, *Hinchenbrook*, in the French and Indian War in August 1776.

Ellis, Bartelot. He served as a soldier under Capt. Samuel Meredith in the Virginia Battalion of Regulars under Col. William Byrd in 1758 in the French and Indian War. He requested his 50 acre warrant 6 April 1780 in Hanover County, Virginia.

Ellis, Mathias, Jr. He was from Sandwich, Massachusetts and served in the late Indian and French wars. He was granted 150 acres 26 September 1739.

Ellis, Patrick. He served as a soldier in the 72nd Regiment in the French and Indian War and petitioned for his land in New York 22 October 1766.

Ellis, Richard. He served as a soldier under Capt. Samuel Meredith in 1758 in the Virginia Regiment under Col. William Byrd in the French and Indian War. Bartelot Ellis requested his 50 acre warrant 6 April 1780 in Hanover County, Virginia since Richard Ellis was too infirm to attend court.

Ellis, William. He was granted 200 acres in Albany County, New York for his service as a sergeant in the 80th Regiment of Foot in the French and Indian War 16 July 1765.

Elmer, Edward. He served in the Pequot War and received a grant of land in Soldiers' Field in Hartford, Connecticut.

Elmor, John. He was granted 50 acres in Albany County, New York for his service as a soldier in the 48th Regiment of Foot in the French and Indian War 21 August 1768.

Elsey, Samuel. He served on the expedition to Canada in 1690. Ephraim Ingalls was admitted to his land in Lyndeboro, Maine in 1736.

Elsley, Isaac. He served in the Narraganset War from Massachusetts in 1685. His son, Capt. William Elsely, received his land in Buxton, Maine.

Elsley, William. He served in the Narraganset War from Massachusetts in 1685. His land was located in Buxton, Maine.

Elsworth, John. He received his 2,000 acres of land in West Florida for his service as a quartermaster in the French and Indian War 29 July 1775.

Elsworth, Verdine. He served as a captain in the French and Indian War and petitioned for his land 30 December 1766 in New York.

Elwell, John. He served in the Narraganset War from Salem, Massachusetts. His son, John Elwell, claimed his land in Amherst, New Hampshire in

1734.

Emerson, Edward. He served on the expedition to Canada and received land in Poland, Maine in 1739.

Emerson, Nathaniel. He served in the Narraganset War from Massachusetts in 1685. His son, Samuel Emerson, received his land in Buxton, Maine.

Emery, Jonathan. He served in the Narraganset War from Massachusetts in 1685. His son, John Emery, received his land in Buxton, Maine.

Emons, Peter. He served in the Narraganset War from Massachusetts in 1685. His land was located in Buxton, Maine.

English, David. He served as a drummer in the 28th Regiment in the French and Indian War and petitioned for his land in New York 17 March 1767.

Enos, Roger. He was granted 2,000 acres in West Florida for his service as a staff officer in the French and Indian War on 13 October 1775.

Enroughty, John. He served as a soldier in the 2nd Virginia Regiment in the French and Indian War. He was from Goochland County, Virginia 6 September 1779. He disposed of his 50 acre warrant.

Epes, Daniel. He served on the expedition to Canada in 1690. He was admitted to his land in Lyndeboro, Maine in 1736.

Eppes, Francis. He served in the French and Indian War as a lieutenant in the regiment under William Byrd. His wife was Elizabeth Hill. His only child, Elizabeth Hill Eppes, married Thomas Woodlief who assigned the warrant for 2,000 acres. It was issued in 1779 in Prince William County, Virginia.

Eppes, Francis. He served as a lieutenant in the 2nd Virginia Regiment in the French and Indian War and assigned his 2,000 acre warrant in Virginia.

Erkley, Henry. He was granted 200 acres in Albany County, New York for his service as a corporal in the 60th Regiment of Foot in the French and Indian War 30 May 1765. He also appeared as Henry Ertley.

Ervin, Samuel. He served as a soldier in Capt. Peter Hogg's Company of Rangers in the French and Indian War and received his 50 acre warrant in Virginia. He proved his service in Augusta County, Virginia 18 May 1780.

Erving, William. He served as a captain in the French and Indian War and petitioned for 3,000 acres in New York 20 September 1764.

Escott, Wills. He received his land in West Florida for his service as a noncommissioned officer in the French and Indian War 12 October 1776. He had served as a sergeant in the 34th Regiment at Mobile.

Esick, Olerick. He was granted 50 acres in Albany County, New York for his

service as a soldier in the 60th Regiment of Foot in the French and Indian War 25 May 1771.

Eskridge, John. He served as a sergeant under Col. William Byrd in the French and Indian War. He proved his service in Westmoreland County, Virginia 30 May 1780.

Estill, Benjamin. He served as a sergeant in a company of rangers in the French and Indian War and received his 200 acre warrant in Virginia.

Estle, Bond. He served as a soldier in 1758 in Capt. William Preston's Company in the French and Indian War and received his 50 acre warrant 15 February 1780 in Greenbrier County, Virginia.

Estle, John. He served as a soldier in Capt. William Preston's Company of Rangers in 1758 in the French and Indian War. He received his 50 acre warrant 15 February 1780 in Greenbrier County, Virginia.

Etherington, James. He served as a sergeant in the Virginia Regiment under Col. George Washington in the French and Indian War. He lost the first warrant for 200 acres and had to have it reissued.

Etherington, Thomas. He was granted 2,000 acres in Albany County, New York for his service as a subaltern in the 47th Regiment of Foot in the French and Indian War 30 October 1765.

Etherington, Thomas. He was granted 2,000 acres in Cumberland County, New York for his service as a lieutenant in the 47th Regiment of Foot in the French and Indian War 8 December 1766.

Euler, George. He was granted 50 acres in Albany County, New York for his service as a soldier in the 60th or Royal American Regiment of Foot in the French and Indian War 28 March 1771.

Eustace, Hancock. He served as a captain in the French and Indian War. He was entitled to 3,000 acres which his heir, John Hancock, desired to locate in Fincastle County, Virginia.

Evans, Amos. He served as a soldier under Capt. James Gunn in Col. William Byrd's Regiment in 1760 in the French and Indian War and received his 50 acre warrant 25 May 1780 in Henry County, Virginia.

Evans, David. He served in the Narraganset War from Providence. His son, David Evans, received his land in Bedford, New Hampshire in 1733.

Evans, John. He was granted 50 acres in Gloucester County, New York for his service as a soldier in the 80th Regiment of Foot in the French and Indian War 5 April 1770.

Evans, Richard. He was granted 50 acres in Albany County, New York for his service as a soldier in the 80th Regiment of Foot in the French and Indian War 18 July 1770.

Evans, Richard. He served as a soldier in 1763 in the French and Indian War.

His warrant for 50 acres was issued to his widow, Elizabeth Evans, 21 February 1780 in Essex County, Virginia since he had no children or blood relation in the country.

Evans, William. For his service in suppressing those involved in Ingle's Insurrection in Maryland, Lord Baltimore granted him a special warrant for a grant for a 400 acre tract on the Isle of Kent jointly with John Jarbo 28 August 1649.

Evans, William. He served as a soldier in a detachment of the Royal Train of Artillery under Capt. David Hays from 1758 to 1760 in the French and Indian War and received his 50 acre warrant in Virginia. He proved his service in Yohogania County, Virginia 28 March 1780.

Evens, Lewis. He was granted 200 acres in Craven County, South Carolina on the King's bounty for his service in the French and Indian War 7 April 1770.

Evens, Richard. He was a veteran of the expedition to Canada in 1690. His brother, Matthias Evens of Dorchester, Massachusetts, at the desire of his eldest brother, Thomas Evens, received the land in Ashburnham, Massachusetts in 1736.

Evins, Edward. He served as a drummer in the French and Indian War and assigned his 200 acre warrant in Virginia. He proved his service as a non-commissioned officer who had served until disbanded in the Virginia Regiment under Col. George Washington after which he served as a non-commissioned officer under Col. Adam Stephen on 6 June 1780 in Frederick County, Virginia. He stated that he had never received more than 200 acres.

Evington, Moses. He served as a sergeant in the French and Indian War and requested his 200 acres 3 January 1774 in Fincastle County, Virginia.

Ewing, John. He was granted 1,000 and 500 acres in Berks County, Pennsylvania for his service as a clergyman in the French and Indian War 7 February 1769.

Faesch, George. He was granted 3,000 acres in Albany County, New York for his service as a captain lieutenant in the 60th Regiment of Foot in the French and Indian War 26 April 1765.

Fagan, Patrick. He was granted 50 acres in Craven County, South Carolina on the King's bounty for his service in the French and Indian War 14 September 1771.

Fairbanks, Abraham. He was granted 50 acres in Albany County, New York for his service as a soldier in the 28th Regiment of Foot in the French and Indian War 21 May 1768.

Fairbanks, Jonathan. He was a veteran of the expedition to Canada in 1690. He served under Capt. Champney. Oliver Wilder of Lancaster, Massachusetts received his land in Ashburnham, Massachusetts in 1736.

Fairlie, Joseph. He was granted 200 acres in Albany County, New York for his service as a miner in the Royal Regiment of Artillery in the French and Indian War 4 July 1770. He also appeared as Joseph Farley.

Fanning, Edmond. He served in the Narraganset War from Connecticut and received land in Voluntown, Connecticut in 1701.

Fanning, Edmond. He served in the Narraganset War from Connecticut and received land in Voluntown, Connecticut in 1701.

Fanning, Jehu. He served as a soldier under Col. William Byrd in the French and Indian War. He proved his service in Halifax County, Virginia 21 April 1780.

Fanning, Thomas. He served in the Narraganset War from Connecticut and received land in Voluntown, Connecticut in 1701.

Farah, Thomas. He served as a soldier in the Virginia Regiment under Col. Adam Stephen in the French and Indian War from Virginia. He applied for his 50 acres of land in King William County, Virginia 16 February 1780.

Farewell, Josiah. He was a lieutenant under Capt. John Lovewell and died in May 1725 in the battle at Pigwacket. He was from Dunstable, Massachusetts, and his land located in Pembroke, New Hampshire was awarded in 1733.

Farguson, William. He was granted 200 acres in Albany County, New York for his service as a corporal in the 77th Regiment of Foot in the French and Indian War 23 March 1765.

Fargusson, James. He served in Capt. Waggoner's Company under Col. George Washington in the Virginia Regiment in the French and Indian War having enlisted 16 June 1757. He proved his service in Chesterfield County, Virginia 7 April 1780.

Faris, Benjamin. He served as a corporal under Capt. Thomas Fleming and Col. William Peachey in the French and Indian War in 1758. He received his 200 acre warrant 6 April 1780 Fluvanna County, Virginia. He also appeared as Benjamin Farriss.

Farmer, Francis. He served as a soldier in the Virginia Regiment under Col. William Byrd in the French and Indian War and petitioned for his 50 acres 18 January 1780 in Washington County, Virginia.

Farmer, Robert. He was granted 3,000 acres in West Florida for his service in the French and Indian War 22 September 1775. He was a major.

Farmer, Thomas. He served in Lovewell's War in Massachusetts and received his land in Petersham, Massachusetts in 1733.

Farnsworth, Ephraim. He served in Lovewell's War in Massachusetts and received his land in Petersham, Massachusetts in 1733.

Farnsworth, Jonathan. He served in the Narraganset War and received land in Templeton, Massachusetts in 1733.

Farnsworth, Reuben. He served in Lovewell's War in Massachusetts and received his land in Petersham, Massachusetts.

Farquahar, William. He was granted 2,000 acres in Albany County, New York for his service as a lieutenant in the 47th Regiment of Foot in the French and Indian War 23 August 1764. He was the son of William Farquahar.

Farr, Joseph. He served in the Narraganset War from Lynn, Massachusetts. His son, Joseph Farr, claimed his land in Amherst, New Hampshire in 1734.

Farra, Joseph. He served under Capt. John Lovewell from Massachusetts and was in battle at Pigwacket in May 1725. He was from Concord and received his land in Pembroke, New Hampshire.

Farrant, Henry. He was granted 2,000 acres in Albany County, New York for his service as a lieutenant in an independent company of foot in the French and Indian War 18 April 1765.

Farrar, Isaac. He served on the expedition to Canada and sought his land in Massachusetts 10 December 1735.

Farrar, Jacob. He served under Capt. John Lovewell from Massachusetts and died in May 1725 at the battle at Pigwacket. He was from Concord, Massachusetts, and his land was located in Pembroke, New Hampshire.

Farrar, John. He served as a sergeant in Capt. James Walker's Company in the Regiment of Col. William Byrd in the French and Indian War. He was in Mecklenburg County, Virginia 13 March 1780. He assigned his 200 acre warrant.

Farrell, Kennedy. He served as wagon master general in the French and Indian War and petitioned for his 3,000 acres of land in New York 27 May 1766.

Farrell, Thomas. He served as a lieutenant in the French and Indian War and received 2,000 acres in Nova Scotia 26 June 1781.

Farrhar, Isaac. He served on the expedition to Canada in 1690 and received his land in Woburn, Massachusetts in 1738.

Farrington, John. He served in the Narraganset War from Lynn, Massachusetts. He applied for his land 4 June 1685. His son, John Farrington, claimed his land in Amherst, New Hampshire in 1734.

Farris, Abraham. He was granted 200 acres in Craven County, South Carolina on the King's bounty 21 June 1765. He served as a midshipman in the French and Indian War.

Farris, John. He was granted land in Virginia for his service in the French and Indian War but disposed of his fifty acre warrant. He was from Goochland County, Virginia 6 September 1779.

Farrow, Ephraim. He served in the Narraganset War from Lynn, Massachusetts. His nephew, Samuel Newhall, claimed his land in Amherst, New Hampshire in 1734. Benjamin Newhall drew same.

Fasset, Joseph. He served in the Narraganset War and received land in Templeton, Massachusetts in 1733.

Fasset, Josiah. He served in the expedition to Port Royal and received his land from Massachusetts 3 December 1735.

Fathy, John. He was granted 50 acres in Albany County, New York for his service as a soldier in the 55th Regiment of Foot in the French and Indian War 17 September 1765.

Fay, Francis. He served as a soldier in the 17th Regiment in the French and Indian War and petitioned for his 50 acres in New York 24 October 1764.

Fay, Jeremiah. He served in the Narraganset War from Boston, Massachusetts. His heir received land in Bedford, New Hampshire in 1733.

Fay, John. He served on the expedition to Canada in 1690. Palmer Golding claimed his right for land in Bethel, Maine in 1767.

Fay, John. He served on the expedition to Canada in 1690. Abner Newton received his land in Bethel, Maine in 1767. It was claimed by Palmer Golding.

Fear, Jacob. He served as a soldier in the 3rd Battalion of the 60th Regiment in the French and Indian War and had his service certified in January 1771 in New York.

Fearis, Robert. He enlisted from Bedford County, Virginia and served three months as a soldier in a ranging company under Capt. Peter Hogg in the French and Indian War. He proved his service in Augusta County, Virginia 17 November 1779.

Fears, Denham. He served as a sergeant in the French and Indian War and petitioned for 100 acres on the King's bounty in South Carolina 6 February 1771.

Feattus, James. He served as a captain in the Royal Navy in the French and Indian War and received 5,000 acres in Nova Scotia 25 January 1779.

Felden, John. He was granted 200 acres in Albany County, New York for his service as a sergeant in the 46th Regiment of Foot in the French and

Indian War 8 June 1771. He also appeared as John Felding.

Fellis, John. He served in the French and Indian War and petitioned for his land in New York 17 March 1767.

Fellows, Isaac. He served in the Narraganset War from Massachusetts in 1685. His son, Jonathan Fellows, received his land in Buxton, Maine.

Fellows, John. He served as a drummer in the 44th Regiment in the French and Indian War and was granted land in New York 16 April 1767.

Fellows, Joseph. He served in the Narraganset War from Massachusetts in 1685. His son, Joseph Fellows, received his land in Buxton, Maine.

Fellows, William. He served in the Narraganset War from Barnstable, Massachusetts and received land in Gorham, Maine in 1733.

Felton, Thomas. He served in the Narraganset War from Yarmouth, Massachusetts and received land in Gorham, Maine in 1733.

Fenan, Benoni. He served in an independent company of rangers in the French and Indian War and petitioned for his land in New York 12 April 1769.

Fendell, Robert. He was granted 2,000 acres in West Florida for his service as a warrant officer in the French and Indian War 22 August 1778.

Fenton, Joseph. He served on the expedition to Canada in 1690. Robert Hale petitioned for his land in Raymond, Maine in 1735.

Fenwick, Edward. He petitioned for 150 acres in St. Bartholomew's Parish on the King's bounty in South Carolina for his service in the French and Indian War 3 May 1768.

Fergey, John. He was granted 50 acres in Gloucester County, New York for his service as a soldier in the 4th Battalion in the 60th Regiment of Foot in the French and Indian War 5 April 1770. He also appeared as John Forgey.

Ferguson, —. Elizabeth Ferguson was granted 200 acres in Colleton County, South Carolina on the King's bounty based on his service in the French and Indian War 4 May 1775.

Ferguson, John. He was granted 50 acres in Charlotte County, New York for his service as a soldier in the 42nd Regiment of Foot in the French and Indian War 1 April 1775.

Fergusson, John. He was granted 3,000 acres in West Florida in 1779 for his service as a lieutenant at the reduction of Louisbourg in the French and Indian War.

Ferrin, Jonathan. He served in Lovewell's War in Massachusetts and received his land in Petersham, Massachusetts in 1733.

Ferris, David. He was granted 50 acres in Albany County, New York for his service as a soldier in the 55th Regiment of Foot in the French and

Indian War 28 October 1765.

Fesch, John Rudolph. He served as a captain in the 60th Regiment in the French and Indian War. His widow was recommended to receive land in New York 29 September 1774. [She may have been the widow Elizabeth Faesch who sought her late husband's land.]

Fidner, James. He served as a soldier in the 1st Virginia Regiment under Col. William Byrd in the French and Indian War. He assigned his right to 50 acres.

Field, —. He served in the expedition to Canada in 1690. George Field received land in Dumbarton, New Hampshire in 1735.

Field, John. He was granted 2,000 acres in Albany County, New York for his service as a surgeon's mate in a military hospital in the French and Indian War 16 April 1765.

Field, John. He received land in Richmond, New Hampshire in 1765 for the service of an unidentified veteran of the expedition to Canada in 1690.

Field, John. He served as a major in a corps of Virginia volunteers under Col. Henry Bouquet on an expedition against the Indians in 1764. Ezekiel Field, his son if he were alive, was to receive his warrant for 5,000 acres. The son received the warrant in Culpeper County, Virginia 16 August 1779.

Field, Samuel. He served in the Indian War. He was awarded 200 acres by Massachusetts 4 December 1735. He was from Deerfield, Massachusetts.

Field, Zachary. He served in the Pequot War and received a grant of land in Soldiers' Field in Hartford, Connecticut.

Fielding, Christopher. He served as a soldier in the 1st Virginia Regiment under Col. George Washington in the French and Indian War. He assigned his right to 50 acres. He was in Culpeper County, Virginia 21 February 1780.

Fielding, John. He served as a soldier in the 28th Regiment in the French and Indian War and had his service certified 19 September 1766 in New York. He was granted 50 acres in Gloucester County, New York 5 April 1770.

Fields, William. He served as a soldier until 1758 in the French and Indian War. He was in Caroline County, Virginia in February 1780. He assigned his right to 50 acres in Virginia.

Figg, Daniel. He was granted 200 acres in Albany County, New York for his service as a noncommissioned officer in the 80th Regiment of Foot in the French and Indian War 8 March 1771.

Finch, Edward. He served in the French and Indian War and petitioned for his land in New York 2 February 1769.

Finch, Henry. He served as a corporal in the French and Indian War and desired to locate his 200 acres in Fincastle County, Virginia 22 April 1774.

Fingle, George. He served as a soldier for six years in the 80th Regiment in the French and Indian War and had his service certified in New York 14 April 1765.

Fink, Alexander. He was granted 50 acres in Albany County, New York for his service as a soldier in the 60th or Royal American Regiment Foot in the French and Indian War 28 March 1771.

Finlay, Patrick. He was a soldier in Capt. Thomas Bullett's Company in the expedition against Fort DuQuesne under Gen. Braddock in 1755 in the French and Indian War. He proved his right to 50 acres in Hampshire County, Virginia 16 October 1779. He assigned his right.

Finlayson, John. He was granted 50 acres in Albany County, New York for his service as a soldier in the 42nd Regiment of Foot in the French and Indian War 30 October 1765.

Finly, Thomas. He served as a soldier in the 44th Regiment in the French and Indian War and petitioned for land 22 October 1766 in New York.

Finney, John. He was granted 50 acres in Albany County, New York for his service as a soldier in the 80th Regiment of Foot in the French and Indian War 5 April 1771.

Finnie, Alexander. He served as a lieutenant in a company of regulars under Capt. DePereony under Col. William Byrd in the 2nd Virginia Regiment in 1755 and as quartermaster in 1758 in the French and Indian War. His son and heir, William Finnie, assigned the two warrants of 4,000 acres in Virginia.

Finnie, Christopher. He served as a soldier in the 1st Virginia Regiment under Col. William Byrd and Col. Adam Stephen in the French and Indian War and received his warrant for 50 acres in December 1779 in Botetourt County, Virginia.

Finnie, John. He served as an ensign in the French and Indian War and received his land warrant for 2,000 acres in Virginia. His brother, William Finnie, assigned the warrant.

Finnie, William. He served as a surgeon in the French and Indian War and received his land warrant for 2,000 acres in Virginia.

Fish, John. He served in the Narraganset War from Connecticut and received land in Voluntown, Connecticut in 1701.

Fish, Samuel. He served in the Narraganset War from Connecticut and received land in Voluntown, Connecticut in 1701.

Fisher, Donald. He was granted 200 acres in Albany County, New York for his service as a corporal in the 77th Regiment of Foot in the French and Indian War 29 October 1765.

Fisher, John. He served as a private in the French and Indian War and petitioned for land in New York 8 July 1772.

Fisher, Moses. He served as a private in a company of rangers under Capt. William Preston in 1757 in the French and Indian War and assigned his 50 acre warrant in Virginia.

Fisher, Patrick. He served as a soldier in Col. William Byrd's Regiment in the French and Indian War. He was in Orange County, Virginia 23 March 1780. He assigned his 50 acre warrant.

Fisher, Thomas. He was granted 50 acres in Albany County, New York for his service as a private in the 60th or Royal American Regiment of Foot in the French and Indian War 8 June 1771.

Fisher, William. He served as a sergeant in the 17th Regiment in the French and Indian War. His widow, Mary Fisher, petitioned for his 200 acres of land in New York 18 June 1772.

Fisher, William. He was granted 50 acres in Albany County, New York for his service as a private in a regiment of foot in the French and Indian War 19 May 1770.

Fisher, William. He was granted five islands consisting of 25 acres in Albany County, New York for his service as a soldier in the 46th Regiment of Foot in the French and Indian War 29 October 1771.

Fishers, Philip. He served as a soldier in the 80th Regiment in the French and Indian War. He was mentioned in a return of a survey for his land 25 October 1765 in Albany County, New York.

Fiske, John. He served in the Narraganset War and was left wounded by Capt. Lathrop. His son, John Fiske of Haddam, Connecticut, petitioned for a regular share.

Fister, Philip. He was granted 50 acres in Albany County, New York for his service as a soldier in the 80th Regiment of Foot in the French and Indian War 28 October 1765.

Fitch, John. He served in the Narraganset War from Attleborough, Massachusetts. His heir, Joseph Brown, claimed his land in Greenwich, Massachusetts in 1737.

Fitch, Rev. James. He served in the Narraganset War from Connecticut and received land in Voluntown, Connecticut in 1701.

Fithey, John. He served as a private in the 55th Regiment in the French and Indian War. His service was certified in New York 20 May 1765.

Fitts, —. He served on the expedition to Canada in 1690. His grandson,

Ephraim Fitts, received his land in Winchendon, Massachusetts in 1736.

Fitts, Abraham. He served in the Narraganset War from Topsfield, Massachusetts. His heirs claimed his land in Amherst, New Hampshire in 1734.

Fitts, John. He was granted 200 acres in Albany County, New York for his service as a corporal in the 47th Regiment of Foot in the French and Indian War 12 July 1765. He also appeared as John Titts.

Fitzgerald, Frederick. He served as a soldier in Capt. William Preston's Company of Rangers in 1762 in the French and Indian War and received his 50 acre warrant 25 May 1780 in Henry County, Virginia.

Fitzgerald, Thomas. He was a soldier in Col. William Byrd's Regiment in 1758 in the French and Indian War. He assigned his 50 acres in Virginia.

Fitzgerral, James. He served as a sergeant in one of the Virginia Regiments under Col. William Byrd in 1759 and 1760 in the French and Indian War. He received his 200 acre warrant in February 1780 in Amherst County, Virginia.

Fitzpatrick, Edward. He served as a private in the French and Indian War and petitioned for his land in New York 8 July 1765.

Fitzpatrick, Joseph. He served as a lieutenant in the French and Indian War and petitioned for his land 30 December 1765 in New York.

Fitzsimmons, Patrick. He was granted 200 acres in Albany County, New York for his service as a corporal in the 28th Regiment of Foot in the French and Indian War 8 June 1771.

Flag, Michael. He served in the Narraganset War from Watertown, Massachusetts. His heirs received his land in Westminster, Massachusetts in 1733.

Flagg, Bartholomew. He served in the Narraganset War from Worcester, Massachusetts. His brother, Benjamin Flagg, claimed his land in Greenwich, Massachusetts in 1737.

Flagg, Eleazer. He served in the Narraganset War. His son, Eleazer Flagg, received his land in Templeton, Massachusetts in 1733.

Flagg, Gershom. He served as a lieutenant in the Narraganset War and received 300 acres of land in Templeton, Massachusetts in 1733.

Flagg, Richard. He served on the expedition to Canada in 1690. Ebenezer Flagg received his land in Bethel, Maine in 1767.

Flagg, Zacheriah. He served under Capt. Davenport in the Narraganset War and received land in Templeton, Massachusetts in 1733.

Flanders, William. He served as a soldier in the Virginia Regiment under Col. William Byrd in the French and Indian War. He desired to locate his

50 acres in Botetourt County, Virginia 14 December 1773.

Fleming, John. He served as a lieutenant in Capt. Kern's Company of Col. Marr's [?] Battalion of Pennsylvania Troops in the French and Indian War and assigned his 2,000 acre warrant in Virginia.

Fleming, Thomas. He served as a captain in the French and Indian War from Virginia and assigned his 3,000 acre land warrant.

Fleming, William. He was appointed Assistant Surgeon in the 1st Virginia Regiment by Gov. Robert Dinwiddie in 1755 and served in the French and Indian War until 1763. He received his warrant for 2,000 acres 2 November 1779 in Kentucky County, Virginia.

Fleming, William. He served as a captain in the 2nd Virginia Regiment in the French and Indian War and received 3,000 acres of land in Fincastle County, Virginia in 1774.

Fletchel, John. He petitioned for 100 acres on the Broad River on the King's bounty in South Carolina for his service in the French and Indian War 3 May 1768.

Fletcher, Angus. He served as a private in the French and Indian War and petitioned for his land in New York 17 March 1767.

Fletcher, Joseph. He was granted 50 acres in Albany County, New York for his service as a soldier in the 60th Regiment of Foot in the French and Indian War 26 July 1765.

Fletcher, Samuel. He served in Lovewell's War in Massachusetts and received his land in Petersham, Massachusetts.

Flinn, John. He was granted 50 acres in Albany County, New York for his service as a soldier in the 60th Regiment of Foot in the French and Indian War 15 August 1766.

Flint, Andrew. He was granted 50 acres in Albany County, New York for his service as a soldier in the 77th Regiment of Foot in the French and Indian War 14 April 1772.

Flintlam, John. He was granted 50 acres in Albany County, New York for his service as a soldier in the 60th Regiment of Foot in the French and Indian War 14 April 1772.

Flood, Noah. He served as a soldier for three years in Capt. Campbell's Company in the 44th Regiment in the French and Indian War and petitioned for a grant of 50 acres in New York 19 August 1766.

Floyd, John. He was a captain and was from Boston, Massachusetts. His descendants, Daniel Floyd, John Floyd, and Samuel Floyd, were awarded 400 acres by Massachusetts 2 December 1735.

Flynt, Thomas. He served in the Narraganset War from Salem, Massachusetts. His son, John Flynt, received his land in Amherst, New Hampshire in

1734.

Focks, Barnaby. He served in the French and Indian War and assigned his right to land to Robert Buchanan 21 January 1767 in New York.

Foe, John. He served as a soldier in the French and Indian War and received 50 acres in Nova Scotia 9 October 1776.

Fogle, John. He was granted 200 acres in West Florida for his service as a noncommissioned officer in the French and Indian War 13 November 1778.

Foley, Edward. He served as a soldier in the 1st Virginia Regiment in the French and Indian War in 1760. He petitioned for his 50 acres in February 1780 in Spotsylvania County, Virginia. He assigned his warrant.

Fomby, Robert. He was granted 50 acres in Berkeley County, South Carolina on the King's bounty for his service in the French and Indian War 1 June 1767.

Fonner, Mathias. He was granted 200 acres in Albany County, New York for his service as a noncommissioned officer in the 16th Regiment of Foot in the French and Indian War 8 October 1765.

Fontenelle, Samuel. He was granted 1,300 acres in West Florida for his service as a surgeon in the French and Indian War 19 December 1779.

Foot, John. He was from Almsbury, Massachusetts and was awarded 200 acres in Methuen for service in the Indian war 12 December 1735. He was a captain.

Foot, John. He served in the French and Indian War. His service was proved in New York 4 April 1768.

Forbes, Alexander. He was granted 200 acres in Albany County, New York for his service as a sergeant in the 42nd Regiment of Foot in the French and Indian War 30 October 1765.

Forbes, Alexander. He was granted 50 acres in Albany County, New York for his service as a soldier in the 42nd Regiment of Foot in the French and Indian War 30 October 1765.

Forbes, Caleb. He served in the Narraganset War from Connecticut and received land in Voluntown, Connecticut in 1701.

Forbes, Charles. He was granted 3,000 acres in Albany County, New York for his service as a captain in the 42nd Regiment of Foot in the French and Indian War 19 October 1765.

Forbes, Duncan. He was granted 2,000 acres in Albany County, New York for his service as a surgeon's mate in a military hospital in the French and Indian War 16 July 1765.

Forbes, John. He was granted 50 acres in Albany County, New York for his

service as a soldier in the 77th Regiment of Foot in the French and Indian War 13 May 1765.

Forbes, William. He served as a corporal in the 55th Regiment in the French and Indian War and petitioned for land in New York 22 March 1771.

Forbes, William. He served as a private in one of the Virginia Regiments in the French and Indian War and received his 50 acre warrant in Virginia. His service was proved in Amherst County, Virginia 7 February 1780.

Ford, Bartlet. He served as a soldier in the French and Indian War and desired to locate his 50 acres in Fincastle County, Virginia 2 June 1774. He assigned the same.

Ford, Edward. He was granted 200 acres in Ulster County, New York for his service as a corporal in the 80th Regiment of Foot in the French and Indian War 23 December 1771.

Ford, James. He served in the Narraganset War from Topsfield, Massachusetts. His heirs claimed his land in Amherst, New Hampshire in 1734.

Ford, James. He served in the French and Indian War and took his land in Fincastle County, Virginia 15 December 1772.

Ford, Nicholas. He served on the expedition to Canada in 1690. Cornelius Tarball was admitted to his land in Lyndeboro, Maine in 1736.

Ford, Richard. He was granted 50 acres in Albany County, New York for his service as a soldier in the 40th Regiment of Foot in the French and and Indian War 15 August 1766.

Ford, Robert. He served in Lovewell's War in Massachusetts and received his land in Petersham, Massachusetts in 1733.

Ford, Samuel. He was granted 50 acres in Albany County, New York for his service as a soldier in the 80th Regiment of Foot in the French and Indian War 5 April 1771.

Ford, Tandy. He served as a soldier in the 2nd Virginia Regiment in the French and Indian War. He was from Goochland County, Virginia 15 November 1779. He assigned his warrant for 50 acres in Virginia.

Ford, Thomas. He was granted 200 acres in Albany County, New York for his service as a corporal in the 4th Battalion in the Royal American or 60th Regiment of Foot in the French and Indian War 27 September 1769.

Formbly, Robert. He served as a private in the French and Indian War and petitioned for 50 acres on the King's bounty in South Carolina 3 December 1766.

Forster, James. He was granted 246 ½ and 218 acres in Cumberland County, Pennsylvania for his service as an ensign in the French and Indian War 3 February 1769.

Fortune, George. He was granted 200 acres in Craven County, South Carolina on the King's bounty for his service in the French and Indian War 26 May 1774.

Fosket, John. He served in the Narraganset War from Charlestown, Massachusetts. His son, Robert Fosket, received his land in Westminster, Massachusetts in 1733.

Fosket, Samuel. He served in the Narraganset War from Charlestown, Massachusetts. His son, Samuel Fosket, received his land in Westminster, Massachusetts in 1733.

Fosson, John. He was granted 50 acres in Gloucester County, New York for his service as a soldier in the 46th Regiment of Foot in the French and Indian War 5 April 1770.

Foster, —. He served in the Narraganset War from Sandwich, Massachusetts. His brother-in-law, Jonathan Morey, received his land in Gorham, Maine in 1733.

Foster, Edmund. He served as a soldier in Capt. Samuel Overton's Company of Rangers in 1756 and in Col. William Byrd's Regiment in 1758 in the French and Indian War. He assigned his right to 50 acres in Virginia.

Foster, Isaac. He was a veteran of the expedition to Canada in 1690. His nephew, Abraham Foster, Jr. of Ipswich, Massachusetts, claimed his land in Winchendon, Massachusetts in 1736.

Foster, James. He served as a soldier under Col. William Byrd in the French and Indian War and assigned his warrant for 50 acres in Virginia.

Foster, Jonathan. He served on the expedition to Canada in 1690. David Foster was admitted to his land in Lyndeboro, Maine in 1736.

Foster, Manuel. He was granted 50 acres in Charlotte County, New York for his service as a private in the 8th Regiment of Foot in the French and Indian War 9 June 1774.

Foster, Peter. He was granted 200 acres in Albany County, New York for his service as a sergeant in the 9th Regiment of Foot in the French and Indian War 18 February 1775.

Foster, Phineas. He served in Lovewell's War in Massachusetts and received his land in Petersham, Massachusetts in 1733.

Foster, Richard. He served as a private in Capt. Samuel Overton's Company of Volunteers in the French and Indian War. He received a warrant for 50 acres 17 January 1780 in Prince Edward County, Virginia.

Foster, Robert. He was granted 200 acres in Gloucester County, New York for his service as a noncommissioned officer in the Royal American Regiment in the French and Indian War 3 February 1775.

Foster, Samuel. He served in the Narraganset War from Walpole, Massachusetts. His son, John Foster, claimed his land in Greenwich,

Massachusetts in 1737.

Foster, Thomas. He served as a soldier under Col. Robert Buchanan in 1758 and 1759 in the French and Indian War. He received his 50 acre warrant in April 1780 in Montgomery County, Virginia.

Foster, William. He served as a soldier in Capt. Samuel Overton's Company of Rangers in 1755 and in 1756 in the French and Indian War. He petitioned for his 50 acres 14 February 1780 in Louisa County, Virginia.

Fotheringham, John. He was granted 50 acres in Albany County, New York for his service as a soldier in the 40th Regiment of Foot in the French and Indian War 9 May 1771.

Fouracres, Richard. He served as a soldier in the 1st Virginia Regiment under Col. George Washington in the French and Indian War and petitioned for his 50 acres in February 1780 in Spotsylvania County, Virginia which he assigned.

Fowle, James. He served on the expedition to Canada in 1690. James Fowle received his land in Bethel, Maine in 1767.

Fowle, James. He served on the expedition to Canada in 1690. His grandson John Fowle, received his land in Woburn, Massachusetts in 1738.

Fowler, Alexander. He served as a lieutenant in Capt. Henry Peyton's Company under Maj. Gen. Sir John Irvin, Colonel of His Majesty's 74th Regiment of Foot in 1759 in the French and Indian War. He received his warrant for 2,000 acres in Virginia. He proved his service in Yohogania County, Virginia 28 February 1780.

Fowler, Alexander. He received 1,000 acres of land in West Florida for his service as a lieutenant in the French and Indian War 10 April 1775. He also had a grant for 1,000 acres 6 May 1776.

Fowler, Matthew. He served as a corporal in the Old Virginia Regiment in the French and Indian War. He proved his service in Ohio County, Virginia 6 March 1780.

Fox, Anthony. He served as a soldier in the 46th Regiment in the French and Indian War and petitioned for land in New York 11 September 1771.

Fox, David. He served on the expedition to Canada in 1690. His kinsman, Eleazer Bateman, received his land in Woburn, Massachusetts in 1738.

Fox, John. He served in the French and Indian War and received his land in Botetourt County, Virginia.

Fox, Joseph. He received his commission as a captain from Robert Dinwiddie and raised a company for service in the French and Indian War. He was awarded 3,000 acres of land 11 October 1779 in Louisa County,

Virginia.

Fox, Nicholas. He served on the expedition to Canada in 1690. James Taylor received his land in Bethel, Maine in 1767.

Fox, Samuel. He served in the Narraganset War from Connecticut and received land in Voluntown, Connecticut in 1701.

Foy, John. He was granted 50 acres in Albany County, New York for his service as a soldier in an independent company of foot in the French and Indian War 28 June 1770.

Francheville, George. He served in the French and Indian War and received his land in Nova Scotia 12 October 1771.

Francis, Charles. He served as a drummer in the French and Indian War and received a warrant for 200 acres.

Francis, Henry. He served as a sergeant in the 1st Virginia Regiment under different commanders in the French and Indian War and was discharged by Col. Adam Stephen having served about six and a half years. He received his 200 acre warrant in May 1780 in Montgomery County, Virginia.

Francis, John. He was granted 200 acres in Albany County, New York for his service as a corporal in the 17th Regiment of Foot in the French and Indian War 8 June 1771.

Francis, John. He served as a soldier in the Virginia Regiment under Col. George Washington and was killed by the Indians in the French and Indian War. His eldest brother and heir, Henry Francis, received his 50 acre warrant in May 1780 in Montgomery County, Virginia.

Francis, Turbutt. He served as a lieutenant in the French and Indian War and was granted land in New York 16 April 1767.

Francis, Turbutt. He was granted 2,775 acres in Berks County and another 1,000 acres in an unspecified county in Pennsylvania for his service as a colonel in the French and Indian War 3 and 4 February 1769.

Francis, Turbutt. He received land in West Florida for his service as a lieutenant in the French and Indian War 12 February 1776.

Francis, William. He served for three years in the 1st Battalion of the Royal Americans in the French and Indian War and died in the service. Henry Francis, his eldest brother and heir, received his 200 acre warrant in May 1780 in Montgomery County, Virginia.

Franklin, John. He served in the French and Indian War and took his land in Fincastle County, Virginia 15 December 1772.

Franklin, Joseph. He was granted 200 acres in Albany County, New York for his service as a sergeant in the 27th Regiment of Foot in the French and Indian War 5 July 1765.

Franks, David. He was granted 500, 500, 500, 500, and 500 acres in unspecified counties and 500 acres in Westmoreland County, Pennsylvania for his service in the French and Indian War 1 April 1769.

Fraris, Denham. He was granted 91 acres and a 9 acre small island in St. Luke's Parish, Granville County, South Carolina on the King's bounty for his service in the French and Indian War 24 August 1770.

Fraser, Alexander. He was granted 50 acres in Albany County, New York for his service as a soldier in the 78th Regiment of Foot in the French and Indian War 1 May 1765.

Fraser, Alexander. He was granted 200 acres in Albany County, New York for his service as a corporal in the 78th Regiment of Foot in the French and Indian War 22 May 1765.

Fraser, Alexander. He was granted 200 acres in Albany County, New York for his service as a sergeant in Capt. Alexander Woods's Company in the 78th Regiment of Foot in the French and Indian War 22 May 1765.

Fraser, Alexander. He was granted 50 acres in Charlotte County, New York for his service as a soldier in the Royal Highland Regiment of Foot in the French and Indian War 12 July 1775.

Fraser, Alexander. He was granted 200 acres in Albany County, New York for his service as a noncommissioned officer in the 60th Regiment of Foot in the French and Indian War 26 April 1765.

Fraser, Duncan. He served as a private in the French and Indian War and petitioned for land in New York 8 July 1772.

Fraser, George. He was granted 2,000 acres in St. Philip Parish, Georgia in two separate tracts for his service as lieutenant in the 78th Regiment of Foot commanded by Col. Simon Frasier at the reduction of Louisbourg and Quebec in the French and Indian War 5 November 1771.

Fraser, George. He served as a lieutenant in the French and Indian War in the Virginia regiment under Col. George Washington. His only daughter and heir at law, Mary Fraser, received his 2,000 acre land warrant in Virginia.

Fraser, Hugh. He served as a private in the French and Indian War and petitioned that his land be laid out in a certain tract 21 January 1767 in New York.

Fraser, John. He served as a soldier in the French and Indian War and assigned his right to 50 acres to William McDonald in Nova Scotia who received the land 7 January 1781.

Fraser, Lewis V. He served as a captain in the 60th Regiment in the French and Indian War and petitioned for his 3,000 acres of land in New York 9

February 1767.

Fraser, Thomas. He served in the 55th Regiment in the French and Indian War and petitioned for his land in New York 21 November 1766. He received 50 acres in Albany County, New York 18 April 1769. He also appeared as Thomas Frazier.

Fraser, William. He was granted 200 acres in Albany County, New York for his service as a sergeant in the 78th Regiment of Foot in the French and Indian War 13 May 1765.

Frasier, Alexander. He served as a sergeant in the 78th Regiment in the French and Indian War. He received 200 acres in Albany County, New York 6 November 1769.

Frasier, Hugh. He was granted 2,000 acres in Albany County, New York for his service as a lieutenant in the 78th Regiment of Foot in the French and Indian War 17 June 1767.

Frasier, John. He was granted 50 acres in Albany County, New York for his service as a soldier in the 42nd Regiment of Foot in the French and Indian War 30 October 1765.

Frasier, Roderick. He was granted 200 acres in Albany County, New York for his service as a corporal in Capt. Hugh Cameron's Company in the 78th Regiment of Foot in the French and Indian War 21 October 1765.

Frazer, Alexander. He was granted 2,000 acres in Albany County, New York for his service as an ensign in the 78th Regiment of Foot in the French and Indian War 25 May 1771.

Frazer, Alexander. He was granted 200 acres in Albany County, New York for his service as a noncommissioned officer in the 42nd Regiment of Foot in the French and Indian War 18 February 1775.

Frazer, Alexander. He was granted 1,000 in West Florida for his service as a subaltern in the French and Indian War 6 January 1778.

Frazer, Daniel. He was granted 50 acres in Albany County, New York for his service as a soldier in the 42nd Regiment of Foot in the French and Indian War 7 October 1771.

Frazer, Donald. He served in the French and Indian War. His service was proved in New York 28 March 1771.

Frazer, Henry. He was granted 50 acres in Albany County, New York for his service as a soldier in the 2nd Battalion in the 42nd Regiment of Foot in the French and Indian War 7 October 1771.

Frazer, John. He was granted 50 acres in Albany County, New York for his service as a soldier in the 78th Regiment of Foot in the French and Indian War 1 May 1765.

Frazer, Thomas. He was granted 50 acres in Albany County, New York for his service as a soldier in the 17th Regiment of Foot in the French and Indian War 28 June 1770.

Frazier, Abraham. He served as a corporal in the 42nd Regiment in the French and Indian War and was granted land in New York 16 April 1774.

Frazier, Alexander. He was granted 50 acres in Albany County, New York for his service as a soldier in the 42nd Regiment of Foot in the French and Indian War 30 October 1765.

Frazier, James. He was granted 50 acres in Albany County, New York for his service as a soldier in the 42nd Regiment of Foot in the French and Indian War 30 October 1765.

Frazier, James. He served as a soldier in the Virginia Regiment under Col. George Washington in the French and Indian War. He was in Rockbridge County, Virginia 5 October 1779. He assigned his 50 acre warrant in Virginia.

Frazier, John. He was granted 300 acres in Pennsylvania for his service in the French and Indian War 1 April 1769.

Freaker, Henry. He was granted 200 acres in Gloucester County, New York for his service as a corporal in the 55th Regiment of Foot in the French and Indian War 5 April 1770.

Fream, David. He served as a soldier in Capt. Christian's Company of Regulars in the French and Indian War. He was in Botetourt County, Virginia in December 1779. He assigned his warrant for 50 acres in Virginia.

Frederick, Andrew. He was granted 200 acres in Albany County, New York for his service as a sergeant in the 4th Battalion in the 60th Regiment of Foot in the French and Indian War 30 May 1765.

Frederick, Richard. He was granted 50 acres in Albany County, New York for his service as a private in the 60th or Royal American Regiment of Foot in the French and Indian War 8 June 1771.

Freeborn, Isaac. He was granted 50 acres in Albany County, New York for his service as a soldier in the 46th Regiment of Foot in the French and Indian War 3 September 1771.

Freeman, —. He served in the expedition to Canada in 1690. His nephew, Nathaniel Clarke, received his land in Winchendon, Massachusetts in 1735.

Freeman, Constant. He served in the expedition to Canada in 1690 and received his land in Dumbarton, New Hampshire in 1735.

Freeman, Edmund. He served in the expedition to Canada in 1690 and received his land in Dumbarton, New Hampshire in 1735.

Freeman, Edmund. He was from Harwich, Massachusetts. He was awarded 300 acres by Massachusetts for his service in the wars with the French and

Indians 16 June 1735. He also appeared as Edward Freeman.

Freeman, John. He served in the Narraganset War from Eastham, Massachusetts and received land in Gorham, Maine in 1733.

Freeman, John. He served as a soldier in Capt. William Phillips's Volunteer Rangers in 1763 in the French and Indian War. He petitioned for 50 acres 13 March 1780 in Louisa County, Virginia.

Freeman, Jonathan. He served in the Narraganset War from Attleborough, Massachusetts. His son, Jonathan Freeman, claimed his land in Greenwich, Massachusetts in 1737.

Freeman, Thomas. He served as a deputy commissary in the French and Indian War. He proved his service in Yohogania County, Virginia 23 May 1780.

French, Ebenezer. He served in the Narraganset War from Connecticut and received his land in Voluntown, Connecticut in 1701.

French, Humphrey. He served on the expedition to Canada in 1690. Nathaniel Gold petitioned for his land in Raymond, Maine in 1735.

French, Samuel. He served as a sergeant in the French and Indian War and assigned his 200 acres in Virginia.

Fricker, William. He was granted 2,000 acres in West Florida for his service as a master's mate in the French and Indian War 8 November 1777.

Fricket, Thomas. He served as a quartermaster in the French and Indian War and returned a survey for 2,000 acres in New York 6 September 1771.

Friend, George. He served as a soldier in the 44th Regiment in the French and Indian War and petitioned for his land in New York 6 August 1774.

Friend, William. He was granted 200 acres in Albany County, New York for his service as a sergeant in Capt. Rudolph Bentick's Company in the 2nd Battalion in the 1st or Royal American Regiment of Foot in the French and Indian War 24 May 1771.

Frink, John. He served as a sergeant in the Narraganset War from Connecticut and received land in Voluntown, Connecticut in 1701.

Frisbie, Samuel. He served in the Narraganset War from Connecticut. His heirs received his land in Voluntown, Connecticut in 1701.

Friswell, John. He was granted 3,000 acres in Albany County, New York for his service as acting lieutenant in the Royal Navy at the siege of Louisbourg and the reduction of Quebec in the French and Indian War 7 May 1765. He served aboard the *Princess Amelia*.

Frogg, John. He served as a sergeant in the 1st Virginia Regiment in the French and Indian War and assigned his 200 acre warrant in Virginia.

Frogg, William. He served as an officer in the French and Indian War and received his 2,000 acre land warrant in Virginia. His service was proved in Augusta County, Virginia 22 March 1780.

Frost, Thomas. He received land in Alstead, New Hampshire in 1771 for the service of an unidentified veteran of the expedition to Canada in 1690.

Frost, William. He was granted 200 acres in Albany County, New York for his service as a corporal in the 60th Regiment of Foot in the French and Indian War 25 May 1771.

Fry, Christopher. He served as a noncommissioned officer in the Old Virginia Regiment under Col. William Byrd in the French and Indian War and received his 200 acre warrant 8 March 1780 in Frederick County, Virginia.

Fry, James. He served in the Narraganset War from Andover, Massachusetts. He claimed his land in Amherst, New Hampshire in 1734.

Fry, John. He served as a captain in Colonel Abijah Willard's Regiment in Massachusetts under Gen. Jeffery Amherst for the reduction of Canada in 1759 in the French and Indian War and assigned his 3,000 acre warrant in Virginia.

Fry, Samuel. He served as an ensign under Capt. Robert Rutherford in a company of rangers in 1758 and 1759 in the French and Indian War. He received a warrant for 2,000 acres 18 November 1779 in Monongalia County, Virginia.

Frye, Jonathan. He served under Capt. John Lovewell from Massachusetts and was killed at the battle at Pigwacket in May 1725. He was from Andover, Massachusetts. His land was located in Pembroke, New Hampshire.

Frye, Thomas. He shared in the grant of East Greenwich, Rhode Island made to those who had rendered service in King Philip's War. The grant was made 31 October 1677.

Fullam, Jacob. He served as sergeant under Capt. John Lovewell from Massachusetts and was killed in battle at Pigwacket in May 1725. He was from Weston, Massachusetts. His land was located in Pembroke, New Hampshire. When his land fell into New Hampshire, Francis Fullam sought to relocate the land in Massachusetts 13 April 1772.

Fuller, Isaac. He served in the expedition to Canada in 1690. Samuel Fuller received his land in Alstead, New Hampshire in 1771.

Fuller, James. He served in the Narraganset War from Massachusetts in 1685. His son, James Fuller, received his land in Buxton, Maine.

Fuller, Joseph. He received land in Alstead, New Hampshire in 1771 for the service of an unidentified veteran of the expedition to Canada in 1690.

Fuller, Josiah. He received land in Alstead, New Hampshire in 1771 for the service of an unidentified veteran of the expedition to Canada in 1690.

Fuller, Dr. Matthew. He served in the Narraganset War from Barnstable, Massachusetts and received land in Gorham, Maine in 1733.
Fuller, Samuel. He served in the Narraganset War from Barnstable, Massachusetts. He received land in Gorham, Maine in 1733.
Fuller, Thomas. He served in the Narraganset War from Barnstable, Massachusetts and received land in Gorham, Maine in 1733.
Fuller, Thomas. He served in the Narraganset War from Salem, Massachusetts. His son, William Fuller, received his land in Amherst, New Hampshire in 1734.
Fuller, Thomas Alexander. He served as aid de camp to the Earl of Albemarle and as major commandant of H. M.'s Corps of German Volunteers in the French and Indian War. His brother, Peeke Fuller, captain of the 46th Regiment, petitioned for his 5,000 acres of land 24 June 1766 in New York.
Fuller, Timothy. He served on the expedition to Canada in 1690 and received land in Dumbarton, New Hampshire in 1735.
Fulton, John. He served as a soldier in Capt. John Dickenson's Company of Rangers in the French and Indian War and received his 50 acre warrant 21 March 1780 in Augusta County, Virginia.
Furgason, Archaball. He served on the expedition to Canada in 1690. Simon Orn was admitted to his land in Lyndeboro, Maine in 1736.
Furnace, John. He served as a soldier in Capt. Peter Hogg's Company of Rangers in 1758 in the French and Indian War. His son and heir, John Furnace, was in Orange County, Virginia. He assigned his 50 acres.
Furniss, Henry. He was granted 50 acres in Gloucester County, New York for his service as a soldier in the 46th Regiment of Foot in the French and Indian War 5 April 1770.
Fuser, Lewis Valentine. He was granted 3,000 acres in Charlotte County, New York for his service as a captain in the 60th Regiment of Foot in the French and Indian War 12 October 1774.
Fusson, John. He had his service as a soldier in the French and Indian War certified 1 July 1766 in New York.
Fuzey, Jacob. He was granted 50 acres in Albany County, New York for his service as a soldier in the 18th Regiment of Foot in the French and Indian War 17 September 1765.
Gaffin, Stephen. He was granted 50 acres in Albany County, New York for his service as a soldier in the 28th Regiment of Foot in the French and Indian War 21 May 1768.
Gage, Henry. He served in the Narraganset War from Yarmouth, Massachusetts and received land in Gorham, Maine in 1733.

Gage, John. He served in the Narraganset War from Yarmouth, Massachusetts and received land in Gorham, Maine in 1733.

Gage, Moses. He served on the expedition to Canada in 1690 and petitioned for his land in Raymond, Maine in 1735.

Gage, William. He served in the Narraganset War from Yarmouth, Massachusetts and received land in Gorham, Maine in 1733.

Gahagan, John. He served as a soldier in the 1st Virginia Regiment in the French and Indian War and assigned his 50 acre warrant in Virginia.

Gahagan, Joseph. He served as a soldier in the Virginia Regiment for seven years in the French and Indian War and assigned his 50 acre warrant in Virginia.

Gaines, James. He served as a soldier under Col. William Byrd in 1760 in the French and Indian War. He was in Orange County, Virginia 27 January 1780. He assigned his right in Virginia.

Gains, Robert. He served in the French and Indian War from Virginia. His heir at law, Henry Gains, received 2,000 acres of land in Yohogania County, Virginia.

Galbreath, Thomas. He served as a soldier in Capt. Peter Hogg's Company in the French and Indian War from Virginia. He received a warrant for 50 acres.

Gale, Stephen. He was granted 50 acres in Albany County, New York for his service as a soldier in the 80th Regiment of Foot in the French and Indian War 6 July 1771.

Gallacher, Arthur. He was granted 200 acres in Charlotte County, New York for his service as a noncommissioned officer in the 44th Regiment of Foot in the French and Indian War 12 October 1774.

Gallaugher, Abraham. He was granted 50 acres in Albany County, New York for his service as a soldier in the 55th Regiment of Foot in the French and Indian War 18 April 1769.

Gallaway, Hugh. He served in the Narraganset War from Massachusetts in 1685. His land was located in Buxton, Maine.

Gallen, Stephen. He served as a private in the French and Indian War and petitioned for his land in New York 20 November 1766.

Gallespy, Alexander. He served as a soldier in Capt. Charles Lewis's Company of Rangers in 1758 in the French and Indian War and proved his service in Augusta County, Virginia 21 March 1780.

Galliver, John. He served as a captain in the expedition to Canada in 1690. At the desire of Jonathan Galliver, Thomas Tilestone of Dorchester, Massachusetts received his land in Ashburnham, Massachusetts in 1736.

Gallop, Adam. He served in the Narraganset War from Connecticut and received land in Voluntown, Connecticut in 1701.

Gallop, John. He was granted 100 acres in Connecticut for his service in the Pequot War 11 May 1671.

Gallop, John. He served in the Narraganset War from Connecticut and received land in Voluntown, Connecticut in 1701.

Gallop, William. He served in the Narraganset War from Connecticut and received land in Voluntown, Connecticut in 1701.

Gallot, Charles. He was granted 2,000 acres in Albany County, New York for his service as a lieutenant in the 60th Regiment of Foot in the French and Indian War 23 August 1764.

Galloway, David, Sr. He served as a sergeant in Capt. John Dickenson's Company of Rangers in 1757 in the French and Indian War. He proved his service in Botetourt County, Virginia 10 February 1780.

Galloway, David, Jr. He served as a soldier in Capt. John Dickerson's Company of Rangers in the French and Indian War and assigned his 50 acre warrant in Virginia. He proved his service in Botetourt County, Virginia 10 February 1780.

Galloway, Patrick. He served in the French and Indian War and took his land in Fincastle County, Virginia 15 December 1772.

Galloway, William. He served in Capt. John Dickenson's Company of Rangers in 1758 in the French and Indian War and proved his service in Botetourt County, Virginia 10 February 1780.

Gamble, James. He was granted 50 acres in Craven County, South Carolina on the King's bounty for his service in the French and Indian War 6 February 1773.

Gamble, Thomas. He was granted 2,000 acres in Cumberland County, New York for his service as a lieutenant in the 50th Regiment of Foot in the French and Indian War 8 February 1770.

Gamble, Thomas. He served in the French and Indian War and received 2,000 acres in Nova Scotia 21 March 1768.

Gamble, Thomas. He was granted 1,000 acres in West Florida for his service as a major in the French and Indian War 13 June 1774.

Gamble, William. He served as a sergeant in the 46th Regiment in the French and Indian War and assigned his right to land in New York 20 May 1767.

Gamblin, Richard. He was granted 50 acres in Gloucester County, New York for his seven years of service as a soldier in the 35th Regiment of Foot in the French and Indian War 5 April 1770.

Gann, James. He was granted 50 acres in Albany County, New York for his

service as a soldier in the 44th Regiment of Foot in the French and Indian War 30 May 1771.

Gannett, Benjamin. He received land in Richmond, New Hampshire in 1765 for the service of an unidentified veteran of the expedition to Canada in 1690.

Gardiner, Valentine. He was granted 3,000 acres in Albany County, New York for his service as a captain in the 55th Regiment of Foot in the French and Indian War 18 October 1765.

Gardner, Joseph. He served as a captain in the Narraganset War from Salem, Massachusetts. His nephew, Habakkuk Gardner, claimed his land in Amherst, New Hampshire in 1734.

Gardner, Joseph. He served on the expedition to Canada in 1690. Joseph Gardner received land in Warwick, Massachusetts in 1738.

Gardner, Samuel. He served in the Narraganset War from Brooklyn. His brother, Joseph Gardner, received land in Bedford, New Hampshire in 1733.

Gardner, Thomas. He served on the expedition to Canada in 1690. Thomas Gardner received land in Warwick, Massachusetts in 1738.

Garland, Peter. He was granted 50 acres in Albany County, New York for his service as a soldier in the 60th or Royal American Regiment of Foot in the French and Indian War 28 March 1771.

Garnet, Leonard. He served as a sergeant in the Virginia Regiment under Col. William Byrd in the French and Indian War and proved his service for 200 acres in King William County, Virginia 18 November 1778.

Garnett, Peter. He was granted 50 acres in Albany County, New York for his service as a soldier in the 55th Regiment of Foot in the French and Indian War 30 May 1771.

Garnier, William. He was granted 5,000 acres 28 May 1779 in West Florida for his service as a commander of an armed ship at the reduction of Quebec in the French and Indian War.

Garrett, Anthony. He served as a soldier in the 1st Battalion in the 60th Regiment in the French and Indian War and petitioned for land 3 March 1766 in New York.

Garrett, James. He served as a sergeant in the French and Indian War and desired to locate his 200 acres in Fincastle County, Virginia.

Garrison, John. He was granted 50 acres in Albany County, New York for his service as a soldier in the 47th Regiment of Foot in the French and Indian War 15 August 1766.

Garrow, John. He was granted 50 acres in Gloucester County, New York for his service as a soldier in an independent of company of foot in the French and Indian War 5 April 1770.

Garrow, Joseph. He received his land in West Florida for his service as a master in the navy on the *Diana* at the reduction of Quebec in the French and Indian War 8 October 1774.

Garvey, James. He was granted 200 acres in St. George Parish, Georgia for his service as a noncommissioned officer in the Royal Regiment of Foot under Lt. Gen. James St. Clair in the French and Indian War 3 May 1768.

Garway, Michael. He was granted 50 acres in Albany County, New York for his service as a soldier in the 80th Regiment of Foot in the French and Indian War 17 September 1765.

Gatchell, John. He served in the Narraganset War from Marblehead, Massachusetts. His nephew, Jeremiah Gatchell, claimed his land in Amherst, Massachusetts in 1734.

Gates, Horatio. He served in the French and Indian War as a field officer. He was entitled to 5,000 acres in Virginia which he assigned.

Gates, Jacob. He served in the Indian War in 1725 from Massachusetts. He was from Stowe, New Hampshire and received his land in Pembroke, New Hampshire. He served under John Lovewell.

Gates, Simon. He served in the Narraganset War from Cambridge, Massachusetts. His son, Jonathan Gates, received his land in Westminster, Massachusetts in 1733.

Gatewood, Joseph. He served as a soldier in the 1st Virginia Regiment under Col. George Washington in the French and Indian War. He was in Essex County, Virginia 21 February 1780. He assigned his right to 50 acres. He also appeared as Joseph Gatwood.

Gatewood, Phillip. He served in the French and Indian War and took his land in Fincastle County, Virginia 15 December 1772.

Gaulding, John. He served as a soldier under Col. William Byrd in the French and Indian War and assigned his warrant for 50 acres in Virginia. He was from Prince Edward County, Virginia.

Gay, John. He served on the expedition to Canada in 1690. John Gay received his land in Warwick, Massachusetts in 1738.

Gay, John. He served as a noncommissioned officer in the French and Indian War and received 200 acres in Nova Scotia 9 October 1776.

Gay, Jonathan. He served in the Narraganset War from Dedham, Massachusetts. His son, Jeremiah Gay, received land in Bedford, New Hampshire in 1733.

Gaylor, Edward. He served as a soldier in one of the Virginia Regiments in the French and Indian War. He produced a certificate from Col. Adam

Stephen. He applied for his 50 acres at Williamsburg, Virginia 15 October 1779.

Gayton, Clark. He received his 5,000 acres of land in West Florida for his service as a captain in the French and Indian War 6 May 1776.

George, James. He served in the Narraganset War from Massachusetts in 1685. His land was located in Buxton, Maine.

George, Samuel. He served on the expedition to Canada in 1690 and received land in Poland, Maine in 1739.

George, William. He was a veteran of the expedition to Canada in 1690. His brother, Joshua George, of Attleborough, Massachusetts, received his land in Ashburnham, Massachusetts in 1736.

Gerhard, Daniel. He was granted 50 acres in Albany County, New York for his service as a soldier in the 60th Regiment of Foot in the French and Indian War 1 May 1765.

Gery, Benjamin. He served in the Narraganset War and received land in Templeton, Massachusetts in 1733.

Gholston, John. He served in the French and Indian War and took his land in Fincastle County, Virginia 15 December 1772.

Gibbs, Francis. He served as a soldier in Capt. Peter Hogg's Company of Rangers in the French and Indian War until 1758. He received his 50 acre warrant in May 1780 in Orange County, Virginia.

Gibbs, Matthew. He served in the Narraganset War from Sudbury, Massachusetts. He received his land in Westminster, Massachusetts in 1733.

Gibbs, Samuel. He served in the Narraganset War from Sandwich, Massachusetts and received land in Gorham, Maine in 1733.

Gibson, Barne. He was granted 200 acres in Albany County, New York for his service as a noncommissioned officer in the 46th Regiment of Foot in the French and Indian War 8 March 1771.

Gibson, Benjamin. He served as a soldier in Col. William Byrd's Regiment of Regulars in the French and Indian War. He received his 50 acre warrant in May 1780 in Chesterfield County, Virginia. He also appeared as Benjamin Gipson.

Gibson, David. He was granted 200 acres in Craven County, South Carolina on the King's bounty 1 June 1767. He served as a noncommissioned officer in the French and Indian War.

Gibson, James. He was granted 50 acres in Albany County, New York for his service as a soldier in the 80th Regiment of Foot in the French and Indian War 5 April 1771.

Gibson, John. He was granted 200 acres in Albany County, New York for his service as a sergeant in the 77th Regiment in the French and Indian War 29 October 1765.

Gibson, John. He was granted 50 acres on Duskins Creek in South Carolina on the King's bounty for his service in the French and Indian War 13 May 1768.

Gibson, John. He served as a deputy commissary at Fort Pitt in 1760 in the French and Indian War and received his 2,000 acre warrant 28 February 1780 in Yohogania County, Virginia.

Gibson, Nathan. He served as a soldier in Capt. Christian's Company of Rangers in 1760 in the French and Indian War. He was in Louisa County, Virginia 8 November 1779. He assigned his right to 50 acres.

Gibson, Peter. He served as a soldier in the French and Indian War and was discharged by Capt. Samuel Overton. He received his warrant for 50 acres in Albemarle County, Virginia in March 1780.

Gibson, William. He was granted 200 acres in Albany County, New York for his service as a corporal in the 60th or Royal American Regiment in the French and Indian War 8 June 1771.

Gibson, William. He served as a soldier in the 1st Virginia Regiment under Col. William Byrd in the French and Indian War. He petitioned for his 50 acres 3 February 1780 in Hanover County, Virginia.

Giddings, —. He served on the expedition to Canada in 1690. His son, Isaac Giddings, of Ipswich received his land in Winchendon, Massachusetts in 1736.

Giddings, —. He served on the expedition to Canada in 1690. His son, Solomon Giddings, received his land in Winchendon, Massachusetts in 1736.

Giddins, John. He served in the Narraganset War from Massachusetts in 1685. His son, Solomon Giddins, received his land in Buxton, Maine.

Gidney, Bartholomew. The General Court of Massachusetts granted him 500 acres in Maine, but the deputies reversed the decision 13 May 1684.

Gilbert, George. He served as a private sentinel in the independent companies in the French and Indian War and sought his 50 acres of land in Georgia 21 March 1769.

Gilbert, John. He served as a soldier in Capt. William Phillips's Company of Volunteer Rangers in the French and Indian War until discharged in 1763. He petitioned for his 50 acres 14 February 1780 in Louisa County, Virginia.

Gilburne, Richard. He served as a sergeant at Louisbourg, Quebec and at the reduction of Montreal in the French and Indian War and had his service certified in New York 28 September 1774.

Gilchrist, Patrick. He was granted 200 acres in Albany County, New York for his service as a corporal in the 80th Regiment of Foot in the French and Indian War 15 August 1765.

Giles, Charles. He served as a master of ordnance on board H.M.S. schooner *Britain* at the siege of Quebec in the French and Indian War and petitioned for his 2,000 acres of land in New York 14 December 1766. He also appeared as Charles Gyles.

Giles, Thomas. He was granted 50 acres on the Savannah River in South Carolina on the King's bounty for his service as a soldier in the French and Indian War 13 May 1768.

Gilispy, Alexander. He served as a soldier in Capt. Charles Lewis's Company in the French and Indian War and received his 50 acre warrant in Virginia.

Gilfird, Paul. He served on the expedition to Canada in 1690. Paul Gilfird received land in Chesterfield, Massachusetts in 1739.

Gill, Edward, Sr. He served as a soldier in the 1st Virginia Regiment under Col. William Byrd and Col. Adam Stephen in the French and Indian War. He received his warrant for 50 acres in December 1779 in Botetourt County, Virginia.

Gill, Robert. He was granted 50 acres in Gloucester County, New York for his service as a soldier in the 28th Regiment of Foot and was drafted into the 44th Regiment in the French and Indian War 5 April 1770.

Gill, Samuel. He served in the Narraganset War from Hingham, Massachusetts and received land in Bedford, New Hampshire in 1733.

Gill, Samuel. He served in the Narraganset War from Dedham, Massachusetts and received land in Bedford, New Hampshire in 1733.

Gill, William. He was granted 50 acres in Albany County, New York for his service as a soldier in the 28th Regiment of Foot in the French and Indian War 3 September 1771.

Gill, William. He served as a soldier in the Old Virginia Regiment in the French and Indian War until he died. His warrant for 50 acres was issued to his heir, Edward Gill, in February 1780 in Botetourt County, Virginia.

Gillespie, Alexander. He served as an armorer and blacksmith in the 1st Virginia Regiment under Col. William Byrd in the French and Indian War. He proved his service in Augusta County, Virginia 21 March 1780.

Gillespie, John. He served as a corporal in the 27th Regiment in the French and Indian War and petitioned for 200 acres land in New York 13 January 1772.

Gillespie, Robert. He served as a sergeant in Capt. John Dickerson's Company of Rangers in 1754 in the French and Indian War. He petitioned for 200 acres in February 1780 in Botetourt County, Virginia.

Gillespie, Thomas. He was granted 200 acres in Albany County, New York for his service as a noncommissioned officer in the 46th Regiment in the French and Indian War 8 March 1771.

Gillet, Nathan. He served in the Narraganset War from Connecticut and received land in Voluntown, Connecticut in 1701.

Gillet, Simon. He served as a soldier in the French and Indian War in the 1st Virginia Regiment under Col. William Byrd. He assigned his right to his 50 acre warrant in Virginia.

Gillett, Nathan. He was granted 50 acres in Connecticut for his service in the Pequot War 11 May 1671.

Gilliam, John. He served as a noncommissioned officer in the French and Indian War and assigned his 200 acre land warrant in Virginia. He also had two other warrants of the same acreage for his deceased brothers. He assigned all three warrants.

Gillilan, William. He served as a soldier in the 35th Regiment in the French and Indian War and petitioned for his land in New York 26 October 1765.

Gilmore, Anthony. He was granted 350 acres in Craven County, South Carolina on the King's bounty for his service in the French and Indian War 27 August 1764.

Gilmore, Robert. He was granted 50 acres in Albany County, New York for his service as a soldier in the 44th Regiment of Foot in the French and Indian War 18 July 1770.

Gilson, John. He served under Capt. John Lovewell from Massachusetts and was in battle at Pigwacket in May 1728. He was from Groton, Massachusetts and received his land in Pembroke, New Hampshire.

Gilson, Joseph. He served under Capt. John Lovewell from Massachusetts and was in battle at Pigwacket in May 1728. He was form Groton, Massachusetts and received his land in Pembroke, New Hampshire.

Gimber, James. He served as a soldier in Col. William Byrd's Regiment in the French and Indian War and petitioned for his 50 acres in February 1780 in Spotsylvania County, Virginia. One of the same name also served under Col. George Washington and assigned his 50 acres.

Gist, Christopher. He served as a captain of rangers in 1756 until 1757 in the French and Indian War. His son and heir, Nathaniel Gist, petitioned for his land in February 1780 in Spotsylvania County, Virginia. He assigned the 3,000 acre warrant.

Gist, Nathaniel. He served as a lieutenant in Capt. Christopher Gist's Company in 1756. He also served as a captain under Col. George Washington in the 1st Virginia Regiment in the French and Indian War. He served lastly as a captain in the regiment under Col. Adam Stephen in 1762. He petitioned for his land in February 1780 in Spotsylvania County, Virginia. He petitioned for three warrants of 3,000, 3,000, and 2,000 acres. His representative, Thomas Gist, received his warrants in 1775.

Gist, Thomas. He served as a cadet in 1757, ensign in 1758, and lieutenant in 1760 in the Virginia Regiment. In 1762 he served as a lieutenant in another regiment in the French and Indian War and received a warrant for 2,000 acres of land in Virginia. He sought additional land in Yohogania County, Virginia 24 April 1780.

Givens, Robert. He served as a soldier in the French and Indian War and received a warrant for 50 acres in Augusta County, Virginia 15 February 1780.

Gladwin, Henry. He was granted 5,000 acres in Albany County, New York for his service as a major in the 80th Regiment of Foot in the French and Indian War 21 October 1765.

Glass, James. He received land in Richmond, New Hampshire in 1765 for the service of an unidentified veteran of the expedition to Canada in 1690.

Glassford, James. He was granted 200 acres in Albany County, New York for his service as a corporal in the 27th Regiment of Foot in the French and Indian War 18 April 1769.

Glazier, Beamsly. He was granted 3,000 acres in Tryon County, New York for his service as a captain in the 4th Battalion in the 60th Regiment of Foot in the French and Indian War 10 September 1772.

Glazier, Frederick. He was granted 200 acres in Colleton County, South Carolina on the King's bounty for his service in the French and Indian War 23 January 1773.

Gleason, William. He served in the Narraganset War from Cambridge, Massachusetts. His son, William Gleason, received his land in Westminster, Massachusetts in 1733.

Glentworth, George. He served as a surgeon's mate in the French and Indian War. His service was proved per certificate in West Florida 7 October 1774.

Gloyd, John. He served in the Narraganset War from Salem, Massachusetts. His son, John Gloyd, claimed his land in Amherst, New Hampshire in 1734.

Goad, Joseph. He served in the Narraganset War from Roxbury, Massachusetts. His son-in-law, John Wilson, received his land in Bedford, New Hampshire in 1733.

Goddard, Ebenezer. He served on the expedition to Canada in 1690. Jonathan Learned received his land in Alstead, New Hampshire in 1771.
Goddard, Josiah. He received his land in Alstead, New Hampshire in 1771 for service of an unidentified veteran of the expedition to Canada in 1690.
Goddin, Amos. He served in the Narraganset War from Massachusetts in 1685. His land was located in Buxton, Maine. He also appeared as Amos Gody.
Godfrey, Samuel. He served on the expedition to Canada in 1690 and received land in Dumbarton, New Hampshire in 1735.
Goff, Daniel. He served in the Narraganset War from Lynn, Massachusetts and petitioned for his land 4 June 1685.
Goffe, John. He served from Massachusetts in the war against the Indians in 1725. He received his land in Pembroke, New Hampshire.
Going, Moses. He served as a soldier in Capt. James Gunn's Company under Col. William Byrd in the French and Indian War and received his 50 acre warrant in Virginia.
Gold, Andrew. He served in the Narraganset War from Salem, Massachusetts. His son-in-law, Ezekiel Marsh, claimed his land in Amherst, New Hampshire in 1734.
Gold, Henry. He served in the Narraganset War from Yarmouth, Massachusetts and received land in Gorham, Maine in 1733.
Gold, John. He served on the expedition to Canada in 1690 and received his land in Woburn, Massachusetts in 1738.
Golding, Patrick. He served on the Canada Expedition in 1690 and petitioned for land.
Goldman, Edward. He served as an ensign in Col. William Byrd's Regiment in the French and Indian War. His elder brother and heir at law, Thomas Goldman, received the 2,000 acres of land 17 February 1780 in Spotsylvania County, Virginia.
Goldsmith, Thomas. He was granted 200 acres in Albany County, New York for his service as a corporal in the 80th Regiment of Foot in the French and Indian War 15 August 1765.
Goldthwaite, Joseph. He was granted 2,000 acres in Charlotte County, New York for his service as a lieutenant in the 50th Regiment of Foot in the French and Indian War 25 March 1775.
Gooch, William. He served as a sergeant in the French and Indian War and assigned his 200 acre warrant in Virginia in 7 May 1774.
Goodale, Isaac. He served on the expedition to Canada in 1690. He petitioned for his land in Raymond, Maine in 1735.
Goodchild, George. He was granted 200 acres in Albany County, New York for

his service as a drummer in the 60th Regiment of Foot in the French and Indian War 15 August 1765.

Goodchild, George. He was granted 50 acres in Albany County, New York for his service as a soldier in a regiment of foot in the French and Indian War 19 May 1770.

Goodhue, William. He was a veteran of the expedition to Canada in 1690. His brother, Joseph Goodhue of Ipswich, Massachusetts claimed his land in Winchendon, Massachusetts in 1736.

Goodin, Abraham. He served as a soldier in Col. William Byrd's Regiment in the French and Indian War and proved his right in Rockbridge County, Virginia 7 September 1779. He assigned his 50 acre warrant in Virginia.

Gooding, Jacob. He served as a captain under Col. George Washington in the French and Indian War and received his 3,000 acre warrant in Virginia.

Gooding, Philip. He served on the expedition to Canada in 1690 under Maj. Wade and received his land in Ashburnham, Massachusetts in 1736.

Goodman, Bartlett. He served as a soldier in Capt. Gabriel Throgmorton's Company of Rangers in the French and Indian War until 1759. He was in Louisa County, Virginia 14 February 1780. He assigned his warrant for 50 acres in Virginia.

Goodman, Bartlett. He served as a soldier in Capt. Thomas Bullet's Company of Rangers in 1762 in the French and Indian War in Virginia and assigned his warrant for 50 acres. He was in Louisa County, Virginia 8 November 1779 when he received his warrant for 50 acres.

Goodman, Richard. He served in the Pequot War and received a grant of land in Soldiers' Field in Hartford, Connecticut.

Goodridge, John. He served in the French and Indian War and petitioned for land in New York 29 May 1770.

Goodson, Thomas. He served as a soldier in Capt. Scott's Company in 1760 in the French and Indian War. He proved his right in Buckingham County, Virginia 13 March 1780. He assigned his 50 acre warrant in Virginia. He also appeared as Thomas Godson.

Goodspeed, Ebenezer. He served in the Narraganset War from Barnstable, Massachusetts and received his land in Gorham, Maine in 1733.

Goodspeed, John. He served in the Narraganset War from Barnstable, Massachusetts and received his land in Gorham, Maine in 1733.

Goodwin, Edward. He served in the French and Indian War and took his land in Fincastle County, Virginia 15 December 1772.

Goodwin, John. He served in the Narraganset War from Boston, Massachusetts.

His son, Nathaniel Goodwin, received his land in Bedford, New Hampshire in 1733.

Goodwin, Lazarus. He served on the expedition to Canada in 1690 and received land in Poland, Maine in 1739.

Goodwin, Robert. He served as a soldier in Capt. William Phillips's Company in 1763 in the French and Indian War. He assigned his right to 50 acres in Virginia.

Goodwin, Timothy. He served on the expedition to Canada and sought land in Massachusetts 10 December 1735.

Goodwin, William. He served as a soldier in the 48th Regiment in the French and Indian War. His service was certified in New York 5 October 1760.

Goold, Arthur. He served in the French and Indian War and received 2,000 acres in Nova Scotia 1 March 1771.

Goold Joseph. He received land in Richmond, New Hampshire in 1765 for the service of an unidentified veteran of the expedition to Canada in 1690.

Gordon, Ann. He was granted 2,000 acres in Albany County, New York for his service as a lieutenant in the 42nd Regiment of Foot in the French and Indian War 23 May 1772.

Gordon, Charles. He served as a corporal in the 28th Regiment in the French and Indian War and petitioned for his land in New York 25 May 1771.

Gordon, Harry. He served as a captain in the French and Indian War and was named in New York 27 January 1768.

Gordon, James. He served as a noncommissioned officer in the French and Indian War and assigned his land warrant of 200 acres in Virginia.

Gordon, John. He was granted 50 acres in Albany County, New York for his service as a soldier in the 47th Regiment of Foot in the French and Indian War 28 October 1765.

Gordon, John. He was granted 3,000 acres in Gloucester County, New York for his service as a captain in an independent company of foot in the French and Indian War 2 August 1774.

Gorham, —. He served as a captain on the expedition to Canada in 1690. John Gorham received his land in Dumbarton, New Hampshire in 1735.

Gorham, —. He served on the expedition to Canada in 1690. Shubal Gorham received land in Dumbarton, New Hampshire in 1735.

Gorham, Jabez. He served in the Narraganset War from Yarmouth, Massachusetts and received land in Gorham, Maine in 1733.

Gorham, John. He served in the Narraganset War from Barnstable, Massachusetts. His son, Shubal Gorham, received his land in Gorham, Massachusetts in 1733.

Gorham, John. He served as a captain in the Narraganset War from Yarmouth, Massachusetts and received his land in Gorham, Massachusetts in 1733.

Gorham, Joseph. He served in the Narraganset War from Yarmouth, Massachusetts and received land in Gorham, Maine in 1733.

Gorman, David. He served in the French and Indian War and took his land in Fincastle County, Virginia 15 December 1772.

Gorrell, James. He was granted 2,000 acres in Albany County, New York for his service as a lieutenant in the 60th Regiment of Foot in the French and Indian War 30 May 1765.

Gorton, Benjamin. He shared in the grant of East Greenwich, Rhode Island made to those who had rendered service in King Philip's War. The grant was made 31 October 1677.

Gorton, John. He shared in the grant of East Greenwich, Rhode Island made to those who had rendered service in King Philip's War. The grant was made 31 October 1677.

Goss, Benjamin. He served as a soldier for fourteen months under Col. William Byrd in 1761 in the French and Indian War. He applied for his warrant in Buckingham County, Virginia 13 March 1780. He assigned his right to 50 acres.

Gould, Joseph. He served on the expedition to Canada in 1690 and received land in Poland, Maine in 1739.

Goulding, James. He served in the French and Indian War and received a land warrant for 50 acres in Virginia which he assigned.

Goulding, Palmer. He was from Worcester, Massachusetts and was awarded 200 acres for his service 12 December 1735.

Gowdey, Andrew. He was granted 50 acres in Albany County, New York for his service as a soldier in the 46th Regiment of Foot in the French and Indian War 30 May 1771.

Gracy, Alexander. He served as a corporal in the 78th Regiment in the French and Indian War and was granted land in New York 13 November 1771. He also appeared as Alexander Gracey.

Graff, Peter. He was granted 200 acres in Albany County, New York for his service as a sergeant in the 3rd Battalion in the 60th Regiment of Foot in the French and Indian War 12 September 1765.

Graham, Colin. He received his 2,000 acres of land in West Florida for his service as a captain in the French and Indian War 21 September 1772 and on 1 February 1775.

Graham, David. He served as a soldier in Capt. William Preston's Company of Rangers in 1758 in the French and Indian War. A warrant for 50 acres was issued to John Graham, the guardian of the only son and heir, Joseph Graham, 21 March 1780 in Augusta County, Virginia.

Graham, John. He served as a captain in the French and Indian War. He received his 3,000 acres of land in Albany County, New York 7 January 1764.

Graham, John. He served in Capt. William Preston's Company of Rangers in 1758 in the French and Indian War. He was dead when his service was proved in Augusta County, Virginia 21 March 1780.

Graham, Patrick. He was granted 200 acres in Albany County, New York for his service as a noncommissioned officer in the 28th Regiment of Foot in the French and Indian War 8 March 1771.

Graham, Robert. He served as a soldier in Capt. William Preston's Company of Rangers in 1758 in the French and Indian War. Maj. Andrew Lockbridge was guardian of his orphans and was issued his warrant for 50 acres 15 February 1780 in Augusta County, Virginia.

Graham, Walter. He was granted 50 acres in Charlotte County, New York for his service as a soldier in the 42nd Regiment of Foot in the French and Indian War 25 January 1773.

Grandidier, James. He was granted 2,000 acres in West Florida for his service as a staff officer in the French and Indian War 8 April 1779.

Granell, James. He served as a sergeant in the 1st Virginia Regiment in the French and Indian War and received his warrant for 200 acres in Goochland County, Virginia 15 November 1779.

Grant, Alexander. He was granted 2,000 acres in Albany County, New York for his service as a subaltern in the 27th Regiment of Foot in the French and Indian War 11 September 1764.

Grant, Alexander. He was granted 2,000 acres in Albany County, New York for his service as a lieutenant in the 77th Regiment of Foot in the French and Indian War 18 October 1765.

Grant, Alexander. He was granted 200 acres in Albany County, New York for his service as a sergeant in the 42nd Regiment of Foot in the French and Indian War 30 October 1765.

Grant, Alexander. He served as commander of H.M.'s vessels on Lake Champlain in the French and Indian War. His service was certified 2 May 1774.

Grant, Allen. He was granted 2,000 acres in Albany County, New York for his service as a lieutenant in the 42nd Regiment of Foot in the French and Indian War 19 October 1765.

Grant, Allen. He was granted 2,000 acres in Albany County, New York for his service as a subaltern in the 60th Regiment of Foot in the French and

Indian War 1 June 1770.

Grant, Allen. He served as a private in the French and Indian War and petitioned for his 50 acres of land in New York 3 June 1772.

Grant, Caleb. He served in the Narraganset War from Weston, Massachusetts. His son-in-law, Ebenezer Boynton, received his land in Westminster, Massachusetts in 1733.

Grant, Christopher. He served in the expedition to Canada in 1690. Christopher Grant, Jr. received his land in Alstead, New Hampshire in 1771.

Grant, Daniel. He was granted 200 acres in Albany County, New York for his service as a sergeant in the 80th Regiment of Foot in the French and Indian War 10 May 1765.

Grant, Evan. He was granted 50 acres in Gloucester County, New York for his service as a soldier in the 78th Regiment of Foot in the French and Indian War 5 April 1770.

Grant, Finley. He was granted 50 acres in Albany County, New York for his service as a soldier in the 42nd Regiment of Foot in the French and Indian War 30 October 1765.

Grant, George. He was granted 2,000 acres in West Florida for his service as a surgeon in the navy in the French and Indian War 1 May 1777.

Grant, Henry. He was granted 200 acres in Albany County, New York for his service as a sergeant in the 44th Regiment of Foot in the French and Indian War 18 February 1775.

Grant, James. He was granted 2,000 acres in Albany County, New York for his service as a lieutenant in the 45th Regiment of Foot in the French and Indian War 11 October 1765.

Grant, James. He was granted 3,000 acres in Albany County, New York for his service as a captain in the 80th Regiment of Foot in the French and Indian War 1 June 1770.

Grant, John. He served as a captain in the French and Indian War and petitioned for land 30 December 1766 in New York.

Grant, John. He was granted 50 acres in Albany County, New York for his service as a soldier in the 80th Regiment of Foot in the French and Indian War 6 July 1771.

Grant, John. He was granted 50 acres in Charlotte County, New York for his service as a soldier in the 42nd Regiment of Foot in the French and Indian War 1 April 1775.

Grant, John. He served as a corporal in the 77th Regiment in the French and Indian War. He received 200 acres in Albany County, New York 6 November 1764.

Grant, John. He served as a captain in the French and Indian War and received 2,000 acres in Nova Scotia 15 July 1783.

Grant, John. He was granted 2,000 acres in West Florida for his service as a master's mate in the navy at the reduction of Louisbourgh in the French and Indian War 9 April 1778.

Grant, Jonah. He served as a soldier in the French and Indian War and received a land warrant for 50 acres in Virginia which he assigned.

Grant, Lewis. He was granted 200 acres in Albany County, New York for his service as a sergeant in the 42nd Regiment of Foot in the French and Indian War 30 October 1765.

Grant, Peter. He was granted 50 acres in Albany County, New York for his service as a soldier in the 42nd Regiment of Foot in the French and Indian War 30 October 1765.

Grant, Robert. He was granted 3,000 acres in Albany County, New York for his service as a captain in the 77th Regiment of Foot in the French and Indian War 7 August 1764.

Grant, Samuel. He served a lieutenant in the Marines in the French and Indian War and received 2,000 acres in Nova Scotia 28 October 1773.

Grant, William. He was granted 3,000 acres in West Florida for his service as a lieutenant in the navy in the French and Indian War 6 May 1776. He also had a grant of 500 acres for his service as a lieutenant in the Royal Regiment of Artillery in the French and Indian War 10 April 1776.

Grath, Daniel. He served as a soldier in the French and Indian War from Virginia and received 50 acres of land.

Grave, William. He served in the French and Indian War and petitioned for his land in New York 2 February 1769.

Graves, Moses. He served from Massachusetts in the campaign against the Indians in 1725. He was from Chelmsford, Massachusetts and received his land in Pembroke, New Hampshire.

Graves, Joseph. He served in the Narraganset War from Sudbury, Massachusetts. His son, Ebenezer Graves, received his land in Westminster, Massachusetts in 1733.

Graves, Samuel. He served in the Narraganset War from Lynn, Massachusetts. He applied for his land 4 June 1685. His son, Samuel Graves, claimed his land in Amherst, New Hampshire in 1734.

Graves, Samuel. He served on the expedition to Canada in 1690 and received his land in Bethel, Maine in 1767.

Graves, William. He served as a lieutenant in the French and Indian War and received 2,000 acres in Nova Scotia 10 September 1781.

Gravis, William. He was granted 200 acres in Albany County, New York for his service as a corporal in 2nd Battalion in the 60th or Royal American Regiment of Foot in the French and Indian War 4 April 1767.

Gray, Alexander. He served as a corporal in the 78th Regiment in the French and Indian War and petitioned for his 200 acres of land in New York 16 April 1771.

Gray, Benjamin. He received his 50 acres of land in West Florida for his service as a private in the French and Indian War 9 April 1777.

Gray, Edward. He served in the Narraganset War from Yarmouth, Massachusetts and received land in Gorham, Maine in 1733.

Gray, George. He served on the expedition to Canada in 1690. George Gray petitioned for his land in Raymond, Maine in 1735.

Gray, Richard. He was granted 50 acres for his service as a soldier in the French and Indian War in West Florida 9 April 1777.

Gray, Robert. He was granted 50 acres in Albany County, New York for his service as a soldier in the 55th Regiment of Foot in the French and Indian War 18 April 1769.

Gray, Robert. He was granted 200 acres in Charlotte County, New York for his service as a noncommissioned officer in the 44th Regiment of Foot in the French and Indian War 12 October 1774.

Gray, William. He served in the Narraganset War from Yarmouth, Massachusetts. His son, William Gray, received land in Gorham, Maine in 1733.

Graydon, Alexander. He was granted 2,000 acres in Cumberland County, New York for his service as a lieutenant in the 2nd Battalion in the 60th Regiment of Foot 4 October 1770.

Greame, Robert. He was granted 50 acres in Albany County, New York for his service as a soldier in the 80th Regiment of Foot in the French and Indian War 26 July 1765.

Greaves, Samuel. He served on the expedition to Canada and sought his land 10 December 1735 in Massachusetts.

Greece, John Charles. He served as a soldier in the French and Indian War and received 50 acres in Nova Scotia 9 October 1776.

Gredon, James. He served as a soldier in the 44th Regiment in the French and Indian War. Mary Gredon, his widow, was certified to be entitled to his land 19 January 1767 in New York.

Greeland, Samuel. He served in the Narraganset War and assigned his land to David Wheeler who received same in Templeton, Massachusetts in 1733.

Greemes, William. He was the master of one of His Majesty's ships of war at the reduction of Louisbourg in the French and Indian War and applied for 2,000 acres. He had twelve months to submit the vouchers to document his service in Georgia 2 July 1771.

Green, John. He served on the expedition to Canada in 1690. John Green received his land in Bethel, Maine in 1767.

Green, Joseph. He served on the expedition to Canada in 1690. Samuel Green received his land in Bethel, Maine in 1767.

Green, Lewis. He was a soldier in the Virginia Regiment under Gen. Braddock in the French and Indian War in 1755. He applied for his 50 acres in Hampshire County, Virginia 10 August 1779. He assigned his right to 50 acres.

Green, Samuel. He was at Kittery when he was awarded 200 acres in York County for his services 3 December 1736 in Massachusetts.

Green, Timothy. He was granted 542 and 616.6 acres in Berks County, Pennsylvania for his service as a captain in the French and Indian War 3 February 1769.

Green, William. He served on the expedition to Canada in 1690. John Green received his land in Bethel, Maine in 1767.

Greenfield, Lewis. He served as a miner in the French and Indian War. He sought his 200 acres of land in New York 14 July 1766.

Greenhold, Henry. He was granted 50 acres in Albany County, New York for his service as a private in the 46th Regiment of Foot in the French and Indian War 8 March 1771.

Greenleaf, Stephen. He served as a captain in the Narraganset War from Massachusetts in 1685. His land was located in Buxton, Maine.

Greenleaf, Stephen. He served as a captain on the expedition to Canada in 1690 and received land in Poland, Maine in 1739.

Greenleaf, Tristrum. He served on the expedition to Canada in 1690 and received land in Poland, Maine in 1739.

Greenshields, Henry. He was granted 200 acres in Albany County, New York for his service as a noncommissioned officer in the 46th Regiment of Foot in the French and Indian War 7 October 1768.

Greer, Edmon. He served on the expedition to Canada in 1690. Edmon Green received land in Chesterfield, Massachusetts in 1739.

Greeter, John. He served as a corporal in the 60th Regiment in the French and Indian War. The survey for his land was returned in New York 1 November 1764.

Gregor, John. He served as a lieutenant in the 42nd Regiment in the French and Indian War. He received 2,000 acres in Albany County, New York.

Gregor, William. He served as a lieutenant in the 42nd Regiment in the French and Indian War. He received 2,000 acres in Albany County, New York.

Gregory, Peter Wharton. He acted as conductor of artillery at the reduction of Canada in the French and Indian War and petitioned for his 2,000 acres of land in New York 22 March 1774. He also appeared as Peter McGregory.

Gregory, Richard. He served as a sergeant in the 60th Regiment in the French and Indian War and petitioned for land in New York 6 April 1772.

Gregory, Richard. He enlisted in 1758 as a soldier in the 1st Virginia Regiment in the French and Indian War until the unit was disbanded after which he served in the 2nd Virginia Regiment until discharged. He proved his service in Frederick County, Virginia 2 May 1780.

Greiner, David. He served as a soldier in Capt. Charles Lewis's Company in the French and Indian War and proved same in Augusta County, Virginia 21 March 1780.

Greley, William Frad. He received his land in West Florida for his service as a noncommissioned officer in the French and Indian War 13 March 1776.

Grey, —. He served on the expedition to Canada in 1690. John Grey received land in Dumbarton, New Hampshire in 1735.

Grezong, Peter. He served as a private in the 17th Regiment in the French and Indian War and petitioned for land 30 May 1766 in New York.

Gridley, Joseph. He served in the Narraganset War from Boston, Massachusetts. His son, John Gridley, received land in Bedford, New Hampshire in 1733.

Gridley, Thomas. His heirs were granted 50 acres in Connecticut for his service in the Pequot War 11 May 1671.

Grierson, Adam. He was granted 200 acres in Charlotte County, New York for his service as a noncommissioned officer in the 4th Battalion of the 60th Regiment of Foot in the French and Indian War 12 October 1774.

Griffin, Benjamin. He shared in the grant of East Greenwich, Rhode Island made to those who had rendered service in King Philip's War. The grant was made 31 October 1677.

Griffin, Leroy. He served as a subaltern in the French and Indian War. His daughter and heir at law, Judith Griffin, received his 2,000 acre land warrant.

Griffin, Matthew. He served in the Narraganset War from Charlestown, Massachusetts. His heir, John Griffin, received his land in Westminster, Massachusetts in 1733.

Griffin, Richard. He served as a soldier in Capt. Robert Mumford's Company of the 1st Virginia Regiment in the French and Indian War. He was from Mecklenburg County, Virginia 14 February 1780. He assigned his 50 acre warrant.

Griffin, Samuel. He served on the expedition to Canada in 1690. Samuel Griffin received land in Warwick, Massachusetts in 1738.

Griffin, William. He served as a private in Capt. Robert Mumford's Company of the 1st Virginia Regiment in the French and Indian War. He was in Charlotte County, Virginia 6 March 1780. He assigned his right to 50 acres.

Griffith, David. He was a surgeon's mate in the Regiment of Provincial Troops raised in New York in the French and Indian War in 1758. Oliver Delancey, Colonel in Chief, and George Brewster, Jr., Captain of the New York Regiment, certified his service. He was the rector of Fairfax Parish, Fairfax County, Virginia when he received his warrant for 2,000 acres in September 1779.

Griffith, David. He served in the French and Indian War and received two warrants for 50 and 100 acres respectively in Virginia.

Grig, Jacob. He served in the Narraganset War from Boston, Massachusetts. His heirs received land in Bedford, New Hampshire in 1733.

Grigg, John. He was granted 50 acres in Albany County, New York for his service as a matross in the Royal Regiment of Artillery in the French and Indian War 27 March 1775.

Grigg, Kenney. He served as a drummer in the 28th Regiment in the French and Indian War and petitioned for his 200 acres in New York 19 January 1775.

Griggs, John. He served in the Narraganset War from Massachusetts and assigned his land to Samuel Chandler who received the land in Templeton, Massachusetts in 1733.

Grimsley, Joseph. He proved his service as a soldier in the 2nd Virginia Regiment in the French and Indian War under Col. William Byrd 21 February 1780 in Culpeper County, Virginia. He assigned his warrant for 50 acres. He also appeared as Joseph Grimsby.

Grind, George. He served in the Narraganset War from Charlestown, Massachusetts. His heirs received his land in Westminster, Massachusetts in 1733.

Grindle, Thomas. He was granted 50 acres in Albany County, New York for his service as a soldier in the 46th Regiment of Foot in the French and Indian War 18 July 1770.

Grindleymer, Phillip. He served as a private in the 4th Battalion Royal Americans in the French and Indian War and petitioned for his 50 acres of land in New York 28 September 1771.

Griswold, John. He served in the Narraganset War from Connecticut and received land in Voluntown, Connecticut in 1701.

Griswold, Matthew. He served in the Narraganset War from Connecticut and received land in Voluntown, Connecticut in 1701.

Griter, John. He was granted 200 acres in Albany County, New York for his service as a noncommissioned officer in the 60th Regiment of Foot in the French and Indian War 13 February 1767.

Grocer, Thomas, Jr. He served as a soldier in the 2nd Virginia Regiment in the French and Indian War but disposed of his warrant.

Groner, Thomas. He served in an independent company of rangers in the French and Indian War and petitioned for his land in New York 12 April 1769.

Grosman, Benjamin. He served in the French and Indian War and had his service certified in New York in January 1767. He also appeared as Benjamin Grosmer.

Grouse, Christian. He served in the French and Indian War and petitioned for his 50 acres of land in New York 16 May 1763.

Grout, Joseph. He served in the Narraganset War from Watertown,

Massachusetts. His son, Joseph Grout, received his land in Westminster, Massachusetts in 1733.

Grover, John. He served as a corporal on the expedition to Canada in 1690. Robert Hale petitioned for his land in Raymond, Maine in 1735.

Grubbs, Daniel. He served as a soldier in Capt. Peter Hogg's Company of Rangers until 1758 during the French and Indian War. He received his 50 acre warrant 24 April 1780 in Rockingham County, Virginia.

Guilford, Paul. He received land in Richmond, New Hampshire for the service of an unidentified veteran of the expedition to Canada in 1690.

Guinn, Robert. He served as a soldier in Capt. William Preston's company in 1758 in the French and Indian War and received a warrant for 50 acres 15 February 1780 in Augusta County, Virginia. He also appeared as Robert Gwinn and Robert Gwin.

Guise, William. He was granted 200 acres in Charlotte County, New York for his service as a sergeant in the 27th Regiment of Foot in the French and Indian War 25 January 1773.

Gullet, Simon. He served as a soldier in the 1st Virginia Regiment under Col. William Byrd in the French and Indian War and received his warrant for 50 acres in James City County, Virginia 3 November 1779.

Gulliver, Jonathan. He served as a captain. He applied for land in Massachusetts 3 December 1735.

Gun, David. He served in the French and Indian War and received his acreage in Albany County, New York 4 April 1774.

Gun, David. He served as a soldier in the French and Indian War and received 50 acres of land in Virginia.

Gun, Henry. He was granted 200 acres in Albany County, New York for his service as a sergeant in the 42nd Regiment of Foot in the French and Indian War 30 October 1765.

Gun, John. He served as a noncommissioned officer in the French and Indian War and received 200 acres in West Florida 8 April 1773.

Gunn, George. He served in the French and Indian War and petitioned for land in New York 8 July 1772.

Gunn, James. He served as a captain in the French and Indian War. He received three warrants for a total of 3,000 acres which he assigned in Virginia.

Gunnell, John. He served as a soldier in Capt. Temple's Company of Regulars in Col. William Byrd's Regiment in the French and Indian War. He received his 50 acre warrant in Virginia.

Gunnis, John. He was granted 200 acres in Albany County, New York for his service as a corporal in the 28th Regiment of Foot in the French and

Indian War 8 June 1771.

Gurnal, Hugh. He was granted 200 acres in Albany County, New York for his service as a corporal in the 28th Regiment of Foot in the French and Indian War 1 April 1772.

Gurnet, Francis. He served in the Narraganset War from Hingham, Massachusetts. His son, Samuel Gurnet, received land in Bedford, New Hampshire in 1733.

Gurney, Francis. He assigned his land for his service in the French and Indian War to Robert Buchanan 9 January 1767 in New York.

Gurney, Zachariah. He served in the Narraganset War from Boston, Massachusetts. He received land in Bedford, New Hampshire in 1733.

Gutteridge, Jeremiah. He served on the expedition to Canada in 1690 and received land in Poland, Maine in 1736.

Guy, Townsend. He was granted 2,000 acres in Albany County, New York for his service as a lieutenant in the 60th Regiment of Foot in the French and Indian War 30 May 1765.

Gwilliams, Edgecomb. He served as a soldier under Capt. Nathaniel Gist in Col. Adam Stephen's Regiment in 1762 in the French and Indian War. He received his 50 acre warrant 25 May 1780 in Henry County, Virginia.

Gwin, James. He served in the French and Indian War and took his land in Fincastle County, Virginia 15 December 1772.

Gwinn, David. He served as a soldier in Capt. Charles Lewis's Company in 1758 in the French and Indian War and received his 50 acre warrant in Virginia.

Haaden, Zopher. He served as a corporal in the French and Indian War and was granted land in New York 1 April 1767.

Hack, William. He was from Taunton, Massachusetts and served on the Canada expedition in 1690. He received his 150 acres of land 31 May 1734.

Hacy, William. He served in the Narraganset War from Boston, Massachusetts. His grandson, William Hacy, received his land in Bedford, New Hampshire in 1733.

Hackley, Francis. He served as a soldier in Col. William Byrd's Regiment in 1758 in the French and Indian War and assigned his 50 acre warrant.

Haddock, William. He served as a private in the 47th Regiment in the French and Indian War and had his service certified in New York 28 January 1767.

Hadley, Edward. He was granted 50 acres in Granville County, South Carolina on the King's bounty for his service in the French and Indian War 13 May 1768.

Hadley, Samuel. He served in the Narraganset War from Massachusetts in 1685. His land was located in Buxton, Maine.

Haff, Peter. He served as a soldier in the French and Indian War from Virginia and received a warrant for 50 acres. His name may have been Peter Hoff.

Hager, John. He served in the Narraganset War from Watertown, Massachusetts. His nephew, Samuel Hager, received his land in Westminster, Massachusetts in 1733.

Haggart, William. He was granted 2,000 acres in Albany County, New York for his service as a lieutenant in the 77th Regiment of Foot in the French and Indian War 19 October 1765. He also appeared as William Hagart.

Haiden, Nathaniel. He served in the Narraganset War from Connecticut. His heirs received land in Voluntown, Connecticut in 1701.

Haight, Jonathan. He served as a captain in the French and Indian War and petitioned for his land 30 December 1765 in New York.

Haist, George. He served as a mate on the ship of war, *Enterprise*, at Louisbourg in the French and Indian War. He applied for 2,000 acres in Georgia in 1772.

Hak, John. He was granted 200 acres in Berkeley County, South Carolina on the King's bounty for his service in the French and Indian War 13 May 1768.

Halbert, Charles. He was granted 200 acres in Albany County, New York for his service as a corporal in the 28th Regiment of Foot in the French and Indian War 25 May 1771. He also appeared as Charles Hulbert.

Halbert, Ebenezer. He served under Capt. John Lovewell from Massachusetts and was in battle at Pigwacket in May 1725. He was from Dunstable, Massachusetts and received land in Pembroke, New Hampshire.

Halbert, Richard. He served as a soldier under Col. William Byrd and Col. Adam Stephen in the French and Indian War and petitioned for his 50 acres 17 February 1780 in Spotsylvania County, Virginia.

Halbrook, Joseph. He served as a private in the French and Indian War and had his service certified in New York in January 1767. He also appeared as Joseph Halbrouk.

Haldane, William. He was granted 2,000 acres in Albany County, New York for his service as an ensign in a corps of rangers in the French and Indian War 15 May 1770.

Haldane, William. He was granted 2,000 acres in Albany County, New York for his service as a subaltern in a corps of rangers in the French and Indian War 1 June 1770.

Haldimand, Frederick. He was granted 1,000 acres in West Florida for his service as a field officer in the French and Indian War 1 August 1772.

Hale, John. He was a clergyman from Beverley, Massachusetts. His grandson, Robert Hale, was granted 300 acres for his service by Massachusetts 1 January 1735/6.

Hale, Samuel. He was granted 50 acres in Connecticut for his service in the Pequot War 11 May 1671. He was from Wethersfield. His heirs were granted 60 acres 13 May 1703.

Hale, Thomas. He was granted 60 acres in Connecticut for his service in the Pequot War 11 May 1671. His heirs were granted 60 acres 13 May 1703.

Hale, Thomas. He served as a captain on the expedition to Canada in 1690 and received land in Poland, Maine in 1739.

Hales, George. He was granted 200 acres in Albany County, New York for his service as a noncommissioned officer in the 46th Regiment of Foot in the French and Indian War 8 March 1771.

Hales, John. He was granted 200 acres in Albany County, New York for his service as a noncommissioned officer in the 28th Regiment of Foot in the French and Indian War 8 March 1771.

Hall, Andrew. He served as a soldier in the French and Indian War and had his service certified in Montgomery County, Virginia for his 50 acres of land 8 March 1780.

Hall, Andrew. He served as a subaltern under Col. Thomas Nash in the expedition against the Shawnee in 1757 in the French and Indian War. He had his service certified in Montgomery County, Virginia for 2,000 acres of land 3 May 1780.

Hall, Benjamin. He served in the Narraganset War from Mansfield, Massachusetts. He claimed his land in Greenwich, Massachusetts in 1737.

Hall, Cornelius. He was from Falmouth, York County, Massachusetts. He was wounded in the ankle in the service. He was awarded 150 acres by Massachusetts 17 June 1735.

Hall, Dennis. He served as a soldier in the 17th Regiment in the French and Indian War and petitioned for his 50 acres in New York 24 October 1764.

Hall, Henry. He served in the Narraganset War from Connecticut and received land in Voluntown, Connecticut in 1701.

Hall, John. His son, Thomas Hall, of Wallingford was granted 50 acres in Connecticut for his services in the Pequot War 13 October 1698.

Hall, John. He was granted 200 acres in Albany County, New York for his service as a sergeant in the 80th Regiment of Foot in the French and Indian War 28 October 1765.

Hall, John. He was granted 2,000 acres in Cumberland County, New York for his service as a lieutenant in the 80th Regiment of Foot in the French and Indian War 7 October 1769.

Hall, John. He served as a soldier in Capt. Alexander Sayers's Company of Volunteers in the French and Indian War and had his service certified in Montgomery County, Virginia for his 50 acres of land 8 March 1780.

Hall, John. He served as a sergeant in the company of Capt. William Phillips's Volunteer Rangers in 1763 in the French and Indian War. His warrant for 200 acres was issued to his coheiresses, Elizabeth Hall and Sarah Hall, 13 March 1780 in Louisa County, Virginia. Their guardian was William Lipscomb.

Hall, Joseph. He served in the Narraganset War from Yarmouth, Massachusetts and received land in Gorham, Maine in 1733.

Hall, Nathaniel. He served in the Narraganset War from Yarmouth, Massachusetts and received land in Gorham, Maine in 1733.

Hall, Preserved. He served on the expedition to Canada in 1690. Preserved Hall received land in Chesterfield, Massachusetts in 1739.

Hall, Richard. He served in Lovewell's War in Massachusetts and received his land in Petersham, Massachusetts.

Hall, Richard. He was a soldier in the Virginia Regiment in the French and Indian War and received his 50 acres of land in Virginia.

Hall, Robert. He served as a soldier in Capt. William Phillips's Company in 1763 in the French and Indian War. His heir at law, David Hall, received his warrant of 50 acres in Virginia.

Hall, Robert. He served as a soldier in Capt. William Preston's Company of Rangers in the French and Indian War and received his 50 acre warrant in Virginia. He proved his service in Augusta County, Virginia 21 March 1780.

Hall, Samuel. He served in the Narraganset War from Yarmouth, Massachusetts and received his land in Gorham, Maine in 1733.

Hall, Stephen. He served on the expedition to Canada and sought his land in Massachusetts 10 December 1735.

Hall, William. He served as a soldier under Col. William Byrd in the French and Indian War. He assigned his warrant for 50 acres in Virginia. He proved his service in Fauquier County, Virginia 22 May 1780.

Hall, William. His service as a soldier in the French and Indian War was proved in Richmond County, Virginia 6 February 1780.

Hall, William. He served as a sergeant in the French and Indian War and received a 200 acre warrant in Virginia.

Halliard, William. He served as a soldier in the 2nd Virginia Regiment under Col. William Byrd in 1758 in the French and Indian War. He received a warrant for 50 acres in King and Queen County, Virginia 14 February 1780.

Halling, John. He was granted 50 acres in Albany County, New York for his service as a soldier in the 60th or Royal American Regiment in the French and Indian War 28 March 1771.

Hallitt, John. He served in the Narraganset War from Yarmouth, Massachusetts and received land in Gorham, Maine in 1733.

Hallum, John J. He served as a midshipman on H. M.S. sloop *Norwich* in the French and Indian War and petitioned for 3,000 acres as a lieutenant in New York 16 November 1767.

Haly, Nathaniel. He served in the Narraganset War from Newton, Massachusetts. He received his land in Westminster, Massachusetts in 1733.

Ham, Jacob. He was granted 50 acres on the southwest side of the Wateree River in South Carolina on the King's bounty for his service in the French and Indian War 21 June 1765.

Hamblet, Jesse. He served as a soldier in the French and Indian War from Virginia and assigned his right to 50 acres.

Hambleton, —. He served on the expedition to Canada in 1690. Thomas Hambleton received land in Dumbarton, New Hampshire 1735.

Hambleton, —. He served under Capt. Noah Wiswall in 1690 in the expedition to Canada as well as several other times. His brother, John Hambleton of Brookfield, petitioned for his land in Massachusetts 13 June 1740.

Hambleton, Daniel. He served on the expedition to Canada in 1690 and received his land in Dumbarton, New Hampshire in 1735.

Hamblin, Bartholomew. He served in the Narraganset War from Barnstable, Massachusetts and received land in Gorham, Maine in 1733.

Hamblin, Eleazer. He served in the Narraganset War from Barnstable, Massachusetts and received land in Gorham, Maine in 1733.

Hamblin, James. He served on the expedition to Canada in 1690 and claimed his land in Dumbarton, New Hampshire in 1735.

Hamilton, Andrew. He served as a soldier in a ranging company under Capt. Walter Cunningham in the French and Indian War and received a warrant for 50 acres 17 November 1779 in Greenbrier County, Virginia.

Hamilton, Archibald. He was granted 3,000 acres in Cumberland County, New

York for his service as a captain in the 108th Regiment of Foot in the French and Indian War 13 August 1766.

Hamilton, Henry. He was granted 50 acres in Berkeley County, South Carolina on the King's bounty for his service in the French and Indian War 15 February 1770.

Hamilton, John. He served as a lieutenant in the 40th Regiment in the French and Indian War and petitioned for 2,000 acres in New York 4 November 1766.

Hamilton, John. He served as a soldier in the French and Indian War and received 50 acres in Nova Scotia 2 March 1778.

Hamilton, John. He served as an ensign in the French and Indian War and assigned his warrant for 2,000 acres to Andrew Hamilton in Virginia.

Hamilton, Robert. He served as a soldier under Col. Henry Bouquet in 1764 and received his 50 acre warrant in Virginia.

Hamilton, Samuel. He served as a sergeant in the French and Indian War in Virginia and assigned his warrant for 200 acres.

Hamilton, Samuel. He served as a soldier for three months in 1757 or 1758 under Col. Andrew Lewis in the French and Indian War. He proved his right in Buckingham County, Virginia 13 March 1780. He assigned his 50 acre warrant in Virginia. He also appeared as Samuel Hambleton.

Hamilton, William. He served as a soldier in the French and Indian War and received 50 acres on the King's bounty in South Carolina 15 February 1770.

Hamilton, William. He served as a soldier in Capt. John Dickeson's Ranging Company in 1758 and 1759 in the French and Indian War. He received his 50 acre warrant 21 March 1780 in Greenbrier County, Virginia.

Hammer, Isaac. He received land in Richmond, New Hampshire in 1765 for the service of an unidentified veteran of the expedition to Canada in 1690.

Hammon, Andrew Snape. He served as a lieutenant in the Royal Navy in the French and Indian War and received 3,000 acres in Nova Scotia 25 May 1776.

Hammond, Eleazer. He served on the expedition to Canada in 1690. Eleazer Hammond received his land in Warwick, Massachusetts in 1738.

Hammond, John. He served as a soldier in the 46th Regiment in the French and Indian War. Mary Hales was certified as his widow 12 December 1766 in New York.

Hammond, Thomas. He was granted 50 acres in Albany County, New York for his service as a soldier in the 1st Regiment of Foot in the French and

Indian War 18 February 1775.

Hanah, Barnaby. He was granted 200 acres in Charlotte County, New York for his service as a noncommissioned officer in the 4th Battalion of the 60th Regiment of Foot in the French and Indian War 12 October 1774.

Hancock, George. He was a soldier in the 2nd Virginia Regiment in the French and Indian War and assigned his right to 50 acres. He also appeared as George Handcock. He was from Goochland County, Virginia 20 September 1779.

Hancock, John. He served in the French and Indian War from Virginia and assigned his warrant.

Hancock, Stephen. He served a soldier in Col. William Byrd's Regiment in 1760 in the French and Indian War and was issued a warrant for 50 acres 1 February 1780 Kentucky County, Virginia. He also appeared as Stephen Handcock.

Handfield, William. He served as a captain in the French and Indian War and petitioned for 3,000 acres in 1766 in New York.

Handley, John. He was granted 50 acres in Granville County, South Carolina on the King's bounty for his service in the French and Indian War 21 October 1765.

Handmore, John. He served in the Narraganset War from Bridgewater, Massachusetts. His son, John Handmore, claimed his land in Greenwich, Massachusetts in 1737.

Hands, John. He served in the Narraganset War from Boston, Massachusetts. His son-in-law, Hugh Calder, received his land in Bedford, New Hampshire in 1733.

Handsforth, Joseph. He served as a sergeant in the 35th Regiment in the French and Indian War and petitioned for his 200 acres in New York 24 October 1764.

Hanson, Thomas. He served in the French and Indian War as a noncommissioned officer from Virginia. He assigned his 200 acre land warrant.

Hapgood, Hezekiah. He served in the Narraganset War and received land in Templeton, Massachusetts in 1733.

Harbison, George. He served as a soldier in Capt. Smith's Company under Col. William Byrd in the French and Indian War in 1760. He proved his service in Montgomery County, Virginia 2 November 1779 and received his 50 acre warrant.

Harboun, William. He was granted 200 acres in Albany County, New York for his service as a musician in the 46th Regiment of Foot in the French and Indian War 25 May 1771. He also appeared as William Harborne and William Harbourne.

Harcourt, William. He was granted 10,000 acres in West Florida for his service as Lieutenant Colonel in the 18th Regiment of Dragoons in the French and Indian War 24 January 1777.

Hardburgher, Frederick John. He was granted 50 acres in Albany County, New York for his service in the 80th Regiment of Foot in the French and Indian War 29 October 1765.

Harding, Isaac. He served as a soldier in the 2nd Virginia Regiment in the French and Indian War and received his 200 acre warrant in Virginia.

Harding, Joseph. He served in the Narraganset War from Eastham, Massachusetts and received land in Gorham, Maine in 1733.

Hardy, Alexander. He was granted 50 acres in Berkeley County, South Carolina on the King's bounty for his service in the French and Indian War 15 February 1770.

Harfield, David. He served as a noncommissioned officer in the French and Indian War and assigned his right to 200 acres in Virginia.

Harket, John. He was granted 200 acres in Craven County, South Carolina on the King's bounty 27 August 1764. He served as a private in the French and Indian War.

Harlow, Joel. He served as a soldier in the French and Indian War and requested his 50 acres 23 April 1774 in Botetourt County, Virginia.

Harlow, Nathaniel. He received land in Richmond, New Hampshire in 1765 for for an unidentified veteran of the expedition to Canada in 1690.

Harman, Adam, Sr. He served as a soldier in the French and Indian War and had his service certified in Montgomery County, Virginia 8 March 1780 for his 50 acres of land.

Harman, Adam. He served as a subaltern in the French and Indian War and had his service certified in Montgomery County, Virginia 8 March 1780 for his 2,000 acres of land.

Harman, Johnson. He served as a colonel against the Indian enemy. He was granted 200 acres in Massachusetts 26 June 1727.

Harman, Thomas. He was granted 50 acres in Albany County, New York for his service as a soldier in the 80th Regiment of Foot in the French and Indian War 26 July 1765.

Harmon, John. He served in the Narraganset War from Scarborough, Massachusetts. He claimed his land in Amherst, New Hampshire in 1734.

Harnes, George. He served as a soldier in the French and Indian War from Virginia and assigned his 50 acres to Andrew Lewis.

Harper, Anthony. He was granted 200 acres in Albany County, New York for his service as a noncommissioned officer in the 35th Regiment of Foot in the French and Indian War 3 September 1771.

Harper, Josiah. He was granted 2,000 acres in Albany County, New York for his service as a surgeon's mate in the 80th Regiment of Foot in the French and Indian War 6 November 1768. He also appeared as Josiah Harpur.

Harpest, Godfrey. He was granted 50 acres in Albany County, New York for his service as a private in a regiment of foot in the French and Indian War 19 May 1770.

Harradaway, Edward. He served in the Narraganset War from Salem, Massachusetts. His heirs claimed his land in Amherst, New Hampshire in 1734.

Harrage, William. He served in the Narraganset War from Abington, Massachusetts and received his land in Gorham, Maine in 1733.

Harringdon, Edward. He served in the Narraganset War from Gloucester, Massachusetts. He claimed his land in Amherst, New Hampshire in 1734.

Harrington, Daniel. He served on the expedition to Canada in 1690. Thomas Harrington received his land in Bethel, Maine in 1767.

Harrington, George. He received land in Alstead, New Hampshire in 1771 for the service of an unidentified veteran of the expedition to Canada in 1690.

Harrington, George, Jr. He received land in Alstead, New Hampshire in 1771 for the service of an unidentified veteran of the expedition to Canada in 1690.

Harrington, Isaac. He was a soldier in 1712 and along with John Tozer and Jonas Smith advanced £30 to redeem their fellow soldier, Daniel Tucker, who was captivated by the Indians in an engagement at Wells. They were awarded 500 acres of land in York County, Massachusetts 8 December 1737.

Harrington, Joseph. He served on the expedition to Canada in 1690. His son, Joseph Harrington, received his land in Bethel, Maine in 1767.

Harris, Bartlet. He was granted 50 acres in Colleton County, South Carolina on the King's bounty for his service in the French and Indian War 23 January 1773.

Harris, Benjamin. He served as a soldier in Capt. Christopher Hudson's Company of Rangers in 1758 in the French and Indian War. His heir, Overton Harris whose guardian was Frederick Harris, petitioned for his 50 acres 14 February 1780 in Louisa County, Virginia.

Harris, David. He was a soldier in the 2nd Virginia Regiment in the French and

Indian War and assigned his right to 50 acres. He was from Goochland County, Virginia 20 September 1779.

Harris, Edward. He served as a soldier in Capt. Samuel Meredith's Company of Rangers in 1760 in the French and Indian War. He received his 50 acre warrant in Virginia.

Harris, George. He served on the expedition to Canada in 1690. Samuel Harris petitioned for his land in Raymond, Maine in 1690.

Harris, Gerreyh. He was granted 200 acres in Albany County, New York for his service as a noncommissioned officer in the 60th Regiment of Foot in the French and Indian War 5 April 1771.

Harris, Giles. He served as a captain in the French and Indian War and applied for land in Massachusetts 9 June 1772. His claim was rejected 1 February 1773.

Harris, James. He was a soldier in the 2nd Virginia Regiment in the French and Indian War. He was in Hanover County, Virginia 4 November 1779 and assigned his warrant of 50 acres.

Harris, John. He served on the expedition to Canada in 1690. He was of Ipswich, Massachusetts when he claimed his land in Winchendon, Massachusetts in 1736.

Harris, Nathanael. He was a soldier at Port Royal under Gen. Nicholson and sought his land in Massachusetts 10 December 1735.

Harris, Robert. He served on the expedition to Canada in 1690. Robert Harris received land in Warwick, Massachusetts in 1738.

Harris, Robert. He was granted 2,000 acres in Orange County, New York for his service as a staff officer in the hospital in the French and Indian War 18 January 1775.

Harris, Samuel. He served in the Narraganset War from Beverly, Massachusetts. His heirs claimed his land in Amherst, New Hampshire in 1734.

Harris, Samuel. He served on the expedition to Canada in 1690. He received land in Bethel, Maine in 1767.

Harris, Thomas. He served on the expedition to Canada in 1690. Stephen Harris received his land in Alstead, New Hampshire in 1771.

Harrison, Burr. He served as an officer in the French and Indian War and received his 2,000 acre land warrant in Virginia.

Harrison, Henry. He served as a captain in the French and Indian War. His son and heir, Henry Harrison, was entitled to a warrant for 3,000 acres which he desired to locate in Fincastle County, Virginia 31 December 1773.

Harrison, John. He was granted 50 acres in Albany County, New York for his service as a soldier in the 80th Regiment of Foot in the French and Indian War 6 June 1765.

Harrison, John. He was granted 200 acres in Albany County, New York for his service as a corporal in the 60th Regiment of Foot in the French and Indian War 1 April 1772.

Harrison, Nicholas. He served as a sergeant in the 47th Regiment in the French and Indian War and was granted 200 acres in New York by 10 October 1774.

Harrison, William. He served as a lieutenant in a ranging company in Lord Dunmore's War in 1774. He proved his service in Yohogania County, Virginia 28 March 1780.

Harrop, Joseph. He was granted 50 acres in Albany County, New York for his service as a soldier in the 60th or Royal American Regiment of Foot in the French and Indian War 30 May 1772.

Harry, Philip. He was granted 50 acres in Gloucester County, New York for his service as a soldier in the 28th Regiment of Foot in the French and Indian War 5 April 1770.

Harson, Samuel. He served as a noncommissioned officer in the French and Indian War and petitioned for 200 acres on the King's bounty in South Carolina 5 June 1771.

Hart, Stephen. He served in the Pequot War and was granted land in Soldiers' Field in Hartford, Connecticut.

Hart, Thomas. He served in the expedition to Canada in 1690. His brother, George Hart of Ipswich, Massachusetts, claimed his land in Winchendon, Massachusetts in 1736.

Hartill, Frederick. He was granted 200 acres in Albany County, New York for his service as a sergeant in the 3rd Battalion of the 60th Regiment of Foot in the French and Indian War 12 September 1765. He also appeared as Frederick Hartel.

Hartshorn, —. He served on the long march in the Narraganset War from Massachusetts and in 1708 moved out of the province to Connecticut. His son, Ebenezer Hartshorn of Concord, Massachusetts, received his 300 acres 4 June 1770.

Hartshorn, David. He was granted 50 acres in Albany County, New York for his service as a soldier in a regiment of foot in the French and Indian War 19 May 1770.

Hartshorn, Ebenezer. He served in Queen Anne's War in 1709 and 1710 and in King George's War in 1722. He received 400 acres. He was in Concord, Massachusetts 15 February 1768.

Hartshorn, Joshua. He was granted 200 acres in Albany County, New York for his service as a sergeant in the 60th Regiment of Foot in the French and Indian War 30 May 1765.

Hartshorne, Thomas. He served on the expedition to Canada in 1690. Thomas Hartshorne received land in Warwick, Massachusetts in 1738.

Hartwell, Samuel. He served in the Narraganset War. His son, Samuel Hartwell, received his land in Templeton, Massachusetts in 1733.

Harvey, Henry. He was a soldier in Capt. Peter Hogg's Company of Rangers in 1758 in the French and Indian War and received a warrant for 50 acres in Orange County, Virginia 25 November 1779 which he assigned.

Harvey, John. He served in the Narraganset War from Massachusetts in 1685. His son, John Harvey, received his land in Buxton, Maine.

Harvey, John. He served as a soldier in the French and Indian War in 1758 and requested his warrant for 50 acres in February 1780 in Caroline County, Virginia.

Harvey, John. He served as a soldier in the 2nd Virginia Regiment of Regulars under Col. William Byrd in 1758 in the French and Indian War and petitioned for his 50 acres 14 February 1780 in King and Queen County, Virginia.

Harvey, Luke. He served as a private in the French and Indian War and petitioned for a warrant for 50 acres in South Carolina 1 May 1764.

Harvey, Philip. He served as a corporal in the 80th Regiment in the French and Indian War and assigned his right to land to Robert Buchanan in New York 21 January 1767.

Harvie, John. He was granted 50 acres in Charlotte County, New York for his service as a soldier in the Royal Highland Regiment of Foot in the French and Indian War 12 July 1775.

Harwood, John. He served as ensign under Capt. John Lovewell from Massachusetts and was killed at Pigwacket in May 1725. He was from Dunstable, Massachusetts. His land was located in Pembroke, New Hampshire.

Hasborne, Thomas. He was granted 200 acres in Albany County, New York for his service as a noncommissioned officer in the 46th Regiment in the French and Indian War 4 July 1770.

Hasborne, Thomas. He was granted 200 acres in Albany County, New York for his service as a corporal in the 46th Regiment of Foot in the French and Indian War 1 April 1772.

Hasely, Francis. He was granted 50 acres in Albany County, New York for his service as a soldier in the 80th Regiment of Foot in the French and Indian War 28 October 1765.

Haskell, —. He served on the expedition to Canada in 1690. His son, William Haskell, received his land in Winchendon, Massachusetts in 1736.

Hassel, Benjamin. He served under Capt. John Lovewell from Massachusetts and was at the battle of Pigwacket in May 1725. He was from Dunstable, Massachusetts and received his land in Pembroke, New Hampshire.

Hastie, Robert. He was granted 200 acres in Albany County, New York for his service as a corporal in the 46th Regiment of Foot in the French and Indian War 8 June 1771. He also appeared as Robert Haisty.

Hastings, Moses. He served on the expedition to Canada in 1690. Nathaniel Stone received his land in Alstead, New Hampshire in 1771.

Hasty, William. He served as a soldier in the 46th Regiment in the French and Indian War. Margaret Hasty was certified as his widow in New York 13 December 1766. His right to land was assigned.

Haswell, Edward. He was granted 200 acres in Albany County, New York for his service as a noncommissioned officer in the 60th Regiment of Foot in the French and Indian War 8 March 1771.

Hatch, Joseph. He served in the Narraganset War from Falmouth, Massachusetts. He claimed his land in Amherst, New Hampshire in 1734.

Hatch, Samuel. He served in the Narraganset War from Scituate, Massachusetts. He received land in Bedford, New Hampshire in 1733.

Hathaway, Abraham. He served in the Narraganset War from Dighton, Massachusetts. His son, Abraham Hathaway, claimed his land in Greenwich, Massachusetts in 1737.

Hathaway, Jacob. He served in the Narraganset War from Taunton, Massachusetts. His heirs claimed his land in Greenwich, Massachusetts in 1737.

Hathaway, John. He served in the Narraganset War from Barnstable, Massachusetts and received land in Gorham, Maine in 1733.

Hathorn, —. He served in the Narraganset War from Lynn, Massachusetts. His widow sought his land 4 June 1685.

Haufield, David. He served as a noncommissioned officer in the French and Indian War from Virginia and received a warrant for 200 acres.

Haven, Richard. He served in the Narraganset War from Lynn, Massachusetts. His son, Joseph Haven, claimed his land in Amherst, New Hampshire in 1734.

Havens, Robert. He shared in the grant of East Greenwich, Rhode Island made to those who had rendered service in King Philip's War. The grant was made 31 October 1677.

Havill, John. He served as a private in the 44th Regiment in the French and Indian War and was granted land in New York 7 March 1770.

Hawcks, John. He served in the Narraganset War from Lynn, Massachusetts and applied for his land 4 June 1685.

Hawford, Richard. He was granted 2,000 acres in West Florida for his service as a master's mate in the navy at the reduction of Louisbourgh in the French and Indian War on 14 May 1778. He served on the *Culloden,* the *Marlborough,* and the *Fonderyard.*

Hawkins, Elijah. He was a soldier under Col. William Byrd in the 2nd Virginia Regiment in the French and Indian War. His land was awarded to his heir at law, Joseph Hawkins, 13 October 1779 at Williamsburg, Virginia.

Hawkins, John. He served in the Narraganset War from Charlestown, Massachusetts. His heirs received his land in Westminster, Massachusetts in 1733.

Hawkins, Joseph. He served as a soldier in the 2nd Virginia Regiment under Col. William Byrd in the French and Indian War. He received his 50 acre warrant 13 October 1779 at Williamsburg, Virginia.

Hawkins, Joseph. He served as a corporal in the 28th Regiment of Foot in the French and Indian War and received 200 acres in Albany County, New York 8 June 1771.

Hawkins, Joseph. He served as a soldier in Capt. McNeal's Company in the 1st Virginia Regiment until discharged in 1762 in the French and Indian War. He proved his service in Augusta County, Virginia 21 December 1779.

Hawkins, Philemon. He served as a soldier under Col. William Byrd in the French and Indian War and received his 50 acre warrant in Virginia.

Hawkins, William. He served in the Narraganset War from Scituate, Massachusetts. Benjamin Turner received his land in Bedford, New Hampshire in 1733.

Hawkins, William. He shared in the grant of East Greenwich, Rhode Island made to those who had rendered service in King Philip's War. The grant was made 31 October 1677.

Hawkinson, Reid. He served as a lieutenant in the Bouquet expedition from Virginia. He received a warrant for 2,000 acres.

Hawley, Thomas. He served in the Narraganset War from Roxbury, Massachusetts. His son-in-law, Edward Dorr, received his land in Bedford, New Hampshire in 1733.

Hawthorn, David. He served in the Narraganset War from Norwich, Connecticut. He claimed his land in Greenwich, Massachusetts in

1737.

Hawthorn, John. He served in the Narraganset War from Norwich, Connecticut. He claimed his land in Greenwich, Massachusetts in 1737.

Hay, Alexander. He served as a lieutenant in the 40th Regiment in the French and Indian War. His son, John Hay, was heir to his 2,000 acres. William Shirreff applied for the land in behalf of his said nephew 11 November 1766 in New York.

Hay, Jehu. He was granted 2,000 acres in Albany County, New York for his service as a lieutenant in the 60th Regiment of Foot in the French and Indian War 28 October 1765.

Hay, John. He served as fort major of the garrison at Detroit in the French and Indian War and had his service certified in New York in April 1774.

Hay, John. He served as a soldier in the French and Indian War and received a warrant for 50 acres of land in Virginia. His name may have been John Hoy.

Hay, William. He was granted 2,500 and 2,000 acres in West Florida for his service as a captain in the navy in the French and Indian War 5 August 1773 and 25 August 1773 respectively.

Hayd, Thomas. He was granted 50 acres in Albany County, New York for his service as a soldier in the 86th Regiment of Foot in the French and Indian War 28 October 1765.

Hayden, William. His heirs were granted 50 acres in Connecticut for his service in the Pequot War 11 May 1671. He also appeared as William Heyden.

Hayle, Thomas. He served as a noncommissioned officer in the 1st Virginia Regiment in the expedition against the Indians in the French and Indian War and received his 200 acre warrant in Virginia. He proved his service in Frederick County, Virginia 4 April 1780.

Haymand, William. He served as a sergeant in the Virginia Regiment in the French and Indian War. He received his 200 acre warrant in November 1779 in Monongalia County, Virginia. He also appeared as William Haymond.

Haynes, John. He served as a soldier in Capt. Gabriel Throgmorton's Company of Regulars in the French and Indian War. He was in Botetourt County, Virginia in March 1780. He assigned his 50 acre warrant.

Hays, Cornelius. He served as a soldier in the 40th Regiment in the French and Indian War and petitioned for his 50 acres in New York 24 October 1764.

Hays, James. He was granted 303 and 334 acres in Berks County, Pennsylvania for his service as a lieutenant in the French and Indian War 3 February 1769.

Hays, John. He served as a soldier in the 1st Virginia Regiment about two years until it was disbanded by Col. Adam Stephen in the French and Indian War. He received his 50 acre warrant in May 1780 in Montgomery County, Virginia.

Hayward, Elisha. He served in the Narraganset War from Bridgewater, Massachusetts. His nephew, Thomas Hayward 3rd, claimed his land in Greenwich, Massachusetts in 1737.

Hayward, Samuel. He applied for his land in Massachusetts 10 December 1735.

Haywood, William. He served as a sergeant in the Old Virginia Regiment in the French and Indian War. He received a warrant for 200 acres in November 1779 in Monongalia County, Virginia.

Hazeless, Henry. He served as a soldier in the 46th Regiment in the French and Indian War and had his service certified 9 July 1766 in New York.

Hazell, Henry. He was granted 50 acres in Gloucester County, New York for his service as a soldier in the 4th Battalion in the French and Indian War 5 April 1770.

Hazen, John. He served in Lovewell's War in Massachusetts and received his land in Petersham, Massachusetts in 1733.

Hazen, Moses. He served in Lovewell's War in Massachusetts and received his land in Petersham, Massachusetts in 1733.

Hazen, Thomas. He served in the Narraganset War from Norwich, Connecticut. He claimed his land in Greenwich, Massachusetts in 1737.

Hazen, William. He served as a subaltern officer in the French and Indian War and received 2,000 acres in Nova Scotia 26 July 1782.

Head, Hadley. He served as a soldier in the French and Indian War and assigned his 50 acre warrant in Virginia.

Heaphey, Jeremiah. He served in the French and Indian War and petitioned for his land in New York 2 February 1769.

Heath, John. He shared in the grant of East Greenwich, Rhode Island made to those who had rendered service in King Philip's War. The grant was made 31 October 1677.

Heath, William. He served on the expedition to Canada in 1690. William Heath received his land in Warwick, Massachusetts in 1738.

Heath, William. He served as a soldier under Col. William Byrd in the French and Indian War. He was in Essex County, Virginia 21 February 1780. He assigned his right to 50 acres to Thomas Hanson.

Heathman, Abraham. He served as a corporal in the French and Indian War and petitioned for his 200 acres in New York 19 January 1775. He also appeared as Abraham Heathorn.

Heaton, James Spry. He served as a Master Mate in the Royal Navy in the French and Indian War and received 2,000 acres in Nova Scotia 2 April 1774.

Heavy, James. He was granted 200 acres in Albany County, New York for his service as a corporal in the 46th Regiment of Foot in the French and Indian War 8 June 1771.

Hebden, James. He served as a soldier in the French and Indian War and assigned his 50 acres 21 April 1774 in Botetourt County, Virginia.

Hedden, Zopher. He was granted 200 acres in Albany County, New York for his service as a sergeant in Capt. Ogden's Independent Company of Rangers in the French and Indian War 25 May 1771.

Hedding, James. He was granted 50 acres in Albany County, New York for his service as a soldier in the 47th Regiment of Foot in the French and Indian War 6 August 1765.

Hedge, —. He served on the expedition to Canada in 1690. Elisha Hedge received land in Dumbarton, New Hampshire in 1735.

Hedge, Joseph. He served as a soldier in 1758 and 1759 in Capt. Robert Rutherford's Company of Rangers in the French and Indian War. He received his 50 acre warrant in March 1780 in Berkeley County, Virginia.

Hedge, Samuel. He served in the Narraganset War from Yarmouth, Massachusetts and received land in Gorham, Maine in 1733.

Hedly, Dennis. He served in the Narraganset War from Sudbury, Massachusetts. He received his land in Westminister, Massachusetts in 1733.

Hencher, Thomas. He served in the Narraganset War from Roxbury, Massachusetts. His nephew-in-law, Zachariah Smith, received his land in Bedford, Massachusetts in 1733.

Henderson, David. He served in the 2nd Virginia Regiment in the French and Indian War and proved his service in Goochland County, Virginia 20 September 1779.

Henderson, Donald. He served as a private in the French and Indian War and petitioned for his land in 1767 in New York.

Henderson, James. He served as a lieutenant in the French and Indian War and petitioned for his 2,000 acres of land in New York 28 January 1767. He was dead by 29 June 1774 when his widow, Elizabeth Henderson, was named.

Henderson, James. He served as an officer in Capt. Christian's Company of

Rangers in the French and Indian War and received his 2,000 acre warrant in Virginia.

Henderson, William. He served as a soldier in Capt. Alexander McClenachan's Company of Independents under Col. Henry Bouquet in 1764. He requested his 50 acres 19 November 1779 in Augusta County, Virginia.

Hendley, Thomas. He served on the expedition to Canada in 1690. Joseph Clough was admitted to his land in Lyndeboro, Maine in 1736.

Hendrick, Israel. He served in the Narraganset War from Norwich, Connecticut. His son, Israel Hendrick, claimed his land in Greenwich, Massachusetts in 1737.

Hendricks, James. He was granted 522 and 639 acres in Berks County, Pennsylvania for his service as a captain in the French and Indian War 3 February 1769.

Hendricks, James. He was a captain in the French and Indian War. He lived in Alexandria, Virginia. He proved his right in Fairfax County, Virginia in September 1779. He assigned his warrant.

Hennery, Benjamin. He served in an independent company of rangers in the French and Indian War and petitioned for land in New York 12 April 1769.

Henry, Hugh. He served as a sergeant in the French and Indian War and petitioned for land in New York 26 December 1769.

Henry, William. He served as a lieutenant in the French and Indian War and received his 2,000 acre land warrant in Virginia.

Henslee, Benjamin. He served as a lieutenant under Col. William Byrd in the Virginia Battalion in the French and Indian War and received his warrant in Augusta County, Virginia in August 1779. He assigned his 2,000 acre warrant.

Hepburn, David. He was granted 2,000 acres in Albany County, New York for his service as a surgeon in the 42nd Regiment of Foot in the French and Indian War 28 October 1765.

Herbert, Charles. He was granted 50 acres in Albany County, New York for his service as a soldier in the 46th Regiment of Foot in the French and Indian War 8 March 1771.

Herbert, Thomas. He served as a noncommissioned officer in the French and Indian War and was entitled to 200 acres in Virginia.

Herin, John. He served in the Narraganset War from Massachusetts in 1685. His land was located in Buxton, Maine.

Hern, John. He served as a soldier under Capt. James Walker in Col. William Byrd's Regiment and received his 50 acre warrant 8 March 1780 in

Mecklenburg County, Virginia.

Hernish, Martin. He was granted 50 acres in Albany County, New York for his service as a private in a regiment of foot in the French and Indian War 19 May 1770.

Heron, David. He served in an independent company of rangers in the French and Indian War and petitioned for land in New York 12 April 1769.

Heron, John. He served in an independent company of rangers in the French and Indian War and petitioned for land in New York 12 April 1769.

Herrick, Jonathan. He served in the expedition to Canada in 1690. Henry Herrick petitioned for his land in Raymond, Maine in 1735.

Herrick, Joseph. He served in the Narraganset War from Salem, Massachusetts. His son, Joseph Herrick, claimed his land in Amherst, New Hampshire in 1734.

Herrick, Joseph. He served on the expedition to Canada in 1690. He petitioned for his land in Raymond, Maine in 1735.

Herring, William. He was granted 200 acres in Albany County, New York for his service as a sergeant in the 60th Regiment of Foot in the French and Indian War 25 May 1771.

Herrington, George. He served in the Narraganset War from Watertown, Massachusetts. His heirs received his land in Westminster, Massachusetts in 1733.

Herrington, John. He served in the Narraganset War from Watertown, Massachusetts. He received his land in Westminster, Massachusetts in 1733.

Herrington, Robert. He served as a soldier under Capt. Hancock Eustace in the 2nd Virginia in the French and Indian War. His service was proved in Fauquier County, Virginia 27 March 1780.

Hersey, Israel. He served on the expedition to Canada in 1690. Israel Hersey received land in Warwick, Massachusetts in 1738.

Hersey, Elisha. He was a veteran of the French and Indian War and applied along with 60 others for a grant of land in recognition of service 28 Dec. 1763. He was from Abington, Massachusetts.

Hervie, John. He was granted 50 acres in Albany County, New York for his service as a soldier in the 44th Regiment of Foot in the French and Indian War 8 October 1771.

Hess, Henry. He served as a corporal of grenadiers in the 2nd Battalion of the 60th Regiment in the French and Indian War and petitioned for his 200 acres in New York 30 January 1775.

Hester, Charles. He served as a soldier in Capt. William Phillips's Company of Volunteer Rangers in 1763 in the French and Indian War. He petitioned for his 50 acres 14 February 1780 in Louisa County, Virginia.

Hewes, Joshua. He served in the Narraganset War from Boston, Massachusetts. Sarah Perkins received his land in Bedford, New Hampshire in 1733.

Hewins, Benjamin. He was a veteran of the expedition to Canada in 1690. William Cooper of Boston, Massachusetts received his land in Ashburnham, Massachusetts in 1736 at the desire of Joseph Hewins, eldest brother of the veteran.

Hewlett, Martin. He served as a corporal in the Virginia Regiment under Col. William Byrd in the French and Indian War. He assigned his warrant for 200 acres in Virginia.

Hews, Peter. He served in the French and Indian War and had his service certified in New York 20 November 1766.

Hibberd, Samuel. He served on the expedition to Canada in 1690. Jonathan Hibberd petitioned for his land in Raymond, Maine in 1735.

Hibbert, John. He served in the Indian wars from 1702 to 1708 and was from Metheun when he was awarded his land by Massachusetts 23 March 1735/6.

Hibden, James. He was a soldier in the French and Indian War. His son, William Hibden, received his warrant for 50 acres in Virginia in 1779. The application was made in Henrico County, Virginia 4 February 1779. He also appeared as James Hibbins.

Hibdon, William. He served as a soldier in the French and Indian War and was entitled to 50 acres in Virginia.

Hickey, Benjamin. He was granted 2,000 acres in West Florida for his service as a warrant officer in the navy in the French and Indian War 26 March 1778.

Hickey, John. He served as a soldier for 13 years ending 19 January 1764 under Capt. James Coldar in one of the independent companies doing duty in South Carolina in the French and Indian War. He sought 50 acres in Georgia 4 February 1771.

Hickey, John. He was granted 50 acres in Amelia Township, South Carolina on the King's bounty for his service in the French and Indian War 21 June 1765.

Hickey, Morris. He was granted 250 acres on a branch on the north side of the Santee River in South Carolina on the King's bounty 21 August 1765. He served as a private in the French and Indian War.

Hicki, George. He had his service in the 46th Regiment in the French and Indian War certified 9 July 1766 in New York.

Hickie, John. He served as a private in the French and Indian War and petitioned for land in New York 8 July 1772.

Hicklen, Thomas. He served as a soldier in Capt. William Preston's Company of Rangers in 1758 in the French and Indian War and received a warrant for 50 acres 15 February 1780 in Augusta County, Virginia.

Hickler, Philip. He was granted 50 acres in Albany County, New York for his service as soldier in the 80th Regiment of Foot in the French and Indian War 28 June 1770.

Hickman, John. He served as a lieutenant in the Virginia Regiment of Regulars under Col. William Peachey in 1759 in the French and Indian War. He petitioned for his land 3 February 1780 in Hanover County, Virginia.

Hickman, Richard. He served as a lieutenant in the French and Indian War. His brother and heir, James Hickman, was issued his warrant for 2,000 acres 15 March 1774 in Fincastle County, Virginia.

Hickman, Richard. He served as a lieutenant in the Virginia Regiment of Regulars under Col. Adam Stephen in 1763 in the French and Indian War. His heir and brother, James Hickman, received his warrant for 2,000 acres 20 January 1780 in King William County, Virginia.

Hickman, Thomas. He served as an ensign in the French and Indian War. His brother and heir, James Hickman, was issued his warrant for 2,000 acres 15 March 1774 in Fincastle County, Virginia.

Hickman, Thomas. He petitioned for 2,000 acres in West Florida for his service as an ensign in the French and Indian War 18 December 1767.

Hicks, George. He served as a sergeant from 1755 to 1761 in the French and Indian War and received his 200 acre warrant in Virginia.

Hicks, Gideon. He was a soldier in the 2nd Virginia Regiment in the French and Indian War and assigned his right to 50 acres. He proved his service in Goochland County, Virginia 29 September 1779. He also appeared as Gideon Hix.

Hicks, John. He was granted 2,000 acres in Albany County, New York for his service as a surgeon in an independent company of foot in the French and Indian War 16 April 1765.

Hicks, Joseph. He served as a noncommissioned officer in the French and Indian War and received a land warrant for 200 acres in Virginia.

Hide, Daniel. He served on the expedition to Canada in 1690. Amos Hide received his land in Bethel, Maine in 1767.

Hide, Eleazer. He served on the expedition to Canada in 1690. Noah Parker received his land in Bethel, Maine in 1767.

Hidgecock, Thomas. He served as a soldier until 1758 in the French and Indian

War and assigned his right to 50 acres. He was in Caroline County, Virginia in February 1780. He also appeared as Thomas Hidgcock.

Hierlihy, Timothy. He received his 3,000 acres of land in West Florida for his service as a major of a brigade in the French and Indian War 30 September 1766.

Hiffernon, Morris. He was granted 200 acres in Albany County, New York for his service as a noncommissioned officer in the 80th Regiment of Foot in the French and Indian War 15 June 1765.

Higgin, Joseph. He served in the Narraganset War from Barnstable, Massachusetts and received his land in Gorham, Maine in1733.

Higgins, —. He served on the expedition to Canada in 1690. Joseph Higgins received land in Dumbarton, New Hampshire in 1735.

Higgins, Eliakim. He served in the Narraganset War from Eastham, Massachusetts and received land in Gorham, Maine in 1733.

Higgins, Jedediah. He served in the Narraganset War from Eastham, Massachusetts and received land in Gorham, Maine in 1733.

Higgins, Joshua. He served on the expedition to Canada in 1690 and received land in Dumbarton, New Hampshire in 1735.

Higgins, Patrick. He was granted 50 acres in Albany County, New York for his service as a private in the 46th Regiment of Foot in the French and Indian War 8 March 1771.

Higginson, John. He served as a private in the French and Indian War and was named in New York 19 July 1771.

Higginson, Samuel. He was granted 200 acres in Albany County, New York for his service as a corporal in the 4th Battalion in the 60th Regiment of Foot in the French and Indian War 2 July 1765.

Hight, Abraham. He served as Deputy Quartermaster under Gen. Braddock in the French and Indian War and received his 2,000 acre warrant in Virginia. He also appeared as Abraham Hite.

Higinson, John. He was granted 50 acres in Albany County, New York for his service as a soldier in the 42nd Regiment of Foot in the French and Indian War 7 October 1771.

Hiland, John. He served as a soldier for four years in the Old Virginia Regiment from 1756 until he was discharged due to infirmities by Col. William Byrd in the French and Indian War. He was in Frederick County, Virginia 8 March 1780. He assigned his right to 50 acres. He also appeared as John Highland.

Hiland, Thomas. He received land in Richmond, New Hampshire in 1765 for the service of an unidentified veteran of the expedition to Canada in 1690.

Hildreth, Ephraim. He served under Capt. William Tyng in 1703 and sought land in Massachusetts 13 December 1734.

Hill, Ebenezer. He served in the Narraganset War from Bridgewater, Massachusetts. His son, Ebenezer Hill, claimed his land in Greenwich, Massachusetts in 1737.

Hill, James. He served as a subaltern in the French and Indian War and assigned his right to 2,000 acres in Virginia.

Hill, James. He served as a noncommissioned officer in the French and Indian War in Virginia and received 200 acres.

Hill, John. He served as a sergeant in the French and Indian War and assigned his warrant for 200 acres in Virginia.

Hill, Joseph. He served in the wars against the Indian under Sir Edmund Andros's government. He received 200 acres in Massachusetts 13 December 1727.

Hill, Robert. He was granted 250 acres on the south side of the Wateree River in South Carolina on the King's bounty 21 June 1765. He served as a sergeant in the French and Indian War.

Hill, Roger. He served as a corporal in the expedition to Canada in 1690. Zebulon Hill petitioned for his land in Raymond, Maine in 1735.

Hill, Samuel. He served in the Narraganset War from Massachusetts in 1685. His land was located in Buxton, Maine.

Hill, Thomas. He served in the French and Indian War and assigned his right to 50 acres of land in Virginia.

Hillard, Henry. He served as a soldier in the French and Indian War and received 50 acres in Nova Scotia 9 October 1776.

Hilliard, David. He served on the expedition to Canada in 1690. Joseph Hilliard was admitted to his land in Lyndeboro, Maine in 1736.

Hilliard, Edward. He served on the expedition to Canada in 1690. Joseph Hilliard was admitted to his land in Lyndeboro, Maine in 1736.

Hilliard, Job. He served as a soldier in the French and Indian War. He assigned his 50 acre warrant in Virginia. He also appeared as Job Hilliar.

Hilliard, Joseph. He served on the expedition to Canada in 1690. Joseph Hilliard was admitted to his land in Lyndeboro, Maine in 1736.

Hilling, James. He served as a soldier in Capt. Thomas Booth's Company of the 2nd Virginia Regiment under Col. William Byrd in the French and Indian War. He assigned his warrant of 50 acres at Williamsburg, Virginia 1 February 1780.

Hills, John. He was granted 50 acres in Connecticut for his service in the Pequot War 11 May 1671.

Hills, Dr. Joseph. He served on the expedition to Canada in 1690 and received land in Poland, Maine in 1739.

Hilton, Lancelot. He was granted 2,000 acres in Albany County, New York for his service as a lieutenant in the 34th Regiment of Foot in the French and Indian War 23 August 1764.

Hilton, Samuel. He served in Lovewell's War in Massachusetts and received his land in Petersham, Massachusetts.

Hincher, Samuel. He served in the Narraganset War and received land in Templeton, Massachusetts in 1733. He also appeared as Samuel Henshaw.

Hinchman, Thomas. He served as captain and garrisoned soldiers in his home at Chelmsford, Massachusetts between 1675 and 1678. He was awarded land there in payment for £83.10.8 on 6 October 1678.

Hincke, Samuel. He commanded Fort Mary at Winter Harbor for about five years. He sought 200 acres in Massachusetts but was rejected 5 December 1727.

Hind, Edmund. He served as a corporal in a company of rangers in the French and Indian War. His son and heir, Edmund Hind, received his 200 acre warrant in Virginia. His service was proved in Augusta County, Virginia 21 March 1780. He also appeared as Edmund Hinds.

Hinds, William. He served in the Narraganset War from Marblehead, Massachusetts and claimed his land in Amherst, New Hampshire in 1734.

Hindson, William. He was granted 2,000 acres in West Florida for his service as a master's mate at the reduction of Louisbourg in the French and Indian War 2 February 1776.

Hinkley, Jacob. He served in the Narraganset War from Barnstable, Massachusetts and received land in Gorham, Maine in 1730.

Hinkley, Samuel. He served in the Narraganset War from Barnstable, Massachusetts and received land in Gorham, Maine in 1733.

Hinkston, John. He served as a lieutenant in Lord Dunmore's War in 1774. He proved his service in Yohogania County, Virginia 28 March 1780.

Hinnaman, Andrew. He was granted 50 acres in Albany County, New York for his service as a soldier in the 77th Regiment of Foot in the French and Indian War 30 October 1766.

Hinsdale, Mahuman. He was from Deerfield, Massachusetts. For his service in the Indian war he was awarded 300 acres by Massachusetts 4 December 1735. He had been carried captive to Canada.

Hinshua, Daniel. He served in the expedition to Canada in 1690. His cousin, Samuel Hinshua of Milton, Massachusetts received his land in

Ashburnham, Massachusetts in 1736.

Hissernon, Morris. He served as a corporal in the 80th Regiment in the French and Indian War. His survey for 200 acres in Albany County, New York was returned 1 June 1765.

Hinton, Richard. He served as a private in the 44th Regiment in the French and Indian War and had a return of a survey for his 50 acres in Albany County, New York 29 October 1765.

Hitchcock, Thomas. He served as a soldier until 1763 in the French and Indian War under Col. William Byrd. He petitioned for his 50 acres in February 1780 in Essex County, Virginia. He assigned his right to Taylor Noell.

Hitchcock, William. He was granted 50 acres in Albany County, New York for his service as a soldier in the 60th Regiment of Foot in the French and Indian War 5 April 1771.

Hite, Abraham. He served as Deputy Quartermaster in the French and Indian War and received 2,000 acres of land in Virginia.

Hix, Samuel. He served on the expedition to Canada in 1690. His sister's husband, Timothy Mossman of Sudbury, claimed his land in Ashburnham, Massachusetts in 1736.

Hobart, Isaac. He served in the Narraganset War from Scituate, Massachusetts. He received land in Bedford, New Hampshire in 1733.

Hobbs, John. He was killed at Bloody Brook 18 September 1675 in the Narraganset War. His nephew and sole heir, Col. Richard Kent, received 300 acres of land, for his own service and that of his late uncle 17 December 1735.

Hobbs, Josiah. He served in the Narraganset War and received land in Templeton, Massachusetts in 1733.

Hobson, John. He served in Narraganset War from Massachusetts in 1685. His son, John Hobson, received his land in Buxton, Maine.

Hobson, Thomas. He was granted 2,000 acres in Tryon County, New York for his service as a lieutenant in the 60th Royal American Regiment in the French and Indian War 5 April 1774.

Hocombe, John. He was granted 1,353 acres in West Florida for his service as a master's mate in the navy in the French and Indian War 29 May 1775.

Hodge, John. He was granted 50 acres in Albany County, New York for his service as a soldier in the 18th Regiment of Foot in the French and Indian War 1 April 1772.

Hodge, Joseph. He served as a soldier in the French and Indian War from Virginia and received 50 acres of land.

Hodges, John. He served as a sergeant under Col. William Byrd in the French and Indian War. His 200 acre warrant was issued to his heiresses, Sarah Hodges and Martha Hodges, in Virginia. Martha Hodges was his relict.

Hodgkins, Ebenezer. He served as a sergeant in the French and Indian War and petitioned for his land in New York in November 1766.

Hodgman, Thomas. He served in the Narraganset War from Reading, Massachusetts. His heirs received his land in Westminster, Massachusetts in 1733.

Hoeg, Benjamin. He served on the expedition to Canada in 1690 and received land in Poland, Maine in 1739.

Hoffman, Valentine. He was granted 50 acres in Albany County, New York for his service as a soldier in the 60th or Royal American Regiment of Foot in the French and Indian War 28 March 1771.

Hogan, William. He served as a major in the French and Indian War and petitioned for land 30 December 1766 in New York.

Hogan, William. He served in the French and Indian War and received his land in Botetourt County, Virginia 15 December 1772.

Hogg, Francis. He served as noncommissioned officer in the French and Indian War and received 200 acres in Nova Scotia 9 October 1776.

Hogg, Peter. He served as an officer in the French and Indian War and was entitled to 3,000 acres. He desired to locate 1,000 acres in Augusta County, Virginia 28 March 1774.

Holbrook, —. He served on the expedition to Canada in 1690. John Holbrook received land in Dumbarton, New Hampshire in 1735.

Holbrook, John. He served on the expedition to Canada in 1690. Ezra Holbrook received land in Bethel, Maine in 1767.

Holbrook, Thomas. He served in the Narraganset War from Braintree, Massachusetts. He received land in Bedford, New Hampshire in 1733.

Holdship, William. He served as a corporal in the 1st Battalion of the 60th Regiment in the French and Indian War. His service was certified 22 April 1765.

Holland, George. He was granted 50 acres in Albany County, New York for his service as a noncommissioned officer in the 46th Regiment of Foot in the French and Indian War 8 March 1771.

Holland, John. He was granted 50 acres in Albany County, New York for his service as a private in the 60th or Royal American Regiment of Foot in the French and Indian War 8 June 1771.

Holland, John. He served on board H.M.S. *Woolwich* and *Bristol* and petitioned for 2,000 acres of land in New York 8 May 1772.

Holland, Joseph. He served on the expedition to Canada in 1690 and received land in Poland, Maine in 1739.

Holland, Matthew. He was granted 50 acres in Albany County, New York for his service as a soldier in the 55th Regiment of Foot in the French and Indian War 18 April 1769.

Holland, Michael. He served as a corporal under Capt. James Gunn in the French and Indian War and died without issue. His heir was his brother, John Holland, who was due his 200 acres in Virginia. He proved his right in Louisa County, Virginia 11 February 1779.

Holland, Stephen. He served as a lieutenant in the French and Indian War and received 2,000 acres in New York 4 July 1764.

Holley, William. He served as a soldier in Capt. Gist's Company of Light Infantry in the French and Indian War. He received his warrant for 50 acres in March 1780 in Botetourt County, Virginia.

Holliard, William. He served as a soldier in the 2nd Virginia Regiment of Regulars under Col. William Byrd in 1758 in the French and Indian War. He petitioned for his 50 acres 16 February 1780 in King and Queen County, Virginia.

Hollice, Edward. He served in the Narraganset War from Salem, Massachusetts. His heirs claimed his land in Amherst, New Hampshire in 1734.

Hollingsworth, Joshua. He served on the expedition to Canada in 1690. Philip English was admitted to his land in Lyndeboro, Maine in 1736.

Hollis, John. He served in the Narraganset War from Weymouth, Massachusetts. His son, Samuel Hollis, received land in Bedford, New Hampshire in 1733.

Holloway, John. He was granted 50 acres in Connecticut for his service in the Pequot War 11 May 1671. He also appeared as John Hallaway.

Holloway, John. He served as sergeant for nearly two years in Massachusetts. His father, William Holloway, administered his estate and received his 150 acres of land 7 May 1662.

Holloway, Malachi. He served in the Narraganset War from Taunton, Massachusetts. He claimed his land in Greenwich, Massachusetts in 1737.

Holloway, Nathan. He served as a soldier until 1762 in the French and Indian War. He petitioned for his 50 acres in March 1780 in Caroline County, Virginia.

Holloway, William. He served as a soldier under Capt. James Walker in the regiment under Col. William Byrd in the French and Indian War. He was in Mecklenburg County 13 March 1780. He assigned his right to 50 acres in Virginia.

Holly, Joseph. He served in the Narraganset War and received land in Templeton, Massachusetts in 1733.

Holmes, Isaac. He served in the Narraganset War from Rochester, Massachusetts. His son, Ebenezer Holmes, claimed his land in Greenwich, Massachusetts in 1737.

Holmes, John. He was granted 200 acres in Charlotte County, New York for his service as a corporal in the 1st or Royal Regiment of Foot in the French and Indian War 30 March 1775.

Holmes, Joseph. He was granted 50 acres in Granville County, South Carolina on the King's bounty for his service in the French and Indian War 25 September 1766.

Holmes, Joshua. He served in the Narraganset War from Connecticut. His heirs received land in Voluntown, Connecticut in 1701.

Holmes, Nathaniel. He received land in Richmond, New Hampshire in 1765 for the service of an unidentified veteran of the expedition to Canada in 1690.

Holmes, Robert. He served in the Narraganset War from Connecticut and received land in Voluntown, Connecticut in 1701.

Holt, Edward. He served as a corporal in the 80th Regiment in the French and Indian War and had his service certified in New York 28 January 1767.

Holt, Nathaniel. He served in the Narraganset War from Connecticut and received land in Voluntown, Connecticut in 1701.

Holton, Joseph. He served in the Narraganset War from Salem, Massachusetts. He claimed his land in Amherst, New Hampshire in 1734.

Honeyman, Thomas. He was granted 50 acres in Albany County, New York for his service as a private in the 55th Regiment of Foot in the French and Indian War 8 March 1771.

Hoobs, Samuel. He was granted 200 acres in Albany County, New York for his service as a sergeant in the 2nd Battalion in the 60th Regiment of Foot in the French and Indian War 17 September 1765.

Hooker, Matthew. He served on the expedition to Canada in 1690. His widow, Mary Hooker of Ipswich, Massachusetts, claimed his land in Winchendon, Massachusetts in 1736.

Hooper, Aaron. He served as a drum major in the 60th Regiment in the French and Indian War and returned the survey for 200 acres in Albany County, New York 14 August 1766.

Hooper, John. He was granted 50 acres in Albany County, New York for his service as a soldier in the 60th Regiment of Foot in the French and Indian War 27 September 1769.

Hooper, John. He served as a soldier under Col. George Washington and as a noncommissioned officer in the French and Indian War. He assigned his 50 acre warrant in Virginia. He proved his service in Frederick County, Virginia 4 April 1780.

Hopkins, John. He was granted 50 acres in Albany County, New York for his service as a soldier in the 80th Regiment of Foot in the French and Indian War 28 October 1765.

Hopkins, Joseph, Jr. He served as a sergeant in Capt. James Gunn's Company of Regulars in 1759 in the French and Indian War. He received his warrant for 200 acres 13 March 1780 in Louisa County, Virginia.

Hopkins, Thomas. He was granted 200 acres in Berkeley County, South Carolina on the King's bounty for his service in the French and Indian War 24 August 1770.

Hopkins, William. He served in the Narraganset War from Taunton, Massachusetts. He claimed his land in Greenwich, Massachusetts in 1737.

Hopson, Thomas. He served as a lieutenant in the French and Indian War and petitioned for his land in New York 28 January 1767.

Horn, John. He served as a noncommissioned officer under Col. Mercer in 1758 in the French and Indian War. His legal representative, John Airs, petitioned for his 200 acres 21 February 1780 in Culpeper County, Virginia. Benjamin Johnston acted in behalf of John Airs.

Horn, Peter. He was granted 200 acres in South Carolina on the King's bounty for his service in the French and Indian War 14 September 1773.

Horsefall, Christopher. He served as a lieutenant in the 80th Regiment in the French and Indian War and petitioned for 2,000 acres in Albany County, New York 27 May 1766.

Horsey, Joseph. He commanded H.M.S. schooner *Huron* on Lake Erie in the French and Indian War. His widow, Hannah Horsey, petitioned for a grant of 2,000 acres and 1,000 for each of her children in New York 12 January 1766.

Horton, Enoch. He was granted 200 acres in West Florida for his service as a noncommissioned officer in the French and Indian War 4 May 1775.

Hough, John. He served in the Narraganset War from Connecticut and received land in Voluntown, Connecticut in 1701.

Hough, Samuel. He was a veteran of the Pequot War. The town of Wallingford, Connecticut granted him land for his service which he devised in his will in 1714.

Hough, Samuel. He served in the Narraganset War from Connecticut and

received land in Voluntown, Connecticut in 1701.

Hough, Timothy. He was granted 50 acres in Albany County, New York for his service as a private in a regiment of foot in the French and Indian War 19 May 1770.

Hough, William. He served in the Narraganset War from Connecticut and received land in Voluntown, Connecticut in 1701.

Houghton, Henry. He served in Lovewell's War in Massachusetts and received his land in Petersham, Massachusetts in 1733.

Houghton, Jacob. He served in the Narraganset War and received land in Templeton, Massachusetts in 1733.

Houghton, James. He served in the Narraganset War. Ebenezer Fisk received his land in Templeton, Massachusetts in 1733.

Houghton, Jonas. He served as a captain in Lovewell's War in Massachusetts and received his land in Petersham, Massachusetts in 1733.

Houghton, Jonas. He served in the Narraganset War and received land in Templeton, Massachusetts in 1733.

Houghton, Jonathan. He served from Massachusetts in the campaign against the Indians in 1725. He was from Lancaster, Massachusetts and received his land in Pembroke, New Hampshire.

Houghton, Stephen. He served in Lovewell's War in Massachusetts and received his land in Petersham, Massachusetts in 1733.

Houghton, William. He was granted 2,000 acres in Albany County, New York for his service as a lieutenant in the Royal Regiment of Artillery in the French and Indian War 3 July 1770.

Houlden, John. He shared in the grant of East Greenwich, Rhode Island made to those who had rendered service in King Philip's War. The grant was made 31 October 1677.

Houseker, Nicholas. He was granted 551 and 609 acres in Berks County, Pennsylvania for his service as a captain in the French and Indian War 3 February 1769.

Houston, John. He served in the French and Indian War and took his land in Fincastle County, Virginia 15 December 1772.

Hovey, Thomas. He served in the Narraganset War from Hadley, Massachusetts. He claimed his land in Greenwich, Massachusetts in 1737.

Hovey, Thomas. He served on the expedition to Canada in 1690 and was of Ipswich, Massachusetts when he claimed his land in Winchedon, Massachusetts in 1736.

How, Nehemiah. He served in the expedition to Port Royal under Gen. Nicholson and was awarded land in Massachusetts 3 December 1735.

How, Samuel. He served in the Narraganset War. His heir, George Farrar, received his land in Templeton, Massachusetts in 1733.

Howard, Eustace. He served as a soldier in the 2nd Virginia Regiment under Col. William Byrd in 1758 in the French and Indian War. Tobias Allen proved his eligibility for 50 acres 28 February 1780 in Middlesex County, Virginia.

Howard, James. He received land in Richmond, New Hampshire in 1765 for the service of an unidentified veteran of the expedition to Canada in 1690.

Howard, John. He served in the Narraganset War from Bridgewater, Massachusetts. His son, Edward Howard, claimed his land in Greenwich, Massachusetts in 1737.

Howard, John. He was granted 50 acres in Albany County, New York for his service as a soldier in the 80th Regiment of Foot in the French and Indian War 26 July 1765.

Howard, John. He was granted 50 acres in Albany County, New York for his service as a soldier in the 4th Regiment of Foot in the French and Indian War 27 September 1769.

Howel, James. He served as a captain in the French and Indian War and petitioned for land 30 December 1766 in New York.

Howell, Charles. He served as a soldier in two campaigns under Col. William Byrd in the French and Indian War and assigned his warrant for 50 acres in Virginia. He was from Prince Edward County.

Howell, Crismus. He was granted 50 acres in Albany County, New York for his service as a soldier in the 60th Regiment of Foot in the French and Indian War 28 June 1770.

Howell, Nicholas. He was granted 50 acres in Albany County, New York for his service as a soldier in the 80th Regiment of Foot in the French and Indian War 26 July 1765.

Howland, John. He served in the Narraganset War from Barnstable, Massachusetts and received land in Gorham, Maine in 1733.

Howlet, Martin. He served as a noncommissioned officer in the French and Indian War and assigned his 200 acre land warrant in Virginia.

Hubbard, Daniel. He served as a soldier in the French and Indian War under Col. William Byrd and assigned his 50 acre land warrant in Virginia.

Hubbert, John. He served as a corporal in the 80th Regiment in the French and Indian War and had his service certified in New York 28 January 1767.

Huber, Jacob. He was granted 200 acres in Albany County, New York for his service as a drummer in the 60th Regiment of Foot in the French and

Indian War 13 October 1767.

Huchins, John. He served in the Narraganset War from Topsfield, Massachusetts. His heirs claimed his land in Amherst, New Hampshire in 1734.

Huckstup, James. He was a soldier in the 2nd Virginia Regiment in the French and Indian War and applied for his warrant in Goochland County, Virginia 29 September 1779. He assigned his land warrant for 50 acres. He also appeared as James Huckstep.

Huddleston, William Orcher. He was granted 2,000 acres in Gloucester County, New York for his service as a captain in the Royal Regiment of Artillery in the French and Indian War 3 February 1775.

Hudgins, Drury. He served as a soldier for six months in Capt. Charles Scott's Company in the Regiment under Col. William Byrd in the French and Indian War. He received his 50 acre warrant 27 March 1780 in Cumberland County, Virginia.

Hudson, Christopher. He served as a captain in the French and Indian War and received two warrants for 2,500 acres in September 1779 in Goochland County, Virginia.

Hudson, Daniel. He served in the Narraganset War from Bridgewater, Massachusetts. He claimed his land in Greenwich, Massachusetts in 1737.

Hudson, David. He served as a soldier in the 2nd Virginia Regiment in the French and Indian War and received his 50 acre warrant in Virginia.

Hudson, Eleazer. He served on the expedition to Canada in 1690 and received land in Poland, Maine in 1739.

Hudson, James. He served in the Narraganset War from Woodstock, Connecticut. His daughter, Sarah Mercy, claimed his land in Greenwich, Massachusetts in 1737.

Hudson, John. He served three enlistments in one of the Virginia Regiments in the French and Indian War. His brother and heir, William Hudson, had his service proved in Essex County, Virginia 21 February 1780.

Hudson, Joseph. He was granted 200 acres in Albany County, New York for his service as a corporal in the 60th or Royal American Regiment in the French and Indian War 8 June 1771.

Huff, John. He served as a noncommissioned officer in the French and Indian War and assigned his 200 acre warrant in Virginia.

Huff, Peter. He was a soldier in Capt. John McNeil's Company in the Virginia Regiment under Gen. Braddock in 1755 in the French and Indian War and assigned his right to 50 acres. He proved his right in Hampshire County, Virginia 10 August 1779.

Hugart, Thomas. He served as adjutant in the French and Indian War and assigned his 2,000 acre warrant in Virginia.

Hugart, William. He served as a lieutenant in the French and Indian War. His heir at law, Thomas Hugart, received his warrant for 2,000 acres in Virginia.

Huggins, Thomas. He served in the Narraganset War from Barnstable, Massachusetts and received land in Gorham, Maine in 1733. He also appeared as Thomas Huckins.

Hughes, Anthony. He served as a soldier in Capt. Charles Scott's Company under Col. William Byrd in 1760 in the French and Indian War. He received his warrant 3 February 1780 in Fluvanna County, Virginia. He assigned his right to 50 acres.

Hughes, Charles. He served as a noncommissioned officer in the French and Indian War and petitioned for his land 7 January 1767 in Albany County, New York.

Hughes, James. He was granted 1,550 acres in West Florida for his service as a lieutenant in the French and Indian War 25 September 1777 and 26 April 1779.

Hughes, John. He served in the French and Indian War and assigned his right to land in New York 22 January 1767.

Hughes, John. He served as a soldier in the French and Indian War and received 50 acres in Virginia.

Hughes, John. He served as an ensign in the 2nd Virginia Regiment in the French and Indian War and assigned his right to 2,000 acres. He was from Goochland County, Virginia 24 September 1779.

Hughes, John. He served as a soldier in Capt. Obediah Woodson's Company in 1755 in the French and Indian War. His heir, William Hughes, received his warrant for 50 acres in Virginia.

Hughes, Robert. He served as a soldier in the Virginia Regiment in the French and Indian War and desired to locate his 50 acres in Fincastle County, Virginia.

Hughes, Sylvester. He served as a soldier in Capt. Robert Stewart's Company under Col. William Byrd in the 2nd Virginia Regiment in the French and Indian War. He assigned his warrant for 50 acres.

Hughes, Thomas. He served as a noncommissioned officer in the French and Indian War from Virginia and received a warrant for 200 acres.

Hughes, William. He served as a lieutenant in the 1st Virginia Regiment in the French and Indian War and was awarded 2,000 acres. He proved his service in York County, Virginia 17 January 1780.

Hughes, William. He served as a major in the rangers in various regiments and in the Virginia Regiment in the French and Indian War. He received a warrant for 2,000 acres. He had previously received 3,000 acres of land as a captain.

Hughes, William. He was appointed Adjutant of Col. Adam Stephen's Regiment by Gov. Francis Fauquier in Virginia 8 June 1762 and also lieutenant in the same 22 May 1762 during the French and Indian War. He had also served as adjutant in the 1st Regiment of Regulars under Col. George Washington 1759-1761 and as a subaltern officer and adjutant in the same unit 1756-1758. He assigned his warrants for 6,000 acres.

Hughes, William. He served as a sergeant in Capt. William Phillips's Company of Volunteer Rangers in 1763. Upon the death of one of the lieutenants, he did duty as an ensign until he was discharged. He had received the warrant for his service as a sergeant. He received a warrant for 2,000 acres 13 March 1780 Louisa County, Virginia.

Hughs, Charles. He was granted 50 acres in Albany County, New York for his service as a private in the 46th Regiment of Foot in the French and Indian War 25 May 1771.

Hughs, Edward. He was granted 50 acres in Albany County, New York for his service as a soldier in the 60th Regiment of Foot in the French and Indian War 26 September 1765.

Hughs, Peter. He was granted 200 acres in Albany County, New York for his service as a corporal in the 4th Battalion in the Royal American or 60th Regiment of Foot in the French and Indian War 27 September 1769.

Hughson, John. He served as a corporal in the 2nd Virginia Regiment in the French and Indian War. He proved his service in Goochland County, Virginia 6 September 1779. He disposed of his warrant in Virginia.

Hulbert, Charles. He served in the French and Indian War. His service was certified in New York in November 1766.

Hulbert, Richard. He served as a soldier in the French and Indian War from Virginia and received 50 acres of land.

Hulet, Sutherland. He was granted 200 acres in Albany County, New York for his service as a sergeant in the 80th Regiment of Foot in the French and Indian War 12 July 1766.

Hull, John. He served in the Narraganset War from Connecticut and received land in Voluntown, Connecticut in 1701.

Hull, John. He served in the Narraganset War from Rehoboth, Massachusetts. His son, Edward Hull, claimed his land in Greenwich, Massachusetts in 1737.

Hull, Joseph. He served in the Narraganset War from Connecticut. His heirs

received land in Voluntown, Connecticut in 1701.

Hull, William. He served as a sergeant in the French and Indian War and received his 200 acre warrant in Virginia.

Hulman, James. He served in a company of Rangers under Capt. William Preston from Virginia in the French and Indian War. His service was proved 5 April 1780 in Montgomery County, Virginia but no warrant was apparently issued.

Hulsey, John. He served as a private in the 60th Regiment in the French and Indian War and was granted his land in New York 16 April 1767.

Human, John. He was granted 50 acres in Albany County, New York for his service as a soldier in the 55th Regiment of Foot in the French and Indian War 28 March 1771.

Humble, Jacob. He served as a soldier in the French and Indian War and had his service certified in Montgomery County, Virginia 8 March 1780 for his 50 acres of land.

Humphrey, Ebenezer. He served on the expedition to Canada in 1690. Ebenezer Humphrey received land in Chesterfield, Massachusetts in 1739.

Humphrey, Elihu. He was granted 2,000 acres in West Florida for his service as a subaltern in the French and Indian War 14 November 1777.

Humphrey, Hopestill. He served in the Narraganset War from Dorchester, Massachusetts. He received his land in Bedford, New Hampshire in 1733.

Humphrey, Nathaniel. He was granted 2,000 acres in West Florida for his service as a subaltern in the French and Indian War 17 January 1778.

Humphrey, Thomas. He was granted 50 acres in Albany County, New York for his service as a soldier in the 48th Regiment of Foot in the French and Indian War 15 August 1766.

Humphreys, James. He served as a soldier in the French and Indian War and had his service certified in Montgomery County, Virginia for his 50 acres of land 8 March 1780.

Humphries, John. He was granted 50 acres in Craven County, South Carolina on the King's bounty for his service in the French and Indian War 25 September 1766.

Humphries, Uriah. He served as a soldier in Capt. John Posey's Company of Regulars in the French and Indian War and received a warrant for 50 acres in March 1780 in Botetourt County, Virginia.

Hunebuss, Henry. He served as a soldier for six months in Capt. Henry Woodward's Company under Col. George Washington in 1758 in the French and Indian War. He proved his service in Cumberland County,

Virginia 22 November 1779.

Hungerford, Thomas. He served in the Narraganset War from Connecticut and received land in Voluntown, Connecticut in 1701.

Hunsiker, Daniel. He served as a lieutenant in Col. French's Pennsylvania Regiment until disbanded in the French and Indian War. He proved his service 7 March 1780 in Frederick County, Virginia.

Hunt, Ephraim. He served on the expedition to Canada in 1690. His heir, Ebenezer Hunt, sought land in Massachusetts 10 December 1735.

Hunt, Jeremiah. He was from Massachusetts and served in the campaign against the Indians in 1725. He was from Billerica, Massachusetts and received his land in Pembroke, New Hampshire.

Hunt, Joel. He served on the expedition to Canada in 1690. Robert Swan was admitted to his land in Lyndeboro, Maine in 1736.

Hunt, John. He applied for his land in Massachusetts 3 December 1735.

Hunt, Joseph. He was granted 200 acres in Albany County, New York for his service as a corporal in the 77th Regiment of Foot in the French and Indian War 15 August 1765.

Hunt, Samuel. He served in 1676 and was granted land by Massachusetts 22 November 1734.

Hunt, Samuel. He served in the Narraganset War from Billerica, Massachusetts. He received his land in Templeton, Massachusetts in 1733.

Hunt, Samuel. He received land in Richmond, New Hampshire in 1765 for the service of an unidentified veteran of the expedition to Canada in 1690.

Hunt, Thomas. He served in the Narraganset War from Boston, Massachusetts. He received land in Bedford, New Hampshire in 1733.

Hunt, Thomas. He served in the Narraganset War from Duxbury, Massachusetts. His nephew, Thomas Hunt, received his land in Gorham, Maine in 1733.

Hunt, Thomas. He was granted 200 acres in Albany County, New York for his service as a corporal in the 27th Regiment of Foot in the French and Indian War 29 October 1765.

Hunter, John. He was granted 200 acres in Ulster County, New York for his service as a corporal in the 45th Regiment of Foot in the French and Indian War 4 August 1774.

Hunter, Samuel. He was granted 609 and 544 acres in Berks County, Pennsylvania for his service as a captain in the French and Indian War 3 February 1769.

Huntly, Aaron. He served in the Narraganset War from Connecticut and received land in Voluntown, Connecticut in 1701.

Huntly, Moses. He served in the Narraganset War from Connecticut and received land in Voluntown, Connecticut in 1701.
Hunton, Richard. He was granted 50 acres in Albany County, New York for his service as a soldier in the 44th Regiment of Foot in the French and Indian War 29 October 1765.
Huntzicker, Daniel. He was granted 292 and 334 acres in Berks County, Pennsylvania for his service as a lieutenant in the French and Indian War 3 February 1769. He assigned his warrant for 2,000 acres in Virginia. He also appeared as Daniel Hunseker.
Hurlbut, Thomas. He was granted 120 acres in Connecticut for his service in the Pequot War 11 May 1671. He also appeared as Thomas Hollybut. His grandson, John Hurlbut, of Middletown requested that the grant be laid out 14 May 1713.
Hurst, George. He served in the French and Indian War and took his land in Fincastle County, Virginia 15 December 1772.
Hurt, Joseph. He served as a soldier under Col. Adam Stephen in 1762 in the French and Indian War and assigned his 50 acre warrant in Virginia. His service was proved in Halifax County, Virginia 18 May 1780.
Huse, Thomas. He served on the expedition to Canada in 1690 and received land in Poland, Maine in 1739.
Huse, William. He served on the expedition to Canada in 1690 and received land in Poland, Maine in 1739.
Hussey, John. He served in the French and Indian War and petitioned for his land in New York 17 March 1767.
Huston, James. He served as an armourer in the Virginia Regiment under Col. William Byrd in the French and Indian War and received a warrant for 50 acres 18 November 1779 in Greenbrier County, Virginia.
Hutcherson, David. He served as a soldier in Capt. John Posey's Company in the Virginia Regiment in the French and Indian War. He was in Charlotte County, Virginia 6 March 1780. He assigned his 50 acre warrant. He also appeared as David Huckeson.
Hutcherson, Thomas. He served as a soldier in the French and Indian War in 1758 and in a different regiment in 1760. He petitioned for two warrants of 50 acres each in March 1780 in Caroline County, Virginia.
Hutcherson, William. He served as a soldier in Capt. William Preston's Company of Rangers in 1759 in the French and Indian War and received his 50 acre warrant in April 1780 in Montgomery County, Virginia.
Hutchings, Charles. He was granted 200 acres in Albany County, New York for

his service as a corporal in the 77th Regiment of Foot in the French and Indian War 13 May 1765.

Hutchins, Joshua. He served in Lovewell's War in Massachusetts and received his land in Petersham, Massachusetts in 1733.

Hutchins, Thomas. He was granted 1,000 and 2,000 acres in West Florida for his service as a field officer and an assistant commissary in the French and Indian War 12 May 1773 and 15 July 1775. He received a third grant for service as paymaster 18 April 1776.

Hutchins, William. He served in Lovewell's War in Massachusetts and received his land in Petersham, Massachusetts in 1733.

Hutchinson, Francis. He was granted 2,000 acres in Albany County, New York for his service as a lieutenant in the 60th Regiment of Foot in the French and Indian War 23 August 1764.

Hutchinson, Francis. He was granted 2,000 acres in West Florida for his service as a lieutenant in the French and Indian War 15 December 1768.

Hutchinson, James. He was granted 200 acres in West Florida for his service as a noncommissioned officer in the navy in the French and Indian War 1 May 1777.

Hutchinson, John. He served in the French and Indian War and received 254 ½ acres in Nova Scotia 22 January 1771.

Hutchinson, Joseph. He served in the Narraganset War from Salem, Massachusetts. His son, Robert Hutchinson, claimed his land in Amherst, New Hampshire in 1734.

Hutchinson, Richard. He served as a private in the 44th Regiment in the French and Indian War. His service was certified in New York 11 November 1766.

Hutchinson, Robert. He served as a sergeant in Capt. Claiton's Company of Pennsylvania Regulars in the French and Indian War at the reduction of Fort Pitt. He was in Botetourt County, Virginia in March 1780. He assigned his warrant for 50 acres in Virginia. He also appeared as Robert Huckeson and Robert Hutcherson.

Hutchinson, Samuel. He served in the Narraganset War from Massachusetts in 1685. His land was located in Buxton, Maine.

Hutchinson, William. He served as a subaltern officer in the French and Indian War and received 2,000 acres in Nova Scotia 21 October 1783.

Hutton, Andrew. He was granted 50 acres in Charlotte County, New York for his service as a soldier in the 42nd Regiment of Foot in the French and Indian War 25 January 1773.

Hutton, Richard. He served in the Narraganset War from Wenham, Massachusetts. His daughter, Elizabeth Fowler, claimed his land in

Amherst, New Hampshire in 1734.

Hutts, Jacob. He served as a soldier under Col. William Byrd in the French and Indian War and received his warrant 8 November 1779 in James City County, Virginia.

Hyns, Francis. He was granted 200 acres in Charlotte County, New York for his service as a noncommissioned officer in the 18th Regiment of Foot in the French and Indian War 12 October 1774.

Huzzey, Jacob. He served as a private in the French and Indian War. His service was certified in New York 8 May 1765.

Huzzey, Thomas. He served as a private in the French and Indian War. His service was certified in New York 8 May 1765.

Ibbit, Moses. He was granted 50 acres in Albany County, New York for his service as a private in a regiment of foot in the French and Indian War 19 May 1770.

Ibbot, Moses. He was granted 200 acres in Albany County, New York for his service as a sergeant in the 55th Regiment of Foot in the French and Indian War 15 June 1765.

Ide, John. He served in the Narraganset War from Rehoboth, Massachusetts. His brother, Timothy Ide, claimed his land in Greenwich, Massachusetts in 1737.

Ilsley, Joseph. He served on the expedition to Canada in 1690 and received land in Poland, Maine in 1739.

Ince, Jonathan. He served in the Pequot War and received a grant of land in Soldiers' Field in Hartford, Connecticut.

Ingalls, Edmond. He served on the expedition to Canada in 1690. His nephew, Samuel Ingalls of Ipswich, Massachusetts claimed his land in Winchedon, Massachusetts in 1736.

Ingalls, Samuel. He served in the Narraganset War from Massachusetts in 1685. His grandson, Samuel Ingalls, received his land in Buxton, Maine.

Ingersoll, Samuel. He served in the Narraganset War from Gloucester, Massachusetts. He claimed his land in Amherst, New Hampshire in 1734.

Ingles, William. He served as a lieutenant in the French and Indian War first for services in 1756 and next from March to July 1763 and was entitled to 3,000 acres. He proved same in Montgomery County, Virginia 7 March 1780. He had already taken 1,000 acres in Fincastle County, Virginia 5 July 1774. He also appeared as William Inglis.

Ingarum, Joseph. He served in the Narraganset War from Connecticut and received land in Voluntown, Connecticut in 1701.

Inwood, John. He served as a sergeant in the French and Indian War and petitioned for his land in New York 17 March 1767.

Irvin, Donald. He was granted 50 acres in Albany County, New York for his service as a soldier in the 78th Regiment of Foot in the French and Indian War 13 May 1765.

Irvin, Francis. He served as a soldier in the French and Indian War until 1758 and petitioned for his 50 acres 17 February 1780 in Spotsylvania County, Virginia. He assigned the warrant.

Irwin, James. He was granted 622 and 547 acres in Berks County, Pennsylvania for his service as a captain in the French and Indian War 3 February 1769.

Irwin, Richard. He served as a corporal in the 26th Regiment in the French and Indian War and petitioned for his land in New York 17 March 1767.

Irwin, Richard. He received his land in West Florida for his service in the French and Indian War 19 March 1777.

Irwin, William. He served as a lieutenant in the French and Indian War in New York and petitioned for his land 28 January 1767. He also appeared as William Irvin.

Isbell, Benjamin. He served as a soldier in the Virginia Regiment in the French and Indian War under Col. William Peachey in 1759. He received a warrant for 50 acres 18 November 1779 in King William County, Virginia.

Isles, Thomas. He was granted 150 acres in Craven County, South Carolina on the King's bounty for his service in the French and Indian War 21 June 1765. He also appeared as Thomas Iles.

Izzard, Richard. He was granted 50 acres in Albany County, New York for his service as a soldier in the 46th Regiment of Foot in the French and Indian War 30 October 1765.

Jacks, James. He was granted 50 acres in Albany County, New York for his service as a soldier in the 55th Regiment of Foot in the French and Indian War 18 April 1769.

Jackson, Caleb. He served in the Narraganset War from Massachusetts in 1685. His son, Joshua Jackson, received his land in Buxton, Maine.

Jackson, Edward. He served on the expedition to Canada in 1690. Samuel Jackson received his land in Alstead, New Hampshire in 1771.

Jackson, Ebenezer. He received land in Richmond, New Hampshire in 1765 for for the service of an unidentified veteran of the expedition to Canada in 1690.

Jackson, George. He served on the expedition to Canada in 1690. Bartholomew Jackson was admitted to his land in Lyndeboro, Maine in 1736.

Jackson, Hugh. He was granted 50 acres in Albany County, New York for his service as a soldier in the 44th Regiment of Foot in the French and Indian War 24 May 1771.

Jackson, Isaac. He served on the expedition to Canada in 1690. Isaac Jackson received his land in Alstead, New Hampshire in 1771.

Jackson, John. He served in the Narraganset War from Massachusetts in 1685. His land was located in Buxton, Maine.

Jackson, Laurence. He served as a soldier in the French and Indian War from Virginia and received a warrant for 50 acres of land.

Jackson, Samuel. He served in the expedition to Canada in 1690 and served as a captain. Samuel Jackson received his land in Alstead, New Hampshire in 1771.

Jackson, Seborn. He served in the Narraganset War from Newton, Massachusetts. His son, Edward Jackson, received his land in Westminster, Massachusetts in 1733.

Jackson, Thomas. He was granted 200 acres in Albany County, New York for his service as a corporal in the 28th Regiment of Foot in the French and Indian War 8 June 1771.

Jackson, William. He served as a soldier in Capt. William Preston's Company of Rangers in 1758 in the French and Indian War. He was issued a warrant for 50 acres 15 February 1780 in Augusta County, Virginia.

Jacob, Peter. He served on the expedition to Canada in 1690. Peter Jacob received land in Chesterfield, Massachusetts in 1739.

Jacobs, John. He served in the Narraganset War from Hingham, Massachusetts. His son, John Jacobs, received his land in Bedford, New Hampshire in 1733.

Jacobs, Maximilian. He served as a captain in the French and Indian War and petitioned for 5,000 acres in New York 6 April 1775.

Jacobs, Maximilian. He served in the French and Indian War and received 5,000 acres in Nova Scotia 16 August 1769.

Jacobs, Richard. He served in the Narraganset War from Massachusetts in 1685. His land was located in Buxton, Maine.

Jacqueri, Daniel. He was granted 2,000 acres in Charlotte County, New York for his service as clerk of stores in the Royal Artillery in the French and Indian War 4 August 1774.

Jacts, John. He served in the Narraganset War from Providence. He received land in Bedford, New Hampshire in 1733.

Jagger, Jeremy. His three sons were granted 20 acres apiece in Connecticut for his service in the Pequot War 11 May 1671. He was from Stamford.

Jahn, Frederick. He served as a sergeant in the 60th Regiment in the French and

Indian War and petitioned for 200 acres of land in New York 18 April 1767.

James, —. He served on the expedition to Canada in 1690. John James received land in Dumbarton, New Hampshire in 1735.

James, Charles. He served in the French and Indian War and took his land in Fincastle County, Virginia 15 December 1772.

James, James. He served as a subaltern in the French and Indian War from Virginia and received 2,000 acres in 1773.

James, Thomas. He served as a major in the French and Indian War and petitioned for a grant of 5,000 acres in New York 23 June 1766.

Jameson, Andrew. He served as a soldier in Capt. John Dickinson's Company of Rangers in the French and Indian War in 1758. He requested his warrant of 50 acres 2 November 1779 in Kentucky County, Virginia.

Jameson, John. He served as a sergeant in the 40th Regiment in the French and Indian War. His service was certified in New York 3 July 1763.

Jameson, John. He served as a soldier under Maj. Robert Stewart in the 1st Virginia Regiment in the French and Indian War and received his 50 acre warrant 15 February 1780 in Greenbrier County, Virginia.

Jaquith, John. He served on the expedition to Canada in 1690. Nathaniel Eames received his land in Bethel, Maine in 1767.

Jarbo, John. For his service in suppressing those involved in Ingle's Insurrection in Maryland, Lord Baltimore granted him a special warrant for 400 acres in conjunction with Lt. William Evans in the Isle of Kent 28 August 1649.

Jarrett, Richard. He served as a noncommissioned officer in the French and Indian War in Virginia and assigned his warrant for 200 acres.

Jefferys, Francis. He served in the Narraganset War from Boxford, Massachusetts. James Curtice claimed his land in Amherst, New Hampshire in 1734.

Jefferys, William. He was a soldier under Col. William Byrd in the French and Indian War and received a warrant for 50 acres in Virginia 19 October 1779.

Jeffrey, Henry. He was granted 200 acres in Albany County, New York for his service as a corporal in the 60th Regiment of Foot in the French and Indian War 10 May 1765.

Jeffrey, Robert. He was granted 200 acres in Gloucester County, New York for his service as a noncommissioned officer in the Royal American Regiment in the French and Indian War 3 February 1775.

Jeffreys, Jethro. He served in the Narraganset War from Newport, Rhode Island. He received land in Bedford, New Hampshire in 1733.

Jeffries, James. He was granted 50 acres in Albany County, New York for his service as a soldier in the 77th Regiment of Foot in the French and Indian War 25 July 1765.

Jefts, John. He served under Capt. John Lovewell from Massachusetts and died in battle at Pigwacket 8 May 1725. He was from Groton, Massachusetts. His land was located in Pembroke, New Hampshire.

Jenkins, Charles. He served as a soldier in Capt. Samuel Overton's Company of Rangers in 1755 in the French and Indian War. He received his warrant in Louisa County, Virginia 14 February 1780. He assigned his right to 50 acres. He also appeared as Charles Jinkins and Charles Jenkings.

Jenkins, Edward. He was granted 2,000 acres in Albany County, New York for his service as a lieutenant in the 60th Regiment of Foot in the French and Indian War 30 May 1765.

Jenkins, John. He was granted 50 acres in Albany County, New York for his service as a soldier in the 48th Regiment of Foot in the French and Indian War 28 October 1765.

Jenkins, William. He served as a soldier in the Old Virginia Regiment in the French and Indian War. He received his 50 acre warrant 2 May 1780 in Frederick County, Virginia.

Jenner, Thomas. He served in the Narraganset War from Charlestown, Massachusetts. His heirs received his land in Westminster, Massachusetts in 1733. He also appeared as Thomas Genner.

Jennick, Michael. He was granted 50 acres in Albany County, New York for his service as a soldier in the 60th Regiment of Foot in the French and Indian War 26 September 1765.

Jennings, Jonathan. He served in the Narraganset War from Connecticut and received land in Voluntown, Connecticut in 1701. He also appeared as Jonathan Gennings.

Jennings, Nicholas. He served in the Pequot War and received a grant of land in Soldiers' Field in Hartford, Connecticut. He also appeared as Nicholas Gennings.

Jennings, Richard. He served in the Narraganset War from Bridgewater, Massachusetts. He claimed his land in Greenwich, Massachusetts in 1737.

Jervis, John. He served as a soldier in the Virginia Regiment in the French and Indian War under Col. George Washington and assigned his right to 50 acres. He also appeared as John Jarvice and John Javis.

Jewett, Benjamin. He was a veteran of the expedition to Canada in 1690. His brother, Jonathan Jewett, Jr. of Rowley, Massachusetts, claimed his land in Winchendon, Massachusetts in 1736.

Jewett, Joseph. He served in the Narraganset War from Massachusetts in 1685. His son, Jonathan Jewett, received his land in Buxton, Maine.

Joans, John. He was a veteran of the expedition to Canada in 1690. His nephew, David Joans of Wrentham, Massachusetts, received his land in Ashburnham, Massachusetts in 1736.

Jewett, Jonathan. He received his land in Massachusetts 10 December 1735.

John, Frederick. He was granted 200 acres in Albany County, New York for his service as a sergeant in the 3rd Battalion in the 60th Regiment of Foot in the French and Indian War 28 June 1770.

Johnson, —. He served in the Narraganset War from Lynn, Massachusetts. Jonathan Johnson claimed his land in Amherst, New Hampshire in 1734.

Johnson, Archibald. He served as a soldier under Lt. Benjamin Temple in the Regular Corps in 1759 and under Capt. John Spears in 1760 against the Indians. He received his warrant for 50 acres 16 March 1780 in Halifax County, Virginia.

Johnson, Daniel. He served in the Narraganset War from Lynn, Massachusetts. He petitioned for his land 4 June 1685.

Johnson, Daniel. He served on the expedition to Canada in 1690. Daniel Johnson received land in Chesterfield, Massachusetts in 1739.

Johnson, Edward. He served in the Narraganset War from Charlestown, Massachusetts. His son, Elezer Johnson, received his land in Westminister, Massachusetts in 1733.

Johnson, Ebenezer. He served as a captain in the Narraganset War from Connecticut and received land in Voluntown, Connecticut in 1701.

Johnson, Eleazer. He served on the expedition to Canada in 1690 and received land in Poland, Maine in 1739.

Johnson, Ezekiel. He served as a soldier in Capt. John Dickerson's Company of Rangers in 1757, 1758, and 1759 in the French and Indian War. He petitioned for his 50 acres February 1780 in Botetourt County, Virginia.

Johnson, Griffing. He served as a soldier under Col. William Byrd until 1758 and again in 1760 in the French and Indian War. He petitioned for two warrants for 50 acres each 21 February 1780 in Essex County, Virginia.

Johnson, Guy. He was granted 2,000 acres in Albany County, New York for his service as a lieutenant in an independent company of foot in the French and Indian War 27 September 1765.

Johnson, Humphrey. He served on the expedition to Canada in 1690.

Humphrey Johnson received land in Chesterfield, Massachusetts in 1739.

Johnson, Ichabod. He served under Capt. John Lovewell and died in battle at Pigwacket 8 May 1725. He was from Woburn, Massachusetts. His land was located in Pembroke, New Hampshire.

Johnson, Isaac. He served as a captain in the Narraganset War from Woodstock, Connecticut. His grandson, Joseph Johnson, claimed his land in Greenwich, Massachusetts in 1737.

Johnson, Jacob. He was granted 50 acres in Albany County, New York for his service as a soldier in the 60th Regiment of Foot in the French and Indian War 7 October 1768.

Johnson, James. He served as a sergeant in Capt. John Reeter's Company in one of the Virginia Regiments in 1758 in the French and Indian War and received 200 acres 21 October 1779 in Virginia.

Johnson, James. He served as a soldier in Capt. Gabriel Throgmorton's Company in the French and Indian War and received his warrant for 50 acres in April 1780 in Botetourt County, Virginia.

Johnson, James. He served as a soldier in Capt. John Dickenson's Company until 1759 in the French and Indian War and received his 50 acre warrant in March 1780 in Greenbrier County, Virginia.

Johnson, John. He was granted 50 acres in Connecticut for his service in the Pequot War 11 May 1671.

Johnson, John. He was from Andover and was awarded 200 acres for his service in the Indian war by Massachusetts 22 March 1735/6.

Johnson, John. He was granted 50 acres in Albany County, New York for his service as a soldier in the 60th Regiment of Foot in the French and Indian War 6 July 1771.

Johnson, John. He was granted 200 acres in Albany County, New York for his service as a corporal in the 55th Regiment of Foot in the French and Indian War 1 April 1772.

Johnson, John. He served as a soldier until 1758 in the French and Indian War. He petitioned for his 50 acres in Caroline County, Virginia.

Johnson, John. He served as a soldier in Capt. Peter Hogg's Company of Rangers in 1758 in the French and Indian War. He applied for his warrant in Louisa County, Virginia 13 March 1780. He assigned his warrant for 50 acres.

Johnson, Joseph. He served on the Canada Expedition in 1690 and petitioned for land in Massachusetts.

Johnson, Josiah. He served under Capt. John Lovewell from Massachusetts and was wounded in his right arm at the battle at Pigwacket in 1725. He was from Woburn, Massachusetts and received his land in Pembroke, New Hampshire.

Johnson, Moses. He served as a sergeant in the Narraganset War from Connecticut and received land in Voluntown, Massachusetts in 1701.

Johnson, Nathaniel. He served on the expedition to Canada in 1690. Nathaniel Johnson received land in Chesterfield, Massachusetts in 1739.

Johnson, Noah. He served as a sergeant under Capt. John Lovewell from Massachusetts and was in battle at Pigwacket in May 1725. He was wounded in both hands and lost the use of them. He was from Dunstable, Massachusetts and received his land in Pembroke, New Hampshire.

Johnson, Raynald. He served in the French and Indian War in the 78th Regiment of Foot for three years; at its reduction he was drafted into the 2nd Battalion of the 60th or Royal American Regiment and completed a total of nine years of service. He petitioned for 100 acres of land in Massachusetts in January 1770.

Johnson, Richard. He served as a lieutenant until 1758 in one regiment and in 1759 in a different regiment in the French and Indian War. He petitioned for 2,000 acres in March 1780 in Caroline County, Virginia. He had already received a warrant for 2,000 acres. [Compare entry with the one for Richard Johnston.]

Johnson, Robert. He was a lieutenant in one of the Virginia Regiments in the French and Indian War and devised his right to 2,000 acres to Robert Johnson, Jr.

Johnson, Robert. He served as a surgeon in the 1st Virginia Regiment under Col. William Byrd in the French and Indian War. The warrant for 2,000 acres was issued in James City County, Virginia 8 November 1779. His executor, William Hughes, assigned his land warrant.

Johnson, Samuel. He served in the Narraganset War from Lynn, Massachusetts. He applied for his land 4 June 1685. His son, Richard Johnson, claimed his land in Amherst, New Hampshire in 1734.

Johnson, Timothy. He was granted 50 acres in Albany County, New York for his service as a private in the 18th Regiment of Foot in the French and Indian War 8 June 1771.

Johnson, William. He served in Narraganset War from Connecticut and received land in Voluntown, Connecticut in 1701.

Johnson, Rev. William. He served on the expedition to Canada in 1690 and received land in Poland, Maine in 1739.

Johnson, William. He was granted 200 acres in Albany County, New York for his service as a corporal in the 77th Regiment of Foot in the French and Indian War 13 February 1767.

Johnson, William. He served in the French and Indian War and took his land in Fincastle County, Virginia 15 December 1772.

Johnston, Wire. He served in the French and Indian War and received his land in Fincastle County, Virginia 15 December 1772.

Johnston, John. He served as a soldier and artificer in Capt. William Preston's Company of Rangers in the French and Indian War and received his 50 acres warrant in Virginia.

Johnston, Joshua. He was granted 350 acres in Craven County, South Carolina on the King's bounty for his service in the French and Indian War 21 June 1765.

Johnston, Laurence. He served as a soldier in the French and Indian War and received his 50 acre warrant in Virginia.

Johnston, Richard. He served as a lieutenant in Col. William Byrd's Regiment in the Cherokee Expedition in 1760 in the French and Indian War. He petitioned for his 2,000 acres 21 April 1780 in Spotsylvania County, Virginia.

Johnston, Richard. He served as a noncommissioned officer in the French and Indian War and received his 200 acre warrant in Virginia.

Johnston, William. He served as a soldier under Capt. William Preston in the French and Indian War and received his 50 acre warrant in Virginia.

Johnstone, George. He received his land in West Florida for his service as a captain in the navy in the French and Indian War 12 January 1778.

Johnstone, William. He was granted 1,000 acres in West Florida for his service as a captain in the Royal Regiment of Artillery in the French and Indian War 5 May 1775 and on 12 September 1775. He was also granted 2,000 acres as Fire Master in the same unit 5 May 1775.

Jones, —. He served on the expedition to Canada in 1690. Cornelius Jones received land in Dumbarton, New Hampshire in 1735.

Jones, Cornelius. He received land in Richmond, New Hampshire in 1765 for the service of an unidentified veteran of the expedition to Canada in 1690.

Jones, Edward. He served as a corporal under Col. George Washington in 1758 in the French and Indian War and died in the service. His legal representative, Lewis Jones, petitioned for his 200 acres 21 February 1780 in Culpeper County, Virginia.

Jones, Evan. He served as a soldier in the 28th Regiment in the French and Indian War and petitioned for his land 18 October 1766 in New York.

Jones, James. He served as a captain in the Narraganset War and received land in Templeton, Massachusetts in 1733.

Jones, James. He served as a soldier in an independent company of foot under Capt. John Epay and sought 50 acres in St. David's Parish, Georgia 7 January 1771.

Jones, James. He was entitled to 2,000 acres in Virginia for his service in the French and Indian War which he assigned.

Jones, John. He served on the expedition to Canada in 1690 and received his land in Bethel, Maine in 1767.

Jones, John. He served as deputy barrack master at Fort George in the French and Indian War and petitioned for 1,000 acres of land in New York 2 March 1772.

Jones, John. He was granted 50 acres in Albany County, New York for his service a private in the 46th Regiment of Foot in the French and Indian War 8 March 1771.

Jones, John. He was granted 200 acres in Charlotte County, New York for his service as a sergeant in the 44th Regiment of Foot in the French and Indian War 10 September 1774.

Jones, John. He served as a drummer in the Virginia Regiment under Col. William Byrd in the French and Indian War. He received his warrant to 200 acres in Hanover County, Virginia 3 February 1780.

Jones, John. He served as an ensign in Col. Thompson's Pennsylvania Regiment in 1757 in the French and Indian War and received his 2,000 acre warrant in Virginia. He proved his service in Frederick County, Virginia 4 July 1780.

Jones, John. He served as a soldier in the Virginia Regiment under Col. George Washington in the French and Indian War. He proved his right to 50 acres in Rockbridge County, Virginia 7 September 1779.

Jones, Josiah. He served under Capt. John Lovewell from Massachusetts and was in the battle at Pigwacket in May 1725. He was from Concord, Massachusetts and received his land in Pembroke, New Hampshire.

Jones, Matthew. He served in the Narraganset War from Connecticut and received land in Voluntown, Connecticut in 1701.

Jones, Matthew. He served in the French and Indian War and took his land in Fincastle County, Virginia 15 December 1772.

Jones, Owen. He served in the French and Indian War and received 3,000 acres in Nova Scotia 23 May 1767.

Jones, Philip. He was granted 200 acres in Albany County, New York for his service as a drummer in the 48th Regiment of Foot in the French and Indian War 28 October 1765.

Jones, Robert. He served in the French and Indian War and took his land in

Fincastle County, Virginia 15 December 1772.

Jones, Samuel. He served in the Narraganset War from Dorchester, Massachusetts. His son, Ebenezer Jones, received his land in Bedford, New Hampshire in 1733.

Jones, Samuel. He served in the Narraganset War from Yarmouth, Massachusetts and received land in Gorham, Maine in 1733.

Jones, Thomas. He had three tours of duty in the French and Indian War. He served as a soldier in Capt. Samuel Overton's Company of Rangers in 1755; as a soldier in Capt. Thomas Fleming's Company of regulars in 1758; and as a soldier in Capt. John Posey's Company of regulars in 1760. He received his warrants in Louisa County, Virginia 14 February 1780. He assigned the three warrants for 50 acres each.

Jones, William. He served in the Narraganset War from Reading, Massachusetts. Samuel Chandler received his land in Westminster, Massachusetts in 1733.

Jones, William. He served as a lieutenant in the French and Indian War and petitioned for his 2,000 acres in Albany County, New York 5 May 1766.

Jones, William. He served as a soldier in the Battalion of Regulars under Col. William Peachey in 1759 in the French and Indian War. He petitioned for his warrant for 50 acres 14 February 1780 in King and Queen County, Virginia.

Jones, William. He served as a soldier under Col. George Washington in 1758 in the French and Indian War and died in the service. His legal representative, Lewis Jones, petitioned for his 50 acres 21 February 1780 in Culpeper County, Virginia.

Jordan, Charles. He served as a soldier in the French and Indian War and assigned his right to land in Virginia.

Jordan, Dominicus. He was from Falmouth, Massachusetts. He was wounded and taken captive by the Indians. He was awarded 300 acres by Massachusetts 24 June 1734.

Jordan, Joshua. He served in the French and Indian War and took his land in Fincastle County, Virginia 15 December 1772.

Joy, Jacob. He served in the Narraganset War from Connecticut and received land in Voluntown, Connecticut in 1701.

Joy, Joseph. He served as an ensign on the expedition to Canada in 1690. Joshua Joy received land in Chesterfield, Massachusetts in 1739.

Joyce, John. He was granted 200 acres in Albany County, New York for his service as a corporal in the 60th or Royal American Regiment in the French and Indian War 8 June 1771.

Joyce, John. He received land in Richmond, New Hampshire in 1765 for the service of an unidentified veteran of the expedition to Canada in 1690.

Judd, James. He was granted 2,000 acres in Albany County, New York for his service as a surgeon's mate in a military hospital in the French and Indian War 16 April 1765.

Judd, Samuel. He served in the Narraganset War from Northampton, Massachusetts. His son, Samuel Judd, claimed his land in Greenwich, Massachusetts in 1737.

Judd, William. He was granted 1,000 acres in West Florida for his service as a lieutenant in the navy in the French and Indian War 15 July 1775.

Judkings, Samuel. He served on the expedition to Canada in 1690. Samuel Judkings received land in Chesterfield, Massachusetts in 1739.

Kaester, Henry Nicholas. He was granted 200 acres in Albany County, New York for his service as a corporal in the 4th Battalion of the 60th Regiment of Foot in the French and Indian War 31 July 1766.

Kainnard, Andrew. He was granted 50 acres in Gloucester County, New York for his six years service as a soldier in the 60th Regiment of Foot in the French and Indian War 5 April 1770.

Kane, John. He was granted 200 acres in Albany County, New York for his service as a sergeant in the 80th Regiment of Foot in the French and Indian War 8 March 1771.

Kays, James He served as a petty officer and linguist under Capt. John Byron on H.M.S. *Fame* from 1759 to 1763 in the French and Indian War and petitioned for land in New York 24 July 1771.

Kearney, Michael. He was granted 3,000 acres in West Florida for his service as a captain in the navy in the French and Indian War 14 November 1777.

Keary, John. He served as as a soldier in the 46th Regiment in the French and Indian War. Elizabeth Keary was certified as his widow 13 December 1766 in New York. She assigned the warrant to Robert Buchanan 21 January 1767.

Keasy, James. He was granted 50 acres in West Florida for his service as a private in the French and Indian War 16 February 1778.

Keating, Garret. He was granted 200 acres in Albany County, New York for his service as a sergeant in the 60th Regiment of Foot in the French and Indian War 15 August 1765.

Keating, John. He was granted 50 acres in Albany County, New York for his service as a private in the 60th or Royal American Regiment of Foot in the French and Indian War 8 June 1771.

Keeling, James. He served as a corporal in the Virginia Regiment of Regulars under Col. George Washington until 1762 in the French and Indian War. He proved his right in Frederick County, Virginia 8 March 1780. He assigned his right to 200 acres.

Keeling, John. He served in the French and Indian War and petitioned for his land 22 November 1766 in New York. He also appeared as John Kelling.

Keene, John. He served in the Narraganset War from Connecticut and received land in Voluntown, Connecticut in 1701. His name was also reported as John Kinne.

Keene, John. He served in Capt. John Dickenson's Company of Rangers in 1756 and 1757 in the French and Indian War. His heir at law was William Keene as proved in Botetourt County, Virginia 11 February 1780.

Keene, Nathaniel. He served in the Narraganset War from Massachusetts in 1685. His land was located in Buxton, Maine.

Keight, Charles. He served as a sergeant in the French and Indian War from Virginia and received a warrant for 200 acres.

Keith, Sir Basil. He was granted 3,000 acres in West Florida for his service as captain in the navy at the reduction of Louisbourgh in the French and Indian War 8 July 1776.

Kellam, Matthew. He was granted 53 acres in Craven County, South Carolina on the King's bounty for his service in the French and Indian War 4 May 1775.

Keller, Adam. He served in the French and Indian War petitioned for his land 10 April 1767 in New York.

Kellet, Richard. He was granted 50 acres in Albany County, New York for his service as a private in the 60th or Royal American Regiment of Foot in the French and Indian War 8 June 1771.

Kellet, Roger. He was granted 2,000 acres in Albany County, New York for his service as a lieutenant in the 44th Regiment of Foot in the French and Indian War 7 August 1764.

Kelley, Peter. He served on the expedition to Canada. His uncle, Benjamin Mansfield, Massachusetts, received his land in Ashburnham, Massachusetts.

Kellogg, Joseph. He was an Indian interpreter and performed other public services for many years. He was from Suffield, Massachusetts when he was granted 200 acres 12 January 1727.

Kells, Daniel. He served as a soldier in the 60th or Royal American Regiment in the French and Indian War and petitioned for his 50 acres in New York 27 April 1765. His name may have been Daniel Kelly.

Kelly, Jacob. He served as a soldier under Col. Adam Stephen in 1762 until he was discharged by Capt. William Fleming in the French and Indian War and assigned his 50 acre warrant in Virginia. He proved his service in Halifax County, Virginia 18 May 1780.

Kelly, Patrick. He was granted 50 acres in Albany County, New York for his service as a private in the 46th Regiment of Foot in the French and Indian War 8 June 1771.

Kelly, Patrick. He was granted 200 acres in West Florida for his service as a noncommissioned officer in the French and Indian War 2 September 1777.

Kelly, Peter. He was granted 200 acres in Albany County, New York for his service as a corporal in the 46th Regiment of Foot in the French and Indian War 23 September 1771.

Kelly, Richard. He was granted 50 acres in Charlotte County, New York for his service as a soldier in the 60th Royal American Regiment of Foot in the French and Indian War 8 August 1774.

Kelly, Thomas. He served as a corporal in Capt. John Dickerson's Company of Rangers in 1757, 1758, and 1759 in the French and Indian War. He petitioned for his 200 acres February 1780 in Botetourt County, Virginia.

Kelly, William. He was a soldier in one of the Virginia regiments in the French and Indian War and assigned his warrant of 50 acres in Virginia.

Kelsey, John. He was a soldier in the Virginia Regiment in Capt. Henry Woodrad's Company under Gen. Braddock in the French and Indian War in 1758 and assigned his right to 50 acres.

Kelsey, Nathaniel. He served as a noncommissioned officer in the 46th Regiment of Foot in the French and Indian War and received 200 acres in Charlotte County, New York 12 October 1774.

Kelsie, Daniel. He served in the Narraganset War from Connecticut and received land in Voluntown, Connecticut in 1701. He also appeared as Daniel Kelsey.

Kelton, Thomas. He was a veteran on the expedition to Canada in 1690. His son, Edward Kelton of Dorchester, Massachusetts, received his land in Ashburnham, Massachusetts in 1736.

Kempton, Thomas. He was granted 50 acres in Gloucester County, New York for his service as a soldier in the 28th Regiment of Foot in the French and Indian War 5 April 1770.

Kendall, Nathaniel. He served in the Narraganset War and received his land in Templeton, Massachusetts in 1733.

Kene, John. He served in the Narraganset War from Massachusetts. He assigned his land to Samuel Chandler, Jr. who received same in Templeton, Massachusetts in 1733.

Kennedy, Alexander. He was granted 200 acres in Albany County, New York for his service as a corporal in the 78th Regiment of Foot in the French and Indian War 23 September 1771.

Kennedy, Archibald. He was granted 50 acres in Charlotte County, New York for his service as a soldier in the 42nd Regiment of Foot in the French and Indian War 1 April 1775.

Kennedy, David. He served a soldier in the Virginia Regiment in the French and Indian War for eight or ten years. He proved his service in Frederick County, Virginia 4 April 1780.

Kennedy, David. He received a warrant for 200 acres for his service in the French and Indian War in Virginia.

Kennedy, David. He served as quartermaster to a troop of light horse under Capt. Robert Steward in the French and Indian War in the French and Indian War. In 1756 he was appointed Deputy Commissary under Dr. Thomas Walker to the troops serving on the frontier. In 1758 he was appointed quartermaster to the Virginia Regiment under Col. George Washington. He also served as ensign in the Virginia Regiment in 1758. In 1762 he served as lieutenant under Col. Adam Stephen. He assigned his eight warrants for 8,000 acres in Virginia.

Kennedy, Duncan. He was granted 50 acres in Albany County, New York for his service as a soldier in the 77th Regiment of Foot in the French and Indian War 15 August 1765.

Kennedy, John. He was granted 2,000 acres in Albany County, New York for his service as a subaltern in the 44th Regiment of Foot in the French and Indian War 7 August 1764.

Kennedy, John. He served as a private in the 55th Regiment in the French and Indian War and had his service certified in July 1771 in New York.

Kennedy, Murdock. He was granted 50 acres in Gloucester County, New York for his service as a soldier for two years in the 42nd Regiment of Foot in the French and Indian War 7 April 1770.

Kennedy, Peter. He was granted 500 acres in West Florida for his service as a warrant officer in the navy in the French and Indian War 17 December 1777.

Kennedy, Robert. He was granted 200 acres in Charlotte County, New York for his service as Assistant Surgeon of Navy Hospitals in the French and Indian War 26 August 1774.

Kennistone, Christopher. He served in the Narraganset War from

Massachusetts in 1685. His land was located in Buxton, Maine.

Kennmere, George. He served as a private in the 44th Regiment in the French and Indian War and petitioned for his land in New York 6 April 1772.

Kenny, Thomas. He served in the Narraganset War from Salem, Massachusetts. His heirs claimed his land in Amherst, New Hampshire in 1734.

Kent, John. He served on the expedition to Canada in 1690 and received land in Poland, Maine in 1739.

Kent, John. He received land in Richmond, New Hampshire in 1765 for the service of an unidentified veteran of the expedition to Canada in 1690.

Kent, Richard. He was from Newbury, Essex County, Massachusetts. He raised a company at his own expense in 1706. They killed twenty-five of the enemy. He was the only heir of his uncle, John Hobbs, who was slain in the Narraganset War. He was awarded 3,000 acres by Massachusetts.

Kenty, Anthony. He served as a soldier in Capt. Samuel Meredith's Company of Rangers under Col. Mercer in 1760 in the French and Indian War. He received his warrant in Louisa County, Virginia 14 February 1780. He assigned his right to 50 acres.

Kenty, Miles. He served as a soldier in Capt. Thomas Fleming's Company of Regulars in 1758 and as a sergeant in Capt. John Posey's Company of Regulars in 1760 in the French and Indian War. His heir, Anthony Kenty, petitioned for his land but assigned the warrants for 50 and 200 acres respectively. The warrants were approved in Louisa County, Virginia in 1780.

Keogh, Michael. He served as a private in the 44th Regiment in the French and Indian War and petitioned for his 50 acres in New York 26 October 1764. He also appeared as Michael Keough.

Kerens, George. He served as a private in the French and Indian War and petitioned for land in New York 9 April 1767. He also appeared as John Kerens.

Kern, Jacob. He was granted 616 ½ and 246 acres in Berks County, Pennsylvania for his service as a captain in the French and Indian War 3 February 1769.

Kernel, William. He served as a soldier in the Virginia Regiment under Col. William Byrd in the French and Indian War. He received the warrant in Essex County, Virginia 21 February 1780. He assigned his right to 50 acres to John Spindle.

Kerns, John. He was granted 50 acres in Albany County, New York for his service as a soldier in the 28th Regiment of Foot in the French and

Indian War 9 May 1771.

Kerns, Peter. He served as a private in the French and Indian War and petitioned for his land in New York 8 July 1765.

Kerns, Robert. He was granted 50 acres in Albany County, New York for his service as a soldier in the 60th Regiment of Foot in the French and Indian War 26 September 1765.

Kertland, Phillip. He served in the Narraganset War from Lynn, Massachusetts and petitioned for his land 4 June 1685.

Ketsbower, George. He was granted 200 acres in Albany County, New York for his service as a noncommissioned officer in the 60th Regiment of Foot in the French and Indian War 30 May 1765.

Keyes, Robert. He was from Princeton, Massachusetts. One of his children was carried to Canada by the Indians. In attempting to recover his child, he spent about £100. He had traveled to Portsmouth, N. H. and also sent to Canada. He learned from an advertisement in the New York paper that his child was among the Mohawks. Last fall he was determined to go for his child, but illness and death in his family prevented him from doing so. Within 60 rods from the door of his house was Watchusett Hill. He prayed for a grant of half of it 29 May 1765.

Keyes, Solomon. He served under Capt. John Lovewell from Massachusetts and was in battle at Pigwacket in May 1725. He was from Marlborough, Massachusetts and received his land in Pembroke, New Hampshire.

Kezee, Arthur. He served as a soldier for six months in 1762 under Capt. Gabriel Throckmorton in the French and Indian War. He proved his service in Halifax County, Virginia 18 May 1780.

Kickler, Philip. He served as a private in the French and Indian War and petitioned for his land in New York 3 January 1770.

Kidder, Benjamin. He served under Capt. John Lovewell from Massachusetts and was in battle at Pigwacket in May 1725. He was from Londonderry, New Hampshire and received his land at Pembroke, New Hampshire.

Killing, John. He was granted 200 acres in Albany County, New York for his service as a corporal in the 4th Battalion in the Royal American or 60th Regiment of Foot in the French and Indian War 27 September 1769.

Killpatrick, John. He was granted 200 acres in Albany County, New York for his service as a noncommissioned officer in the 28th Regiment of Foot in the French and Indian War 8 March 1771.

Killpatrick, Terrence. He served as a corporal in the 28th Regiment in the French and Indian War and had his service certified in New York 28 January 1767.

Kills, Robert. He served as a soldier in the French and Indian War and received 50 acres in Nova Scotia 9 October 1776.

Kimball, Aaron. He was a veteran of the expedition to Canada in 1690. His brother, Moses Kimball of Ipswich, Massachusetts, claimed his land in Winchendon, Massachusetts in 1736.

Kimball, Caleb. He served in the Narraganset War from Massachusetts in 1685. His land was located in Buxton, Maine.

Kimball, Henry. He served in the Narraganset War from Massachusetts in 1685. His land was located in Buxton, Maine.

Kimpton, Thomas. He served as a private in the 28th Regiment in the French and Indian War and had his service certified 19 September 1766 in New York.

Kincade, William. He served as a soldier in Capt. Charles Lewis's Company under Col. Henry Bouquet in 1764. He requested his 50 acres 18 January 1780 in Augusta County, Virginia.

Kinck, Sebastian. He was granted 50 acres in Albany County, New York for his service as a soldier in the 60th Regiment of Foot in the French and Indian War 17 September 1765.

Kindrick, Thomas. He served in the Narraganset War from Rehoboth, Massachusetts. His heirs claimed his land in Greenwich, Massachusetts in 1737.

King, Daniel. He served on the expedition to Canada in 1690. William King was admitted to his land in Lydeboro, Maine in 1736.

King, Duncan. He was granted 200 acres in Albany County, New York for his service as a noncommissioned officer in the 77th Regiment of Foot in the French and Indian War 13 May 1765.

King, Gilbert. He was granted 2,000 acres in Albany County, New York for his service as a lieutenant in the 80th Regiment of Foot in the French and Indian War 18 November 1769.

King, Hezekiah. He served as an ensign in the French and Indian War and received 2,000 acres in Nova Scotia 7 October 1763.

King, John. He served on the expedition to Canada in 1690. Samuel King was admitted to his land in Lydeboro, Maine in 1736.

King, John. He served as a lieutenant in the French and Indian War and was entitled to 2,000 acres which he desired to locate in Augusta County, Virginia 27 May 1774. He assigned the warrant.

King, John. He served as a soldier in the 2nd Virginia Regiment of Col. William Byrd in the French and Indian War and assigned his 50 acre warrant in Virginia. He applied in King William County, Virginia in April 1780.

King, Josiah. He served as an ensign in the French and Indian War and received 2,000 acres in Nova Scotia 13 July 1772.

King, Richard. He served on the expedition to Canada in 1690. Samuel Hide received his land in Alstead, New Hampshire in 1771.

King, William. He served as a soldier in the 1st Virginia Regiment in Capt. Christopher Hudson's Company under Col. George Washington in the French and Indian War and petitioned for his 50 acres 3 February 1780 in Hanover County, Virginia.

Kingsbury, Thomas. He served in the Narraganset War from Massachusetts in 1685. His land was located in Buxton, Maine.

Kingman, John. He received land in Richmond, New Hampshire in 1765 for the service of an unidentified veteran of the expedition to Canada in 1690.

Kingsley, Edward. He served as a private in the French and Indian War and was granted land in New York 5 February 1772.

Kinkaid, Thomas. He served as a sergeant in a company of rangers under Capt. William Christian and received a warrant for 200 acres 17 November 1779 in Greenbrier County, Virginia. He also appeared as Thomas Kincade.

Kinkead, John. He served as a private under Capt. William Preston in the French and Indian War and proved his right to 50 acres in Augusta County, Virginia 15 February 1780.

Kinkead, Thomas. He served as a soldier in Capt. Charles Lewis's Company under Col. Henry Bouquet in 1764 and was granted a warrant for 50 acres 15 February 1780 in Augusta County, Virginia.

Kinkead, Thomas. He served as a soldier in 1758 and 1759 in Capt. William Preston's Company of Rangers in the French and Indian War and received his 50 acre warrant 21 March in 1780 in Greenbrier County, Virginia.

Kinkead, William. He served as a soldier in Capt. Charles Lewis's Company under Col. Henry Bouquet in 1764 and was granted a warrant for 50 acres 15 February 1780 in Augusta County, Virginia.

Kinked, John. He served as a soldier in Capt. William Preston's Company of Rangers in 1758 in the French and Indian War. He was issued a warrant for 50 acres 15 February 1780 in Augusta County, Virginia. He also appeared as John Kinkead and John Kenkedd.

Kinney, Joseph. He was granted 200 acres in Albany County, New York for his service as a sergeant in the French and Indian War 8 June 1771.

Kinsmon, Robert. He served in the Narraganset War from Massachusetts in 1685. His son, Joseph Kinsmon, received his land in Buxton, Maine.

Kirby, Joseph. He served as a corporal in the French and Indian War and petitioned for his 200 acres in New York 30 January 1775.

Kirk, Alexander. He served as a soldier in an independent company under Col. Henry Bouquet in 1764 and received a warrant for 50 acres 17 November 1779 in Augusta County, Virginia.

Kirkman, Michael. He was granted 1,000 acres in West Florida for his service as a lieutenant in the 21st Regiment of Foot in the French and Indian War 16 August 1768.

Kirkpatrick, John. He was granted 200 acres in Albany County, New York for his service as a sergeant in the 60th Regiment of Foot in the French and Indian War 28 October 1765.

Kitchen, John. He served as a soldier under Col. George Washington in the French and Indian War. He died without any children or blood relation in the United States. His widow, Lucy Kitchen, received the warrant in Essex County, Virginia 21 February 1780 and assigned same.

Kitchen, Richard. He was granted 50 acres in Albany County, New York for his service as a soldier in the 45th Regiment of Foot in the French and Indian War 18 February 1775.

Kittle, Jonathan. He served in the Narraganset War from Charlestown, Massachusetts. His son, James Kittle, received his land in Westminster, Massachusetts in 1733.

Kittredge, Jonathan. He served under Capt. John Lovewell from Massachusetts and was killed in battle at Pigwacket 8 May 1725. He was from Billerica, Massachusetts. His land was located in Pembroke, New Hampshire.

Knap, Isaac. He served on the expedition to Canada in 1690. Isaac Knap was admitted to his land in Lyndeboro, Maine in 1736.

Knap, James. He served on the expedition to Canada in 1690. Isaac Knap was admitted to his land in Lyndeboro, Maine in 1736.

Knap, Joseph. He received land in Richmond, New Hampshire in 1765 for the service of an unidentified veteran of the expedition to Canada in 1690.

Kneeland, Samuel. He served in the Narraganset War from Massachusetts in 1685. His land was located in Buxton, Maine.

Knight, Charles. He served as a sergeant in the French and Indian War until 1758 and petitioned for his land in February 1780 in Spotsylvania County, Virginia. He assigned the 200 acres. He also appeared as Charles Night.

Knight, James. He was granted 50 acres in Albany County, New York for his service as a soldier in the 60th Regiment of Foot in the French and Indian War 17 September 1765.

Knight, Richard. He shared in the grant of East Greenwich, Rhode Island made to those who had rendered service in King Philip's War. The grant was made 31 October 1677.

Knight, Samuel. He served in the Narraganset War from New London, Connecticut. His niece, Madam Livingstone, received land in Bedford, New Hampshire in 1733.

Knight, Samuel. He was granted 50 acres in Gloucester County, New York for his service as a soldier in the 28th Regiment of Foot in the French and Indian War 5 April 1770.

Knights, William. He served in the Narraganset War from Connecticut and received land in Voluntown, Connecticut in 1701.

Knott, Dr. Richard. He served in the Narraganset War from Marblehead, Massachusetts. Thomas Martin claimed his land in Amherst, New Hampshire in 1734.

Knott, Samuel. He served in the Narraganset War from Sandwich, Massachusetts. His nephew, Samuel Toby, received his land in Gorham, Maine in 1733.

Knowles, Andrew. He served as a private in the French and Indian War. His service was certified in New York in November 1766.

Knowles, Andrew. He received his 2,000 acres of land in West Florida for his service as a warrant officer in the French and Indian War 7 November 1776.

Knowles, John. He served in the Narraganset War from Eastham, Massachusetts and received land in Gorham, Maine in 1733.

Knowles, John. He shared in the grant of East Greenwich, Rhode Island made to those who had rendered service in King Philip's War. The grant was made 31 October 1677.

Knowlton, Daniel. He served as an ensign in the French and Indian War and received 2,000 acres in Nova Scotia 7 June 1783.

Knowlton, William. He served in the Narraganset War from Massachusetts in 1685. His land was located in Buxton, Maine.

Kong, John Jacob. He served as a soldier in the 25th Regiment in the French and Indian War and had his service certified 13 October 1766.

Lacells, Edward. He was granted 50 acres in Albany County, New York for his service as a soldier in the 55th Regiment of Foot in the French and Indian War 26 July 1765.

Lackoy, George. He was granted 50 acres on a branch of the Edisto River in South Carolina on the King's bounty for his service in the French and Indian War 21 June 1765.

Lad, Daniel. He served in the Narraganset War from Massachusetts in 1685.

His land was located in Buxton, Maine.

Lafell, Philip. He was granted 50 acres in Gloucester County, New York for his service as a soldier in the 28th Regiment of Foot in the French and Indian War 5 April 1770.

Lahones, Benjamin. He served as a soldier in the French and Indian War and assigned his 50 acre warrant in Virginia. His name also appeared as Benjamin Lehone.

Lain, Dumas. He served as a soldier in Capt. Christian's Company of Rangers in 1760 in the French and Indian War. He proved his right in Louisa County, Virginia 11 October 1779. He assigned his warrant for 50 acres. He also appeared as Dumas Lane.

Lain, Ephraim. He served in the Narraganset War from Hingham, Massachusetts. His son, Ephraim Lain, received land in Bedford, Massachusetts in 1733.

Lain, Joshua. He served in the Narraganset War from Boston, Massachusetts. His son, John Lain, received land in Bedford, New Hampshire in 1733.

Lain, Samuel. He served in the Narraganset War from Suffield, Massachusetts. His son, Samuel Lain, claimed his land in Greenwich, Massachusetts in 1737.

Laing, Thomas. He was granted 200 acres in Albany County, New York for his service as a drummer in the 55th Regiment of Foot in the French and Indian War 26 July 1765.

Laird, David. He served as a corporal in Capt. Peter Hogg's Company of Rangers in 1757 until discharged at Bedford in the French and Indian War. He received his warrant for 200 acres 28 March 1780 in Buckingham County, Virginia.

Lake, Richard. He served in the Narraganset War from Yarmouth, Massachusetts and received land in Gorham, Maine in 1733.

Lakin, Isaac. He served under Capt. John Lovewell from Massachusetts and was at the battle of Pigwacket in May 1725. He was from Groton, Massachusetts and received his land in Pembroke, New Hampshire.

Lamar, Thomas. He served in the French and Indian War and petitioned for 100 acres on the King's bounty in South Carolina 2 June 1767.

Lamb, —. He served on the expedition to Canada in 1690. Huldah Lamb received land in Warwick, Massachusetts in 1738.

Lamb, Abiell. He served in the Narraganset War from Oxford, Massachusetts. His son, Abiell Lamb, claimed his land in Greenwich, Massachusetts in 1737.

Lamb, Archibald. He served as a soldier in the Virginia Regiment in the

French and Indian War from 1759 to 1762 and assigned his 50 acre warrant in Virginia. He proved his service in Bedford County, Virginia 24 January 1780.

Lamb, John. He was granted 200 acres in Albany County, New York for his service as a corporal in the 78th Regiment of Foot in the French and Indian War 8 October 1771.

Lamb, John. He served as a soldier in Col. William Byrd's Regiment in 1758 in the French and Indian War. He proved his right in Orange County, Virginia 24 February 1780. He assigned his right to 50 acres.

Lamb, Joseph. He was granted 200 acres in West Florida for his service as a a noncommissioned officer in the French and Indian War 2 March 1779.

Lamb, Richard. He served as a soldier in Col. William Byrd's Regiment in 1758 in the French and Indian War. He applied in Orange County, Virginia 24 February 1780. He assigned his right to 50 acres.

Lambert, James. He served as a soldier under Col. Mercer in the 2nd Virginia Regiment in the French and Indian War and assigned his 50 acre warrant in Virginia.

Lambert, John. He received land in Richmond, New Hampshire in 1765 for the service of an unidentified veteran of the expedition to Canada in 1690.

Lambert, Jonathan. He served in the Narraganset War from Salem, Massachusetts. Ephraim Ingalls drew his land in Amherst, Massachusetts in 1734.

Lambert, Joseph. He served as a corporal in the French and Indian War and petitioned for land in New York 17 March 1767.

Lambert, Joseph. He served as a noncommissioned officer under Maj. Stewart and Col. Adam Stephen in the French and Indian War. He proved his right in Mecklenburg County, Virginia 8 May 1780. He assigned his 200 acre warrant.

Lambert, Philip. He was granted 200 acres in Albany County, New York for his service as a corporal in the 46th Regiment of Foot in the French and Indian War 10 March 1772.

Lambert, Samuel. He served on the expedition to Canada in 1690. Joseph Lambert was admitted to his land in Lyndeboro, Maine in 1736.

Lambeth, John. He served as a sergeant until he was discharged in 1762 in the French and Indian War and received a warrant for 200 acres in Virginia which he assigned.

Lamont, Archibald. He served as a lieutenant in the French and Indian War and petitioned for his 2,000 acres in Tryon County, New York 1 November 1774.

Lampling, Jacob. He was granted 50 acres in Albany County, New York for his service as a soldier in the 60th Regiment of Foot in the French and Indian War 26 September 1765.

Lampton, William. He served as a soldier in the French and Indian War. He petitioned for his land in February 1780 in Spotsylvania County, Virginia.

Lamson, Samuel. He served in the Narraganset War from Reading, Massachusetts. He applied for his land 4 June 1685. His son, Samuel Lamson, received his land in Westminster, Massachusetts in 1733. He also appeared as Samuel Lambson.

Lancaster, Henry. He was granted 42 and 58 acres in Granville County, South Carolina on the King's bounty for his service in the French and Indian War 4 May 1775.

Landon, David. He served in the Narraganset War from Boston, Massachusetts. His son, Benjamin Landon, received his land in Bedford, New Hampshire in 1733.

Lane, Dumas. He served as a soldier in Capt. Christian's Company of Rangers in 1760 in the French and Indian War from Virginia and assigned his 50 acre warrant.

Lane, Joseph. He served in an independent company of rangers in the French and Indian war and petitioned for land in New York 12 April 1769.

Lane, Littleberry. He served as a soldier in Capt. Peter Hogg's Company in Col. William Byrd's Regiment in Virginia in the French and Indian War in 1758. He received a warrant for 50 acres 23 March 1780 in Orange County, Virginia.

Lang, Thomas. He was granted 200 acres in Gloucester County, New York for his service as a drummer in the 55th Regiment of Foot in the French and Indian War 5 April 1770.

Langkster, John. He was granted 200 acres in Albany County, New York for his service as a noncommissioned officer in the 80th Regiment of Foot in the French and Indian War 30 May 1765.

Langley, John. He served in the Narraganset War from Hingham, Massachusetts. His son, John Langley, received land in Bedford, New Hampshire in 1733.

Langor, John. He served in the Narraganset War from Hingham, Massachusetts and petitioned for his land 4 June 1685.

Lankford, James. He served as a private in Capt. Christopher Hudson's Company in 1758 in the French and Indian War. He proved his right to a 50 acre warrant in Goochland County, Virginia 20 September 1779. He was in Hanover County, Virginia in June 1780.

Larabe, John. He served in the Narraganset War from Connecticut and received land in Voluntown, Connecticut in 1701.

Larey, Darbey. He was granted 50 acres in Williamsburg Township, South Carolina on the King's bounty for his service in the French and Indian War 24 August 1770.

Larkin, Edward. He served in the Narraganset War from Connecticut and received land in Voluntown, Connecticut in 1701.

Larned, Isaac. He served in the Narraganset War and received land in Templeton, Massachusetts in 1733.

Larned, Jeremiah. He served as a lieutenant in Col. Abijah Willard's Regiment raised in Massachusetts under General Jeffery Amherst for the reduction of Canada in 1759 in the French and Indian War and assigned his 2,000 acre warrant in Virginia.

Larrabee, Benjamin. He spent upwards of 30 years in service against the enemy Indians. He received 100 acres in Massachusetts 11 June 1728.

Larrance, —. He served on the expedition to Canada in 1690. Samuel Larrance received land in Dumbarton, New Hampshire in 1735.

Lason, Henry. He was granted 200 acres in Albany County, New York for his service as a noncommissioned officer in the 61st Regiment of Foot in the French and Indian War 18 February 1775.

Lassley, John. He served in the 2nd Battalion of the 1st Regiment as a private in the French and Indian War and petitioned for his land in New York 30 January 1775.

Latham, John. He served in the Narraganset War from Connecticut and received land in Voluntown, Connecticut in 1701.

Lathrop, Benjamin. He served in the Narraganset War from Charlestown, Massachusetts. His nephew, Nathaniel Goodwin, received his land in Westminister, Massachusetts in 1733.

Lathrop, John. He served in the Narraganset War from Connecticut and received land in Voluntown, Connecticut in 1701.

Lathrop, Samuel. He served in the Narraganset War from Connecticut and received land in Voluntown, Connecticut in 1701.

Latrot, James. He served in the French and Indian War and took his land in Fincastle County, Virginia 15 December 1772.

Laulb, John. He served as a corporal in the French and Indian War and was granted land in New York 7 March 1770.

Laughlin, Robert. He was granted 300 acres in Pennsylvania for his service in the French and Indian War 1 April 1769.

Law, Michael. He was granted 50 acres in Albany County, New York for his service as a soldier in the 3rd Battalion in the 60th Regiment of Foot in the French and Indian War 28 June 1770.

Lawler, John. He served as a soldier in the French and Indian War and assigned his 50 acre warrant in Virginia.

Lawler, Thomas. He served as a soldier in the French and Indian War and had his service certified in Montgomery County, Virginia for his 50 acres of land 8 March 1780.

Lawrence, Daniel. He served on the expedition to Canada in 1690. Daniel Lawrence received land in Warwick, Massachusetts in 1738.

Lawrence, Edward. He was granted 200 acres in Gloucester County, New York for his service as a corporal in the 4th Battalion in the 60th Regiment of Foot in the French and Indian War 5 April 1770.

Lawrence, Edward. He served as a soldier in the 28th Regiment in the French and Indian War. He petitioned for his land 6 August 1774 in New York.

Lawrence, Edward. He was granted 200 acres in Albany County, New York for his service as a corporal in the 60th or Royal American Regiment in the French and Indian War 8 June 1771.

Lawrence, Edward. He served as a soldier in the 4th Battalion of Royal Americans in the French and Indian War and petitioned for his land 22 October 1766 in New York.

Lawrence, Jonathan. He served in the Narraganset War and received land in Templeton, Massachusetts in 1733.

Lawrence, Joseph. He was granted 200 acres in Albany County, New York for his service as a sergeant in a regiment of foot in the French and Indian War 19 May 1770.

Lawrence, Zechariah. He served in the Narraganset War and received land in Templeton, Massachusetts in 1733.

Lawson, Henry. He served as a sergeant in 61st Regiment in the French and Indian War and was granted land in New York 11 November 1772.

Lawson, John. He served as a lieutenant in the French and Indian War from Virginia and was entitled to 2,000 acres which he desired to locate on the Large Buffalo Lick on the southwest side of Povisa River 18 miles from the Ohio River.

Lawson, Peter. He served as a soldier in the French and Indian War and received a 50 acre land warrant in Virginia.

Lay, Edward. He shared in the grant of East Greenwich, Rhode Island made to those who had rendered service in King Philip's War. The grant was made 31 October 1677. His name also appeared as Edward Day.

Layman, Henry. He served as a soldier in the 60th Regiment in the French and Indian War. His widow, Rachel Layman, petitioned for his land in

New York 14 December 1767.

Lazell, Joshua. He served in the Narraganset War from Hingham, Massachusetts and applied for his land 4 June 1685 .

Lea, Charles. He served as a lieutenant and captain in the 44th Regiment of Foot from 1755 to the reduction of Canada in 1760 in the French and Indian War. He was afterwards promoted to Major in the 103rd Regiment of Foot and served to the close of the war. He received a warrant for 5,000 acres in Frederick County, Virginia 2 November 1779. He also appeared as Charles Lee.

Lea, John. He was a soldier in Capt. Christian's Company of Rangers in 1760 in the French and Indian War. He was awarded 50 acres 11 October 1779 in Louisa County, Virginia. He also appeared as John Lee.

Leaberry, William. He served as a noncommissioned officer in the French and Indian War and received 200 acres in Nova Scotia 9 October 1776.

Leach, John. He served in the Narraganset War from Boston, Massachusetts. His son, John Leach, received land in Bedford, New Hampshire in 1733.

Leader, Edward. He was granted 200 acres in Albany County, New York for his service as a sergeant in the 46th Regiment of Foot in the French and Indian War 1 April 1772.

Leake, Robert. He was granted 5,000 acres in Albany County, New York for his service as a Inspector General of Provisions and Paymaster of the Carriage in the French and Indian War 22 May 1770.

Learned, David. He served on the expedition to Canada in 1690. Elisha Learned received his land in Alstead, New Hampshire in 1771.

Learned, Jonathan. He received land in Alstead, New Hampshire in 1771 for the service of an unidentified veteran of the expedition to Canada in 1690.

Leary, Patrick. He was granted 50 acres in Albany County, New York for his service as private in a regiment of foot in the French and Indian War 19 May 1770.

Leatherdale, William, Jr. He served as a soldier in Capt. Thomas Bullett's Company of Regulars in the Old Virginia Regiment in the French and Indian War and received a warrant for 50 acres in February 1780 in Botetourt County, Virginia.

Leatherman, Casper. He was granted 50 acres in Albany County, New York for his service as a private in a regiment of foot in the French and Indian War 19 May 1770.

LeBauch, Peter. He was granted 50 acres in Albany County, New York for his service as a private in a regiment of foot in the French and Indian War

19 May 1770.

Lechmere, Charles. He was granted 5,000 acres in West Florida for his service as Commissary of General Stores and Provisions in the French and Indian War 4 August 1777.

Ledbetter, Henry. He served in the Narraganset War from Dorchester, Massachusetts. His heirs received land in Bedford, New Hampshire in 1733.

Lee, Charles. He served as a lieutenant and a captain in the 44th Regiment in 1755 to the reduction of Canada in 1760. He was afterwards promoted to Major in the 103rd Regiment until the end of the French and Indian War. He had his service certified 2 November 1779 in Frederick County, Virginia. He received 5,000 acres.

Lee, John. He served on the expedition to Canada in 1690. John Lee, Jr. petitioned for his land in Raymond, Maine in 1735.

Lee, John. He was granted 200 acres in Albany County, New York for his service as a sergeant in an independent company of foot in the French and Indian War 30 October 1765.

Lee, Samuel. He served under Col. John March and was wounded at Port Royal. His wound shortened his life. He was from Gloucester. His widow, Ruth Lee, was awarded 150 acres by Massachusetts 3 December 1735.

Lee, Thomas. He served in the expedition to Canada in 1690. John Lee, Jr., applied for his land in Raymond, Maine in 1735.

Lee, Thomas. He was granted 200 acres in Albany County, New York for his service as a drum major in the 80th Regiment of Foot in the French and Indian War 15 August 1765.

Lee, William. He served in the Narraganset War from Connecticut and received land in Voluntown, Connecticut in 1701.

Leekie, Peter. He served in the French and Indian War and assigned his right to 50 acres in New York 24 October 1764. He also appeared as Peter Leckie.

Leeson, John. He served in the French and Indian War and petitioned for his land in New York 29 June 1774.

Leffingwell, Thomas. He served as a lieutenant in the Narraganset War from Connecticut and received land in Voluntown, Connecticut in 1701.

Lefler, Conrad. He served as a soldier in the 60th or Royal American Regiment in the French and Indian War and petitioned for his 50 acres in New York 29 October 1764.

Legge, Francis. He served as a captain in the French and Indian War. He petitioned for 5,000 acres in New York 12 May 1767.

Legrand, Alexander. He served as a sergeant in a company of volunteers which joined the detachment of regulars under Maj. Andrew Lewis and served six months in the French and Indian War. He received a warrant for 200 acres 17 January 1780 in Prince Edward County, Virginia.

Legroe, John. He served on the expedition to Canada in 1690. Daniel Epes, Jr. was admitted to his land in Lyndeboro, Maine in 1736.

Legus, William. He was granted 50 acres in Albany County, New York for his service as a soldier in the 55th Regiment of Foot in the French and Indian War 1 July 1771.

LeHunt, George. He served as a major by brevet in the 80th Regiment in the French and Indian War and petitioned for 5,000 acres in New York 29 29 January 1766.

Leighton, Cheney. He was a veteran of the expedition to Canada in 1690. His nephew, John Leighton of Ipswich, claimed his land in Winchendon, Massachusetts in 1736.

Leighton, John. He served in the Narraganset War from Massachusetts in 1685. His son, John Leighton, received his land in Buxton, Maine. He also appeared as John Laighton.

Leland, John. He was granted 5,000 acres in Gloucester County, New York for his service as a major under Col. Gray in the 98th Regiment of Foot in the French and Indian War 4 October 1775.

Lemay, John. He served as a soldier in a volunteer company of rangers under Capt. William Phillips in 1763 in the French and Indian War. He proved his right to 50 acres in Essex County, Virginia 14 February 1780.

Lemmon, Samuel. He served in the Narraganset War from Charlestown, Massachusetts. His heirs received his land in Westminster, Massachusetts in 1733.

Lemmons, John. He served as a soldier in the Virginia Regiment under Col. William Byrd in the French and Indian War. He proved his right in Washington County, Virginia 18 January 1780. He assigned his right to 50 acres.

Lemon, Alexander. He served as a soldier in 1758 and 1759 in Capt. Robert Rutherford's Company of Rangers in the French and Indian War. He received his 50 acre warrant in March 1780 in Berkeley County, Virginia. [Compare with Alexander Semon.]

Lemon, Thomas. He served as a lieutenant under Capt. William Fox in a company of rangers under Col. Adam Stephen in the French and Indian War. He received a 2,000 acre warrant 3 October 1779 in

Virginia.

Lems, Christopher. He was granted 623.7 acres in Berks County, Pennsylvania for his service as a captain in the French and Indian War 3 February 1769.

Lendall, James. He served in the Narraganset War from Boston, Massachusetts. His heirs received land in Bedford, New Hampshire in 1733.

Leonard, Isaac. He served in the Narraganset War from Bridgewater, Massachusetts. In 1737 his son, Isaac Leonard, claimed his land in Greenwich, Massachusetts.

Leonard, Samuel. He served in Lovewell's War in Massachusetts and received his land in Petersham, Massachusetts in 1733.

Leonard, Timothy. He served as a private in the 80th Regiment in the French and Indian War and petitioned for his land in New York 22 May 1765.

Leslie, Alexander. He served as a drummer in the 1st Regiment in the French and Indian War and was granted land in New York 5 February 1772.

Leslie, Alexander. He was granted 50 acres in Albany County, New York for his service as a soldier in the 60th Regiment of Foot in the French and Indian War 14 April 1772.

Leslie, Thomas. He was granted 50 acres in Albany County, New York for his service as a soldier in the 55th Regiment of Foot in the French and Indian War 28 October 1765.

Leslie, William. He was granted 2,000 acres in Albany County, New York for his service as a lieutenant in the 60th Regiment of Foot in the French and Indian War 30 October 1765.

Lester, Gilbert. He served as a surgeon's mate in the French and Indian War and had his service certified in New York 28 January 1765.

Leuach, George. He served in the French and Indian War and petitioned for land in New York 17 March 1767.

Leuze, Robert. He was granted 200 acres in Albany County, New York for his service as a noncommissioned officer in the 80th Regiment of Foot in the French and Indian War 15 August 1765.

Leviston, John. He served in Lovewell's War in Massachusetts and received his land in Petersham, Massachusetts in 1733.

Leviston, John. He served in the French and Indian War. His service was certified in New York 14 February 1771.

Leviston, Richard. He served in the French and Indian War. His service was certified in New York 14 February 1771.

Lewelling, Freeman. He served as a private in the French and Indian War under Col. William Byrd. He was in Prince Edward County, Virginia in February 1780. He assigned his 50 acre warrant.

Lewis, Aaron. He served as a sergeant in the French and Indian War and received his 200 acre warrant in Virginia.

Lewis, Andrew. He served as a major in the French and Indian War and received land warrants for 2,000 and 3,000 acres in Virginia.

Lewis, Benjamin. He served in the Narraganset War from Sandwich, Massachusetts. His brother, John Lewis, received his land in Gorham, Maine in 1733.

Lewis, Charles. He served as a captain in the 1st Virginia Regiment in the French and Indian War. His 3,000 acres of land was awarded to his sons, John Lewis, Andrew Lewis, and Charles Lewis, and received by their guardian, Joseph Jones, 29 October 1779 in Spotsylvania County, Virginia. He was a native of Virginia.

Lewis, Charles. He served as a captain in a company of independents under Col. Henry Bouquet in 1764. His executor, William Lewis, received his warrant for 2,000 acres 17 November 1779 Augusta County, Virginia. An earlier warrant for 2,000 acres for his service as a lieutenant under Capt. William Preston had been issued.

Lewis, Francis. He served as Commissary of Stores and Provisions in America in the French and Indian War and petitioned for his 3,000 acres in New York 8 October 1764.

Lewis, George. He served in the Narraganset War from Barnstable, Massachusetts and received land in Gorham, Maine in 1733.

Lewis, Isaac. He served in the Narraganset War from Charlestown, Massachusetts. His nephew, Thomas Skinner, received his land in Westminster, Massachusetts in 1733.

Lewis, James. He served on the expedition to Canada in 1690 and received land in Dumbarton, New Hampshire in 1735.

Lewis, John. He served in the Narraganset War from Connecticut and received land in Voluntown, Connecticut in 1701.

Lewis, John. He served in the Narraganset War from Lynn, Massachusetts. His grandson, Edmund Lewis, claimed his land in Amherst, New Hampshire in 1734.

Lewis, John. He served in the Narraganset War from Barnstable, Massachusetts. His heirs received his land in Gorham, Maine in 1733.

Lewis, John. He served on the expedition to Canada in 1690 and received land in Dumbarton, New Hampshire in 1735.

Lewis, John. He was granted 200 acres in Albany County, New York for his service as a noncommissioned officer in the 46th Regiment of Foot in the French and Indian War 8 March 1771.

Lewis, John. He served as a private in the French and Indian War and petitioned for 50 acres on the King's bounty in South Carolina 7 April 1767.

Lewis, John. He was a sergeant in the 2nd Virginia Regiment in the French and Indian War. He proved his right to 200 acres in Goochland County, Virginia 20 September 1779. He assigned his warrant.

Lewis, John. He served as a subaltern in the French and Indian War from Virginia and received 2,000 acres of land which was surveyed 30 June 1774.

Lewis, Jonathan. He served as a surgeon in the French and Indian War and petitioned for land 30 December 1766 in New York.

Lewis, Robert. He served as a sergeant in the French and Indian War and received 200 acres in Albany County, New York 13 August 1765.

Lewis, Samuel. He served as a private in the French and Indian War and petitioned for his land in New York in January 1766.

Lewis, Thomas. He served in the Narraganset War from Haddam, Massachusetts. He claimed his land in Greenwich, Massachusetts in 1737.

Lewis, Thomas. He served as a noncommissioned officer in the French and Indian War in Virginia and assigned his 200 acres.

Lewis, Zachary. During the French and Indian War he was a lieutenant in 1756 and a recruiting officer. He enlisted 30 men whom he passed at a general rendezvous at Winchester in 1758. He failed in getting a commission of captain. He was issued a warrant for 2,000 acres 13 March 1780 in Louisa County, Virginia.

Lewiston, Richard. He served in the French and Indian War and petitioned for his land in New York 17 March 1767. *Vide* Richard Leviston.

Ley, Andries. He served as a sergeant in the 60th Regiment in the French and Indian War. He petitioned for 200 acres in Albany County, New York 2 November 1764.

Liah, John. He served on the expedition to Canada in 1690. Robert Hale petitioned for his land in Raymond, Maine in 1735.

Lightfoot, Francis. He served as a sergeant in the French and Indian War in Col. Mercer's Company in 2nd Virginia Regiment. He proved his service 8 May 1780 in Mecklenburg County, Virginia.

Lightfoot, John. He served as a lieutenant in the French and Indian War and received his land warrant for 2,000 acres in Virginia.

Lilly, Henry. He shared in the grant of East Greenwich, Rhode Island made to those who had rendered service in King Philip's War. The grant was made 31 October 1677.

Lilly, Reuben. He served on the expedition to Canada in 1690. His grandson,

Reuben Lilly a minor, received his land in Woburn, Massachusetts in 1738.

Linch, Joseph. He was granted 50 acres in Albany County, New York for his service as a soldier in the 40th Regiment of Foot in the French and Indian War 28 March 1771.

Lincoln, John. He served on the expedition to Canada in 1690. John Lincoln received land in Chesterfield, Massachusetts in 1739.

Lincoln, Samuel. He served in the Narraganset War from Hingham, Massachusetts. He applied for his land 4 June 1685. His son, Samuel Lincoln, received land in Bedford, New Hampshire in 1733.

Lind, Joseph. He served in the Narraganset War from Charlestown, Massachusetts. His heirs received his land in Westminster, Massachusetts in 1733.

Lindale, William. He was granted 200 acres in Albany County, New York for his service as a noncommissioned officer in the 60th Regiment of Foot in the French and Indian War 8 March 1771.

Lindsey, James. For his service as a sergeant in suppressing those involved in Ingle's Insurrection in Maryland, Lord Baltimore granted him a warrant for the 2,000 acre manor of Snow Hill in conjunction with Richard Willan 28 August 1649.

Lindsey, John. He served in the Narraganset War from Lynn, Massachusetts. He applied for his land 4 June 1685. His son-in-law, Joseph Farr, claimed his land in Amherst, New Hampshire in 1734. He also appeared as John Lynzey.

Lindsey, Robert. He was a soldier in Col. Adam Stephen's Regiment in the French and Indian War from Virginia. His heir at law, John Lindsey, received his warrant for 50 acres 18 November 1779 in Greenbrier County, Virginia.

Lingfield, Edward. He served under Capt. John Lovewell from Massachusetts in the campaign against the Indians. He was in battle at Pigwacket in May 1725. He was from Dunstable, Massachusetts and received his land in Pembroke, New Hampshire.

Linnell, Samuel. He served in the Narraganset War from Barnstable, Massachusetts and received land in Gorham, Maine in 1733.

Linnet, —. He served on the expedition to Canada in 1690. Jonathan Linnet received land in Dumbarton, New Hampshire in 1735.

Linthwaite, William. He was granted 200 acres in Albany County, New York for his service as a sergeant in the 58th Regiment of Foot in the French and Indian War 8 October 1765.

Lithgow, Robert. He served in the 5th Regiment as a soldier in the French and

Indian War. He sought his land in New York 2 February 1767. He also appeared as Robert Lethgow.

Lithgow, William. He was granted 50 acres in Berkeley County, South Carolina on the King's bounty for his service in the French and Indian War 2 October 1767.

Little, Charles. He served as a lieutenant in the French and Indian War and received 2,000 acres in Nova Scotia 7 October 1771.

Little, John. He served as a captain in the French and Indian War and petitioned for his land in New York 28 February 1770.

Little, Moses. He served in the Narraganset War from Massachusetts in 1685. His land was located in Buxton, Maine.

Little, William. He was granted 200 acres in Albany County, New York for his service as a corporal in the 46th Regiment of Foot in the French and Indian War 8 June 1771.

Littleale, John. He served on the expedition to Canada in 1690 and received land in Poland, Maine in 1739.

Littlepage, John Dickinson. He served as an ensign in the French and Indian War in Virginia. He desired to locate his 2,000 acres in Fincastle County, Virginia 31 January 1774.

Littlewood, John. He was granted 200 acres in Albany County, New York for his service as a corporal in the 60th Regiment of Foot in the French and Indian War 30 March 1771.

Littlewood, John. He was granted 200 acres in Albany County, New York for his service as a drummer in the 60th Regiment of Foot in the French and Indian War 30 October 1765.

Littlewood, William. He was granted 200 acres in Albany County, New York for his service as a noncommissioned officer in the 42nd Regiment of Foot in the French and Indian War 30 October 1765.

Livermore, David. He received land in Alstead, New Hampshire in 1771 for the service of an unidentified veteran of the expedition to Canada in 1690.

Livermore, Oliver. He served in the expedition to Canada in 1690. Amos Livermore received his land in Alstead, New Hampshire in 1771.

Livers, Christopher. He was granted 50 acres in Albany County, New York for his service as a soldier in the 60th or Royal American Regiment of Foot in the French and Indian War 30 May 1771.

Livingston, Donald. He was granted 50 acres in Albany County, New York for his service as a soldier in the 78th Regiment of Foot in the French and Indian War 13 May 1765.

Livingston, James. He was granted 50 acres in Charlotte County, New York for

for his service as a soldier in the Royal Highland Regiment of Foot in the French and Indian War 12 July 1775.

Livingston, Malcolm. He was granted 50 acres in Albany County, New York for his service as a soldier in the 42nd Regiment of Foot in the French and Indian War 30 October 1765.

Livingston, Peter Van Brugh. He received his land in West Florida for his service as a commissary in the French and Indian War 22 July 1776.

Lloyd, James. He served as a soldier in the 2nd Virginia Regiment of Regulars in 1758 under Col. William Byrd in the French and Indian War and petitioned for his 50 acre land warrant 14 February 1780 in King and Queen County, Virginia.

Lloyd, Thomas. He served as surgeon to Capt. William Preston's Company of Rangers in 1755 until disbanded in June 1756. He served a second time under the same officer with the rank of a sergeant in the French and Indian War. He received his 200 and 1,000 acre warrants in Virginia. He also received a warrant for 1,800 acres. His name also appeared as Thomas Loyd.

Lloyd, William. He served in the French and Indian War and received 1,000 acres in Nova Scotia 12 October 1771.

Loafman, Edward. He served as a soldier under Capt. Charles Lewis and Col. Adam Stephen for six months in the French and Indian War. He proved his service in Chesterfield County, Virginia 2 June 1780.

Loafman, John. He served as a soldier under Capt. Charles Lewis and Col. Adam Stephen for six months in the French and Indian War. He proved his service in Chesterfield County, Virginia 2 June 1780.

Lobdell, Nathaniel. He served on the expedition to Canada in 1690. Nathaniel Lobdell received land in Chesterfield, Massachusetts in 1739.

Lock, Joshua. He was granted 2,000 acres in Charlotte County, New York for his service as a lieutenant in a corps of rangers in the French and Indian War 23 November 1775.

Lock, Samuel. He fought under Capt. Noah Wiswall at Lamprey River and received 150 acres land from Massachusetts in 1735.

Lockart, Charles. He served as a scout to Capt. Walter Cunningham's Company of Rangers in the French and Indian War. His heir, Jacob Lockart, received the warrant for 50 acres 18 November 1779 in Greenbrier County, Virginia. He also appeared as Charles Lockheart.

Lockhart, Archibald. He served as a soldier in the 1st Virginia Regiment in the French and Indian War. He proved his right in Kentucky County, Virginia 1 February 1788. He assigned his warrant for 50 acres. He also appeared as Archibald Lockett.

Lockhart, Patrick. Since he did not serve in any corps other than the militia in the French and Indian War, it was proved in Botetourt County, Virginia 13 April 1780 that he was ineligible for bounty land.

Lockheart, James. He served as a soldier in the French and Indian War and received a warrant for 50 acres in Virginia which he assigned.

Logan, Samuel. He was granted 200 acres in Albany County, New York for his service as a corporal in the 80th Regiment of Foot in the French and Indian War 17 July 1766.

Loggins, James. He served as a corporal in Maj. William Peachey's Company in the 1st Virginia Regiment in the French and Indian War. His assignee, Martin Loggins, petitioned for his land in February 1780 in Charlotte County, Virginia.

Loggins, Richard. He served as a corporal in Capt. James Gunn's Company in the French and Indian War and assigned his right to 200 acres in Virginia to Martin Loggins.

Lomax, Daniel. He was granted 200 acres in Albany County, New York for his service as a noncommissioned officer in the 60th Regiment of Foot in the French and Indian War 8 March 1771.

Lomax, John. He served as a lieutenant under Col. William Peachey in the 1st Virginia Regiment of Regulars in the French and Indian War. His warrant for 2,000 acres was issued to his heir at law, Thomas Lomax, 2 November 1779 at Williamsburg, Virginia.

Long, David. He served as a subaltern in the French and Indian War and received his 2,000 acre land warrant in Virginia which he assigned.

Long, Henry. He was granted 50 acres for his service as a soldier in the French and Indian War. He proved his right in Montgomery County, Virginia in September 1779.

Long, John Christopher. He served as a drummer in the 48th Regiment in the French and Indian War and petitioned for 200 acres in Ulster County, New York 20 August 1766.

Long, Philip. He shared in the grant of East Greenwich, Rhode Island made to those who rendered service in King Philip's War. The grant was made 31 October 1677.

Long, William. He served as a lieutenant in the Virginia Regiment in the French and Indian War and assigned his 2,000 acre warrant in Virginia.

Longdon, Robert. He served in the French and Indian War and took his land in Fincastle County, Virginia 15 December 1772.

Longest, Dudley. He served as a soldier in the 2nd Virginia Regiment under Col. George Washington in the French and Indian War. His brother and heir, Timothy Longest, proved his right in Essex County, Virginia 21 February 1780.

Longest, Richard. He served as a soldier in the 2nd Virginia Regiment of Col. William Byrd in the French and Indian War in 1758. His brother and heir, Timothy Longest, petitioned for his 50 acres 21 February 1780 in Essex County, Virginia.

Longest, Timothy. He served as a soldier in the 2nd Virginia Regiment under Col. William Byrd in the French and Indian War. He petitioned for a warrant for 50 acres 21 February 1780 in Essex County, Virginia.

Longfellow, Stephen. He served on the expedition to Canada in 1690 and received land in Poland, Maine in 1739.

Longfellow, Stephen. He served on the expedition to Canada in 1690 and received land in Poland, Maine in 1739.

Longley, John. He served in the Narraganset War and received land in Templeton, Massachusetts in 1733.

Lood, Casper. He was granted 50 acres in Albany County, New York for his service as a soldier in the 60th or Royal American Regiment of Foot in the French and Indian War 28 March 1771.

Looker, Jonathan. He served in the Narraganset War from Lynn, Massachusetts. He applied for his land 4 June 1685 and assigned his right to land to Elnathan Jones who received same in Templeton, Massachusetts in 1733.

Looney, Peter. He served as a sergeant in Capt. Smith's Company and was a a prisoner of the French and Indians for two years from 1756 in the French and Indian War. He never returned. His heir, Peter Looney, received his warrant of 200 acres in March 1780 in Botetourt County, Virginia.

Lord, Richard. He served in the Narraganset War from Connecticut and received land in Voluntown, Connecticut in 1701.

Lord, Robert. He served in the Narraganset War from Connecticut and received land in Voluntown, Connecticut in 1701.

Lord, Saund. He served on the expedition to Canada in 1690. His nephew, Thomas Lord, Jr. at the request of his father, John Lord, received his land in Winchendon, Massachusetts in 1736.

Lord, Samuel. He was a veteran of the expedition to Canada in 1690. His nephew, Nathaniel Lord of Ipswich, Massachusetts, claimed his land in Winchendon, Massachusetts in 1736.

Lorimer, John. He was granted 2,000 acres in West Florida for his service as a surgeon in the French and Indian War 6 May 1776.

Loring, Joshua. He served as a captain in the royal navy and petitioned for

5,000 acres in New York 30 December 1765.

Loring, Josiah. He served on the expedition to Canada in 1690. Josiah Loring received land in Chesterfield, Massachusetts in 1739.

Losscon, Peter. He was a soldier in the 2nd Virginia Regiment in the French and Indian War. His heir, David Losscon, assigned his right to 50 acres. He also appeared as Peter Lawson.

Lothrop, —. He served on the expedition to Canada in 1690. Nathaniel Lothrop received land in Dumbarton, New Hampshire in 1735.

Lothrop, Thomas. He served as a captain and was in battle with the Indians in 1675 between Deerfield and Hatfield when he and upwards of three score were killed in 1675. His heirs were awarded land in Massachusetts 30 December 1735.

Lothrop, Mark. He received land in Richmond, New Hampshire in 1765 for the service of an unidentified veteran of the expedition to Canada in 1690.

Love, Edward. He was granted 50 acres in Albany County, New York for his service as a soldier in the 46th Regiment of Foot in the French and Indian War 3 October 1765.

Love, Philip. He served as a commander in the French and Indian War and received his 2,000 acre land warrant in Virginia.

Love, William. He served as a private in the 2nd Troops of Rangers under Capt. James Edward Powell. His application for 50 acres in Georgia was rejected 5 May 1767.

Lovel, John. He served in the Narraganset War from Massachusetts in 1685. His land was located in Buxton, Maine.

Lovell, Thomas. He served as a drummer in the Virginia Regiment from 1754 to 1762 in the French and Indian War. He assigned his warrant for 200 acres in Virginia. He applied in Kentucky County, Virginia 2 November 1779.

Lovell, William King. He was granted 200 acres in Tryon County, New York for his service as a sergeant in the Royal Regiment of Artillery in the French and Indian War 10 September 1774.

Lovewell, John. He served as a captain from Massachusetts on the expedition against the Indians and was slain in battle at Pigwacket 8 May 1725. He was from Groton, Massachusetts. His land was located in Pembroke, New Hampshire.

Low, Abraham. He served as a lieutenant in the French and Indian War and petitioned for 2,000 acres in Albany County, New York 24 January 1764.

Low, Arthur. He received land in Richmond, New Hampshire in 1765 for the service of an unidentified veteran of the expedition to Canada in 1690.

Low, David. He was a veteran of the expedition to Canada in 1690. He was of Ipswich, Massachusetts when he claimed his land in Winchendon, Massachusetts in 1736.

Low, Edward. He served in the 44th Regiment in the French and Indian War from New York. His service was certified in New York 9 August 1765.

Low, George. He was granted 3,000 acres in West Florida for his service as a captain in the French and Indian War 6 August 1779.

Low, Thomas. He served in the Narraganset War from Massachusetts in 1685. His land was located in Buxton, Maine.

Lowcas, Daniel. He was granted 50 acres in Albany County, New York for his service as a soldier in the 55th Regiment of Foot in the French and Indian War 26 May 1772.

Lowden, James. He served in the Narraganset War from Charlestown, Massachusetts. He received his land in Westminster, Massachusetts in 1733.

Lowe, Edward. He served as a private in the 46th Regiment in the French and Indian War. His survey for 50 acres was returned in New York 3 October 1765.

Lowell, Gideon. He served on the expedition to Canada in 1690 and received land in Poland, Maine in 1739.

Lowne, Thomas. He was granted 50 acres in Albany County, New York for his service as a soldier in the 35th Regiment of Foot in the French and Indian War 4 July 1770.

Lowrey, Thomas. He served as a private in the 35th Regiment in the French and Indian War and petitioned for land in New York 16 May 1770.

Lowrie, Gavin. He was granted 200 acres in Albany County, New York for his service as a sergeant in the 1st Regiment of Foot in the French and Indian War 18 February 1775.

Lowry, William. He served in the French and Indian War and took his land in Fincastle County, Virginia 15 December 1772.

Lubeken, Albert Minert. He was granted 2,000 acres in Albany County, New York for his service as a surgeon's mate in His Majesty's hospital in the French and Indian War 8 June 1771.

Lucas, Burton. He served as a subaltern officer in Col. William Byrd's Regiment in 1758 or 1759 in the French and Indian War. He assigned the 2,000 acre warrant received from Gov. Dunmore to Matthew Ritchie and William Bruce in Yohogania County, Virginia 27 September 1779.

Lucas, Edward. He served as a sergeant in Capt. Robert Rutherford's Company of Rangers in the French and Indian War. He received his 200 acre warrant in March 1780 in Berkeley County, Virginia.

Lucas, Daniel. He served as a private in the 55th Regiment in the French and Indian War and received 50 acres of land in New York.

Lucas, John. He served as a soldier in Col. William Byrd's Regiment in 1758 in the French and Indian War. He proved his right in Orange County, Virginia 25 November 1779. He received a warrant for 50 acres which he assigned.

Ludlow, James. He served in the French and Indian War and took his land in Fincastle County, Virginia 15 December 1772.

Ludwick, Edward. He served as a soldier in the 1st Virginia Regiment in the French and Indian War and petitioned for his 50 acres 21 April 1780 in Spotsylvania County, Virginia.

Luessner, William. He was granted 50 acres in Albany County, New York for his service as a private in the 48th Regiment of Foot in the French and Indian War. He also appeared as William Lussner.

Lufkin, Jacob. He was a veteran of the expedition to Canada in 1690. His sister, Mary Lufkin of Ipswich, Massachusetts claimed his land in Winchendon, Massachusetts in 1736 at which time Thomas Lufkin was "her next friend."

Lufkin, John. He was a veteran of the expedition to Canada in 1690. His brother, Thomas Lufkin of Ipswich, Massachusetts, claimed his land in Winchendon, Massachusetts in 1736.

Lufkin, Timothy. He served in the Narraganset War from Salem, Massachusetts. His son, Thomas Lufkin, claimed his land in Amherst, New Hampshire in 1734.

Lum, Nicholas. He served in the Narraganset War from Reading, Massachusetts. Thomas Bancroft claimed his land in Amherst, New Hampshire in 1734.

Lumbert, Caleb. He served in the Narraganset War from Barnstable, Massachusetts and received land in Gorham, Maine in 1733.

Lumbert, Jedediah. He served in the Narraganset War from Barnstable, Massachusetts and received land in Gorham, Maine in 1733. His name was originally mis-entered as Jonathan Lumber.

Lumbert, Jonathan. He served in the Narraganset War from Tisbury, Massachusetts and received land in Gorham, Maine in 1733.

Lummis, John. He served in the Narraganset War from Connecticut and received land in Voluntown, Connecticut in 1701.

Lund, William. He was from Dunstable, Massachusetts. He was on an alarm in September 1724 when he was taken captive by Indians, taken to Canada, and released in July 1725. He was granted 400 acres by

Massachusetts 5 December 1734.

Lunt, John. He served on the expedition to Canada in 1690 and received land in Poland, Maine in 1739.

Lurkin, John. He was granted 200 acres in Albany County, New York for his service as a noncommissioned officer in the 46th Regiment of Foot in the French and Indian War 8 March 1771.

Luson, John. He was granted 200 acres in Albany County, New York for his service as a drummer in the 55th Regiment of Foot in the French and Indian War 1 April 1772.

Lutnie, Peter. He served as a soldier in the French and Indian War and petitioned for his 50 acres in New York 15 October 1764.

Lydson, John. He was dangerously wounded by the Indians in 1693 and had his thigh broken. He applied for 300 acres of land in Massachusetts 30 May 1744 at which time he had been confined to his home for the last three years.

Lyford, Christopher. He was granted 50 acres in Albany County, New York for his service as a soldier in the 4th Battalion of the 60th Regiment of Foot in the French and Indian War 21 May 1768.

Lyle, David. He served as a sergeant in the 2nd Virginia Regiment of Col. William Byrd in the French and Indian War and received his 200 acre warrant in April 1780 in King William County, Virginia. He also appeared as David Lysle.

Lyllie, Aaron. He was granted 50 acres in Albany County, New York for his service as a soldier in the 80th Regiment of Foot in the French and Indian War 6 July 1771.

Lynam, Andrew. He served as a subaltern in the French and Indian War and had his service certified in Montgomery County, Virginia 8 March 1780.

Lynch, Owen. He served as a soldier in the 55th Regiment in the French and Indian War and had his service certified 3 October 1766 in New York.

Lyon, Eliab. He served on the expedition to Canada in 1690. Hezekiah Barber of Dorchester, Massachusetts received his land in Ashburnham, Massachusetts. He did so at the desire of Zachariah Lyon, son of Nathaniel Lyon, who was the eldest brother of the veteran.

Lyon, Henry. He was a veteran of the expedition to Canada in 1690. His nephew, Thomas Lyon, Jr. of Dorchester, Massachusetts, the son of Thomas Lyon who was the eldest brother of the veteran, received his land in Ashburnham, Massachusetts in 1736.

Lyon, Joseph. He served in the Narraganset War from Woodstock, Connecticut. His son, Joseph Lyon, claimed his land in Greenwich, Massachusetts in 1737.

Lyon, Michael. He was granted 50 acres in Albany County, New York for his service as a soldier in the 46th Regiment of Foot in the French and Indian War 7 October 1771.

Lyon, William. He served in the Narraganset War from Boston, Massachusetts. His son, Samuel Lyon, received land in Bedford, New Hampshire in 1733.

Lyscom, —. He served on the expedition to Canada in 1690. His son, Samuel Lyscom, received his land in Bethel, Maine in 1767.

Mabuss, John. He was granted 200 acres in Albany County, New York for his service as a corporal in the 1st Battalion in the Royal American Regiment in the French and Indian War 15 October 1765. He also appeared as John Mabeess.

McAdam, Gilbert. He was granted 3,000 acres in Albany County, New York for his service as a captain and aide de camp to the commander in chief in the French and Indian War 19 November 1771.

McAlester, James. He served as a lieutenant in the Pennsylvania Regiment in 1763. He produced his certificate of service signed by Gov. James Hamilton of Pennsylvania. He proved his service in Frederick County, Virginia 8 March 1780.

McAllister, James. He served in the French and Indian War and had his service certified in August 1767 in New York.

McAlpine, Daniel. He was granted 2,000 acres in Charlotte County, New York for his service as a captain the 2nd Battalion of the 60th Regiment under Gen. James Oglethorpe in the French and Indian War 7 October 1773.

McAnulty, William. He served in the French and Indian War and received his land in Botetourt County, Virginia.

McArthur, Allan. He was granted 50 acres in Albany County, New York for his service as a soldier in the 78th Regiment of Foot in the French and Indian War 13 May 1765.

McArthur, Duncan. He served as a private in the 78th Regiment in the French and Indian War and petitioned for his land in New York 23 March 1767.

McAshlin, Dougal. He was granted 200 acres in Charlotte County, New York for his service as a corporal in the 42nd Regiment of Foot in the French and Indian War 7 May 1772. He also appeared as Douglas McAsland.

McAtley, Barnaby. He was granted 50 acres in Albany County, New York for his service as a soldier in the 80th Regiment of Foot in the French and Indian War 30 May 1765.

McBaine, Lewis. He was granted 50 acres in Charlotte County, New York for his service as a soldier in the 42nd Regiment of Foot in the French and Indian War 1 April 1775. He also appeared as Lewis McBean.

McBean, Malcolm. He was granted 50 acres in Albany County, New York for his service as a soldier in the 42nd Regiment of Foot in the French and Indian War 30 October 1765.

McBride, Hugh. He was granted 50 acres in Albany County, New York for his service as a soldier in the 45th Regiment of Foot in the French and Indian War 1 June 1770.

McBride, James. He was granted 200 acres in Albany County, New York for his service as a sergeant in the 47th Regiment of Foot in the French and Indian War 23 April 1765.

McCabe, Ross. He was granted 50 acres in Albany County, New York for his service as a soldier in the 80th Regiment of Foot in the French and Indian War 28 June 1770.

McCaber, John. He was granted 50 acres in Albany County, New York for his service as a soldier in the 44th Regiment of Foot in the French and Indian War 1 April 1772.

Maccaboy, Thomas. He served in the French and Indian War in the 47th British Regiment and produced a certificate signed by William Russell, Colonel Commandant, that he had been discharged unfit for duty. He proved his service in Fauquier County, Virginia 27 March 1780.

Macado, John. He was granted 50 acres in Albany County, New York for his service as a soldier in the 47th Regiment of Foot in the French and Indian War 7 October 1765.

Maccay, John. He served in the French and Indian War and petitioned for land in New York 17 March 1767.

McCall, Duncan. He served as a private in the French and Indian War and petitioned for his 50 acres of land 3 June 1772 in New York.

McCallister, James. He was granted 340.82 acres in Berks County, Pennsylvania for his service as a lieutenant in the French and Indian War 3 February 1769.

McCann, John. He was granted 50 acres in Albany County, New York for his seven years of service as a soldier in an independent of company of foot in the French and Indian War 15 August 1766.

McCann, Thomas. He served as a soldier in the French and Indian War and and petitioned for 50 acres on the King's bounty in South Carolina 10 August 1764.

Maccantosh, John. He served on the expedition to Canada in 1690. John Maccantosh received land in Warwick, Massachusetts in 1738.

McCarmick, George. He served as an ensign in the Company of Rangers under Col. Henry Bouquet. He proved his right in Yohogania County, Virginia in February 1780. He assigned his warrant for 2,000 acres.

McCarter, Duncan. He was granted 50 acres in Albany County, New York for his service as a soldier in the 77th Regiment of Foot in the French and Indian War 7 May 1767.

McCarthy, Charles. He was granted 50 acres in Albany County, New York for his service as a soldier in the 80th Regiment of Foot in the French and Indian War 26 July 1765.

McCarthy, John. He served as a sergeant in the 40th Regiment in the French and Indian War and petitioned for his 200 acres in New York 24 October 1764.

Macarty, Charles. He shared in the grant of East Greenwich, Rhode Island made to those who had rendered service in King Philip's War. The grant was made 31 October 1677.

McCarty, Daniel. He served as a private in the Virginia Regiment under Col. William Byrd in the French and Indian War. Sarah Raines was his sister and heiress, and her husband, Giles Raines, received the warrant for 50 acres in Virginia.

McCarty, John. He was granted 200 acres in Albany County, New York for his service as a drummer in the 80th Regiment of Foot in the French and Indian War 8 October 1771.

McCarty, Thomas. He served as a sergeant in the 2nd Battalion of the 60th Regiment in the French and Indian War and petitioned for 200 acres in New York 19 August 1766.

McCauley, Neal. He served as a soldier in Capt. John Field's Company in Col. William Byrd's Regiment in 1758 in the French and Indian War. He petitioned for his warrant for 50 acres 21 February 1780 in Culpeper County, Virginia. He also appeared as Neil McCauley.

McCauley, Thomas. He served as a corporal in the 2nd Virginia Regiment in the French and Indian War and received his 50 acre warrant 13 April 1780 Albemarle County, Virginia. He also appeared as Thomas McCawley.

McChombeck, Duncan. He was granted 200 acres in Albany County, New York for his service as a sergeant in the 42nd Regiment in the French and Indian War 30 October 1765.

McClanachan, Alexander. He served as a lieutenant in the 1st Virginia Regiment in the French and Indian War and later as a captain of volunteers in Col. Henry Bouquet's expedition against the Indians in 1764. He received 3,000 acres in Virginia.

McClanachan, John. He served as a lieutenant under Capt. Charles Lewis in a company of independents on the expedition against the Indians under Col. Henry Bouquet in 1764. His warrant for 1,000 acres was issued to his orphaned heir, John McClanachan, in care of his guardians, Alexander McClanachan and Alexander Sinclair, 18 November 1779 in Augusta County, Virginia.

McClanachan, Robert. He served as a sergeant in Capt. Alexander McClanachan's Company of Independents under Col. William Byrd in the expedition against the Indians in 1764. His children, John McClanachan and Robert McClanachan, received his warrant for 200 acres 19 November 1779 in Augusta County, Virginia. Alexander McClanachan was the administrator of his estate.

McClanahan, John. He served as a subaltern in the French and Indian War in Virginia. His heir, John McClanahan, received his warrant for 1,000 acres in Virginia.

McClarron, Charles. He was granted 50 acres in Charlotte County, New York for his service as a soldier in the 70th Regiment of Foot in the French and Indian War 18 October 1775.

McClay, David. He was granted 200 acres in Albany County, New York for his service as a corporal in the 73rd Regiment of Foot in the French and Indian War 18 April 1769.

McClayland, Daniel. He served as a soldier in Col. William Byrd's Regiment in 1758 in the French and Indian War and received a warrant for 50 acres 28 October 1779 in Orange County, Virginia. He also appeared as Daniel McClelland.

McClean, John. He was granted 200 acres in Albany County, New York for his service as a noncommissioned officer in the French and Indian War 7 October 1765.

McCloud, Murdock. He received his 50 acres of land in West Florida for his service as a private in the French and Indian War 9 April 1777.

McClung, Charles. He served as a captain in the 3rd Pennsylvania Regiment under Col. Hugh Mercer in the French and Indian War. His heir, James McClung, received three warrants for 1,000 acres each in Virginia. James McClung had been an inhabitant of Virginia for above 30 years.

McClung, Joseph. He served as a sergeant under Col. William Byrd against the Cherokee in 1760 in the French and Indian War and received his 50 acre warrant 21 March 1780 in Greenbrier County, Virginia.

McClure, John. He served as an ensign in the 1st Pennsylvania Regiment in 1760 in the French and Indian War. He proved his service in

Yohogania County, Virginia 28 March 1780.

McColl, Donald. He was granted 50 acres in Albany County, New York for his service as a soldier in the 77th Regiment of Foot in the French and Indian War 13 May 1765.

McColl, John. He was granted 50 acres in Charlotte County, New York for his service as a soldier in the Royal Regiment of Foot in the French and Indian War 12 July 1775.

McCollester, James. He served as a lieutenant in the French and Indian War in 1763 in the Pennsylvania Regiment. He was commissioned by Gov. James Hamilton of Pennsylvania and stated he had been a resident of Virginia four years. He assigned his 2,000 acre warrant in March 1780 in Frederick County, Virginia.

Maccomber, John. He served in the Narraganset War from Taunton, Massachusetts. His son, Thomas Maccomber, claimed his land in Greenwich, Massachusetts in 1737.

McConacky, Robert. He served as a corporal in the 78th Regiment in the French and Indian War and petitioned for land in New York 11 September 1771. He also appeared as Robert McConnachy.

McConey, John. He was granted 200 acres in Albany County, New York for his service as a noncommissioned officer in the 60th Regiment of Foot in the French and Indian War 5 April 1771.

McConkey, David. He served as a corporal in the 77th Regiment in the French and Indian War and received 200 acres of land in Albany County, New York 9 November 1764.

McCorin, Moses. He served as a soldier about six months in the 1st Virginia Regiment in the Cherokee Expedition in 1760 in the French and Indian War. His heir and daughter, Mary McCorin, received his 50 acre warrant in May 1780 in Montgomery County, Virginia.

McCormac, Caesar. He served as an ensign in the French and Indian War and petitioned for 2,000 acres in New York 5 November 1766.

McCormack, William. He served as a lieutenant in a company of rangers under Col. Henry Bouquet. He proved his right in Yohogania County, Virginia 28 February 1780. He assigned his warrant for 2,000 acres.

McCormick, George. He served as an ensign in a ranging company in 1764 and proved his service in Yohogania County, Virginia 28 February 1780.

McCown, Moses. He served about six months in the additionals to the 1st Virginia Regiment in the Cherokee Expedition in 1760 in the French and Indian War. His daughter, Mary McCown, received his 50 acre warrant in Virginia in 1780 in Montgomery County, Virginia.

McCoy, Finley. He served as a noncommissioned officer in the French and Indian War and was entitled to 200 acres in Virginia which he assigned.

McCoy, James. He served as a corporal in the French and Indian War and was entitled to 200 acres in Virginia which he assigned.

McCoy, John. He served as a soldier in the company of volunteer rangers under Capt. William Phillips in 1763 in the French and Indian War. He proved his right in Louisa County, Virginia 14 February 1780. He assigned his right to 50 acres.

McCra, John. He served as a noncommissioned officer in the French and Indian War and received 200 acres in Nova Scotia 24 January 1777.

McCrindle, James. He was granted 200 acres in Albany County, New York for his service as a sergeant in the 4th Battalion in the Royal American Regiment of Foot in the French and Indian War 9 December 1769.

McCubbins, Robert. He served as a soldier in the 4th Battalion Royal Americans in the French and Indian War and petitioned for his land 22 October 1766 in New York.

McCubbons, Joseph. He served in the French and Indian War as a noncommissioned officer and assigned his land 20 May 1767.

McCullough, Philip. He was granted 50 acres in Albany County, New York for his service as a soldier in the 55th Regiment of Foot in the French and Indian War 21 May 1768.

McCullock, Kenneth. He served as an ensign in the 78th Regiment in the French and Indian War and petitioned for 2,000 acres of land in New York 27 April 1768.

McCullock, Nathaniel. He was granted 2,000 acres in Albany County, New York for his service as a lieutenant in the 42nd Regiment of Foot in the French and Indian War 3 May 1765.

McCullock, Robert. He was granted 200 acres in Albany County, New York for his service as a sergeant in the 60th Regiment of Foot in the French and Indian War 25 May 1771. He also appeared as Robert McCullogh.

McCullum, William. He was granted 50 acres in Albany County, New York for his service as a soldier in the 60th Regiment of Foot in the French and Indian War 17 September 1765.

McCutchen, James. He served as a soldier in Capt. John Blagg's Company in Col. William Byrd's Regiment in 1760 in the French and Indian War. He received his 50 acre warrant in May 1780 in Henry County, Virginia.

McCutchen, Samuel. He served as a soldier in Lewis's Rangers in the French and Indian War. He proved his service in Augusta County, Virginia 21

March 1780.

Mackdafillin, Robert. He served on the expedition to Canada in 1690. Daniel Mackdafilling received his land in Bethel, Maine in 1767.

McDiffit, John. He served as a sergeant in the French and Indian War and received 200 acres of land in Virginia.

McDonald, Alexander. He was granted 50 acres in Albany County, New York for his service as a soldier in the 42nd Regiment of Foot in the French and Indian War 30 October 1765.

McDonald, Alexander, Jr. He was granted 50 acres in Albany County, New York for his service as a soldier in the 42nd Regiment of Foot in the French and Indian War 30 October 1765.

McDonald, Alexander. He was granted 200 acres in Charlotte County, New York for his service as a noncommissioned officer in the 42nd Regiment of Foot in the French and Indian War 1 April 1775.

McDonald, Alexander. He served as a captain lieutenant in the French and Indian War and petitioned for 3,000 acres in New York 10 April 1764.

McDonald, Alexander. He served as a lieutenant in the French and Indian War and was entitled to 2,000 acres which he assigned in Virginia.

McDonald, Alexander. He served as a soldier under Capt. Israel Christian in the French and Indian War and had his service certified in Montgomery County, Virginia 3 May 1780. He had proved his service in Botetourt County, Virginia 9 March 1780.

McDonald, Angus. He served as a private in the 78th Regiment in the French and Indian War and petitioned for his 50 acres in New York.

McDonald, Angus. He served as a noncommissioned officer at the battle of the Meadows and afterwards as a noncommissioned officer under Col. George Washington when he was promoted to ensign in the regiment under Col. Adam Stephen until the regiment was reduced. He also served as commissary at Red Stone Fort for two or three years. His service was proved in Frederick County, Virginia 4 April 1780.

McDonald, Angus. He served a lieutenant in Capt. George Berkeley's Company under Maj. Gen. Sir John Irvin, Colonel of His Majesty's 74th Regiment of Foot, in the French and Indian War. He assigned his 2,000 acre warrant in Virginia.

McDonald, Donald. He was granted 200 acres in Albany County, New York for his service as a corporal in the 77th Regiment of Foot in the French and Indian War 13 May 1765.

McDonald, Donald. He was granted 50 acres in Albany County, New York for his service as a soldier in the 42nd Regiment of Foot in the French and Indian War 30 October 1765.

McDonald, John. He served in the French and Indian War and qualified for 50 acres of land in Nova Scotia which he transferred to William McDonald 7 January 1781.

McDonald, Donald. He was granted 2,000 acres in West Florida for his service as a major in the French and Indian War 29 April 1778.

McDonald, Finley. He was granted 50 acres in Albany County, New York for his service as a soldier in the 42nd Regiment of Foot in the French and Indian War 30 October 1765.

McDonald, George. He was granted 50 acres in Albany County, New York for his service as a private in the 28th Regiment of Foot in the French and Indian War 8 June 1771.

McDonald, Hanson. He served in the French and Indian War in the Old Virginia Regiment. He proved his right in 1779 in Greenbrier County, Virginia and received a warrant for 50 acres of land 17 November 1779. He also appeared as Hanson McDowell.

McDonald, Isaac. He served as a soldier under Maj. McNiel in Col. Adam Stephen's Regiment in the French and Indian War in 1762. He proved his right in Henry County, Virginia 25 March 1780. He assigned his right to 50 acres.

McDonald, James. He served as a sergeant in the 80th Regiment in the French and Indian War and had his service certified in New York in January 1768.

McDonald, James. He was granted 50 acres in Charlotte County, New York for his service as a soldier in the Royal Regiment of Foot in the French and Indian War 12 July 1775.

McDonald, James. He served as a lieutenant in the 60th Regiment in the French and Indian War and petitioned for his 2,000 acres in New York 24 September 1765.

McDonald, John. He was granted 50 acres in Albany County, New York for his service as a soldier in the 78th Regiment of Foot in the French and Indian War 1 May 1765.

McDonald, John. He was granted 50 acres in Albany County, New York for his service as a soldier in the 78th Regiment of Foot in the French and Indian War 13 May 1765.

McDonald, John. He was granted 200 acres in Albany County, New York for his service as a corporal in the 77th Regiment of Foot in the French and Indian War 23 March 1765.

McDonald, John. He served as a soldier in the French and Indian War and assigned his right to William McDonald who located the 50 acres in Nova Scotia 7 January 1781.

McDonald, John. He was granted 2,000 acres in Albany County, New York for his service as a noncommissioned officer in the 80th Regiment of Foot in the French and Indian War 28 October 1765.

McDonald, John. He was granted 50 acres in Albany County, New York for his service as a soldier in the 55th Regiment of Foot in the French and Indian War 28 October 1765.

McDonald, John. He was granted 50 acres in Albany County, New York for his service as a soldier in the 42nd Regiment of Foot in the French and Indian War 30 October 1765.

McDonald, John. He served as a soldier in the French and Indian War and assigned his right to William McDonald who located the 50 acres in Nova Scotia 7 January 1781.

McDonald, John. He served as a soldier under Capt. John Field in Gen. Forbes's expedition in 1758 in the French and Indian War. He proved his right in Culpeper County, Virginia 18 October 1779. He received a warrant for 50 acres which he assigned.

McDonald, John. He served as a soldier in the French and Indian War in 1760. He assigned his right to 50 acres in Virginia. He proved his right in Caroline County, Virginia in February 1780.

McDonald, Malcolm. He was granted 50 acres in Charlotte County, New York for his service as a soldier in the 42nd Regiment of Foot in the French and Indian War 1 April 1775.

McDonald, Malcolm. He was granted 50 acres in Charlotte County, New York for his service as a soldier in the Royal Highland Regiment of Foot in the French and Indian War 12 July 1775.

McDonald, Murdock. He was granted 50 acres in Charlotte County, New York for his service as a soldier in the 42nd Regiment of Foot in the French and Indian War 12 October 1774.

McDonald, Neil. He was granted 200 acres in Albany County, New York for his service as a noncommissioned officer in the 55th Regiment of Foot in the French and Indian War 28 March 1771.

McDonald, Norman. He was granted 50 acres in Albany County, New York for his service as a soldier in the 42nd Regiment of Foot in the French and Indian War 30 October 1765.

McDonald, Roderick. He was granted 200 acres in Albany County, New York for his service as a sergeant in the 77th Regiment of Foot in the French and Indian War 3 October 1765.

McDonald, Ronald. He was granted 50 acres in Albany County, New York for his service as a soldier in the 42nd Regiment of Foot in the French and Indian War 30 October 1765.

McDonald, Theodosius. He served as an ensign in the Virginia Regiment in the French and Indian War. His brother and heir, Daniel McDonald, received his land warrant for 2,000 acres in Virginia.

McDonald, William. He was granted 50 acres in Albany County, New York for his service as a soldier in the 77th Regiment of Foot in the French and Indian War 6 August 1765.

McDonald, William. He was granted 50 acres in Albany County, New York for his service as a soldier in the 60th or Royal American Regiment of Foot in the French and Indian War 8 June 1771.

McDonald, William. He served in the French and Indian War and received land in Nova Scotia 7 January 1781.

McDougal, George. He was granted 2,000 acres in Albany County, New York for his service as a lieutenant in the 60th Regiment of Foot in the French and Indian War 21 October 1765.

McDougal, John. He was granted 200 acres in Albany County, New York for his service as a noncommissioned officer in the 4th Battalion in the Royal American Regiment of Foot in the French and Indian War 8 July 1771.

McDougall, John. He received his 2,000 acres of land in West Florida for his service as a warrant officer in the French and Indian War 7 November 1776.

McDowell, James. He served as an officer in the French and Indian War. His heir, James McDowell, received his 2,000 acre warrant in Virginia.

McDowell, Samuel. He served as an officer in the French and Indian War. He received his 2,000 acre warrant in Virginia.

McDugall, Dugall. He served as a soldier in the 40th Regiment in the French and Indian War and petitioned for his land 28 October 1766 in New York.

McDugall, Henry. He served as a private in the French and Indian War and petitioned for his land in New York in November 1766. He also appeared as Henry McDougal.

McDugald, Angus. He was granted 200 acres in Albany County, New York for his service as a noncommissioned officer in the 42nd Regiment of Foot in the French and Indian War 26 April 1765.

McEkron, John. He was granted 50 acres in Albany County, New York for his service as a soldier in the 80th Regiment of Foot in the French and Indian War 26 July 1765.

McFadden, Pharrel. He served as a soldier for six months under Col. William Peachey in the French and Indian War and received his 50 acre warrant 8 November 1779 in Buckingham County, Virginia.

McFall, Hoseah. He was granted 50 acres in Albany County, New York for his service as a soldier in the 28th Regiment of Foot in the French and Indian War 23 September 1771.

McFall, Patrick. He was granted 50 acres in Albany County, New York for his service as a soldier in the 80th Regiment of Foot in the French and Indian War 26 July 1765.

McFarlan, John. He was granted 200 acres in Albany County, New York for his service as a sergeant in the 80th Regiment of Foot in the French and Indian War 28 June1765.

McFarland, Daniel. He served as a captain in Col. Abijah Willard's Regiment raised in Massachusetts under Gen. Jeffery Amherst for the reduction of Canada in 1760 in the French and Indian War and received his 3,000 acre warrant in Virginia.

McFarlane, Alexander. He was granted 50 acres in Charlotte County, New York for his service as a soldier in the Royal Highland Regiment of Foot in the French and Indian War 12 July 1775.

McFarlane, Archibald. He was granted 50 acres in Albany County, New York for his service as a soldier in the 60th Regiment of Foot in the French and Indian War 28 June 1770.

McFarlane, Parlane. He was granted 50 acres in Charlotte County, New York for his service as a soldier in the 42nd Regiment of Foot in the French and Indian War 1 April 1775.

McFarlane, Walter. He was granted 200 acres in Albany County, New York for his service as a corporal in the 42nd Regiment of Foot in the French and Indian War 20 January 1769.

McFarran, Martin. Since he did not serve in any corps other than the militia in the French and Indian War, he was not eligible for bounty land as proved in Botetourt County, Virginia 13 April 1780.

McFee, John. He served in the French and Indian War as a soldier. His service in behalf of his heirs was certified in Montgomery County, Virginia 8 March 1780.

McGarrah, John. He was granted 200 acres in Albany County, New York for his service as a sergeant in the 28th Regiment of Foot in the French and Indian War 18 February 1775.

McGarry, John. He was granted 200 acres in Albany County, New York for his service as a sergeant in the 28th Regiment of Foot in the French and Indian War 18 February 1775.

McGauley, James. He served as a private in the French and Indian War and petitioned for 50 acres on the King's bounty in South Carolina 7 April 1767.

McGavock, James. He served as a captain of a company of volunteers against the Shawnee under Col. Thomas Nash in 1757. He served four months in the French and Indian War. He received 3,000 acres 6 April 1780 in Montgomery County, Virginia. He also appeared as James McGarvock.

McGee, John. He served in the 28th Regiment in the French and Indian War and petitioned for his land 18 October 1766 in New York.

McGee, William. He was granted 200 acres in Albany County, New York for his service as a sergeant in the 28th Regiment of Foot in the French and Indian War 18 February 1775.

McGehee, James. He served as a soldier under Capt. William Phillips in the French and Indian War in 1763 and received a warrant for 50 acres in Virginia.

McGehee, William. He served as a soldier under Capt. William Phillips in the French and Indian War in 1763 and received his 50 acre warrant in Virginia.

McGilorary, Fargher. He served as a soldier in the French and Indian War and received 50 acres in Nova Scotia 30 April 1781.

McGilvary, John. He was granted 50 acres in Albany County, New York for his service as a soldier in the 78th Regiment in the French and Indian War 13 May 1765.

McGinnis, John. He was granted 200 acres in Albany County, New York for his service as a corporal in the 60th Regiment of Foot in the French and Indian War 1 April 1772.

McGlashan, Leonard. He was granted 200 acres in Charlotte County, New York for his service as a noncommissioned officer in the 42nd Regiment of Foot in the French and Indian War 7 July 1773.

McGowen, James. He was granted 50 acres in Albany County, New York for his service as a soldier in the 46th Regiment of Foot in the French and Indian War 4 July 1770.

McGreeger, Thomas. He served as a soldier in Capt. William Preston's Company of Rangers in the French and Indian War. He assigned his 50 acres in Virginia. He proved his service in Augusta County, Virginia 18 November 1779.

McGreever, John. He served as a private in the French and Indian War and petitioned for the laying out of his land 21 January 1767 in New York.

McGregor, Alexander. He was granted 200 acres in Berkeley County, South Carolina on the King's bounty 6 February 1773. He served as a noncommissioned officer in the French and Indian War.

McGregor, John. He served as a corporal in the 1st or Royal Regiment in the

French and Indian War and was at the sieges of Louisbourg and Isle au Nou. He had his service certified 13 January 1767 in New York.

McGregor, John. He served as a soldier in the French and Indian War and assigned his right to William McDonald who received the 50 acres in Nova Scotia 7 January 1781.

McGregor, Patrick. He was granted 200 acres in Charlotte County, New York for his service as a corporal in the 78th Regiment of Foot in the French and Indian War 18 July 1774.

McGregor, William. He was granted 50 acres near Fort Charlotte, South Carolina on the King's bounty for his service in the French and Indian War 13 May 1768.

McGrowder, Peter. He was granted 50 acres in Albany County, New York for his service in the 46th Regiment of Foot in the French and Indian War 15 August 1766.

McGuire, James. He served as a noncommissioned officer in the French and Indian War and petitioned for his land in New York 19 February 1772.

McGuire, James. He served in Capt. Christian's Company of Regulars in the 2nd Virginia Regiment under Col. William Byrd in the French and Indian War. He proved his service in Botetourt County, Virginia 9 December 1779.

McGuire, Patrick. He served as a soldier in the Old Virginia Regiment in the French and Indian War and proved his service in Frederick County, Virginia 3 August 1780.

McGuire, Thomas. He was granted 200 acres in Albany County, New York for his service as a corporal in the 80th Regiment of Foot in the French and Indian War 17 August 1765.

McHarge, Alexander. He was granted 50 acres in Albany County, New York for his service as a soldier in the 1st Regiment of Foot in the French and Indian War 26 July 1765.

McInnis, Donald. He was granted 50 acres in Albany County, New York for his service as a soldier in a regiment of foot in the French and Indian War 19 May 1770.

McIntire, Donald. He was granted 200 acres in Albany County, New York for his service as a corporal in the 78th Regiment of Foot in the French and Indian War 13 May 1765.

McIntire, John. He was granted 50 acres in Albany County, New York for his service as a soldier in the 78th Regiment of Foot in the French and Indian War 10 May 1765.

McIntire, John. He was granted 200 acres in Albany County, New York for his service as a corporal in the 77th Regiment of Foot in the French and Indian War 29 October 1765.

McIntosh, Alexander. He was granted 3,000 acres in Albany County, New York for his service as a captain in the 77th Regiment of Foot in the French and Indian War 7 August 1764.

McIntosh, Alexander. He was granted 50 acres in Charlotte County, New York for his service as a soldier in the 42nd Regiment of Foot in the French and Indian War 1 April 1775.

McIntosh, Alexander. He was granted 200 acres in West Florida for his service as a noncommissioned officer in the French and Indian War 9 October 1777.

McIntosh, Daniel. He was granted 200 acres in Albany County, New York for his service as a sergeant in the 80th Regiment of Foot in the French and Indian War 6 July 1771.

McIntosh, Daniel. He was granted 200 acres in Albany County, New York for his service as a noncommissioned officer in the 42nd Regiment of Foot in the French and Indian War 14 April 1772. He was probably the Donald McIntosh who served as a corporal in the 42nd or Royal Highland Regiment.

McIntosh, Donald. He served as a corporal in the 42nd Regiment in the French French and Indian War. His service was certified in New York 17 November 1767.

McIntosh, Duncan. He served in the French and Indian War and petitioned for 50 acres of land in New York 15 December 1773.

McIntosh, Hugh. He was granted 50 acres in Albany County, New York for his service as a soldier in the 77th Regiment of Foot in the French and Indian War 13 May 1765.

McIntosh, James. He was granted 50 acres in Berkeley County, South Carolina on the King's bounty for his service in the French and Indian War 11 August 1774.

McIntosh, John. He was granted 50 acres in Albany County, New York for his service as a soldier in the 78th Regiment of Foot in the French and Indian War 10 May 1765.

McIntosh, Lachlan. He was granted 1,500 acres in St. David Parish, Georgia for his service as a lieutenant in an independent company in South Carolina under Captain Raymond Demerie in the French and Indian War 3 November 1772.

McIntosh, Robert. He served as a soldier in the 42nd Regiment in the French and Indian War and had his service certified 13 October 1766 in New York. He assigned his right to Robert Buchanan 20 January 1767.

McIntosh, William. He was granted 2,000 acres in Albany County, New York for his service as a lieutenant in the 27th Regiment of Foot in the French and Indian War 7 May 1765.

McIntosh, William. He was granted 50 acres in Charlotte County, New York for his service as a soldier in the Royal Highland Regiment of Foot in the French and Indian War 12 July 1775.

McIntosh, William. He received 1,766 and 724 acres of land in West Florida for his service as a lieutenant in the French and Indian War 11 May 1774.

McIntyre, Archibald. He served as a corporal in the 40th Regiment in the French and Indian War and petitioned for land 28 October 1766 in New York.

McIntyre, Duncan. He was granted 50 acres in Charlotte County, New York for his service as a soldier in the 42nd Regiment of Foot in the French and Indian War 1 April 1775.

MacIntyre, Peter. He was granted 50 acres in Albany County, New York for his service as a soldier in the 42nd Regiment of Foot in the French and Indian War 30 October 1765.

Macinven, Angus. He was granted 50 acres in Albany County, New York for his service as a soldier in the 42nd Regiment of Foot in the French and Indian War 30 October 1765.

McIver, John. He served as a soldier in the French and Indian War and assigned his right to William McDonald who received the 50 acres in Nova Scotia 7 January 1781.

McKachan, Andrew. He was granted 200 acres in Albany County, New York for his service as a corporal in the 42nd Regiment of Foot in the French and Indian War 30 October 1765. He also appeared as Andrew McKachern.

McKaga, Alexander. He was granted 50 acres in Albany County, New York for his service as a soldier in the 60th Regiment of Foot in the French and Indian War 29 May 1765. He was disbanded after he returned from Niagara to Philadelphia.

Mackay, Aeneas. He was granted 200 acres in Ulster County, New York for his service as a sergeant in the 60th Regiment of Foot in the French and Indian War 3 October 1771.

McKay, Aeneas. He served as Deputy Commissary under General Commissary Leake in 1771 and 1772. He proved his service in Yohogania County, Virginia 28 February 1780.

McKay, Angus. He served as a soldier in the 42nd Regiment of Foot in the French and Indian War and received 50 acres in Charlotte County,

New York 12 October 1774.

McKay, Colin. He served as a soldier in the French and Indian War and received 50 acres in Nova Scotia 9 December 1777.

Mackay, Donald. He was granted 50 acres in Albany County, New York for his service as a soldier in the 42nd Regiment of Foot in the French and Indian War 30 October 1765.

McKay, Donald. He was granted 164 acres in Albany County, New York for his service as a corporal in the 42nd or Royal Highland Regiment of Foot in the French and Indian War 2 May 1770.

McKay, Finlay. He served as a corporal in a troop of light horse under Robert Stewart in 1755, in the Old Virginia Regiment under Col. George Washington, then under Col. Adam Stephen, then assistant commissary at Fort Cumberland for 18 months, and lastly for nine months under Dr. Thomas Walker. He proved his service in Frederick County, Virginia 4 April 1780.

MacKay, Francis. He served in the French and Indian War and petitioned for his land in New York 11 June 1771.

McKay, Hugh. He was granted 100 acres in Granville County, South Carolina on the King's bounty for his service in the French and Indian War 6 February 1773.

McKay, John. He was granted 50 acres in Albany County, New York for his service as a soldier in an independent company of foot in the French and Indian War 30 October 1765.

MacKay, Samuel. He served in the French and Indian War and petitioned for his land in New York 11 June 1771.

McKee, Alexander. He served as a captain in the French and Indian War and petitioned for his 2,000 acres in New York 28 February 1770.

McKee, Alexander. He was granted 500 acres in Pennsylvania for his service in the French and Indian War 14 February 1769.

McKee, Nathanael. He served under Lt. Gershom Flagg at Lamprey River. He assigned his land to Nicholas Bartlet who received it in Massachusetts 9 January 1735.

McKendree, John. He served as a sergeant in the 2nd Virginia Regiment under Col. William Byrd in 1758 in the French and Indian War. He petitioned for 200 acres 14 February 1780 in King and Queen County, Virginia.

McKenley, Brian. He served in the French and Indian War and petitioned for his land in New York in November 1766.

McKennin, Kenneth. He was granted 50 acres in Albany County, New York for his service as a soldier in the 77th Regiment of Foot in the French and Indian War 10 May 1765.

McKenny, Dennis. He was granted 50 acres in Granville County, South Carolina on the King's bounty 6 February 1773. He served as a private in the French and Indian War.

McKenny, John. He was granted 200 acres in Albany County, New York for his service as a soldier in the 40th Regiment of Foot in the French and Indian War 13 May 1765.

McKensie, John. He served as a sergeant in the 1st Virginia Regiment in the French and Indian War and received his 200 acre warrant 2 November 1780 in Kentucky County, Virginia.

McKenzie, Alexander. He was granted 200 acres in Albany County, New York for his service as a sergeant in the 48th Regiment of Foot in the French and Indian War 29 October 1765.

McKenzie, Alexander. He was granted 200 acres in Albany County, New York for his service as a corporal in the 42nd Regiment of Foot in the French and Indian War 30 October 1765.

McKenzie, Alexander. He was granted 50 acres in Albany County, New York for his service as a soldier in the 42nd Regiment of Foot in the French and Indian War 9 May 1771.

McKenzie, Alexander. He served as a soldier in the 78th Regiment in the French and Indian War. His service was certified in New York 2 March 1766.

McKenzie, Alexander. He served as a captain under Maj. Grant in the French and Indian War and was killed near Pittsburgh. He was born in North Britain [i.e. Scotland]. His legal representatives, Alexander McKay and his wife Jane McKay, received his 3,000 acre warrant in Virginia. Jane McKay was his second cousin and only heir in America. His service was proved in Bedford County, Virginia 22 May 1780.

McKenzie, Hector. He was granted 200 acres in Charlotte County, New York for his service as a noncommissioned officer in the 4th Battalion of the Royal American Regiment in the French and Indian War 4 August 1774.

McKenzie, John. He was granted 200 acres in Albany County, New York for his service as a sergeant in the 77th Regiment of Foot in the French and Indian War 6 June 1765.

McKenzie, John. He was granted 50 acres in Charlotte County, New York for his service as a soldier in the 42nd Regiment of Foot in the French and Indian War 12 October 1774.

McKenzie, John. He was granted 150 acres on the Saludy River in South Carolina on the King's bounty 21 June 1765. He served as a private in the French and Indian War.

McKenzie, Kenneth. He was granted 200 acres in Albany County, New York for his service as a noncommissioned officer in the 77th Regiment of Foot in the French and Indian War 26 April 1765.

McKenzie, Kenneth. He was granted 50 acres in Albany County, New York for his service as a soldier in the 78th Regiment of Foot in the French and Indian War 13 May 1765.

McKenzie, Kenneth. He served as a soldier in the French and Indian War and assigned his right to William McDonald who located the 50 acres in Nova Scotia 7 January 1781.

McKenzie, Robert. He served in the French and Indian War and received a warrant for 3,000 acres in Virginia.

McKenzie, Roderick. He was granted 50 acres in Albany County, New York for his service as a soldier in the 55th Regiment of Foot in the French and Indian War 28 June 1770.

McKenzie, Roderick. He served as a sergeant in the French and Indian War and was killed. His legal representatives, Alexander McKay and his wife Jane McKay, received his 200 acre warrant in Virginia. Jane McKay was his second cousin and only heir in America. His service was proved in Bedford County, Virginia 22 May 1780.

McKenzie, William. He was granted 50 acres in Albany County, New York for his service as a soldier in the 55th Regiment of Foot in the French and Indian War 28 October 1765.

McKercher, Donald. He served in the French and Indian War and petitioned for his land in Albany County, New York in April 1774.

MacKey, Aneas. He was granted 300 acres in Pennsylvania for his service in the French and Indian War 1 April 1769.

Mackey, Angus. He was granted 50 acres in Albany County, New York for his service as a soldier in the 42nd Regiment of Foot in the French and Indian War 30 October 1765.

Mackey, Daniel. He served on the expedition to Canada in 1690. Norman Clark received his land in Bethel, Maine in 1767.

McKinnin, Neil. He was granted 200 acres in Albany County, New York for his service as a corporal in the 77th Regiment of Foot in the French and Indian War 31 May 1771. He also appeared as Neal McKinnon.

McKinsey, John. He was granted 200 acres in Albany County, New York for his service as a sergeant in the 55th Regiment of Foot in the French and Indian War 1 April 1772.

McKintosh, John. He served as a lieutenant in the 42nd Regiment in the French and Indian War and petitioned for his 2,000 acres of land in New

York 27 February 1769.

MacKintosh, Robert. He served in the Royal Highland Regiment of Foot as a private sentinel and sought 50 acres in Georgia 7 February 1769.

Mackintosh, William. He served as a private in the French and Indian War and petitioned for 50 acres on the King's bounty in South Carolina 3 July 1764.

MacKintosh, William. He served as a corporal in an independent company in South Carolina in the French and Indian War and applied for 200 acres of land in Georgia 2 November 1769.

McKintosh, William. He was granted 50 acres in Craven County, South Carolina on the King's bounty for his service as a private in the French and Indian War 21 June 1765.

McKinvin, John. He was granted 50 acres in Albany County, New York for his service as a soldier in the 78th Regiment of Foot in the French and Indian War 13 May 1765.

McKoy, Hugh. He served in the French and Indian War and took his land in Fincastle County, Virginia 15 December 1772.

McLane, Laughlen. He served in the French and Indian War from Virginia and received a warrant for 100 acres.

McLaran, David. He was granted 350 acres on the north side of the Saludy River in South Carolina on the King's bounty for his service in the French and Indian War 21 June 1765.

McLaren, James. He was granted 50 acres in Albany County, New York for his service as a soldier in the 55th Regiment of Foot in the French and Indian War 28 October 1765.

McLaughlan, Edward. He served as a sergeant in the 3rd Battalion of the Pennsylvania Regiment of Gen. Forbes in the French and Indian War. He received his 200 acre warrant in Virginia.

McLaughlan, James. He served as a sergeant major in the 3rd Battalion of the Pennsylvania Regiment under Gen. Forbes in the French and Indian War. His heir, Edward McLaughlan, received his 200 acre warrant in Virginia.

McLaughlan, John. He served as a sergeant in the 3rd Battalion of the Pennsylvania Regiment in the French and Indian War. He assigned his 200 acre warrant to Edward McLaughlan in Virginia.

McLaughlin, Michael. He served as a lieutenant in the French and Indian War and petitioned for land 30 December 1765 in New York.

McLean, David. He served as a soldier in the French and Indian War in the 78th Regiment in New York. He sought his land in February 1764.

McLean, Donald. He was granted 200 acres in Albany County, New York for his service as a sergeant in the 42nd Regiment of Foot in the French and Indian War 30 October 1765.

McLean, Donald. He was granted 2,000 acres in Albany County, New York for his service as a surgeon in the 77th Regiment of Foot in the French and Indian War 11 November 1768.

McLean, Francis. He was granted 50 acres in Albany County, New York for his service as a soldier in the 17th Regiment of Foot in the French and Indian War 28 October 1765.

McLean, Hugh. He was granted 50 acres in Charlotte County, New York for his service as a soldier in the 42nd Regiment of Foot in the French and Indian War 1 April 1775.

McLean, James. He served as a corporal in the 60th Regiment in the French and Indian War and petitioned for his land in New York 17 March 1767.

McLean, John. He was granted 50 acres in Charlotte County, New York for his service as a soldier in the Royal Highland Regiment of Foot in the French and Indian War 12 July 1775.

McLean, John. He served as a corporal in the 77th Regiment in the French and Indian War and petitioned for his 200 acres in Albany County, New York 2 November 1764.

McLean, Neal. He was granted 2,000 acres in Albany County, New York for his service as a lieutenant in the 47th Regiment of Foot in the French and Indian War 11 November 1768.

McLean, William. He served as a private in the 42nd Regiment in the French and Indian War and petitioned for his 50 acres of land 3 June 1772 in New York.

McLelland, John. He prayed for a grant of land for service in the French and Indian War in New York 1 July 1767.

McLennan, William. He was granted 50 acres in Charlotte County, New York for his service as a soldier in the 42nd Regiment of Foot in the French and Indian War 1 April 1775.

McLeod, Donald. He served in the French and Indian War and petitioned for 50 acres of land in New York 8 December 1773.

McLeod, Donald. He served as a soldier in the French and Indian War and assigned his right to William McDonald who received the 50 acres in Nova Scotia 7 January 1781.

McLeod, Norman. He was granted 3,000 acres in Albany County, New York for his service as a captain in the 80th Regiment of Foot in the French and Indian War 29 September 1770.

McLeod, Robert. He served in the French and Indian War. His service was certified in New York 14 February 1771.

McLeod, Roderick. He was granted 200 acres in Charlotte County, New York for his service as a corporal in the Royal Highland Regiment of Foot in the French and Indian War 12 July 1775.

McLoud, Norman. He was granted 200 acres in Albany County, New York for his six years of service as a sergeant in the 77th Regiment of Foot in the French and Indian War 10 May 1765.

McLoud, Norman. He was granted 50 acres in Albany County, New York for his service as a soldier in the 40th Regiment of Foot in the French and Indian War 13 May 1765.

McMahon, John. He served as a soldier in Capt. Peter Hogg's Company of Rangers in the French and Indian War. He requested his 50 acres 17 November 1779 in Augusta County, Virginia.

McMann, William. He was granted 50 acres in Albany County, New York for his service as a soldier in the 60th Regiment of Foot in the French and Indian War 17 September 1765.

McMean, William. He was granted 216 and 248 acres in Cumberland County, Pennsylvania for his service as an ensign in the French and Indian War 3 February 1769.

McMillan, Andrew. He served as a colonel in the French and Indian War and received 2,000 acres in Conway, New Hampshire in 1765. He was from Concord.

McMillan, Hector. He was granted 50 acres in Albany County, New York for his service as a soldier in the 42nd Regiment of Foot in the French and Indian War 30 October 1765.

McMullan, Patrick. He was granted 50 acres in Albany County, New York for his service as a soldier in the 55th Regiment of Foot in the French and Indian War 26 July 1765.

McMullin, Edward. He served as a soldier in Capt. John Dickerson's Company of Rangers in 1758 and 1759 in the French and Indian War. He petitioned for his 50 acres in February 1780 in Botetourt County, Virginia.

McMullin, John. He served as a soldier in Capt. John Dickerson's Company of Rangers in 1758 in the French and Indian War. He petitioned for his 50 acres in February 1780 in Botetourt County, Virginia.

McNab, James. He was granted 200 acres in Albany County, New York for his service as a sergeant in the 42nd Regiment of Foot in the French and Indian War 30 October 1765.

McNabb, Finley. He was granted 200 acres in the fork of the Santee and Wateree Rivers in South Carolina on the King's bounty 10 January 1771. He served as a corporal in the French and Indian War.

McNabb, Hugh. He served in the 80th Regiment in the French and Indian War. His petition was referred to the surveyor general in New York 22 April 1774.

McNeal, Angus. He served as a lieutenant in Capt. George Berkeley's Company under Maj. Gen. Sir John Irvin, Colonel of His Majesty's 74th Regiment of Foot, in the French and Indian War and assigned his 2,000 acre warrant in Virginia. He proved his service in Yohogania County, Virginia 28 February 1780. He also appeared as Anguish McNeill.

McNeal, Hugh. He was granted 200 acres in Charlotte County, New York for his service as a noncommissioned officer in the 80th Regiment of Foot in the French and Indian War 18 July 1774.

McNeal, John. He was granted 50 acres in Gloucester County, New York for his service as a soldier in the 44th Regiment of Foot in the French and Indian War 5 April 1770.

McNeil, Hector. He was granted 50 acres in Albany County, New York for his service as a soldier in the 80th Regiment of Foot in the French and Indian War 28 October 1765.

McNeill, Hugh. He served as a drummer in the Old Virginia Regiment under Capt. Gabriel Throgmorton in the French and Indian War. He proved his right in Botetourt County, Virginia in March 1780. He assigned his warrant for 50 acres.

McNelly, John. He served as a noncommissioned officer in the French and Indian War. His legal representative, Sarah Gibbs, received his 200 acre warrant in Virginia.

McNicholl, John. He was granted 200 acres in Albany County, New York for his service as a corporal in the 77th Regiment of Foot in the French and Indian War 15 August 1765.

MacPharland, John. He was granted 50 acres in Albany County, New York for his service as a soldier in the 42nd Regiment of Foot in the French and Indian War 30 October 1765.

McPherson, Alexander. He was granted 50 acres in Albany County, New York for his service as a soldier in the 1st Regiment of Foot in the French and Indian War 26 July 1765.

McPherson, Alexander. He was granted 200 acres in Albany County, New York for his service as a sergeant in the 42nd Regiment of Foot in the French and Indian War 30 October 1765.

McPherson, Donald. He was granted 200 acres in Albany County, New York for his service as a drummer in the 42nd Regiment of Foot in the French and Indian War 30 October 1765.

McPherson, Evan. He served as a corporal in the French and Indian War and petitioned for a grant of 200 acres in New York 2 July 1766.

McPherson, Hugh. He was granted 50 acres in Albany County, New York for his service as a soldier in the 42nd Regiment of Foot in the French and Indian War 30 October 1765.

McPherson, John. He was granted 200 acres in Albany County, New York for his service as a corporal in the 42nd Regiment of Foot in the French and Indian War 28 June 1765.

McPherson, John. He was granted 200 acres in Albany County, New York for his service as a noncommissioned officer in the 42nd Regiment of Foot in the French and Indian War 30 October 1765.

McPherson, John. He was granted 200 acres in Albany County, New York for his service as a sergeant in the 77th Regiment of Foot in the French and Indian War 7 May 1767.

McPherson, John. He was granted 50 acres in Albany County, New York for his service as a private in a regiment of foot in the French and Indian War 19 May 1770.

McPherson, Robert. He served as a private in the French and Indian War and petitioned for land in New York 8 July 1772.

McPherson, Thomas. He was granted 50 acres in Albany County, New York for his service as a soldier in the 78th Regiment of Foot in the French and Indian War 13 May 1765.

McQueen, James. He was granted 50 acres in St. George Parish, Georgia for his service in the 78th Regiment of Foot commanded by Col. Simon Fraser in the French and Indian War 19 January 1773. He was discharged in Quebec.

McQuery, William. He served as a soldier in Col. William Byrd's Regiment in the French and Indian War in 1758. He asked for his 50 acres 18 March 1783 in Lincoln County, Virginia [i.e. Kentucky].

McQuin, Daniel. He was granted 50 acres in Albany County, New York for his service as a soldier in the 17th Regiment of Foot in the French and Indian War 28 June 1770.

McTartin, Archy. He served as a soldier in the French and Indian War and petitioned for his land in New York 3 January 1770.

McTavish, John. He served as a lieutenant in the Highland Regiment in the French and Indian War and petitioned for land 4 April 1766 in New New York. His son, Simon McTavish, petitioned for the land in behalf of his father.

McVae, John. He was granted 200 acres in Albany County, New York for his service as a corporal in the 60th or Royal American Regiment in the

French and Indian War 8 June 1771. He also appeared as John McVee.

McVicar, Archibald. He was granted 200 acres in Albany County, New York for his service as a sergeant in the 77th Regiment in the French and Indian War 10 May 1765.

McVicar, Dougal. He served as a private in the 55th Regiment in the French and Indian War and petitioned for his land in New York 10 December 1773.

McVicar, Duncan. He was granted 2,000 acres in Albany County, New York for his service as a quartermaster in the 55th Regiment of Foot in the French and Indian War 12 July 1765.

McWilliams, Thomas. He was granted 200 acres in Charlotte County, New York for his service as a corporal in the 55th Regiment of Foot in the French and Indian War 25 January 1773.

Madison, Humphrey. He served as a captain and an ensign in Capt. John Dickerson's Company in 1756 and lost his life in the French and Indian War. His heiress, Catherine Arbuckle the wife of William Arbuckle, received his 2,000 acre land warrant in Virginia.

Madison, John. He served as a sergeant in the French and Indian War and was entitled to a 200 acre warrant which he assigned in Virginia in 1774.

Madison, John. He served as a captain of a company of volunteers on the expedition under Col. Thomas Nash against the Shawnee in 1757 in the French and Indian War and served four months until the unit was disbanded. He made his petition in 1780 in Montgomery County, Virginia. He received 3,000 acres of land.

Madison, William. He served as a corporal in the Virginia Regiment under Col. William Byrd in the French and Indian War. His heir, Thomas Arburthnott, received his warrant for 200 acres.

Madocks, John. He was from Watertown, Massachusetts and sought 100 acres for his former service. His application was rejected 27 August 1726.

Maginnis, Robert. He served as a captain in the French and Indian War and petitioned for land 30 December 1766 in New York.

Mahan, Peter. He was granted 50 acres in Albany County, New York for his service as a private in the 80th Regiment of Foot in the French and Indian War 5 April 1771.

Maid, John. He served in the French and Indian War and took his land in Fincastle County, Virginia 15 December 1772.

Mailey, Barney. He was granted 50 acres in Albany County, New York for his service as a private in the 18th Regiment of Foot in the French and Indian War 8 June 1771.

Mair, Charles. He served as a sergeant in the 42nd Regiment in the French and Indian War and petitioned for his 200 acres in New York 19 January 1775.

Maitland, Richard. He was granted 5,000 acres in Albany County, New York for his service as Adjutant General to the troops in Quebec in the French and Indian War 23 June 1767.

Majory, Joseph. He served in the Narraganset War from Marblehead, Massachusetts. His son, Joseph Majory, claimed his land in Amherst, New Hampshire in 1734.

Maker, —. He served on the expedition to Canada in 1690. James Maker received land in Dumbarton, New Hampshire in 1735.

Maker, James. He served in the Narraganset War from Yarmouth, Massachusetts and received land in Gorham, Maine in 1733.

Malco, Frederick. He was granted 200 acres in Albany County, New York for his service as a noncommissioned officer in the 60th or Royal American Regiment in the French and Indian War 28 March 1771.

Malcomb, George. He served in the French and Indian War and took his land in Fincastle County, Virginia 15 December 1772.

Mallato, Richard. He was granted 50 acres in Albany County, New York for his service as a soldier in the 80th Regiment of Foot in the French and Indian War 26 July 1765. He also appeared as Richard Mallats.

Mallett, Jonathan. He was granted 3,000 acres in Albany County, New York for his service as a surgeon in a military hospital in the French and Indian War 28 October 1765.

Mallett, Stephen. He served as a soldier in Capt. James Gunn's Company in the French and Indian War in Virginia. He proved his right in Mecklenburg County, Virginia 14 February 1780. He assigned his right to 50 acres.

Malone, Cornelius. He served as a private in the 2nd Battalion 60th Regiment in the French and Indian War and petitioned for his 50 acres of land in New York 2 March 1774.

Malone, Thomas. He served as a soldier in the New Jersey Regiment under Col. Peter Schuyler. He proved his service in Fauquier County, Virginia 28 February 1780 at which time he had been an inhabitant of Virginia seven years.

Man, Richard. He served in the Narraganset War from Hebron, Connecticut. He claimed his land in Greenwich, Massachusetts in 1737.

Man, Thomas. He served in the Narraganset War from Wrentham, Massachusetts. His son, John Man, claimed his land in Greenwich, Massachusetts in 1737.

Manley, William. He served in the Narraganset War from Boston, Massachusetts. He received land in Bedford, New Hampshire in 1733.
Manlove, Christopher. He served as an apothecary's mate in the French and Indian War and petitioned for his 3,000 acres in New York 6 September 1764.
Mann, John. He served as an ensign in Capt. Cunningham's Company under Col. Henry Bouquet in 1764. It was proved that Moses Mann was his heir at law in Botetourt County, Virginia 10 February 1780.
Mann, Thomas C. He served as a staff officer in the French and Indian War petitioned for his land in New York 24 December 1774.
Mann, Thomas. He served as a soldier in Capt. John Dickerson's Company of Rangers in 1759 in the French and Indian War. His service was proved in February 1780 in Botetourt County, Virginia. His heir was Moses Mann, the son of John Mann.
Mann, William. He served as a sergeant in Col. William Peachey's Battalion in the French and Indian War. His eldest son and heir, Moses Mann, assigned his 200 acre warrant in Virginia.
Manning, Nicholas. He served in the Narraganset War from Salem, Massachusetts. His nephew, Samuel Manning, claimed his land in Amherst, New Hampshire in 1734.
Manone, Jacob. He was granted 50 acres in Albany County, New York for his service as a private in the 60th Regiment of Foot in the French and Indian War 5 April 1771. He also appeared as Jacob Marrone.
Mansfield, Joseph. He served in the Narraganset War from Lynn, Massachusetts and petitioned for his land 4 June 1685.
Manson, William. He served as a private in the French and Indian War and petitioned for his land in New York 2 May 1768.
Mant, Thomas Pocock. He served in the French and Indian War and had his service certified in New York 14 July 1764.
Marble, Gershom. He received land in Richmond, New Hampshire in 1765 for the service of an unidentified veteran of the expedition to Canada in 1690.
March, John. He served on the expedition to Canada in 1690 and received land in Poland, Maine in 1739.
March, John. He served as a colonel and was from Newbury. His only son, Capt. John March, received 400 acres for his father's and his own land in Massachusetts 3 December 1736.
Marchan, Lazarus. He served as a private in the French and Indian War and petitioned for land in New York 17 March 1767.
Marchel, John. He served in the French and Indian War and petitioned for

land in New York 17 March 1767.

Mark, —. He served on the expedition to Canada in 1690. James Mark received land in Dumbarton, New Hampshire in 1735.

Markham, William. He was granted 5,000 acres in Tryon County, New York for his service as a field officer in the 47th Regiment of Foot in the French and Indian War 5 April 1774.

Markin, Thomas. He was granted 50 acres in Albany County, New York for his service as a soldier in the 46th Regiment of Foot in the French and Indian War 8 March 1771.

Markle, Jacob. He served as a soldier in the French and Indian War and received 50 acres in Nova Scotia 21 May 1781.

Marr, John. He was granted 1,500 acres in West Florida for his service as a warrant officer in the navy in the French and Indian War at the reduction of Quebec 23 September 1778.

Marr, John. He served as a soldier in one of the Virginia Regiments and died in service in the French and Indian War. His heir, Daniel Marr, received his warrant for 50 acres 27 March 1780 in Fauquier County, Virginia.

Marra, Dennis. He was granted 50 acres in Albany County, New York for his service as a soldier in the 86th Regiment of Foot in the French and Indian War 28 October 1765.

Marscraft, John. He served on the expedition to Canada in 1690. John Marscraft received land in Warwick, Massachusetts in 1736.

Marsh, Jonathan. He served on the expedition to Canada in 1690 and received land in Poland, Maine in 1739.

Marsh, Zacheriah. He served on the expedition to Canada in 1690. His heirs received land in Chesterfield, Massachusetts in 1739.

Marshall, Alexander. He was granted 200 acres of land in Albany County, New York for his service as a corporal in the 28th Regiment of Foot in the French and Indian War 25 May 1771.

Marshall, John. He served as a private in the 60th Regiment in the French and Indian War and was granted land in New York 16 April 1767.

Marshall, Roger. He was granted 600 acres at Pamunkey in Virginia for his service as commander of Fort Royal and for garrisoning same at his own expense 14 March 1649/50. He had kept ten men there for the past three years.

Marshall, William. He received his land in West Florida for his service as a staff officer in the French and Indian War 26 March 1774 and on 21 October 1774.

Marston, John. He served in the Narraganset War from Sudbury,

Massachusetts. He received his land in Westminster, Massachusetts in 1733.

Martain, Jesse. He served as an ensign in the Virginia Regiment in 1758 in the French and Indian War and received his 2,000 acre warrant in March 1780 in Ohio County, Virginia. He also appeared as Jesse Martin.

Martain, Richard. He served as a private in Capt. Mordecai Buckner's Company in the 1st Virginia Regiment in the French and Indian War. He proved his right in Charlotte County, Virginia 7 February 1780. He assigned his 50 acres. He also appeared as Richard Martin.

Martin, Brotherton. He served as a subaltern in the French and Indian War and received 2,000 acres in Nova Scotia 7 June 1783.

Martin, George. He served as a soldier under Capt. William Preston in the French and Indian War and received his 50 acre warrant in Virginia. He proved his service in Washington County, Virginia 21 March 1780.

Martin, Jasper. He was granted 50 acres in Albany County, New York for his service as a soldier in the 80th Regiment of Foot in the French and Indian War 18 July 1770.

Martin, Jesse. He served as an ensign in the French and Indian War in the Virginia Regiment in 1758. He had his service certified 6 March 1780 in Yohogania County, Virginia. On the same date he or a man of the same name proved that he served as an artificer in 1760.

Martin, John. He served on the expedition to Canada in 1690. Peter Martin was admitted to his land in Lyndeboro, Maine in 1736.

Martin, John. He served in the Narraganset War in Massachusetts in 1685. His land was located in Buxton, Maine.

Martin, John. He served in the Narraganset War from Rehoboth, Massachusetts. His son, John Martin, claimed his land in Greenwich, Massachusetts in 1737.

Martin, John. He served as a lieutenant in the French and Indian War and petitioned for his 2,000 acres in New York 16 January 1764.

Martin, Josiah. He served as Lieutenant Colonel of the 68th Regiment in the French and Indian War and petitioned for his 20,000 acres of land in New York 2 September 1774. He was governor of North Carolina.

Martin, Peter. He served as a soldier in the 28th Regiment in the French and Indian War and petitioned for his land in New York 6 August 1774.

Martin, Thomas. He was granted 50 acres in Albany County, New York for his service as a soldier in the 80th Regiment of Foot in the French and Indian War 28 June 1765.

Martin, Thomas. He was a soldier in the French and Indian War and received his warrant for 50 acres in November 1779 in Montgomery County, Virginia. His name may have been Thomas Mastin.

Masdam, Robert. He served as a private in the 60th Regiment in the French and Indian War and petitioned for his land in New York 6 April 1772.

Mason, John. He was granted 500 acres in Connecticut for his service in the Pequot War 5 January 1641/2. He served as a captain.

Mason, John. He was granted 50 acres in Gloucester County, New York for his service as a soldier in the 28th Regiment of Foot in the French and Indian War 5 April 1770.

Mason, Joseph. He served on the expedition to Canada in 1690. Nehemiah Mason received his land in Alstead, New Hampshire in 1771.

Mason, Robert. He served as a soldier in the French and Indian War and proved his service in Frederick County, Virginia 6 June 1780.

Mason, Sampson. He served in the Narraganset War from Rehoboth, Massachusetts. He claimed his land in Greenwich, Massachusetts in 1737.

Mason, Thomas. He was granted 200 acres in Albany County, New York for his service as a sergeant in the Inniskilling Regiment of Foot in the French and Indian War 8 April 1771.

Mason, Thomas. He served as a drummer in the Virginia Battalion under Col. William Byrd in 1758 in the French and Indian War. He received his 200 acre warrant 6 April 1780 in Hanover County, Virginia.

Massey, John. He was granted 2,000 acres in West Florida for his service as a surgeon in the French and Indian War 9 June 1776.

Masten, Thomas. He served as a soldier in the French and Indian War and proved his right to 50 acres in Montgomery County, Virginia 2 August 1780.

Matheson, Robert. He was granted 200 acres in Albany County, New York for his service as a corporal in the 42nd Regiment of Foot in the French and Indian War 30 October 1765.

Mathews, James. He was granted 50 acres in Albany County, New York for his service as a soldier in the 15th Regiment of Foot in the French and Indian War 30 October 1765.

Mathews, Richard. He served as a soldier in Capt. Christopher Hudson's Company of Regulars in 1758 and as a corporal in Capt. Samuel Meredith's Company of Regulars in 1760 in the French and Indian War. He applied in Louisa County, Virginia 14 February 1780. He assigned his right to two warrants for 250 acres.

Mathews, Robert. He was granted 200 acres in Gloucester County, New York for his service as a noncommissioned officer in an independent company of foot in the French and Indian War 5 April 1770.

Mathews, Thomas. He served as a soldier in the 80th Regiment in the French and Indian War and petitioned for 50 acres in New York 3 October 1766.

Mathewson, Donald. He was granted 50 acres in Albany County, New York for his service as a soldier in the 77th Regiment of Foot in the French and Indian War 6 August 1765.

Matthews, Daniel. He served in the Narraganset War from Boston, Massachusetts. His daughter, Rebecca Hannan, received land in Bedford, New Hampshire in 1733.

Matthews, John. He served in the Narraganset War from Yarmouth, Massachusetts and received land in Gorham, Maine in 1733.

Matthews, John. He served as a soldier in the French and Indian War and received 50 acres in Nova Scotia 9 October 1776.

Matthews, Thomas. He served as a soldier under Capt. James Gunn in the French and Indian War in Virginia. He proved his right in Mecklenburg County, Virginia 13 March 1780. He assigned his right to 50 acres.

Matts, William. He was granted 200 acres in Charlotte County, New York for his service as a noncommissioned officer in the 18th Regiment of Foot in the French and Indian War 12 October 1774.

Maturin, Peter. He was granted 50 acres in Albany County, New York for his service as a private in the 60th or Royal American Regiment of Foot in the French and Indian War 8 June 1771.

Maudesley, Samuel. He served as a captain the Narraganset War from Boston, Massachusetts. His son-in-law, Jonathan Williams, received land in Bedford, New Hampshire in 1733.

Maunsel, John. He was granted 5,000 acres in Albany County, New York for his service as a lieutenant colonel in the 72nd Regiment of Foot in the French and Indian War 7 March 1771.

Maxey, John. He served as a soldier in the French and Indian War and was discharged in 1756 by Col. George Washington after six months of service. He received his 50 acre warrant 20 April 1780 in Powhatan County, Virginia.

Maxey, Marcus. He was granted 200 acres in Charlotte County, New York for his service as a noncommissioned officer in the 4th Battalion of the 60th Regiment of Foot in the French and Indian War 12 October 1774. He also appeared as Marcus Mackey.

Maxey, William. He served as a soldier for six months under Capt. James Gunn in 1760 in the French and Indian War. He proved his right in

Buckingham County, Virginia 8 November 1779. He assigned his 50 acre warrant.

Maxwell, John. He served as a sergeant in the artillery train in the French and Indian War. His 200 acre warrant was issued to his heir, John Maxwell, in Virginia who had been an inhabitant of Virginia for twenty years.

Maxwell, William. He was granted 2,000 acres in Charlotte County, New York for his service as Deputy Commissary of Stores and Provisions in the French and Indian War 12 June 1775.

Maxwell, William. He served as a sergeant in the 35th Regiment in the French and Indian War. He received his 200 acre warrant in May 1780 in Rockbridge County, Virginia. He had been discharged at Quebec 6 October 1759.

May, James. He served as a soldier under Col. George Washington from 1756 to 1762 in the French and Indian War. He petitioned for 50 acres 9 March 1780 in Warwick County, Virginia.

May, Jesse. He served as a soldier in the French and Indian War and received a warrant for 50 acres in Virginia 19 October 1779. Capt. Thomas Bullit certified his service.

May, John. He served as a lieutenant and adjutant in the Virginia Regiment under Col. Adam Stephen in the French and Indian War in 1762. He requested his 2,000 acres 10 January 1780 in James City County, Virginia.

Mayn, Ezekiel. He served in the Narraganset War from Connecticut and received land in Voluntown, Connecticut in 1701.

Mays, John. He served as a corporal in the Old Virginia Regiment in the French and Indian War and received a warrant for 200 acres 21 February 1780 in Goochland County, Virginia.

Mays, Jonathan. He served on the expedition to Canada in 1690. Jonathan Mays received land in Chesterfield, Massachusetts in 1739.

Meachen, William. He was granted 50 acres in Albany County, New York for his service as a soldier in the 17th Regiment of Foot in the French and Indian War 1 April 1771.

Mead, Abiel. He served as a soldier under Col. William Byrd in 1760 in the French and Indian War. He received a warrant for 50 acres 23 August 1779 in Bedford County, Virginia.

Meade, James. He served on the expedition to Canada in 1690. Henry Hale petitioned for his land in Raymond, Maine in 1735.

Means, John. He served in the Narraganset War from Boston, Massachusetts. He received land in Bedford, New Hampshire in 1733.

Meany, William. He served in the French and Indian War and received his land in Nova Scotia 12 October 1771.

Mease, Richard. He served as a private in the 60th Regiment in the French and Indian War and had his service certified in New York 8 March 1774.

Meaton, John. He was granted 50 acres in Albany County, New York for his service as a soldier in the 44th Regiment of Foot in the French and Indian War 28 March 1771.

Mechum, John. He served under Col. William Byrd in 1760 in the French and Indian War. He proved his service in Bedford County, Virginia 27 March 1780.

Medcalf, Valentine. He was granted 200 acres in Albany County, New York for his service as a drummer in the 55th Regiment of Foot in the French and Indian War 1 April 1771.

Medscar, Henry. He served as a private in the French and Indian War and petitioned for 50 acres on the King's bounty in South Carolina 3 December 1766.

Mee, Francis. He was granted 50 acres in Albany County, New York for service as a soldier in the 80th Regiment in the French and Indian War 29 October 1765.

Meeks, William. He was granted 50 acres in Gloucester County, New York for his service as a soldier in the 28th Regiment in the French and Indian War 5 April 1770.

Meisinger, Conrad. He was granted 50 acres in Gloucester County, New York for his service as a soldier in the 4th Battalion of the 60th Regiment in the French and Indian War 5 April 1770.

Mekel, John. He was granted 45 acres in Tryon County, New York for service as a soldier in the 2nd Battalion of the Royal American Regiment in the French and Indian War 30 December 1774.

Meldrum, James. He was granted 200 acres in Albany County, New York for his service as a corporal in the 42nd Regiment of Foot in the French and Indian War 30 October 1765.

Melton, James. He served as a soldier in Capt. Samuel Overton's Company of Rangers in 1756 and in Capt. John Posey's Company in 1758 in the French and Indian War. He proved his right in Louisa County, Virginia 11 October 1779. He assigned his right to two warrants for 50 acres each.

Melton, James. He served as a soldier in Capt. Christian's Company in the French and Indian War from Virginia and obtained 50 acres of land.

Melton, William. He served as a soldier under Capt. Samuel Overton in 1756, Capt. Christopher Hudson in 1758, and a ranger under Capt. Christian

1760 in the French and Indian War. He proved his rights in Louisa County, Virginia 11 October 1779. He assigned each of his warrants for 50 acres.

Melvin, David. He served as a lieutenant under Capt. John Lovewell from Massachusetts and was in the battle of Pigwacket in May 1725. He was from Concord, Massachusetts and received his land in Pembroke, New Hampshire.

Melvin, Eleazer. He served under Capt. John Lovewell from Massachusetts and was in the battle of Pigwacket in May 1725. He was from Concord, Massachusetts and received his land in Pembroke, New Hampshire.

Mennis, Robert. He served as a soldier in Capt. William Christian's Company under Col. William Byrd in the French and Indian War. He received his warrant for 50 acres 28 March 1780 in Buckingham County, Virginia.

Menott, George. He was a veteran of the expedition to Canada in 1690. His nephew, Mr. William Cooper of Boston, Massachusetts, received his land in Ashburnham, Massachusetts in 1736.

Menyard, John. He served as a soldier in the 48th Regiment in the French and Indian War. His survey for 50 acres was returned 25 October 1765 in New York.

Menzie, Alexander. He was granted 50 acres in Charlotte County, New York for his service as a soldier in the Royal Highland Regiment of Foot in the French and Indian War 12 July 1775.

Menzies, Alexander. He was granted 2,000 acres in Albany County, New York for his service as a lieutenant in the 77th Regiment of Foot in the French and Indian War 11 September 1764.

Menzies, Charles. He served as a lieutenant in the 42nd Regiment in the French and Indian War from New York and petitioned for his 2,000 acres of land 2 November 1764.

Menzies, Thomas. He was granted 2,000 acres in Albany County, New York for his service as a lieutenant in the 77th Regiment of Foot in the French and Indian War 11 September 1764.

Mercer, George. He served as a captain in 1754 in the French and Indian War under Col. Joshua Fry. In 1755 he was on the expedition against Fort DuQuesne under Capt. Robert Stewart. He commanded an independent company. He was promoted to the rank of lieutenant colonel in the 2nd Virginia Regiment under Col. William Byrd until it was reduced. His warrants for 14,000 acres were issued 22 March 1780 in Richmond, Virginia.

Mercer, Hugh. He served as a colonel in the 3rd Battalion of the Pennsylvania

Regiment in the French and Indian War and received his 5,000 acre land warrant in Virginia. His heirs were mentioned 1 September 1780.

Mercer, James. He was an officer of a company in the expedition in 1754 against Cartagena and returned in 1755 in the French and Indian War. He was a captain in the 18th Regiment of Foot under Col. Dunbar against Fort DuQuesne where he was a major. His heir was his brother, John Mercer, of Stafford County when James Mercer died in 1768. His brother's son was John Francis Mercer, an infant. He received three warrants for 5,000 acres 22 March 1780 in Richmond, Virginia.

Mercer, John Fenton. He served as a ensign in 1754 in the French and Indian War under Col. Joshua Fry. In 1755 he was on the expedition against Fort DuQuesne. He was appointed lieutenant of horse under Capt. Robert Stewart. He was killed by the enemy. His warrants totaling 5,000 acres were assigned to his brother, George Mercer, 22 March 1780 in Richmond, Virginia.

Mercer, Robert. He served as a private in the French and Indian War and was granted land in New York 1 April 1767.

Meriam, Robert. He served on the expedition to Canada in 1690. Joseph Meriam received his land in Bethel, Maine in 1767.

Meridith, Samuel. He served as a captain in the Virginia Regiment under Col. William Byrd in the French and Indian War and desired to locate his warrant for 3,000 acres in Fincastle County, Virginia in1774.

Merrett, Nicholas. He served on the expedition to Canada in 1690. Joseph Blany was admitted to his land in Lyndeboro, Maine in 1736.

Merrill, Steven. He served in Lovewell's War in Massachusetts and received his land in Petersham, Massachusetts in 1733.

Merriman, Nathaniel. He served as a lieutenant in the Narraganset War. The town of Wallingford, Connecticut granted him 10 acres for his services 26 January 1684/5. On 14 February 1686 the town granted him 8 acres of soldier's land. His son, John Merriman, of Wallingford, Connecticut was granted 50 acres 13 October 1698 for his father's service.

Merriman, Nathaniel. He served in the Narraganset War and was slain. The town of Wallingford, Connecticut granted his brothers 5 acres 26 January 1684/5.

Metcalf, Thomas. He served on the expedition to Canada in 1690. Joseph Metcalf requested Edward Eveleth to receive his land in Winchendon, Massachusetts in 1736.

Metcalf, Valentine. He served as a drummer in the 55th Regiment in the

French and Indian War and petitioned for land in New York 4 April 1768.

Meuvenbeldt, Peter. He served as a sergeant in the French and Indian War and petitioned for his 200 acres in New York 18 October 1766.

Meyers, —. His widow was granted 300 acres in Pennsylvania for his service in the French and Indian War 1 April 1769.

Michael, John. He served in the French and Indian War. His service was certified in New York 1 September 1774.

Michael, Peter. He was granted 50 acres in Gloucester County, New York for his service as a soldier in the 4th Battalion in the 60th Regiment of Foot in the French and Indian War 5 April 1770.

MickelJohn, Walter. He was granted 200 acres in Albany County, New York for his service as a noncommissioned officer in the 55th Regiment of Foot in the French and Indian War 28 March 1771.

Midden, Walter. He served as a private in the 46th Regiment in the French and Indian War and had his service certified in New York in January 1767. He also appeared as Walter Middon.

Middleton, Peter. He was granted 5,000 acres in Albany County, New York for for his service as Surgeon General in the expedition against Crown Point in the French and Indian War 24 February 1770.

Middleton, Robert. He was granted 50 acres in Albany County, New York for his service as a soldier in the 60th Regiment of Foot in the French and Indian War 25 May 1771.

Milbank, William. He was granted 200 acres on a branch of the Little Saludy River in South Carolina on the King's bounty for his service in the French and Indian War 15 February 1770.

Miles, Samuel. He served in the Narraganset War and received his land in Templeton, Massachusetts in 1733.

Millbank, William. He was granted 200 acres in St. Paul Parish, Georgia for his service as a sergeant in the 3rd Battalion of the 16th or Royal American Regiment commanded by Brig. Gen. William Haverland 3 January 1775. He had been discharged at Havana.

Milledge, John. He served as a captain in the 1st Troop of Rangers and sought 3,000 acres in Georgia. His application was rejected 5 May 1767.

Millen, James. He served as a soldier in the French and Indian War from Virginia and received 50 acres of land. He also appeared as James Millens.

Miller, Charles. He was granted 200 acres in Albany County, New York for his service as a sergeant in the 60th Regiment of Foot in the French and Indian War 16 October 1765.

Miller, Francis. He received land in West Florida for his service as a captain commandant of an independent company in the French and Indian War on 18 April 1776 and 22 July 1776.

Miller, Humphrey. He served in the Narraganset War from Charlestown, Massachusetts. His heirs received his land in Westminster, Massachusetts in 1733.

Miller, Jacob. He served in the French and Indian War and petitioned for his land in New York 14 November 1774.

Miller, James. He was granted 50 acres in Albany County, New York for his service as a soldier in the 60th Regiment of Foot in the French and Indian War 26 September 1765.

Miller, James. He served in the 2nd Virginia Regiment under Col. William Byrd in 1758 in the French and Indian War. Christopher Miller proved his service in Middlesex County, Virginia 27 March 1780.

Miller, John. He served in the Narraganset War from Milton, Massachusetts. His brother, Samuel Miller, received his land in Bedford, New Hampshire in 1733.

Miller, John. He was granted 200 acres in Albany County, New York for his service as a corporal in the 28th Regiment of Foot in the French and Indian War 8 March 1771.

Miller, John. He was granted 200 acres in Albany County, New York for his service as a corporal in the 28th Regiment of Foot in the French and Indian War 25 May 1771.

Miller, John. He was granted 50 acres in Albany County, New York for his service as a soldier in the 55th Regiment of Foot in the French and Indian War 1 April 1772.

Miller, John. He served as a noncommissioned officer in the French and Indian War and received 200 acres in Nova Scotia 9 December 1777.

Miller, John. He served as a soldier in Capt. William Preston's Company in 1758 and 1759 in the French and Indian War and received his 50 acre acre warrant 22 March 1780 in Greenbrier County, Virginia.

Miller, Patrick. He served as a soldier in Capt. William Preston's Company of Rangers in 1758 in the French and Indian War. He received a warrant for 50 acres 15 February 1780 in Augusta County, Virginia.

Miller, Paul. He was granted 200 acres in Albany County, New York for his service as a corporal in the 60th Regiment of Foot in the French and Indian War 29 October 1765.

Miller, Paul. He served as a corporal in the French and Indian War and petitioned for 200 acres in South Carolina 1 October 1765.

Miller, Robert. He was a soldier in the French and Indian War and received a warrant for 50 acres in October 1779 in Montgomery County, Virginia.

Miller, Samuel. He served as a soldier in one of the Virginia regiments under Col. William Byrd in the French and Indian War and received his 50 acre warrant 17 February 1780 in Amherst County, Virginia.

Miller, Thomas. He served in the Narraganset War from Milton, Massachusetts and received land in Bedford, New Hampshire in 1733.

Miller, Thomas. He served as a soldier in Capt. Christian's Company of Rangers in 1756 in the French and Indian War. He proved his right in Botetourt County, Virginia in March 1780. He assigned his warrant for 50 acres.

Miller, William. He was granted 50 acres in Albany County, New York for his service as a soldier in the 28th Regiment of Foot in the French and Indian War 26 July 1765.

Miller, William. He served as a private in the French and Indian War and petitioned for 50 acres in South Carolina 3 September 1765.

Miller, William. He served as a soldier in the Virginia Regiment under Col. William Byrd in the French and Indian War. He was killed in the service by Indians. His only heir was Sarah Hiland. She also appeared as Sarah Highland and was his remarried widow. She proved his service in Frederick County, Virginia 4 April 1780 and 2 January 1781.

Millet, Thomas. He was granted 200 acres in Albany County, New York for his service as a sergeant in the 46th Regiment of Foot in the French and Indian War 10 March 1772.

Millian, William. He served as a soldier in the French and Indian War from Virginia and received 50 acres of land.

Millican, Tolly. He served as a soldier in the French and Indian War and had his service certified in Montgomery County, Virginia for his 50 acres of land 8 March 1780.

Milligan, George. He was granted 4,000 acres in Granville County, South Carolina on the King's bounty 5 May 1773. He served as an ensign and as a surgeon in an independent company in the French and Indian War.

Milligan, James. He served as a soldier in Capt. Peter Hogg's Company of Rangers in 1754 in the French and Indian War. He received his 50 acre warrant 21 March 1780 in Greenbrier County, Virginia.

Milligan, Robert. He was granted 50 acres in Albany County, New York for his service as a soldier in the 80th Regiment of Foot in the French and Indian War 17 September 1765.

Milligen, John. He served as a lieutenant in the Royal Navy in the French and Indian War and received 3,000 acres in Nova Scotia 2 February 1779.

Milliken, James. He was granted 200 acres in Charlotte County, New York for his service as a noncommissioned officer in the 44th Regiment of Foot in the French and Indian War 12 October 1774.

Millins, James. He served as a soldier in Capt. John Posey's Regulars for six months in 1761 and twelve months in 1762 under Capt. John Blagg in the French and Indian War and assigned his 50 acre warrant in Virginia. He proved his service in Botetourt County, Virginia 9 March 1780. He also appeared as James Milling and James Melling.

Mills, George. He served as a sergeant in the 40th Regiment of Foot commanded by Gen. Armerger and was at the reduction of Havana. He had lost his discharge. He sought his 100 acre land grant in Georgia 1 October 1771.

Mills, James. He was a soldier under Capt. Thomas Bullitt in one of the Virginia regiments in the French and Indian War and was awarded a warrant for 50 acres 19 October 1779 in Virginia.

Mills, John. He served in an independent company of rangers in the French and Indian War and petitioned for land in New York 12 April 1769.

Mills, William. He served as a private in the French and Indian War and petitioned for his 50 acres on the King's bounty in South Carolina 7 October 1766.

Mills, William Henry. He was granted 1,040 acres in Craven County, South Carolina on the King's bounty for his service in the French and Indian War 23 March 1773.

Mills, William Henry. He was granted 293 and 48 acres in Craven County, South Carolina on the King's bounty for his service in the French and Indian War 23 March 1774.

Millson, Donald. He served as a private in the French and Indian War and petitioned for his land in New York 2 May 1768. He was granted 50 acres in Albany County, New York for his service as a soldier in the 55th Regiment of Foot in the French and Indian War 18 April 1769.

Milward, Francis. He served in the French and Indian War and had his service certified in New York in April 1768.

Miner, Ephraim. He served in the Narraganset War from Connecticut and received land in Voluntown, Connecticut in 1701.

Miner, Joseph. He served in the Narraganset War from Connecticut and received land in Voluntown, Connecticut in 1701.

Miner, Manasseth. He served in the Narraganset War from Connecticut and received land in Voluntown, Connecticut in 1701.

Miner, Samuel. He served in the Narraganset War from Connecticut. His heirs received land in Voluntown, Connecticut in 1701.

Miner, Thomas. He served as a lieutenant in the Narraganset War from Connecticut and received land in Voluntown, Connecticut in 1701.

Minor, Clement. He served in the Narraganset War from Connecticut and received land in Voluntown, Connecticut in 1701.

Mintor, John. He served in Narraganset War from Connecticut and received land in Voluntown, Connecticut in 1701.

Minyard, John. He was granted 50 acres in Albany County, New York for his service as a soldier in the 48th Regiment of Foot in the French and Indian War 28 October 1765.

Mirick, Samuel. He served in the Narraganset War from Taunton, Massachusetts. His son, Samuel Mirick, claimed his land in Greenwich, Massachusetts in 1737.

Mitchell, Hill. He was granted 50 acres in Albany County, New York for his service as a private in the 60th Regiment of Foot in the French and Indian War 5 April 1771.

Mitchell, John. He served in the Narraganset War from Massachusetts in 1685. His daughter, Mary Mitchell, received his land in Buxton, Maine.

Mitchell, John. He served on the expedition to Canada in 1690. Robert Warner petitioned for his land in Raymond, Maine in 1735.

Mitchell, John. He served in Capt. William Piper's Company of Light Horse from Pennsylvania in the French and Indian War and came to Virginia in 1772. He proved his service in Berkeley County, Virginia 21 March 1780.

Mitchell, Robert. His application for his service in an engagement with the enemy at sea was rejected by Massachusetts 23 March 1735/6.

Mitchell, Roger. He was from Kittery and saw action against the Indians in 1734. His land claim was rejected by Massachusetts 2 March 1735.

Mitchell, William. He was granted 50 acres in Albany County, New York for his service as a soldier in the 46th Regiment of Foot in the French and Indian War 1 April 1771.

Mitchell, William. He was granted 24 acres in Charlotte County, New York for his service as a soldier in the 35th Regiment of Foot in the French and Indian War 20 April 1775.

Mitchell, William. He was a soldier in the French and Indian War in 1758. He petitioned for his 50 acres in February 1780 in Caroline County, Virginia.

Mitting, Thomas. He was granted 50 acres in Albany County, New York for his service as a soldier in the 55th Regiment of Foot in the French and

Indian War 27 September 1769.

Mixer, John. He served on the expedition to Canada in 1690 and received his land in Bethel, Maine in 1767.

Mixer, Josiah. He received land in Alstead, New Hampshire in 1771 for the service of an unidentified veteran of the expedition to Canada in 1690.

Modsley, Yonnite. He served on the expedition to Canada in 1690. His brother, Thomas Modsley, desired that Hezekiah Barber of Dorchester, Massachusetts receive the veteran's land in Ashburnham, Massachusetts in 1736.

Moffet, James. He was granted 200 acres in Albany County, New York for his service as a sergeant in the 46th Regiment of Foot in the French and Indian War 8 June 1771. He also appeared as James Moffat.

Moffett, George. He served in the French and Indian War and received his 2,000 acre land warrant in Virginia.

Moncrieff, Thomas. He was granted 2,000 acres in Cumberland County, New York for his service as a lieutenant in the 50th Regiment of Foot in the French and Indian War 10 June 1772.

Monday, John. He served as a soldier in the French and Indian War in 1758. His legatee, Reuben Monday, petitioned for his 50 acres in February 1780 in Caroline County, Virginia.

Monday, Reuben. He served as a soldier from Virginia in the French and Indian War until he was discharged in 1760. He proved his right in Caroline County, Virginia 10 February 1780. He assigned his warrant for 50 acres to his brother, James Munday. He also appeared as Reuben Munday.

Monk, Elias. He was a veteran of the expedition to Canada in 1690 and was of Stoughton, Massachusetts. Joseph Warren of Roxbury, Massachusetts received his land in Ashburnham, Massachusetts in 1736.

Monn, George. He served in the French and Indian War and petitioned for land in New York 8 July 1772.

Monroe, George. He served as a sergeant in the French and Indian War and was named in New York 20 February 1765.

Monroe, Edmund. He served as an ensign in the French and Indian War and petitioned for 2,000 acres of land in Albany County, New York 12 June 1766.

Monroe, Hugh. He was granted 122 acres in Albany County, New York for his service as a noncommissioned officer in the 77th Regiment of Foot in the French and Indian War 15 July 1768.

Monroe, Jacob. He served as a private in the 46th Regiment in the French and Indian War and was granted land in New York 11 November 1772.

Monroe, Robert. He served as a corporal in the 47th Regiment in the French and Indian War and petitioned for his land in New York 8 July 1765.

Monson, William. He was granted 50 acres in Albany County, New York for his service as a soldier in the 44th Regiment of Foot in the French and Indian War 1 April 1772.

Montgomery, Archibald. He was granted 50 acres in Albany County, New York for his service as a soldier in the 80th Regiment of Foot in the French and Indian War 29 October 1765.

Montgomery, Hugh. He was granted 50 acres in Albany County, New York for his service as a soldier in the 80th Regiment of Foot in the French and Indian War 26 July 1765.

Montgomery, James, Jr. He served as a soldier in the French and Indian War and had his service certified in Montgomery County, Virginia for 50 acres of land 8 March 1780.

Montgomery, James, Sr. He served as a soldier in the French and Indian War and had his service certified in Montgomery County, Virginia for 50 acres of land 8 March 1780.

Montgomery, John. He and Alexander Montgomery were granted 1,000 acres in Washington and Westmoreland Counties and 1,000 acres in Westmoreland County, Pennsylvania for their service in the French and Indian War 9 February 1769.

Montgomery, John. He served as a captain of a company of volunteers incorporated with a part of the Virginia Regiment on the Shawnee Expedition under Maj. Andrew Lewis in the French and Indian War in 1756. He received his 3,000 acre warrant in April 1780 in Montgomery County, Virginia.

Montgomery, John. He served as a soldier in the French and Indian War and received 50 acres in Virginia. He may have been the one of the name who served in Capt. Charles Lewis's Company of Rangers in 1758 as proved in Augusta County, Virginia 15 February 1780.

Montgomery, Joseph. He served as a soldier in Capt. John Montgomery's Company incorporated with part of the Virginia Regiment on the Shawnee Expedition in 1756 under the command of Maj. Andrew Lewis in the French and Indian War. He received his 50 acre warrant in April 1780 in Montgomery County, Virginia.

Montgomery, Robert. He served as a soldier in the French and Indian War and had his service certified in Montgomery County, Virginia for his 50 acres of land 8 March 1780.

Montgomery, Samuel. He served in Capt. John Montgomery's Company of Volunteers in the Virginia Regiment in the expedition against the

Shawnee in 1756 in the French and Indian War. He received his 50 acre warrant in April 1780 in Montgomery County, Virginia.

Montgomery, William. He served as a soldier in Capt. John Montgomery's Company of Volunteers incorporated with the Virginia Regiment under Maj. Andrew Lewis in the expedition against the Shawnee in 1756 in the French and Indian War. He received his 50 acre warrant in April 1780 in Montgomery County, Virginia.

Montour, Henry. He served as a captain in the French and Indian War and petitioned for land in New York 28 February 1770.

Montressor, James. He served as colonel and director of engineers in North America in the French and Indian War and prayed a warrant for 10,000 acres in New York 28 July 1766.

Montressor, John. He served as a colonel in the French and Indian War and had his petition for land dismissed because his selection was within the Hardenbergh Patent in New York 20 March 1771.

Montressor, John. He served as a lieutenant in the 48th Regiment in the French and Indian War and had his petition for land dismissed because his selection was within the Hardenbergh Patent 20 March 1771. He was granted land 2 September 1774 in New York.

Moody, Caleb. He served on the expedition to Canada in 1690 and received land in Poland, Maine in 1739.

Moody, Joshua. He served on the expedition to Canada in 1690 and received land in Poland, Maine in 1739.

Moody, Samuel. He served in the expedition to Port Royal and Louisbourg. His children, Joseph Moody and Mary Emerson, the wife of Rev. Joseph Emerson of Malden, applied for the land due their father in Massachusetts 20 January 1763.

Moon, John. He served as a corporal in the 60th Regiment in the French and Indian War and was granted land in New York 16 April 1767.

Mooney, David. He was granted 2,000 acres in Albany County, New York for his service as a lieutenant in the 60th Regiment of Foot in the French and Indian War 28 October 1765.

Moor, Caleb. He served in the Narraganset War from Boston, Massachusetts. His son, Ephraim Moor, received land in Bedford, New Hampshire in 1733.

Moor, Jacob. He served on the expedition to Canada in 1690. Daniel Moor received his land in Bethel, Maine in 1767.

Moor, Joseph. He served on the expedition to Canada in 1690. John Woodward received his land in Bethel, Maine in 1767.

Moor, Thomas. He was granted 50 acres in Albany County, New York for his service as a soldier in the 80th Regiment in the French and Indian War 28 October 1765.

Moore, Abraham. He served as a soldier in Capt. Thomas Bullet's Company of Regulars in the French and Indian War. He proved his right in Botetourt County, Virginia in March 1780. He assigned his 50 acre warrant.

Moore, Benoni. He was awarded 200 acres by Massachusetts for his service 13 January 1735/6.

Moore, Charles. He was granted 200 acres in Albany County, New York for his service as a noncommissioned officer in the 60th Regiment of Foot in the French and Indian War 5 April 1771.

Moore, Charles. He served as clerk to the hospital in the French and Indian War and petitioned for his 2,000 acres in New York 24 January 1776.

Moore, Henry. He served as a sergeant in the French and Indian War and petitioned for his land in New York 26 April 1765.

Moore, James. He served as a soldier in the 80th Regiment in the French and Indian War from New York. His service was certified 5 December 1764.

Moore, John. He served in the French and Indian War and petitioned for land in New York 17 March 1767.

Moore, Samuel. He served in the campaign against the Indians in 1725. He was from Dunstable, Massachusetts and received his land in Pembroke, New Hampshire.

Moore, Samuel. He was granted 200 acres in Albany County, New York for his service as a sergeant in the 80th Regiment of Foot in the French and Indian War 21 May 1768.

Moore, Thomas. He was granted 50 acres in Albany County, New York for his service as a soldier in the 55th Regiment of Foot in the French and Indian War 18 April 1769.

Moore, Thomas. He served as a soldier in the 80th Regiment in the French and Indian War. His survey was returned in New York 26 October 1765.

Moore, Thomas. He served as a soldier in the French and Indian War and had his service certified in Montgomery County, Virginia for his 50 acres of land 8 March 1780.

Moors, John. He served in an independent company of rangers in the French and Indian War and petitioned for land in New York 12 April 1769.

Moors, Jonathan. He served as a lieutenant in the Narraganset War from Massachusetts in 1685. His land was awarded in Buxton, Maine.

Moors, Thomas. He served in the Narraganset War from Boston, Massachusetts. His son, John Moors, received land in Bedford, New

Hampshire in 1733.

Morarty, Daniel. He served as a sergeant in the 44th Regiment in the French and Indian War and petitioned for his 200 acres in New York 26 April 1765.

Morden, James. He served as a lieutenant in the 72nd Regiment of Foot in the French and Indian War and received 2,000 acres in Nova Scotia 22 July 1778.

More, Abel. He served in the Narraganset War from Connecticut and received land in Voluntown, Connecticut in 1701.

More, Joseph. He served in the Narraganset War from Sudbury, Massachusetts. His son, John More, received his land in Westminster, Massachusetts in 1733.

More, William. He was granted 200 acres in Albany County, New York for his service as a sergeant in the 80th Regiment of Foot in the French and Indian War 16 July 1765. He also appeared as William Moore.

Moreton, William. He served in one of the Virginia Regiments in the French and Indian War. He proved his service in Essex County, Virginia 21 February 1780.

Morey, James. He was a veteran of the expedition to Canada in 1690. His daughter, Martha Morey, married a Blake, and her son, William Blake of Milton, Massachusetts, received his grandfather's land in Ashburnham, Massachusetts in 1736.

Morey, Thomas. He served in the Narraganset War from Roxbury, Massachusetts. His son, John Morey, received land in Bedford, New Hampshire in 1733.

Morfett, Thomas. He was granted 50 acres in Craven County, South Carolina on the King's bounty 13 May 1768 for his service as a private in the French and Indian War.

Morgan, Daniel. He served as an officer in the French and Indian War and received his 2,000 acre warrant in Virginia.

Morgan, Haynes. He served as Sergeant Major in the 80th Regiment for seven years in the French and Indian War in 1758. He was a native of Virginia. Montague Wilmott commanded the regiment, and James Grant, Captain Commandant, signed his discharge. The unit was reduced in New York in 1764. He petitioned for his 200 acres 18 April 1780 in Pittsylvania County, Virginia. He also submitted a certificate from Thomas Gage, Commander in Chief to all the King's governors in North America authorizing the granting of land to reduced officers and soldiers. He proved his right in Pittsylvania County, Virginia 18 April 1780.

Morgan, James. He served in the Narraganset War from Connecticut and received land in Voluntown, Connecticut in 1701.

Morgan, John. He served on the expedition to Canada in 1690. John Morgan petitioned for his land in Raymond, Maine in 1735.

Morgan, John. He served as a corporal in the 4th Battalion of the Royal American or 60th Regiment in the French and Indian War and petitioned for his 200 acres in New York 1 May 1770.

Morgan, Joseph. He served on the expedition to Canada in 1690 and petitioned for his land in Raymond, Maine in 1735.

Morgan, Joseph. He served in the Narraganset War from Connecticut and received land in Voluntown, Connecticut in 1701.

Morgan, Joseph. He served in the Narraganset War from Beverly, Massachusetts. His son, Joseph Morgan, claimed his land in Amherst, New Hampshire in 1734.

Morgan, Samuel. He served on the expedition to Canada in 1690. John Morgan petitioned for his land in Raymond, Maine in 1735.

Morison, Henry. He was granted 50 acres in Craven County, South Carolina on the King's bounty for his service in the French and Indian War 15 February 1770.

Morrell, William. He was granted 200 acres in Colleton County, South Carolina on the King's bounty for his service in the French and Indian War 28 January 1771.

Morrett, John. He served as a noncommissioned officer in the French and Indian War and petitioned for 200 acres on the King's bounty in South Carolina 5 May 1772.

Morrice, Robert. He served in the French and Indian War and assigned his right to land to Robert Buchanan 20 January 1767 in New York.

Morris, Edward. He served on the expedition to Canada in 1690. Edward Morris received land in Warwick, Massachusetts in 1738.

Morris, Isaac. He served in the Narraganset War from Killingly, Connecticut. His brother, Samuel Morris, claimed his land in Greenwich, Massachusetts in 1737.

Morris, Jacob. He served as a sergeant in the French and Indian War in Virginia and was entitled to 200 acres which he desired to locate in Fincastle County, Virginia 14 February 1774.

Morris, John. He served as a lieutenant in the French and Indian War and petitioned for 2,000 acres in New York 27 January 1775.

Morris, Richard. He served in the French and Indian War and took his land in Fincastle County, Virginia 15 December 1772.

Morris, Thomas. He served as a soldier until 1759 in the French and Indian

War. He petitioned for his 50 acres in February 1780 in Orange County, Virginia.

Morris, William. He served as a lieutenant in the French and Indian War and received a warrant for 2,000 acres in September 1779 in Goochland County, Virginia.

Morrison, Daniel. He served as a surgeon in the French and Indian War and had his service certified 4 April 1766 in New York.

Morrison, Donald. He served as a soldier in the French and Indian War and petitioned for 50 acres of land in New York 15 December 1773.

Morrison, Edward. He was granted 200 acres in Dutchess County, New York for his service as a sergeant in the 35th Regiment of Foot in the French and Indian War 24 November 1772.

Morrison, Henry. He served as a noncommissioned officer in the French and Indian War and received 200 acres of land in West Florida 12 February 1776.

Morrison, Hugh. He was granted 200 acres in Charlotte County, New York for his service as a noncommissioned officer in the Highland Regiment in the French and Indian War 18 July 1774.

Morrison, Kenneth. He was granted 200 acres in Albany County, New York for for his service as a sergeant in the 55th Regiment of Foot in the French and Indian War 26 May 1772.

Morrison, Robert. He was granted 2,000 acres in Albany County, New York for his service as a conductor in the Royal Regiment of Artillery in the French and Indian War 13 July 1770.

Morrison, Samuel. He was granted 50 acres in Charlotte County, New York for for his service as a soldier in the 27th Regiment of Foot in the French and Indian War 25 January 1773.

Morrow, James. He was granted 217 ½ acres in Cumberland County, Pennsylvania for his service as an ensign in the French and Indian War 3 February 1769.

Mors, John. He served in the Narraganset War from Boston, Massachusetts. His grandson, John Gridley, received land in Bedford, New Hampshire in 1733.

Morse, John. He served as a commissary. His widow and relict, Elizabeth Morse, received his land for herself and her children in Massachusetts 15 October 1679.

Morse, Joseph. He served on the expedition to Canada in 1690. Joseph Morse received his land in Bethel, Maine in 1767.

Morse, Nathaniel. He served on the expedition to Canada in 1690 and received his land in Bethel, Maine in 1767.

Morse, Nathaniel. He served on the expedition to Canada in 1690. Joshua Fuller received his land in Bethel, Maine in 1767.

Morseman, Timothy. He served on the expedition to Canada in 1690. Timothy Morseman received land in Warwick, Massachusetts in 1738.

Morton, Bryant. He served in the expedition to Louisbourg in 1745 and applied for land in Massachusetts 10 April 1770.

Morton, John. He served as a lieutenant in a company of volunteers which joined Maj. Andrew Lewis's detachment form the 1st Virginia Regiment of Regulars in the French and Indian War. He received a warrant for 2,000 acres 17 January 1780 in Prince Edward County, Virginia.

Morton, Oliver. He served as a soldier under Col. Adam Stephen in the French and Indian War from Virginia and received 50 acres of land.

Morton, Thomas. He received land in Richmond, New Hampshire in 1765 for the service of unidentified veteran of the expedition to Canada in 1690.

Morton, Thomas. He served as a 2nd lieutenant in the company of volunteers which joined Maj. Andrew Lewis's detachment of regulars in the 1st Virginia Regiment in the French and Indian War. He received a warrant for 2,000 acres 17 January 1780 in Prince Edward County, Virginia.

Morton, William. He served as a soldier under Capt. William Daingerfield in Col. Adam Stephen's Regiment in the French and Indian War. He was discharged unfit for duty due to dropsy. He proved his right in Essex County, Virginia 21 February 1780. He assigned his right for 50 acres.

Moss, James. He served as a soldier in the French and Indian War and petitioned for his 50 acres which he desired to locate in Fincastle County, Virginia.

Moss, John. He served in the Narraganset War. The town of Wallingford, Connecticut granted him 5 acres of land 14 February 1686.

Moss, Richard. He served as a corporal in the French and Indian War and petitioned for land in New York 17 March 1767.

Moss, Thomas. He served as a drummer in 1754 in the French and Indian War. He proved his right in Caroline County, Virginia in February 1780 and assigned his right to four 50 acres warrants.

Mossman, William. He was granted 50 acres in Granville County, South Carolina on the King's bounty for his service in the French and Indian War 15 February 1770.

Mothershead, George. He served as a soldier in the 2nd Virginia Regiment under Col. William Byrd in 1759 in the French and Indian War.

He received his 50 acre warrant 28 March 1780 in Westmoreland County, Virginia.

Moulton, Ebenezer. He served as a noncommissioned officer in the French and Indian War and received 200 acres in Nova Scotia 29 September 1772.

Moulton, Jeremiah. He served as a captain in the Indian wars and was in battle at Nerridgawock. He received 100 acres in York County, Massachusetts 28 November 1726.

Mount, Thomas. He was granted 50 acres in Albany County, New York for his service as a soldier in the Royal American or 60th Regiment of Foot in the French and Indian War 18 July 1770.

Mountfort, John. He served as a sergeant in the French and Indian War and petitioned for his land in New York 2 May 1768.

Mountfort, Joseph. He was granted 200 acres in Albany County, New York for his service as a noncommissioned officer in the 46th Regiment of Foot in the French and Indian War 10 May 1770.

Mountfort, Joseph. He was granted 200 acres in Albany County, New York for his service as a noncommissioned officer in the 4th Battalion in the 60th Regiment of Foot in the French and Indian War 18 July 1770.

Mountgomery, John. He served as a soldier in a company of rangers in the French and Indian War and received his 50 acre warrant in Virginia.

Mouret, John. He was granted 200 acres in St. Matthew's Parish, South Carolina on the King's bounty for his service in the French and Indian War 14 February 1772.

Mourning, Dominick. He was a soldier in the 1st Virginia Regiment under Col. George Washington in the French and Indian War. He proved his right to 50 acres in Rockbridge County, Virginia 8 October 1779. He seems to be the same person who appeared as Dominick Moran.

Mourning, Thomas. He served as a soldier in the Virginia Regiment under Col. William Byrd in 1758 in the French and Indian War. He proved his right in Hanover County, Virginia 2 March 1780. He assigned his right to 50 acres.

Mousley, John. He served in the Narraganset War from Charlestown, Massachusetts. His heirs received his land in Westminster, Massachusetts in 1733.

Mowat, John. He was granted 3,000 acres in Albany County, New York for his service as Secretary to Admiral Durrell at the time of the reduction of Louisbourg and Quebec in the French and Indian War 10 May 1770.

Mower, John. He served in the Narraganset War from Lynn, Massachusetts. His son, Richard Mower, claimed his land in Amherst, New

Hampshire in 1734.

Mowers, Samuel. He served in the Narraganset War from Lynn, Massachusetts and petitioned for his land 4 June 1685.

Mowrey, Benjamin. He shared in the grant of East Greenwich, Rhode Island made to those who had rendered service in King Philip's War. The grant was made 31 October 1677.

Mowrey, Joseph. He shared in the grant of East Greenwich, Rhode Island made to those who had rendered service in King Philip's War. The grant was made 31 October 1677.

Mudge, George. He served in the Narraganset War from Charlestown, Massachusetts. His heirs received his land in Westminster, Massachusetts in 1733.

Mudge, John. He served in the Narraganset War from Malden, Massachusetts. He received his land in Westminster, Massachusetts in 1733.

Muerenbeldt, Peter. He was granted 200 acres in Albany County, New York for his service as a sergeant in the 3rd Battalion in the 60th Regiment of Foot in the French and Indian War 1 June 1770.

Mulcaster, Frederick George. He was granted 1,000 acres in West Florida for his service as a lieutenant of engineers in the French and Indian War 24 March 1779.

Mulford, Thomas. He served in the Narraganset War from Eastham, Massachusetts and received land in Gorham, Maine in 1733.

Mullen, Thomas. He served as a corporal in the Virginia Regiment under Col. William Byrd in the French and Indian War. He assigned his warrant for 200 acres in Virginia.

Muller, Jacob. He was granted 3,000 acres in Orange County, New York for his service as a captain in the 60th Regiment of Foot in the French and Indian War 18 January 1775.

Mullican, Tully. He served as a soldier in a company of rangers in 1757 in the French and Indian War in Virginia and assigned his 50 acre warrant.

Mullins, James. He served as a soldier in Capt. Pray's Company of Regulars in 1759 in the French and Indian War. He proved his service in Botetourt County, Virginia in April 1780 and received a warrant for 50 acres.

Mulreany, Patrick. He was granted 50 acres in Albany County, New York for his service as a private in a regiment of foot in the French and Indian War 19 May 1770.

Mumford, Robert. He applied for 3,000 acres of land in Georgia. He served as a captain in the 2nd Virginia Regiment in 1758 in the expedition against Fort DuQuesne in the French and Indian War. His application was rejected 5 May 1767. He also appeared as Robert Munford.

Mundell, John. He was granted 250 acres on the south side of the Edisto River in South Carolina on the King's bounty for his service in the French and Indian War 15 February 1770.

Munn, Benjamin. He served in the Pequot War and received a grant of land in Soldiers' Field in Hartford, Connecticut.

Munro, Daniel. He served as Commissary of Stores and Provisions at Fort Edward in the French and Indian War and petitioned for 2,000 acres of land in New York 6 June 1775.

Munroe, Donald. He served as a sergeant in the 60th Regiment in the French and Indian War and was granted land in New York 22 April 1772.

Munro, Donald. He was granted 200 acres in Albany County, New York for his service as a noncommissioned officer in the 77th Regiment of Foot in the French and Indian War 13 May 1765.

Munro, Donald. He was granted 200 acres in Albany County, New York for his service as a corporal in the 42nd Regiment of Foot in the French and Indian War 30 October 1765.

Munro, Donald. He served as a sergeant in the 4th Battalion of the Royal American Regiment in the French and Indian War. He petitioned for his 200 acres in New York 20 January 1772.

Munro, Hugh. He was granted an island of 42 acres in the Hudson River in New York for his service as sergeant in the 77th Regiment of Foot in the French and Indian War 5 August 1766.

Munro, John, Sr. He served in the 48th Regiment in the French and Indian War and petitioned for his land in New York 20 May 1771.

Munro, John, Jr. He served in the 48th Regiment in the French and Indian War and petitioned for his land in New York 20 May 1771.

Munro, Robert. He was granted 200 acres in Albany County, New York for his service as a noncommissioned officer in the 78th Regiment of Foot in the French and Indian War 22 May 1765. He also appeared as Robert Monro.

Munro, Samuel. He served in the 48th Regiment in the French and Indian War and petitioned for his land in New York 20 May 1771.

Munro, William. He served as quartermaster in the French and Indian War and petitioned for his 2,000 acres in New York 24 January 1764.

Munroe, Alexander. He was granted 200 acres in Albany County, New York for his service as a sergeant in the 55th Regiment of Foot in the French and Indian War 2 July 1765.

Munroe, Duncan. He was granted 50 acres in Albany County, New York for his service as a soldier in the 42nd Regiment of Foot in the French and Indian War 30 October 1765.

Munroe, George. He was granted 3,000 acres in Albany County, New York for his service as a physician in a military hospital in the French and Indian War 28 October 1765.

Munroe, Harry. He was granted 2,000 acres in Albany County, New York for his service as a chaplain in the 77th Regiment of Foot in the French and Indian War 7 August 1764. He also appeared as Henry Munroe.

Munroe, Henry. He served as a lieutenant in the French and Indian War. He received his second 500 acres in Nova Scotia 6 May 1778.

Munroe, John. He was a soldier under Capt. Noah Wiswall at Lamprey River. He was awarded 150 acres by Massachusetts 28 November 1735.

Munroe, Robert. He was granted 200 acres in Albany County, New York for his service as a corporal in the 47th Regiment of Foot in the French and Indian War 12 July 1765.

Munroe, William. He was from Lexington and served in the war against the French and Indians. He applied for his land in Massachusetts 25 March 1736.

Munsell, Jeffrey. He served as a soldier in the Virginia Regiment in the French and Indian War and was entitled to 50 acres which he assigned.

Munson, Thomas. He served in the Pequot War and received a grant of land in Soldiers' Field in Hartford, Connecticut.

Munster, Herbert. He received 5,000 acres of land in West Florida for his service as a lieutenant colonel in the French and Indian War 1 May 1772.

Murdock, James. He was granted 2,000 acres in Albany County, New York for his service as a surgeon's mate in the 42nd Regiment of Foot in the French and Indian War 28 June 1771.

Murffey, James. He served in the Narraganset War from Connecticut and received land in Voluntown, Connecticut in 1701. He also appeared as James Murphey.

Murphey, Edward. He was a soldier in the 2nd Virginia Regiment in the French and Indian War. He proved his right in Goochland County, Virginia 29 September 1779. He assigned his right to 50 acres.

Murphy, James. He was granted 200 acres in Albany County, New York for his service as a sergeant in the 60th Regiment of Foot in the French and Indian War 29 October 1765.

Murphy, Luke. He was granted 50 acres in Charlotte County, New York for his service as a soldier in the 45th Regiment of Foot in the French and Indian War 18 October 1775.

Murphy, Robert. He served in the French and Indian War and received his land in Botetourt County, Virginia.

Murphy, Thomas. He was granted 200 acres in Ulster County, New York for his service as a corporal in the 80th Regiment of Foot in the French and Indian War 23 December 1771.

Murphy, Thomas. He served as a soldier in 1758 under Gen. Forbes in the French and Indian War. He proved his right in Culpeper County, Virginia 17 January 1780. He assigned his right to 50 acres.

Murray, George. He was granted 200 acres in Albany County, New York for his service as a corporal in the 77th Regiment of Foot in the French and Indian War 13 May 1765.

Murray, George. He was granted 200 acres in Gloucester County, New York for his service as a noncommissioned officer in the 42nd Regiment of Foot in the French and Indian War 23 October 1775.

Murray, John. He was granted 200 acres in Albany County, New York for his service as a corporal in the 4th Battalion in the 60th Regiment of Foot in the French and Indian War 18 July 1770.

Murray, John. He was granted 50 acres in Charlotte County, New York for his service as a soldier in the Royal Highland Regiment of Foot in the French and Indian War 12 July 1775.

Murray, John. He served as a soldier in the 78th Regiment in the French and Indian War and petitioned for his 50 acres in New York 6 August 1774.

Murray, William. He served as an officer in the French and Indian War and received his 2,000 acre warrant in Virginia.

Murrell, Jeffrey. He served as a soldier in the Virginia Regiment in the French and Indian War and was eligible for a 50 acre warrant in Virginia which his heir, William Murrell, assigned.

Murrell, William. He served as a sergeant in the Virginia Regiment in the French and Indian War and assigned his warrant for 200 acres in Virginia.

Murry, John. He served as an ensign in Capt. Alexander McClenachan's Company of Independents under Col. Henry Bouquet in 1764. His widow and heir, Elizabeth Murry, requested his 2,000 acres 21 December 1779 in Augusta County, Virginia. She also appeared as Elizabeth Murray.

Muse, George. He served as a lieutenant colonel in the French and Indian War in 1754. He petitioned for warrants of 300, 50, 1,000, 250, and 950 acres in February 1780 in Caroline County, Virginia. He assigned his right to other warrants for 300, 500, 200, 500, 500, and 500 acres.

Musgro, Jabez. He served in the Narraganset War from Massachusetts in 1685. His land was located in Buxton, Maine.

Mustard, James. He was granted 200 acres in Albany County, New York for his service as a drummer in the 55th Regiment of Foot in the French and Indian War 11 October 1765.

Muzzy, John. He served in the Narraganset War and received land in Templeton, Massachusetts in 1733.

Myer, Michael. He was granted 50 acres in Albany County, New York for his service as a soldier in the 60th Regiment of Foot in the French and Indian War 26 September 1765.

Myers, George. He was granted 200 acres in Albany County, New York for his service as sergeant in the 60th Regiment of Foot in the French and Indian War 29 October 1765.

Myles, John. He was slain in the service in battle with a French privateer in July 1709. His heirs, John Myles, Sarah Price, and Anne Cresse, were granted 600 acres for his service as a captain in Massachusetts 14 December 1734.

Myrick, John. He served in the Narraganset War from Eastham, Massachusetts and received land in Gorham, Maine in 1733.

Nairn, William. He served as a soldier in the French and Indian War and received 50 acres in Nova Scotia 9 December 1777.

Nall, Martin. He served in an independent corps under Maj. John Field in 1764 and Col. Henry Bouquet against the Shawnee. He received a warrant for 50 acres of land in Culpeper County, Virginia 18 October 1779. He also appeared as Martin Nalle.

Nalor, Thomas. He was granted 50 acres in Albany County, New York for his service as a soldier in the 46th Regiment of Foot in the French and Indian War 28 October 1765.

Napier, James. He served as inspector and director general of H. M.'s military hospital in North America in the French and Indian War. His survey in Albany County, New York was returned 24 October 1765.

Napp, Thomas. He served in the French and Indian War and took his land in Botetourt County, Virginia. His widow, Margaret Napp, proved that he served in the whole war and died after the war. Their son, John Nap, was a soldier in the Continental Army when she proved her late husband's service in Frederick County, Virginia 2 May 1780. He also appeared as Thomas Nap.

Nash, Abner. He served as a lieutenant in 2nd Virginia Regiment under Col. William Byrd in the French and Indian War. His right was proved in York County, Virginia 17 January 1780. His two warrants for 1,000 acres were assigned.

Nash, James. He served as a sergeant in Capt. John Field's Company in Col.

William Byrd's Regiment in the French and Indian War and received his warrant for 200 acres 17 August 1779 in Culpeper County, Virginia.

Nash, John. He was granted 50 acres in Albany County, New York for his service as a soldier in the 46th Regiment in the French and Indian War 8 June 1771.

Nash, John. He was a soldier under Capt. James Gunn in the French and Indian War. He proved his right in Louisa County, Virginia 11 October 1779. He assigned his right to 50 acres of land.

Nash, John. He served as a sergeant under Capt. John Field in the French and Indian War. He proved his right in Culpeper County, Virginia 16 August 1779.

Nash, John. He served as a sergeant for seven and a half years in Capt. Henry Woodward's Company in Col. George Washington's Regiment in the French and Indian War. He proved his right in Cumberland County, Virginia 27 March 1780. He assigned his 200 acre warrant.

Nash, Marvel. He served as a sergeant in Capt. James Gunn's Company under Col. William Byrd in the French and Indian War and received his 200 acre warrant in Virginia.

Naye, Simon. He was granted 50 acres in Albany County, New York for his service as a soldier in the 60th Regiment of Foot in the French and Indian War 13 February 1767.

Neal, James. He was granted 3,000 acres in Gloucester County, New York for his service as a captain in a corps of rangers in the French and Indian War 14 July 1774.

Neal, Jeremiah. He served in the Narraganset War from Salem, Massachusetts. His son, Jeremiah Neal, claimed his land in Amherst, New Hampshire in 1734.

Neal, John. He served as a private in the French and Indian War and petitioned for his land in New York in November 1766.

Nealand, John. He was a veteran of the expedition to Canada in 1690. His brother, Edward Nealand of Ipswich, Massachusetts, claimed his land in Winchendon, Massachusetts in 1736.

Neavit, Henry. He served as a soldier in the Virginia Regiment in the French and Indian War and received a warrant for 50 acres.

Needham, John. He served in the Narraganset War. His son, John Needham, received his land in Templeton, Massachusetts in 1733.

Needham, Sebastian. He served as a noncommissioned officer in the French and Indian War and petitioned for his 200 acres of land in Albany County, New York 20 December 1773.

Neeves, Edward. He served as a soldier in the 80th Regiment in the French and Indian War and petitioned for his land 22 October 1766 in New York.

Neill, Charles. He served as a soldier in the Old Virginia Regiment in the French and Indian War for the whole war. He proved his service in Frederick County, Virginia 5 September 1780.

Nelson, Edward. He served in the 46th Regiment in the French and Indian War. Rebecca Nelson was certified as his widow 13 December 1766 in New York.

Nelson, John. He served in the Narraganset War from Boston, Massachusetts and received land in Bedford, New Hampshire in 1733.

Nelson, John. His heir, Temple Nelson, received his land in Massachusetts 26 March 1736.

Nelson, Robert. He served on the expedition to Canada in 1690. Joseph Annable received his land in Winchendon, Massachusetts in 1736.

Nevelt, John. He was granted 50 acres in Albany County, New York for his service as a soldier in the 46th Regiment of Foot in the French and Indian War 8 March 1771.

Nevils, Henry. He was a soldier in the Virginia Regiment under Col. George Washington in the French and Indian War. He proved his right in Rockbridge County, Virginia 7 September 1779 and assigned his 50 acres.

Newberry, Samuel. He served as a soldier in the French and Indian War and received a warrant for 50 acres in November 1779 in Montgomery County, Virginia.

Newcombe, Henry. He served in the French and Indian War and petitioned for land in New York 2 February 1769.

Newell, Samuel. He served in the Narraganset War from Charlestown, Massachusetts. His nephew, Samuel Long, received his land in Westminster, Massachusetts in 1733.

Newell, Samuel. He served on the expedition to Canada in 1690. Samuel Newell received land in Warwick, Massachusetts in 1738.

Newgen, John. He was granted 200 acres in Albany County, New York for his service as a corporal in the 22nd Regiment of Foot in the French and Indian War 8 June 1771. He also appeared as John Newgan.

Newhall, John. He served in the Narraganset War from Lynn, Massachusetts. He claimed his land in Amherst, New Hampshire in 1734.

Newhall, John. He served on the expedition to Canada in 1690. John Newhall received land in Chesterfield, Massachusetts in 1739.

Newhall, Samuel. He served on the expedition to Canada in 1690. Samuel Newhall received land in Chesterfield, Massachusetts in 1739.

Newland, Edmund. He served as a lieutenant in the 80th Regiment in the French and Indian War and petitioned for his land in New York 26 October 1771.

Newland, John. He served as a noncommissioned officer in the 55th Regiment in the French and Indian War and petitioned for his 200 acres of land in New York 4 April 1768.

Newland, Trevor. He served as a lieutenant in the French and Indian War and petitioned for his 2,000 acres of land in New York 9 May 1770.

Newland, William. He was granted 200 acres in Albany County, New York for his service as a noncommissioned officer in the 60th or Royal American Regiment of Foot in the French and Indian War 28 March 1771.

Newman, Benjamin. He served in the Narraganset War from Massachusetts in 1685. His land was located in Buxton, Maine.

Newman, Joseph. He served as a soldier in one of the Virginia Regiments in 1755 under Gen. Braddock in the French and Indian War. He proved his right in Amherst County, Virginia in April 1780. He assigned his 50 acre warrant.

Newman, Nimrod. He served as a fifer in the Old Virginia Regiment under Col. William Byrd in the French and Indian War and received a warrant for 50 acres in September 1779 in Bedford County, Virginia.

Newmarch, Zaccheus. He served in the Narraganset War from Massachusetts in 1685. His son, John Newmarch, received his land in Buxton, Maine.

Newton, Hibbert. He served in the French and Indian War and received 2,000 acres of land in Nova Scotia 16 January 1767.

Niblet, Benjamin. He served as a corporal in the 55th Regiment in the French and Indian War and petitioned for his land in New York 22 March 1771.

Nice, John. He was granted 334 and 370 acres in Berks County, Pennsylvania for his service as a lieutenant in the French and Indian War 3 February 1769.

Nicholls, Charles. He was granted 200 acres on the south side of the Saludy River in South Carolina on the King's bounty for his service in the French and Indian War 21 June 1765.

Nichols, Ebenezer. For his service in former wars Col. Nichols was granted 300 acres of land in Massachusetts 16 March 1758.

Nichols, Thomas. He served in the Narraganset War from Reading, Massachusetts. He received his land in Westminster, Massachusetts in 1733.

Nichols, Thomas. He served as a sergeant and shared in the grant of East

Greenwich, Rhode Island made to those who had served in King Philip's War. The grant was made 31 October 1677.

Nicholson, John. He served as a soldier in the Virginia Regiment under Col. William Byrd in the French and Indian War. He proved his service in Fauquier County, Virginia 27 March 1780.

Nicholson, Robert. He served in the Narraganset War from Chatham, Massachusetts. His son, Robert Nicholson, claimed his land in Amherst, New Hampshire in 1734.

Nicolls, James. He served in the Narraganset War from Reading, Massachusetts and petitioned for his land 4 June 1685.

Nicolls, Nathaniel. He served in the Narraganset War from Pembrook, Massachusetts. He claimed his land in Greenwich, Massachusetts in 1737.

Nixon, Henry. He was a soldier in 1758 in Capt. John Field's Company in Gen. Forbes's expedition in the French and Indian War. He proved his service in Culpeper County, Virginia 18 October 1779. He assigned his right to 50 acres.

Nixon, John. He served as a sergeant in the French and Indian War in Virginia. He proved his right in Botetourt County, Virginia in March 1780. He assigned his warrant for 200 acres.

Noble, James. He served as a sergeant in the 1st Highland Battalion of 77th Regiment under Col. Archibald Montgomery in the French and Indian War and was discharged in New York. He applied for 200 acres land in Georgia 4 August 1772.

Noble, John. He was granted 200 acres in Albany County, New York for his service as a corporal in the 80th Regiment of Foot in the French and Indian War 8 June 1771.

Noble, Joseph. He was a native of Virginia and served in the 2nd Virginia Regiment under Gen. Forbes in 1758 in the French and Indian War. His service was proved in Amelia County, Virginia 25 November 1779. He sold his rights to Robert Goode of Prince Edward Co., Va.

Noble, Mark. He served as a lieutenant in the French and Indian War and petitioned for his 2,000 acres in New York 22 January 1776.

Noice, Walter. He served in the Narraganset War from Marshfield, Massachusetts. He claimed his land in Greenwich, Massachusetts in 1737.

Noise, Rev. Moses. He served in the Narraganset War from Connecticut and received land in Voluntown, Connecticut in 1701.

Noland, James. He served in the Old Virginia Regiment under Col. George Washington in the 1755 and under Col. William Byrd in 1762 in the

French and Indian War. He proved his service in Bedford County, Virginia 27 March 1780.

Noland, Samuel. He served as a soldier in or about 1758 in the Old Virginia Regiment under Col. William Byrd and later under Col. Adam Stephen. He proved his service in Frederick County, Virginia 2 May 1780.

Norcross, Jeremiah. He served in the Narraganset War from Weston, Massachusetts. Nathaniel Norcross received his land in Westminster, Massachusetts in 1733.

Nordbergh, John. He was granted 2,000 acres in Cumberland County, New York for his service as a lieutenant in the 60th or Royal American Regiment in the French and Indian War 5 December 1766.

Norman, Benjamin. He served on the expedition to Canada in 1690. William Hine was admitted to his land in Lyndeboro, Maine in 1736.

Norman, John. He was granted 200 acres in Albany County, New York for his service as a corporal in the 28th Regiment of Foot in the French and Indian War 9 May 1771.

Norman, William. He served on the expedition to Canada in 1690. Simon Orn was admitted to his land in Lyndeboro, Maine in 1736.

Norris, John. He served in the Old Virginia Regiment in the French and Indian War. He proved his right in Botetourt County, Virginia in April 1780. He assigned his warrant for 50 acres.

North, Joshua. He served as a drummer in the French and Indian War and prayed for land in New York 23 September 1766.

Northcut, William. He served as a soldier for eight months under Col. William Byrd in the French and Indian War. He proved his right in Buckingham County, Virginia 13 March 1780. He assigned his 50 acre warrant.

Northrop, Joseph. He served in the Narraganset War from Connecticut and received land in Voluntown, Connecticut in 1701.

Norton, John. He was granted 300 acres in Craven County, South Carolina on the King's bounty 21 June 1765. He served as a sergeant in the French and Indian War.

Nourse, Robert. He served as a lieutenant in His Majesty's Navy in the French and Indian War and was entitled to 3,000 acres which he desired to locate in Fincastle County, Virginia 1 March 1775.

Nourse, William. He served as a soldier in the French and Indian War from Virginia and received 50 acres of land.

Nowland, James. He served as a soldier under Col. George Washington in 1755 and Col. William Byrd in 1762 in the French and Indian War and received a warrant for 50 acres in March 1780 in Bedford County, Virginia. He also appeared as John Noland.

Nowland, John. He was granted 200 acres in Albany County, New York for his service as a noncommissioned officer in the 55th Regiment of Foot in the French and Indian War 1 April 1772.

Nowlson, Charles. He was granted 200 acres on Log Creek, South Carolina on the King's bounty 1 June 1767. He served as a sergeant in the French and Indian War.

Noyes, Rev. James. He served in the Narraganset War from Connecticut and received land in Voluntown, Connecticut in 1701.

Noyes, Moses. He served on the expedition to Canada in 1690. Joseph Noyes received his land in Bethel, Maine in 1767.

Noyes, Thomas. He served as lieutenant under Capt. Hugh Mason and received 250 acres of land in Massachusetts 19 October 1664. He was from Sudbury, Massachusetts.

Nunn, Joseph. He was granted 3,000 acres in West Florida for his service as a lieutenant in the navy in the French and Indian War 10 May 1779.

Nutcher, Richard. He was granted 450 acres in Granville County, South Carolina on the King's bounty 21 June 1765. He served as a sergeant in the French and Indian War.

Oaks, Frederick. He was granted 50 acres in Amelia Township, South Carolina on the King's bounty for his service in the French and Indian War 21 June 1765.

Oates, Manuill. He served in the French and Indian War and petitioned for his land in New York 17 March 1767.

Oats, Edmond. He was granted 200 acres in Albany County, New York for his service as a corporal in the 4th Battalion in the Royal American or 60th Regiment of Foot in the French and Indian War 27 September 1769.

Oats, Edward. He was granted 200 acres in Craven County, South Carolina on the King's bounty 6 February 1773. He served as a midshipman in the French and Indian War.

O'Brien, James. He was granted 50 acres in St. Paul Parish, Georgia for his service as a soldier in the 1st Battalion in the 60th or Royal American Regiment of Foot in the French and Indian War in 1771.

Offill, John. He served as a noncommissioned officer in the French and Indian War and assigned his 200 acre warrant in Virginia.

Ogden, Amos. He was granted 3,000 acres in West Florida for his service as a captain in the French and Indian War 6 May 1774. In 1760 he raised a company at his own expense and marched from Albany, New York to Quebec. In 1761 he saw action in the West Indies. He was discharged in New York in 1762.

Ogden, John. He served as a corporal in the French and Indian War and petitioned for 200 acres on the King's bounty in South Carolina 5 February 1765.

Ogden, Jonathan. He served as a captain in the French and Indian War and petitioned for land 30 December 1765 in New York.

Ogilvie, Alexander. He was granted 200 acres in Albany County, New York for his service as a corporal in the 40th Regiment of Foot in the French and Indian War 30 May 1771.

Ogilvie, John. He was granted 2,000 acres in Charlotte County, New York for his service as a staff officer in the 4th Battalion in the 60th Regiment of Foot in the French and Indian War 26 May 1772.

Ogilvie, John. He served as chaplain in the 4th Battalion Royal American Regiment in the French and Indian War and petitioned for 2,000 acres in Albany County, New York 28 March 1767.

Oglesby, William. He served as a soldier under Col. William Byrd in the French and Indian War and assigned his 50 acres in Virginia.

Olcott, Thomas. He served in the Pequot War and received a grant of land in Soldiers' Field in Hartford, Connecticut.

Old, Robert. He served in the Narraganset War from Connecticut and received land in Voluntown, Connecticut in 1701.

Oliphant, John. He was granted 50 acres in Colleton County, South Carolina on the King's bounty for his service in the French and Indian War 23 January 1773.

Oliver, Benjamin. He served as a soldier in the French and Indian War until 1758. He petitioned for 50 acres 10 February 1780 in Caroline County, Virginia.

Oliver, James. Massachusetts granted land to Nathaniel Barnes for the use of Capt. James Oliver 14 October 1687.

Oliver, James. He served as a captain in the Narraganset War from Boston, Massachusetts. His nephew, Daniel Oliver, received land in Bedford, New Hampshire in 1733.

Oliver, Thomas. He was granted 200 acres in Gloucester County, New York for his service as a noncommissioned officer in the 46th Regiment for twenty-six years and in the French and Indian War 5 April 1770.

Olmstead, Richard. He served in the Pequot War and received a grant of land in Soldiers' Field in Hartford, Connecticut.

Omohundro, Richard. He served as a corporal in the French and Indian War and received his 200 acre land warrant in Virginia which he assigned.

O'Neal, James. He was granted 50 acres in Craven County, South Carolina on the King's bounty 21 June 1765. He served as a private in the French and Indian War.

O'Neal, John. He served as a soldier in the Virginia Regiment under Col. William Peachey in the French and Indian War. He petitioned for his 50 acres in February 1780 in King William County, Virginia.

O'Neal, Lodowick. He served in Col. William Byrd's Regiment in the French and Indian War until 1758 and petitioned for his land in February 1780 in Spotsylvania County, Virginia.

O'Neil, John. He was granted 200 acres in Albany County, New York for his service as a corporal in the 60th Regiment of Foot in the French and Indian War 10 May 1775. He received his discharge after he returned from Detroit to Philadelphia.

Oram, James. He served as a bombardier in the French and Indian War and received 200 acres in Nova Scotia 17 July 1776.

Ormsby, John. He was granted 300 acres in Pennsylvania for his service in the French and Indian War 1 April 1769.

Ormsby, John, Jr. He was granted 300 acres in Pennsylvania for his service in the French and Indian War 1 April 1769.

Ormsby, John. He served as a commissary in the French and Indian War in 1758, 1759, and 1760 which he had certified 28 February 1780 in Yohogania County, Virginia. He received 2,000 acres of land. He also served as paymaster.

Ormsby, Oliver. He was granted 300 acres on the Monongahela River, Pennsylvania for his service in the French and Indian War 1 April 1769.

Orris, Roger. He served in the Narraganset War from Connecticut and received land in Voluntown, Connecticut in 1701.

Osborn, William. He served in the Narraganset War from Salem, Massachusetts. His son, William Osborn, claimed his land in Amherst, New Hampshire in 1734.

Osborn, William. He was granted 200 acres in Charlotte County, New York for his service as a noncommissioned officer in the French and Indian War 12 October 1774.

Osborne, Richard. He was granted 80 acres of land in Connecticut for his service in the Pequot War 11 May 1671. He was from Fairfield.

Osburn, James. He was granted four islands in the Hudson River containing 22 acres in Albany County, New York for his service as a soldier in the 60th Regiment of Foot in the French and Indian War 18 July 1770.

Osbourne, John. He served as a soldier in Capt. Robert Mumford's Company in the French and Indian War. He proved his right in Mecklenburg

County, Virginia 14 February 1780. He assigned his right to 50 acres.

Osgood, Joseph. He served on the expedition to Canada in 1690 and received his land in Poland, Maine in 1739.

Osland, John. He served on the expedition to Canada in 1690 and received his land in Bethel, Maine in 1767.

Oswell, John. He was granted 50 acres in Gloucester County, New York for his service as a soldier in an independent company of foot in the French and Indian War 5 April 1770.

Outerbridge, White. He was granted 2,000 acres in St. Mary Parish, Georgia for his service as an ensign in Gen. James Oglethorpe's Regiment and afterwards as a lieutenant in an independent company in South Carolina in the French and Indian War 1 November 1768.

Overton, Samuel. He served as a captain in the French and Indian War and received his 3,000 acre land warrant in Virginia.

Owen, Ebenezer. He served in the Narraganset War from Taunton, Massachusetts. His son-in-law, John Woodward, claimed his land in Greenwich, Massachusetts in 1737. His grandson, Thomas Owen, claimed the right.

Owen, Henry. He was granted 200 acres in Albany County, New York for his service as a sergeant in the 46th Regiment of Foot in the French and Indian War 5 April 1771.

Owen, James. He served as a soldier in Capt. James Gunn's Company in the French and Indian War. He proved his right in Mecklenburg County, Virginia 14 February 1780. He assigned his right to 50 acres.

Pace, Henry. He served in the French and Indian War and received his land in Nova Scotia 24 October 1767.

Pace, John. He served in the French and Indian War and received his land in Nova Scotia 24 October 1767.

Packer, John. He served in the Narraganset War from Connecticut and received land in Voluntown, Connecticut in 1701. He also appeared as John Parker.

Packer, Samuel. He served in the Narraganset War from Connecticut and received land in Voluntown, Connecticut in 1701. He also appeared as Samuel Parker.

Packett, William Stewart. He served as a sergeant about three years in the French and Indian War and received a warrant for 500 acres in Virginia 19 October 1777. Capt. Thomas Bullitt certified his service.

Paddleford, —. He served in the Narraganset War and received land in Templeton, Massachusetts in 1733.

Page, Adam. He served on the expedition to Canada in 1690. Moses Gage petitioned for his land in Raymond, Maine in 1735.

Page, Alexander. He served as a soldier in the 1st Virginia Regiment about three years until he was discharged by Col. Adam Stephen during the French and Indian War. He received his 50 acre warrant in May 1780 in Montgomery County, Virginia.

Page, John. He served on the expedition to Canada in 1690. His heirs received land in Chesterfield, Massachusetts in 1739.

Page, Samuel. He served on the expedition to Canada in 1690. Ebenezer Corey received his land in Bethel, Maine in 1767.

Pain, —. He served on the expedition to Canada in 1690. James Pain, clerk, received land in Dumbarton, New Hampshire in 1735.

Paine, Thomas. He served in the Narraganset War from Eastham, Massachusetts and received land in Gorham, Maine in 1733.

Palemon, —. He served as a sergeant in the French and Indian War and petitioned for 200 acres in the fork of the Saluda on the King's bounty in South Carolina 7 August 1765.

Palmer, Edward. He was a major in the Narraganset War from Connecticut and received land in Voluntown, Connecticut in 1701.

Palmer, Elnathan. He received land in Richmond, New Hampshire in 1756 for the service of an unidentified veteran of the expedition to Canada in 1690.

Palmer, Gershom. He served in the Narraganset War from Connecticut and received land in Voluntown, Connecticut in 1701.

Palmer, Thomas. He served in the Narraganset War from Massachusetts in 1685. His son, Timothy Palmer, received his land in Buxton, Maine.

Palmer, William. He served in the Indian Wars first under Capt. Jonathan Selleck and next under Capt. Minor. His third period of service was under Maj. John Senn to Albany. He applied for land 2 May 1719 from Greenwich, Connecticut.

Panter, Frederick. He was granted 50 acres in Albany County, New York for his service as a soldier in the 80th Regiment of Foot in the French and Indian War 28 March 1771.

Panton, Francis. He was granted 2,000 acres in Charlotte County, New York for his service as a store keeper in the hospital in the French and Indian War 18 October 1775.

Parish, James. He was a soldier in one of the Virginia Regiments in the French and Indian War. He assigned his warrant for 50 acres. He also appeared as James Parrish.

Parish, Joseph. He served as a sergeant in the 2nd Virginia Regiment in the French and Indian War in 1758 and petitioned for his 200 acres in

February 1780 in Spotsylvania County, Virginia. He assigned his right. He also appeared as Joseph Parrish.

Park, John. He served in the Narraganset War from Newton, Massachusetts. His son, John Park, received his land in Westminster, Massachusetts in 1733.

Park, John. He served as a noncommissioned officer in the French and Indian War and assigned his warrant for 200 acres in New York 20 May 1767.

Park, Nathaniel. He served in the Narraganset War from Connecticut and received land in Voluntown, Connecticut in 1701.

Park, Richard. He served on the expedition to Canada in 1690. William Park received his land in Alstead, New Hampshire in 1771.

Park, Richard. He served in the expedition to Canada in 1690. Samuel Fuller received his land in Bethel, Maine in 1767.

Park, Robert. He served in the Narraganset War from Connecticut and received land in Voluntown, Connecticut in 1701.

Park, Thomas. He served in the Narraganset War from Connecticut. His heirs received land in Voluntown, Connecticut in 1701.

Parker, —. He served on the expedition to Canada in 1690. Thomas Parker received land in Dumbarton, New Hampshire in 1735.

Parker, Benjamin. He served in the campaign against the Indians in 1725. He was from Groton, Massachusetts and received his land in Pembroke, New Hampshire.

Parker, Eben. He served in the Narraganset War and received his land in Templeton, Massachusetts in 1733.

Parker, Isaac. He was on the expedition to Port Royal in 1710 and was awarded 150 acres by Massachusetts 5 January 1735/6.

Parker, John. He served on the expedition to Canada in 1690. John Parker received land in Warwick, Massachusetts in 1738.

Parker, John. He served in the Narraganset War from Andover, Massachusetts and claimed his land in Amherst, New Hampshire in 1734.

Parker, John. He served in the 17th Regiment in the French and Indian War and had his service certified in New York 28 January 1767.

Parker, John. He shared in the grant of East Greenwich, Rhode Island made to those who had rendered service in King Philip's War. The grant was made 31 October 1677.

Parker, Jonathan. He served in the Narraganset War from Reading, Massachusetts. His nephew, Nathaniel Parker, received his land in Westminster, Massachusetts in 1733.

Parker, Jonathan. He served on the expedition to Canada in 1690 and received his land in Bethel, Maine in 1767.

Parker, Nathaniel. He received land in Richmond, New Hampshire in 1765 for the service of an unidentified veteran of the expedition to Canada in 1690.

Parker, Richard. He was a soldier under Capt. John Field in Col. William Byrd's Regiment in 1758 in the French and Indian War and received 50 acres. He was in Culpeper County, Virginia 16 August 1779.

Parker, Zacheriah. He served under Capt. John Lovewell from Massachusetts and was in the battle at Pigwacket in May 1725. He was from Concord, Massachusetts and received his land in Pembroke, New Hampshire.

Parkes, James. He served as an artificer in 1760 in the French and Indian War. He proved his service in Yohogania County, Virginia 6 March 1780.

Parkhurst, John. He served in the Narraganset War from Sudbury, Massachusetts. His son, John Parkhurst, received his land in Westminster, Massachusetts in 1733.

Parkhurst, Samuel. He served on the expedition to Canada in 1690. Joseph Stone received his land in Bethel, Maine in 1767.

Parkinson, James. He was granted 2,000 acres in Charlotte County, New York for his service as a cornet in a troop of light horse raised at Havana in the French and Indian War 18 October 1775. He also appeared as James Perkinson.

Parmelle, Robert. He served in an independent company of rangers in the French and Indian War and petitioned for land in New York 12 April 1769.

Parmer, Jonathan. He served as a captain in Col. Clapham's Pennsylvania Regiment for one year in the French and Indian War. He proved his service in Frederick County, Virginia 6 June 1780.

Parmeter, John. He served in the Narraganset War from Connecticut and received land in Voluntown, Connecticut in 1701.

Parmeter, Joseph. He served in the Narraganset War from Sudbury, Massachusetts. His brother, Benjamin Parmeter, received his land in Westminster, Massachusetts in 1733.

Parmeter, William. He served in the Narraganset War from Watertown, Massachusetts. His son, George Parmeter, received his land in Westminster, Massachusetts in 1733.

Parrish, Moses. He served as a soldier in the French and Indian War and assigned his 50 acres in Virginia.

Parsinger, Abraham. He served as a soldier in Capt. John Dickinson's Company of Rangers in 1757 in the French and Indian War and died underage. His father, Jacob Parsinger, assigned his right to 50 acres in Virginia.

Parsinger, Jacob, Sr. He served as a soldier in Capt. John Dickinson's Company of Rangers in 1757 in the French and Indian War. He assigned his right to 50 acres in Virginia.

Parsinger, Philip. He served as a soldier in Capt. John Dickinson's Company of Rangers in 1757 in the French and Indian War. He died underage. His father, Jacob Parsinger, assigned his right to 50 acres in Virginia.

Parson, Benjamin. He served in the Narraganset War from Massachusetts in 1685. His land was located in Buxton, Maine. He may have been Benjamin Pearson.

Parsons, Thomas. His sons, Ebenezer Parsons and Samuel Parsons, were granted 50 acres in Connecticut for his service in the Pequot War 13 October 1698.

Patch, Thomas. He served on the expedition to Canada in 1690 and petitioned for his land in Raymond, Maine in 1735.

Paterson, Matthew. He served as a captain or foreman of a company of carpenters in the French and Indian War and petitioned for land in New York in 1767.

Patrick, Hugh. He was granted 200 acres in Albany County, New York for his service as a sergeant in the 44th Regiment of Foot in the French and Indian War 5 January 1768.

Patterson, Donald. He was granted 50 acres in Albany County, New York for his service as a soldier in the 77th Regiment of Foot in the French and Indian War 15 August 1765.

Patterson, Andrew. He served on the expedition to Canada in 1690. James Patterson received his land in Bethel, Maine in 1767.

Patterson, Mark. He served as a lieutenant in the French and Indian War and petitioned for his land in New York 28 January 1767.

Patterson, Moses. He was granted 200 acres in Albany County, New York for his service as a drummer in the 55th Regiment of Foot in the French and Indian War 1 April 1772.

Patterson, Walter. He served as a lieutenant in the French and Indian War and was granted land in New York 28 January 1767.

Patterson, William. He was granted 200 acres in Albany County, New York for his service as a noncommissioned officer in the 80th Regiment of Foot in the French and Indian War 17 August 1765.

Patterson, William. He was granted 200 acres in Albany County, New York for his service as a noncommissioned officer in the 80th Regiment of Foot in the French and Indian War 6 July 1771.

Pattison, James. He served in the Narraganset War. His son, James Pattison, received his land in Templeton, Massachusetts in 1733.

Paul, Christmas. He was granted 2,000 acres in West Florida for his service as warrant officer in the French and Indian War 9 July 1772.

Paul, Hugh. He served in the French and Indian War and took his land in Fincastle County, Virginia 15 December 1772.

Paul, William. He was granted 200 acres in Albany County, New York for his service as a corporal in the 55th Regiment of Foot in the French and Indian War 26 July 1765.

Paul, William. He received his 50 acres of land in West Florida for his service as a private in the French and Indian War 9 April 1777.

Pauling, Henry. He was a soldier in the Virginia Regiment under Col. William Byrd in 1760 in the French and Indian War and proved his service in Botetourt County, Virginia 10 February 1780.

Paull, Audley. He served as a captain in the French and Indian War and received his 2,000 acre land warrant in Virginia.

Pavie, Richard. He served in the French and Indian War and petitioned for land 22 November 1766 in New York. He assigned his right to Robert Buchanan 20 January 1767.

Pawlett, William. He served as a captain in the 59th Regiment in the French and Indian War and received 3,000 acres in Nova Scotia 15 March 1774.

Payne, John. He served as a lieutenant in the Frontier Battalion under Col. William Byrd in the French and Indian War. He assigned his right to his 2,000 acres of land in Virginia. He also appeared as John Payn and John Payton.

Payne, John. He was granted 2,000 acres in West Florida for his service as a master's mate in the navy in the French and Indian War 12 December 1776.

Payson, John. He served in the Narraganset War from Roxbury, Massachusetts. His son, John Payson, received land in Bedford, New Hampshire in 1733.

Peabody, William. He served in the Narraganset War from Boxford, Massachusetts. His son, Stephen Peabody, claimed his land in Amherst, New Hampshire in 1734.

Peachy, William. He served as paymaster to the 2nd Virginia Regiment in the French and Indian War in 1758 and received a warrant for 1,000 acres 18 November 1779 in King William County, Virginia.

Peachy, William. He had a warrant for 5,000 acres for service as Lieutenant Colonel Commandant of the Frontier Battalion in 1759 in the French and Indian War which he received 6 March 1780 in Richmond

County, Virginia. He also had a warrant for 3,000 acres for his service as a captain in the Regiment of Col. George Washington in 1755, 1756, and 1757 in the French and Indian War which he received 6 March 1780 in Richmond County, Virginia.

Peacock, Isaac. He was granted 200 acres in Charlotte County, New York for his service as a noncommissioned officer in the 60th Regiment of Foot in the French and Indian War 18 October 1775.

Peacock, Samuel. He served on the expedition to Canada in 1690. Samuel Peacock received land in Warwick, Massachusetts in 1738.

Peal, George. He served on the expedition to Canada in 1690. Jonathan Peal was admitted to his land in Lyndeboro, Maine in 1736.

Pearce, —. He served on the expedition to Canada in 1690. Thomas Boardman received his land in Winchendon, Massachusetts in 1736.

Pearce, John. He served as a sergeant in the French and Indian War and petitioned for his 200 acres of land in New York 7 February 1764.

Pearce, Gyles. He shared in the grant of East Greenwich, Rhode Island made to those who had rendered service in King Philip's War. The grant was made 31 October 1677.

Pearce, John. He was a mason. He shared in the grant of East Greenwich, Rhode Island made to those who had rendered service in King Philip's War. The grant was made 31 October 1677.

Pearce, William. He served as a private in the French and Indian War and was named in New York 1 April 1767.

Pearcy, Charles. He served as a soldier in Col. William Byrd's Regiment in 1759 in the French and Indian War. He received his warrant for 50 acres 23 March 1780 in Orange County, Virginia.

Pearse, Edward. He served as a noncommissioned officer in the 2nd Battalion of the Royal Regiment of Artillery in the French and Indian War and petitioned for land 11 June 1766 in New York.

Pearse, Henry. He served as a sergeant of miners in the 2nd Battalion of the Royal Regiment of Artillery in the French and Indian War and petitioned for land 11 June 1766 in New York.

Peart, Griffin. He served as an ensign in the French and Indian War and received 2,000 acres of land in Virginia.

Pecher, Samuel. He served in the Narraganset War from Bridgewater, Massachusetts. His son, Samuel Pecher, claimed his land in Greenwich, Massachusetts in 1737.

Peckham, John. He shared in the grant of East Greenwich, Rhode Island made to those who had rendered service in King Philip's War. The grant was made 31 October 1677.

Peckham, Stephen. He shared in the grant of East Greenwich, Rhode Island made to those who had rendered service in King Philip's War. The grant was made 31 October 1677.

Peckham, Thomas. He shared in the grant of East Greenwich, Rhode Island made to those who had rendered service in King Philip's War. The grant was made 31 October 1677.

Pedley, Nathaniel. He served as a private in an independent company of foot in the French and Indian War and was discharged the second time in New York 16 November 1763. He had previously been discharged as unfit for duty due to blindness 8 December 1759.

Peirce, Isaac. He served in the Narraganset War from Middleborough, Massachusetts. He claimed his land in Greenwich, Massachusetts in 1737.

Peirce, Samuel. He served in the Narraganset War from Massachusetts in 1685. His land was located in Buxton, Maine. He also appeared as Samuel Parse.

Pembleton, —. He served as a captain in the Narraganset War from Connecticut and received land in Voluntown, Connecticut in 1701. He also appeared as — Pendleton.

Pence, Adam. He served as a soldier and corporal in the 60th Regiment in the French and Indian War. William Gilliland filed a petition in his behalf for his land in New York 17 April 1773.

Pence, Jacob. He served as a soldier in the French and Indian War in Capt. Peter Hogg's Company of Rangers in 1757 until disbanded at Bedford. He received his warrant for 50 acres 28 March 1780 in Buckingham County, Virginia.

Pendall, William. He served in the Narraganset War from Connecticut and received land in Voluntown, Connecticut in 1701.

Pendergrass, Garrett. He served under Col. Adam Stephen as the second in command under General Forbes in 1758 and under General Stanwix in 1759 in the French and Indian War. He received pay as a lieutenant and was an inhabitant of Virginia at the time of his enlisting. His widow was Margaret Pendergrass, and his infant son and heir was Jesse Pendergrass. His service was proved in Jefferson County, Virginia [Kentucky] 7 March 1781.

Penell, August. He was granted 50 acres in Albany County, New York for his service as a soldier in the 60th or Royal American Regiment in the French and Indian War 28 March 1771.

Pengally, John. He served in the Narraganset War from Suffield, Massachusetts. He claimed his land in Greenwich, Massachusetts in

1737.

Penix, Edward. He served as a soldier under Col. William Byrd in the French and Indian War. He died after he left the service. His warrant was issued in Prince Edward County, Virginia 7 February 1780. His heir, Jeremiah Penix, assigned his right to 50 acres.

Penix, John. He served as a soldier in Capt. Samuel Overton's Company of Rangers in 1756 in the French and Indian War. He assigned his 50 acre warrant.

Penn, Adam. He served as a corporal in the 3rd Battalion in the 60th Regiment in the French and Indian War and petitioned for land 3 March 1766 in New York.

Penn, Gabriel. He served as a sergeant in the Virginia Regiment in the French and Indian War under Col. William Byrd. He proved his right in Amherst County, Virginia 1 November 1779. He received a warrant for 200 acres which he assigned.

Penn, Jacob. He served as a soldier in the French and Indian War from Virginia and received a warrant for 50 acres.

Pennecuff, Philip. He was granted 50 acres in Gloucester County, New York for his service as a soldier in the 80th Regiment of Foot in the French and Indian War 5 April 1770.

Penny, William. He was granted 50 acres in Albany County, New York for his service as a soldier in the 55th Regiment of Foot in the French and Indian War 27 September 1769.

Perkins, Abraham. He was a veteran of the expedition to Canada in 1690 and was of Ipswich, Massachusetts when he claimed his land in Winchendon, Massachusetts in 1736.

Perkins, Joseph. He served in the Narraganset War from Wenham, Massachusetts. William Rogers and Joseph Perkins claimed his land in Amherst, New Hampshire in 1734.

Perkins, Samuel. He served in the Narraganset War from Topsfield, Massachusetts. His heirs claimed his land in Amherst, New Hampshire in 1734.

Perkins, Zaccheus. He served in the Narraganset War from Topsfield, Massachusetts and claimed his land in Amherst, New Hampshire in 1734.

Perley, Jacob. He served in Lovewell's War in Massachusetts and received his land in Petersham, Massachusetts in 1733.

Perley, Jeremiah. He served in Lovewell's War in Massachusetts and received his land in Petersham, Massachusetts.

Perrie, John. He served as a sergeant in the French and Indian War and received 200 acres of land in Virginia which he assigned.

Perrin, James. He served as a sergeant in Capt. John McNeal's Company in the 1st Virginia Regiment in the French and Indian War. He proved his right in Charlotte County, Virginia 7 February 1780. He assigned his right to 200 acres.

Perrin, Thomas. He was a veteran of the expedition to Canada in 1690. He was of Rowley, Massachusetts when he claimed his land in Winchendon, Massachusetts in 1736.

Perry, Josiah. He served in the Narraganset War from Rehoboth, Massachusetts. His son, Josiah Perry, claimed his land in Greenwich, Massachusetts in 1737.

Perry, Mervyn. He was granted 2,000 acres in Albany County, New York for his service as an ensign in an independent company of foot or the Queen's Royal American Regiment in the French and Indian War 2 November 1764.

Perry, Richard. He was granted 50 acres in Albany County, New York for his his service as a soldier in the 46th Regiment of Foot in the French and Indian War 28 October 1765.

Perry, Samuel. He served on the expedition to Canada in 1690. Samuel Perry received land in Warwick, Massachusetts in 1738.

Persloe, Henry. He was granted 200 acres in Albany County, New York for his his service as a corporal in the 80th Regiment of Foot in the French and Indian War 15 June 1765.

Persons, John. He was granted 50 acres in Albany County, New York for his service as a soldier in the 80th Regiment of Foot in the French and Indian War 26 July 1765.

Petchlett, George. He was granted 50 acres in Albany County, New York for his service as a soldier in the 60th Regiment of Foot in the French and Indian War 29 October 1765.

Peters, Andrew. He served in the Narraganset War from Andover, Massachusetts. His son, Andrew Peters, claimed his land in Amherst, New Hampshire in 1734.

Peters, Edmund. He served as a sergeant under Col. William Byrd in Capt. Thomas Fleming's Company for eight months in 1758 in the French and Indian War. He received his 50 acre warrant 13 March 1780 in Buckingham County, Virginia.

Peters, Joseph. He served in the French and Indian War and received 500 acres of land in Nova Scotia 9 July 1771.

Peters, Richard. He served on the expedition to Canada in 1690. Joseph Killiard was admitted to his land in Lyndeboro, Maine in 1736.

Peterson, Henry. He served in the Narraganset War from Connecticut and received land in Voluntown, Connecticut in 1701. He also appeared as Henry Paterson.

Petrie, Andrew. He served as a private in the French and Indian War and petitioned for 50 acres on the King's bounty in South Carolina 5 April 1768.

Pettit, Isaac. He served as an ensign in Capt. Hunt's Company of Rangers in the French and Indian War and assigned his 400 acre and 1,600 acre warrants in Virginia.

Petty, Joseph. He was awarded 200 acres by Massachusetts for his service 13 January 1735/6.

Petry, David. He had his service as a soldier in the 46th Regiment in the French and Indian War certified 11 December 1766 in New York. He assigned his right to land to Robert Buchanan 21 January 1767.

Petry, Robert. He served in the 46th Regiment in the French and Indian War. Hannah Petry was certified as his widow in New York 12 December 1766. She assigned her right to the land to Robert Buchanan 21 January 1767.

Peyton, Francis. He served as a subaltern in the French and Indian War from Virginia and received 2,000 acres of land.

Pfister, Francis. He served as a lieutenant in the 1st Battalion of the Royal Americans in the French and Indian War and petitioned for 2,000 acres 18 February 1766 in New York.

Phelon, Edward. He served in the French and Indian War and received his land in Nova Scotia 12 October 1771.

Phelps, Edward. He served in the Narraganset War and received land in Templeton, Massachusetts in 1733.

Phelps, Robert. He served from Massachusetts in the campaign against the Indians in 1725. He was from Lancaster, Massachusetts and received his land in Pembroke, New Hampshire.

Phelps, Samuel. He served in the Narraganset War from Andover, Massachusetts and claimed his land in Amherst, New Hampshire in 1734.

Pheney, Robert. He received land in Richmond, New Hampshire in 1765 for the service of an unidentified veteran of the expedition to Canada in 1690.

Philips, Alexander. He served in the Narraganset War from Charlestown, Massachusetts. His heirs received his land in Westminster, Massachusetts in 1733.

Philips, Andrew. He served as a lieutenant in the French and Indian War and received 2,000 acres in New York.

Philips, James. He was granted 50 acres in Albany County, New York for his service as a soldier in the 44th Regiment of Foot in the French and Indian War 3 September 1771.

Philips, James. He was entitled to 200 acres of land for his service as a noncommissioned officer in Virginia. John Philips, relationship not indicated, assigned the land in Virginia.

Philips, John. He was granted 200 acres in Albany County, New York for his service as a drummer in the 76th Regiment of Foot in the French and Indian War 18 February 1775.

Phillips, —. He served on the expedition to Canada in 1690. Michael Phillips received land in Dumbarton, New Hampshire in 1735.

Phillips, Henry. He served as a subaltern in the French and Indian War and petitioned for his 2,000 acres in New York 22 January 1776.

Phillips, Richard. He served as a soldier in Capt. Joseph Fox's Company in 1755 in the French and Indian War. He petitioned for his 50 acres 12 March 1780 in Louisa County, Virginia.

Phillips, John. He served as a lieutenant in the French and Indian War and petitioned for his 2,000 acres of land in New York 5 September 1764.

Phillips, Timothy. He served in the Indian war. His only surviving son, John Phillips of Charlestown, was awarded 200 acres by Massachusetts 6 January 1735/6.

Phillips, William. He served as a soldier in the Pequot War and received a grant in Soldiers' Field in Hartford, Connecticut.

Phillips, William. He served as an ensign in the French and Indian War and petitioned for his 2,000 acres in New York 22 January 1776.

Phillips, William. He served as a soldier in the 2nd Virginia Regiment under Col. William Byrd in 1760 in the French and Indian War. He petitioned for his 50 acres 14 February 1780 in King and Queen County, Virginia.

Phillips, William. He served as a soldier in a company of rangers under Capt. Joseph Fox in 1755 in the French and Indian War. He petitioned for his 50 acres 13 March 1780 in Louisa County, Virginia.

Phillips, William. He served as a subaltern in the French and Indian War and received 3,000 acres in Kentucky County, Virginia.

Phillips, Zephaniah. He served as a non-commissioned officer in Gen. Braddock's campaign in the French and Indian War. He proved his service in Frederick County, Virginia 3 September 1782.

Phinney, —. He served on the expedition to Canada in 1690. Edward Phinney received land in Dumbarton, New Hampshire in 1735.

Phinney, —. He served on the expedition to Canada in 1690. Robert Phinney received land in Dumbarton, New Hampshire in 1735.

Phinney, John. He served in the Narraganset War from Barnstable, Massachusetts and received his land in Gorham, Maine in 1733.

Phipps, David. He served as Master and Commander in His Majesty's Navy in the French and Indian War and received 5,000 acres in Nova Scotia 21 August 1783.

Phipps, William. He served as a soldier in the French and Indian War and had his service certified in Montgomery County, Virginia 5 October 1779 for his 50 acres of land.

Phyn, George. He was granted 2,000 acres in Albany County, New York for his service as a lieutenant in the 44th Regiment of Foot in the French and Indian War 14 October 1765.

Pickard, John. He served in the Narraganset War from Massachusetts in 1685. His grandson, Jonathan Pickard, received his land in Buxton, Maine.

Picket, Elias. He served in the Narraganset War from Beverly, Massachusetts. His son, Joseph Picket, claimed his land in Amherst, New Hampshire in 1734.

Pickworth, John. He served on the expedition to Canada in 1690. Daniel Epes was admitted to his land in Lyndeboro, Maine in 1736.

Pickworth, Samuel. He served in the Narraganset War from Salem, Massachusetts. His heirs claimed his land in Amherst, New Hampshire in 1734.

Pierce, Jeremiah. He served as a corporal in the French and Indian War and was entitled to 200 acres. He received his warrant in October 1779 in Montgomery County, Virginia. His name may have been Jeremiah Prince.

Pierce, John. He served in the Pequot War and received a lot north of Soldiers' Field in Hartford, Connecticut.

Pierce, Joseph. He served on the expedition to Canada in 1690. His brother, James Pierce, received his land in Woburn, Massachusetts in 1738.

Pierce, Moses. He was a veteran of the expedition to Canada in 1690. His nephew, Moses Wells of Ipswich, claimed his land in Winchendon, Massachusetts in 1736.

Pierce, Thomas. He served on the expedition to Canada in 1690. His brother, John Pierce, received his land in Woburn, Massachusetts in 1738.

Pierce, William. He was granted 50 acres in Albany County, New York for his service as a private in the 44th Regiment of Foot in the French and Indian War 8 June 1771.

Pigg, Henry. He served as a private in the 2nd Virginia Regiment of Regulars in the French and Indian War and received a warrant for 50 acres 17 January 1780 in Prince Edward County, Virginia.

Piggot, Robert. He was granted 50 acres in Albany County, New York for his service as a soldier in the 80th Regiment of Foot in the French and Indian War 17 September 1765.

Pike, Elias. He received his land form Massachusetts 3 December 1735.

Pike, James. He served in the Narraganset War from Reading, Massachusetts. He applied for his land 4 June 1685. His son, Onesiphorous Pike, received his land in Westminster, Massachusetts in 1733.

Pike, Joseph. He served on the expedition to Canada in 1690 and received land in Poland, Maine in 1739.

Pike, Samuel. He served in the late wars and was granted 200 acres land in Massachusetts.

Pindar, —. He served on the expedition to Canada in 1690. His son, John Pindar, received his land in Winchendon, Massachusetts in 1736.

Pinhorne, John. He served as a lieutenant in the 45th Regiment in the French and Indian War. His widow, Gertrude Pinhorne, petitioned for 2,000 acres of land in his right in New York 4 September 1775.

Pinier, Peter. He served as a lieutenant in the French and Indian War and petitioned for his 2,000 acres of land in New York 18 February 1772.

Pinmore, John. He served as a soldier in the Virginia Regiment in the French and Indian War and assigned his right to 50 acres in Virginia. His widow, Rebecca Pinmore, assigned the warrant in 1775. He also appeared as John Penmire.

Pinney, Jonathan. He received his land in West Florida for his service as a subaltern in the French and Indian War 26 October 1776.

Pinney, William. He served in the French and Indian War and had his service certified 20 November 1766 in New York.

Pintard, Samuel. He had his service as a captain in the 30th Regiment in the French and Indian War certified in New York 11 September 1773.

Piper, William. He was granted 553 and 609 acres in Berks County, Pennsylvania for his service as a captain in the French and Indian War 3 February 1769.

Piper, William. He was granted 247 ½ acres in Cumberland County, Pennsylvania for his service as an ensign in the French and Indian War 3 February 1769.

Pitt, Thomas. He was granted 200 acres in West Florida for his service as a midshipman in the Royal Navy at the reduction of Quebec in the French and Indian War 29 September 1778.

Pitts, William. He served as a corporal in the French and Indian War and petitioned for land in New York 17 March 1767.

Pittifer, Samuel. He received land in Richmond, New Hampshire in 1765 for the service of an unidentified veteran of the expedition to Canada in 1690.

Plank, Henry. He served as a soldier in the French and Indian War and petitioned for his land in New York in November 1766.

Plant, John. He served in the Narraganset War from Connecticut. His heirs received land in Voluntown, Connecticut in 1701.

Platts, John. He served on the Canada Expedition in 1690 and petitioned for land in Massachusetts in 1736.

Pless, Clement. He was granted 50 acres in Albany County, New York for his service as a soldier in the 3rd Battalion of the 60th Regiment of Foot in the French and Indian War 30 May 1765.

Plimbly, Thomas. He served in the Narraganset War from Boston, Massachusetts. His heirs received land in Bedford, New Hampshire in 1733.

Plumb, John. He served in the Narraganset War from Connecticut and received land in Voluntown, Connecticut in 1701.

Plumbly, John. He served as a soldier in Capt. Christian's Company of Regulars in the French and Indian War. He proved his right in Botetourt County, Virginia in March 1780. He assigned his warrant for 50 acres.

Plummer, Joseph. He served in the Narraganset War from Massachusetts in 1685. His grandson, John Plummer, received his land in Buxton, Maine.

Plunket, William. He was granted 547 and 619 acres in Berks County, Pennsylvania for his service as a captain in the French and Indian War 3 February 1769.

Plunkett, John. He served as a drummer in the French and Indian War and petitioned for 200 acres on the King's bounty in South Carolina 30 May 1764.

Plunkett, John. He served in Capt. John Dickenson's Company of Rangers in 1759 in the French and Indian War and proved his service in Augusta County, Virginia 21 March 1780.

Plunkett, William. He served in the French and Indian War and petitioned for 200 acres on the King's bounty in South Carolina 30 May 1764.

Plyer, John. He was granted 200 acres in Albany County, New York for his service as a drum major in the 60th Regiment of Foot in the French and Indian War 30 October 1765.

Plympton, John. He served in the Narraganset War from Medfield,

Massachusetts. His son, John Plympton, received land in Bedford, New Hampshire in 1733.

Poe, David. He served as a soldier in the 1st Virginia Regiment under Col. William Byrd in the French and Indian War. He proved his right in James City County, Virginia 3 November 1779. He received a warrant for 50 acres which he assigned.

Poe, Samuel. He served as a sergeant in the 1st Virginia Regiment in the French and Indian War. He proved his right in James City County, Virginia 8 November 1779. He assigned his 200 acre warrant to Robert Goode of Prince Edward County, Virginia. He was a native of Virginia and served under Gen. Forbes in 1758. His service was also proved in Amelia County, Virginia 25 November 1779.

Poe, Thomas. He was a soldier under Col. William Byrd in the 1st Virginia Regiment in the French and Indian War and assigned his warrant for 50 acres in Virginia.

Poindexter, John. He was a soldier in Capt. Joseph Fox's Company in the French and Indian War and received a warrant for 50 acres 12 October 1779 in Louisa County, Virginia.

Poindexter, Richard. He was a soldier under Capt. Joseph Fox in the French and Indian War. His warrant for 50 acres was issued to his brother, Capt. John Poindexter, as guardian of one of the coheirs 12 October 1779 in Louisa County, Virginia.

Poland, Samuel. He was a veteran of the expedition to Canada in 1690. He was of Ipswich, Massachusetts when he claimed his land in Winchendon, Massachusetts in 1736.

Polard, Samuel. He served in the Narraganset War from Boston, Massachusetts. His grandson, Samuel Kneeland, received land in Bedford, New Hampshire in 1733.

Pollard, John. He served from Massachusetts in the campaign against the Indians in 1725. He was from Billerica, Massachusetts and received his land in Pembroke, New Hampshire.

Pollard, Oliver. He served in Lovewell's War in Massachusetts and received his land in Petersham, Massachusetts in 1733.

Polson, John. He was granted 50 acres in Charlotte County, New York for his service as a soldier in the Royal Highland Regiment of Foot in the French and Indian War 12 July 1775.

Polson, John. He co-patented land in Botetourt County, Virginia 15 December 1772 for having encouraged men to enlist in the French and Indian War.

Pond, William. He served as a sergeant in the 46th Regiment in the French and

Indian War and had his service certified 13 December 1766 in New York. He assigned his right to land to Robert Buchanan 20 January 1767.

Ponder, Tobias. He served as a private in the 60th Regiment in the French and Indian War and petitioned for his land in New York 7 April 1768. He also appeared as Tobias Pounder.

Ponset, John. He served as a sergeant in the 55th Regiment in the French and Indian War and petitioned for 200 acres of land in New York 3 July 1775. He also appeared as John Pounset.

Ponston, Richard. He served as a soldier in the French and Indian War and assigned his 50 acre warrant in Virginia. [His name was Reinhart Punstein.]

Poo, Thomas. He served in the French and Indian War as a soldier and received a warrant for 50 acres 17 May 1774 in Virginia. He seems to be a different soldier than Thomas Poe, *quo vide.*

Poole, John. He served on the expedition to Canada in 1690. Jonathan Poole petitioned for his land in Raymond, Maine in 1735.

Poole, Jonathan. He served on the expedition to Canada in 1690. His son, Jonathan Poole, received his land in Woburn, Massachusetts in 1738.

Poole, Samuel. He served on the expedition to Canada and received land in Massachusetts 10 December 1735.

Poole, William. He served as a private in the 35th Regiment in the French and Indian War and petitioned for his 50 acres in New York 30 January 1775.

Poor, Charles. He served as a soldier in the Virginia Regiment under Col. William Byrd in 1759 in the French and Indian War. He received his 50 acre warrant in February 1780 in Westmoreland County, Virginia.

Poore, Henry. He served in the Narraganset War from Massachusetts in 1685. His son, Samuel Poore, received his land in Buxton, Maine.

Poore, Samuel. He served in the Narraganset War from Massachusetts in 1685. His land was located in Buxton, Maine.

Pope, Ebenezer. He served on the expedition to Canada in 1690. His brother, Ralph Pope, received his land in Ashburnham, Massachusetts in 1736.

Pope, John. He was a veteran of the expedition to Canada in 1690. His eldest daughter, Susanna Pope, married Thomas Wilder of Lancaster, Massachusetts who received his land in Ashburnham, Massachusetts in 1736.

Porter, Benjamin. He was granted 200 acres in Albany County, New York for his service as a sergeant in the 27th Regiment of Foot in the French and Indian War 5 July 1765.

Porter, John. He served on the expedition to Canada in 1690. John Porter received land in Chesterfield, Massachusetts in 1739. He also appeared as John Potter.

Porter, Nathaniel. He served on the expedition to Canada in 1690 and petitioned for his land in Raymond, Maine in 1735.

Porter, Noah. He was granted 2,000 acres in Charlotte County, New York for his service as a lieutenant in a corps of rangers in the French and Indian War 23 November 1775.

Porter, Robert. He served in the late Indian War and received his land in Massachusetts 4 June 1685. He was from Lynn, Massachusetts.

Porter, Thomas. He was granted 200 acres in Albany County, New York for his service as a sergeant in the 28th Regiment of Foot in the French and Indian War 8 March 1771.

Posey, Francis. He served as a soldier under Col. Adam Stephen in the French and Indian War and received his 50 acre warrant in Virginia.

Posey, John. He served as a captain in the French and Indian War and was entitled to 3,000 acres of land in Virginia which he assigned.

Potes, William. He served on the expedition to Canada in 1690. Thomas Cloutman was admitted to his land in Lyndeboro, Maine in 1736.

Potter, Benjamin. He served as a sergeant in the French and Indian War and petitioned for 200 acres in New York 9 July 1764.

Potter, Edmund. He served in the Narraganset War from Massachusetts in 1685. His land was located in Buxton, Maine.

Potter, Robert. He served in the Narraganset War from Lynn, Massachusetts. He applied for his land 4 June 1685. His son, Benjamin Potter, claimed his land in Amherst, New Hampshire in 1734.

Potter, William. He served as a soldier in the French and Indian War under Col. William Byrd and received 50 acres in Virginia.

Potts, Alexander. He was granted 2,000 acres in Albany County, New York for his service as a surgeon in the 60th Regiment of Foot in the French and Indian War 23 August 1764.

Potts, William. He served in the Narraganset War from Connecticut and received land in Voluntown, Connecticut in 1701.

Potts, William. He was granted 2,000 acres in Albany County, New York for his service as a lieutenant in the 60th Regiment of Foot in the French and Indian War 26 April 1765.

Pouder, Tobias. He was granted 50 acres in Albany County, New York for his service as a soldier in the 60th Regiment of Foot in the French and Indian War 25 May 1771.

Poulter, William. He served as a soldier in the Virginia Regiment under Col.

William Byrd in 1759 in the French and Indian War. He proved his right in Culpeper County, Virginia 20 December 1779. He assigned his warrant for 50 acres.

Powel, Ambrose. He served as a staff officer in the French and Indian War in 1755 and received his 2,000 acre warrant 27 April 1780 in Orange County, Virginia.

Powel, Benjamin. He served as a sergeant in Col. William Byrd's Regiment in 1758 in the French and Indian War. He proved his service in Orange County, Virginia 23 September 1779. He assigned his 50 acres.

Powell, John. He served as a private in H.M.'s Royal Regiment in the French and Indian War and petitioned for land 30 May 1766 in New York.

Powell, John. He served as a soldier in the French and Indian War until discharged in 1758. He proved his right in Caroline County, Virginia in March 1780. He assigned the warrant for 50 acres.

Powell, Simon. He served as a sergeant in Capt. Peter Hogg's Company of Rangers in the French and Indian War. His warrant was issued to his coheiresses, Elizabeth Jennet Head, the wife of James Head, and Sally Riddle, wife of Lewis Riddle, 23 December 1779 in Orange County, Virginia.

Powell, Thomas. He was a soldier in Col. William Byrd's Regiment in the French and Indian War in 1758. He proved his right in Orange County, Virginia 25 November 1779. He assigned his 50 acre warrant. He also appeared as Thomas Powal.

Power, Giles. He was granted 50 acres in Albany County, New York for his service as a soldier in the 80th Regiment of Foot in the French and Indian War 6 July 1771.

Powers, Jonathan. He received his land from Massachusetts 3 December 1735.

Prator, Thomas. He was granted 200 acres in Albany County, New York for his service as a bombardier in the Royal Regiment of Artillery in the French and Indian War 30 May 1765.

Pratt, James. He was granted 50 acres in Albany County, New York for his service as a soldier in the 47th Regiment in the French and Indian War 30 May 1771.

Pratt, Joseph. He served in the Narraganset War from Charlestown, Massachusetts. His heirs received his land in Westminster, Massachusetts in 1733.

Pratt, Marshall. He served in the French and Indian War and took his land in Fincastle County, Virginia 15 December 1772.

Pratt, William. He served in the Pequot War and received a grant of land in Soldiers' Field in Hartford, Connecticut.

Preble, Jedediah. He served as a Brigadier General in the French and Indian War and applied for land in Massachusetts 25 June 1771.

Prentice, Henry. He was from Cambridge and applied for his land in Massachusetts 10 December 1735.

Prentice, Thomas. He served as a captain in the Narraganset War from Newton, Massachusetts. His heirs received his land in Westminster, Massachusetts in 1733.

Presberry, Stephen. He served on the expedition to Canada in 1690 and received land in Dumbarton, New Hampshire in 1735.

Prescote, Peter. He served in the Narraganset War. Because his name was omitted by neglect, Massachusetts granted land in the town of Boxford for the support of his widow.

Prescott, Benjamin. He served as a colonel in the Narraganset War and received land in Templeton, Massachusetts in 1733.

Presson, John. He served in the Narraganset War from Andover, Massachusetts. He claimed his land in Amherst, New Hampshire in 1734.

Preston, William. He served as a captain of a company of regulars in the French and Indian War from 14 July 1755 to 24 June 1756. He then served under Col. James Patton until the latter was killed; he then served under the governor and Maj. Andrew Lewis. He was allowed his land by Lord Dunmore in December 1773. He also commanded a company of rangers from 8 June 1757 to 4 May 1759 under the governor (to May 1758) and Maj. Andrew Lewis. He applied for additional land 5 April 1780 in Montgomery County, Virginia. His second application was rejected.

Prevoost, Augustine. He was granted 5,000 acres in Albany County, New York for his service as a field officer in the 3rd Battalion of the 60th Regiment of Foot in the French and Indian War 10 March 1768.

Prevost, Augustine. He was granted 2,000 acres in Albany County, New York for his service as a lieutenant colonel in the 60th Regiment of Foot in the French and Indian War 22 August 1768.

Prevost, Augustine. He was granted 1,000 acres in West Florida for his service as a lieutenant in the French and Indian War 16 January 1778. He also received 5,000 acres as a military governor 31 December 1776. He received a third grant of 2,000 acres for his service as adjutant 30 March 1778. He was the son of Lt. Col. Augustine Prevost.

Prevost, James Marcus. He received his land in West Florida for his service as a major of a brigade and also as a captain in the French and Indian War 9 July 1778.

Prevost. James Marcus. He was granted 5,000 acres in Orange County, New York for his service as a major in the French and Indian War 18 January 1775.

Prevost, Mark. He served as a captain in the French and Indian War and was granted land in New York 16 April 1774.

Price, Jeremiah. He served in the French and Indian War as a corporal and proved his right to 200 acres in Montgomery County, Virginia 9 September 1779.

Price, Joseph Stores. He served as a soldier for one year in 1758 under Col. George Washington in the French and Indian War. He received his 50 acre warrant 13 March 1780 in Buckingham County, Virginia. He also appeared as Joshua Stores Price.

Price, Leonard. He served as a captain in one of the Virginia Regiments in the French and Indian War and was awarded 3,000 acres which was issued to his executors, Thomas Mann Randolph and Joseph Woodson, in Henrico County, Virginia 7 September 1779.

Price, Richard. He served as 4th lieutenant aboard H.M.S. *Fame* in the French and Indian War and petitioned for 3,000 acres of land in New York 12 June 1771.

Price, Thomas. He was granted 50 acres in Albany County, New York for his service as a soldier in the 60th Regiment of Foot in the French and Indian War 29 October 1765.

Price, Thomas. He was granted 50 acres in Gloucester County, New York for his service as a soldier in the 1st Battalion in the 60th Regiment of Foot in the French and Indian War 5 April 1770.

Price, Thomas. He served as a captain in the Pennsylvania Regiment under Col. Mercer in the French and Indian War. He wanted to locate his 3,000 acres in Fincastle County, Virginia.

Price, William. He was granted 200 acres in Albany County, New York for his service as a sergeant in the 60th Regiment of Foot in the French and Indian War 1 April 1772.

Pricket, Richard. He was granted 50 acres in Albany County, New York for his service as a soldier in the Inniskilling Regiment of Foot in the French and Indian War 7 October 1771.

Priest, John. He served in the Narraganset War and received land in Templeton, Massachusetts in 1733.

Priest, Joseph. He served in the Narraganset War from Watertown, Massachusetts. His son, Joseph Priest, received his land in Westminster, Massachusetts in 1733.

Priest, William. He served in the Narraganset War from Ashfield,

Massachusetts. His son, William Priest, claimed his land in Greenwich, Massachusetts in 1737.

Prince, Charles. He was granted 3,000 acres in Craven County, South Carolina on the King's bounty for his service in the French and Indian War 6 January 1775.

Prince, Isaac. He served in the Narraganset War from Boston, Massachusetts. His heirs received land in Bedford, New Hampshire in 1733.

Prince, Richard. He served in the Narraganset War from Salem, Massachusetts. His nephew, Joseph Prince, claimed his land in Amherst, New Hampshire in 1734.

Pringle, George. He was granted 50 acres in Albany County, New York for his service as a soldier in the 55th Regiment of Foot in the French and Indian War 1 July 1771.

Prior, Joseph. He received land in Richmond, New Hampshire in 1765 for the service of an unidentified veteran of the expedition to Canada in 1690.

Proctor, Benjamin. He served on the expedition to Canada in 1690. John Proctor was admitted to his land in Lyndeboro, Maine in 1736.

Proctor, John. He was granted 300 acres in Pennsylvania for his service as a captain in the French and Indian War 1 April 1769.

Proctor, Jonathan. He was granted 200 acres in Albany County, New York for his service as a noncommissioned officer in the 46th Regiment of Foot in the French and Indian War 8 March 1771.

Proctor, Thomas. He served as a bombardier in H.M.'s Royal Regiment of Artillery in the French and Indian War. His survey for his 200 acres of land was returned in New York 30 May 1765.

Proudfoot, Christopher. He was granted 150 acres in Craven County, South Carolina on the King's bounty for his service in the French and Indian War 24 August 1770.

Prout, Ebenezer. He served in the Narraganset War from Middletown, Massachusetts. He claimed his land in Greenwich, Massachusetts in 1737.

Proute, Richard. He served in the Narraganset War from Scituate, Massachusetts. His son, John Proute, received land in Bedford, New Hampshire in 1733.

Provinder, John. He served in the Narraganset War. Benjamin Muzzey drew his land in Templeton, Massachusetts in 1733.

Provo, William. He served as a soldier in the 2nd Virginia Regiment under Capt. Hancock Eustace in the French and Indian War as proved by certificate from Lt. Charles Mynn Thurston. He applied for his 50 acre warrant 27 March 1780 in Fauquier County, Virginia.

Provoost, Adam. He was granted 50 acres in Charlotte County, New York for his service as a soldier in the Royal Highland Regiment of Foot in the French and Indian War 12 July 1775.

Provost, John. He was granted 200 acres in Craven County, South Carolina on the King's bounty 6 February 1773. He served as a sergeant in the French and Indian War.

Prush, John. He was granted 50 acres in Albany County, New York for his service as a soldier in the 55th Regiment of Foot in the French and Indian War 27 September 1769. He also appeared as John Prusk.

Pryce, David. He served as agent to transports in America in the French and Indian War and petitioned for his 5,000 acres of land in New York in 1764.

Pryor, John. He served as a soldier in Capt. William Preston's Company of Rangers in 1756, 1757, and 1758 in the French and Indian War. He proved his service in Botetourt County, Virginia in April 1780. He assigned his right to 50 acres.

Puckett, Drury. He served as a sergeant in the Virginia Regiment under Col. William Byrd in the French and Indian War. He proved his service in Washington County, Virginia 18 January 1780 and assigned his right to 200 acres.

Pugsley, John. He served in the Narraganset War from Yarmouth, Massachusetts and received land in Gorham, Maine in 1733.

Pulcepher, Benedictus. He was a veteran of the expedition to Canada in 1690. His nephew, Ebenezer Pulcepher of Gloucester, Massachusetts claimed his land in Winchendon, Massachusetts in 1736.

Pullin, Loftus. He served as a soldier in Capt. William Preston's Company of Rangers in the French and Indian War. He was issued a warrant for 50 acres 15 February 1780 in Augusta County, Virginia.

Purcel, Edward. He served as a soldier in the Virginia Regiment in the French and Indian War under Col. George Washington. He proved his right in Hampshire County, Virginia 10 August 1779. He sold his 50 acre warrant.

Purcel, John. He was a soldier in the Virginia Regiment under Gen. Braddock in 1755 in the French and Indian War. He assigned his right to 50 acres.

Purcell, John. He was granted 200 acres on a branch of the Saludy River in South Carolina on the King's bounty 21 June 1765. He served as a sergeant in the French and Indian War.

Purchase, John. He served in the Pequot War and received a grant of land in Soldiers's Field in Hartford, Connecticut. He also appeared as John

Purkas.

Purdee, John. He was granted 50 acres on Wilson Creek in South Carolina on the King's bounty for his service in the French and Indian War 28 January 1771.

Purviance, Samuel, Jr. He was granted 2,000 and 4,000 acres in Pennsylvania for his service in the French and Indian War 4 February 1769 and 4,000 acres on 9 February 1769.

Putnam, Eleazer. He served on the expedition to Canada in 1690. Samuel Putnam petitioned for his land in Raymond, Maine in 1735.

Putnam, James. He was granted 50 acres in Charlotte County, New York for his service as a soldier in the 27th Regiment of Foot in the French and Indian War 25 January 1773.

Putnam, Jonathan. He was in two expeditions to Port Royal and applied for land in Massachusetts 25 March 1736.

Putnam, Thomas. He served in the Narraganset War from Salem, Massachusetts. His son, Thomas Putnam, claimed his land in Amherst, Massachusetts in 1734.

Putton, William. He served in the 48th Regiment in the French and Indian War and petitioned for his land in New York 20 May 1771.

Quarles, John. He served a captain of militia and commanded a company of militia from April 1758 to January 1759 in the French and Indian War. He proved his service in Bedford County, Virginia 27 March 1780.

Quin, Patrick. He served as a private in the French and Indian War and petitioned for his land in New York in November 1766.

Quin, Peter. He served as a soldier in the 4th Battalion of the 60th Regiment in the French and Indian War and had his service certified in New York 17 January 1774.

Quinbee, Benjamin. He was from Almsbury, Massachusetts and was awarded 200 acres for his service in the Indian war 12 December 1735.

Quinier, Thomas. He received land in Alstead, New Hampshire in 1771 for the service of an unidentified veteran of the expedition to Canada in 1690.

Quinn, Edward. He was granted 50 acres in Albany County, New York for his service as a soldier in the 4th Battalion in the 60th Regiment in the French and Indian War 18 July 1770. He also appeared as Edward Quin.

Raab, John. He was granted 50 acres in Albany County, New York for his service as a soldier in the 60th or Royal American Regiment of Foot in the French and Indian War 28 March 1771.

Ragon, Timothy. He served in the 48th Regiment in the French and Indian War and petitioned for his land in New York 20 May 1771.

Ragsdale, William. He served five years in the French and Indian War. He served against the Indians in 1760. He was in the company of Capt. John McNeal under Col. Andrew Lewis. He was a native of Virginia and received his 50 acre warrant 16 May 1780 in Pittsylvania County, Virginia.

Railey, Miles. He served in an independent company of rangers in the French and Indian War and petitioned for land in New York 12 April 1769.

Rainbird, Thomas. He was granted 200 acres in Albany County, New York for his service as a corporal in the light horse in the French and Indian War 8 June 1771.

Rains, Giles. He served as a sergeant in the Virginia Regiment under Col. William Byrd in the French and Indian War. He received a warrant for 200 acres 6 May 1774 in Virginia.

Ralf, Michael. He served as a private in the 55th Regiment in the French and Indian War and had his service certified 26 November 1766 in New York. He also appeared as Michael Ralph.

Ramsay, John. He served in the French and Indian War and took his land in Fincastle County, Virginia 15 December 1772.

Ramsdell, Aquilla. He served in the Narraganset War from Lynn, Massachusetts. His son, Benjamin Ramsdell, claimed his land in Amherst, New Hampshire in 1734.

Ramsdell, Daniel. He served in the Narraganset War from Middleborough, Massachusetts. His son, Thomas Ramsdell, claimed his land in Greenwich, Massachusetts in 1737.

Ramsdell, William. He served in the Narraganset War from Enfield. He claimed his land in Greenwich, Massachusetts in 1737.

Ramsey, Augustine. He served as a soldier in the French and Indian War. His sisters, Mary Ramsey, Margaret Ramsey, Milley Ramsey, and Anne Ramsey, were entitled to his 50 acres 25 February 1780 in Essex County, Virginia.

Ramsey, Charles. He was granted 50 acres in Albany County, New York for his service as a soldier in the 60th Regiment of Foot in the French and Indian War 28 June 1770.

Ramsey, James. He was granted 2,000 acres in Albany County, New York for his service as a lieutenant in the 77th Regiment of Foot in the French and Indian War 19 October 1765. He also appeared as James Rumsey.

Ran, John. He was granted 50 acres in Gloucester County, New York for his service as a soldier in the 28th Regiment of Foot in the French and Indian War 5 April 1770.

Rand, —. He served in the Narraganset War from Lynn, Massachusetts. His son, Robert Rand, claimed his land in Amherst, New Hampshire in 1734.

Rand, William. He served on the expedition to Canada in 1690 and petitioned for his land in Massachusetts in 1735.

Randall, Samuel. He received land in Alstead, New Hampshire in 1771 for the service of an unidentified veteran of the expedition to Canada in 1690.

Randle, David. He served as a lieutenant in the French and Indian War and was killed on the field of battle. His heiress, Bathsheba Randle, proved his service in Ohio County, Virginia 3 April 1780.

Randle, Joseph. He was granted 200 acres in Albany County, New York for his service as a gunner in the Royal Artillery Regiment in the French and Indian War 30 May 1771. He also appeared as Joseph Randall.

Randolph, John Henry. He was granted 50 acres in Albany County, New York for his service as a soldier in the 60th or Royal American Regiment of Foot in the French and Indian War 30 May 1772.

Rankin, Moses. He served as a noncommissioned officer in the French and Indian War and received his 200 acre warrant 24 April 1780 in Fauquier County, Virginia.

Ranolds, John. He was granted 50 acres in Albany County, New York for his service as a soldier in the 42nd Regiment of Foot in the French and Indian War 30 October 1765.

Ratliff, James. He served as a soldier in Capt. Samuel Overton's Company of Rangers in 1755 in the French and Indian War. He proved his right in Louisa County, Virginia 14 February 1780. He assigned his right to 50 acres.

Ratliff, James. He served as a soldier in Capt. William Phillips's Company of Volunteer Rangers in the French and Indian War in 1763. He proved his right in Louisa County, Virginia 14 February 1780. He received his 50 acre land warrant.

Ratliff, John. He served as a soldier in the French and Indian War in Capt. Spotswood's Company of Rangers in 1757. He petitioned for his 50 acres 14 February 1780 in Louisa County, Virginia.

Ratzer, Bernard. He served as an assistant engineer in the French and Indian War and petitioned for land in New York 6 June 1770.

Ray, James. He served in the Narraganset War from Haddam, Massachusetts. He claimed his land in Greenwich, Massachusetts in 1737.

Ray, James. He served as a lieutenant in Virginia Regiment under Col. William Byrd in the French and Indian War and received his 2,000 acre land warrant in Virginia.

Ray, Joseph. He served in the Virginia Regiment as a cadet and marched up to Fort Ligonier where he was appointed superintendent of a company of artificers under Gen. Stanwix. He received the pay of a captain and continued in the same until 1759 when the army returned to winter quarters. He received six warrants for 500 acres each 17 November 1779 in Augusta County, Virginia.

Ray, William. He was granted 200 acres in Albany County, New York for his service as a noncommissioned officer in the 80th Regiment of Foot in the French and Indian War 5 April 1771.

Rayburn, Robert. He served in the French and Indian War in Virginia. He wished to locate his 100 acres of land in Fincastle County, Virginia.

Rayment, John. He served on the expedition to Canada in 1690. Nathaniel Rayment petitioned for his land in Raymond, Maine in 1735.

Rayment, Nathaniel. He served on the expedition to Canada in 1690 and petitioned for his land in Raymond, Maine in 1735.

Rayment, Thomas. He served in the Narraganset War from Beverly, Massachusetts. He applied for his land 4 June 1685. He claimed his land in Amherst, New Hampshire in 1734. He also appeared as Thomas Raymond.

Rayment, William. He served on the expedition to Canada in 1690. Josiah Batchelder petitioned for his land in Raymond, Maine in 1735.

Rayment, William. He served in the Narraganset War from Beverly, Massachusetts. He applied for his land 4 June 1685. His heirs claimed his land in Amherst, New Hampshire in 1734. Ebenezer Rayment drew his land. He also appeared as William Raymond.

Raymond, John, Jr. He served in the Narraganset War from Beverly, Massachusetts and petitioned for his land 4 June 1685.

Rea, Daniel. He was in two expeditions to Port Royal and applied for his land in Massachusetts 25 March 1736.

Rea, Richard. He served as a captain in the French and Indian War and petitioned for land 30 December 1766 in New York.

Reaburne, John. He served as a soldier in Capt. Peter Hogg's Company of Rangers until disbanded in 1759 in the French and Indian War. He received his warrant for 50 acres in April 1780 in Botetourt County, Virginia.

Read, Hankinson. He was a lieutenant in an independent company in Col. Henry Bouquet's expedition against the Shawnee in 1764. He received a warrant for 2,000 acres in Virginia.

Read, Jonathan. He was granted 200 acres in Albany County, New York for his service as a corporal in the 77th Regiment of Foot in the French and

Indian War 5 July 1765.

Read, Joseph. He served on the expedition to Canada in 1690 and received his land in Woburn, Massachusetts in 1738.

Read, Samuel. He served in the Narraganset War from Charlestown, Massachusetts. He received his land in Westminster, Massachusetts in 1733.

Read, Thomas. He served a lieutenant in the French and Indian War and petitioned for his 2,000 acres in New York 22 January 1776.

Realy, James. He served as a corporal in the 55th Regiment in the French and Indian War and received his 200 acres in Albany County, New York 15 May 1770.

Reamer, Isaac. He served as a corporal in the 48th Regiment in the French and Indian War and petitioned for his 200 acres in New York 12 October 1764. He also appeared as Isaac Reemer.

Reasoner, Michael. He served as a soldier in the French and Indian War in Virginia and assigned his 50 acres.

Reasoner, Michael. He served as a private in Col. William Byrd's Regiment in the French and Indian War in 1758. He requested his fifty acres 18 March 1783 in Lincoln County, Virginia [i.e. Kentucky].

Reaston, William. He was granted 115 acres in Granville County, South Carolina on the King's bounty for his service in the French and Indian War 23 May 1771.

Records, John. He received land in Richmond, New Hampshire in 1765 for the service of an unidentified veteran of the expedition to Canada in 1690.

Redman, Charles. He was a veteran of the expedition to Canada in 1690. His son, Robert Redman of Stoughton, Massachusetts, received his land in Ashburnham, Massachusetts in 1736.

Redmiller, Martin. He was granted 50 acres in Albany County, New York for his service as a soldier in the 60th Regiment of Foot in the French and Indian War 13 February 1767.

Reed, John. He served in the Narraganset War from Barrington. His son, John Reed, claimed his land in Greenwich, Massachusetts in 1737.

Reed, John. He was granted 5,000 acres in Charlotte County, New York for his service as a field officer in the 42nd Regiment of Foot in the French and Indian War 12 October 1774.

Reed, Joseph. He served in Lovewell's War in Massachusetts and received his land in Petersham, Massachusetts.

Reed, Patrick. He was granted 50 acres in Albany County, New York for his service as a soldier in the 80th Regiment of Foot in the French and Indian War 6 July 1771.

Reed, Thankful. He served in the Narraganset War. Nehemiah Abbot received his land in Templeton, Massachusetts in 1733.

Reed, William. He served in the 28th Regiment in the French and Indian War and petitioned for his land 18 October 1766 in New York.

Reen, John. He was granted 200 acres in Albany County, New York for his service as a noncommissioned officer in the 77th Regiment of Foot in the French and Indian War 8 March 1771.

Reeves, John. He served as a soldier in the Virginia Regiment in Capt. John Blagg's Company in Col. Adam Stephen's Regiment for five years in the French and Indian War. He was at Fort Lewis in 1762. His service was proved in Buckingham County, Virginia 14 February 1780. His son-in-law, Samuel Howard, assigned his right to 50 acres.

Regar, Lawrence. He was granted 200 acres in Albany County, New York for his service as a corporal in the 43rd Regiment of Foot in the French and Indian War 17 October 1766.

Regley, Peter. He served in the French and Indian War and had his service certified in New York in January 1767.

Reid, Alexander. He was granted 50 acres in Albany County, New York for his service as a soldier in the 42nd Regiment of Foot in the French and Indian War 28 June 1770.

Reid, Christopher. He served in the Narraganset War from Beverly, Massachusetts. He claimed his land in Amherst, New Hampshire in 1734.

Reid, David. He served as a private in the 21st Regiment in the French and Indian War and was named in New York 14 June 1769.

Reid, David. He was granted 200 acres in Albany County, New York for his service as a noncommissioned officer in the 42nd Regiment of Foot in the French and Indian War 28 June 1770.

Reid, David. He was granted 100 acres in Dutchess County, New York for his service as a sergeant in the 42nd Regiment of Foot in the French and Indian War 4 June 1772.

Reid, David. He was granted 200 acres in Charlotte County, New York for his service as a noncommissioned officer in the 42nd or Royal Highland Regiment of Foot in the French and Indian War 18 October 1775.

Reid, James. He was granted 50 acres in Albany County, New York for his service as a soldier in the 44th Regiment of Foot in the French and Indian War 15 August 1766.

Reid, John. He was granted 200 acres in Albany County, New York for his service as a corporal in the 77th Regiment of Foot in the French and Indian War 10 May 1765.

Reid, John. He was granted 200 acres in Albany County, New York for his service as a noncommissioned officer in the 42nd Regiment of Foot in the French and Indian War 30 October 1765.

Reid, Peter. He was granted 50 acres in Albany County, New York for his service as a private in the 60th Regiment of Foot in the French and Indian War 25 May 1771.

Reid, William. He received his 50 acres of land in West Florida for his service as a private in the French and Indian War 9 April 1777.

Reiley, Peter. He was granted 50 acres in Albany County, New York for his service as a private in an independent company of foot in the French and Indian War 8 June 1771.

Reilley, Bartholomew. He received his 50 acres of land in West Florida for his service as a private in the French and Indian War 9 April 1777.

Reilly, Thomas. He served as a corporal in the 60th Regiment in the French and Indian War and petitioned for land in New York 4 April 1768.

Reinard, Jean. He served as a soldier in the French and Indian War and received 50 acres of land in Nova Scotia 9 October 1770.

Reinerd, Thurston. He served in the Narraganset War from Connecticut and received land in Voluntown, Connecticut in 1701.

Rellings, William. He was granted 50 acres on the north side of the Santee River in South Carolina on the King's bounty 21 June 1765. He served as a private in the French and Indian War.

Remick, Abraham. He served on the expedition to Canada in 1690 and received his land in Dumbarton, New Hampshire in 1735.

Remington, John. He shared in the grant of East Greenwich, Rhode Island made to those who had rendered service in King Philip's War. The grant was made 31 October 1677.

Remington, Jona. He served in the Narraganset War from Cambridge, Massachusetts. His son, Jonathan Remington, received his land in Westminster, Massachusetts in 1733.

Rennol, Benjamin. He served as a soldier in the French and Indian War in 1758 under Col. George Washington. He petitioned for his 50 acres in February 1780 in Caroline County, Virginia. He also appeared as Benjamin Runnolds.

Rennolds, William. He served as a soldier until 1758 in the French and Indian War. He proved his service in Caroline County, Virginia in March 1780. He assigned his right to 50 acres.

Reordan, Timothy. He was granted 250 acres on a branch of Turkey Creek in South Carolina on the King's bounty for his service in the French and Indian War 21 June 1765. He also appeared as Timothy Riordan.

Reyley, John. He served as a soldier in the Old Virginia Regiment under Maj. Andrew Lewis in the French and Indian War and received his 50 acre warrant 19 April 1780 in Greenbrier County, Virginia.

Reynolds, Ellexander. He served in the Narraganset War from Middleborough, Massachusetts. He claimed his land in Greenwich, Massachusetts in 1737.

Reynolds, John. He served as a soldier in the Old Virginia Regiment in the French and Indian War and proved his service in Frederick County, Virginia 2 May 1780. He assigned his 50 acre warrant.

Reynolds, Richard. He served as a soldier in Col. William Byrd's Regiment in the French and Indian War until 1760 and petitioned for his 50 acres in February 1780 in Spotsylvania County, Virginia. He assigned his warrant for 50 acres in Virginia.

Reynolds, Thomas. He served in the Narraganset War from Connecticut and received land in Voluntown, Connecticut in 1701.

Rhoad, Michael. He was granted 50 acres in Albany County, New York for his service as a soldier in the 80th Regiment of Foot in the French and Indian War 30 May 1765.

Rhoades, Henry. He served in the Narraganset War from Lynn, Massachusetts and petitioned for his land 4 June 1685.

Rhodes, James. He served as a private in the French and Indian War and petitioned for 50 acres on the King's bounty in South Carolina 8 May 1765.

Ribbeath, Thomas. He served as a soldier in Capt. Peter Hogg's Company of Rangers in the French and Indian War. He proved his service in Augusta County, Virginia 18 November 1779.

Rice, Caleb. He was from Marlborough and received his land in Massachusetts 3 December 1735.

Rice, David. He served as a private in a ranging company under Capt. Evan Shelby in Maryland in 1759 in the French and Indian War. He enlisted from Virginia. He also served as a pack horse driver in 1764. He proved his service in Yohogania County, Virginia 24 April 1780.

Rice, Ebenezer. He served on the expedition to Canada in 1690. Ebenezer Rice received his land in Bethel, Maine in 1767.

Rice, George. He served as a captain of brigade of pack horse men in the Bouquet Expedition and received a warrant for 2,000 acres 8 March 1780 in Frederick County, Virginia.

Rice, John. He served in the Narraganset War from Needham. He received land in Bedford, New Hampshire in 1733.

Rice, Joseph. He served on the expedition to Canada in 1690. He applied for his land in Massachusetts 10 December 1735. His nephew, Isaac Rice, received his land in Bethel, Maine in 1767.

Rice, Michael. He served as a noncommissioned officer under Col. William Byrd in 1758 in the French and Indian War. He proved his service in Orange County, Virginia 25 November 1779. He assigned his right to 200 acres.

Rice, Moses. He received his land from Massachusetts 3 December 1735.

Rice, Phineas. He applied for his land in Massachusetts 10 December 1735.

Rice, Timothy. He served in the Narraganset War from Watertown, Massachusetts. His son-in-law, Thomas Herrington, received his land in Westminster, Massachusetts in 1733.

Rich, David. He served in an independent company of rangers in the French and Indian War and petitioned for land in New York 12 April 1769.

Richard, James. He served as a corporal in the French and Indian War and assigned his right to land to Robert Buchanan 20 January 1767 in New York.

Richards, James. He served as a soldier in the 1st Virginia Regiment in the French and Indian War and petitioned for his 50 acres 21 April 1780 in Spotsylvania County, Virginia.

Richards, John. He served in the Narraganset War from Lynn, Massachusetts. His son, John Richards, received land in Bedford, New Hampshire in 1733.

Richards, Joseph. He served in the Narraganset War from Bridgewater, Massachusetts. Benjamin Richards claimed his land in Greenwich, Massachusetts in 1737.

Richards, Peter. He served as a soldier in the French and Indian War. He received a warrant for 50 acres in Virginia which he assigned. He also appeared as Peter Richardson.

Richards, Philip. He served three years as a soldier in the French and Indian War and petitioned for his land in New York 27 April 1765.

Richardson, Caleb. He served in the Narraganset War from Massachusetts in 1685. His land was located in Buxton, Maine.

Richardson, Ezekiah. He served as a drum major in the 1st Virginia Regiment in 1758 and in 1760 under Col. Adam Stephen in the French and Indian War. His service was proved 21 April 1780 in Spotsylvania County, Virginia. His warrant for 200 acres was issued to his widow and relict, Mary Richardson.

Richardson, James. He was granted 337 acres in Orange County, New York for his service as a corporal in the 46th Regiment of Foot in the French and Indian War 22 March 1770. He was granted the tract with Augustine

Stine.

Richardson, James. He was granted 200 acres in Albany County, New York for his service as a corporal officer in the 46th Regiment of Foot in the French and Indian War 1 April 1772.

Richardson, James. He served in the French and Indian War and assigned his right to land in New York to Robert Buchanan 20 January 1767.

Richardson, John. He served on the expedition to Canada in 1690. His son, John Richardson who was *non compos* and on whose behalf his guardian, Nathan Richardson, received the land in Woburn, Massachusetts in 1738.

Richardson, Joseph. He was granted 50 acres in Albany County, New York for his service as a soldier in the 55th Regiment of Foot in the French and Indian War 27 September 1769.

Richardson, Joshua. He served in the Narraganset War and received land in Templeton, Massachusetts in 1733.

Richardson, Nicholas. He served in the Narraganset War from Massachusetts in 1685. His land was located in Buxton, Maine.

Richardson, Samuel. He was granted 200 acres in Albany County, New York for his service as a miner in the Royal Regiment of Artillery in the French and Indian War 21 October 1765.

Richardson, Thomas. He served under Capt. John Lovewell from Massachusetts and was at the battle at Pigwacket in May 1725. He was from Woburn, Massachusetts and received his land in Pembroke, New Hampshire.

Richardson, Timothy. He served under Capt. John Lovewell from Massachusetts and was wounded at the battle of Pigwacket in May 1725. He was from Woburn, Massachusetts and received his land in Pembroke, New Hampshire 23 April 1733.

Richardson, Turner. He served as a sergeant in the French and Indian War and was entitled to 200 acres which he assigned in Virginia.

Richarson, Samuel. He served in the Narraganset War from Connecticut and received land in Voluntown, Connecticut in 1701. He also appeared as Samuel Richardson.

Richeson, Holt. He served as a lieutenant in the Virginia Battalion of Regulars under William Peachey in 1759 in the French and Indian War. He petitioned for 1,000, 500, and 500 acre warrants 2 March 1780 in Hanover County, Virginia. He also appeared as Holt Richardson.

Richeson, Stephen. He served in the Narraganset War from Connecticut and received land in Voluntown, Connecticut in 1701. He also appeared as Stephen Richardson.

Richey, David. He was granted 50 acres in Albany County, New York for service as a soldier in the 47th Regiment of Foot in the French and Indian War 28 October 1765.

Richie, Thomas. He was granted 200 acres in Albany County, New York for his service as a noncommissioned officer in the 55th Regiment of Foot in the French and Indian War 28 March 1771.

Richmond, Edward. He shared in the grant of East Greenwich, Rhode Island made to those who had rendered service in King Philip's War. The grant was made 31 October 1677.

Rick, John. He served as a soldier in the French and Indian War and received 50 acres in Nova Scotia 9 October 1776.

Rickman, William. He served in the French and Indian War and received 2,000 acres in Nova Scotia 3 August 1769.

Rickout, Paul. He served as an aide de camp in the French and Indian War and filed his memorial for 5,000 acres in New York 6 September 1767.

Ridaway, John. He served in the Narraganset War from Rehoboth, Massachusetts. His son, James Ridaway, claimed his land in Greenwich, Massachusetts in 1737.

Riddle, James. He served as a noncommissioned officer in Capt. Peter Hogg's Company of Rangers in 1758 in the French and Indian War. He proved his service in Orange County, Virginia 24 February 1780. He assigned his four warrants for 50 acres each.

Riddle, Matthew. He served as a private in the 2nd Virginia Regiment in the French and Indian War. He disposed of his warrant for 50 acres.

Riddle, Richard. He served as a soldier in 1758 under Col. George Washington in the French and Indian War. He proved his right in Caroline County, Virginia in February 1780. He assigned his right to 50 acres in Virginia.

Ridenburgh, Jacob. He was granted 50 acres in Albany County, New York for his service as a soldier in the 60th or Royal American Regiment of Foot in the French and Indian War 28 March 1771.

Rider, —. He served on the expedition to Canada in 1690. Samuel Rider received land in Dumbarton, New Hampshire in 1735.

Ridout, Richard. He served as a corporal in the French and Indian War and petitioned for his 200 acres on the King's bounty in South Carolina 3 July 1764.

Rieley, Thomas. He was granted 200 acres in Albany County, New York for his service as a noncommissioned officer in the 60th Regiment of Foot in the French and Indian War 1 April 1772.

Riley, Barney. He served as a soldier in the 1st Virginia Regiment in the French and Indian War and received his warrant for 50 acres 1 February 1780 in Kentucky County, Virginia. He also appeared as Barney Ryley.

Riley, Francis. He served as a private in Capt. William Preston's Company of Rangers in the French and Indian War. His administrator, James Rowland, received his warrant for 50 acres in December 1780 in Botetourt County, Virginia.

Riley, John. He served as a soldier in the Old Virginia Regiment under Col. William Byrd in the French and Indian War. He received his 50 acre warrant in May 1780 in Rockbridge County, Virginia.

Ring, Daniel. He served as a captain in the Narraganset War from Massachusetts in 1685. His land was located in Buxton, Maine.

Ring, Samuel. He served on the expedition to Canada in 1690. Charles Richardson received his land in Bethel, Maine in 1767.

Ring, Thomas. He was a veteran of the expedition to Canada in 1690. His brother, John Ring of Gloucester, Massachusetts claimed his land in Winchedon, Massachusetts in 1736.

Ring, William. He served in the Narraganset War from Plymouth, Massachusetts and received land in Gorham, Maine in 1733.

Rion, James. He served as a soldier under Col. William Byrd in the French and Indian War and received his warrant 8 November 1779 in James City County, Virginia.

Ripley, George. He served in the Narraganset War from Boston, Massachusetts. Moses Ayres received his land in Bedford, New Hampshire in 1733.

Ripley, Jeremiah. He served in the Narraganset War from Windham. His son, Joshua Ripley, claimed his land in Greenwich, Massachusetts in 1737.

Ripley, Peter. He served on the expedition to Canada in 1690. Peter Ripley received land in Chesterfield, Massachusetts in 1739.

Risdel, William. He was granted 50 acres in Albany County, New York for his service as a soldier in the Royal American or 60th Regiment of Foot in the French and Indian War 18 July 1770.

Ritchey, John. He applied for 1,500 acres in West Florida for his service as a lieutenant in the 49th Regiment in the French and Indian War. He was rejected 16 August 1768.

Ritchie, James. He served as a soldier in Capt. Christian's Company of Rangers on the Cherokee Expedition under Col. William Byrd in the French and Indian War in 1760. He requested his 50 acres in December 1779 in Botetourt County, Virginia.

Ritchie, Patrick. He served as a soldier in the 2nd Virginia Regiment under Col. George Washington in the French and Indian War. He proved his service in Culpeper County, Virginia 21 February 1780. He assigned his right to 50 acres.

Roach, Peter. He received land in Richmond, New Hampshire in 1765 for the service of an unidentified veteran of the expedition to Canada in 1690.

Roach, Price. He was granted 200 acres in Albany County, New York for his service as a corporal in the 77th Regiment of Foot in the French and Indian War 4 July 1770.

Robanel, Thomas. He was granted 200 acres in Charlotte County, New York for his service as a noncommissioned officer in the Battalion of the 60th Regiment of Foot in the French and Indian War 12 October 1774.

Robards, Thomas. He served on the expedition to Canada in 1690. Thomas Robards received land in Chesterfield, Massachusetts in 1739.

Robarts, Matthew. He was a soldier in the 1st Virginia Regiment under Col. William Byrd in the French and Indian War. He assigned his warrant for 50 acres in Virginia.

Robbins, Daniel. He received land in Alstead, New Hampshire in 1771 for the service of an unidentified veteran of the expedition to Canada in 1690.

Robbins, Jonathan. He served as a lieutenant under Capt. John Lovewell from Massachusetts and was killed in battle at Pigwacket 8 May 1725. He was from Dunstable, Massachusetts. His widow, Margaret Robbins, and five children, the last of whom was posthumous, received his land in Pembroke, New Hampshire.

Robbins, Robert. He served in the Narraganset War and received land in Templeton, Massachusetts in 1733.

Robbins, William. He served in the Narraganset War from Reading, Massachusetts and applied for his land 4 June 1675.

Roberts, Benjamin. He was granted 200 acres in Albany County, New York for his service as a lieutenant in the 46th Regiment of Foot in the French and Indian War 29 September 1770.

Roberts, David. He served in the Narraganset War and received land in Templeton, Massachusetts in 1733.

Roberts, Francis. He served as a private in Capt. John McNeal's Company in the 1st Virginia Regiment in the French and Indian War. He proved his service in Charlotte County, Virginia 7 February 1780. He assigned his right to 50 acres.

Roberts, Matthew. He was a free Negro. He served as a soldier in the 1st Virginia Regiment in the French and Indian War. He proved his service in James City County 8 November 1779 assigned his right to 50 acres in Virginia.

Roberts, Morris. He served as a soldier in a company of rangers under Capt. Joseph Fox in 1756 in the French and Indian War. He proved his right in Louisa County, Virginia 14 February 1780. He assigned his right to

50 acres.

Roberts, Samuel. He served in the Narraganset War from Connecticut and received land in Voluntown, Connecticut in 1701.

Roberts, Thomas. He was granted 50 acres in Albany County, New York for his service as a private in the 46th Regiment of Foot in the French and Indian War 8 March 1771.

Roberts, Thomas. He served as a soldier in the 1st Battalion of the 60th Regiment in the French and Indian War and petitioned for his 50 acres of land in New York 3 March 1766.

Roberts, William. He served in the Narraganset War from Connecticut and received land in Voluntown, Connecticut in 1701.

Robertson, Alexander. He served as a private in the 78th Regiment in the French and Indian War. His service was certified in New York 18 January 1767.

Robertson, Charles. He was granted 200 acres in Albany County, New York for his service as a corporal in the 42nd Regiment of Foot in the French and Indian War 30 October 1765.

Robertson, Charles. He was granted 50 acres in Charlotte County, New York for his service as a soldier in the 42nd Regiment of Foot in the French and Indian War 1 April 1775.

Robertson, Daniel. He served as a lieutenant in the French and Indian War and petitioned for his 2,000 acres of land in New York 2 June 1767.

Robertson, Donald. He was granted 50 acres in Charlotte County, New York for his service as a soldier in the Royal Highland Regiment of Foot in the French and Indian War 12 July 1775.

Robertson, George. He served as a private in the 22nd Regiment in the French and Indian War and petitioned for his 50 acres in New York 21 September 1766.

Robertson, James. He served as a lieutenant colonel in the French and Indian War and received his land in New York 7 November 1766.

Robertson, James. He served as a deputy quartermaster general in the French and Indian War and petitioned for 5,000 acres in Cumberland County, New York 21 August 1766. He was granted 5,000 acres in Cumberland County, New York 31 March 1767.

Robertson, James. He was granted 2,000 acres in West Florida for his service as a lieutenant in the French and Indian War 16 June 1777.

Robertson, James. He served as a subaltern in a company of enlisted men on the frontier of Augusta [County] until the autumn of 1764 under various captains under the command of Col. Andrew Lewis. He received 2,000 acres in April 1780 in Montgomery County, Virginia.

Robertson, John. He was granted 50 acres in Albany County, New York for his service as a soldier in the 42nd Regiment of Foot in the French and Indian War 9 May 1771.

Robertson, James. He served as a sergeant in the French and Indian War and received his 200 acre land warrant in Virginia in 1774.

Robertson, Joseph. He was granted 300 acres in Albany County, New York for his service as a noncommissioned officer in the 55th Regiment of Foot in the French and Indian War 4 January 1775.

Robertson, William. He served as a sergeant in the French and Indian War. His service was proved in Caroline County, Virginia in March 1780. His warrant for 200 acres was issued to his heir at law, John Robertson.

Robeson, Benjamin. He was granted 200 acres in Gloucester County, New York for his service as a corporal in the 55th Regiment of Foot in the French and Indian War 5 April 1770.

Robins, —. He served on the expedition to Canada in 1690. James Robins received land in Dumbarton, New Hampshire in 1735.

Robins, —. He served on the expedition to Canada in 1690. Ziniro Robins received land in Dumbarton, New Hampshire in 1735.

Robins, Joseph. He was granted 50 acres in Colleton County, South Carolina on the King's bounty for his service in the French and Indian War 15 February 1770.

Robins, William. He served in the Narraganset War from Walpole, Massachusetts. His son, William Robins, claimed his land in Greenwich, Massachusetts in 1737. He also appeared as William Robbins.

Robinson, —. He served on the expedition to Canada in 1690. John Robinson received land in Dumbarton, New Hampshire in 1735.

Robinson, Alexander. He served in the 42nd Regiment as a soldier. He assigned his right to land for service in the French and Indian War to Robert Buchanan 20 January 1767 in New York.

Robinson, Benjamin. He served as a miner in the French and Indian War and was named in New York 20 February 1765.

Robinson, David. He was a lieutenant in a company under Capt. Alexander Sayers from July 1763 to March 1764 under Col. Andrew Lewis in the French and Indian War in Virginia and received a warrant for 2,000 acres in April 1780 in Montgomery County, Virginia.

Robinson, Edmond. He was granted 200 acres in Gloucester County, New York for his service as a noncommissioned officer in the 60th Regiment of Foot in the French and Indian War 3 February 1775.

Robinson, George. He was granted 50 acres in Albany County, New York for his service as a soldier in the 55th Regiment of Foot in the French and Indian 27 September 1769.

Robinson, George. He served as a soldier in the French and Indian War under Col. George Washington until 1758. His brother and heir at law, William Robertson, inherited the right and his heir at law, John Robertson, transferred the right to the 50 acres in Virginia. His service was proved in Essex County, Virginia 21 February 1780.

Robinson, James. He was a veteran of the expedition to Canada in 1690. John Robinson, Jr. of Dorchester, Massachusetts, whose father John Robinson, was the eldest brother of the veteran, received his land in Ashburnham, Massachusetts in 1736.

Robinson, James. He served as a subaltern in the French and Indian War and received 2,000 acres of land in Virginia.

Robinson, James. He served as a soldier in the 46th Regiment in the French and Indian War and had his service certified 11 December 1766 in New York. He assigned his right to land to Robert Buchanan 20 January 1767.

Robinson, James. He served as a sergeant in Capt. Peter Hogg's Company of Rangers in the French and Indian War in 1758. He received a 200 acre warrant 11 November 1779 in Botetourt County, Virginia.

Robinson, John. He served as a corporal in the 80th Regiment in the French and Indian War and was named in New York 16 May 1774.

Robinson, John. He served as boatswain on board H.M.S. *Onondaga* in the French and Indian War and petitioned for 2,000 acres of land in New York 31 July 1771.

Robinson, John. He served as a captain under Lord Dunmore in 1774. He proved his service in Yohogania County, Virginia 28 March 1780.

Robinson, John. He was granted 2,000 acres in West Florida for his service as a staff officer in the navy in the French and Indian War 15 July 1775.

Robinson, Jonathan. He served as a lieutenant and was slain in the campaign against the Indians. His widow, Margaret Robinson, and his five children received land in Massachusetts 30 July 1728.

Robinson, Joseph. He served as a corporal in the 55th Regiment in the French and Indian War and petitioned for his land in New York 15 November 1774. He also appeared as Joseph Robertson.

Robinson, Robert. He served as a miner in the French and Indian War and was named in New York 20 February 1765.

Robinson, Samuel. He served as a private in the French and Indian War and had his petition for land granted in New York 7 August 1771.

Robinson, Samuel. He served as a sergeant in the regiment under Col. George

Washington in the French and Indian War. His brother and heir was William Robinson who assigned the right to 200 acres in Virginia. His service was proved in Essex County, Virginia 21 February 1780.

Robinson, Thomas. He served as captain of H.M.S. packet *Hariot* in the French and Indian War and petitioned for his land in New York 15 July 1766.

Robinson, William. He served on the expedition to Canada in 1690. In 1736 Abel Robinson was admitted to his land in Lyndeboro, Maine.

Robinson, William. He served as a lieutenant in the company of Capt. Alexander Sayers and Col. Andrew Lewis from July 1763 to March 1764 on the frontiers of Augusta in the French and Indian War. He received his warrant for 2,000 acres in April 1780 in Montgomery County, Virginia.

Robottom, Matthew. He served as a soldier in one of the Virginia Regiments in the French and Indian War in Capt. Thomas Bullitt's Company under Col. Adam Stephen and was discharged 8 March 176[?]. He assigned his warrant of 50 acres in Virginia. He was deceased by 1779.

Robson, Benjamin. He was granted 200 acres in Albany County, New York for his service as a miner in the Royal Regiment of Artillery in the French and Indian War 29 October 1765. He also appeared as Benjamin Robinson.

Robson, Robert. He was granted 200 acres in Albany County, New York for his service as a miner in the Royal Regiment of Artillery in the French and Indian War 29 October 1765. He also appeared as Robert Robinson.

Roch, Edward. He was granted 50 acres in Albany County, New York for his service as a soldier in the 47th Regiment of Foot in the French and Indian War 6 August 1765. He also appeared as Edward Roache.

Rochet, Peter. He was granted 2,000 acres in West Florida for his service as a staff officer in the French and Indian War 24 July 1772.

Rock, John. He served in the French and Indian War and received his land in Nova Scotia 12 October 1771.

Rockenfoos, John. He was granted 200 acres in Gloucester County, New York for his service as a soldier in the 4th Battalion in the 60th Regiment of Foot in the French and Indian War 5 April 1770.

Rocket, Benjamin. He was awarded 150 acres by Massachusetts 23 March 1735/6 for his service in the Indian war at Black Point when Capt. Sweet was killed. He was from Wrentham.

Rockley, George. He served in the French and Indian War and petitioned for land in New York 2 February 1769.

Rocksteur, Paul. He was granted 50 acres in Albany County, New York for his service as a soldier in the 60th or Royal American Regiment of Foot in the French and Indian War 28 March 1771.

Rockwell, Daniel. He served as a lieutenant in the French and Indian War and received 2,000 acres in Nova Scotia in 1781.

Rockwood, Benjamin. He was from Wrentham, Massachusetts and petitioned for land for his service against the Indians. He received 200 acres in 1737.

Rodgers, George. He was granted 50 acres in Albany County, New York for his service as a soldier in the 27 Regiment of Foot in the French and Indian War 30 October 1765.

Rodgers, James. He was granted 200 acres in Charlotte County, New York for his service as a noncommissioned officer in the 60th Regiment of Foot in the French and Indian War 18 October 1775.

Rodney, Sir George Brydges, Baronet. He was granted 5,000 acres in West Florida as a post captain in the French and Indian War 13 October 1775.

Roe, James. He served as a soldier in the 1st Virginia Regiment in Capt. Mordecai Buckner's Company until discharged in February 1762 by Col. Adam Stephen in the French and Indian War. He received his 50 acre warrant 11 May 1780 in Southampton County, Virginia.

Rogers, Arthur. He was granted 200 acres in Albany County, New York for his service as a corporal in the 80th Regiment of Foot in the French and Indian War 25 May 1771.

Rogers, Edward. He was granted 50 acres in Albany County, New York for his service as a soldier in the 60th Regiment of Foot in the French and Indian War 28 June 1770.

Rogers, Gamaliel. He served in the Narraganset War from Boston, Massachusetts. His son, Simon Rogers, received land in Bedford, New Hampshire in 1733.

Rogers, George. He was granted 200 acres in Albany County, New York for his service as a corporal in the 27th Regiment of Foot in the French and Indian War 1 June 1770.

Rogers, James. He was granted 50 acres in Connecticut for his service in the Pequot War 11 May 1671.

Rogers, James. He was granted 3,000 acres in Albany County, New York for his service as a captain in an independent company of rangers in the French and Indian War 30 May 1765.

Rogers, James. He was granted 200 acres in Albany County, New York for his service as a sergeant in the 28th Regiment of Foot in the French and Indian War 25 May 1771.

Rogers, Nathaniel. He served in the Narraganset War from Billerica, Massachusetts and received land in Templeton, Massachusetts in 1733.

Rogers, Robert. He served as a captain in the French and Indian War and received 3,000 acres in New York 4 July 1764.

Rogers, Samuel. He served in the Narraganset from Connecticut and received land in Voluntown, Connecticut in 1701.

Rogers, Thomas. He served in the Narraganset War from Massachusetts in 1685. His land was located in Buxton, Maine.

Rogers, William. He served as a soldier under Col. William Byrd in 1758 in the French and Indian War. He proved his right in Orange County, Virginia 25 November 1779. He assigned his right to 50 acres.

Rolf, Daniel. He served in the Narraganset War from Massachusetts in 1685. His land was located in Buxton, Maine.

Rolfe, Benjamin. He was a clergyman. He, his wife, and daughter were slain in the attack on Haverhill in August 1708 by the Indians. His son, Benjamin Rolfe, was awarded 600 acres by Massachusetts 17 June 1735.

Rolfe, Thomas. He was granted 400 acres on the Chickahominy Ridge in Virginia for his service as commander of Fort James and for garrisoning said fort at his own expense 8 August 1653.

Rollins, Nicholas. He served in the Narraganset War from Massachusetts in 1685. His land was located in Buxton, Maine.

Rollins, Vincent. He served as a soldier in the 2nd Virginia Regiment under Capt. Hancock Eustace in the French and Indian War as proved by certificate from Lt. Charles Mynn Thurston. He received his 50 acre warrant 27 March 1780 in Fauquier County, Virginia.

Rood, Thomas. He served in the Narraganset War from Connecticut and received land in Voluntown, Connecticut in 1701.

Rooker, Abraham. He was granted 50 acres in Gloucester County, New York for his service as a soldier in the 28th Regiment of Foot in the French and Indian War 5 April 1770.

Roost, Leonard. He was granted 200 acres in Albany County, New York for his service as a noncommissioned officer in the French and Indian War 28 March 1771.

Root, Thomas. He served in the Pequot War and received a grant of land in Soldiers' Field in Hartford, Connecticut.

Rose, Hugh. He served as a lieutenant in the French and Indian War. His widow, Anna Rose, petitioned for 2,000 acres in Albany County, New York in May 1765.

Rose, James. He was granted 50 acres in Albany County, New York for his service as a sergeant in the 55th Regiment of Foot in the French and Indian War 28 March 1771. He also appeared as James Rosse.

Rose, Joseph. He served in the Narraganset War from Massachusetts in 1685. His land was located in Buxton, Maine.

Rose, Robert. He served in the Pequot War and received a grant of land in Connecticut which he gave to his son-in-law in 1679.

Rose, Thomas. He served in the Narraganset War from Connecticut and received land in Voluntown, Connecticut in 1701. He also appeared as Thomas Ross.

Roseboom, Barent. He served as a lieutenant in the French and Indian War and petitioned for land 30 December 1766 in New York.

Roseboom, Mydert. He served as a lieutenant colonel in the French and Indian War and petitioned for land 30 December 1766 in New York.

Roser, John. He served as a noncommissioned officer in the French and Indian War and received a warrant for 200 acres in Virginia which he assigned. He also appeared as John Rosser.

Rosewell, Lewis. He served as drumbeater in the 46th Regiment in the French and Indian War and petitioned for land in New York 30 December 1771.

Roskruge, Thomas. He served as a lieutenant in the Royal Artillery in the French and Indian War and petitioned for his 2,000 acres of land in New York 6 May 1765.

Ross, Alexander. He served as a sergeant in the 1st Battalion of the Royal American Regiment in the French and Indian War and petitioned for his land in New York 15 April 1765.

Ross, Alexander. He served as a noncommissioned officer in the French and Indian War and received 200 acres in Nova Scotia 9 October 1776.

Ross, Alexander. He was granted 2,000 acres in West Florida for his service as a staff officer in the French and Indian War 19 November 1777.

Ross, Alexander. He was entitled to 2,000 acres for his service as a subaltern in the French and Indian War. His warrant was issued in Virginia.

Ross, James. He was granted 2,000 acres in Albany County, New York for his eight years of service as an apothecary's mate in a military hospital in the French and Indian War 16 April 1765.

Ross, James. He was granted 200 acres in Albany County, New York for his service as a corporal in the 55th Regiment of Foot in the French and Indian War 1 July 1771.

Ross, James. He was granted 2,000 acres in Charlotte County, New York for his service as a staff officer in the hospital in the French and Indian

War 20 April 1775.

Ross, James. He served as sergeant in the 78th Regiment under Capt. McConnell in the French and Indian War and petitioned for his land in New York 8 July 1766.

Ross, John. He was a veteran of the expedition to Canada in 1690 and was of Ipswich, Massachusetts when he claimed his land in Winchendon, Massachusetts in 1736.

Ross, John. He served in the Narraganset War from Salem, Massachusetts. His son-in-law, Jonathan March, claimed his land in Amherst, New Hampshire in 1734.

Ross, John. He was granted 3,000 acres in Albany County, New York for his service as a captain in the 95th Regiment of Foot in the French and Indian War 19 November 1771.

Ross, John. He served in the French and Indian War and received 600 acres in Nova Scotia 23 December 1772.

Ross, Joseph. He served in the Narraganset War from Marshfield, Massachusetts. He claimed his land in Greenwich, Massachusetts in 1737.

Ross, Philip. He served as a lieutenant in an independent company in Col. Henry Bouquet's expedition against the Shawnee in 1764. He received 2,000 acres 28 October 1779 in Virginia.

Ross, Robert. He served as a soldier under Col. Henry Bouquet. He proved his service in Augusta County, Virginia 22 March 1780. He assigned his warrant for 50 acres.

Ross, William. He served as a soldier in the 1st Virginia Regiment in the French and Indian War and petitioned for his land in February 1780 in Spotsylvania County, Virginia. He assigned the warrant for 50 acres.

Rossbottom, James. He was granted 200 acres in Albany County, New York for his service as a sergeant in the 55th Regiment of Foot in the French and Indian War 1 April 1772.

Rosson, Joseph. He served as a soldier in the 4th Battalion Royal Americans in the French and Indian War and petitioned for his land 22 October 1766 in New York.

Rote, Andrew. He served as a private in a Virginia Regiment in the French and Indian War. He proved his service in Yohogania County, Virginia 27 March 1780.

Rothwell, Claiborne. He served as a soldier in Capt. William Phillips's Company of Volunteer Rangers in 1763 in the French and Indian War. He proved his service in Louisa County, Virginia 14 February 1780. He assigned his warrant for 50 acres. He also appeared as Claiborne

Routhwell.

Rothwell, William. He served in the French and Indian War and petitioned for his land in New York 29 September 1775.

Rotstone, John. He served as a corporal in the 80th Regiment in the French and Indian War and was granted land in New York 16 April 1767.

Roulson, John. He was granted 200 acres in Albany County, New York for his service as a noncommissioned officer in the 80th Regiment of Foot in the French and Indian War 6 July 1771.

Rouse, John. He served as a sergeant in a company of Rangers under Capt. Robert Rutherford in the French and Indian War in 1758 and 1759. He proved his service in Berkeley County, Virginia in March 1780 and received a warrant for 200 acres.

Row, Bannister. He served as a sergeant in the Virginia Regiment in the French and Indian War and received 200 acres which William Row located in Fincastle County, Virginia in March 1774.

Row, Benjamin. He served as a soldier in the French and Indian War and desired to locate his 50 acres in Botetourt County, Virginia in January 1774.

Row, Henry. He served in the Narraganset War from Gloucester, Massachusetts. His son, Jacob Row, claimed his land in Amherst, New Hampshire in 1734.

Row, Stephen. He served as a private in the French and Indian War and petitioned for his land in New York in November 1766.

Rowan, John. He served as a sergeant in the 60th Regiment in the French and Indian War and returned his survey for 200 acres in Albany County, New York 14 August 1766.

Rowland, Hugh. He served in the Narraganset War from Connecticut and received land in Voluntown, Connecticut in 1701.

Rowland, Thomas. He served in the French and Indian War and received 500 acres of land in Virginia.

Rowley, David. He served as a soldier in the 72nd Regiment in the French and Indian War and petitioned for his land 22 October 1766 in New York.

Rowley, John. He served on the expedition to Canada in 1690 and received land in Dumbarton, New Hampshire in 1735.

Roy, James. He served as a lieutenant under Col. William Peachey in the 1st Virginia Regiment in the French and Indian War. His children and devisees, Lunsford Lomax Roy and Ralph Lomax Roy, received his warrant for 2,000 acres 12 October 1779 in Louisa County, Virginia. Thomas Lomax was the guardian of the two children.

Roy, Peter. He served as a soldier in Col. William Peachey's Virginia Regiment for eight months in 1759 in the French and Indian War. He proved his service in Buckingham County, Virginia 14 February 1780. He assigned his 50 acre warrant.

Rudd, John. He served as a soldier in Col. William Byrd's Regiment of Regulars in the French and Indian War and received his 50 acre warrant 5 May 1780 in Chesterfield County, Virginia.

Rudd, Jonathan. He served in Narraganset War from Connecticut and received land in Voluntown, Connecticut in 1701.

Ruff, Daniel. He served in Narraganset War from Massachusetts in 1685. His land was located in Buxton, Maine.

Ruger, Frederick. He was granted 50 acres in Albany County, New York for his service as a soldier in the 60th Regiment of Foot in the French and Indian War 28 March 1771.

Ruggles, —. He served in the Narraganset War from Boston, Massachusetts. His son, John Ruggles, received land in Bedford, New Hampshire in 1733.

Ruggles, John. He served on the expedition to Canada in 1690. John Ruggles received land in Warwick, Massachusetts in 1738.

Rumsey, James. He served as a lieutenant in the 78th Regiment in the French and Indian War and petitioned for his land in New York 16 January 1764.

Rumsey, James. He was granted 1,000 acres in West Florida for his service as a lieutenant in the French and Indian War 26 March 1774. He had a second warrant for 1,000 acres.

Rush, Jacob. He served as a soldier in 1758 and 1759 under Capt. Robert Rutherford in the French and Indian War and received his 50 acre warrant in March 1780 in Berkeley County, Virginia.

Rusk, Andrew. He served as a private in the French and Indian War and petitioned for his 50 acres in New York 2 September 1766.

Rushton, William. He served in the French and Indian War. His service was certified in New York 4 January 1768.

Rusken, George. He served as a soldier under Col. William Byrd in 1760 in the French and Indian War and received a warrant for 50 acres in September 1779 in Bedford County, Virginia. His name may have been George Rustin. He also appeared as George Rusher.

Russel, Robert. He was granted 200 acres in Charlotte County, New York for his service as a corporal in the 55th Regiment of Foot in the French and Indian War 30 March 1775.

Russell, —. He was granted 2,000 acres in West Florida for his service as a lieutenant in the French and Indian War 19 December 1764.

Russell, Benjamin. He served in the Narraganset War from Concord, Massachusetts. His grandson, James Russell, received his land in Templeton, Massachusetts in 1733.

Russell, Henry. He served as a subaltern in the French and Indian War. His heir, William Russell, received his 2,000 acre land warrant in Virginia.

Russell, James. He served as a soldier in the French and Indian War in 1760. He petitioned for his 50 acres in February 1780 in Caroline County, Virginia.

Russell, John. He was a surgeon from Barnstable, Massachusetts and served on the expedition to Port Royal under Col. March. He petitioned for and received 200 acres of land 18 August 1737.

Russell, John. He served on the expedition to Canada in 1690. His son, John Russell, received his land in Woburn, Massachusetts in 1738.

Russell, John. He was granted 200 acres in Gloucester County, New York for his service as a corporal in the 55th Regiment of Foot in the French and Indian War 5 April 1770.

Russell, William. He served in the Narraganset War from Cambridge, Massachusetts and received his land in Westminster, Massachusetts in 1733.

Russell, William. He served as a captain in the French and Indian War and received a warrant for 3,000 acres 14 March 1774 in Montgomery County, Virginia.

Russell, William. He served as a sergeant in Capt. James Gunn's Company under Col. William Byrd against the Indians in 1760 in the French and Indian War. He received his 200 acre warrant 21 March 1780 in Pittsylvania County, Virginia.

Russet, James. He was granted 50 acres in Albany County, New York for his service as a soldier in the 55th Regiment of Foot in the French and Indian War 27 September 1769.

Rust, —. He served on the expedition to Canada in 1690. His widow, Rachel Rust, claimed his land in Winchendon, Massachusetts in 1736.

Ruston, William. He was granted 50 acres in Albany County, New York for his service as a soldier in the Royal American or 60th Regiment of Foot in the French and Indian War 18 July 1770.

Rutherford, David Lord. He served as a lieutenant in the navy in the French and Indian War and received a warrant for 1,200 acres in West Florida 19 November 1777.

Rutherford, Robert. He served as an officer in the French and Indian War and was entitled to a 3,000 acre warrant in Virginia.

Rutter, Thomas. He served in the Narraganset War from Sudbury, Massachusetts. His son, Joseph Rutter, received his land in Westminster, Massachusetts in 1733.

Ruxter, Paul. He served in the French and Indian War and petitioned for land in New York 10 April 1767.

Ryalty, Daniel. He served as a soldier for five years under Col. George Washington and Col. William Byrd in the French and Indian War and received his 50 acre warrant in Virginia.

Ryan, James. He served as a soldier under Col. Adam Stephen in 1758 in the French and Indian War. His service was proved in Caroline County, Virginia 9 March 1780 at which time he was deceased. His warrant for 50 acres was assigned.

Rydout, Richard. He was granted 200 acres in Amelia Township, South Carolina on the King's bounty for his service in the French and Indian War 21 June 1765.

Ryeant, Paul. He served as a major in the 17th Regiment in the French and Indian War and petitioned for land in New York 12 February 1767. He also appeared as Paul Rycant.

Ryles, Jonathan. He was granted 50 acres in Charlotte County, New York for his service as a private in the French and Indian War 9 June 1774.

Rymes, Jonathan. He served as a soldier in the French and Indian War and petitioned for his land in New York 3 January 1770.

Ryner, John. He was granted 50 acres in Albany County, New York for his service as a soldier in the 60th Regiment of Foot in the French and Indian War 26 September 1765.

S —, Timothy. He served on the expedition to Canada in 1690. Thomas Macke [or Macoy] received his land in Bethel, Maine in 1767.

Sabin, Jeremiah. He served in the Narraganset War from Pomfret, Connecticut. His nephew, Jeremiah Sabin, claimed his land in Greenwich, Massachusetts in 1737.

Sadler, Abiel. He served in the Narraganset War from Massachusetts in 1685. His land was located in Buxton, Maine.

Sage, Joseph. He served on the expedition to Canada in 1690 and received his land in Poland, Maine in 1739.

St. Clair, Arthur. He served as a lieutenant in H. M.'s Independents and petitioned for a grant of 2,000 acres 25 April 1766 in New York.

St. Clair, Arthur. He was granted 300 acres in Pennsylvania for his service in the French and Indian War 9 February 1769.

St. Clair, Sir John, Baronet. His son, John St. Clair, by his testamentary guardians, Richard Maitland and Andrew Elliott, was granted 5,000 acres in Albany County, New York for the father's service as a field officer in the French and Indian War 8 June 1771.

St. Clair, Robert. He was granted 200 acres in Albany County, New York for his service as a corporal in the 4th Battalion in the 60th Regiment of Foot in the French and Indian War 25 May 1771.

St. Clear, Peter. He served as a corporal in the French and Indian War and petitioned for his land in New York in November 1766. He also appeared as Peter St. Clair.

St. Leger, John. He served as a sergeant in the 80th Regiment in the French and Indian War and petitioned for his 200 acres in New York 19 August 1766.

Sailor, George. He served as a soldier in the French and Indian War and received 50 acres in Nova Scotia 9 October 1776.

Sale, John. He served as a sergeant major in the 1st Virginia Regiment under Col. William Byrd in the French and Indian War in 1760. He received 200 acres. He was in Amherst County, Virginia 4 October 1779.

Sallard, John. He served as a subaltern in 1759, 1760, and 1761 in the 1st regiment of Col. William Byrd and in the 2nd Virginia Regiment in the French and Indian War. He proved his service in Richmond County, Virginia 6 March 1780. He assigned his right to the 2,000 acres.

Sallis, Nicholas. He served as a soldier in the 1st Virginia Regiment in the French and Indian War and assigned his right to 50 acres in Virginia. He proved his service in Augusta County, Virginia 21 December 1779.

Salmon, Jacob. He served as a sergeant in Col. William Peachey's Battalion in one of the Virginia Regiments in the French and Indian War. He received a warrant for 200 acres 17 November 1779 in Greenbrier County, Virginia.

Sample, Samuel. He served as a captain in the 1st Pennsylvania Regiment under Col. John Armstrong in 1764 in the French and Indian War and received his 3,000 acre warrant in Virginia.

Sampson, George. He served in the Narraganset War from Plympton, Massachusetts. He claimed his land in Greenwich, Massachusetts in 1737.

Sampson, John. He served as a soldier in the French and Indian War in 1758. He petitioned for his 50 acres in February 1780 in Caroline County, Virginia.

Sampson, Stephen. He served in the Narraganset War from Duxbury, Massachusetts and received land in Gorham, Maine in 1733.

Sampson, William. He served as a soldier in the French and Indian War from

Virginia and received 50 acres of land.

Samson, —. He served on the expedition to Canada in 1690. Jeremiah Samson received land in Dumbarton, New Hampshire in 1735.

Samuel, James. He served as a soldier in the French and Indian War in 1754. He proved his service in Caroline County, Virginia in February 1780. He assigned his right to 50 acres.

Sanders, Hopestill. He served on the expedition to Canada in 1690. Thomas Tilestone of Dorchester, Massachusetts in behalf of John Sanders, received his land in Ashburnham, Massachusetts in 1736.

Sanders, John. He served on the expedition to Canada in 1690. William Royal of Stoughton, Massachusetts received his land in the right of Samuel Sanders in behalf of John Sanders in 1736.

Sanders, John. He served as a corporal under Capt. John Field in Col. William Byrd's Regiment in 1758 in the French and Indian War. He received 200 acres. He applied in Culpeper County, Virginia 16 August 1779.

Sanders, John. He served as a soldier in the company of volunteer rangers under Capt. William Phillips in the French and Indian War. He proved his service in Louisa County, Virginia 14 February 1780. He assigned his right to 50 acres.

Sanders, Robert. He served as a corporal in the French and Indian War until 1760. He petitioned for his 200 acres 17 February 1780 in Spotsylvania County, Virginia.

Sanders, Samuel. He served on the expedition to Canada in 1690. William Royal of Stoughton in behalf of John Sanders received his land in Ashburnham, Massachusetts in 1736.

Sanders, Thomas. He served as a soldier in the 2nd Virginia Regiment under Capt. John Lightfoot in the French and Indian War. He petitioned for his 50 acres 9 March 1780 in New Kent County, Virginia.

Sanderson, William. He was granted 250 acres in Craven County, South Carolina on the King's bounty for his service in the French and Indian War 27 August 1764.

Sandfort, Robert. He served in the Narraganset War from Duxbury, Massachusetts. His son, Robert Sandfort, received his land in Gorham, Maine in 1733.

Sands, Daniel. He was granted 150 acres in Craven County, South Carolina on the King's bounty for his service as a soldier in the French and Indian War 21 June 1765.

Sanford, John. He shared in the grant of East Greenwich, Rhode Island made to those who had rendered service in King Philip's War. The grant was made 31 October 1677.

Sanger, David. He served on the expedition to Canada in 1690. David Sanger received his land in Alstead, New Hampshire in 1771.

Sanger, Nathaniel. He served in the Narraganset War from Woodstock, Connecticut. He claimed his land in Greenwich, Massachusetts in 1737.

Sangster, John. He served as a corporal in the 80th Regiment French and Indian War had a survey for 200 acres in Albany County, New York 31 May 1765.

Sansome, Richard. He served as a corporal in Capt. James Gunn's Company in the 1st Virginia Regiment in the French and Indian War and served to the end of the war. He assigned his 200 acre warrant in Virginia.

Sapeteen, Charles. He was granted 50 acres in Albany County, New York for his service as a soldier in the 77th Regiment of Foot in the French and Indian War 16 July 1765.

Sargent, Andrew. He served in the Narraganset War from York, Massachusetts. His son, Dennison Sargent, claimed his land in Amherst, New Hampshire in 1734.

Sargent, Jonathan. He served in the Canada Expedition in 1690 when Gen. Nicholson was drowned. His son, John Sargent of Gloucester, was awarded 200 acres in York County, Massachusetts 3 December 1735.

Sarson, Paul. He was granted 200 acres in Albany County, New York for his service as a corporal in the 80th Regiment of Foot in the French and Indian War 4 July 1770.

Satterwhite, James. He served as a soldier in the French and Indian War until 1758. He proved his service in Caroline County, Virginia in February 1780. He assigned his right to 50 acres.

Saunders, Robert. He was granted 200 acres in Albany County, New York for his service as a miner in the Royal Regiment of Artillery in the French and Indian War 25 January 1773.

Saunders, Robert. He served as a corporal under Col. William Byrd and Col. Adam Stephen in the French and Indian War and petitioned for his 200 acres in February 1780 in Spotsylvania County, Virginia.

Saunders, Thomas. He was granted 200 acres in Albany County, New York for his service as a miner in the Royal Regiment of Artillery in the French and Indian War 21 October 1765.

Saunders, Thomas. He served as a drummer in the French and Indian War and assigned his 50 acre warrant in Virginia.

Saunders, Thomas. He served in the French and Indian War and had his service certified in Montgomery County, Virginia for his 200 acres of land 8 March 1780.

Saunders, William. He was granted 40 acres in Orange County, New York for his service as a soldier in the 4th Battalion in the 60th Regiment of Foot in the French and Indian War 15 May 1770.

Saunders, William. He served as a soldier in the 2nd Virginia Regiment in the French and Indian War. He proved his service in Goochland County, Virginia 6 September 1779. He assigned his warrant for 50 acres of land.

Sautell, Joseph. He was granted 300 acres for his services and sufferings in the Indian Wars by Massachusetts. He also appeared as Josiah Sartell.

Savage, James. He served as an ensign in the 76th Regiment in the French and Indian War and petitioned for 2,000 acres of land in New York 21 June 1769.

Savage, John. He served as an officer in the French and Indian War and assigned his warrant for 3,000 acres in Virginia.

Savage, Perez. He served in the Narraganset War from Boston, Massachusetts. His heirs received land in Bedford, New Hampshire in 1733.

Savery, Samuel. He served in the Narraganset War from Plymouth, Massachusetts. His son, Thomas Savery, received his land in Gorham, Maine in 1733.

Savory, Robert. He served on the expedition to Canada in 1690 and received land in Poland, Maine in 1739.

Sawen, Thomas. He served in the Narraganset War from Watertown, Massachusetts. His son, John Sawen, received his land in Westminster, Massachusetts in 1733.

Sawyer, Ephraim. He served in the Narraganset War. Caleb Sawyer received his land in Templeton, Massachusetts in 1733 and was probably his brother.

Sawyer, Ezra. He served in Lovewell's War in Massachusetts and received his land in Petersham, Massachusetts.

Sawyer, Fenwick. He served in the Narraganset War from Pomfret, Connecticut. His son, Fenwick Sawyer, claimed his land in Greenwich, Massachusetts in 1737.

Sawyer, John. He served in Lovewell's War in Massachusetts and received his land in Petersham, Massachusetts in 1733.

Sawyer, Samuel. He served in Lovewell's War in Massachusetts and received his land in Petersham, Massachusetts.

Sawyer, William. He served in the Narraganset War from Massachusetts in 1685. His son, Francis Sawyer, received his land in Buxton, Maine.

Sawyers, James. He served as a sergeant in a ranging company under Col. Henry Bouquet. He proved his service in Augusta County, Virginia 17

November 1779.

Saxon, Joseph. He was granted 200 acres in Ulster County, New York for his service as a bombardier in the Royal Regiment of Artillery in the French and Indian War 6 December 1774.

Sayers, David. He served as a sergeant in Capt. Alexander Sayers's Company in 1758 and was stationed on the frontier in the French and Indian War. He received his 200 acre warrant in May 1780 in Montgomery County, Virginia.

Sayers, Alexander. He was an officer in a company incorporated with a detachment of the Virginia Regiment under Maj. Andrew Lewis on two different occasion in the French and Indian War. His son and heir, Robert Sayers, received a warrant for 2,000 acres in August 1779 in Montgomery County, Virginia.

Sayers, John. He was entitled to 2,000 acres for his service as an ensign in the Virginia Regiment under Col. William Byrd in 1758 in the French and Indian War. It was assigned to Alexander Woodrow, administrator with the will annexed of said Sayers, in Virginia. He also appeared as John Seayers. His heir was his son Thomas Sayers who was underage. The service was proved in Essex County, Virginia 20 March 1780.

Sayers, William. He served as an ensign in Capt. John Buchanan's Company from April 1758 to May 1759 in the French and Indian War. He received his 2,000 acre warrant in April 1780 in Montgomery County, Virginia.

Sayward, Joseph. He was awarded 200 acres by Massachusetts for his service 23 March 1735/6. He was from York County.

Schlatter, Michael. He was granted 2,000 acres in Albany County, New York for his service as a clerk [i.e. a chaplain] in the 60th Regiment of Foot in the French and Indian War 30 May 1765.

Schneider, George. He was granted 2,000 acres in Albany County, New York for his service as a lieutenant in the 60th Regiment of Foot in the French and Indian War 23 August 1764.

Schuyler, Cortland. He served as a captain in the French and Indian War. His heir at law, John C. Schuyler, had a memorial for 3,000 acres in Albany County, New York 22 October 1765.

Scill, Joseph. He served as a captain in the Narraganset War from Medford, Massachusetts. His son-in-law, John Hall, received his land in Westminster, Massachusetts in 1733.

Scoffel, Samuel. He was granted 200 acres in Albany County, New York for his service as a drummer in the 80th Regiment of Foot in the French and Indian War 28 June 1765.

Scot, John. He served in the Narraganset War from Roxbury, Massachusetts. His son, Joseph Scot, received land in Bedford, New Hampshire in 1733.

Scott, Charles. He served as a private, corporal, sergeant, and ensign in the 1st Virginia Regiment in the French and Indian War. He assigned his warrants of 1,000, 200, 200, 50, and 1,000 acres in Virginia.

Scott, Edward. He served as a sergeant in the 2nd Virginia Regiment in the French and Indian War. His heir, Charles Scott, assigned his warrant of 200 acres in Virginia.

Scott, Francis. He served as a soldier in the French and Indian War and was entitled to 50 acres which he assigned in Virginia.

Scott, Hugh. He was granted 50 acres in Albany County, New York for his service as a soldier in the 44th Regiment of Foot in the French and Indian War 1 April 1771.

Scott, James. He was granted 200 acres in Albany County, New York for his service as a drummer in the 55th Regiment of Foot in the French and Indian War 11 August 1768.

Scott, James. He was granted 50 acres in Albany County, New York for his service as a soldier in the 44th Regiment of Foot in the French and Indian War 24 May 1771.

Scott, John. He was granted 50 acres in Albany County, New York for his service as a soldier in the 80th Regiment of Foot in the French and Indian War 5 April 1771.

Scott, John. He served as a sergeant in the 60th Regiment in the French and Indian War and petitioned for his 200 acres in New York 30 January 1775.

Scott, Nicholas. He was a soldier in the French and Indian War and was entitled to 50 acres in Virginia which he proved in 1774. He later assigned the warrant.

Scott, Thomas. He was granted 200 acres in Albany County, New York for his service as a sergeant in the 80th Regiment in the French and Indian War 6 July 1771.

Scott, Thomas. He served as a soldier in ranging company under Capt. Charles Lewis against the Indians in 1764. He requested his 50 acres 17 November 1779 in Augusta County, Virginia.

Scott, William. He served as a soldier in the French and Indian War and received 50 acres in Nova Scotia 9 October 1776.

Scott, William. He served as a drummer in the 1st Virginia Regiment in the French and Indian War. He proved his service in Greenbrier County, Virginia 21 March 1780. He assigned his 200 acre warrant.

Scottow, Joshua. The heirs of his daughters, Elizabeth Savage, Rebecca Blackman, and Mary Cheakly, were awarded 2,600 acres by Massachusetts 14 Jan. 1735/6. Joseph Wadsworth and his wife Elizabeth Wadsworth filed the application on behalf of the more than fifty heirs. Scottow had spent upwards of £204 and more than twice that amount in fortifying his home.

Scouten, John. He was granted 50 acres in Albany County, New York for his service as a soldier in the 80th Regiment of Foot in the French and Indian War 26 July 1765.

Scruber, Charles. He was granted 200 acres in Craven County, South Carolina on the King's bounty 27 August 1764. He served as a corporal in the French and Indian War.

Scully, Michael. He served in the French and Indian War and took his land in Fincastle County, Virginia 15 December 1772.

Sealy, Christopher. He was granted 200 acres on the Saludy River in South Carolina on the King's bounty for his service in the French and Indian War 28 January 1771.

Seamon, Jonathan. He served as a corporal in 1758 and 1759 in Capt. Robert Rutherford's Company of Rangers in the French and Indian War. He received his 50 acre warrant in March 1780 in Berkeley County, Virginia.

Searl, Thomas. He served on the expedition to Canada in 1690. Benjamin Goodhue was admitted to his land in Lyndeboro, Maine in 1736.

Searles, William. He was granted 50 acres in Albany County, New York for his service as a soldier in the 80th Regiment of Foot in the French and Indian War 26 July 1765.

Seaton, Sir Henry, Baronet. He was granted 3,000 acres in Albany County, New York for his service as aid-de-camp to Major General Monckton in the French and Indian War 18 July 1767.

Seaver, John. He served on the expedition to Canada in 1690. John Seaver received land in Warwick, Massachusetts in 1738.

Seaver, Shubal. He served on the expedition to Canada in 1690. Shubal Seaver received land in Warwick, Massachusetts in 1738.

Sedwell, Thomas. He served as a matross in the 2nd Battalion Royal Regiment of Artillery in the French and Indian War and petitioned for his 50 acres in New York 24 October 1764.

Seiffer, Christopher. He served as a soldier in the French and Indian War and petitioned for his land 20 November 1766 in New York.

Self, Francis. He served as a soldier in 1754 in the French and Indian War. He proved his service in Caroline County, Virginia in February 1780 and assigned his right to 50 acres.

Self, Jeremiah. He served as a sergeant in Capt. John McNeal's Company of Regulars in the French and Indian War in 1759 and received a warrant for 200 acres in Virginia.

Semon, Alexander. He served in the French and Indian War from Virginia and received a warrant for 50 acres. [Compare with Alexander Lemon.]

Semple, Samuel. He served as a captain of a corps of rangers in Pennsylvania in the French and Indian War. He proved his service in Yohogania County, Virginia 28 February 1780.

Senter, John. He served in the Narraganset War from Charlestown, Massachusetts. His son, John Senter, received his land in Westminster, Massachusetts in 1733.

Sergeant, John. He served as a captain on the expedition to Canada in 1690 and received his land in Poland, Maine in 1739.

Sergeant, John. He served as a captain on the expedition to Canada in 1690 and received his land in Poland, Maine in 1739.

Sergeant, Samuel. He served on the expedition to Canada in 1690 and received his land in Poland, Maine in 1739.

Severance, Joseph. He was from Deerfield and received 200 acres of land in Massachusetts 3 December 1735.

Severns, Mathews. He served in an independent company of rangers in the French and Indian War and petitioned for land in New York 12 April 1769.

Severry, Edmund. He served on the expedition to Canada in 1690. Thomas Porter petitioned for his land in Raymond, Maine in 1735.

Sewell, William. He served in the Narraganset War from Weymouth, Massachusetts. His son-in-law, Nicholas Phillips, received land in Bedford, New Hampshire in 1733.

Sexton, Joseph. He served as a bombardier in the French and Indian War and petitioned for his land in New York 21 August 1772.

Shackleford, Henry. He served as a soldier in Capt. Peter Hogg's Company of Rangers in 1758 in the French and Indian War. He proved his service in Orange County, Virginia 25 November 1779. He assigned his 50 acre warrant.

Shaddock, Samuel. He served in an independent company of rangers in the French and Indian War and petitioned for land in New York 12 April 1769.

Shadon, Ludowick. He served as a sergeant under Col. Henry Bouquet until discharged 15 November 1762 in the French and Indian War. His executor and only heir, Jacob Doran, assigned his warrant for 200 acres in Virginia. His service was proved in Augusta County, Virginia 22 March 1780.

Shakespear, John. He was granted 250 acres in Granville County, South Carolina on the King's bounty for his service in the French and Indian War 28 January 1771.

Shane, Bartholomew. He was granted 50 acres in Albany County, New York for his service as a soldier in the 60th Regiment of Foot in the French and Indian War 17 September 1765.

Shaply, David. He served in the Narraganset War from Marblehead, Massachusetts. His son, Richard Shaply, claimed his land in Amherst, New Hampshire in 1734.

Sharp, Jacob. He served as a soldier in the French and Indian War and assigned his warrant for 50 acres in Virginia.

Sharp, John. He served on the expedition to Canada in 1690. John Sharp received land in Warwick, Massachusetts in 1738.

Sharp, Peter. He served as a sergeant in the 55th Regiment in the French and Indian War and petitioned for his 200 acres of land in New York 20 January 1772.

Sharp, Robert. He was from Brookline and received land from Massachusetts 3 December 1735.

Sharp, Robert. He served on the expedition to Canada in 1690 and received land in Warwick, Massachusetts in 1736.

Sharp, William. He served on the expedition to Canada in 1690. William Sharp received land in Warwick, Massachusetts in 1738.

Sharp, William. He was granted 200 acres in Albany County, New York for his service as a miner in the Royal Regiment of Artillery in the French and Indian War 21 October 1765.

Shattuck, Nathaniel. He received land in Alstead, New Hampshire in 1771 for the service of an unidentified veteran of the expedition to Canada in 1690.

Shattuck, Samuel. He served in Lovewell's War in Massachusetts and received his land in Petersham, Massachusetts.

Shattuck, William. He served in the Narraganset War and received land in Templeton, Massachusetts in 1733.

Shattuck, William. He served in the Narraganset War from Watertown, Massachusetts. He received his land in Westminster, Massachusetts in 1733.

Shautam, —. He served on the expedition to Canada in 1690. Elimas Shautam received land in Dumbarton, New Hampshire in 1735.

Shaw, Alexander. He served as a lieutenant in the French and Indian War and applied for his land in West Florida 17 May 1779 having removed there from Virginia.

Shaw, Daniel. He served in the Narraganset War from Connecticut and received land in Voluntown, Connecticut in 1701.

Shaw, Daniel. He served as a sergeant in the 108th Company of Marines in the French and Indian War and had his service certified in New York 17 February 1763.

Shaw, David. He had his service in the French and Indian War certified in New York 12 December 1766.

Shaw, James. He served as a sergeant in the 77th Regiment in the French and Indian War and petitioned for his land in New York 3 November 1764.

Shaw, James. He served as a soldier in Capt. Peter Hogg's Company of Rangers in 1757 in the French and Indian War. He received his 50 acre warrant 19 April 1780 in Greenbrier County, Virginia.

Shaw, John. He served in the Narraganset War from Connecticut and received land in Voluntown, Connecticut in 1701.

Shaw, John. He served as a drummer in H. M.'s Royal Regiment in the French and Indian War and petitioned for land 30 May 1766 in New York.

Shaw, John. He served as a lieutenant in the French and Indian War and received 2,000 acres in West Florida 12 February 1777.

Shaw, Joshua. He was granted 50 acres in Albany County, New York for his service as a soldier in an independent of foot in the French and Indian War 8 June 1771.

Shaw, Richard. He was granted 50 acres in Albany County, New York for his service as a soldier in the 55th Regiment of Foot in the French and Indian War 18 April 1769.

Shaw, William. He served as a lieutenant in the 40th Regiment of Foot in the French and Indian War and received 2,000 acres in Nova Scotia 1 March 1778.

Sheal, Arnold. He served in the 1st Battalion of the Royal American Regiment of Foot in the French and Indian War and was entitled to 200 acres which he assigned in Virginia.

Sheapard, John. He served in the Narraganset War from Massachusetts in 1685. His grandson, Timothy Sheapard, received his land in Buxton, Maine.

Sheapard, Solomon. He served in the Narraganset War from Massachusetts in 1685. His son, Solomon Sheapard, received his land in Buxton, Maine.

Sheather, Samuel. He served in the Narraganset War from Connecticut. His heirs received land in Voluntown, Connecticut in 1701.

Shedd, John. He served in the Narraganset War. His son, Benjamin Shedd, received land in Templeton, Massachusetts for his father who was still alive.

Sheels, William. He served as a private in the French and Indian War and petitioned for his land in New York in November 1766.

Sheffield, William. He served on the expedition to Canada in 1690. Isaac Sheffield received his land in Bethel, Maine in 1767.

Shehan, William. He served as deputy commissary of stores and provisions in the French and Indian War and petitioned for his 2,000 acres in New York 25 October 1774.

Shelby, Evan. He served in the French and Indian War. He was entitled to 3,000 acres for his service as a captain. He desired to locate the last 1,000 acres in Fincastle County, Virginia 7 January 1774. On 20 October 1779 he proved his service as a major of a detachment of Rangers and received 4 warrants for 500 acres each.

Shelby, John. He received 2,000 acres for his service in the French and Indian War which he desired to locate in Fincastle County, Virginia 7 January 1774.

Sheldon, John. He was an ensign in Deerfield when it was destroyed by Indians in 1703. His children, Ebenezer Sheldon and Mary wife of Samuel Clap, each received 150 acres of land from Massachusetts in 1734.

Sheldon, John. He served in the Narraganset War. His son, Samuel Sheldon, received his land in Templeton, Massachusetts in 1733.

Shelley, Joseph. He received land in Richmond, New Hampshire in 1765 for the service of an unidentified veteran of the expedition to Canada in 1690.

Shelton, John. He served as a noncommissioned officer in the 1st Virginia Regiment under Col. George Washington in the French and Indian War. He was granted 200 acres at Williamsburg, Virginia 12 October 1779. He also appeared as John Skelton.

Shepherd, John. He served in the Narraganset War from Charlestown, Massachusetts. His heirs received his land in Westminster, Massachusetts in 1733.

Shepherd, John. He served on the expedition to Canada in 1690. His nephew, John Shepherd of Stoughton, Massachusetts received his land in Ashburnham, Massachusetts in 1736.

Shepherd, John. He served on the expedition to Canada in 1690. John Shepherd received land in Warwick, Massachusetts in 1738.

Shepherd, Joseph. He was a soldier in the 2nd Virginia Regiment in the French and Indian War. He proved his service in Henrico County, Virginia 4 February 1779 and assigned his right to 50 acres.

Shepperson, John. He served as a soldier in Capt. Christopher Hudson's Company in 1758 in the French and Indian War. He proved his service in Louisa County, Virginia 11 October 1779. He assigned his warrant for 50 acres.

Shepperson, John. He served as a soldier in Capt. Samuel Overton's Company of Rangers in 1756 in the French and Indian War. He assigned the warrant for 50 acres in Virginia.

Shepperson, William. He served as a soldier in the French and Indian War and assigned his warrant of 50 acres in Virginia. Col. Samuel Meredith certified his service. He proved his service in Henrico County, Virginia in November 1779.

Sherbourn, Benjamin. He served under Col. John March and Capt. Thomas Nichols in March 1707. He was captivated by the Indians at Casco Bay. He sought 200 acres in Massachusetts 28 November 1729.

Sheriff, Charles. He was granted 2,000 acres in Charlotte County, New York for his service as a lieutenant in the 45th Regiment of Foot in the French and Indian War 18 October 1775. His brother, Capt. William Sheriff, had petitioned for the land in his behalf 31 October 1765.

Sheriff, William. He served as a captain in the 47th Regiment in the French and Indian War from New York and received 3,000 acres in Albany County, New York 14 October 1765. He also appeared as William Shireff.

Sherington, Robert. He served as a soldier in the 2nd Virginia Regiment under Capt. Hancock Eustace in the French and Indian War as proved by a certificate from Lt. Charles Mynn Thurston dated 11 October 1774. He received his 50 acre warrant 27 March 1780 in Frederick County, Virginia.

Sherman, John. He received his land from Massachusetts 3 December 1735.

Sherman, John. He served in the Narraganset War from Watertown, Massachusetts. His nephew, John Sherman, received his land in Westminster, Massachusetts in 1733.

Sherwin, Samuel. He served as an ensign in the 2nd Virginia Regiment under Col. William Byrd in the French and Indian War. He received 2,000 acres on 12 October 1779.

Shields, Hugh. He was granted 50 acres in Albany County, New York for his seven years of service as a soldier in the 35th Regiment of Foot in the French and Indian War 26 September 1765.

Shields, John. He served as a soldier in Capt. John Dickenson's Company of

Rangers in 1759 in the French and Indian War. He received his 50 acre warrant in Virginia. He proved his service in Augusta County, Virginia 21 March 1780.

Shields, William. He served as a soldier in Capt. John Dickenson's Company of Rangers in 1759 in the French and Indian War. He received his 50 acre warrant in Virginia. He proved his service in Augusta County, Virginia 21 March 1780.

Shiflett, Thomas. He served as a soldier in the 2nd Virginia Regiment in the French and Indian War and received his 50 acre warrant 13 April 1780 in Albemarle County, Virginia.

Shine, John. He was granted 50 acres in Albany County, New York for his service as a soldier in the 80th Regiment of Foot in the French and Indian War 18 July 1770.

Shingleton, John. He was a soldier in Col. William Byrd's Regiment in the French and Indian War in 1758 and received 50 acres. He was in Culpeper County, Virginia 20 September 1779.

Shipman, Edward. He served in the Narraganset War from Connecticut and received land in Voluntown, Connecticut in 1701.

Shipley, John. He served under Capt. William Tyng in 1703 and sought land from Massachusetts 13 December 1734.

Shirley, James. He served as a soldier in 1758 and 1759 in Capt. Robert Rutherford's Company of Rangers in the French and Indian War. He received his 50 acre warrant in March 1780 in Berkeley County, Virginia.

Shirley, Jervice. He served as a soldier in 1758 and 1759 in Capt. Robert Rutherford's Company of Rangers in the French and Indian War. He received his 50 acre warrant in March 1780 in Berkeley County, Virginia.

Shirley, Walter. He served as a soldier under Capt. Robert Rutherford in 1758 and 1759 in the French and Indian War. He received his 50 acre warrant in March 1780 in Berkeley County, Virginia.

Shivers, James. He was granted 50 acres in Craven County, South Carolina on the King's bounty for his service in the French and Indian War 12 December 1768.

Shonnard, Frederick. He was granted 50 acres in Charlotte County, New York for his service as a soldier in the 4th Battalion in the 60th Regiment of Foot in the French and Indian War 25 January 1773.

Shoudreau, John. He was granted 50 acres in Saxe Gotha Township, South Carolina for his service as a private in the French and Indian War on the King's bounty 21 June 1765. He had petitioned for the land 30

May 1764. He also appeared as John Schroodreau.

Short, Joseph. He served on the expedition to Canada in 1690 and received land in Poland, Maine in 1739.

Showler, George. He served as a private in the 45th Regiment in the French and Indian War and was granted land in New York 11November 1772.

Shumway, Peter. His son, Peter Shumway of Topsfield, Massachusetts, petitioned on 25 March 1749/50 for the land due his father for service in the Narraganset War and the taking of the fort there.

Sidwell, Thomas. He served as a private in the 42nd Regiment in the French and Indian War and petitioned for his 50 acres of land in New York 24 October 1764.

Sidwell, Thomas. He served as a matross in the 2nd Battalion of the Royal American Regiment of Artillery in the French and Indian War. His service was certified in New York 29 January 1764.

Sill, Joseph. He was a captain and was granted 200 acres out of that taken from the enemy. The deputies reversed the General Court of Massachusetts because a plantation of eight miles square had been set aside for those who had been in the late Indian war 17 November 1685.

Silver, Samuel. He served on the expedition to Canada in 1690 and received land in Poland, Maine in 1739.

Silvester, John. He received land in Richmond, New Hampshire in 1765 for the service of an unidentified veteran of the expedition to Canada in 1690.

Silvester, Jos[eph]. He received land in Richmond, New Hampshire in 1765 for the service of an unidentified veteran of the expedition to Canada in 1690.

Simmonds, Thomas. He was a soldier under Gen. Braddock in the Virginia troops on the expedition to Fort DuQuesne in 1755 in the French and Indian War. He proved his service in Hampshire County, Virginia 10 August 1779. He assigned his right to 50 acres.

Simmons, John. He served on the expedition to Canada in 1690. John Simmons received land in Chesterfield, Massachusetts in 1739.

Simmons, John. He served on the expedition to Canada in 1690 and received his land in Bethel, Maine in 1767.

Simmons, Moses. He received land in Richmond, New Hampshire in 1765 for the service of an unidentified veteran of the expedition to Canada in 1690.

Simon, John. He was granted 50 acres in Albany County, New York for his service as a private in the 80th Regiment of Foot in the French and Indian War 5 April 1771.

Simon, Joseph. He served as a soldier in the French and Indian War and applied for his land in New York 24 October 1764.

Simon, Ludwig. He was granted 50 acres in Gloucester County, New York for his service as a soldier in the 44th Regiment of Foot in the French and Indian War 5 April 1770.

Simon, Philip. He served as a corporal in the Royal American Regiment in the French and Indian War and petitioned for his 200 acres in New York 24 October 1764.

Simonds, James. He served in the Narraganset War and received land in Templeton, Massachusetts in 1733.

Simonds, Jonathan. He served in the Narraganset War and received land in Templeton, Massachusetts in 1733.

Simpkins, Pilgrim. He served in the Narraganset War from Boston, Massachusetts. His sons, Thomas Simpkins and John Simpkins, received his land in Bedford, New Hampshire in 1733.

Simpson, Alexander. He was granted 50 acres in Albany County, New York for his service as a soldier in the 55th Regiment of Foot in the French and Indian War 18 April 1769.

Simpson, Daniel. He served as a corporal in 1760 in the 1st Virginia Regiment in the French and Indian War and petitioned for his land 17 February 1780 in Spotsylvania County, Virginia which he assigned.

Simpson, Donald. He was granted 200 acres in Orange County, New York for his service as a sergeant in the 42nd Regiment of Foot in the French and Indian War 16 January 1776.

Simpson, Donald. He was granted 200 acres in Granville County, South Carolina on the King's bounty for his service in the French and Indian War 6 February 1773.

Simpson, John. He received his land in Massachusetts 10 December 1735.

Simpson, John. He was granted 50 acres in Albany County, New York for his service as a soldier in the 78th Regiment of Foot in the French and Indian War 10 May 1765.

Simpson, John. He was granted 50 acres in Albany County, New York for his service as a soldier in the 46th Regiment of Foot in the French and Indian War 25 May 1771.

Simpson, John. He was granted 200 acres in Charlotte County, New York for his service as a noncommissioned officer in the 17th Regiment of Foot in the French and Indian War 12 October 1774.

Simpson, Solomon. He served as a soldier in the 1st Virginia Regiment in the French and Indian War under Col. William Byrd and Col. Adam Stephen and received his warrant for 50 acres in December 1779 in

Botetourt County, Virginia.

Simpson, William. He served as a soldier in the 1st Virginia Regiment under Col. George Washington in the French and Indian War and died in the service. His heir, Solomon Simpson, received his 50 acre warrant in February 1780 in Botetourt County, Virginia. The name of the veteran may have been William Simpkins.

Sims, George. He served as a soldier in Capt. Samuel Overton's Company of Rangers in 1755 in the French and Indian War. He proved his right in Louisa County, Virginia 14 February 1780. He assigned his right to 50 acres.

Simson, Thomas. He served as a noncommissioned officer in the 46th Regiment of Foot in the French and Indian War and received 200 acres in Charlotte County, New York 12 October 1774.

Sinclair, Daniel. He served as a soldier in the 55th Regiment in the French and Indian War. His service was certified in New York 7 December 1764.

Skeggs, Richard. He received his land in West Florida for his service as a soldier in the French and Indian War 27 March 1776.

Skene, Andrew Philip. He served as a lieutenant in the 72nd Regiment in the French and Indian War and petitioned for his 2,000 acres of land in New York 22 April 1769.

Skene, David. He served as a lieutenant in the 108th Regiment in the French and Indian War and petitioned for his 2,000 acres 28 October 1766 in New York.

Skene, Philip. He was granted 3,000 acres in Albany County, New York for his service as captain or town mayor at Havana in the French and Indian War 6 July 1771.

Skillern, George. He served as a sergeant in the French and Indian War and received a warrant for 200 acres 2 November 1779 in Montgomery County, Virginia.

Skillern, William. He served as a sergeant in the regular additional troops in the Cherokee Expedition under Col. William Byrd in 1760 in the French and Indian War. He received a warrant for 200 acres 13 August 1779 in Botetourt County, Virginia.

Skillern, William. He served as an ensign in Capt. Robert Breckinridge's Company in Augusta County raised on the order of Col. William Byrd to garrison Fort Chiswell in the absence of the army on expedition against the Cherokee in 1760 in the French and Indian War. He received his warrant for 2,000 acres 13 August 1780 in Botetourt County, Virginia.

Skillings, Samuel. He served in the Narraganset War from Norton,

Massachusetts. His daughter, Mehitable Tucker, claimed his land in Greenwich, Massachusetts in 1737.

Skinner, Abraham. He served in the Narraganset War from Malden, Massachusetts. His son, Abraham Skinner, received his land in Westminster, Massachusetts in 1733.

Skinner, John. He served as a captain in the French and Indian War and petitioned for his land in New York 28 January 1767.

Skinner, John. He served as a captain in the French and Indian War and received 3,000 acres in Nova Scotia 8 February 1782.

Skinner, Samuel. He was granted 50 acres in Albany County, New York for his service as a soldier in the 60th Regiment of Foot in the French and Indian War 29 October 1765.

Skinner, Thomas. He served as a private in the French and Indian War and was granted land in New York 1 April 1767.

Slaughter, George. He was a soldier in an independent company in Col. Henry Bouquet's expedition against the Shawnee in 1764. He received a warrant for 50 acres in Virginia.

Slingsby, Edward. He was granted 50 acres in Albany County, New York for his service as a soldier in the 60th Regiment of Foot in the French and Indian War 14 April 1772.

Small, John. He was granted 3,000 acres in Albany County, New York for his service as a captain in the 42nd Regiment of Foot in the French and Indian War 22 October 1765.

Small, John. He was granted 2,100 acres in West Florida for his service as a brigade major in the French and Indian War 27 September 1773. He was also granted 1,000 acres on 25 August 1773.

Small, Matthew. He served as a soldier in Capt. William Christian's Company in Col. William Byrd's Regiment in the French and Indian War and received his 50 acre warrant in Virginia.

Smallman, Thomas. He served as a captain in the French and Indian War and petitioned for his land in New York 28 February 1770.

Smallman, Thomas. He served as an ensign in 1756, lieutenant in 1756, lieutenant of calvary in 1757, captain in 1760, and Indian agent at Fort Chartres in 1761 from Pennsylvania in the French and Indian War. He proved his service in Yohogania County, Virginia 28 February 1780. He received 5,000 acres.

Smallman, Thomas. He served as a lieutenant and quartermaster in the 1st Battalion in a Pennsylvania Regiment in 1758 in the French and Indian War. He proved his service in Yohogania County, Virginia 26 October 1779.

Smallwood, Thomas. He served as a captain under Col. John Armstrong in the 1st Pennsylvania Battalion in 1759 in the French and Indian War and received his 3,000 acre warrant in Virginia.

Smart, George. He was granted 200 acres in Albany County, New York for his service as a noncommissioned officer in the Royal Regiment of Artillery in the French and Indian War 4 August 1774.

Smart, John. He served as a private in the French and Indian War and petitioned for his land in New York in November 1766.

Smart, Robert. He was granted 50 acres in the fork of the Broad and Saludy Rivers in South Carolina on the King's bounty for his service in the French and Indian War 6 February 1773.

Smedley, John. He was granted 50 acres in Gloucester County, New York for his service as a soldier in the 46th Regiment of Foot in the French and Indian War 5 April 1770.

Smeed, —. He was in the fight with the Indians at Deerfield, Massachusetts. His son, John Smeed of Poquaig, Worcester County, Massachusetts, was granted 200 acres for recompense of his honored father, deceased, on 14 June 1743.

Smeeton, Joseph. He was granted 120 acres in Albany County, New York for his service as a sergeant in the 47th Regiment of Foot in the French and Indian War 13 April 1768.

Smith, Adam. He was granted 200 acres in Craven County, South Carolina on the King's bounty 27 August 1764. He served as a private in the French and Indian War.

Smith, Benjamin. He served in the Narraganset War and received land in Templeton, Massachusetts in 1733.

Smith, Benjamin. He served as a private in a company of rangers in 1757. He assigned his 50 acre warrant in Virginia.

Smith, Charles. He served as a sergeant in Capt. William Preston's Company of Rangers in the French and Indian War and received his 200 acre warrant in Virginia. He proved his service in Augusta County, Virginia 21 March 1780.

Smith, Charles. He served as a soldier in the French and Indian War and assigned his 50 acre warrant in Virginia. The service of a man of his name was proved in Berkeley County, Virginia 23 March 1780.

Smith, David. He was granted 200 acres in Albany County, New York for his service as a sergeant in the 60th Regiment of Foot in the French and Indian War 5 April 1771.

Smith, Ebenezer. He served on the expedition to Canada in 1690. Ebenezer Smith received land in Warwick, Massachusetts in 1738.

Smith, Edward. He received land in Richmond, New Hampshire in 1765 for the service of an unidentified veteran of the expedition to Canada in 1690.

Smith, Edward. He was granted 50 acres in Albany County, New York for his service as a soldier in the 60th Regiment of Foot in the French and Indian War 1 May 1765.

Smith, Edward. He was granted 200 acres in Albany County, New York for his service as a noncommissioned officer in the 60th Regiment of Foot in the French and Indian War 5 April 1771.

Smith, Edward. He served as a commissary in the French and Indian War and petitioned for his 3,000 acres of land in New York 24 December 1774.

Smith, Francis. He served in the Narraganset War from Connecticut and received land in Voluntown, Connecticut in 1701.

Smith, Francis. He served as a lieutenant in a company on the frontiers of Augusta County from July 1763 to December 1764 under several captains. He received a warrant for 2,000 acres in April 1780 in Montgomery County, Virginia.

Smith, Frederick. He was granted 50 acres in Orange County, New York for his service as a soldier in the 4th Battalion in the 60th Regiment of Foot in the French and Indian War 15 May 1770.

Smith, Frederick. He was granted 358 acres in Amelia Township, South Carolina on the King's bounty 21 June 1765. He served as a private in the French and Indian War.

Smith, Gabriel. He was granted 200 acres in Albany County, New York for his service as a corporal in the 28th Regiment of Foot in the French and Indian War 1 April 1772.

Smith, George. He was granted 200 acres in Albany County, New York for his service as a noncommissioned officer in the 60th Regiment of Foot in the French and Indian War 29 October 1765.

Smith, George. He served as a major in the French and Indian War and received 2,000 acres of land in Virginia in 1774.

Smith, George. He served as a soldier under Col. William Byrd in the French and Indian War and proved his service in Bedford County, Virginia 27 March 1780.

Smith, Hazadiah. He served as a sergeant on the expedition to Canada in 1690. Samuel Smith petitioned for his land in Raymond, Maine in 1735.

Smith, Henry. He was granted 80 acres in Connecticut for his service in the Pequot War 11 May 1671.

Smith, James. He served in the Narraganset War from Charlestown, Massachusetts. His heir, Jonathan Call, received his land in Westminster, Massachusetts in 1733.

Smith, James. He was granted 50 acres in Albany County, New York for his service as a soldier in the 44th Regiment of Foot in the French and Indian War 11 August 1768.

Smith, James. He served as a soldier in the 48th Regiment in the French and Indian War and petitioned for his 50 acres in New York 27 April 1765.

Smith, James. He was granted 200 acres in Albany County, New York for his service as a noncommissioned officer in the 80th Regiment of Foot in the French and Indian War 6 July 1771.

Smith, James. He served as a soldier in the French and Indian War in Capt. William Phillips's Volunteer Rangers in 1763. His service was proved in Louisa County, Virginia 14 February 1780. His heir, William Smith, assigned the warrant for 50 acres.

Smith, Jeremiah. He served in the Narraganset War from Eastham, Massachusetts. His son, Jeremiah Smith, received his land in Gorham, Maine in 1733.

Smith, John. He served in the Narraganset War from Connecticut and received land in Voluntown, Connecticut in 1701.

Smith, John. He served in the Narraganset War from Cambridge, Massachusetts. His heirs received his land in Westminster, Massachusetts in 1733.

Smith, John. He was a soldier under Capt. Noah Wiswall. He was awarded 150 acres by Massachusetts 28 November 1735. He was from Woburn, Massachusetts.

Smith, John. He served on the expedition to Canada in 1690. William Webb was admitted to his land in Lyndeboro, Maine in 1736.

Smith, John. He was granted 200 acres in Albany County, New York for his service as a miner in the Royal Regiment of Artillery in the French and Indian War 21 October 1765.

Smith, John. He served as a soldier in the 42nd and 76th Regiments in the French and Indian War and petitioned for his land in New York 27 April 1765.

Smith, John. He served as a sergeant in the 1st Battalion Royal American Regiment in the French and Indian War and petitioned for 200 acres in New York 24 October 1764.

Smith, John. He served as soldier in the 48th Regiment in the French and Indian War and petitioned for his 50 acres in New York 27 April 1765.

Smith, John. He served as drum beater in the 60th Regiment in the French and Indian War and petitioned for his land in New York 24 October 1764.

Smith, John. He served as a sergeant in Col. William Preston's Company of Rangers in the French and Indian War. His heir at law, Thomas Smith, received his warrant for 200 acres 18 November 1779 in Augusta County, Virginia.

Smith, John. He served as a soldier in the 2nd Virginia Regiment in the French and Indian War and assigned his warrant for 50 acres.

Smith, John. He served as a lieutenant in Capt. John Smith's Company of Rangers in 1756 in the French and Indian War and was killed at Fort Vause. His heir and brother, Abraham Smith, petitioned for his 2,000 acres 23 November 1779 in Rockingham County, Virginia.

Smith, John. He served as a captain of the new levies in the French and Indian War. He was entitled to 3,000 acres in Virginia per a certificate from Lord Dunmore 16 December 1773.

Smith, John. He served as a soldier in the French and Indian War and received a warrant for 50 acres. He proved his service in Goochland County, Virginia 15 November 1779.

Smith, Jon. He served in the Narraganset War from Yarmouth, Massachusetts and received land in Gorham, Maine in 1733.

Smith, Jonathan. He served in the Narraganset War from Watertown, Massachusetts. His son, Zechariah Smith, received his land in Westminster, Massachusetts in 1733.

Smith, Jonathan. He served as a lieutenant in the Regulars under Col. William Byrd in the French and Indian War. He received his warrant for 2,000 acres in March 1780 in Prince Edward County, Virginia.

Smith, Jonas. He was a soldier in 1712 who with others advanced £30 to redeem Daniel Tucker from the Indian enemy. He, John Tozer, and Isaac Harrington were granted 500 acres in York County 8 December 1737 by Massachusetts.

Smith, Joseph. He served in the Narraganset War from Cambridge, Massachusetts. His heirs received his land in Westminster, Massachusetts in 1733.

Smith, Joseph. He served in the Narraganset War from Watertown, Massachusetts. His son, Joseph Smith, received his land in Westminster, Massachusetts in 1733.

Smith, Lawrence. He was granted 50 acres in Albany County, New York for his service as a soldier in the 60th Regiment of Foot in the French and Indian War 17 September 1765.

Smith, Laurence. He was from Gloucester County, Virginia and proposed that within 15 months from April 1679 that he settle 50 men on the Rappahannock River fitted out with arms to defend the frontier plus up to 200 additional men. In return he was to be granted land along the river and back into the woods. He served as a major.

Smith, Nathaniel. He served in the Narraganset War from Cambridge, Massachusetts. His heirs received his land in Westminster, Massachusetts in 1733.

Smith, Nathaniel. He received land in Alstead, New Hampshire in 1771 for the service of an unidentified veteran of the expedition to Canada in 1690.

Smith, Nehemiah. He served in the Narraganset War from Connecticut and received land in Voluntown, Connecticut in 1701.

Smith, Nicholas. He served in a company of Rangers under Capt. William Preston in the French and Indian War from Virginia. He assigned his warrant of 50 acres.

Smith, Richard. He served in the Narraganset War from Connecticut and received his land in Voluntown, Connecticut in 1701.

Smith, Richard. He served in the Narraganset War from Connecticut and received land in Voluntown, Connecticut in 1701.

Smith, Richard. He served in the French and Indian War and took his land in Fincastle County, Virginia 15 December 1772.

Smith, Richard. He was granted 50 acres of land in West Florida for his service as a private in the French and Indian War 21 September 1776.

Smith, Robert. He served as a soldier in the 1st Virginia Regiment under Lt. Col. Adam Stephen in the French and Indian War. His heir, William Smith, received his 50 acre warrant 27 March 1780 in Fauquier County, Virginia.

Smith, Roger. He was granted 200 acres in Albany County, New York for his service as a sergeant in the 55th Regiment of Foot in the French and Indian War 17 September 1765.

Smith, Samuel. He served in the Narraganset War from Cambridge, Massachusetts. His nephew, Samuel Smith, received his land in Westminster, Massachusetts in 1733.

Smith, Samuel. He served on the expedition to Canada in 1690 and received his land in Poland, Maine in 1739.

Smith, Samuel. He served in the French and Indian War and had his service certified in New York 23 January 1767.

Smith, Stephen. He served as a soldier in the 2nd Virginia Regiment under Col. William Byrd in the French and Indian War. He petitioned for his 50 acres 16 February 1780 in King William County, Virginia.

Smith, Thomas. He served in the Narraganset War from Massachusetts in 1685. His land was located in Buxton, Maine.

Smith, Thomas. He had his service in the 46th Regiment in the French and

Indian War certified in New York 11 December 1766. He assigned his land 21 January 1767.

Smith, Thomas. He served as a soldier in 1758 and 1760 in the French and Indian War. He proved his right in Caroline County, Virginia 10 February 1780. He assigned his right to 50 acres.

Smith, Thomas. He served in Capt. Dunlop's Company in the French and Indian War and proved his service in Augusta County, Virginia 15 February 1780.

Smith, William. He was granted 200 acres in Albany County, New York for his service as a noncommissioned officer in the 3rd Battalion in the 60th Regiment of Foot in the French and Indian War 13 December 1765.

Smith, William. He was granted 200 acres in Albany County, New York for his service as a corporal in the 4th Battalion of the 60th or Royal American Regiment in the French and Indian War 13 December 1768.

Smith, William. He was granted 200 acres in Charlotte County, New York for his service as a noncommissioned officer in the 28th Regiment of Foot in the French and Indian War 12 October 1774.

Smith, William. He was granted 50 acres in Albany County, New York for his service as a private in the 18th Regiment of Foot in the French and Indian War 8 June 1771.

Smith, William, D.D. He served as acting chaplain to the regiments in America in the French and Indian War and petitioned for 2,000 acres of land in New York 4 September 1775.

Smith, William. He was granted 200 acres in Craven County, South Carolina on the King's bounty 27 August 1764. He served as a drummer in the French and Indian War.

Smith, William. He was granted 200 acres in St. Bartholomew Parish, Colleton County, South Carolina on the King's bounty 21 June 1765. He served as a sergeant in the French and Indian War.

Smith, William. He served as a soldier in Capt. Peter Hogg's Company of Rangers in the French and Indian War in 1758 and assigned his warrant for 50 acres 25 May 1780 in Orange County, Virginia.

Smith, William. He served as a noncommissioned officer in the 1st Virginia Regiment in the French and Indian War and received a warrant for 200 acres 27 March 1780 in Fauquier County, Virginia.

Smither, William, Sr. He served as a soldier in the 1st Virginia Regiment under Col. George Washington in the French and Indian War until 1760. He petitioned for his 50 acres 10 February 1780 in Caroline County, Virginia.

Smither, William. He served as a soldier in the 1st Virginia Regiment under

Col. George Washington in the French and Indian War and received his warrant for 50 acres in Caroline County, Virginia.

Smitten, Joseph. He served as a sergeant in the 47th Regiment in the French and Indian War. His service was certified 23 October 1765 in New York.

Snell, Thomas. He received land in Richmond, New Hampshire in 1765 for the service of an unidentified veteran of the expedition to Canada in 1690.

Snethen, Barrack. He served as a captain in the French and Indian War and petitioned for land 30 December 1765 in New York.

Snow, —. He served on the expedition to Canada in 1690. Lt. Jabez Snow received land in Dumbarton, New Hampshire in 1735.

Snow, Herman. He was granted 50 acres in Albany County, New York for his service as a private in a regiment of foot in the French and Indian War 19 May 1770.

Snow, Jabez. He served as a captain in the French and Indian War and received 3,000 acres in Nova Scotia 10 September 1781.

Snow, James. He served in the Narraganset War from Marshfield, Massachusetts. Isaac Winslow claimed his land in Greenwich, Massachusetts in 1737. [*n.b.* The name of the claimant is extremely difficult to read.]

Snow, James. He received land in Richmond, New Hampshire in 1765 for the service of an unidentified veteran of the expedition to Canada in 1690.

Snow, Thomas. He served on the expedition to Canada in 1690 and received land in Dumbarton, New Hampshire in 1735.

Snow, Zacheriah. He served in the Narraganset War. Nathan Brooks received his land in Templeton, Massachusetts in 1733.

Snowden, George. He was granted 50 acres in Albany County, New York for his service as a soldier in the 80th Regiment of Foot in the French and Indian War 28 October 1765.

Snowden, James. He was granted 50 acres in Albany County, New York for his service as a soldier in the 55th Regiment of Foot in the French and Indian War 18 April 1769.

Snowden, Jonas. He served in the 55th Regiment in the French and Indian War and had his service certified 2 May 1764 in New York.

Snyder, Jacob. He was granted 50 acres in Albany County, New York for his service as a soldier in the 80th Regiment of Foot in the French and Indian War 26 July 1765.

Snyder, Peter. He served as a sergeant in the 60th Regiment in the French and Indian War and returned his survey for 200 acres in Albany County, New York 12 August 1766.

Snyder, William. He was granted 50 acres in Albany County, New York for his service as a soldier in the 60th Regiment of Foot in the French and Indian War 26 September 1765.

Soams, Joseph. He served in the Narraganset War from Salem, Massachusetts. His nephew, Nathaniel Soams, claimed his land in Amherst, New Hampshire in 1734.

Solomon, Martin. He was granted 150 acres in St. John's Parish, Berkeley County, South Carolina on the King's bounty 21 June 1765. He served as a private in the French and Indian War.

Solomon, Simon. He served in the 28th Regiment in the French and Indian War and petitioned for his land 18 October 1766 in New York.

Somerby, William. He served on the expedition to Canada in 1690. In 1735 Joseph Herrick, Jr. petitioned for his land in Raymond, Maine.

Somes, John. He served in the Narraganset War from Connecticut and received land in Voluntown, Connecticut in 1701.

Sommers, John. He was granted 2,000 acres in West Florida for his service as an assistant surgeon in the French and Indian War 2 August 1773.

Somner, Ezekiel. He served as a lieutenant of rangers in the French and Indian War. His service was certified in New York 7 December 1769.

Soper, Thomas. He received land in Richmond, New Hampshire in 1765 for the service of an unidentified veteran of the expedition to Canada in 1690.

Sorrall, William. He was deceased. Lt. Col. George Hackett proved that Sorrall was discharged in 1755 in the French and Indian War. James Sorrall, son and heir, received his warrant for 50 acres 21 February 1780 in Culpeper County, Virginia.

Sortin, Thomas. He served on the expedition to Canada in 1690. John Bartell was admitted to his land in Lyndeboro, Maine in 1736.

Soudran, William. He had lived in Virginia upwards of 40 years. He served as a sergeant in the 1st Virginia Regiment in Capt. Thomas Bullet's Company in the French and Indian War. He lost his discharge from Col. Adam Stephen. He assigned his warrant for 200 acres.

Southack, Cyprian. He was from Boston, Massachusetts and served upwards of thirty years in the late wars. He was awarded 500 acres 2 July 1734.

Southall, James. He served as a subaltern in the French and Indian War and assigned his 2,000 acre land warrant in Virginia.

Southall, Turner. He served as a lieutenant under Col. William Byrd in the Virginia Regiment in the French and Indian War and received 2,000 acres of land in Virginia which he assigned.

Southall, William. He was granted 200 acres in West Florida for his service as a noncommissioned officer in the French and Indian War 26 March 1774.

Southwell, John. He was granted 1,900 acres in West Florida for his service as a quartermaster in the French and Indian War 2 August 1773.

Spafford, John. He was captivated by the Indians and held for 15 months in Canada. The Indians destroyed two of his mills by fire. He was granted two rights plus another 100 acres in Charlestown, New Hampshire.

Spaight, William. He was granted 2,000 acres in Albany County, New York for his service as a master on board the *Portmahon* at the reduction of Louisbourg and Quebec in the French and Indian War 6 November 1768.

Spalding, Leonard. He received his land in Massachusetts 10 December 1735.

Spalding, Timothy. He served in the Narraganset War and received land in Templeton, Massachusetts in 1733.

Sparham, Thomas. He served as a surgeon's mate in the French and Indian War and had his service certified in New York 22 June 1773.

Sparhawk, Nathaniel. He served on the expedition to Canada in 1690. Nathaniel Sparhawk received his land in Bethel, Maine in 1767.

Sparks, Samuel. He served as a soldier in 1754 in the French and Indian War. He was at the battle of the Meadows and afterwards in the Old Virginia Regiment under Col. George Washington. He proved his service in Frederick County, Virginia 9 March 1780. He assigned his right to 50 acres.

Sparks, Thomas. He served in the Narraganset War from Massachusetts in 1685. His land was located in Buxton, Maine.

Sparrow, Jonathan. He served in the Narraganset War from Eastham, Massachusetts and received land in Gorham, Maine in 1733.

Spaulding, William. He served in Lovewell's War in Massachusetts and received his land in Petersham, Massachusetts.

Speake, George. He served as a subaltern in the Virginia Regiment in the French and Indian War. His son and heir, Lawson Speake, received his 2,000 acre warrant which he desired to locate in Fincastle County, Virginia in 1774.

Spears, Robert. He was granted 500 acres in West Florida for his service as a warrant officer in the French and Indian War 29 November 1776. He also received land on 19 March 1777.

Speers, Hugh. He was granted 50 acres in Albany County, New York for his service as a soldier in the 4th Battalion in the 60th Regiment of Foot in the French and Indian War 18 July 1770.

Spence, Peter. He was granted 2,000 acres in Orange County, New York for his service as a surgeon's mate in the 60th Regiment of Foot in the French and Indian War 18 January 1775.

Spencer, Benjamin. He served a soldier in the French and Indian War and received 50 acres of land in Virginia which he assigned.

Spencer, John. He served as a sergeant. He shared in the grant of East Greenwich, Rhode Island made to those who had rendered service in King Philip's War. The grant was made 31 October 1677.

Spencer, Thomas. He was granted 60 acres in Connecticut for his service as a sergeant in the Pequot War 11 May 1671.

Spicer, Peter. He served in the Narraganset War from Connecticut. His heirs received land in Voluntown, Connecticut in 1701. He also appeared as Peter Spiser.

Spicer, Stephen. He served a soldier in the French and Indian War in 1758. He petitioned for his 50 acres 21 April 1780 in Spotsylvania County, Virginia.

Spiers, Hugh. He served in the French and Indian War. His service was certified in New York 4 January 1768.

Spiers, Robert. He was granted 50 acres in Albany County, New York for his service as a private in the 60th or Royal American Regiment in the French and Indian War 8 June 1771.

Spofford, John. He served in the Narraganset War from Massachusetts in 1685. His land was located in Buxton, Maine.

Spooner, Ralph. He was granted 200 acres in Albany County, New York for his service as a miner in the Royal Regiment of Artillery in the French and Indian War 21 October 1765.

Spooney, Edward. He served under Capt. John Lovewell from Massachusetts and was in battle at Pigwacket in May 1725. He was from Dunstable, Massachusetts and received his land in Pembroke, New Hampshire.

Spotswood, Alexander. He served as an officer in the French and Indian War and received 3,000 acres of land in Virginia.

Spotswood, Robert. He served in the French and Indian War from Virginia. He was deceased when his heir at law, Alexander Spotswood Dandridge, received his warrant for 3,000 acres.

Sprague, Jonathan. He served in the Narraganset War from Charlestown, Massachusetts. His son, John Sprague, received his land in Westminster, Massachusetts in 1733.

Sprague, Nathanael. He was from Rochester, Massachusetts. In 1726 he and Samuel Duty were on a fishing voyage on a sloop to Cape Sable. They put in the harbor at Malligast to water when the Indians in a piratical manner carried them away. He was awarded 300 acres by Massachusetts 23 March 1735/6.

Sprague, Richard. He was granted 500 acres in Maine 13 May 1684 by Massachusetts.

Sprague, Samuel. He received land in Richmond, New Hampshire in 1765 for the service of an unidentified veteran of the expedition to Canada in 1690.

Sprigg, Edward. He served as a captain in the regiment of Col. George Washington in the French and Indian War, and lost his life in the service. His son, Edward Sprigg, received his 4,000 acre warrant in Virginia.

Spring, Henry. He served in the French and Indian War and was in much reduced circumstances. On 24 January 1774 in Massachusetts he applied for a grant of 171 acres west on the Farmington River which no one desired.

Spring, John. He served on the expedition to Canada in 1690. Jonathan Williams, Jr. received his land in Alstead, New Hampshire in 1771.

Spring, Nathaniel. He received land in Alstead, New Hampshire for the service of an unidentified veteran of the expedition to Canada in 1690.

Springauff, Rudolph. He served as a noncommissioned officer in the French and Indian War and received 200 acres in Nova Scotia 10 October 1777.

Springer, Denis. He served in the Narraganset War from Connecticut and received land in Voluntown, Connecticut in 1701. He also appeared as Dempsy Springer.

Springer, Joseph. He was granted 50 acres in Gloucester County, New York for his service as a soldier in the 28th Regiment of Foot in the French and Indian War 5 April 1770.

Spry, Sir Richard. He received his land in West Florida for his service as a post captain in the French and Indian War 9 March 1776.

Spry, William. He served as captain lieutenant in the French and Indian War and received 3,000 acres in Nova Scotia 2 April 1774.

Spurr, John. He served in the Narraganset War from Taunton, Massachusetts. He claimed his land in Greenwich, Massachusetts in 1737.

Spurr, William. He served as a soldier in Capt. Samuel Overton's Company of Rangers in the French and Indian War and proved his service in King William County, Virginia 16 February 1780. He assigned his right to 50 acres. Samuel Meredith certified his service.

Stackpole, John. He was from Biddeford, York County, Massachusetts and sought land for his extraordinary sufferings in captivity on 4 June 1736.

Stadle, Christian. He was granted 200 acres in Albany County, New York for his service as a sergeant under Capt. Winepress in the 55th Regiment of Foot in the French and Indian War 26 July 1765.

Stadler, John. He served as a lieutenant in the Pennsylvania Regiment under Col. Armstrong in the French and Indian War and was entitled to 2,000 acres in Virginia. He also appeared as John Sadler.

Stafford, Thomas. He served as a corporal in the 4th Battalion 60th or Royal American Regiment in the French and Indian War and petitioned for his 200 acres in New York 26 April 1765.

Stair, Douglas. He was granted 5,000 acres in West Florida for his service as a captain in the navy in the French and Indian War 2 June 1777.

Stalker, Peter. He was granted 50 acres in Albany County, New York for his service as a soldier in the 55th Regiment of Foot in the French and Indian War 1 July 1771.

Standish, Thomas. He was granted 50 acres in Connecticut for his service in the Pequot War 11 May 1671.

Standley, Edward. He received land in Richmond, New Hampshire in 1765 for the service of an unidentified veteran of the expedition to Canada in 1690.

Standley, Thomas. He served as a corporal in the 2nd Virginia Regiment under Col. William Byrd in the French and Indian War. His heir, William Standley, petitioned for his 200 acres 16 February 1780 in King William County, Virginia.

Stanford, David. He served as a private in the French and Indian War in the 2nd Virginia Regiment. He disposed of his warrant of 50 acres.

Stanley, John. He served as a corporal in the 4th Battalion of the Royal American Regiment in the French and Indian War. His service was certified in New York 15 October 1769.

Stanley, John. He served as a private in the French and Indian War in the 2nd Virginia Regiment. He disposed of his warrant of 50 acres.

Stanton, Daniel. He served in the Narraganset War from Connecticut and received land in Voluntown, Connecticut in 1701.

Stanton, John. He served as a captain in the Narraganset War from Connecticut and received land in Voluntown, Connecticut in 1701.

Stanton, Joseph. He served in the Narraganset War from Connecticut and received land in Voluntown, Connecticut in 1701.

Stanton, Richard. He served as a sergeant in the French and Indian War and proved his service in Washington County, Virginia 18 January 1780.

Stanton, Robert. He served in the Narraganset War from Connecticut and received land in Voluntown, Connecticut in 1701.

Stanton, Samuel. He served in the Narraganset War from Connecticut and

received land in Voluntown, Connecticut in 1701.

Stanton, Thomas. He served in the Pequot War and received a grant of land in Soldiers' Field in Hartford, Connecticut.

Staples, Daniel. He served in the Virginia Regiment in the French and Indian War and took his land in Fincastle County, Virginia 15 December 1772. His widow, Christian Go[?]ff claimed his land in Frederick County, Virginia 2 May 1780. She said he had no relations in this country to her knowledge.

Stark, Aaron. He served in the Narraganset War from Connecticut. His heirs received his land in Voluntown, Connecticut in 1701.

Stark, Archibald. He served as a lieutenant in the French and Indian War and received 2,000 acres in New Hampshire 31October 1765. He was from Dunbarton.

Stark, John. He served in the Narraganset War from Connecticut. His heirs received his land in Voluntown, Connecticut in 1701.

Stark, John. He served as a captain in the French and Indian War and petitioned for a grant of 3,000 acres in New York 3 July 1766.

Stark, Samuel. He served as a lieutenant in the French and Indian War. He was from Derryfield, New Hampshire and received 2,000 acres in New Hampshire 31 October 1765.

Starlman, Daniel. He served as a private in the French and Indian War and petitioned for 50 acres on the King's bounty in South Carolina 5 April 1768.

Starr, Thomas. He served as surgeon in one of the companies against the Pequot. His widow and eight small children applied for 400 acres of land 10 October 1658 from Massachusetts. Benjamin Starr of New London in behalf of the heirs and descendants was granted the plat for the tract on 9 June 1735 in Massachusetts. Comfort Starr had also sought the land on 13 June 1728.

Staunton, Richard. He served as a noncommissioned officer in the Virginia Regiment under Col. William Byrd in the French and Indian War. He proved his service in Washington County, Virginia 18 January 1780. He assigned his 200 acres.

Staunton, Robert. He served as a soldier for two years in the 1st Virginia Regiment under Col. William Byrd in the French and Indian War and received his 50 acre warrant in May 1780 in Montgomery County, Virginia.

Steal, Arnold. He served as a sergeant in the French and Indian War from Virginia and received a warrant for 200 acres.

Stearns, Charles. He served on the expedition to Canada in 1690. Samuel

Stearns petitioned for his land in Raymond, Maine in 1735.

Stebbins, Benjamin. He went to the relief of Deerfield in February 1703/4 and applied for his land in Massachusetts 12 December 1735.

Stedman, Caleb. He served on the expedition to Canada in 1690. Caleb Stedman received land in Warwick, Massachusetts in 1738. Because the land later fell within New Hampshire, John Williams was re-granted the land in 1765.

Steeker, Jabez. He served as a soldier in the French and Indian War and received a warrant for 50 acres of land in Virginia.

Steel, Henry. He was a sergeant in the 1st Virginia Regiment under Col. George Washington in 1755 under Gen. Braddock in the French and Indian War. He proved his service in Hampshire County, Virginia 10 August 1779 and assigned his right to 200 acres.

Steel, Robert. He served as a soldier in the 80th Regiment in the French and Indian War. His service was certified in New York 5 December 1764.

Steel, Samuel. He served as a lieutenant in the 42nd Regiment in the French and Indian War and petitioned for land in New York 28 January 1767.

Steel, William Snow. He was granted 2,000 acres in Cumberland County, New York for his service as a subaltern in the 55th Regiment of Foot in the French and Indian War 7 March 1770.

Steele, George. He served in the Pequot War and received a grant of land in Soldiers' Field in Hartford, Connecticut.

Steelman, James. He served as a soldier in the French and Indian War and assigned his 50 acre warrant in Virginia.

Steenbergen, Peter. He served as a lieutenant in the French and Indian War and received his 2,000 land warrant in Virginia.

Stephen, Adam. He was appointed eldest captain under Col. Joshua Fry in 1754 in the French and Indian War. He was promoted to the rank of major or lieutenant colonel in the said corps after Col. Joshua Fry's death. He was appointed paymaster to the troops raised in the winter of 1754 and the spring of 1755 until Mr. Boyd was appointed in April. He served under Gen. Braddock as captain commandant and eldest officer at that time in Virginia service. He was lieutenant colonel under George Washington and served until the spring of 1763 under Col. William Byrd. He commanded the Virginia Regiment in 1762. He proved his service in Frederick County, Virginia 8 March 1780. He received warrants for 5000, 2000, 3000, 2000, 5000, and 3000 acres.

Stephen, Alexander. He served as a lieutenant in the French and Indian War and received 2,000 acres of land in Virginia which he assigned.

Stephens, Henry. He served in the Narraganset War from Connecticut and

received land in Voluntown, Connecticut in 1701.

Stephens, John. He served in the Narraganset War from Connecticut and received land in Voluntown, Connecticut in 1701.

Stephens, Samuel. He served in the Narraganset War from Connecticut and received land in Voluntown, Connecticut in 1701.

Stephenson, Hugh. He served as a captain in 1764 in Henry Bouquet's campaign. He was entitled to 3,000 acres in Virginia. He assigned 1,000 acres to Richard Yeates. He proved his service in Yohogania County, Virginia 27 September 1779.

Stephenson, James. His son, Capt. James Stephenson, petitioned for the land 2 August 1764. He was granted 3,000 acres in Charlotte County, New York for his deceased father's service as Commissary of Stores in the French and Indian War 7 December 1775. The veteran received his commission 1 September 1756. He also appeared as James Stevenson.

Stephenson, John. He served as a soldier in Capt. McClanahan's Independent Company in Col. Henry Bouquet's Campaign in the French and Indian War and received his warrant for 50 acres in March 1780 in Buckingham County, Virginia.

Stephenson, John. He served as a captain of ranging company in Dunmore's War in 1774. He proved his service in Yohogania County, Virginia 28 March 1780.

Stephenson, William. He served as a soldier in the French and Indian War and received a warrant for 50 acres of land in Virginia which he assigned.

Stephinson, William. He was granted 200 acres in Albany County, New York for his service as a corporal in the 55th Regiment of Foot in the French and Indian War 26 May 1772.

Sterling, Hugh. He served as a lieutenant in the French and Indian War and received 2,000 acres in New Hampshire 31 October 1765. He was from Londonderry.

Sterling, Robert. He received his 2,000 acres of land in West Florida for his service as a subaltern in the French and Indian War 26 May 1777.

Stern, John. He served in the Narraganset War under Capt. Prentice from Billerica, Massachusetts. His heirs claimed land in Templeton, Massachusetts in 1733.

Sterns, Samuel. He served on the expedition to Canada in 1690. Samuel Sterns received land in Warwick, Massachusetts in 1736.

Sterns, Shubal. He served in the Narraganset Expedition in 1675. He was late of Lynn when Samuel Frail of Salem, aged 85, proved his service so that his grandson, Timothy Sterns could obtain his land from Massachusetts 23 November 1749.

Stetson, John. He received land in Richmond, New Hampshire in 1765 for the service of an unidentified veteran of the expedition to Canada in 1690.

Stetson, Matthew. He received land in Richmond, New Hampshire in 1765 for the service of an unidentified veteran of the expedition to Canada in 1690.

Stevens, Jacob. He received his land in Massachusetts 3 December 1735.

Stevens, John. He served from Massachusetts in the campaign against the Indians in 1725. He was from Groton, Massachusetts and received his land in Pembroke, New Hampshire.

Stevens, Joseph. He served on the expedition to Canada in 1690. Joseph Stevens received land in Warwick, Massachusetts in 1738.

Stevens, Joseph. He served as a major and engineer until 1758 in the French and Indian War. His son and heir, Richard Stevens, was due his warrants of 2,000 and 3,000 acres 9 March in 1780 Caroline County, Virginia.

Stevens, Samuel. He received his land from Massachusetts 3 December 1735.

Stevens, Samuel. He was granted 2,000 acres in Albany County, New York for his service as a lieutenant in a corps of rangers in the French and Indian War 1 June 1770.

Stevens, Simon. He served as a captain in one of H. M.'s independent companies in the French and Indian War and petitioned for 3,000 acres in New York 19 November 1765. He was from Charlestown, New Hampshire.

Stevens, Willard. He served as a lieutenant in the French and Indian War and petitioned for his 2,000 acres in Albany County, New York 12 June 1766.

Stevenson, James. He was granted 200 acres in Albany County, New York for his service as a corporal in the 2nd Battalion in the 60th Regiment in the French and Indian War 1 June 1770.

Stevenson, James. He was granted 2,000 acres in Cumberland County, New York for his service as an ensign in the 50th Regiment of Foot in the French and Indian War 13 October 1772.

Stevenson, James. He served as a lieutenant in a ranging company in Dunmore's War in 1774. He proved his service in Yohogania County, Virginia 28 March 1780.

Stevenson, John. He served as an officer in the French and Indian War and received his 2,000 acre warrant in Virginia.

Stevenson, Marcus. He served as an ensign in a ranging company in Dunmore's War in 1774. He proved his service in Yohogania County, Virginia 28 March 1780.

Stevenson, Samuel. He served as a sergeant in the 56th Regiment in the French and Indian War and petitioned for his land in New York 29 June 1774.

Steward, Donald. He was granted 50 acres in Charlotte County, New York for his service as a soldier in the Royal Highland Regiment of Foot in the French and Indian War 12 July 1775.

Steward, John. He served on the Canada Expedition in 1690 and petitioned for land in Massachusetts 9 December 1736.

Steward, Malcolm. He was granted 50 acres in Charlotte County, New York for his service as a soldier in the Royal Highland Regiment of Foot in the French and Indian War 12 July 1775.

Stewart, —. He served on the expedition to Canada in 1690. James Stewart received land in Dumbarton, New Hampshire in 1735.

Stewart, Alexander. He was granted 200 acres in Albany County, New York for his service as a corporal in the 42nd Regiment of Foot in the French and Indian War 30 October 1765.

Stewart, Alexander. He served as a soldier in the 42nd Regiment in the French and Indian War and assigned his right to land to Robert Buchanan in New York 9 January 1767.

Stewart, Alexander. He served as a soldier in the 80th Regiment in the French and Indian War. His service was certified in New York 5 November 1766.

Stewart, Alexander. He was granted 1,000 acres in Cumberland County, Pennsylvania for his service in the French and Indian War 17 February 1769. He was also granted 1,000 and 1,000 acres with John Montgomery in Washington and Westmoreland Counties 9 February 1769.

Stewart, Alexander. He served as a noncommissioned officer in the French and Indian War and assigned his warrant for 200 acres in Virginia.

Stewart, Angus. He was granted 50 acres in Albany County, New York for his service as a soldier in the 42nd Regiment of Foot in the French and Indian War 30 October 1765.

Stewart, Charles. He was granted 340.6 and 288 acres in Berks County, Pennsylvania for his service as lieutenant in the French and Indian War 3 February 1769.

Stewart, David. He was granted 200 acres in Charlotte County, New York for his service as a noncommissioned officers in the 42nd Regiment of Foot in the French and Indian War 12 October 1774.

Stewart, David. He served as a principal commissary in Col. Andrew Lewis's expedition against the Indians in 1758 in the French and Indian War.

His son and heir, John Stuart, petitioned for his 2,000 acres in February 1780 in Greenbrier County, Virginia.

Stewart, Donald. He was granted 50 acres in Albany County, New York for his service as a soldier in the 55th Regiment of Foot in the French and Indian War 28 October 1765.

Stewart, Donald. He was granted 50 acres in Albany County, New York for his service as a soldier in the 42nd Regiment of Foot in the French and Indian War 30 October 1765.

Stewart, James. He was granted 50 acres in Charlotte County, New York for his service as a soldier in the 46th Regiment of Foot in the French and Indian War 26 May 1772.

Stewart, John. He was granted 50 acres in Albany County, New York for his service as a soldier in the 77th Regiment of Foot in the French and Indian War 13 May 1765.

Stewart, John. He was granted 50 acres in Albany County, New York for his service as a soldier in the 42nd Regiment of Foot in the French and Indian War 30 October 1765.

Stewart, John. He served in an independent company of rangers in the French and Indian War and petitioned for land in New York 12 April 1769.

Stewart, John. He served in an independent company of rangers in the French and Indian War and petitioned for land in New York 12 April 1769. [second of the name]

Stewart, John. He served as a sergeant in the 28th Regiment in the French and Indian War and was granted land in New York in 1767.

Stewart, Joseph. He served in an independent company of rangers in the French and Indian War and petitioned for land in New York 12 April 1769.

Stewart, Lodewick. He was granted 200 acres in Charlotte County, New York for his service as a corporal in the 55th Regiment of Foot in the French and Indian War 25 January 1773.

Stewart, Neil. He was granted 200 acres in Albany County, New York for his service as a corporal in the 77th Regiment of Foot in the French and Indian War 13 May 1765.

Stewart, Patrick. He served in the French and Indian War and petitioned for his land in New York 28 January 1775.

Stewart, Peter. He was granted 2,000 acres in Albany County, New York for his service as a master's mate in the Royal Navy on the *Shannon* and *Shrewsbury* at the reduction of Louisbourg and Quebec in the French and Indian War 7 May 1765.

Stewart, Robert. He was granted 50 acres in Albany County, New York for his service as a soldier in the 42nd Regiment of Foot in the French and Indian War 7 October 1771.

Stewart, Robert. He was granted 200 acres in Albany County, New York for his service as a noncommissioned officer in the 77th Regiment of Foot in the French and Indian War 14 May 1772.

Stewart, Robert. He served in the French and Indian War and took his land in Botetourt County, Virginia. He was probably the one who proved service in Capt. John Dickenson's Company in 1758 in Augusta County, Virginia 18 May 1780.

Stewart, Samuel. He served in an independent company of rangers in the French and Indian War and petitioned for land in New York 12 April 1769.

Stewart, Thomas. He was granted 200 acres in Albany County, New York as a corporal in the 42nd Regiment of Foot in the French and Indian War 30 October 1765.

Stewart, Walter. He was granted 2,000 acres in Albany County, New York for his service as a lieutenant in the Welsh Fusileers in the French and Indian War 7 September 1771.

Stewart, Walter. He served as a sergeant in the 44th Regiment in the French and Indian War and received 200 acres of land in Virginia.

Stewart, William. He was granted 700 acres in Williamsburg Township, South Carolina on the King's bounty for his service in the French and Indian War 13 May 1768.

Stewart, William. He served as a soldier in Capt. William Preston's Company of Rangers in 1758 in the French and Indian War and received his 50 acre warrant in Virginia. He was probably the William Stuart who proved his service in Augusta County, Virginia 21 March 1780.

Stickney, John. He served in the Narraganset War from Massachusetts in 1685. His son, Samuel Stickney, received his land in Buxton, Maine.

Stickney, Samuel. He served in Lovewell's War from Massachusetts and received his land in Petersham, Massachusetts in 1733.

Stiell, William. He was granted 2,000 acres in West Florida for his service as a lieutenant in the French and Indian War 8 November 1777. He received 2,000 acres for his service as adjutant 30 March 1778 and 1,000 acres 27 August 1779.

Stilson, Henry. He was granted 50 acres in Albany County, New York for his service as a soldier in the 80th Regiment of Foot in the French and Indian War 15 April 1771.

Stimson, George. He served in the Narraganset War from Massachusetts in 1685. His son, Richard Stimson, received his land in Buxton, Maine.

Stine, Augustine. He was granted 337 acres in Orange County, New York for his service as a sergeant in the 4th Battalion in the 60th or Royal American Regiment in the French and Indian War 22 March 1770 for seven years and two months. He was granted the tract with James Richardson.

Stine, Augustine. He was granted 246 and 232.75 acres in Cumberland County, Pennsylvania for his service as an ensign in the French and Indian War 3 February 1769.

Stinson, John. He was granted 200 acres in Albany County, New York for his service as a sergeant in the 80th Regiment of Foot in the French and Indian War 4 July 1770.

Stobo, Robert. He served in the French and Indian War. His representative, David Richardson, took his land in Botetourt County, Virginia.

Stockley, Francis. He served as a soldier under Col. William Byrd in 1758 in the French and Indian War. He proved his service in Orange County, Virginia 25 November 1779. He assigned his warrant for 50 acres.

Stoddard, John. He was from Northampton, Massachusetts when he was granted 1,000 acres 12 December 1734.

Stoggle, Ambrose. He served as a soldier in the 2nd Virginia Regiment in the French and Indian War. He proved his service in Goochland County, Virginia 20 September 1779. He assigned his right to 50 acres.

Stoke, John. He served as a sergeant in the French and Indian War and petitioned for 200 acres on the King's bounty in South Carolina 3 December 1766.

Stolt, John. He served as a captain in the French and Indian War and received his 3,000 acre warrant in Virginia.

Stone, Daniel. He served on the expedition to Canada in 1690. Michael Stone received his land in Bethel, Maine in 1767.

Stone, David. He was granted 2,000 acres in Charlotte County, New York for his service as a lieutenant in a corps of rangers in the French and Indian War 23 November 1775.

Stone, Jonathan. He served on the expedition to Canada in 1690. Samuel Stone petitioned for his land in Raymond, Maine in 1690.

Stone, Leonard. He was granted 100 acres in Colleton County, South Carolina and 100 acres on the north side of the Broad River on the King's bounty for his service in the French and Indian War 9 November and 8 December 1774.

Stone, Nathaniel. He received land in Alstead, New Hampshire in 1771 for the service of an unidentified veteran of the expedition to Canada in 1690.

Stone, Patrick. He was granted 200 acres in Albany County, New York for his service as a sergeant in the 2nd Battalion of the 1st Regiment of Foot in the French and Indian War 15 August 1765.

Stone, Samuel. He was granted a farm in Connecticut for his service in the Pequot War. He was from Hartford. His widow, Eliza Stone and his son, Samuel Stone, were granted 500 acres of upland and 50 or 60 acres of meadow, in lieu of the former grant 8 October 1663.

Stone, Samuel. He served in the Narraganset War and received land in Templeton, Massachusetts in 1733.

Stone, Simon. He served in the Narraganset War and received land in Templeton, Massachusetts in 1733.

Stone, Samuel. He served on the expedition to Canada in 1690 and received his land in Bethel, Maine in 1767.

Stone, Thomas. He served as a sergeant in the 48th Regiment in the French and Indian War and petitioned for 200 acres land in New York 9 June 1766.

Storer, Seth. He served in the Narraganset War from Massachusetts in 1685. His son, Seth Storer, received his land in Buxton, Maine.

Storm, John. He was granted 2,000 acres in Albany County, New York for his service as a surgeon's mate in the 60th Regiment of Foot in the French and Indian War 16 July 1765.

Stott, John. He served as a captain in the French and Indian War from Virginia and received a warrant for 3,000 acres. [His surname is indistinct in the record.]

Stoughton, John. He was granted 2,000 acres in Albany County, New York for his service as a lieutenant in an independent company in the French and Indian War 25 July 1764.

Stowel, John. He received land in Alstead, New Hampshire in 1771 for the service of an unidentified veteran of the expedition to Canada in 1690.

Stowel, Samuel. He served on the expedition to Canada in 1690. Edmund Barnard received his land in Alstead, New Hampshire in 1771.

Stowel, William. He served on the expedition to Canada in 1690. He received land in Chesterfield, Massachusetts in 1739.

Strange, John. He shared in the grant of East Greenwich, Rhode Island made to those who had rendered service in King Philip's War. The grant was made 31 October 1677.

Stratton, John. He proved his service as a soldier under Col. William Byrd in the French and Indian War in one of the Virginia Regiments in 1760 in Amherst County, Virginia 6 March 1780.

Stricker, John. He served as a soldier in the 2nd Virginia Regiment in the French and Indian War. He proved his service in Goochland County,

Virginia 7 September 1779. He disposed of his right to 50 acres of land.

Stringer, Samuel. He was granted 2,000 acres in Albany County, New York for his service as an apothecary's mate in the military hospital in the French and Indian War 20 January 1769.

Strong, John. He served as a soldier in the French and Indian War. He proved his service in Goochland County, Virginia 21 September 1779 and assigned his warrant for 50 acres.

Strong, Sherwood. He served as a soldier in the French and Indian War. He was deceased. His service was proved in Goochland County, Virginia 21 September 1779. His warrant for 50 acres was assigned.

Strowles, George. He was granted 50 acres in Albany County, New York for his service as a soldier in the 45th Regiment of Foot in the French and Indian War 18 February 1775.

Strugnal, John. He served as a corporal in the 46th Regiment in the French and Indian War. It was certified that his widow was entitled to land 15 December 1766 in New York. His land was assigned 22 January 1767.

Stuart, Charles. He was granted 2,000 acres near Natchez, West Florida for his service as an officer in the French and Indian War 3 February 1767.

Stuart, Charles. He was granted 4,000 acres in West Florida for his service as Agent of Transport and a lieutenant in the 78th Regiment of Foot in the French and Indian War 31 July 1775.

Stuart, David. He was granted 2,150 acres on Rocky Creek in South Carolina on the King's bounty 16 July 1765. He served as a lieutenant in the French and Indian War.

Stuart, Duncan. He was granted 200 acres in Albany County, New York for his service as a sergeant in the 77th Regiment of Foot in the French and Indian War 7 May 1767.

Stuart, Ebenezer. He served on the expedition to Canada in 1690 and received land in Poland, Maine in 1739.

Stuart, George. He was granted 50 acres in Albany County, New York for his service as a soldier in the 78th Regiment of Foot in the French and Indian War 1 May 1765.

Stuart, James. He served as a private in the French and Indian War and petitioned for land in New York 8 July 1772.

Stuart, John. He received his land in West Florida for his service as a captain in the French and Indian War 16 August 1768, 12 November 1776, and 4 March 1777 for 2,500 acres.

Stuart, Malcolm. He served as a private in the French and Indian War and petitioned for land in New York 8 July 1772.

Stuart, Patrick. He was granted 1,000 acres in West Florida for his service as a lieutenant in the French and Indian War 11 July 1777.

Stuart, William. He was granted 300 acres in Williamsburg Township, South Carolina on the King's bounty for service in the French and Indian War 21 June 1765.

Stubbins, Daniel. He served in the Narraganset War from Connecticut and received land in Voluntown, Connecticut in 1701.

Stubblefield, George. He served as a cadet under Col. Adam Stephen in the French and Indian War in 1758 and received his 50 acre warrant 15 June 1780 in Spotsylvania County, Virginia.

Stubbs, Butler. He served as a lieutenant in Capt. George Berkeley's Company under Maj. Gen. Sir John Irvin, Colonel of His Majesty's 74th Regiment of Foot, in the French and Indian War. He proved his service in Yohogania County, Virginia 28 February 1780. He assigned his 2,000 acre warrant.

Studholme, Gilfred. He served as a subaltern officer in the French and Indian War and received 2,000 acres in Nova Scotia 26 July 1782.

Studley, Joseph. He received land in Richmond, New Hampshire in 1765 for the service of an unidentified veteran of the expedition to Canada in 1690.

Stupart, Alexander. He received his 3,000 acres of land in West Florida for his service as a master in the navy on the *Alcide* in the French and Indian War 3 June 1776.

Sturgis, Joseph. He served on the expedition to Canada in 1690 and received land in Dumbarton, New Hampshire in 1735.

Suiter, Charles. He served as a soldier in the French and Indian War from Virginia under Col. William Byrd and received a warrant for 50 acres. He also appeared as Charles Sueter.

Sullivan, James. He served in the French and Indian War and was issued a warrant for 300 acres in South Carolina on the King's bounty. He was robbed of the warrant and applied for a new one 6 June 1764.

Sullivan, James. He served in the French and Indian War. He received 1,000 acres of land in Virginia.

Sullivan, John. He served as a sergeant in the 40th Regiment in the French and Indian War and assigned his right to for 200 acres in New York 27 July 1765.

Sullivan, Peter. He served as a soldier in the 47th Regiment in the French and Indian War and petitioned for his 50 acres in New York 26 October 1764.

Sumers, Henry. He served in the Narraganset War from Charlestown, Massachusetts. He received his land in Westminster, Massachusetts in 1733.

Sumersby, Daniel. He served in the Narraganset War from Massachusetts in 1685. His land was located in Buxton, Maine.

Summers, John. He served as a sergeant in the 2nd Virginia Regiment under Col. William Byrd in the French and Indian War. He assigned his warrant for 200 acres in Virginia.

Summers, John. He served as an officer in the French and Indian War and received 2,000 acres in West Florida.

Sumner, Ebenezer. He served on the expedition to Canada in 1690. His nephew, Bartholame Gold of Boston, Massachusetts, received his land in Ashburnham, Massachusetts in 1736.

Sumner, Hezekiah. He was granted 2,000 acres in Albany County, New York for his service as a lieutenant in a company of foot in the French and Indian War 2 May 1770.

Sumner, Jethro. He served as a subaltern in the French and Indian War and received 2,000 acres of land in Virginia.

Sumner, Josianiah. He was a veteran of the expedition to Canada in 1690. His nephew, Seth Sumner of Milton, Massachusetts at the desire of his uncle, William Sumner, received his land in Ashburnham, Massachusetts in 1736.

Sumner, Samuel. He served on the expedition to Canada in 1690. His nephew, Edward Sumner of Roxbury, Massachusetts received his land in Ashburnham, Massachusetts in 1736.

Sumner, Samuel. He served on the expedition to Canada in 1690. His son, Samuel Sumner of Taunton, Massachusetts received his land in Ashburnham, Massachusetts in 1736.

Sumner, William. He served on the expedition to Canada in 1690. His brother, Benjamin Sumner of Milton, Massachusetts, received his land in Ashburnham, Massachusetts in 1736.

Sumner, William. He served on the expedition to Canada in 1690. He was the son of Increase Sumner. The veteran's cousin, William Sumner of Milton, Massachusetts, received his land in Ashburnham, Massachusetts in 1736.

Sumpter, Francis. He was granted 50 acres in Albany County, New York for his service as a private in the 60th or Royal American Regiment in the French and Indian War 8 June 1771.

Sunderland, John. He served as a sergeant in the 55th Regiment in the French and Indian War and received 200 acres in Albany County, New York which was surveyed 13 August 1765.

Surft, James. He served as a soldier in the 28th Regiment in the French and Indian War and had his service certified 19 September 1766 in New York.

Sutherland, Aeneas. He served as a noncommissioned officer in the French and Indian War and received 200 acres in Nova Scotia 23 June 1780.

Sutherland, Alexander. He received his 200 acres of land in West Florida for his service as a noncommissioned officer in the French and Indian War 17 October 1774.

Sutherland, Andrew. He was granted 200 acres in Albany County, New York for his service as a noncommissioned officer in the 55th Regiment of Foot in the French and Indian War 15 August 1765.

Sutherland, Erick. He was granted 2,000 acres in Albany County, New York for his service as a lieutenant in an independent company in the French and Indian War 5 September 1764.

Sutherland, George. He was granted 50 acres in Albany County, New York for his service as a soldier in the 77th Regiment of Foot in the French and Indian War 13 May 1765.

Sutherland, George. He was granted 50 acres in Albany County, New York for his service as a soldier in the 28th Regiment of Foot in the French and Indian War 8 October 1771.

Sutherland, George. He served as a soldier in the French and Indian War and assigned his right to William McDonald who received the 50 acres in in Nova Scotia 7 January 1781.

Sutherland, James. He was granted two warrants for 1,500 acres each in West Florida for his service as a lieutenant in the navy in the French and Indian War 23 September 1778.

Sutherland, John. He was granted 50 acres in Albany County, New York for his service as a soldier in the 77th Regiment of Foot in the French and Indian War 10 May 1765.

Sutherland, John. He was granted 50 acres in Albany County, New York for his service as a soldier in the 78th Regiment of Foot in the French and Indian War 7 May 1767.

Sutherland, John. He served as master's mate in the navy in the French and Indian War and received two warrants for 500 acres each in West Florida 8 September 1780.

Sutherland, Nicholas. He was granted 3,000 acres in Albany County, New York for his service as a captain in the 77th Regiment of Foot in the French and Indian War 7 August 1764. He also appeared as Nicholas Southerland.

Sutherland, William. He was granted 200 acres in Albany County, New York for his service as a corporal in the 77th Regiment of Foot in the French and Indian War 28 October 1771.

Sutherland, William. He served as an ensign in the 95th Regiment of Foot under Col. Burton in the French and Indian War and received his 2,000 acre land warrant in Virginia.

Sutten, Benjamin. He received land in Richmond, New Hampshire in 1765 for the service of an unidentified veteran of the expedition to Canada in 1690.

Sutton, Benjamin. He served on the expedition to Canada in 1690 and received land in Chesterfield, Massachusetts in 1739.

Sutton, Edward. He petitioned for a warrant for 50 acres for his service as a private in the 1st Virginia Regiment in the French and Indian War in 1760 in Spotsylvania County, Virginia in February 1780 which he assigned.

Sutton, John. He served as a corporal in the Royal Regiment of Artillery in the French and Indian War and petitioned for his 200 acres of land in New York 24 January 1775.

Sutton, Thomas. He served as a private in the French and Indian War and petitioned for land in New York in November 1766.

Swaddle, Jesse. He was granted 50 acres in Orange County, New York for his service as a soldier in the 4th Battalion in the 60th Regiment of Foot in the French and Indian War 15 May 1770.

Swain, Henry. He served in the Narraganset War from Boston, Massachusetts. His son, Benjamin Swain, received land in Bedford, New Hampshire in 1733.

Swain, Jeremiah. He served as a major in the Narraganset War from Reading, Massachusetts and petitioned for his land 4 June 1685. His heirs received his land in Westminster, Massachusetts in 1733.

Swan, John. He served in the Narraganset War and received land in Templeton, Massachusetts in 1733.

Swan, Joshua. He was from Methuen, Essex County, Massachusetts and was awarded 160 acres for his sufferings and service in the Indian war 23 March 1735/6.

Swan, Robert. He served in the Narraganset War from Massachusetts in 1685. His son, Richard Swan, received his land in Buxton, Maine.

Swasey, Stephen. He served on the expedition to Canada in 1690. Samuel Swacy was admitted to his land in Lyndeboro, Maine in 1736.

Swearengen, Van. He served as a subaltern in the French and Indian War. He proved his service in Yohogania County, Virginia 24 April 1780.

Swearingan, Thomas. He served as an officer in the French and Indian War and was entitled to 2,000 acres which he assigned in Virginia.

Sweat, Elisha. He served on the expedition to Canada in 1690 and received his land in Poland, Maine in 1739.

Sweat, Joseph. He served on the expedition to Canada in 1690. Joseph Sweat was admitted to his land in Lyndeboro, Maine in 1736.

Sweat, Stephen. He served in the Narraganset War from Marblehead, Massachusetts. His brother, Joseph Sweat, claimed his land in Amherst, New Hampshire in 1734.

Sweedland, Christopher. He served as a staff officer in the Royal Artillery in the French and Indian War and petitioned for his 2,000 acres in New New York 30 December 1774.

Sweeny, Walter. He was granted 200 acres in Albany County, New York for his service as a sergeant in the 60th Regiment of Foot in the French and Indian War 15 August 1765.

Sweet, Benjamin. He served as a captain and was slain by the enemy. His son, Stephen Sweet, was awarded 200 acres by Massachusetts 12 December 1735.

Sweet, Moses. He was a veteran of the expedition to Canada in 1690. His son, Jabez Sweet of Ipswich, Massachusetts, claimed his land in Winchedon, Massachusetts in 1736.

Swietzer, Godlieb. He was granted 200 acres in Albany County, New York for his service as a sergeant in the 60th Regiment of Foot in the French and Indian War 3 October 1771.

Swift, Francis. He was granted 200 acres in Charlotte County, New York for his service as a noncommissioned officer in the 4th Battalion of the 60th Regiment of Foot in the French and Indian War 12 October 1774.

Swift, James. He was a veteran of the expedition to Canada in 1690. His brother, Obadiah Swift of Dorchester, Massachusetts, received his land in Ashburnham, Massachusetts in 1736.

Swift, James. He was granted 50 acres in Gloucester County, New York for his service as a soldier in the 28th Regiment of Foot in the French and Indian War 5 April 1770.

Swift, John. He was granted 50 acres in Albany County, New York for his service as a soldier in the 60th Regiment of Foot in the French and Indian War 28 June 1770.

Swift, Paul. He served in the 28th Regiment in the French and Indian War and petitioned for his land 18 October 1766 in New York.

Swift, William. He was a veteran of the expedition to Canada in 1690. John Swift, Jr. of Framingham, Massachusetts in the right of his father Mr.

John Swift, eldest brother to the veteran, received his land in Ashburnham, Massachusetts in 1736.

Swoop, Joseph, Sr. He served in Capt. Dickenson's Company of Rangers in 1758 in the French and Indian War. It was proved in Botetourt County, Virginia 10 February 1780 that his heirs were Patrick Carragun and Joseph Swoop.

Swords, Thomas. He was granted 3,125 acres in Albany County, New York for his service as a lieutenant in the 55th Regiment of Foot in the French and Indian War 7 October 1767.

Syfard, Christopher. He served as a private in the 60th Regiment in the French and Indian War and was granted land in New York 2 March 1768.

Symmes, Zechariah. He served in the Narraganset War from Massachusetts and received his land in Templeton, Massachusetts in 1733.

Symonds, James. He served on the expedition to Canada in 1690. His son, James Symonds, received his land in Woburn, Massachusetts in 1738.

Syrutscheck, John. He served as a soldier in the French and Indian War and petitioned for 50 acres of land in New York 3 October 1766.

Taft, Thomas. He served on the expedition to Canada in 1690. Thomas Taft received land in Warwick, Massachusetts in 1738.

Talbert, Haly. He served as a sergeant in 1760 in Capt. James Gunn's Company in Col. William Byrd's Regiment of Regulars in the French and Indian War. He received his 200 acre warrant 21 March 1780 in Chesterfield County, Virginia. He also appeared as Halley Tolbot and Haley Talbot.

Talbot, Peter. He served in the Narraganset War from Stoughton, Connecticut. His son, George Talbot, received land in Bedford, New Hampshire in 1733.

Taley, John. He served in the Narraganset War and assigned his right to land to Samuel Chandler who received it in Templeton, Massachusetts in 1733.

Tally, Stephen. He received his 50 acres of land in West Florida for his service as a private in the French and Indian War 9 April 1777.

Tapley, John. He served on the expedition to Canada in 1690. William Tapley was admitted to his land in Lyndeboro, Maine in 1736.

Tapley, Robert. He served on the expedition to Canada in 1690. William Tapley was admitted to his land in Lyndeboro, Maine in 1736.

Tapper, William. He was granted 50 acres in Albany County, New York for his service as a soldier in the 80th Regiment of Foot in the French and Indian War 7 October 1768.

Tarbel, John. He served in the Narraganset War from Salem, Massachusetts. His heirs claimed his land in Amherst, New Hampshire. Cornelius

Tarbel, drew same.

Tarbell, Thomas. He served at Port Royal and received his land in Massachusetts 10 December 1735.

Tarble, Thomas. He served in the Narraganset War and received land in Templeton, Massachusetts in 1733.

Tarbol, Samuel. He served in Lovewell's War in Massachusetts and received his land in Petersham, Massachusetts in 1733.

Tarbot, Nicholas. He served in the Narraganset War from Massachusetts in 1685. His land was located in Buxton, Maine.

Tarbox, Jonathan. He served on the expedition to Canada in 1690. Jonathan Tarbox received land in Chesterfield, Massachusetts in 1739.

Tarbox, Samuel. He served in the Narraganset War from Lynn, Massachusetts. He applied for his land 4 June 1685. His heirs claimed his land in Amherst, New Hampshire in 1734. Thomas Tarbox drew the land.

Tarlow, Charles. He was granted 50 acres in Albany County, New York for his service as a private in the 46th Regiment of Foot in the French and Indian War 5 April 1771.

Tate, Charles. He was granted 200 acres in Albany County, New York for his service as a noncommissioned officer in the Royal Regiment of Artillery in the French and Indian War 4 August 1774.

Tate, James. He served as a lieutenant in the French and Indian War and received 2,000 acres in New York 4 July 1764.

Tattingham, Elisha. He served in the Narraganset War and received land in Templeton, Massachusetts in 1733.

Tatum, John. He served as a sergeant in Capt. Stewart's Company of Regulars in Virginia under Col. William Byrd in the French and Indian War. He requested his land in April 1780 in Botetourt County, Virginia.

Taylor, Abraham. He served in the Narraganset War and received his land in Templeton, Massachusetts in 1733.

Taylor, Charles. He was granted 1,320 acres in Orangeburg, South Carolina on the King's bounty for service in the French and Indian War 23 January 1774. He served as a lieutenant in a company of foot.

Taylor, Daniel. He was granted 200 acres in Albany County, New York for his service as a corporal in the 80th Regiment of Foot in the French and Indian War 9 May 1771.

Taylor, David. He was granted 200 acres in Albany County, New York for his service as a corporal in the 55th Regiment of Foot in the French and Indian War 19 July 1766.

Taylor, Francis. He was granted 50 acres in Albany County, New York for his service as a private in the 46th Regiment of Foot in the French and

Indian War 8 June 1771.

Taylor, George, Jr. He served as an ensign in the French and Indian War. His heir, James Taylor, received his 2,000 acre warrant in Virginia.

Taylor, Isaac. He was granted 200 acres in Albany County, New York for his service as a drummer in the 60th Regiment of Foot in the French and Indian War 1 April 1772.

Taylor, James. He served on the expedition to Canada in 1690 and received his land in Bethel, Maine in 1767.

Taylor, James. He served as an ensign in Capt. Peter Hogg's Company of Rangers in 1758 in the French and Indian War. He petitioned for his 2,000 acres 9 March 1780 in Caroline County, Virginia.

Taylor, James. He served as a soldier in Capt. Charles Scott's Company under Col. William Byrd against the Indians in 1760 in the French and Indian War. He was a native of Virginia. He received his 50 acre warrant 21 March 1780 in Pittsylvania County, Virginia.

Taylor, John. He served in the Narraganset War from Yarmouth, Massachusetts and received land in Gorham, Maine in 1733.

Taylor, John. He served in the Narraganset War from Concord, Massachusetts. His heir, William Clark, received his land in Templeton, Massachusetts in 1733.

Taylor, John. He was granted 200 acres in Albany County, New York for his service as a noncommissioned officer in the 46th Regiment of Foot in the French and Indian War 8 March 1771.

Taylor, John. He served as a soldier in the French and Indian War and received 50 acres in Nova Scotia 9 October 1776.

Taylor, John. He served as a soldier in Capt. John Dickerson's Company of Ranger in the French and Indian War. He proved his service in Botetourt County, Virginia in April 1780. He assigned his 50 acre warrant.

Taylor, Joseph. He served in the Narraganset War from Barnstable, Massachusetts and received his land in Gorham, Maine in 1733.

Taylor, Richard. He served in the Narraganset War from Sudbury, Massachusetts. His son, Richard Taylor, received his land in Westminster, Massachusetts in 1733.

Taylor, Richard. He served in the Narraganset War from Yarmouth, Massachusetts and received his land in Gorham, Maine in 1733.

Taylor, Samuel. He served in the Narraganset War from Massachusetts in 1685. His land was located in Buxton, Maine.

Taylor, Samuel. He served in the Narraganset War from Pomfret, Connecticut. He claimed his land in Greenwich, Massachusetts in 1737.

Taylor, Samuel. He served as a soldier under Col. William Byrd until 1758 in the French and Indian War. He proved his service in Caroline County, Virginia in March 1780 and assigned his right to 50 acres.

Taylor, Sebred. He served in the Narraganset War from Sudbury, Massachusetts. His son, Thomas Taylor, received his land in Westminister, Massachusetts in 1733.

Taylor, Zachary. He served in the French and Indian War as a sergeant in the 2nd Virginia Regiment. He received his 200 acre land warrant in Virginia which he assigned.

Teatham, John. He served as a sergeant in Capt. Stewart's Company of Regulars under Col. William Byrd in the French and Indian War. He proved his service in Botetourt County, Virginia in April 1780. He assigned his warrant for 200 acres.

Teator, George. He served as a soldier in the French and Indian War in Capt. Gist's Company of the 1st Virginia Regiment. He received a warrant for 50 acres in December 1779 in Botetourt County, Virginia.

Teator, George. He served as a sergeant in Col. William Byrd's Regiment in the French and Indian War and received a warrant for 200 acres 1 February 1780 in Kentucky County, Virginia.

Teeson, Daniel. He was granted 200 acres in Albany County, New York for his service as a corporal in the 80th Regiment of Foot in the French and Indian War 14 June 1765.

Temple, Abraham. He served in the Narraganset War from Massachusetts. His son, Benjamin Temple, received his land in Templeton, Massachusetts in 1733.

Temple, Benjamin. He served as a lieutenant in the Virginia Battalion of Regulars under Col. William Peachey in 1759 in the French and Indian War. He petitioned for 2,000 acres 2 March 1780 in Hanover, County, Virginia.

Temple, Richard. He served on the expedition to Canada in 1690. His son, John Temple, received his land in Bethel, Maine in 1767.

Temple, William. He served on the expedition to Canada in 1690. His son, Jabez Temple of Wilmington, received his land in Woburn, Massachusetts in 1738.

Tenny, Daniel. He served in the Narraganset War from Massachusetts in 1685. His son, Daniel Tenny, received his land in Buxton, Maine.

Tenny, Thomas. He served in the Narraganset War from Massachusetts in 1685. His land was located in Buxton, Maine.

Tennyson, William. He sought 600 acres in West Florida for his service as an officer in the French and Indian War 17 May 1779.

Tenor, Richard. He was granted 200 acres in Albany County, New York for his service as a corporal in the 4th Battalion in the 60th Regiment of Foot in the French and Indian War 25 May 1771.

Terpley, James. He was granted 50 acres in Albany County, New York for his service as a soldier in the 44th Regiment of Foot in the French and Indian War 21 May 1768. He also appeared as James Tarpley.

Terry, Jeremiah. He was granted 2,000 acres in West Florida for his service as an officer in the French and Indian War 28 July 1766.

Terry, John. He served as a captain in the French and Indian War and received 3,000 acres in Nova Scotia 2 December 1771.

Terry, Joseph. He served as a sergeant under Capt. William Phillips under Col. Andrew Lewis against the Indians in 1763 in the French and Indian War. He received his 200 acre warrant 21 March 1780 in Pittsylvania County, Virginia.

Terry, Thomas. He served in the French and Indian War and was entitled to 200 acres in Virginia which he assigned.

Terry, William. He served as a soldier in Capt. Joseph Fox's Company under Col. Andrew Lewis in 1755 in the French and Indian War. He received his 50 acre warrant 21 March 1780 in Pittsylvania County, Virginia.

Thallay, Thomas. He was granted 50 acres in Albany County, New York for his service as a soldier in the 55th Regiment of Foot in the French and Indian War 18 April 1769.

Thatcher, John. He served in the Narraganset War from Yarmouth, Massachusetts and received his land in Gorham, Maine in 1733.

Thaxter, —. He served as a colonel on the expedition to Canada in 1690. Col. Thaxter received land in Chesterfield, Massachusetts in 1739.

Thaxter, Thomas. He served in the Narraganset War from Hingham, Massachusetts. His brother, Samuel Thaxter, received land in Bedford, New Hampshire in 1733.

Thesslewood, Benjamin. He served as a soldier in the 4th Battalion Royal Americans in the French and Indian War and petitioned for land 22 October 1766 in New York.

Thodey, Francis. He served as a captain in the French and Indian War and petitioned for land 30 December 1766 in New York.

Thodey, Michael. He served as a colonel in the French and Indian War and petitioned for land 30 December 1766 in New York.

Thomas, James. He was granted 50 acres in Albany County, New York for his service as a private in the 15th Regiment of Foot in the French and Indian War 28 March 1771.

Thomas, John. He served as a private in the French and Indian War and petitioned for land in New York 17 March 1767.

Thomas, John. He served as an officer in the Royal Regiment of Artillery in the French and Indian War and received 1,000 acres in West Florida 3 February 1768.

Thomas, Morris. He served as a soldier in the 46th Regiment in the French and Indian War. Mary Thomas was certified as his widow 15 December 1766 in New York. She assigned the warrant to Robert Buchanan 21 January 1767.

Thomas, Samuel. He served as a corporal under Col. George Washington in the French and Indian War and received a warrant for 50 acres which he assigned in Virginia. He proved his service in Frederick County, Virginia 6 June 1780.

Thomas, Samuel. He served in the Narraganset War from Yarmouth, Massachusetts and received land in Gorham, Maine in 1733.

Thomas, Somerset. He served as a soldier in the 28th Regiment in the French and Indian War and petitioned for his land in New York 6 August 1764.

Thompson, —. He served on the expedition to Canada in 1690. His son, John Thompson, received his land in Winchendon, Massachusetts in 1736.

Thompson, Alexander. He served as a soldier in the French and Indian War and received 50 acres on the King's bounty in South Carolina 1 December 1772.

Thompson, Archibald. He served as a sergeant in the French and Indian War and received a warrant for 200 acres in November 1779 in Montgomery County, Virginia.

Thompson, Charles. He was a soldier in Capt. Mordecai Buckner's Company in the Virginia Regiment in the French and Indian War and received his land 3 March 1774.

Thompson, David. He served as a sergeant in Col. William Byrd's Regiment in 1758 in the French and Indian War and assigned his 200 acres.

Thompson, George. He was granted 50 acres in Albany County, New York for his service as a soldier in the 42nd Regiment of Foot in the French and Indian War 30 October 1765.

Thompson, James. He was granted 200 acres in Albany County, New York for his service as a sergeant in the 55th Regiment of Foot in the French and Indian War 1 July 1771.

Thompson, James. He served as a soldier in one of the Virginia Regiments in 1758 under Gen. Forbes during the French and Indian War. He received his 50 acre warrant in March 1780 in Amherst County,

Virginia.

Thompson, Jeremiah. He was granted 50 acres in Gloucester County, New York for his service as a soldier in the 4th Battalion in the 60th Regiment of Foot in the French and Indian War 5 April 1770.

Thompson, John. He was granted 2,000 acres in Charlotte County, New York for his service as a lieutenant in the 95th Regiment of Foot in the French and Indian War 3 August 1774.

Thompson, John. He served as a soldier in Capt. Joseph Fox's Company in the French and Indian War and received a warrant for 50 acres 12 October 1779 in Louisa County, Virginia.

Thompson, Richard. He was granted 200 acres in Albany County, New York for his service as a corporal in the 40th Regiment of Foot in the French and Indian War 29 October 1765.

Thompson, Robert. He was granted 300 acres in Pennsylvania for his service in the French and Indian War 1 April 1769.

Thompson, William. He was granted 200 acres in Albany County, New York for his service as a corporal in the 60th or Royal American Regiment in the French and Indian War 8 June 1771.

Thompson, William. He served as a captain in the French and Indian War and petitioned for his land in New York 28 February 1770.

Thompson, William. He was granted 300 acres in Pennsylvania for his service in the French and Indian War 1 April 1769.

Thompson, William. He was granted 50 acres on the Long Canes in South Carolina on the King's bounty for his service as a private in the French and Indian War 13 May 1768.

Thompson, William. He was granted 50 acres in Craven County, South Carolina on the King's bounty for his service in the French and Indian War 1 December 1772.

Thompson, William. He served as a soldier in the Virginia Regiment under Col. George Washington from 1757 to the end of the French and Indian War and received his 50 acre warrant in March 1780 in Amherst County, Virginia.

Thompson, William. He served as a sergeant under Capt. Henry Harrison and Col. Adam Stephen in the French and Indian War. He proved his service in Halifax County, Virginia 18 May 1780.

Thomson, Anthony. He served as a soldier in a company of rangers under Capt. Joseph Fox in 1756 in the French and Indian War. He petitioned for a warrant for 50 acres 14 February 1780 in Louisa County, Virginia.

Thomson, Anthony. He served as a sergeant in Capt. Samuel Overton's Company in the French and Indian War and received a warrant for

200 acres.

Thomson, Joseph. He served in the Narraganset War. His son, Benjamin Thomson, received his land in Templeton, Massachusetts in 1733.

Thomson, William. He served as a captain in the French and Indian War from Virginia and was entitled to 3,000 acres which he desired to locate in Fincastle County, Virginia in 1774.

Thorley, John. He served as a private in the French and Indian War and petitioned for land in New York in November 1766.

Thorn, Joseph. He served in the Narraganset War from Hingham, Massachusetts and received land in Bedford, New Hampshire in 1733.

Thornbury, John. He was granted 200 acres in Albany County, New York for his service as a noncommissioned officer in the 80th Regiment of Foot in the French and Indian War 8 March 1771.

Thornton, George. He served as a fifer in Col. Adam Stephen's Regiment in the French and Indian War and received a warrant for 200 acres 18 November 1779 in Greenbrier County, Virginia.

Thornton, Thomas. He served in the Narraganset War from Yarmouth, Massachusetts and received land in Gorham, Maine in 1733.

Thorp, Samuel. He served on the expedition to Canada in 1690 and received land in Warwick, Massachusetts in 1736.

Thorp, John. He served six months under Gen. Forbes in 1758 in the French and Indian War and departed this life. His heir, William Thorp, received his 50 acre warrant in January 1780 in Bedford County, Virginia.

Thorp, Thomas. He served on the expedition to Canada in 1690. Thomas Thorp received land in Warwick, Massachusetts in 1738.

Thorp, Thomas. He served as a corporal from 1759 until 1760 under Col. William Byrd in the French and Indian War. His service was proved in Caroline County, Virginia in March 1780. He assigned his warrant for 200 acres to Edmund Thorp in Virginia. He was a native of Virginia. A man of the same name and rank proved his service in Bedford County, Virginia 24 April 1780.

Thorp, William. He served as a sergeant from 1755 until 1762 in the French and Indian War. He received his 200 acre warrant in December 1779 in Bedford County, Virginia. He was a native of Virginia.

Thracey, William. He served as a soldier in the French and Indian War and petitioned for his 50 acres in New York in 1771.

Throckmorton, Gabriel. He served as a lieutenant in the regiment of Col. William Byrd in 1758 until 1759 and a captain in the battalion under Col. William Peachey in the French and Indian War. He proved his service in Frederick County, Virginia 8 March 1780. He received warrants for 5,000 acres which he assigned.

Thrall, William. He was granted 50 acres in Connecticut for his service in the Pequot War 11 May 1671. He also appeared as William Trall.

Thresher, John. He served in the Narraganset War from Taunton, Massachusetts. He claimed his land in Greenwich, Massachusetts in 1737.

Thruston, Charles Mynn. He served as a lieutenant in the Virginia Regiment in the French and Indian War and assigned his 2,000 acres of land.

Thurlo, John. He served on the expedition to Canada in 1690 and received land in Poland, Maine in 1739.

Thursting, William. He was granted 200 acres in Albany County, New York for his service as a drummer in the 80th Regiment of Foot in the French and Indian War 6 July 1771.

Thurston, Daniel. He served in the Narraganset War from Massachusetts in 1685. His son, Daniel Thurston, and his grandson, John Thurston, received his land in Buxton, Maine.

Thwaite, Robert. He was granted 50 acres in Craven County, South Carolina on the King's bounty for service as a private in the French and Indian War 6 February 1773.

Tibbals, Thomas. He was granted 50 acres in Connecticut for his service as a sergeant in the Pequot War 11 May 1671. He was from Milford.

Tileston, Timothy. He served in the Narraganset War from Dorchester, Massachusetts. His son, Thomas Tileston, received land in Bedford, New Hampshire in 1733.

Tilestone, Cornelius. He served on the expedition to Canada in 1690. Timothy Tilestone of Dorchester, Massachusetts his brother, received his land in Ashburnham, Massachusetts in 1736.

Tilestone, Thomas. He was from Dorchester and received 200 acres of land in Massachusetts 9 January 1735. He served in several expeditions against the Indians. In 1695 he was under Col. Church; he commanded a company under Col. Marsh; he later commanded a company at Castle William. He also appeared as Thomas Tileston.

Tilghman, James. He was granted 5,000 and 500 acres in Pennsylvania for his service in the French and Indian War 4 February 1769.

Tilton, Abraham. He was a veteran of the expedition to Canada in 1690 and and was of Ipswich, Massachusetts when he claimed his land in Winchendon, Massachusetts in 1736.

Tilman, Daniel. He served as a sergeant in Capt. Thomas Fleming's Company under Col. William Peachey in the Frontier Battalion in 1758 in the

French and Indian War. He received his 200 acre warrant 6 April 1780 in Fluvanna County, Virginia. He also appeared as Daniel Tilmon.

Tilsey, John. He was granted 200 acres in Albany County, New York for his service as a drummer in the 77th Regiment of Foot in the French and Indian War 28 June 1770.

Timberlake, Epaphroditus. He served as a sergeant under Capt. Hancock Eustace in the French and Indian War and received a warrant for 200 acres 25 October 1779 in Fauquier County, Virginia. He had also served as an acting ensign.

Timberlake, Henry. He served in the Narraganset War from Boston, Massachusetts. His heirs received land in Bedford, New Hampshire in 1733.

Timberlake, Henry. He served as a lieutenant under Col. Samuel Meredith in the 2nd Virginia Regiment in the French and Indian War. His 1,000 acres were awarded to his heir, Richard Timberlake, in Henrico County, Virginia in December 1779.

Timberlake, Richard. He served six months as a soldier in 1758 under Gen. Forbes in the French and Indian War and received his 50 acre warrant in May 1780 in Bedford County, Virginia. He was a native of Virginia.

Tinder, James. He served as a soldier in Col. William Byrd's Regiment in 1758 in the French and Indian War and obtained his 50 acre warrant 14 February 1780 in Louisa County, Virginia.

Ting, Edward. He served in the Narraganset War from Boston, Massachusetts. His son, Edward Ting, received his land in Bedford, New Hampshire in 1733.

Tingle, George. He served as a noncommissioned officer in the French and Indian War and petitioned for his 200 acres in New York 22 April 1765.

Tingle, George. He served in the French and Indian War. His service was proved in Berkeley County, Virginia 23 March 1780.

Tinkham, Peter. He served in the Narraganset War from Plymouth, Massachusetts. His son, Peter Tinkham, received his land in Gorham, Maine in 1733.

Tinnison, Barnett. He was granted 200 acres in Albany County, New York for his service as a sergeant in a regiment of foot in the French and Indian War 19 May 1770.

Tinsley, William. He served as a soldier in the Virginia Regiment under Col. William Byrd in the French and Indian War and petitioned for his 50 acres in February 1780 in Spotsylvania County, Virginia.

Tisdale, Joshua. He served in the Narraganset War from Freetown, Massachusetts. His son, Samuel Tisdale, claimed his land in Greenwich, Massachusetts in 1737.

Titcomb, Abraham. He served on the expedition to Canada in 1690 and received land in Poland, Maine in 1739.

Toalman, John. He was a veteran of the expedition to Canada in 1690. His son, John Toalman, Jr., received his land in Ashburnham, Massachusetts in 1736.

Tobin, Peter. He served as sergeant in the 48th Regiment in the French and Indian War. His petition for land was deposited in New York in October 1767. He petitioned for his land 31 October 1770.

Toby, —. He served on the expedition to Canada in 1690. Timothy Toby received land in Dumbarton, New Hampshire in 1735.

Tolten, William. He was granted 200 acres in Albany County, New York for his service as a corporal in the 4th Battalion in the Royal American or 60th Regiment of Foot in the French and Indian War 27 September 1769. He also appeared as William Totten.

Tomkins, Charles. He served as a scout and ensign in the French and Indian War. William Peachey, a field officer in the 2nd Virginia Regiment, certified his service. He received four warrants for 500 acres in Virginia 19 October 1779. He also appeared as Charles Tomkies.

Tomlin, Thomas. He was granted 200 acres in Charlotte County, New York for his service as a corporal officer in the 44th Regiment of Foot in the French and Indian War 26 May 1772.

Tomlinson, Daniel. He was granted 200 acres in Ulster County, New York for his service as a corporal in the 9th Regiment of Foot in the French and Indian War 6 December 1774.

Tommy, Matthew. He served as a private in the French and Indian War and assigned his right to 50 acres in Virginia.

Tonyn, Anthony. He served in the French and Indian War and received 500 acres in Nova Scotia 30 September 1767.

Tool, John. He was granted 50 acres in Albany County, New York for his service as a soldier in the 44th Regiment of Foot in the French and Indian War 1 April 1772.

Toppon, James. He served on the expedition to Canada in 1690 and received land in Poland, Maine in 1739.

Torrey, James. He served as lieutenant of the train band in Scituate, Plymouth Colony and had gone to the home of Mrs. Tickner where the magazine was kept. He opened two barrels of gunpowder to dry. There was an accidental explosion. Badly burned, he died the next day on 6 July 1665. The town granted 200 acres to his four younger sons, William Torrey, Joseph Torrey, Jonathan Torrey, and Josiah Torrey, on 2 October 1665. Their guardian was their uncle, Capt. William Torrey.

Totman, Stephen. He received land in Richmond, New Hampshire in 1765 for the service of an unidentified veteran of the expedition to Canada to 1690.

Towel, Henry. He was granted 50 acres in Albany County, New York for his service as a soldier in the 17th Regiment of Foot in the French and Indian War 7 October 1768. *Vide* Henry Towl.

Tower, Daniel. He served on the expedition to Canada in 1690. Daniel Tower received land in Chesterfield, Massachusetts in 1739.

Towers, James. He served in the French and Indian War. His representative, John Baynes, took his land in Botetourt County, Virginia.

Towl, Henry. He was granted 50 acres in Albany County, New York for his service as a soldier in the 17th Regiment of Foot in the French and Indian War 30 May 1771. *Vide* Henry Towel.

Townsend, Andrew. He served in the Narraganset War from Lynn, Massachusetts. He applied for his land 4 June 1685. His heirs claimed his land in Amherst, New Hampshire in 1734.

Townsend, Henry. He served as a soldier in the French and Indian War and assigned his 50 acre warrant in Virginia.

Townsley, John. He was granted 200 acres in Albany County, New York for his service as a corporal in the 28th Regiment of Foot in the French and Indian War 8 June 1771.

Tozer, John. He was a soldier in 1712 and helped advance £30 for the redemption of Daniel Tucker from the Indian enemy. He, Jonas Smith, and Isaac Harrington were granted 500 acres in York County by Massachusetts 8 December 1737.

Tozer, Richard. He was awarded 200 acres by Massachusetts for his service in the Indian wars. He was from Berwick, York County.

Tracy, Daniel. He served in the Narraganset War from Connecticut and received land in Voluntown, Connecticut in 1701.

Tracy, Solomon. He served in the Narraganset War from Connecticut and received land in Voluntown, Connecticut in 1701.

Trask, Nathaniel. He served in the Narraganset War and received land in Templeton, Massachusetts in 1733.

Trask, William. He served on the expedition to Canada in 1690. Samuel Trask petitioned for his land in Raymond, Maine in 1735.

Trask, William. He served in the Narraganset War from Salem,

Massachusetts. His son, John Trask, claimed his land in Amherst, New Hampshire in 1734.

Trask, William. He served on the expedition to Canada in 1690. Edward Trask was admitted to his land in Lyndeboro, Maine in 1736.

Travis, Charles. He served as a drummer in the French and Indian War. He proved his right in Richmond County, Virginia 6 February 1780. He assigned his 200 acre land warrant in Virginia. He also appeared as Charles Travers.

Travis, John. He served as a sergeant in the 80th Regiment in the French and Indian War and assigned his warrant for 200 acres in New York 20 May 1767.

Traylor, John. He enlisted in 1758 in Capt. Thomas Fleming's Company and Col. William Peachey's Regiment of Regulars in the French and Indian War. He received his 50 acre warrant 7 April 1780 in Chesterfield County, Virginia.

Treat, Malachi. He was granted 2,000 acres in Albany County, New York for his service as a surgeon's mate in the 47th Regiment of Foot in the French and Indian War 11 November 1768.

Treby, John. He was granted 3,000 acres in Albany County, New York for his service as a captain in the 80th Regiment of Foot in the French and Indian War 21 October 1765.

Tredway, John. He served as a soldier in the French and Indian War and was recruited in Virginia. He received his 50 acre warrant in Virginia.

Tredwell, Elisha. He was a veteran of the expedition to Canada in 1690. His brother, Thomas Tredwell of Ipswich, Massachusetts, claimed his land in Winchendon, Massachusetts in 1736.

Tree, Joseph. His heirs were granted 1,095 acres for his service in the Canada Expedition in 1690 by Massachusetts on 24 June 1773.

Trescott, Samuel. He served on the expedition to Canada in 1690. His sister, Elizabeth Trescott of Milton, Massachusetts, received his land in Ashburnham, Massachusetts in 1736.

Tresfall, Andrew. He was granted 200 acres in Albany County, New York for his service as a noncommissioned officer in the 60th Regiment of Foot in the French and Indian War 5 April 1771.

Trickett, Thomas. He was granted 2,000 acres in Albany County, New York for his service as quartermaster in the 44th Regiment of Foot in the French and Indian War 7 October 1771.

Trigg, Daniel. He served as a subaltern in the French and Indian War and assigned his land in Virginia.

Trigg, John. He served as a sergeant in the 1st Virginia Regiment under Col.

George Washington in the French and Indian War. He assigned his 200 acre warrant in Virginia. He proved his service in Berkeley County, Virginia 15 August 1780.

Trigg, William. He served as a subaltern in the French and Indian War from Virginia and received a warrant for 2,000 acres 19 March 1774.

Trigger, William. He was granted 50 acres in Orange County, New York for his service as a soldier in the 4th Battalion in the 60th Regiment of Foot in the French and Indian War 15 May 1770.

Triscot, John. He served in the Narraganset War from Boston, Massachusetts. Samuel Kneeland received his land in Bedford, New Hampshire in 1733.

Triscott, Joseph. He was a veteran of the expedition to Canada in 1690. His son, Joseph Triscott of Dorchester, Massachusetts, received his land in Ashburnham, Massachusetts in 1736.

Trissell, James. He served on the expedition to Canada in 1690. James Trissell received land in Warwick, Massachusetts in 1738.

Trivet, Henry. He served on the expedition to Canada in 1690. His heirs received land in Chesterfield, Massachusetts in 1739.

Trotter, John. He served as commissary in the French and Indian War and petitioned for his 3,000 acres of land in New York 24 December 1774.

Trotter, Meier. He was granted 200 acres in Albany County, New York for his service as a sergeant in a regiment of foot in the French and Indian War 19 May 1770.

Trotter, Richard. He served in the French and Indian War and took his land in Fincastle County, Virginia 15 December 1772.

Trow, George. He served on the expedition to Canada in 1690 and petitioned for his land in Raymond, Maine in 1735.

Trow, Tobias. He served on the expedition to Canada in 1690. Benjamin Trow petitioned for his land in Raymond, Maine in 1735.

Trowbridge, Caleb. He served on the expedition to Canada in 1690. Thaddeus Trowbridge received his land in Alstead, New Hampshire in 1771.

Trowbridge, William. He served on the expedition to Canada in 1690. Thaddeus Trowbridge received his land in Alstead, New Hampshire in 1771.

Trull, Samuel. He served in Lovewell's War in Massachusetts and received his land in Petersham, Massachusetts.

Truman, Joseph. He served as a private in Capt. Obediah Woodson's Company of Volunteers which joined Maj. Andrew Lewis's detachment from the 1st Virginia Regiment in the French and Indian War. He served six months. He received a warrant for 50 acres in January 1780 in Prince Edward County, Virginia. He also appeared as Joseph Trueman.

Trumble, Joseph. He served on the expedition to Canada in 1690. William Trow petitioned for his land in Raymond, Maine in 1735.

Trumbul, John. He served in the Narraganset War from Charlestown, Massachusetts. His heirs received his land in Westminister, Massachusetts in 1733.

Trumbull, Joseph. He served on the expedition to Canada in 1690. Joseph Trumbull received his land in Bethel, Maine in 1767.

Tubbs, Samuel. He served in the Narraganset War from Connecticut. His heirs received land in Voluntown, Connecticut in 1701.

Tucker, Samuel. He served on the expedition to Canada in 1690. Samuel Tucker received land in Warwick, Massachusetts in 1738.

Tuckerman, John. He served in the Narraganset War from Boston, Massachusetts and received land in Bedford, New Hampshire in 1733.

Tudor, Edward. He served as a lieutenant in the 85th Regiment in the French and Indian War and petitioned for his 2,000 acres of land in New York 28 April 1770.

Tull, William. He served as a soldier in Capt. John Field in Gen. Forbes's expedition in the French and Indian War and received a warrant for 50 acres 18 October 1779 in Culpeper County, Virginia.

Tully, Thomas. He served in the French and Indian War and had his service certified in New York in August 1767.

Tumblin, Thomas. He was granted 50 acres in Gloucester County, New York for his service as a soldier in the 44th Regiment of Foot in the French and Indian War 5 April 1770. He also appeared as Thomas Tumlin.

Tumbull, John. He was granted 50 acres in Albany County, New York for his service as a soldier in the 60th Regiment of Foot in the French and Indian War 26 September 1765.

Tunley, John. He served as a soldier in Capt. Christian's Company of Rangers in 1760 under Col. William Byrd against the Cherokee in the French and Indian War. He received a warrant for 50 acres in December 1779 in Botetourt County, Virginia.

Tunstall, Robert. He served in the French and Indian War and took his land in Fincastle County, Virginia 15 December 1772.

Tupper, —. He served on the expedition to Canada in 1690. Elisha Tupper received land in Dumbarton, New Hampshire in 1735.

Turner, Benjamin. He served as a soldier in Col. William Byrd's Regiment in the French and Indian War. He was deceased when there was a petition for his 50 acres in February 1780 in Spotsylvania County,

Virginia.

Turner, Charles. He served as a soldier in the 2nd Virginia Regiment of Regulars under Col. William Byrd in 1758 in the French and Indian War. He petitioned for his 50 acres 14 February 1780 in King and Queen County, Virginia.

Turner, George. He served as a soldier in the 1st Virginia Regiment in the French and Indian War under Col. George Washington. He petitioned for his 50 acres 18 February 1780 in Caroline County, Virginia.

Turner, James. He served as a sergeant in the 2nd Virginia Regiment under Capt. Christopher Hudson in the French and Indian War. He received his 200 acre warrant 21 February 1780 in Goochland County, Virginia.

Turner, John Baker. He served as a soldier in the 1st Virginia Regiment under Col. George Washington in the French and Indian War. He proved his right in Culpeper County 21 February 1780. He assigned his right to 50 acres in Virginia.

Turner, Lazarus. He received land in Richmond, New Hampshire in 1765 for the service of an unidentified veteran of the expedition to Canada in 1690.

Turner, Thomas. He was granted 50 acres in Albany County, New York for his service as a private in the 55th Regiment of Foot in the French and Indian War 8 March 1771.

Turner, Thomas. He was granted 50 acres in Albany County, New York for his service as a soldier in the 17th Regiment of Foot in the French and Indian War 30 May 1771.

Turner, Thomas. He was granted 200 acres in Albany County, New York for his service as a corporal in the 46th Regiment of Foot in the French and Indian War 30 May 1771.

Turner, William. He served as a soldier in the French and Indian War in Col. William Byrd's Regiment and petitioned for his 50 acres in February 1780 in Spotsylvania County, Virginia. He assigned his right.

Turney, Charles. He was granted 200 acres in Berkeley County, South Carolina on the King's bounty for his service in the French and Indian War 6 February 1773. He served as a sergeant.

Tute, James. He served as a captain in one of H. M.'s independent companies in the French and Indian War and petitioned for 3,000 acres in New York 25 November 1765.

Tutt, William. He served as a soldier in 1758 under Capt. John Field and Gen. Forbes in the French and Indian War. His service was proved 18 October 1779 in Culpeper County, Virginia. He received a warrant for

50 acres of land.

Twentyman, John. He served as a soldier in the French and Indian War and assigned his 50 acre land warrant in Virginia.

Twitchell, Edward. He served on the expedition to Canada in 1690. Ebenezer Twitchell received his land in Bethel, Maine in 1767.

Twitchell, Ephraim. He served in the Narraganset War and received land in Templeton, Massachusetts in 1733.

Twitchell, Joseph. He served on the expedition to Canada in 1690. Ephraim Twitchell received his land in Bethel, Maine in 1767.

Twopence, James. He served as a soldier in a company of rangers in 1763 under Capt. William Phillips in the French and Indian War. He proved his service in Louisa County, Virginia 14 February 1780. He assigned his right to 50 acres.

Twopence, James. He served as a soldier in Capt. Christian's Company of Rangers in 1760 in the French and Indian War. He proved his service in Louisa County, Virginia 14 February 1780. He assigned his right to 50 acres.

Tygart, John. He served as a soldier in the Old Virginia Regiment in the French and Indian War. He proved his service in Botetourt County, Virginia in April 1780. He assigned his right to his 50 acre warrant. He also appeared as John Taggart.

Tyler, Daniel. He served as a corporal in the French and Indian War and petitioned for land in New York 9 April 1767.

Tyler, Francis. He served as a lieutenant in a ranging company on an expedition against the Ohio Indians in the French and Indian War. He was in Stafford County, Virginia in August 1779.

Tyler, John. He served on the expedition to Canada in 1690. He petitioned for land from Massachusetts.

Tyler, Roger. He served in the Narraganset War. The town of Wallingford, Connecticut granted him 5 acres of land 9 April 1688 for his services.

Tyler, Samuel. He served in the Narraganset War from Andover, Massachusetts. His son, Ebenezer Tyler, claimed his land in Amherst, New Hampshire in 1734.

Tyng, Edward. He served as a colonel from Massachusetts, was taken prisoner in 1690, and died in a dungeon in France, Edward Tyng of Boston received his land.

Tyng, Edward. He was granted 2,000 acres in West Florida for his service as a subaltern in the French and Indian War 29 November 1776.

Tyre, Tobias. He was granted 50 acres in Albany County, New York for his service as a soldier in the 60th Regiment of Foot in the French and

Indian War 6 July 1771.

Tyser, John. He was granted 200 acres in Albany County, New York for his service as a noncommissioned officer in the 46th Regiment of Foot in the French and Indian War 5 April 1771.

Ually, Andrew. He was granted 50 acres in Albany County, New York for his service as a soldier in the 42nd Regiment of Foot in the French and Indian War 30 October 1765.

Uhhaurinausaussmut, Solomon. He served as a captain in the French and Indian War and was an Indian. He petitioned for land 16 April 1773. He also appeared as Solomon Uhkaunoaunahnmut. His petition was rejected because the Royal Proclamation did not extend to American Indians.

Underhill, John. He was granted 200 acres in Albany County, New York for his service as a corporal in the 80th Regiment of Foot in the French and Indian War 15 August 1765.

Underweg, Casper. He was granted 200 acres in Ulster County, New York for his service as a sergeant in the Royal American Regiment of Foot in the French and Indian War 6 December 1774.

Underwood, George. He was granted 50 acres in Albany County, New York for his service as a soldier in the 80th Regiment of Foot in the French and Indian War 4 July 1770.

Underwood, George. He served as a noncommissioned officer in the French and Indian War. He assigned his right to 200 acres in Virginia.

Unselt, George. He served as a soldier in the 60th Regiment in the French and Indian War. His service was certified in New York 17 January 1764.

Updike, James. He served in the Narraganset War from North Kingston. He claimed his land in Greenwich, Massachusetts in 1737.

Upham, Phineas. He served in the Narraganset War from Malden, Massachusetts. Samuel Kneeland, his assignee, received his land in Westminster, Massachusetts in 1733.

Upham, Phineas. He served in the Narraganset War from Reading, Massachusetts. His son, Richard Upham, received his land in Westminster, Massachusetts in 1733.

Upton, Thomas. He served as a soldier in one of the Virginia Regiments under Col. William Byrd in 1760 in the French and Indian War and received his 50 acre warrant in Virginia. His service was proved in Amherst County, Virginia 6 March 1780.

Urquhart, Donald. He was granted 50 acres in Albany County, New York for his service as a soldier in the 77th Regiment of Foot in the French and Indian War 10 May 1765.

Urhard, John. He was granted 50 acres in Charlotte County, New York for his service as a soldier in the 42nd Regiment of Foot in the French and Indian War 25 January 1773.

Usher, Alexander. He was granted 50 acres in Colleton County, South Carolina on the King's bounty for his service in the French and Indian War 28 January 1771.

Usher, Robert. He served under Capt. John Lovewell from Massachusetts and was killed in the battle at Pigwacket in May 1725. He was from Dunstable, Massachusetts. His land was in Pembroke, New Hampshire.

Vachob, John. He served as a soldier in Capt. William Preston's Company of Rangers in 1758 in the French and Indian War. He received his 50 acre warrant 2 March 1780 in Augusta County, Virginia. He also appeared as Jacob Vachob.

Vaham, John. He proved his service in the French and Indian War in Augusta County, Virginia 21 March 1780.

Valandigham, George. He served as a lieutenant in Dunmore's War in 1774. He proved his service in Yohogania County, Virginia 28 March 1780.

Vallet, Jacquet. He was granted 100 acres in Hillsborough Township, South Carolina on the King's bounty for his service in the French and Indian War 13 May 1768.

Vanbraam, Jacob. He served in the French and Indian War and took his land in Botetourt County, Virginia.

VanBushkirk, Michael. He served as an ensign by a commission from Gov. Horatio Sharp of Maryland dated 2 May 1756 in a corps raised by Alexander Bealle in the French and Indian War. He proved his service in Yohogania County, Virginia 27 October 1779. He assigned his 2,000 acre warrant in Virginia. He also appeared as Michael VanBuscark and Michael VanBuskkirk.

Vance, John. He served as a sergeant in the French and Indian War. His claim to 200 acres was certified in Washington County, Virginia 15 May 1781.

Vandill, Adam. He served as a soldier in the 3rd Battalion of the 60th Regiment in the French and Indian War. His service was certified in New York 24 August 1774.

VanFuser, Lewis. He was a captain in the French and Indian War and was named in an order concerning a grant in New York 13 March 1771.

Vanmeter, Joseph. He served as a soldier in a ranging company under Capt. Robert Rutherford in 1758 and 1759 in the French and Indian War and received his 50 acre warrant in Virginia. He proved his service in

Ohio County, Virginia 5 June 1780.

VanSchaick, Goose. He served as a lieutenant colonel in the French and Indian War and petitioned for land 30 December 1766.

Varlo, Weston. He was granted 5,000 acres in West Florida for his service as a captain in the navy at the reduction of Quebec in the French and Indian War 13 November 1777.

Varnum, John. He served in Lovewell's War in Massachusetts and received his land in Petersham, Massachusetts in 1733.

Varnum, Joseph. He was from Dracut, Massachusetts and petitioned for 200 acres of land 18 March 1735.

Vashon, James. He received his 2,000 acres of land in West Florida for his service as a warrant officer in the navy in the French and Indian War 19 November 1776.

Vass, Rubin. He served as a lieutenant in the Regiment of Regulars of Col. William Byrd in 1758 and 1762 in the French and Indian War. He gave a power of attorney to Vincent Vass to receive his three warrants of 250, 250, and 500 acres in Virginia. Two 500 acre warrants were also assigned. He had another four warrants for 500 acres each which he also assigned. His service was proved in Caroline County, Virginia 10 February 1780.

Vaughan, Andrew. He served as a sergeant in the Virginia Regiment in 1755 in the French and Indian War. He proved his service in Yohogania County, Virginia 27 March 1780.

Vaughan, George. He served as a soldier in Capt. John Lightfoot's Company against Fort DuQuesne in 1758 in the French and Indian War and received his 50 acre warrant in Virginia. He proved his service in Halifax County, Virginia 16 March 1780.

Vaughan, John. He was granted 50 acres in Albany County, New York for his service as a private in the 58th Regiment of Foot in the French and Indian War 8 June 1771.

Vaughan, John. He served as a lieutenant colonel in the French and Indian War and petitioned for a grant of 1,000 acres in addition to the 5,000 acres to which he was entitled on 20 December 1765 in New York. He had petitioned for the latter on 20 November 1765.

Vaughan, Shadrack. He served as a subaltern under Col. William Byrd in the French and Indian War from Virginia and received his 2,000 acre land warrant.

Vaughn, Daniel. He shared in the grant of East Greenwich, Rhode Island made to those who had rendered service in King Philip's War. The grant was made 31 October 1677.

Vaughn, George. He shared in the grant of East Greenwich, Rhode Island made to those who had rendered service in King Philip's War. The grant was made 31 October 1677.

Vaughter, William. He was a sergeant in Capt. Peter Hogg's Company of Rangers in the French and Indian War in 1758 and assigned his 200 acres. He proved his service in Orange County, Virginia 28 October 1779. He also appeared as William Vawter.

Verey, Benjamin. He served in the Narraganset War from Massachusetts in 1685. His land was located in Buxton, Maine.

Verey, Jonathan. He served in the Narraganset War from Massachusetts in 1685. His land was located in Buxton, Maine.

Verey, Samuel. He served in the Narraganset War from Massachusetts in 1685. His land was located in Buxton, Maine.

Vernon, Richard. He served as a wagon master, forage master, and assistant commissary under Generals Braddock, Forbes, and Stanwix in 1755, 1756, 1757, 1758, and 1759 in the French and Indian War. He received his 2,000 acre warrant in May 1780 in Culpeper County, Virginia.

Verry, John. He served on the expedition to Canada in 1690. Jonathan Verry was admitted to his land in Lydeboro, Maine in 1736.

Verry, Samuel. He served in the Narraganset War from Salem, Massachusetts. His son, Jonathan Verrey, claimed his land in Amherst, New Hampshire in 1734.

Viand, John. He served as a soldier and corporal in 3rd Battalion 60th Regiment in the French and Indian War and petitioned for 200 acres in New York 24 October 1764.

Vickery, George. He served in the Narraganset War from Hingham, Massachusetts. His son, Israel Vickery, received land in Bedford, New Hampshire in 1733.

Vignolles, Francis. He served as a captain in the French and Indian War and sought 2,000 acres in West Florida 26 May 1766.

Vining, —. He was slain in the war by the Indians. His son, William Vining of Sutton, Worcester County, was awarded 150 acres by Massachusetts 16 June 1735.

Vose, Thomas. He served in the Narraganset War from Milton, Massachusetts. His heirs received land in Bedford, New Hampshire in 1733.

Wade, Andrew. He served as a sergeant under Lt. James Walker in 1759 in the French and Indian War and received his 200 acre warrant in Virginia. He proved his service in Bedford County, Virginia 16 March 1780.

Wade, John Utley. He was a soldier in the 2nd Virginia Regiment in the French and Indian War and assigned his right to 50 acres. He proved his service in Goochland County, Virginia 29 September 1779.

Wade, Jonathan. He was a veteran of the expedition to Canada in 1690 and was of Ipswich, Massachusetts when he claimed his land in Winchedon, Massachusetts in 1736.

Wade, Robert, Jr. He served as a lieutenant in the 1st Virginia Regiment under Capt. James Gunn and Col. William Byrd in the French and Indian War. He proved his service in Halifax County, Virginia 18 May 1780.

Wadsworth, Samuel. He served as a captain in the Narraganset War from Boston, Massachusetts. His son, Joseph Wadsworth, received land in Bedford, New Hampshire in 1733.

Waggoner, Edmund. He served as a subaltern officer in the Virginia Regiment in the French and Indian War. His heir, Andrew Waggoner, assigned his 1,000 acre warrant in Virginia.

Waggoner, Thomas. He served as a captain in the French and Indian War and received a 3,000 acre land warrant in Virginia.

Waight, —. He served in the Narraganset War. Thomas Hapgood received his land in Templeton, Massachusetts in 1733.

Waight, John. He served as a soldier in the French and Indian War from Virginia and received 50 acres of land.

Wainwright, John His daughter Anne Cushing and her husband James Cushing, his daughter Abigail Hale and her husband, Moses Hale, and their under aged siblings Bedford Wainwright, Mehitable Wainwright, and Hannah Wainwright on 7 January 1735/6 applied for the land due their father as well as the land due their paternal grandfather, Capt. Samuel Wainwright, who was slain by the Indians in Haverhill, Massachusetts in August 1703.

Wainwright, John. He served as a captain. He lived at Haverhill, Massachusetts when he died. His father was Capt. Simon Wainwright who also served against the Indians. The children and grandchildren received 1,000 acres of land from Massachusetts.

Wainwright, Simon. *Vide supra.*

Wait, Thomas. He served in the Narraganset War from Massachusetts in 1685. His land was located in Buxton, Maine.

Waite, Benjamin. He served as an ensign in the French and Indian War and petitioned for 2,000 acres of land in Albany County, New York 12 June 1766.

Waite, Joseph. He served as a captain in the French and Indian War and petitioned for 3,000 acres of land in Albany County, New York 12 June 1766.

Walcot, John. He served in the Narraganset War from Marblehead, Massachusetts. His son, Jonathan Walcot, claimed his land in Amherst, New Hampshire in 1734.

Walden, James. He served as a soldier in the 2nd Virginia Regiment under Col. William Byrd in 1760 in the French and Indian War. He petitioned for his 50 acres 14 February 1780 in King and Queen County, Virginia.

Wales, Eliazer. He served in the expedition to Canada in 1690. His nephew, Samuel Burch of Dorchester, Massachusetts, received his land in Ashburnham, Massachusetts.

Walk, John. He served on the expedition to Canada in 1690. Samuel Osgood was admitted to his land in Lyndeboro, New Hampshire in 1736.

Walker, Asaph. He served as a soldier for six months under Col. William Bryd in the French and Indian War. He proved his service in Buckingham County, Virginia 13 March 1780 and assigned his 50 acre warrant.

Walker, Benjamin. He served in Lovewell's War in Massachusetts and received his land in Petersham, Massachusetts.

Walker, Daniel. He served on the expedition to Canada in 1690 and received his land in Bethel, Maine in 1767.

Walker, Edward. He served in the Narraganset War from Brookfield, Massachusetts. He claimed his land in Greenwich, Massachusetts in 1737.

Walker, George. He served on the expedition to Canada in 1690. James Moor received his land in Bethel, Maine in 1767.

Walker, Henry. He was a soldier in an independent company in Col. Henry Bouquet's expedition against the Shawnee in 1764. He received a warrant for 50 acres in Virginia.

Walker, John. He was granted 3,000 acres in Cumberland County, New York for his service as Captain Lieutenant of a Company of Rangers under Maj. Joseph Gorham in the French and Indian War 9 February 1770.

Walker, John. He was a soldier in the 2nd Virginia Regiment in the French and Indian War and assigned his 50 acres. He proved his service in Goochland County, Virginia 29 September 1779.

Walker, John. He served in the Narraganset War from Eastham, Massachusetts and received his land in Gorham, Maine in 1733.

Walker, Joseph. He served in the 46th Regiment in the French and Indian War. Margaret Walker was certified as his widow 12 December 1766 in New York. His right was assigned to Robert Buchanan 21 January 1767.

Walker, Robert. He was granted 300 acres in Craven County, South Carolina on the King's bounty for his service in the French and Indian War 27 August 1764.

Walker, Thomas. He served as a soldier in Capt. Peter Hogg's Company of Rangers in 1758 in the French and Indian War. He was in Orange County, Virginia 23 September 1779. He received a warrant for 50 acres of land.

Walker, Thomas. He received his 50 acres of land in West Florida for his service as a private in the French and Indian War 9 April 1777.

Walker, Thomas. He served as commissary general for seven years in the French and Indian War and assigned his 2,000 acre warrant in Virginia. He proved his service in Botetourt County, Virginia 10 August 1780.

Walker, William. He served as a soldier in the 2nd Virginia Regiment in the French and Indian War and assigned his right to 50 acres. He proved his service in Goochland County, Virginia 20 September 1779.

Wall, Adam. He served as a soldier in the French and Indian War and had his service certified in Montgomery County, Virginia for his 50 acres of land 8 March 1780.

Wall, Conrad. He served as a soldier in the French and Indian War and had his service certified in Montgomery County, Virginia for his 50 acres of land 8 March 1780.

Wall, James. He served as a lieutenant in Gen. James Oglethorpe's Regiment and was allotted 500 acres on Great Ochechee in Georgia about 1748 and another 250 acres on St. Simon's Island. He later relinquished his claims.

Wallace, Hugh. He was granted 2,000 acres in Albany County, New York for his service as a lieutenant in an independent company of foot in the French and Indian War 21 October 1765.

Wallace, John. He served in an independent company of rangers in the French and Indian War and petitioned for his land 12 April 1769.

Waller, John. He served as a private in the French and Indian War in New York and had his service certified 23 January 1767. He also appeared as John Walter.

Waller, John. He served as a lieutenant in the 2nd Virginia Regiment in the French and Indian War and received his 2,000 acre land warrant in Virginia.

Waller, Philip. He was granted 50 acres in Gloucester County, New York for his service as a soldier in the 44th Regiment of Foot in the French and Indian War 5 April 1770.

Wallingford, Thomas. He served as a captain on the expedition to Canada in

1690 and received land in Poland, Maine in 1739.

Walsh, Lewis. He served as a corporal in the 80th Regiment in the French and Indian War and received 200 acres in Albany County, New York.

Walsh, Peter. He was granted 924 acres in West Florida for his service as a staff officer in the French and Indian War 18 September 1777 and 585 acres 26 April 1779.

Walyart, Frederick. He was granted 50 acres in Albany County, New York for his service as a soldier in the 60th Regiment of Foot in the French and Indian War 30 May 1765.

Walton, Joseph. He and twenty-three other soldiers in the French and Indian War petitioned for land in Albany County, New York 26 January 1763.

Wansley, William. He served as a soldier in Capt. James Gunn's Company of Regulars in 1758 and in Capt. Samuel Meredeth's Company of Rangers in 1759 in the French and Indian War. He proved his service in Louisa County, Virginia 14 February 1780. He assigned his right to 50 acres in Virginia. He also appeared as William Wamsley.

Ward, —. He served as a major on the expedition to Canada in 1690. Dr. Nicholas Noyes received his land in Winchendon, Massachusetts in 1736.

Ward, Benjamin. He served as an officer in the French and Indian War and was awarded 2,000 acres in West Florida 3 February 1768.

Ward, Edmund. He suffered from great fatigues and hardships in the Indian wars and was incapable of further service. He sought 200 acres in Massachusetts 14 June 1728.

Ward, Edward. He served on the expedition to Canada in 1690 and received his land in Bethel, Maine in 1767.

Ward, Edward. He served as a lieutenant 1756 and 1757, captain in 1757 and 1758 in the 1st Battalion of the Pennsylvania Regiment under Col. John Armstrong, and Indian agent in 1760, 1761, and 1762 in the French and Indian War and received his 2,000 acre warrant in Virginia. He proved his service in Yohogania County, Virginia 27 March 1780.

Ward, Edward. He had command of Fort Pitt in 1754 and surrendered to the French in the French and Indian War. He proved his service in Yohogania County, Virginia 26 October 1779 at which time he bore the title of major.

Ward, Eleazer. He was from Newton, Massachusetts. He served on six expeditions against the Indians and suffered much from a wound in his arm. He had three grown sons and did not have enough land to provide for them. He was granted 150 acres by Massachusetts 10 December 1734.

Ward, James. He served as a lieutenant in Capt. Alexander McClanachan's Independent Company under Col. Henry Bouquet in the expedition against the Indians in 1764. His son, William Ward, received five warrants of 400 acres each 6 March 1780 in Williamsburg, Virginia.

Ward, James. He served in Capt. John Dickenson's Company of Rangers in 1756 and 1757 in the French and Indian War. His service was proved in Botetourt County, Virginia 14 January 1780.

Ward, John. He served on the expedition to Canada in 1690. John Ward received land in Chesterfield, Massachusetts in 1739.

Ward, John. He served as a soldier in the French and Indian War and petitioned for 50 acres in New York in 1771.

Ward, Joseph. He served in Capt. John Dickenson's Company of Rangers in 1756 and 1757 in the French and Indian War. His service was proved in Botetourt County, Virginia 14 January 1780.

Ward, Nahum. He received his land in Massachusetts 10 December 1735.

Ward, Nicholas. He served as a lieutenant in the 80th Regiment in the French and Indian War and petitioned for his land in New York 26 October 1771.

Ward, Obediah. He served on the expedition to Canada in 1690. Richard Ward received his land in Bethel, Maine in 1767.

Ward, Samuel. He served as an ensign in Col. Abijah Willard's Regiment in Massachusetts under Gen. Jeffery Amherst for the reduction of Canada in 1759 in the French and Indian War and received his 2,000 acre warrant in Virginia.

Ward, William. He served as a sergeant in Capt. John Dickerson's Company of Rangers on the Frontier in 1756 and 1757 in the French and Indian War. He received a warrant for 200 acres in August 1779 in Botetourt County, Virginia.

Ward, William. He served as a lieutenant in Capt. Robert Breckinridge's Company of Rangers which was incorporated with detachments of the 1st Virginia Regiment in 1760 under Col. William Byrd against the Cherokee in the French and Indian War. He received a warrant for 2,000 acres in February 1780 in Botetourt County, Virginia.

Wardwell, Elihu. He served in the Narraganset War from Topsfield, Massachusetts. His heirs claimed his land in Amherst, New Hampshire in 1734.

Ware, John. He served as a captain in the French and Indian War and received his 3,000 acre land warrant in Virginia.

Warner, John. He was granted 50 acres in Connecticut for his service in the Pequot War 11 May 1671.

Warner, John. He served as a soldier in Col. William Byrd's Regiment in 1758 in the French and Indian War. He proved his service in Orange County, Virginia 28 October 1779. He assigned his 50 acres.

Warner, Samuel. He served in the Narraganset War and received land in Templeton, Massachusetts in 1733.

Warren, —. He served in the Narraganset War from Boston, Massachusetts. His widow, Sarah Warren, received land in Bedford, New Hampshire in 1733.

Warren, Daniel. He served in the Narraganset War from Weston, Massachusetts. He received his land in Westminster, Massachusetts in 1733.

Warren, Jabez. He received land in Richmond, New Hampshire in 1765 for the service of an unidentified veteran of the expedition to Canada in 1690.

Warren, James. He served on the expedition to Canada in 1690 under Joseph Sylvester and petitioned for his land in Massachusetts in 1735.

Warren, Robert. He served on the expedition to Canada in 1690 and petitioned for his land in Raymond, Maine in 1735.

Warren, Thomas. He received his land in West Florida for his service as a surgeon in the French and Indian War 7 October 1776.

Warrenstaff, Charles. He served as an ensign in the Pennsylvania Regiment in the French and Indian War and received his land warrant for 2,000 acres in Virginia.

Warrin, Thomas. He served as ensign under Capt. Cresap in Dunmore's War in 1774. He proved his service in Yohogania County, Virginia 28 March 1780.

Warwick, John. He was a soldier under Henry Bouquet in the expedition in 1764. He proved his service in Augusta County, Virginia 18 May 1780.

Washburn, Jonathan. He served in the Narraganset War from Bridgewater, Massachusetts. His son, Benjamin Washburn, claimed his land in Greenwich, Massachusetts in 1737.

Washington, George. He patented three tracts in Botetourt County, Virginia of 2,448, 4,395, and 2,314 acres and one tract in Fincastle County of 10,990 acres of land for having encouraged men to enlist in the French and Indian War 15 December 1772.

Watcock, Richard. He was granted 50 acres in Albany County, New York for his service as a soldier in the Royal American or 60th Regiment of Foot in the French and Indian War 18 July 1770.

Waterhouse, John. He served in the Narraganset War from Connecticut and received his land in Voluntown, Connecticut in 1701.

Waterhouse, John. He served as a surgeon's mate in the French and Indian War and petitioned for his 2,000 acres of land in New York 8 May 1765.

Waterhouse, Joseph. He served in the Narraganset War from Connecticut and received his land in Voluntown, Connecticut in 1701.

Waters, Anthony. He served as a captain in the French and Indian War and petitioned for his land 30 December 1766 in New York.

Waters, Hugh. He was granted 200 acres in Charlotte County, New York for his service as a noncommissioned officer in the 28th Regiment of Foot in the French and Indian War 12 October 1774.

Watken, Thomas. He served as a soldier in the French and Indian War from Virginia and received a warrant for 50 acres. [His name is difficult to interpret.]

Watkins, Andrew. He served in the Narraganset War from Ashfield, Massachusetts. His son, Andrew Watkins, claimed his land in Greenwich, Massachusetts in 1737.

Watkins, John. He was granted 2,000 acres in Charlotte County, New York for his service as a ensign in the 80th Regiment of Foot in the French and Indian War 2 March 1775.

Watkins, Philip. He served as a soldier in Capt. John Montgomery's Company of Volunteers in the Virginia Regiment in the Sandy Creek Expedition against the Shawnee in 1756 under Maj. Andrew Lewis in the French and Indian War. He proved his service in Botetourt County, Virginia 10 March 17380. He received his 50 acre warrant in April 1780 in Montgomery County, Virginia.

Watkins, Robert. He served as a soldier in the Virginia Regiment under Col. William Byrd in the French and Indian War. He proved his service in Bedford County, Virginia 25 July 1780.

Watson, Donald. He was granted 200 acres in Albany County, New York for his service as a corporal in the 42nd Regiment of Foot in the French and Indian War 30 October 1765.

Watson, Henry. He served as a lieutenant in the French and Indian War and petitioned for 2,000 acres in New York 9 July 1764.

Watson, John. He served in the Narraganset War from Roxbury, Massachusetts. His nephew, Caleb Stedman, received his land in Bedford, New Hampshire in 1733.

Watson, William. He served in the French and Indian War and had his service certified in New York in January 1767.

Watson, William. He served as a soldier in Capt. Samuel Overton's Company of Regulars in 1763 in the French and Indian War. He assigned his 50 acre warrant in Virginia.

Watts, Arthur. He served in the French and Indian War. His representative took his land in Botetourt County, Virginia.

Watts, Charles. He served as a soldier in 1758 in Col. William Byrd's Regiment in the French and Indian War. The warrant was issued to his heir, David Watts, 23 March 1780 in Orange County, Virginia.

Watts, John. He served as a commissary in the French and Indian War. His widow, Susanna Reilly, petitioned for his 3,000 acres of land in New York 1 March 1774.

Watts, John. He was granted 200 acres in Albany County, New York for his service as a sergeant in a regiment of foot in the French and Indian War 19 May 1770.

Watts, John. He was granted 200 acres in Charlotte County, New York for his his service as a noncommissioned officer in the 48th Regiment of Foot in the French and Indian War 26 May 1772.

Watts, Samuel. He served as a soldier in the 1st Virginia Regiment under Capt. Thomas Bullet in the French and Indian War. He received his 50 acre warrant 21 April 1780 in Halifax County, Virginia.

Watts, William. He served as a soldier under Capt. John Smith in the French and Indian War in Virginia and proved his service in Mecklenburg County, Virginia 13 March 1780. He assigned his right to 50 acres.

Waugh, Alexander, Jr. He served as a lieutenant in the Virginia forces under Col. William Byrd in the French and Indian War in 1758. He received his 2,000 acres 17 April 1780 in Culpeper County, Virginia.

Waugh, David. He was granted 1,000 acres in West Florida for his service as a commissary in the French and Indian War 11 March 1776.

Waugh, John. He was granted 200 acres in Albany County, New York for his service as a sergeant in the 55th Regiment of Foot in the French and Indian War 6 June 1765.

Way, Richard. He served in the Narraganset War from Boston, Massachusetts. His heirs received land in Bedford, New Hampshire in 1733. Massachusetts re-granted the land to his representative, Rev. Mr. Hull Abbot, in 1765 since the land was no longer within Massachusetts but in New Hampshire.

Weaver, Clement. He shared in the grant of East Greenwich, Rhode Island made to those who had rendered service in King Philip's War. The grant was made 31 October 1677. [**n.b.** The printed law gives two men of this name.]

Weaver, John. He shared in the grant of East Greenwich, Rhode Island made to those who had rendered service in King Philip's War. The grant was made 31 October 1677.

Weaver, Milk. He was granted 50 acres in Albany County, New York for his service as a soldier in the 60th or Royal American Regiment of Foot in the French and Indian War 28 March 1771.

Webb, Buckridge. He was granted 50 acres in Albany County, New York for his service as a soldier in the 60th Regiment of Foot in the French and Indian War 1 May 1765.

Webb, Julius. He served as a soldier in Capt. Gabriel Throgmorton's Company of Regulars in the French and Indian War. He proved his service in Botetourt County, Virginia in March 1780. He assigned his warrant for 50 acres.

Webb, Martin. He served as a soldier in the Virginia Regiment under Col. William Peachey in the French and Indian War. He proved his service in Buckingham County, Virginia 8 November 1779. He assigned his 50 acre warrant.

Webster, James. He was granted 50 acres in Albany County, New York for his service as a soldier in the 35th Regiment of Foot in the French and Indian War 8 June 1771.

Webster, Joseph. He served as a soldier in Capt. James Gunn's Company under Col. William Byrd in 1760 in the French and Indian War and received his 50 acre warrant 25 May 1780 in Henry County, Virginia.

Webster, Joshua. He served in Lovewell's War in Massachusetts and received his land in Petersham, Massachusetts.

Webster, Thomas. He was granted 50 acres in Albany County, New York for his service as a soldier in the 4th Battalion in the 60th Regiment of Foot in the French and Indian War 18 July 1770.

Webster, William. He was granted 550 acres in Granville County, South Carolina on the King's bounty for his service in the French and Indian War 21 August 1765.

Wedan, Edward. He served in the Narraganset War from Boston, Massachusetts. His daughter, Rebecca Foster, received his land in Bedford, New Hampshire in 1733.

Wedderman, Christian. He was granted 50 acres in Albany County, New York for his service as a soldier in the 60th Regiment of Foot in the French and Indian War 26 September 1765.

Weedg, Elijah. He was granted 50 acres in Tryon County, New York for his service as a private in the Major Joseph Gorham's Corps in the French and Indian War 10 September 1774. He also appeared as Elijah Wedg and Elijah Weedy.

Weeks, Ammiel. He was a veteran of the expedition to Canada in 1690. His son, George Weeks, desired that Samuel Kneeland of Boston, Massachusetts receive his land in Ashburnham, Massachusetts in 1736.

Weeks, Joseph. He was a veteran of the expedition to Canada in 1690. His sister, Mary Weeks, married Joseph Leads of Dorchester, Massachusetts who received his land in Ashburnham, Massachusetts in 1736.

Weeks, Thomas. He was a veteran of the expedition to Canada in 1690. His brother, Joseph Weeks of Dorchester, Massachusetts, received his land in Ashburnham, Massachusetts in 1736.

Weelyart, Frederick. He served as a soldier in the 3rd Battalion of the 60th Regiment in the French and Indian War. The survey for his land was returned 3 May 1765 in New York.

Weems, Thomas. He was granted 50 acres on Lynch's Creek in South Carolina on the King's bounty for his service in the French and Indian War 4 May 1775.

Wefield, John. He was granted 200 acres in Albany County, New York for his service as a corporal in a regiment of foot in the French and Indian War 19 May 1770.

Weir, Duncan. He served as a sergeant in the French and Indian War and petitioned for land in New York 17 March 1767.

Weir, Gilbert. He was granted 122 acres in Ulster County, New York for his service as corporal in the 55th Regiment of Foot in the French and Indian War 13 October 1775.

Welch, James. He served in the Narraganset War from Connecticut and received his land in Voluntown, Connecticut in 1701.

Welch, James. He served as a sergeant in the Queen's independent company of Royal American Rangers under Capt. Joseph Hopkins in the French and Indian War and petitioned for a grant of 200 acres 16 December 1765 in New York.

Welch, John. He was granted 50 acres in Albany County, New York for his service as a private in a regiment of foot in the French and Indian War 19 May 1770.

Welch, Lewis. He served as a corporal in the French and Indian War. His service was certified in New York 8 May 1765.

Welch, Thomas. He served in the Narraganset War from Charlestown, Massachusetts. His heirs received his land in Westminster, Massachusetts in 1733.

Weld, John. He was granted 50 acres in Albany County, New York for his service as a private in the Inniskilling Regiment in the French and Indian War 30 May 1772.

Weld, Samuel. He served on the expedition to Canada in 1690. Samuel Weld received his land in Warwick, Massachusetts in 1738.

Weld, Thomas. He served in the Narraganset War from Roxbury, Massachusetts. His son, Edmond Weld, received land in Bedford, New Hampshire in 1733.

Welden, Joseph. He served in the Narraganset War from Yarmouth, Massachusetts and received land in Gorham, Maine in 1733.

Wells, Agrippa. He served in an independent company of rangers in the French and Indian War and petitioned for land in New York 12 April 1769.

Wells, Edward. He served as a private in the 2nd Virginia Regiment in the French and Indian War and received 50 acres. He was from Goochland County, Virginia 29 September 1779.

Wells, James. He served as a soldier in one of the Virginia Regiments in 1760 under Col. William Byrd in the French and Indian War and received his 50 acre warrant in March 1780 in Amherst County, Virginia.

Wells, Jonathan. He went to the relief of the Deerfield in February 1703/4 and applied for land in Massachusetts 12 December 1735.

Wells, Joseph. He served in the Narraganset War from Topsfield, Massachusetts. His heirs claimed his land in Amherst, New Hampshire in 1734.

Wells, Michael. He was granted 50 acres in Charlotte County, New York for his service as a soldier in the 48th Regiment of Foot in the French and Indian War 26 May 1772.

Wells, Richard. He was granted 2,000 acres in West Florida for his service as a master's mate in the navy at the reduction of Quebec in the French and Indian War 6 January 1778.

Wells, William. He was granted 50 acres in Albany County, New York for his service as a soldier in the 55th Regiment of Foot in the French and Indian War 5 April 1771.

Welman, Isaac. He served in the Narraganset War from Reading, Massachusetts. His heirs received his land in Westminster, Massachusetts in 1733.

Welsh, John. He served as a soldier in the 1st Virginia Regiment in the French and Indian War and proved his service in Augusta County, Virginia 21 March 1780.

Welsh, William. He served in the French and Indian War and received his land in Nova Scotia 12 October 1771.

Welt, Henry. He served as a sergeant in the 60th Regiment in the French and

Indian War and was granted land in New York 6 June 1770.

Wensell, William. He was granted 50 acres in Albany County, New York for his service as a soldier in the 60th Regiment of Foot in the French and Indian War 26 September 1765.

Wesson, Samuel. He served on the expedition to Canada in 1690. John Wesson received his land in Bethel, Maine in 1767.

West, Edward. He was granted 50 acres in Colleton County, South Carolina on the King's bounty for his service in the French and Indian War 23 June 1774.

West, Evan. He was granted 200 acres in Albany County, New York for his service as a corporal in the 46th Regiment of Foot in the French and Indian War 8 June 1771.

West, Francis. He proved his service as a soldier under Col. William Byrd in one of the Virginia regiments in the French and Indian War in Amherst County, Virginia 6 March 1780.

West, George. He was a sergeant in the 2nd Virginia Regiment in the French and Indian War and proved his service in Goochland County, Virginia 20 September 1779. He assigned his 200 acres.

West, Henry. He was granted 50 acres in Albany County, New York for his service as a soldier in the 40th Regiment of Foot in the French and Indian War 15 August 1766.

West, James. He was granted 50 acres in Albany County, New York for his service as a soldier in the 60th or Royal American Regiment in the French and Indian War 8 June 1771.

West, John, Jr. He served as an officer in the French and Indian War and was entitled to 2,000 acres which he assigned in 1775 in Virginia.

West, Thomas. He was granted 200 acres in Albany County, New York for his service as a corporal in the 80th Regiment of Foot in the French and Indian War 15 August 1765.

Weston, William. He served as a private in the French and Indian War and was named in New York 16 May 1774.

Wetherel, John. He received land in Richmond, New Hampshire in 1765 for the service of an unidentified veteran of the expedition to Canada in 1690.

Wetherell, Theophilus. He served in the Narraganset War from Dighton, Massachusetts. His son-in-law, Edward Shove, claimed his land in Greenwich, Massachusetts in 1737.

Wetherell, William. He served in the Narraganset War from Norton, Massachusetts. His son, John Wetherell, claimed his land in Greenwich, Massachusetts in 1737.

Wethers, Richard. He was granted 200 acres in Albany County, New York for his service as a noncommissioned officer in the 60th Regiment of Foot in the French and Indian War 5 April 1771.

Weymouth, Thomas. He served in the Narraganset War from Boston, Massachusetts. His heirs received his land in Bedford, New Hampshire in 1733.

Wharton, John. He was granted 3,000 acres in Albany County, New York for his service as a captain in the 60th Regiment of Foot in the French and Indian War 15 April 1765.

Whayne, Humphrey. He served as a sergeant in 1755 in the French and Indian War and died in the service. Tabitha Whayne swore that John Whayne was his heir and received his 200 acre warrant in April 1780 in King and Queen County, Virginia.

Whayne, William. He served as a soldier in 1755 in the French and Indian War and died in the service. John Whayne was his heir and received his 50 acre warrant in April 1780 King and Queen County, Virginia.

Wheat, Moses. He served in the Narraganset War. Joseph Wheat received his land in Templeton, Massachusetts in 1733.

Wheeden, Nathan. He served as a corporal in the 2nd Virginia Regiment in the French and Indian War. He proved his service in Goochland County, Virginia 17 April 1780. He assigned his warrant for 200 acres in Virginia.

Wheedon, George. He served as a captain lieutenant in the 1st Virginia Regiment and as a captain under Col. Adam Stephen in the French and Indian War. He petitioned for his land in February 1780 in Spotsylvania County, Virginia and received six warrants for 500 acres each. He also appeared as George Weedon.

Wheeler, —. He served in the Narraganset War. Daniel Gates received his land in Templeton, Massachusetts in 1733.

Wheeler, David. He received his 200 acres of land in West Florida for his service as noncommissioned officer in the French and Indian War 21 September 1776.

Wheeler, Isaac. He served in the Narraganset War from Connecticut and received his land in Voluntown, Connecticut in 1701.

Wheeler, James. He was granted 150 acres on the southwest side of Lynch's Creek in South Carolina on the King's bounty for his service as a private in the French and Indian War 21 June 1765.

Wheeler, John. He served in the Narraganset War from Connecticut and received his land in Voluntown, Connecticut in 1701.

Wheeler, John. He served in the Narraganset War. His son, Ebenezer Wheeler, received his land in Templeton, Massachusetts in 1733.

Wheeler, John. He served on the expedition to Canada in 1690. Thomas Hill petitioned for his land in Raymond, Maine in 1735.

Wheeler, John. He served as a soldier from 1758 to his death in the French and Indian War. His 50 acres were issued to his heir, Moses Wheeler, 13 March 1780 in Louisa County, Virginia.

Wheeler, Joseph. He served in the Narraganset War from Connecticut and received his land in Voluntown, Connecticut in 1701.

Wheeler, Joseph. He served in the Narraganset War. His brother, John Wheeler, received his land in Templeton, Massachusetts in 1733.

Wheeler, Samuel. He served on the expedition to Canada in 1690 under Maj. Nathaniel Wade. His nephew, Joseph Wilder of Lancaster, Massachusetts, received his land in Ashburnham, Massachusetts.

Wheeler, William. He served in the Narraganset War from Connecticut and received his land in Voluntown, Connecticut in 1701.

Wheeler, William. He served in the Narraganset War and received his land in Templeton, Massachusetts in 1733.

Wheeler, William. He served as a private in the French and Indian War and petitioned for land in New York 17 March 1767.

Wheeler, William. He served as a soldier from 1758 to his death in the French and Indian War. His heir was Moses Wheeler 13 March 1780 in Louisa County, Virginia.

Wheelock, Abel. He served as a lieutenant in the French and Indian War and received 2,000 acres in Nova Scotia 3 August 1769.

Wheelock, Joseph. He served in the Narraganset War and received land in Templeton, Massachusetts in 1733.

Wheelock, Joseph. He served from Massachusetts in the campaign against the Indians in 1725. He was from Lancaster, Massachusetts and received his land in Pembroke, New Hampshire.

Wheelock, Timothy. He served on the expedition to Canada in 1690. His nephew, Joseph Wheelock of Lancaster, Massachusetts, received his land in Ashburnham, Massachusetts in 1736.

Wheely, Benjamin. He served as a soldier in the 2nd Virginia Regiment of Regulars under Col. William Byrd in 1758 in the French and Indian War. He petitioned for his 50 acres 14 February 1780 in King and Queen County, Virginia.

Wheeton, John. He served in the Narraganset War from Swanzy, Massachusetts. He claimed his land in Greenwich, Massachusetts in 1737.

Whiddam, John. He served in the 2nd Virginia Regiment in the French and

Indian War. He was deceased when his rights were assigned in Goochland County, Virginia 20 September 1779.

Whipple, —. He served on the expedition to Canada in 1690. Simonds Epes received his land in Winchendon, Massachusetts in 1736. Epes called him father.

Whitcomb, John. He served in the Narraganset War and received land in Templeton, Massachusetts in 1733.

Whitcomb, Jonathan. He served in the Narraganset War and received land in Templeton, Massachusetts in 1733.

Whitcomb, Joseph. He served in the Lovewell's War in Massachusetts and received his land in Petersham, Massachusetts.

White, Alexander. He served as a captain in the French and Indian War and petitioned for his land in New York 30 December 1765.

White, Anthony. He was granted 50 acres on the King's bounty in Amelia Township, Berkeley County, South Carolina for his service as a private in the French and Indian War 25 September 1765.

White, Augustine. He served as a soldier in the Virginia Regiment under Col. William Byrd in or about 1758 until disbanded after which he served under Col. Adam Stephen in the French and Indian War and assigned his 290 acre warrant in Virginia. He proved his service in Frederick County, Virginia 2 May 1780.

White, Benjamin. He served on the expedition to Canada in 1690 and received his land in Warwick, Massachusetts in 1736.

White, Benjamin. He was a veteran of the expedition to Canada in 1690 and and was of Ipswich, Massachusetts when he claimed his land in Winchendon, Massachusetts in 1736.

White, Benjamin. He served in the Narraganset War from Brooklyn. His heirs received his land in Bedford, New Hampshire in 1733.

White, Chapman. He served under Capt. William Phillips in the French and Indian War from Virginia. His heir at law, Moses White, petitioned for his 50 acres 14 February 1780 in Louisa County, Virginia.

White, Charles. He was granted 200 acres in Granville County, South Carolina on the King's bounty for his service in the French and Indian War 15 February 1770.

White, Daniel. He served in the Narraganset War and received his land in Templeton, Massachusetts in 1733.

White, Daniel. He was granted 200 acres in Albany County, New York for his service as a sergeant in the 60th or Royal American Regiment of Foot in the French and Indian War 30 May 1771.

White, Ebenezer. He received land in Richmond, New Hampshire for the service of a veteran of the expedition to Canada in 1690.

White, Edward. He served on the expedition to Canada in 1690. Edward White received his land in Warwick, Massachusetts in 1738.

White, Elisha. He served as a lieutenant in Capt. Joseph Fox's Company of Rangers in 1755 in the French and Indian War and received his warrant for 200 acres 13 March 1780 in Louisa County, Virginia.

White, George. He was granted 200 acres in Albany County, New York for his service as a sergeant in the 28th Regiment of Foot in the French and Indian War 8 June 1771.

White, George. He served as a soldier until 1758 in the French and Indian War. His widow, Mary White, obtained his warrant in Caroline County, Virginia in February 1780. She assigned her right to 50 acres in Virginia.

White, James. He served as a subaltern in the French and Indian War and received 2,000 acres in Nova Scotia 26 July 1782.

White, John. He served in Lovewell's War in Massachusetts and received his land in Petersham, Massachusetts in 1733.

White, John. He served as a private in the 28th Regiment in the French and Indian War. His service was certified in New York 18 October 1766.

White, Jonathan. He served in the Narraganset War from Yarmouth, Massachusetts and received land in Gorham, Maine in 1733.

White, Joseph. He served in the Narraganset War from Taunton, Massachusetts. His son, Joseph White, claimed his land in Greenwich, Massachusetts in 1737.

White, Philip. He was granted 50 acres in Albany County, New York for his service as a soldier in the 44th Regiment of Foot in the French and Indian War 1 April 1772.

White, Return. He received land in Richmond, New Hampshire in 1765 for the service of an unidentified veteran of the expedition to Canada in 1690.

White, Samuel, Jr. He served as a corporal in the 2nd Virginia Regiment under Col. William Byrd in the French and Indian War and died in the service. His heir, Elias White, petitioned for his 200 acres 21 February 1780 in King William County, Virginia.

White, Thomas. He served on the expedition to Canada in 1690. Joseph White was admitted to his land in Lyndeboro, New Hampshire in 1736.

White, Timothy. He served in the Narraganset War from Scituate, Massachusetts. His son, Timothy White, received his land in Gorham, Maine in 1733.

White, William. He was a soldier in the Virginia troops in Capt. Thomas Bullet's Company under Gen. Braddock on the expedition against

Fort DuQuesne in 1755 in the French and Indian War. He proved his right in Hampshire County, Virginia 10 August 1779. He assigned his 50 acres.

Whitefield, William. He was granted 200 acres in Albany County, New York for his service as a corporal in the 55th Regiment of Foot in the French and Indian War 15 May 1770.

Whitehead, Samuel. He was granted 50 acres in Connecticut for his service in the Pequot War 11 May 1671. He was from New Haven.

Whitehouse, John. He was granted 150 acres on the Savannah River in South Carolina on the King's bounty 21 June 1765. He served as a private in the French and Indian War.

Whitehouse, Joseph. He was granted 200 acres in Albany County, New York for his service as a corporal in the Royal Regiment of Artillery in the French and Indian War 17 October 1766.

Whitehouse, Samuel. He served as a corporal in the French and Indian War in New York and had his service certified 23 January 1767.

Whiteman, John. He served as a sergeant in the French and Indian War and petitioned for 200 acres on the King's bounty in South Carolina 3 July 1764.

Whiten, Thomas. He served as a sergeant in the 55th Regiment in the French and Indian War and petitioned for his land in New York 22 March 1771.

Whiting, Nathan. He was granted 3,000 acres in Cumberland County, New York for his service as a captain in an independent company of foot in the French and Indian War 15 August 1766.

Whiting, Samuel. He served in the expedition against the Indians in Massachusetts in 1725. He received his land in Pembroke, New Hampshire. He was from Dracut, Massachusetts.

Whitlock, Achilles. He served as a soldier in the French and Indian War until he was discharged in 1758. His service was proved in Caroline County, Virginia in March 1780. His oldest son, John Whitlock, assigned the warrant for 50 acres in Virginia.

Whitlow, Joseph. He served as a private in the 2nd Virginia Regiment in the French and Indian War. He disposed of his 50 acre warrant.

Whitman, John. He served in the expedition to Canada in 1690 under Sir William Phipps. He received his land in Massachusetts [Henniker, New Hampshire today] 10 December 1735.

Whitmarsh, John. He served in the Narraganset War from Weymouth, Massachusetts. Gideon Terrel received his land in Bedford, New Hampshire in 1733.

Whitmore, John. He served in the Narraganset War from Medford, Massachusetts. His son, John Whitmore, received his land in Westminster, Massachusetts in 1733.

Whitney, Benjamin. He served in the Narraganset War and received land in Templeton, Massachusetts in 1733.

Whitney, David. He served in the Narraganset War and received land in Templeton, Massachusetts in 1733.

Whitney, David. He served on the expedition to Canada in 1690. Ezekiel Whitney received his land in Alstead, New Hampshire in 1771.

Whitney, Isaac. He served under Capt. John Lovewell from Massachusetts and was in battle at Pigwacket in May 1725. He was from Concord, Massachusetts and received his land in Pembroke, New Hampshire.

Whitney, John. He served on the expedition to Canada in 1690. Abraham Whitney received his land in Alstead, New Hampshire in 1771.

Whitney, Jonathan. He served in the Narraganset War and received land in Templeton, Massachusetts in 1733.

Whitney, Moses. He served under Capt. Davenport in the Narraganset War and received land in Templeton, Massachusetts in 1733.

Whitney, Samuel. He served under Capt. John Lovewell from Massachusetts and was in battle at Pigwacket in May 1725. He was from Dunstable and received his land in Pembroke, New Hampshire.

Whitney, Samuel. His son-in-law, John Fish, of Watertown applied for land in Massachusetts. His petition was rejected.

Whitney, Timothy. He served on the expedition to Canada in 1690. Timothy Whitney received land in Warwick, Massachusetts in 1738.

Whittemore, Henry. He was from Cambridge, Massachusetts and sought his land 10 December 1735.

Whood, Gabriel. He served on the expedition to Canada in 1690. He applied for his land in Raymond, Maine in 1735.

Whorry, Robert. He served as a private in the French and Indian War and petitioned for his land in New York in November 1766.

Wiat, Edward. He served on the expedition to Canada in 1690. His niece, Waitstill Lyon of Dorchester, Massachusetts, received his land in Ashburnham, Massachusetts in 1736.

Wickham, Benjamin. He served as a lieutenant in the French and Indian War and petitioned for 2,000 acres in New York 13 March 1765.

Wickham, Benjamin. He served as a lieutenant in the 47th Regiment of Foot in the French and Indian War per certificate in West Florida.

Wicks, William. He served in the 80th Regiment in the French and Indian War and had his service certified 27 September 1766.

Wickwier, John. He served in the Narraganset War from Connecticut and received land in Voluntown, Connecticut in 1701.

Wicomb, Daniel. He served in the Narraganset War from Norwich, Connecticut. His son, Daniel Wicomb, claimed his land in Greenwich, Massachusetts in 1737.

Widdershine, Daniel. He was granted 50 acres in Albany County, New York for his service as a soldier in the 60th or Royal American Regiment in the French and Indian War 28 March 1771.

Widsell, John. He was granted 200 acres in Gloucester County, New York for his service as a drummer in the 4th Battalion in the 60th Regiment of Foot in the French and Indian 5 April 1770.

Wier, Archibald. He was granted 200 acres in Albany County, New York for his service as a sergeant in the Royal Regiment of Artillery in the French and Indian War 18 February 1775.

Wier, James. He was granted 200 acres in Albany County, New York for his service as a corporal in the 1st or Royal Regiment of Foot in the French and Indian War 12 September 1765.

Wifreld, John. He served as a corporal in the 80th Regiment in the French and Indian War and was granted land in New York 31 December 1770.

Wiggins, Thomas. He was granted 301.4 and 339.1 acres in Berks County, Pennsylvania for his service as a lieutenant in the French and Indian War 3 February 1769.

Wilbore, William, Jr. He shared in the grant of East Greenwich, Rhode Island made to those who had rendered service in King Philip's War. The grant was made 31 October 1677.

Wild, Jonathan. He served in the Narraganset War from Topsfield, Massachusetts. His heirs claimed his land in Amherst, New Hampshire in 1734. John Wild drew the land.

Wild, Thomas. He received land in Richmond, New Hampshire in 1765 for the service of an unidentified veteran of the expedition to Canada in 1690.

Wilder, James. He served as a lieutenant in the 60th Royal American Regiment in the French and Indian War and petitioned for a grant of 2,000 acres on 20 January 1766 in New York.

Wilder, John. He served in Lovewell's War in Massachusetts and received his land in Petersham, Massachusetts in 1733.

Wiley, John. He was granted 200 acres in Albany County, New York for his service as a noncommissioned officer in the 80th Regiment of Foot in the French and Indian War 15 June 1765.

Wiley, John. He served as a soldier in Capt. John Dickinson's Company of Rangers from Virginia in the French and Indian War in Botetourt

County, Virginia 9 March 1780.

Wiley, John. He served as a soldier in the Virginia Regiment on the Cherokee Expedition in 1760 under Col. William Byrd in the French and Indian War and received his 50 acre warrant in April 1780 in Botetourt County, Virginia.

Wiley, Peter. He served as a soldier in Capt. John Dickinson's Company of Rangers in the French and Indian War and received his 50 acre warrant in May 1780 in Montgomery County, Virginia.

Wilkerson, Edward. He served as a sergeant in the French and Indian War in Virginia. He assigned his warrant for 200 acres.

Wilkinson, James. He served as a soldier in the 2nd Virginia Regiment in the French and Indian War. He proved his service in Goochland County, Virginia 21 February 1780. He assigned his warrant for 50 acres in Virginia. He also appeared as James Wilkerson.

Willan, Richard. For his service in suppressing those involved in Ingle's Insurrection in Maryland, Lord Baltimore granted him a warrant for the 2,000 acre manor of Snow Hill in conjunction with Sgt. James Lindsey 28 August 1649.

Willard, Jacob. He served in the Narraganset War from Newton, Massachusetts. His son, Jonathan Willard, received his land in Westminster, Massachusetts in 1733.

Willard, Samuel. He served as a captain in Lovewell's War in Massachusetts and received his land in Petersham, Massachusetts in 1733.

Willard, Simon. He served as a major. He was granted 500 acres of land by the Massachusetts Bay Colony for his service in the Indian Wars. He and Daniel Gookin were granted another 500 acres together. His widow and relict, Mary Noyes, in behalf of his six minor children, petitioned for 1,000 acres for the said children as they came of age 11 May 1681.

Willey, John. He served in the Narraganset War from Connecticut. His heirs received his land in Voluntown, Connecticut in 1701.

Williams, Charles. He was granted 2,000 acres in Gloucester County, New York for his service as a subaltern officer in the 80th Regiment of Foot in the French and Indian War 2 August 1774.

Williams, Anthony. He was granted 50 acres in Albany County, New York for his service as a soldier in the 80th Regiment of Foot in the French and Indian War 21 May 1768.

Williams, Anthony. He was granted 200 acres in Albany County, New York for his service as a corporal in the 80th Regiment of Foot in the French and Indian War 1 July 1771.

Williams, Benjamin. He served in the Narraganset War from Boston,

Massachusetts. His heirs received his land in Bedford, New Hampshire in 1733.

Williams, Charles. He served as a lieutenant in the 80th Regiment in the French and Indian War and petitioned for his 2,000 acre land grant in New York 26 December 1771.

Williams, Ebenezer. He served in the Narraganset War from Dorchester, Massachusetts. He received his land in Bedford, New Hampshire in 1733.

Williams, George. He served as a sergeant in the 28th Regiment in the French and Indian War and petitioned for his land 18 October 1766 in New York.

Williams, Henry. He served as lieutenant in the French and Indian War and was entitled to 2,000 acres in Virginia which he assigned.

Williams, Hilliard. He served on the expedition to Canada in 1690. Thomas Trott was admitted to his land in Lyndeboro, Maine in 1736.

Williams, Jacob. He was a soldier in Col. William Byrd's Regiment in 1758 in the French and Indian War and assigned his right to 50 acres in Virginia. He proved his service in Orange County, Virginia 26 September 1779.

Williams, James. He served as a soldier in the French and Indian War and received 50 acres in Nova Scotia 9 October 1776.

Williams, James. He served as a corporal in one of the Virginia Regiments in the French and Indian War and received a warrant for 50 acres 17 November 1779 in Greenbrier County, Virginia.

Williams, John. He was a minister from Deerfield, Massachusetts. Eleazar Williams, Stephen Williams, and Warham Williams for themselves and the other heirs sought the 700 acres due their deceased father 13 June 1735.

Williams, John. He served in the Narraganset War from Massachusetts in 1685. His land was located in Buxton, Maine.

Williams, John. He served as a private in the French and Indian War and was named in New York 8 July 1765.

Williams, John. He was granted 200 acres in Albany County, New York for his service as a corporal in the 17th Regiment of Foot in the French and Indian War 8 June 1771.

Williams, John. He served as a major in the French and Indian War and petitioned for 5,000 acres of land in New York 17 January 1764.

Williams, John. He proved his service as a soldier in the French and Indian War in Goochland County, Virginia 6 September 1779.

Williams, John. He served as a soldier in Col. William Byrd's Regiment in

1758 in the French and Indian War and transferred his right to land in Virginia. He proved his service in James City County 8 November 1779.

Williams, John. He served as a soldier in Col. William Byrd's Regiment in 1758 in the French and Indian War and received 50 acres which he assigned in Virginia.

Williams, John. He served as a soldier in Col. William Byrd in the French and Indian War and received his warrant 8 November 1779 in James City County, Virginia.

Williams, John. He served in the French and Indian War. He received a warrant for 50 acres in Virginia which he assigned.

Williams, Jonathan. He served on the expedition to Canada in 1690. Isaac Williams was admitted to his land in Lyndeboro, Maine in 1736.

Williams, Joseph. He served as a captain in the 50th Regiment in the French and Indian War and petitioned for his land in New York 20 March 1767.

Williams, Lewis Powell. He was granted 1,325 acres in Albany County, New York for his service as a surgeon's mate in a military hospital in the French and Indian War 7 October 1772.

Williams, Nathaniel. He was awarded 100 acres for his service as a commissary in Massachusetts 15 October 1679.

Williams, Nathaniel. He served in the Narraganset War from Eastham, Massachusetts and received his land in Gorham, Maine in 1733.

Williams, Richard. He was granted 2,000 acres in Albany County, New York for his service as a lieutenant in the 80th Regiment of Foot in the French and Indian War 18 November 1769.

Williams, Samuel. He served from Deerfield, Massachusetts in the late war against the Indians as a lieutenant. Elijah Williams in behalf of his three brothers, two sisters, and himself sought the land due their late brother 21 June 1738.

Williams, Samuel. He served in the Narraganset War from Roxbury, Massachusetts and received his land in Bedford, New Hampshire in 1733.

Williams, Thomas. He served in the Narraganset War from Connecticut and received his land in Voluntown, Connecticut in 1701.

Williams, William. He served in the Narraganset War from Connecticut and received his land in Voluntown, Connecticut in 1701.

Williams, William. He served on the expedition to Canada in 1690. Jonathan Williams received his land in Alstead, New Hampshire in 1771.

Williams, William. He was granted 3,000 acres in Albany County, New York for his service as a captain in the 52nd Regiment of Foot in the French and Indian War 29 October 1765.

Williamson, Caleb. He served on the expedition to Canada in 1690 and received his land in Dumbarton, New Hampshire in 1735. He was a corporal.

Williamson, George. He was granted 50 acres in Albany County, New York for his service as a soldier in the 40th Regiment of Foot in the French and Indian War 30 October 1765.

Williamson, John. He served as a noncommissioned officer in the 46th Regiment in the French and Indian War and petitioned for his 200 acres in New York 26 April 1765.

Williamson, Richard. He was a soldier in the Col. William Byrd's Regiment in the French and Indian War and was awarded 50 acres. He was in Rockbridge County, Virginia 7 September 1779.

Williamson, Smith. He served as a soldier under Col. William Byrd in the French and Indian War. He proved his service in Rockbridge County, Virginia in September 1779. He assigned his 50 acre warrant.

Williamy, Leonard. He served as a soldier in 3rd Battalion of the 60th Regiment in the French and Indian War and petitioned for his land in Albany County, New York 3 March 1766.

Willington, Benjamin. He served in the Narraganset War from Watertown, Massachusetts. His heirs received his land in Westminster, Massachusetts in 1733.

Willington, John. He served in the Narraganset War from Cambridge, Massachusetts. His nephew, Thomas Willington, received his land in Westminster, Massachusetts in 1733.

Willington, Dr. Palgrave. He served in the Narraganset War from Watertown, Massachusetts. His heirs received his land in Westminster, Massachusetts in 1733.

Wallis, Caleb. He served on the expedition to Canada in 1690. Caleb Wallis applied for his land in Raymond, Maine in 1735.

Willis, Edward. He served as a soldier in the 2nd Virginia Regiment of Regulars in the French and Indian War. He proved his service in Goochland County, Virginia 29 September 1779. He assigned his 50 acre warrant.

Willis, John. He was granted 200 acres in Mecklenburg County, North Carolina for his service as noncommissioned officer in the French and Indian War 3 March 1775. He had formerly lived in Orange County, North Carolina. He had originally obtained the warrant about August 1772 and had given it to Capt. John Pfifer to carry it to the Secretary's office. It was destroyed in a fire at Pfifer's premises.

Willis, John. He served on the expedition to Canada in 1690 under Capt. Savage. His son-in-law, Nathan Heywood of Lunenburg, Massachusetts, received his land in Ashburnham, Massachusetts.

Willis, Joseph. He served as a soldier in Capt. John Dickinson's Company of Rangers in 1758 in the French and Indian War. He received his 50 acre warrant 1 February 1780 in Kentucky County, Virginia.

Willis, Samuel. He was granted 200 acres in Tryon County, New York for his service as a sergeant in the 15th Regiment of Foot in the French and Indian War 10 September 1774.

Willis, Thomas. He served in the Narraganset War from Medfield, Massachusetts. His son, William Willis, received his land in Westminster, Massachusetts in 1733.

Willit, James. He served in the Narraganset War from Connecticut and received his land in Voluntown, Connecticut in 1701.

Willmarth, Jonathan. He served in the Narraganset War from Rehoboth, Massachusetts. He claimed his land in Greenwich, Massachusetts in 1737.

Wills, Justinian. He served as a sergeant major under Col. William Byrd in 1758 in the French and Indian War and received a warrant for 200 acres in March 1780 in Bedford County, Virginia. He also appeared as Justinian Wells.

Willshire, Richard. He was a soldier in Capt. John McNeil's Company of Grenadiers in the Virginia Regiment in the French and Indian War, He proved his service in Rockbridge County, Virginia in 1779. He assigned his 50 acres.

Willson, Benjamin. He served on the expedition to Canada in 1690 and received his land in Warwick, Massachusetts in 1736.

Willson, Donald. He served in the French and Indian War and had his service certified in New York in August 1767.

Willson, John. He served as an ensign in H. M.'s Independents and petitioned for a grant of 4,000 acres in New York 24 April 1766.

Willson, John. He served as a private in the 4th Battalion of the 60th Regiment in the French and Indian War. The survey of his land was returned in New York 22 April 1765.

Willson, Richard. He was granted 100 acres in Craven County, North Carolina in part for the 200 acres due him as a sergeant in the 22nd Regiment of Foot in the French and Indian War on 6 March 1775. He was at the reduction of Havana and was discharged by Major Loftus.

Wilmot, John. He was granted 200 acres in Albany County, New York for his service as a noncommissioned officer in the 60th Regiment of Foot in the French and Indian War 15 August 1765.

Wilper, John David. He served in the French and Indian War and took his land in Botetourt County, Virginia in 1773.

Wilson, Alexander. He was granted 200 acres in Albany County, New York for his service as a corporal in the 77th Regiment of Foot in the French and Indian War 7 May 1767.

Wilson, Alexander. He was granted 200 acres in Colleton County, South Carolina on the King's bounty 23 June 1774. He served as a corporal in the French and Indian War.

Wilson, Edward. He served in the Narraganset War and received land in Templeton, Massachusetts in 1733.

Wilson, Edward. He served in the French and Indian War from New York and assigned his right to his land to Robert Buchanan 22 January 1767.

Wilson, James. He served in the French and Indian War and assigned his land in New York in January 1767.

Wilson, James. He was granted 200 acres in Albany County, New York for his service as a corporal in the 28th Regiment of Foot in the French and Indian War 25 May 1771.

Wilson, John. He served as a captain in the 59th Regiment in the French and Indian War and petitioned for land in New York 17 March 1767.

Wilson, John. He was granted 50 acres in Albany County, New York for his service as a soldier in the 78th Regiment of Foot in the French and Indian War 1 May 1765.

Wilson, John. He served in the French and Indian War and took his land in Fincastle County, Virginia 15 December 1772.

Wilson, Joseph. He served in Lovewell's War in Massachusetts and received his land in Petersham, Massachusetts in 1733.

Wilson, Paul. He served in the Narraganset War from Roxbury, Massachusetts. His son, Henry Wilson, received land in Bedford, New Hampshire in 1733.

Wilson, Peter. He served as a soldier in Capt. Stephens's Company in the French and Indian War in 1761 and received his 50 acre warrant in Virginia. He proved his service in Augusta County, Virginia 20 June 1780.

Wilson, Richard. He served as a soldier in the 1st Virginia Regiment in the French and Indian War. He proved his service in Fauquier County, Virginia 28 February 1780.

Wilson, Robert. He was granted 200 acres on Fishing Creek in South Carolina on the King's bounty for service in the French and Indian War 15

February 1770.

Wilson, Samuel. He served under Capt. Prentice in the Narraganset War and received his land in Templeton, Massachusetts in 1733.

Win, Edward. He served in the Narraganset War and received land in Templeton, Massachusetts in 1733.

Winders, Samuel. He was granted 50 acres in Albany County, New York for his service as a soldier in the 55th Regiment of Foot in the French and Indian War 17 September 1765.

Wing, Annanias. He served in the Narraganset War from Yarmouth, Massachusetts and received land in Gorham, Maine in 1733.

Wing, Bacheldor. He served on the expedition to Canada in 1690 and received land in Dumbarton, New Hampshire in 1735.

Wing, Nathaniel. He served in the Narraganset War from Sandwich, Massachusetts. His son, Nathaniel Wing, received his land in Gorham, Maine in 1733.

Winn, John. He enlisted and served his time in the French and Indian War. His son and heir, Thomas Winn, proved his service in Lunenburg County, Virginia 10 February 1780.

Winslow, Benjamin. He served as an ensign under Col. William Byrd in the French and Indian War in 1760 and received four warrants for 500 acres 18 October 1779 in Culpeper County, Virginia.

Winslow, John. He served in the Narraganset War from Malden, Massachusetts. His son, John Winslow, received his land in Westminster, Massachusetts in 1733.

Winslow, Josiah. He served in the Narraganset War from Marshfield, Massachusetts. His son, Isaac Winslow, claimed his land in Greenwich, Massachusetts in 1737.

Winston, Joseph. He served as a lieutenant in Capt. Samuel Overton's Company of Rangers in the French and Indian War. His son, Edmund Winston, received his 2,000 acres of land in Virginia.

Winter, John. He served in the French and Indian War and petitioned for his land in New York 16 May 1763.

Winter, Joseph. He served on the expedition to Canada in 1690. Joshua Fuller received his land in Bethel, Maine in 1767.

Winterbottom, James. He was granted 50 acres in Albany County, New York for his service as a soldier in the 80th Regiment of Foot in the French and Indian War 6 July 1771.

Winthrop, Wait. He served as a major in the Narraganset War from Connecticut and received his land in Voluntown, Connecticut in 1701.

Wire, Archibald. He served as a noncommissioned officer in the French and

Indian War and petitioned for his land in New York 29 June 1774.

Wise, —. He served on the expedition to Canada in 1690. His son, Henry Wise, received his land in Winchendon, Massachusetts in 1736.

Wise, John. He was the minister of Chebacco Parish in Ipswich, Massachusetts and had served on the Canada Expedition in 1690. His son, Ammi-uhamah Wise of Ipswich, received 300 acres of land in 1736.

Wise, Jeremiah. He lived in Berwick and petitioned for 200 acres of land in Massachusetts.

Wiseman, John. He was granted 50 acres in Albany County, New York for his service as a soldier in the 60th Regiment of Foot in the French and Indian War 25 May 1771.

Wite, Samuel. He served on the expedition to Canada in 1690. Samuel Wite received land in Warwick, Massachusetts in 1738.

Withers, William. He was granted 200 acres in Granville County, South Carolina on the King's bounty for his service in the French and Indian War 21 June 1765.

Witherspoon, David. He was granted 100 acres in the township of Williamsburg in Craven County, South Carolina 26 June 1736. His grant stated for "service of militia commences...."

Withington, John. He served as a captain in the expedition to Canada in 1690. His son, Richard Withington of Dorchester, received his land in Ashburnham, Massachusetts in 1736.

Witt, Henry. He was granted 200 acres in Albany County, New York for his service as a noncommissioned officer in the 60th Regiment of Foot in the French and Indian War 23 September 1771.

Wixum, Barnabus. He served as a corporal on the expedition to Canada in 1690 and received land in Dumbarton, New Hampshire in 1735.

Woller, John. He served in the Narraganset War from Connecticut and received land in Voluntown, Connecticut in 1701. His name may have been John Waller.

Wollper, John David. He served as an officer in Col. Andrew Lewis's Regiment of Regulars from Virginia in the French and Indian War. He proved his service 22 January 1780 and received a warrant for 2,000 acres.

Wolly, Benony. He received land in Richmond, New Hampshire in 1765 for the service of an unidentified veteran of the expedition to Canada in 1690.

Wolverton, John. He served as a lieutenant in Capt. Benjamin's Company in Col. Abraham Vancamp's Regiment under General Webb in 1757 in the French and Indian War and assigned his 2,000 acre warrant in Virginia.

Wood, —. He served on the expedition to Canada in 1690. Benjamin Wood received land in Dumbarton, New Hampshire in 1735.

Wood, Abraham. He was granted 600 acres at the fall of the Appomattox in Virginia for his service as the commander of Fort Henry and for garrisoning same at his own expense 9 June 1653.

Wood, Anthony. He served on the expedition to Canada in 1690. Deacon Israel Wood petitioned for his land in Raymond, Maine in 1735.

Wood, John. He served in the Narraganset War and received his land in Templeton, Massachusetts in 1733.

Wood, John. He served in the Narraganset War. John Overing received land for him in Templeton, Massachusetts in 1733.

Wood, Jonathan. He was granted 250 acres on a branch of Bush River in South Carolina on the King's bounty 21 June 1765. He served as a corporal in the French and Indian War.

Wood, Joseph. He was a veteran of the expedition to Canada in 1690. His nephew, John Wood of Ipswich, Massachusetts in the room of and by the consent of his father, claimed his land in Winchendon, Massachusetts in 1736.

Wood, Joseph. He served in the Narraganset War and received his land in Templeton, Massachusetts in 1733.

Wood, Nathaniel. He served in the Narraganset War from Topsfield, Massachusetts. He claimed his land in Amherst, New Hampshire in 1734.

Wood, Thomas. He served in the French and Indian War and received 2,000 acres in Nova Scotia 1 August 1767.

Wood, Thomas. He shared in the grant of East Greenwich, Rhode Island made to those who had rendered service in King Philip's War. The grant was made 31 October 1677.

Wood, William. He served on the expedition to Canada in 1690. Anthony Wood petitioned for his land in Raymond, Maine in 1735.

Wood, William. He was granted 2,000 acres in Albany County, New York for his service as clerk of stores to ordnance in the French and Indian War 13 July 1770.

Wood, William. He served as a lieutenant in Capt. Breckinridge's Rangers incorporated into the 1st Virginia Regiment in 1760 on the expedition against the Cherokee under Col. William Byrd in the French and Indian War. He proved his right to 2,000 acres in Botetourt County, Virginia in February 1780.

Woodberry, Joseph. He served as a corporal on the expedition to Canada in 1690. Joseph Woodberry petitioned for his land in Raymond, Maine in 1735.

Woodberry, Richard. He served as a sergeant on the expedition to Canada in 690. Richard Woodberry petitioned for his land in Raymond, Maine in 1735.

Woodford, William. He served as a lieutenant in the French and Indian War and received his 2,000 acre land warrant in Virginia.

Woodin, John. He served in the Narraganset War from Massachusetts in 1685. His land was located in Buxton, Maine.

Woodman, John. He served as a soldier in the Inniskilling Regiment in the French and Indian War and had his service certified in New York 24 June 1765.

Woodrum, John. He served in the French and Indian War. His warrant was assigned 20 September 1779 in Goochland County, Virginia at which time he was deceased.

Woodrow, Andrew. He served in the French and Indian War. He received 900 acres of land in Virginia.

Woodrow, Thomas. He was granted 50 acres in Albany County, New York for his service as a soldier in the 80th Regiment of Foot in the French and Indian War 29 October 1765.

Woods, —. He served on the expedition to Canada in 1690. His nephew, Daniel Woods, received his land in Bethel, Maine in 1767.

Woods, Daniel. He served under Capt. John Lovewell from Massachusetts and was killed at the battle at Pigwacket in May 1725. He was from Groton, Massachusetts. His land was located in Pembroke, New Hampshire.

Woods, Gabriel. He was granted 50 acres in Albany County, New York for his service as a soldier in the 46th Regiment of Foot in the French and Indian War 11 August 1768.

Woods, Nathaniel. He served as a sergeant under Capt. John Lovewell from Massachusetts and was at the battle at Pigwacket in May 1725. He was from Groton, Massachusetts and received his land in Pembroke, New Hampshire.

Woods, Thomas. He served under Capt. John Lovewell from Massachusetts and was killed at the battle of Pigwacket in May 1725. He was from Groton, Massachusetts. His land was located in Pembroke, New Hampshire.

Woodson, John. He served in the French and Indian War from Virginia and assigned his right to 50 acres.

Woodward, Daniel. He served in the Narraganset War and received land in Templeton, Massachusetts in 1733.

Woodward, Ebenezer. He served in the expedition to Port Royal under Gen. Nicholson and received his land in Massachusetts 3 December 1735.

Woodward, Ezekiel. He served in the Narraganset War from Massachusetts in 1685. His land was located in Buxton, Maine.

Woodward, William. He was granted 50 acres in Colleton County, South Carolina on the King's bounty for his service in the French and Indian War 14 September 1771.

Woodward, William. He was granted 250 acres in West Florida 1 September 1777 for his service as a soldier in the French and Indian War.

Woodworth, Benjamin. He served in the Narraganset War from Lebanon, Connecticut. He claimed his land in Greenwich, Massachusetts in 1737.

Woodworth, James. He was granted 200 acres in Albany County, New York for his service as a corporal in the 60th Regiment of Foot in the French and Indian War 1 April 1772.

Woody, Henry. He was a native of Virginia and served as a soldier under Col. William Byrd in 1760 in the French and Indian War. He proved his service in Bedford County, Virginia 25 October 1779.

Wool, John. He served as a soldier in the 80th Regiment in the French and Indian War and petitioned for his land in New York 6 August 1764.

Woolrick, Nicholas. He was granted 50 acres in Albany County, New York for his service as a soldier in the 44th Regiment of Foot in the French and Indian War 18 July 1770.

Wooster, David. He was granted 3,000 acres in Albany County, New York for his service as a captain in the 51st Regiment of Foot in the French and Indian War 11 October 1765.

Wooster, David. He served as colonel of a regiment from Connecticut in the French and Indian War. He sought 1,000 acres for himself and each of his associates in New York 3 September 1763.

Wooster, Thomas. He served in the Narraganset War from Connecticut and received land in Voluntown, Connecticut in 1701.

Wooten, John. He served as a soldier in the 1st Virginia Regiment in Capt. James Gunn's Company in the French and Indian War and received his 50 acre warrant in Virginia. He proved his service in Halifax County, Virginia 18 May 1780.

Wooten, John. He served as a soldier under Sgt. Andrew Wade in the French and Indian War in 1759. He proved his service in Halifax County, Virginia 16 March 1780.

Wooten, Joseph. He served as a soldier in the 2nd Virginia Regiment under Capt. Gabriel Throckmorton in 1760 in the French and Indian War and received his 50 acre warrant in Virginia. He proved his service in Halifax County, Virginia 21April 1780.

Wormstrof, Charles. He served as an ensign in the Pennsylvania Regiment in the French and Indian War and patented 2,000 acres of land in Fincastle County, Virginia 16 December 1773.

Wormwood, William. He served on the expedition to Canada in 1690. His heirs received land in Chesterfield, Massachusetts in 1739.

Worth, James. He received his 50 acres of land in West Florida for his service as a soldier in the French and Indian War 27 March 1776.

Wriesberg, Daniel. He was granted 2,000 acres in Albany County, New York for his service as a lieutenant in the 60th Regiment of Foot in the French and Indian War 18 April 1765.

Wright, Benjamin. He spent nearly 40 years in service against the enemy Indians. He was from Falmouth, Massachusetts and sought 100 acres 5 June 1728.

Wright, Ebenezer. He served from Massachusetts in the campaign against the Indians in 1725. He was from Chelmsford, Massachusetts and received his land in Pembroke, New Hampshire.

Wright, Jacob. He served in the Narraganset War. John Tyler received his land in Templeton, Massachusetts in 1733.

Wright, John. He was granted 200 acres in Albany County, New York for his service as a sergeant the 80th Regiment of Foot in the French and Indian War 28 June 1765.

Wright, John. He served as a soldier under Col. William Byrd in 1758 in the French and Indian War and received his warrant for 50 acres in March 1780 in Bedford County, Virginia. He also appeared as John Right.

Wright, Joseph. He served on the expedition to Canada in 1690. His son, Jacob Wright, received his land in Woburn, Massachusetts in 1738.

Wright, Joseph, Jr. He served on the expedition to Canada in 1690. His son, Moussell Wright, received his land in Woburn, Massachusetts in 1738.

Wright, Joseph. He served from Massachusetts in the campaign against the Indians in 1725. He was from Dracut, Massachusetts and received his land in Pembroke, New Hampshire.

Wright, Peter. He was granted 50 acres in Albany County, New York for his service as a soldier in the 55th Regiment of Foot in the French and Indian War 28 October 1765.

Wright, Peter. He served as a soldier in Capt. John Dickenson's Company of Rangers in the French and Indian War and had his service certified in Botetourt County, Virginia 10 February 1780. He received his warrant in Montgomery County, Virginia for his 50 acres of land 7 March

1780.

Wright, Samuel. He received his land in Massachusetts 10 December 1735.

Wright, William. He served as a soldier in the 2nd Virginia Regiment under Capt. Hancock Eustace in the French and Indian War. He proved his service by a certificate from Lt. Charles Mynn Thurston dated 11 October 1774. He received his 50 acre warrant 27 March 1780 in Fauquier County, Virginia.

Wright, Zadock. He served as a sergeant in a ranging company in 1764 and a lieutenant in Dunmore's War in 1774. He proved his service in Yohogania County, Virginia 28 March 1780.

Wrightson, John. He served as major of the 27th or Inniskilling Regiment in the reduction of Canada in the French and Indian War and sought his 5,000 acres of land 7 January 1766.

Write, Joseph. He served as a soldier in the 28th Regiment in the French and Indian War and petitioned for his land in New York 6 August 1764.

Wyatt, George. He served on the expedition to Canada in 1690. George Wyatt petitioned for his land in Raymond, Maine in 1735.

Wylie, Alexander. He served as a soldier in the French and Indian War and had his service certified in Montgomery County, Virginia 8 March 1780 for his 50 acres of land.

Wyman, Benjamin. He served in the Narraganset War and received land in Templeton, Massachusetts in 1733.

Wyman, John. He served under Capt. Prentice in the Narraganset War and was killed at Narraganset. John Wyman, his son, received his land in Templeton, Massachusetts in 1733.

Wyman, John, Jr. He served on the expedition to Canada in 1690. His son, Jabez Wyman, received his land in 1738 in Woburn, Massachusetts.

Wyman, John. He served on the expedition to Canada in 1690. His son, Nathan Wyman, received his land in 1738 in Woburn, Massachusetts.

Wyman, Jonathan. He served in the Narraganset War and received land in Templeton, Massachusetts in 1733.

Wyman, Samuel. He served on the expedition to Canada in 1690. His son, Samuel Wyman, received his land in 1738 in Woburn, Massachusetts.

Wyman, Seth. He served as a captain from Massachusetts in the campaign against the Indians and died of disease 5 September 1725. He was from Woburn, Massachusetts. His land was in Pembroke, New Hampshire.

Wynn, Increase. He served on the expedition to Canada in 1690. His son, Edward Wynn, received his land in Woburn, in 1738 in Massachusetts.

Wynn, Joseph. He served on the expedition to Canada in 1690. His son, Timothy Wynn, received his land in 1738 in Woburn, Massachusetts.

Yarrow, Edward. He served as a corporal in the French and Indian War and petitioned for his land in New York in November 1766.

Yates, Andrew. He served as a private in the French and Indian War and petitioned for land in New York 8 July 1772.

Yeaman, Joseph. He was granted 50 acres in Albany County, New York for his service as a private in the 80th Regiment of Foot in the French and Indian War 5 April 1771.

Yeates, Christopher. He served as a captain in the French and Indian War and petitioned for land 30 December 1766 in New York.

Yeates, John. He served as a corporal in the 77th Regiment in the French and Indian War and had his service certified 11 December 1766. He assigned his land in New York in January 1767.

Yeomans , Samuel. He served in the Narraganset War from Connecticut and received land in Voluntown, Connecticut in 1701.

York, James. He served in the Narraganset War from Connecticut. His heirs received land in Voluntown, Connecticut in 1701.

Young, Alexander. He served as a corporal in the 77th Regiment in the French and Indian War and had his service certified 24 January 1765 in New York.

Young, Edward. He served as a soldier in Capt. John Posey's Company in the French and Indian War. He proved his service in Botetourt County, Virginia 9 March 1780.

Young, Francis. He served in the Narraganset War from Massachusetts in 1685. His land was located in Buxton, Maine.

Young, James. He served as a sergeant in the French and Indian War. His 200 acre warrant was awarded to his heirs at law, James Young and Joseph Young, in October 1779 in Montgomery County, Virginia.

Young, James. He served as a soldier in the Virginia Regiment under Col. William Byrd in the French and Indian War for three years. He was discharged in March 1762. He proved his service in Montgomery County, Virginia in April 1780 and received a warrant for 50 acres.

Young, John. He was granted 2,000 acres in Albany County, New York for his service as a provost marshal in the French and Indian War 14 June 1765.

Young, John. He was granted 50 acres in Charlotte County, New York for his service as a soldier in the 60th Regiment of Foot in the French and Indian War 18 October 1775.

Young, John. He served as a soldier in the Virginia Regiment in the French and Indian War and had his service certified in Montgomery County, Virginia 7 March 1780 for his 50 acres of land.

Young, John. He served as a private for three years under Col. William Byrd in the French and Indian War and was discharged in March 1762. He received his warrant for 50 acres in April 1780 in Montgomery County, Virginia.

Young, John. He served as a private in Capt. James Gunn's Company of the 1st Virginia Regiment in the French and Indian War and received his warrant for 50 acres 6 March 1780 in Charlotte County, Virginia.

Young, Moses. He was granted 50 acres in Albany County, New York for his service as a private in the 80th Regiment of Foot in the French and Indian War 5 April 1771.

Young, Moses. He served as a soldier in the French and Indian War and received 50 acres of land in Virginia.

Young, Mouttray. He was granted 200 acres in Albany County, New York for his service as a corporal in the 42nd Regiment of Foot in the French and Indian War 30 October 1765.

Young, Patrick. He received his 2,000 acres of land in West Florida for his service as a staff officer in the French and Indian War 1 February 1775.

Young, Samuel. He served as a sergeant in Capt. Robert Rutherford's Company of Rangers in 1758 and 1759 in the French and Indian War. He received a warrant for 200 acres in Louisa County, Virginia 11 October 1779 which he later assigned.

Young, William. He served as a surgeon in H. M.'s Hospital in North America in the French and Indian War and petitioned for 3,000 acres in Albany County, New York 31 May 1766.

Younker, George. He was granted 50 acres in Albany County, New York for his service as a private in a regiment of foot in the French and Indian War 19 May 1770.

Zimmerman, Henry. He was granted 50 acres in Albany County, New York for his service as a soldier in the 60th or Royal American Regiment in the French and Indian War 28 March 1771.

Index

The index includes the names of individuals and ships appearing within the individual entries in the text. Females are entered under maiden and married surnames if both are known.

www.ingramcontent.com/pod-product-compliance
Ingram Content Group UK Ltd.
Pitfield, Milton Keynes, MK11 3LW, UK
UKHW020128290926
15471UKWH00003B/351

9 780806 317809